11/04

Queen

THE LIFE AND MUSIC OF

Dinah Washington

NADINE COHODAS

 PANTHEON BOOKS · NEW YORK

All rights reserved under International and Pan-American Copyright
Conventions. Published in the United States by Pantheon Books, a division
of Random House, Inc., New York, and simultaneously in Canada by
Random House of Canada Limited, Toronto.

Pantheon Books and colophon are registered trademarks of
Random House, Inc.

Library of Congress Cataloging-in-Publication Data
Cohodas, Nadine.
Queen : the life and music of Dinah Washington / Nadine Cohodas.
p. cm.
Includes bibliographical references and index.
ISBN 0-375-42148-3
1. Washington, Dinah, 1924–1963. 2. Singers—United States—Biography.
I. Title: Life and music of Dinah Washington. II. Title.
ML420.W2C65 2004
782.42164'092—dc22
[B]   2003070766

www.pantheonbooks.com

Printed in the United States of America
First Edition

2 4 6 8 9 7 5 3 1

FOR CHARLES WALTON, WHO SHOWED ME THE WAY

CONTENTS

Queen

George Gershwin wouldn't know his own song when I'm through with it. I can't stay hidebound to any melody.

— DINAH WASHINGTON

I t was a Saturday night in February 1961 on Chicago's South Side. The patrons at Roberts Show Lounge were in a festive mood— the men in sharp business suits, the women dressed somewhere between Sunday church and New Year's Eve. A few whites were scattered among the tables; the rest were black Chicagoans waiting expectantly for the show to begin even though most of them had seen the star attraction many times.

That didn't matter. When Dinah Washington was in town, the music was always good and always different. No one knew when something unusual might happen. What would she sing? What would she wear? What was new in the offstage life that raised eyebrows and made headlines?

Dinah had just married her sixth husband, a slight, handsome actor twelve years her junior. But it was a good bet she'd have a story about the good-looking man who'd caught her eye the other day. She might tell a few jokes, too. And if the patrons were noisy when she sang, Dinah's sharp tongue would silence them. It was grand to watch as a spectator, though less inviting to be on the other end of her momentary annoyance.

Shortly after ten the announcer came over the loudspeaker: "Ladies and gentlemen, Miss D—Dinah Washington."

She walked to the microphone with a slow, confident gait, sizing up this night's audience as they took her in from their seats. She was just over five feet but seemed much taller. It wasn't the high-heeled dress shoes but her command of the space and the moment. She turned to the band and signaled the key. The piano player hit the opening notes. The bass and drums came in a split second later, and Dinah was off. She opened upbeat, then sang some ballads, finally some blues, first the bawdy tunes and then the ones that made her cry with those lines about love gone sour and life all alone.

At the end the audience, on their feet, cheered for more.

Dinah treasured those moments, hard earned and savored in the early morning hours when the applause had faded. They were the culmination of the silent, even furtive dreams of the young girl born Ruth Jones far away from the glory of center stage and the fans who would one day call her Queen.

1.

Tuscaloosa

1900–1928

Tuscaloosa lies at the heart of Alabama's natural riches. In the 1920s, iron ore, a key ingredient for making steel, was plentiful. So was limestone. The hills and valleys were full of hard and soft timber for mill and factory. Rail service was more than adequate, and because the city was built on the banks of the Black Warrior—the literal translation of Tuscaloosa, the Choctaw name of a tribal chief—manufactured products could be shipped south to the port city of Mobile and on to faraway markets.

Between 1890 and 1923 the city's population had more than tripled, to 18,500 at last count. With outlying communities included the population was close to 30,000. The latest chamber of commerce brochure, a mixture of pride and boosterism, listed ninety-nine reasons why new business should come to this growing and prosperous southern city. Forty-seven new firms had opened in the previous year; five miles of new streets had been paved; an eleven-story office building had been completed and occupied by a bank. Thirty acres had been added to the golf course; Tuscaloosa ranked fourth in Alabama in the number of automobiles within its city limits.

The newest city directory gushed over Tuscaloosa's "many beautiful homes and her broad streets and avenues which are arched with giant shade trees. It has long been known as a city of culture and refinement." The University of Alabama, "the seat of education" for the state, was in the center of town, and the estimable William Jennings Bryan had recently spoken on campus.

Accurate as they were, these descriptions were only a partial portrait. Nearly half of Tuscaloosa was black. Older residents had been slaves; most others were the children and grandchildren of slaves. None lived in the Tuscaloosa of big homes, broad streets, and "culture and refinement," and although they kept those big homes clean and their occupants well fed and cared for, they were absent from the city's civic life. The chamber of commerce made no reference to black Tuscaloosa in its publicity brochure, but by indirection the city directory provided a glimpse of their world: blacks and black-operated businesses were identified by an asterisk before their names. The street-by-street listings of residents and shops, asterisks in place, showed most living in two places: the west-southwest part of town not far from the railroad tracks, an area known as Shacktown, and the small town of Northport just over the Black Warrior River. The occupations listed after the asterisked names testified to the circumscribed opportunities in black Tuscaloosa: chauffeur, cook, engine cleaner, gardener, laborer, laundress, porter, though there were also a half-dozen barbers who had their own shops and a few residents who taught at the all-black schools. "Both male and female white help may be had in any number wanted, and such colored labor as may be needed in the boiler room and like places may be had," said one brochure that served both as recruitment tool and a guide to local custom.

The number of black churches was striking—seventeen. Half were Baptist, but whatever the denomination, they reflected the central truth that the church was a place of community and comfort in an otherwise difficult world, a place to find joy and release, strength and renewal. Decades later, a book on the history of the oldest black church in Tuscaloosa, Hunter's Chapel AME Zion founded in 1866, was appropriately titled *How Firm a Foundation*.

Rufus and Matilda Williams were more fortunate than many of the families in the black community. Though they lived in the outlying hamlet of Sylvan, some twenty miles south of the city limits, they had moved closer in after their daughter, Asalea, was born September 23, 1905. They owned a small farm, which freed them from the constant indebtedness of sharecropping, but like the tenant farmers, they, too, worried about good soil, good weather, and a good yield. In a county where nearly half of the black population and a quarter of the white residents were illiterate, the Williamses could read and write. They were intent on making sure their daughter could, too, and sent her to St. Paul's Lutheran, one of the all-black schools. Perhaps a reversal of fortune required Asalea to stop her formal schooling after she finished eighth grade at St. Paul's. She did not attend high school, and that most likely accounted for an appreciation of education that would last her entire life.

Though Rufus and Matilda were twenty-one and twenty when they got married, Rufus nonetheless teased Asalea when she turned seventeen because she hadn't yet found a husband. But by the time she was nineteen she had met Ollie Jones, the handsome, rakish son of Ike and Mattie Jones, who lived nearby in Northport. Ollie, who was fourteen months older than Asalea, was one of six children—five boys, one girl. Ike was a tenant farmer; Mattie took care of the children. Neither could read or write. The boys—Chapp, Richard, Albert, known as "Snow," Ollie, and Willie—were charmers. Years later their children would admit that all the Jones men—even their grandfather Ike—were "womanizers."

On February 23, 1924, Asalea and Ollie went to the Tuscaloosa county courthouse and applied for their marriage license. They were married the next day.

By now Ollie was working for the Kaul Lumber Company, one of Tuscaloosa's most prominent employers. The couple had moved into a two-room wood frame house in Tuscaloosa on 24th Street, which was just a dirt road that ran through a wooded area. No records indicate that the couple owned the house, and most likely they rented it. Like their neighbors, the Joneses had a well in the yard to get water and a privy out back. The white-owned sanitation company hired black employees to go through the alleys of black Tuscaloosa once a week and pick up the waste.

One of the advantages of living in a rural setting was the abundance of food that grew literally within arm's reach: peaches, pears, figs, pecans. All were harvested and eaten or stored for later use. Many families made their own molasses from the sugarcane that grew wild in nearby fields. This natural bounty was supplemented by a steady diet of biscuits and fried pork.

Asalea took a different kind of nourishment from Elizabeth Baptist Church, which was just around the bend from her house. Founded in 1888, it was, along with Hunter's Chapel, one of the oldest in the black community. When it relocated to 24th Street in 1913, it became such a significant landmark that the surrounding area became known as Elizabeth Quarters. If Ollie was less interested in religion than Asalea, her enthusiasm and participation were enough for both. She did more than just attend Sunday services; she played the piano and sang in the Elizabeth Baptist Choir.

On August 29, 1924, Asalea gave birth to a daughter. Though Peoples Hospital, which served black Tuscaloosa, was a few blocks away on 15th Street, the custom was to give birth at home with the assistance of a midwife. The baby was named Ruth Lee, for Asalea's father, Rufus, and she in fact took after the Williams side of the family: dark-skinned, compact, and chubby with big, expressive eyes.

Ollie's steady job at the lumber mill was apparently enough to meet family expenses. Asalea did not work outside their home, and she surely considered herself lucky given the options available to a young black woman. Her friend, Viola Finney Gamble, another Elizabeth Baptist parishioner, was a laundress at one of the hotels and took in white families' laundry at home to make extra money to feed her own growing family. It was arduous work—pumping water into a wide iron tub, boiling it over a fire, scrubbing the clothes on a handmade washboard, hanging each piece out to dry, and then pressing and folding everything. Several hours' work yielded $2.

Though life in Tuscaloosa was bearable, black families were always looking for better circumstances. World War I had created new demands for labor in the North, and by 1916 northern companies, particularly those in and around Chicago, were sending recruiting agents south to entice blacks with promises of good jobs. Some even carried free train tickets in their pockets as a special inducement. In 1917 so many blacks had left Tuscaloosa that the city commission, in an unsuccessful effort to stem the loss of labor, slapped a $300 license fee on any labor agent wanting to recruit new workers. Montgomery, the state capital, imposed fines and in some cases jail sentences on any "person, firm or corporation" found guilty of "enticing, persuading, or influencing" residents to leave the city.

Prodding the migration was the *Chicago Defender,* a popular weekly of surprisingly wide circulation. Editor Robert S. Abbott, a Georgia transplant, published articles and editorials to support a "Great Northern Drive," scoffing at southern white promises to improve conditions for blacks. "Turn a deaf ear to everybody," he counseled. "You see they are not lifting their laws to help you, are they? . . . To their section of the country we have said, as the song goes, 'I hear you calling me,' and have boarded the train singing, 'Good-bye, Dixie Land.' "

Little in Tuscaloosa proved Abbott wrong. The Ku Klux Klan, moribund in the early years of the twentieth century, was on the rise again, though its emphasis was now slightly different. While blacks were still victimized, this resurgent Klan was equally concerned about the increase in immigrants—Italians, Russians, Greeks, Poles—who threatened the native-born white community. By coincidence, Tuscaloosa Klan activities formed sobering markers to significant events in Asalea and Ollie's early life together. A few days after they were married, the Klan held a "special Klonklave" to induct new members, who wore the robes and hoods of an earlier era. Four days before Ruth was born, more than a thousand Klansmen and their wives gathered for another rally, whose centerpiece was a speech about "The State, the Klan, and the Church."

There is no evidence that Asalea and Ollie or any members of their immediate families were ever threatened, but the pervasive fear of the Klan was one more element that restricted their lives. By 1928, with Ruth now four years old, it seemed a good time to move north. Asalea's uncle Henry already was in Chicago. So was Ollie's older brother Snow, his wife, Lela, and their son, George Albert, who was three months older than Ruth. At least there would be family to welcome them when they arrived in their new city.

In the ensuing years Ollie never lost touch with Tuscaloosa, where his younger siblings still lived. But Asalea, who changed her name to the more conventional Alice, never looked back. Ruth was too young to have any memories. The most important thing about the city in her young life was leaving it.

2.

Lift Every Voice

By the late 1920s, 60th and Wentworth on Chicago's South Side was also the southernmost edge of the city's expanding black belt, which began on 31st Street, extended fifteen blocks east to Lake Michigan, and then turned southwest to stretch down Cottage Grove Avenue to 65th Street. The housing around this Wentworth corner, situated near railroad property, was hardly the most desirable, but Snow Jones had found a place in a two-story building big enough to accommodate him, his wife, Lela, and George and to welcome Ollie, Alice, and Ruth when they arrived. A short time later they made room for one more person, James Doss, a family friend from Tuscaloosa who had attended St. Paul's Lutheran School with Alice.

There was more than familial affinity in the living arrangements. Combining families and taking in a boarder were ways to share expenses in a section of the city where demand for housing was greater than supply. Rents reflected that reality, and even if it didn't sound like much, the $1.50 per week that a landlord might charge could be difficult to find when $1.50 was often a quarter of a family's weekly income.

The two Jones families and Doss lived on the first floor of their building; another family lived above them. The main impetus for leaving Tuscaloosa was the promise of better jobs, but the housing the families found in Chicago proved to be better, too. This one was cramped, but it had running water and indoor plumbing. It was fortunate the children were so young. While each family had its separate room, Ruth and George shared a bed when it came time for their daily naps.

This new setting was a world apart from Alabama. Even though Ruth and her family had lived within Tuscaloosa's city limits, the rhythms of their life had been essentially rural. Now they were in the midst of constant activity—congestion, crowds, hubbub. Perhaps as striking, there was no sign of white people in the everyday course of life as there had been down south. Some adults ventured out to jobs at factories, the stockyards, or the homes of white families. But the children stayed in their self-contained community.

George and Ruth were fast friends, playing together every day and, once they turned five, starting school at Carter Elementary a few blocks away on Michigan Avenue. The families shared meals; Lela and Alice both loved to cook and were good at it. Ollie had better luck than his brother Snow when he found employment at the Byrd Roofing Company doing maintenance work, a job he would keep for fifty years. While Snow moved from job to job, Lela found steady work with a family in the white neighborhood known as Hyde Park and home to the University of Chicago. Alice did not work outside the home in these early days. Ollie's wages were enough for them to make ends meet, and unlike her sister-in-law, Alice was not willing to clean for white people.

Sixtieth and Wentworth proved to be a temporary location for both Jones families. Like other recent arrivals, they moved frequently, always looking for something better or more economical. By the end of 1930 the two families had moved several miles north to Aldine Square, a neighborhood in the heart of the black belt, 37th and Vincennes. Ten years earlier, the two- and three-story houses here with their handsome stone fronts and decorative trim had been owned by prosperous whites, businessmen, doctors, and lawyers and their families. Now they were almost all occupied by the black families streaming into the city. Absentee white landlords who had moved to other parts of Chicago or out of the city entirely had divided many of the homes into apartments, and three or four families might be living where only one had before.

The Aldine Square apartment, with its larger rooms, was a step up. Neither family had a phone, but there was one in the building that could be used for a nickel a call; once a month the children could watch the coins cascading out of the machine into a bucket when the man from the phone company came out to empty the box.

The two Jones families were certainly not well off, but they took pride in their ability to keep up their home and to make sure the children had what they needed. If one family had a moment of distress, the other was there to help out, George recalled. Years later he scoffed at the notion that he and his cousin Ruth lived amid rats and roaches in the city's most downtrodden neighborhood.

For Alice one of the advantages of living at 37th and Vincennes was its proximity to St. Luke Baptist Church a few blocks away. Her devotion to religion had not abated in the move to Chicago. It most likely intensified during turbulent periods with Ollie, when there were intermittent estrangements and reconciliations between them. After one of the latter, their son, Harold Kirkland, was born in 1936. Two more daughters would arrive before Ollie and Alice went their separate ways for good, Clarissa in 1939, when the family had moved to an apartment at 28th and Indiana, and Estrellita in 1944. Alice spread religion to nephew George, too, making time to teach him his first Easter verse when he turned six.

ALTHOUGH THERE WERE MORE than 130 Baptist churches in Chicago's black community, St. Luke, established in 1917, was among the better known and largest with a tradition of hiring well-educated, well-known pastors to lead its congregation. In 1938, the Reverend S. A. Grayson was called to the pulpit. The son of a pastor, the junior Grayson had already made a name for himself as a striking orator with an easy command of the ministry at Mount Olive Baptist Church in Columbus, Ohio. He flavored his services with such topics as "Christ Our Life" and "Bystanders and Standbys at the Cross." His old congregation thought enough of him that he was invited back to install his replacement. His new parishioners, equally pleased, celebrated his one-year anniversary with a festive dinner and his third with a week's worth of pastoral and music programs. He and his wife had three sons, and Robert, the middle one, known as Bobby, was a year younger than Ruth.

At an established church like St. Luke there could be as many as three or four different choirs: the senior choir, which sang hymns and anthems, the often elaborate presentations that set Bible verses to music; the young people's choir, for the junior members of the congregation; and the gospel choir. The latter was a relatively recent addition and reflected the growing popularity of a new kind of church music that was more visceral than the usual church fare. It was plainly emotional, a dialogue between singer and his or her God. It had rhythm, and it had a beat, the feel of blues but in the service of sacred themes. The chief practitioner of this new hybrid was Thomas A. Dorsey. In more youthful days, when he was known as "Georgia Tom," he played the piano for the great blues innovator Ma Rainey and wrote entertaining blues songs spiced with double entendres, even though his childhood had been steeped in religion. Dorsey's father was a preacher, his mother a church organist and a Sunday school teacher.

In 1921 Dorsey broke from his blues career after a spiritual awakening at the National Baptist Convention. His conversion proved short-lived, however, and he returned to a secular career with the Whispering Syncopations. By 1928 Dorsey felt the pull of the church again, and this time his conversion held. Two years earlier he had tried his hand at a gospel song, "If You See My Savior, Tell Him That You Saw Me," but it took until 1930 before the song caught on. By that time he was writing one choir song after another—"songs of hope and faith," in his words—and those with an optimistic bent became popular as an antidote to hard economic times.

"I wrote to give them something to lift them out of that Depression," Dorsey recalled years later. "They could sing at church but the singing had no life, no spirit. The preacher would preach till his collar would melt down around his neck, but there wouldn't be no money in the oblations."

Dorsey's music caught on after he joined forces with Sallie Martin, a singer who was a better businesswoman than musician. "She can't sing a lick, but she can get over anywhere in the world,"

Dorsey observed, because she understood the power of the music and its message. "All right, ushers," she might say during a service, "clear the one-way street for Jesus." Sallie knew there was money to be made if Dorsey could get his compositions out to churches, who in turn could train their choirs to sing them. Before long ads for "All Gospel Songs" started appearing in newspapers serving black communities across the country listing such Dorsey titles as "Peace Is Wonderful" and "When the Last Mile Is Finished" for 10 cents a copy. Readers were advised to send their orders and cash to Dorsey's office on Oakwood Boulevard, one of the main thoroughfares on the South Side. In 1932 a gathering of all the choirs using Dorsey's music filled one of Chicago's largest churches. Five years later Dorsey and his own gospel choir were broadcasting locally over WCFL.

The St. Luke choir was as adept as any in singing Dorsey's music, and combined with dynamic ministers and innovative programs every week, church worship evolved into a kind of spiritual theater. Rev. Grayson encouraged such special events as Mother's Day pageants, "Jesus Light of the World," a candlelight service with all the congregants participating, and gospel rallies that drew choirs and ministers from other Chicago churches.

The musical life at St. Luke had become a source of financial as well as spiritual sustenance for Alice. Given her experience at Elizabeth Baptist in Tuscaloosa, she could make a little money helping organize the programs in her new church. And in a community with so many other churches, Alice could also lend her talents to other congregations, whether Baptist or not. Greater Walters AME Zion was one such place, where Alice became director of the gospel choir. The *Defender* announced that she "triumphed" in her first solo recital there May 31, 1938.

Alice's passion for music meant that music was all around her daughter all of the time. It didn't take long for Alice and Ollie to realize that Ruth had musical ability, both singing and at the piano. She could master anything she heard, from hymns to Haydn, and her cousin George sometimes walked her to her weekly piano lessons just a few blocks away at the pastor's house.

When Alice turned her attention to the gospel choir at St. Luke, she recruited her sister-in-law Lela and added daughter Ruth as soon as she was old enough. The minute Ruth learned the songs she liked to teach them to younger children. She got a special kick out of teaching the neighborhood kids she called "my little cousins" who had recently moved to Chicago. They were the daughters of James Doss, her parents' good friend from Tuscaloosa, and the first song Ruth taught the girls was a duet, "Oh, We're Heavenly Father's Children."

THOUGH THERE WERE DOZENS and dozens of choirs around Chicago and hundreds of young people who sang in the weekend gospel get-togethers, Ruth stood out right away. Perhaps it was an intuitive feel for the words that allowed her to phrase passages with a maturity beyond her years and her experience. Maybe it was the pure quality of the sound she produced. Whatever it was she was making a name for herself around the city though still a teenager. On April 28, 1940, Ruth gave a recital at St. Luke with her mother. The program almost surely included "Precious Lord Take My Hand," Dorsey's most popular song and already a standard, "He Knows How Much We Can Bear," "Just a Closer Walk with Thee," "He'll Understand and Say Well Done," and one of Alice's favorites, "Christ Is All." Ruth and her mother repeated the program two and a half weeks later at the First Church of Divine Science.

When it ran an advance on the recitals, the *Defender* noted in a respectful caption under Ruth's picture—smiling and wearing her choir robe—that "Miss Jones, although only 15 years old, is well known among the gospel singers of Chicago."

Ruth's ascension as a gospel singer coincided with an important change in Sallie Martin's life. Successful as her relationship with Dorsey had been, there were personality clashes between Sallie and some of his singers, and it spilled over to her dealings with Dorsey. Though the two had given a recital together at the Morningstar Baptist Church in the fall of 1939 and Sallie had helped organize an elaborate fortieth birthday celebration for Dorsey at Pilgrim Baptist, disagreements came to a head early in 1940, and Sallie walked out, determined to go it alone.

Sallie had already done a number of recitals around Chicago and knew Alice and her talented daughter through the gospel circle. Sallie also knew that Ruth played the piano for one or another of the St. Luke choirs and sometimes for her mother when Alice sang in recital. Though Ruth had taken formal piano lessons with their emphasis on classical fare, what she loved even more was the way Roberta Martin, another Chicago gospel singer, accompanied her singers with a deft array of chords that fit just so with the melody. There didn't need to be much, but when it was right, you couldn't miss the majesty of it all. Ruth had gotten a firsthand look at Roberta Martin's talents when at fourteen she attended a gospel choir convention in Brooklyn.

When Sallie needed an accompanist for her own solo performances, she occasionally used Ruth. Sallie also tapped her sometime in 1940 when she put together the first group of women who eventually became known as the Sallie Martin Singers. Little of their initial itinerary is known, but a photograph survives from 1940 with Sallie and three other singers, Ruth, Necie Morris, and Sarah Daniels, dressed in choir robes as they posed for a picture at a Virginia revival.

They also went further south to Atlanta, to perform at the Greater Mount Calvary Baptist Church, where the Reverend Dr. B. J. Johnson, Dorsey's brother-in-law, presided. Dorsey and his choir had come for a performance not long before the Martin Singers arrived, and he had packed the church. A smaller crowd showed up for the Martin quartet, and Sallie let Rev. Johnson know how unhappy she was with the turnout.

Rev. Johnson's daughter, Lena, loved these performances, and with a father and a famous uncle in the church, she had seen the best of the gospel choirs, who regularly made stops in Atlanta. She admitted being partial to "Uncle Ted," as the family called Dorsey, but she liked the Sallie Martin Singers, too. Ruth was not much older than she was, and when the group was onstage, she paid special attention to her. "Ruth could sing," Lena recalled years later. "But I don't think she liked the robe. She was in the group but not of it."

The Martin Singers also traveled to New Jersey to perform at a weeklong gathering in Newark at the Church of God and Christ. Although it was the custom for the singers to stay together with one parishioner, Ruth spent a couple of nights at the home of Ann Littles, who was two years younger and was the great-granddaughter of the church's founder, Cora Hayes. While Ann was one of the stars in the Sunday school, winning many a Bible contest, she couldn't sing a note, which made her all the more admiring of her new friend. Ruth confided to Ann that she was determined to be a singer, and a lead singer at that.

"I WANNA BE A SHOWGIRL," Ruth told her mother more than once. And Sallie Martin could see that her young protégée was drawn more to the secular than the sacred. "Shoot, she'd catch the eye of some man and she'd be out the church before the minister finished off the doxology," Sallie told Anthony Heilbut in his seminal *The Gospel Sound: Good News and Bad Times.*

The chance to expand her horizons came when Ruth, like other young teenagers in the neighborhood, went from grammar school to Wendell Phillips High, a handsome three-story brick building with architectural detail that suggested a Greek temple. The school's namesake had been an abolitionist before and during the Civil War. Phillips was all white when it opened in 1905. Reflecting Chicago's evolving demography, it was now all black, and by 1939 it had the city's first black high school principal, Maudelle B. Bousfield, who had also broken the color bar when she was named principal at Douglas Grammar School.

The atmosphere of a church was welcoming and familial, congregants united in the central purpose of worship. A public high school was a different arena, which highlighted rather than obscured the various social strata—athletics, academics, and the piquant fact of skin color. It was no secret that those who were "light, bright but not quite white" had the most opportunity to be leaders, heading student government, being cheerleaders, setting the social pace. There were constant reminders that this was so. The *Defender* carried weekly ads for hair-straightening products and Nadinola Bleaching Cream, the latter promising that with regular applications the user could "enjoy lighter, smoother, softer skin!" The paper's society pages favored pictures of debutantes with light skin and softly curling hair just like the white women were wearing. An oft-told joke, barbed and rueful, was that the women and men who made it into the *Defender* had passed the "blue vein" test: skin so light that a blue vein could be seen through the surface. For teenagers in high school a special talent like the ability to throw a football or toss a basketball through a hoop or the confidence that comes from superior academic achievement could overcome the perceived stigma of dark skin and tight curly hair, which was a description that fit the teenage Ruth.

Some classmates remembered her as "plain-looking." Others were less generous. "She didn't have nothin' glamorous happening," said Charles Walton, a year behind her. "The cats wanted to get a fair-skinned girlfriend. The girls liked to get fair-skinned boyfriends with slick hair."

If this hierarchy of skin color caused private hurt, in public Ruth was all bravado. "She could out-cuss most people," recalled Melvin Gaynor, two classes ahead of her. And Vera Hamb, a high school chum, described Ruth as "already stormy" when they met. "She was wild . . . boy crazy."

Ruth got in plenty of tussles, too, and later joked that "they used to send for my mother so often they thought she was a student." Some of the pretty, light-skinned girls pointedly kept their distance. Hamb did not: "I was fair-skinned, but she was my friend." The two regularly walked to school together because they lived just a block apart, and Hamb enjoyed listening to Ruth talk about her hopes and plans for a life in music. It was not the gospel music that already had put her on the pages of the *Defender*, however, but the music that was all around her outside the church.

It was no exaggeration to say that the neighborhoods within a mile of 28th and Indiana, where the Jones family now lived, throbbed with nightlife. At the Platinum Lounge longtime local favorite Jimmie Noone and his band backed an assortment of singers including a young Joe Williams. At Eugene's 33 Club blues singer Rosetta Howard held forth. The Manchester Grill hosted singer Lil Green, who later gained fame with "In the Dark." A few blocks south, at the Pioneer Lounge, Tommy Powell and his Hi-De-Ho-Boys were featured along with regular appearances by the Cats and the Fiddle, a popular young quartet with a national following. Enthralled by the sounds they heard spilling out of the clubs, teenagers huddled in the alleys behind the buildings so they could listen a bit longer. They might even see famous musicians—at least famous to them—out back having a cigarette. That made the adventure all the more alluring.

Then there was radio, a medium that had its racial distinctions in programming but not in audience. In the privacy of one's home, it was at once a matter of choice and an opportunity to cross racial barriers, though in this moment, because of the few black-oriented programs, it was black listeners who most often tuned into a white world and not vice versa.

Although Alice could be strict, she allowed Ruth and later her other children to be exposed to a variety of things. "She didn't mind us listening. She was a music lover," Clarissa remembered. "She just didn't want us to participate" in music not made in—or for—the church.

On the South Side, the radio was as essential as a refrigerator or a stove. Jack L. Cooper, the first prominent black disc jockey, had made it so. Broadcasting over WSBC with a diction and intonation devoid of dialect, he started his on-air rise in November 1929 with the *All-Negro Hour,* which featured short comedy routines and up-beat musical numbers. By the mid-1930s that one hour had evolved into many hours of programming that included religious music and church services on Sunday mornings and evenings with such gospel disc jockey shows as *Song of Zion.* During the summer there were sports programs that featured interviews with black sports heroes.

On weekdays music dominated, a blend of the established black and white swing bands and vocalists whose tunes were available on record from Cooper's suppliers. *Search for Missing Persons,* a popular weekly program launched with the cooperation of the Chicago police, helped more than twenty thousand blacks reunite with family members during the great migration from the South. It was no surprise that by the late 1930s, half the homes in black Chicago were tuned in to Cooper's program.

At other points on the radio dial, WCFL, for example, Ruth could hear Chick Webb's orchestra. On WBBM there was Benny Goodman, on WMAQ, the other T. Dorsey, Tommy, the white trombone player and bandleader. Fletcher Henderson came over the airwaves on WENR, Cab Calloway on WIND. This was the big band era, and these groups invariably featured vocalists, male and female, performing ballads, blues, and swing numbers. Chick Webb was atop the charts with Ella Fitzgerald singing "A-Tisket A-Tasket." And it was probably on radio that Ruth first heard the singer who most intrigued her, Billie Holiday, singing with Count Basie and his band in 1937 and with Artie Shaw for a time in 1938 in those broadcasts from the Hotel Lincoln in New York.

One could understand the special attraction to Holiday's music. It wasn't that far from the underlying spirit of Thomas Dorsey. The subject matter might be secular, but the goal was the same: to put across a feeling—and you didn't have to wear a robe. It is easy to picture the teenage Ruth at home, listening to Holiday and singing along with the band as though she, too, were onstage.

"Ruth could do Billie better than Billie," said classmate James Duke Davis. "She would swing the whole time." Yvonne Buckner wasn't Ruth's closest friend, but she knew that music was her salvation at Phillips. "Ruth was not pretty as we thought of pretty at the time. But she was talented. All she had to do was sing."

IN OCTOBER 1940, two months after her sixteenth birthday, Ruth obtained a Social Security card so she could work at a nightclub, not as a singer but as a waitress. She got a job at Dave's Cafe at 343 East Garfield. "I loved my parents, but I itched to get away from the house where everything was geared to the church and old fashion strictness," Ruth told an interviewer years later, explaining how eager she was to be on her own.

Dave's was one of the better-known nightspots on the South Side. As a "black and tan"—the slang for nightspots with black entertainment but an integrated audience—Dave's featured a revue format, often with elaborate productions. In the late 1930s the club had changed hands and changed names, to Swingland, but early in 1940 it had fallen on hard times. A relative of the original owner took it over, changed the name back to Dave's, refurbished the place with a $2,000 kitchen, and took out regular ads in the *Defender* touting its popularity and its policy of no cover charge and no drink minimum.

On her off nights Ruth may have sung with trumpeter Walter Fuller's band at the Grand Terrace, which had reopened the previous September after a hiatus. Years later Fuller spoke about Ruth being part of the group he had assembled for a few months in 1940, but she didn't merit any notice in ads the Grand Terrace took out in the *Defender* nor in stories about Fuller's run.

Sometime in these months of 1940, however, Ruth won an amateur contest at the Regal Theater, located at 47th and South Park and the premier entertainment spot in black Chicago. Grand and or-nate in Spanish baroque style, it hosted such stars as Duke Ellington, Louis Armstrong, and Ella Fitzgerald. In the spring of 1938, the theater managers decided to follow the practice of some of the smaller South Side clubs and host a weekly amateur hour. They recruited the nearby South Center department store, the most popular in black Chicago, to help sponsor the program. Unlike the club shows, however, the Regal amateur hour would be broadcast over WIND, from 8:30 to 9:30 P.M. every Wednesday, complete with a master of ceremonies and the house orchestra led by Tiny Parham.

Competition was open to anyone; entry blanks could be picked up at the theater lobby or at the South Center store. Hopefuls would audition and then be notified whether they were selected to perform. Two months after the first show the *Defender* proclaimed the idea a success. "They are actually finding obscure talent and starting them on their way to success," the paper said. By then seven hundred individuals had auditioned. Seventy-four were presented, covering a mix of acts from the conventional—singing, dancing, instrumentals by trios and quartets—to the unusual. (One young man did an impression of how a chicken would sing "The One Rose.") Heeding the cheers from the audience, the theater put together a late August evening built around all the winners, "New Radio Stars of 1938."

Ruth wanted to be on one of those early shows and recalled in a 1957 interview that she was denied the opportunity. She tried again when she was sixteen—by then the shows ran from 8:00 to 9:00 P.M. and had switched to WCFL—and this time, she not only got a slot but won her contest. She performed "I Can't Face the Music," a song in the repertoire of her favorite, Billie Holiday. That night Ruth was competing against singers from nearby rival DuSable High School, and it was a sweet moment for her and for Phillips High when she won. Vera Hamb was among those in the audience, and recalled years later how happy she was that her mother had let her go to cheer on her friend.

Winning the Regal contest is probably what propelled Ruth into her first official nongospel singing job. She was hired to be in a revue that opened in February 1941 at Dave's Cafe. This surely signaled the end of her association with Martin after barely a year. The worlds of gospel and secular music were distinct. Practitioners of the former had disdain—even disapproval—for the latter. One either sang for the church or for a paying audience in clubs or theaters—

even Thomas Dorsey. (When Sarah Vaughan made a recording of "The Lord's Prayer," some in the church community accused her of being sacrilegious.) Ruth's last church-related performance was probably March 30, 1941, at Allen Temple AME, where she performed with her mother on a program that featured some of the city's best-known gospel choirs.

On February 22, 1941, Dave's used its regular ad in the *Defender* to highlight the latest act, "direct from New York—a spectacular and completely new Harlem Revue." The rest of the ad listed the names of the performers. Sixth on the roster was Ruth Jones, though her role was not specified. (Management was apparently unconcerned that not *all* of the revue members were from New York.) Ruth kept the job through the middle of April when Dave's installed a new show starring Coleman Hawkins and his orchestra and featuring the comedian Dusty Fletcher.

IN THE SUMMER of 1941 Alice and Ollie and their children moved again. The city of Chicago had just opened an impressive new housing project, the Ida B. Wells Homes, which could accommodate sixteen hundred families—roughly seven thousand individuals who would be living in more than eight hundred apartments and a nearly equal number of row houses. The project, which, coincidentally, was on some of the land that had been Aldine Square, was named for one of the earliest civil rights advocates, a woman born into slavery in Mississippi who devoted her adult life to battling discrimination. The Joneses, which now included Ruth's much younger siblings Harold and Clarissa, qualified for a four-and-a-half-room, two-story row house after going through a laborious application process that reflected a singular fact: public housing in this moment was a clear step up from the kind of rentals that most black families could find. To qualify, a family had to consent to an office interview by a social worker, employment verification, checks for any police record, and a home visit by a Housing Authority investigator. The Joneses' rent, according to the agency formula, was $21 a month. Whatever Alice and Ollie were earning, it could not exceed $88 a month, which was the maximum the Housing Authority set for a family of five.

The row house at 661 East 37th Street had a kitchen, living

room, and utility room on the first floor and two bedrooms on the second floor. One was for Alice and Ollie—when he was around. The other was for the children; Harold had a single bed, Ruth and Clarissa shared a double bed. Ruth listed 37th Street as her address when she obtained a second Social Security card in July 1941. When the family finally got a private telephone, it was listed in Alice's name, no doubt a sign of who was in charge.

Making a life in music was Ruth's consuming passion. So much so that to her mother's chagrin, she dropped out of Phillips. What she wanted to learn wasn't going to be taught in the classroom. At the same time, she met a young man six years older than she, John Young. He "talked my language," Ruth explained, "and said he'd help me get into show business. I figured this was my opportunity."

Whether it was romance or convenience—perhaps some combination of the two—John and Ruth decided to get married. They got their license on June 24, 1942. Apparently birth certificates were not required to verify ages. Ruth was listed as eighteen, though her eighteenth birthday was two months away.

The couple was married a month later by Rev. Grayson of St. Luke Baptist. The bride wore a long white dress with a train that trailed down from a flowered headpiece. The groom wore a formal cutaway jacket with wide satin lapels and tuxedo pants. St. Luke parishioners and their children were invited. Six-year-old Belle Green was the flower girl.

One of the wedding photographs, taken in front of the Jones family's home on 37th Street, is both revealing and poignant in its innocence. The couple is standing next to each other but not quite touching. Ruth's arms are folded in front of her, John's are behind his back. Each of them is strikingly aloof from the other.

3.

Is There Anyone Finer?

While being Mrs. John Young might have changed the way friends and family looked at Ruth, this new status did nothing to change her ambition. She wanted to be out every night to find work in the clubs and hoped to get noticed, even if she was unbilled and played only for tips. From his promises of help, Ruth assumed John shared her dream, but he wanted a stay-at-home wife. The chilly look of their wedding picture was prescient. When John went into the army three months after their wedding, the marriage was over. "He didn't think I should be an entertainer, and this is what I wanted," Ruth recalled with matter-of-factness. "I knew we were through, and I guess he did, too."

Determined to be "a showgirl," Ruth now set her sights on something grander than the South Side venues: Randolph Street, forty blocks north and the heart of nightlife for white Chicago. By 1942 the two blocks of Randolph from State Street running west to Clark were full of clubs, restaurants, showrooms, and movie theaters lit up with neon signs that glittered into the predawn dark of a new day. Film enthusiasts talked about the Randolph Rialto; music writers, noting the jazz venues, compared Randolph to New York City's legendary 52nd Street. The area was anchored on the east by the Chicago Theater and the Capitol Lounge, a prominent jazz spot, right next to it. Across the street was the State-Lake Theater. Next door was Elmer's, a cocktail lounge known for its jazz pianists. Down the block at Randolph and Dearborn two movie houses faced each other, the imposing Oriental on one side of the street and the equally grand United Artists Theater on the other. The anchor of the next corner, Randolph and Clark, was the Sherman Hotel. The Panther Room, its well-known nightclub, drew some of the biggest names: Benny Goodman, Duke Ellington, Cab Calloway, Glenn Miller, Jimmy Dorsey, Harry James, Fats Waller.

If this area was Chicago's White Way, the description referred more to the audience than the entertainment. Like the Panther Room the other venues featured the most acclaimed black performers. But there were precious few black patrons to hear them; even if they could afford it, they were given a cold shoulder.

That black musicians would play Randolph Street highlighted the trade-offs they had to make day after day. Playing here was a mark of achievement in status and pay, but the performers' lives were circumscribed by the racial divide. Chicago was as segregated as any southern city, where separation of the races was written into law, and "separate but equal" was a concept with no content. Separate was not equal in Atlanta or Memphis or Chicago in schools, housing, jobs, grocery stores, and all the other activities that made up daily life. Benny Goodman, Harry James, and Glenn Miller could stay at the Sherman when they finished up at the Panther Room. Duke Ellington and Cab Calloway found their hotel rooms on the South Side. Unappealing, even demeaning as these things were, the black artists found their own ways to make peace with conditions beyond their control. What they could control—the music and the performance—was paramount. Race mattered, but the music mattered even more. The equation was understood—perhaps it was closer to a private bargain—and accepted.

Playing at the Garrick Building on Randolph was a case in point. Joe Sherman, a wily, irascible ex-boxer, operated two clubs there, the Downbeat Room, which was belowground and the larger of the two, and the Stagebar, which was at street level. Some jazz fans considered Sherman a cartoonish figure, striding up and down the street to corral customers with little appreciation for the music inside. They loved to tell the story that when he first hired Billie Holiday, he thought she was a man.

Sherman booked more black talent than white, but he never hid the fact that he wanted only whites in the audience. He didn't want the black musicians fraternizing with them either. When some of the musicians complained, their union local called Sherman in to explain himself. He admitted that he tried to discourage blacks from coming in by seating them in the back. If they didn't complain, he charged them the same drink prices as he charged white customers. But if they insisted on a better seat, he put an X on the back of their drink tickets, and they were charged more than the usual price. He hoped they wouldn't come back. Sherman wasn't prejudiced, he insisted. He was only trying to stay in business, and he argued that he simply could not afford to cater to a mixed clientele.

In late September 1942 Sherman got into more trouble with the union after a scrap with Mel Draper, the drummer in Jimmie Noone's trio. Draper was walking out after the night's performance, his arms full of equipment, when he said Sherman threw a punch at him. Sherman claimed self-defense, but the drummer said he was just following Sherman's directive that "if you don't like the way I treat you, you can get out," which Draper said was exactly what he was doing.

The union retaliated by ordering all its members to refuse to play the Garrick. Billie Holiday had just opened at the Downbeat Room for an extended engagement, and though she was not covered by the union order, she walked out of a subsequent performance in sympathy with Draper and his bandmates. The white musicians who were asked to fill in also refused to play when they learned of the incident, an unusual show of solidarity in a city that segregated its musicians unions. Sherman eventually paid the $700 the club owed the trio and another $50 to cover Draper's medical bills.

Just as Holiday was opening at the Garrick, Ruth's luck changed. She was hired to play the piano at the Three Deuces, a small club not quite in the Randolph Street orbit but within striking distance at Wabash and Van Buren. Though it was roughly a half-mile southeast of the entertainment hub, the Three Deuces still rated attention from the city's music literati, white and black. *Down Beat,* Chicago's earnest jazz magazine staffed by white men and a few women who all loved the music, noted who was coming and going. So did the *Defender*. In one issue *Down Beat* even chastised the club for featuring second-rate entertainment, if that: "It's a shame to see such acts where good ones used to play."

Martha Davis was one of the many talented young piano players in the city, and she had befriended Ruth, even giving her a dress for her first publicity shot. Davis invited Ruth to one of Holiday's shows at the Downbeat Room sometime in November. The Cats and the Fiddle were playing in the smaller Stagebar. Though Ruth knew of them from their South Side dates and radio shows, Davis probably knew them personally from working the clubs where she was already making a name for herself. Fats Waller had been impressed enough to give her a couple of piano lessons.

Perhaps it was Davis who urged Sherman to let Ruth sing, knowing that he was always looking for new acts. He sometimes employed five different groups to alternate in the two showrooms. Or maybe Ruth stepped forward herself during a moment of introduction. However it happened that night, Ruth sang the Jimmy Dorsey hit "I Understand" with the Cats and the Fiddle, and detractors aside, Sherman showed that he had an ear when it counted. He hired her right away at $50 a week and made sure *Down Beat* knew that he was "knocked out over a singing find" who would work the Stagebar with the Cats.

Ruth was on her way.

AS RUTH WAS SETTLING into the Garrick, Lionel Hampton and his sixteen-piece band were getting ready for a weeklong stay at the Regal that would include a gala Christmas and New Year's performance with Billie Holiday. It was a heady time for a group that was barely two years old and was riding a wave of ecstatic reviews and sold-out houses. The band had recently made its first recording for Decca.

"Hamp," as he was universally known, was a consummate showman, a fireplug of energy who inspired his bandmates and thrilled his audiences. "Let it jump, but keep it mellow," he liked to say. Hampton had started out as a drummer for Louis Armstrong. In 1930, when he was just twenty-two, Armstrong asked him to ex-

periment on the vibraharp, a relatively new instrument that resembled a xylophone but was electrified to give it more kick. Hampton
never looked back, though he enjoyed taking a turn on the drums or
piano as the spirit moved him.

In 1936 Hampton followed pianist Teddy Wilson into Benny
Goodman's group, making a trio a quartet. It was the first integrated
jazz combo—at once a wonderful and sobering experience, the
chance to make great music with great exposure but with the constant reminder of racial prejudice. "I don't know how many times
Teddy and I were mistaken for servants—Mr. Goodman's valet or
the water boy for the Benny Goodman orchestra," Hampton recalled in his autobiography, *Hamp*. He praised Goodman for trying to
protect his musicians as best he could, insisting that they be treated
like their white colleagues. On a cross-country trip from Los Angeles
to Atlantic City—Hampton's first ever plane ride—he composed
"Flying Home," the up-tempo instrumental that became his signature song and an audience favorite.

By the late summer of 1940 Hampton was ready to form his
own band, encouraged by his wife, Gladys, who was as much partner as mate. She found the musicians, negotiated for instruments,
picked the uniforms, got the train tickets, secured hotel rooms, handled the money, and took care of Hampton off the bandstand. It was
a partnership that endured even in the early days when, Hampton
(something of a philanderer) confessed, "I was a bad boy."

The band had introduced itself to Chicago in February 1941
when they came for what was supposed to be a six-week stay at the
Grand Terrace. On opening night more than a thousand customers
were turned away, and the six weeks turned into a four-month
engagement. In the fall, Hampton and band returned to Chicago,
this time to play the Panther Room. Different venue, different
audience—same response. They were a hit. "From seven-thirty until
nine, Hamp played music soft but with jump. From nine on they
tore it up," said *Down Beat*, which dubbed Hampton "the jumping
jack vibe king."

Hampton was using singers sporadically, though he had asked
Billie Holiday to sing with him full-time. She declined because she
wanted to be on her own but agreed to do occasional guest appearances. By the end of 1941 Hampton had hired a Chicago man, Rubel

Blakey, a singer well-known on the city's club circuit. Periodically Hampton brought in women singers, too, and when he got to the Regal for the December 1942 run, Lois Anita was on the bill with Blakey even though Holiday was set to do another guest spot. Joe Glaser, who owned Associated Booking Corporation and handled Hampton's schedule, had been after the bandleader to hire a regular "girl singer," as Hampton put it. Finally Hampton was giving the idea serious consideration.

In December 1942 he and Ruth were in the same city but they were playing in different worlds. Hampton was on a grand theater stage, Ruth in the second-tier showroom of a small club, albeit on Randolph Street. One was a household name, the other an un-known, not even billed when she sang, not sure what would follow when the Garrick job was over. But if timing is everything, Ruth's was impeccable. She was ready to be noticed when Hampton was looking.

Many people take credit for the match: Joe Glaser, the comedian Slappy White, and Hampton band member Snooky Young all claim to have suggested that Hampton go to the Garrick to hear Ruth sing. Hampton remembered—erroneously—that Ruth was the wash-room attendant who came out into the club every chance she could to sing with whatever band was playing. In a 1952 interview Ruth herself recalled that Joe Sherman brought Joe Glaser to hear her, and that the next night Glaser returned with Hampton.

Whatever the impetus, one night in late December, after his show at the Regal, Hampton went the fifty blocks north to the Gar-rick. On the small stage, Ruth was finishing her set with the Cats and the Fiddle. She had made good use of her time at the Stagebar, going downstairs every chance she could to watch Holiday in the Downbeat Room. With her gospel background, Ruth already had her own sound, but there was much to be learned about phrasing and emphasis and the intangibles that make a performance memo-rable. At some point Hampton asked her to sing "Sweet Georgia Brown."

It would have been understandable to be nervous. The stakes couldn't be any higher. But Ruth didn't lack confidence. Although she had just turned eighteen, she had been singing in front of other people since she was ten and began giving solo recitals at fifteen.

Now was the time to draw on that experience. This was her moment. By the time she got to "It's been said she knocks 'em dead when she lands in town," Ruth had done just that. Hampton was sold.

Even in such an informal audition he appreciated her talent. "I knew she was the girl I was looking for," Hampton said. He liked her "gutty style." It wasn't that she was brassy. Her voice was too crisp and clear for that. But she sang with conviction, direct yet with feeling. Hampton was certain she could be heard "even with my blazing band in the background."

Hampton invited Ruth to be part of the year-end show at the Regal, which was an hours-long gala each night packaging Hampton's music with two comedy acts, the Two Zephyrs and Butterbeans and Suzy, one of the most popular duos on the circuit. Billie Holiday was a guest star. Patrons who wanted to see the weekly movie were treated to *Eyes in the Night* starring Edward Arnold, Ann Harding, and Donna Reed along with a newsreel of *All-American Negro News*.

There was one more matter. If she was going to sing with a big band, and a hot one at that, the plain and pedestrian "Ruth Jones" would not do. Hampton and Glaser claim credit for giving Ruth a new name. But verifiable chronology suggests it was Joe Sherman who came up with "Dinah Washington." "You ought to have something that rolls off people's tongues, like rich liquor," he explained, and to him "Dinah Washington" fit the bill.

Why "Dinah"? Perhaps it came to mind in tribute to Ethel Waters, a heroine in the black community: successful singer, success in movies and on Broadway. A decade earlier she had had a hit with the single "Dinah." More recently, Dinah Shore, the popular white singer, had just signed a movie deal and was in the news. So "Dinah" would strike a chord with blacks and whites.

Why "Washington"? Like Lincoln and Roosevelt, it was the name of a president, thus a name of distinction and not unusual to find in either the white or black community. Together the two words had rhythm, indeed the same rhythm as the names of two current stars, Billie Holiday and Ella Fitzgerald: two-syllable first name, three-syllable last. "Dinah Washington" it would be. Trumpeter Red Allen, who was playing at the Downbeat Room, remembered introducing the young singer, "burlesque style as 'Dynamite Washington.' "

Two years earlier Ruth had left the Regal stage as an amateur, walking off with the few silver dollars the winner took home. Now she was back as Dinah Washington, a professional determined to make the most of it. "She walked out on that stage like she owned it," Hampton recalled.

A writer for *Down Beat* happened to take in the show. The next issue included a short article on page four about the performance. "Dinah Washington Has South Side Debut," said the headline. The story said the audience "was greeted with a surprise introduction when Dinah Washington previewed at the Regal for her first South Side appearance." "Dianah [sic], currently at the Stagebar in the Loop, showed remarkable ability on all fronts." Though only one paragraph, the story gave the moment official status, committing to the permanent record the creation of Dinah Washington from the raw material of eighteen-year-old Ruth Jones.

After the show Hampton asked Dinah to go on the road with him. She didn't hesitate a moment to say yes. And there was more good news: she would get a raise, to $75 a week.

4.

The "Find" of the Year

January–July 1943

Alice had not been happy when her daughter moved away from gospel music. She was even more unhappy when she dropped out of school to work in Chicago clubs. And when Dinah announced she was going to sing with Lionel Hampton, Alice knew she couldn't stop her even if she wanted to. Dinah had already moved out when she married John Young. On top of that Alice had plenty to handle in her own life: two young children to take care of, six-year-old Harold and Clarissa, who had just turned three, and an unreliable if genial husband.

Though mother and daughter had a shared passion for music, they took divergent paths to express it. This moment crystallized the difference: Alice was increasingly busy as a church recitalist—a performance at Mount Joy Baptist was her most recent—just as Dinah embarked on her secular career.

Everything was happening so fast for Dinah, she barely had time to take care of a few basic details. She didn't have suitable luggage so she bought suitcases on credit after two friends signed for her. Given the turn of events, she knew she could pay off the debt.

Hampton had had a terrific week at the Regal. He and the band broke the attendance record—more than twenty thousand jammed the theater over the seven days, dozens of them standing along the walls each night because they couldn't find seats.

Finished in Chicago, the group headed to Detroit for a week-long stay at the Paradise Theater. After that were dates in Boston, Newark, and a military base in Massachusetts. Dinah was to join them before Hampton and the band headed to New York for an engagement at the fabled Apollo Theater.

While Ruth Jones the gospel singer had traveled in the cocoon of the church, chaperoned by older women keeping an eye on her, Dinah Washington the big band singer was on her own. Earl "Fatha" Hines and his group happened to be in the same city as the Hampton band—most likely Newark, where Hampton played the Laurel Garden—when the bandleader told the musicians he had hired a new singer who would be joining them shortly. "They thought a great big beautiful girl was going to walk out," recalled George Dixon, one of Hines's sidemen, "and when they saw Dinah everybody covered their head up."

If Dinah saw the unkind gestures, it had to have hurt even if she tried to laugh it off. Skin color still mattered, even with talent, and Dinah didn't fit the stereotype of the showgirl. She was short—just over five feet tall—and a bit plump. Her face was oval with almond-shaped eyes that set off high cheekbones. Her eyebrows had a natural arch. Her smile lit up her face. She had beautiful hands with long slender fingers, and she was learning to use them to expressive advantage onstage.

Slappy White, the comedian, was the exception to male musicians who were rude to Dinah. He took her under his wing and consoled her in the lonely moments. "She was a nice girl," he recalled, "just a struggling girl working on the job." He gave her his hotel room on one of those first nights on the road after he found her alone on the band's bus, crying because she didn't have a place to stay. The other band members, seasoned travelers all, had scattered to the rooming houses that took in visiting musicians with no thought of their new young singer. White knew why. "She wasn't the best-looking girl in the world," he said, "so the band boys—wasn't nobody hitting on her. You know because she was just jive—you know, another girl. They were looking for the girl around the stage door."

Joe Wilder, one of Hampton's trumpeters who was not much older than Dinah, hadn't paid much attention to her at first because she was so shy. But they got to know each other on the bus— Dinah's seat was right in front of his. She had trouble getting used to the rhythm of the road, Wilder recalled, and was usually sound asleep when the band stopped for a middle-of-the-night break to get food. No one thought to get her anything in her first few weeks with the band, and she often woke up hungry.

Wilder learned that Dinah liked cheeseburgers, so once he understood the situation, he would buy one for her and save it until she woke up. Dinah appreciated the gesture. "She was always nice to me," Wilder said. Dinah was probably also grateful because he never teased her about her appearance the way some of the other men did.

Dinah got her first official notice when the *New York Amsterdam News* ran a story February 13 about Hampton's current week at the Apollo Theater. She was mentioned as vocalist along with Rubel Blakey. It was hard to believe the whirlwind of the last six months: a new bride in August, separated by October, playing an uptown club by November, at the Regal with Hampton in December. Now, the Apollo at 125th Street in Harlem, the entertainment palace of legend and legends. The audiences were knowledgeable and tough. You bathed in their affection if they liked you. If they didn't, the cat-calls rained down with unembarrassed gusto, especially from the second balcony, known appropriately as "the Buzzard's Roost."

But Dinah was ready. When Hampton called her to the stage for her New York debut, she opened with "The Man I Love." Then she did a few traditional blues tunes. The audience loved her—the thunderous applause told her that. So did the critics. "Foremost among the surprises was the new girl singer with the Lionel Hampton band," said *Metronome,* the New York equivalent of *Down Beat.* "When she finished the blues numbers, she properly brought down the house. She sang much like Billie Holiday, in a languorous style in a relaxed voice and with an authority that is amazing in a girl of nineteen," the review added. In fact Dinah was only eighteen. And if she read the notice, she probably didn't mind that *Metronome* had misspelled her name throughout, calling her "Diana."

Variety liked "her spiffy style and voice," and seemed to like the way she looked, too. "Her fortissimo is socko in a blues speciality that stamps the comely femme as a comer."

By the time the band returned to Newark for another evening at Laurel Garden, word about Hampton's new singer had traveled across the Hudson River. The *Newark Afro-American* promised on its entertainment page February 27 that "the newest sensation in the field of vivacious vocalists" would be part of the Hampton program. In prose that bubbled off the page, the paper said "Delightful Dinah" had a voice full of "sweetness, mirth and pathos that will make her the 'find' of the year."

A Hampton show had a certain pace and format. The band might open with "Lady Be Good," and then move into its swing version of "Nola." "Stompology," "Bouncing at the Beacon," or "As Time Goes By" were usually featured with Hampton taking an extended solo, and of course the audience would demand to hear "Flying Home." Spaced between the numbers would be the comedy routines and the vocals. By the time the band got to Boston the third week in March, Hampton understood that Dinah was no ordinary singer. He shifted her place in the lineup from the nondescript middle to the slot right before his big finish because she was stopping the show every time she performed. "I had to put her next to closing because nobody and no one could follow her," he explained. Hampton believed the audiences were responding to the new way Dinah sang familiar songs, with gospel inflections that showcased an understated passion for the music, powerful but devoid of distracting artifice. He had been correct in his initial assessment that Dinah could be heard over the band, which never had to cut back its robust, propulsive sound when she was onstage.

From Boston, where Joe Williams, another Chicago singer, had joined the revue, Hampton and the band went to Baltimore and then Philadelphia. After Philadelphia was Cleveland, where Dinah got billing in the newspaper as a featured singer in letters only slightly smaller than Hampton's.

Though Hampton had been plenty successful before he added Dinah to the show, the benefits of her presence were evident. The *Amsterdam News* reported in a mid-March dispatch that the band had broken revenue records in the past few dates and had played overlong shows because of the audience demand for encores.

. . .

WHILE GENUINE ABILITY was the prerequisite for a successful singing career, it was not the only element. Image was important, too—how a singer dressed and carried herself onstage. Dinah was a natural talent with an intuitive sense of showmanship. But she hadn't had the opportunity to develop a look. Hampton had plucked her out of the Garrick Stagebar and taken her out on the road without any advance planning. She was "raggedy," he admitted, and it was true that Dinah didn't have fancy dresses and the accessories to go with them. Back in Chicago, she confided to friends, she had had to borrow her mother's nylon stockings every now and then when she was trying to get jobs in the clubs.

By the late spring of 1943, it was time for Dinah to have a new publicity photograph to go along with her new status, and she needed to look the part.

Gladys Hampton probably helped Dinah prepare for the shoot at the studio of celebrity photographer James Kriegsmann. She was taking an interest in the young singer now and had much to offer when it came to matters of image and style. Before marrying Hampton, she had worked as a seamstress for a movie studio in California, and her designs had caught the attention of such stars as Joan Crawford and Marion Davies. She also had a taste for shoes, and because of Hampton's success, which she helped make possible, the means to buy as many pairs as she wanted. Though the two women were built differently, Gladys was able to remake some of her evening dresses for the young singer. Because they had the same size feet, Dinah was also the recipient of shoes that Gladys had already tired of wearing, all of them in good shape.

For the photo shoot, Dinah wore a dress with a light flowered pattern and a full skirt with a slit in the front that could be swept to the side to reveal her legs. Her black high-heeled pumps had a bit of decorative trim on the front. In the studio Kriegsmann sat Dinah on a stool facing left but with her head turned back to the right so she looked out front and center, smiling. The photograph is sharp enough to reveal the careful makeup—mascara and eyebrow pencil—that sets off her eyes. A long strand of beads hangs around her neck. She is wearing a large white flower in her hair in homage to Billie Holiday and her ever-present gardenia.

If the new wardrobe enhanced Dinah's image onstage, it also brought her new attention from the men in the band. Some of the dresses were short, just above the knee, and they showed off Dinah's slender legs. "What was interesting after Gladys went to work, the guys in the band started noticing Dinah's legs and feet," Hampton recalled, "and they nicknamed her 'Legs.' " He thought the good-natured joshing made Dinah feel better about herself. Perhaps so. But such moments were double-edged, reminders of the wounding slights from high school and how far she now was from the church, where "the importance and creative capacity of women" was paramount, as gospel historian Anthony Heilbut put it. That was a matriarchy, but now Dinah was very much in a man's world.

Like other singers, Dinah sat onstage awaiting her turn at the mike. One band member, a superstitious Southerner whose seat was near hers, wasn't so thrilled with the shorter skirts. "Please tell that girl not to cross her legs or I'll have seven years bad luck," he begged no one in particular, unnerved at seeing more of Dinah's legs than he thought proper and provoking chuckles from his more admiring bandmates.

The first week in June the band made a side trip south to Norfolk, Virginia, to perform Saturday night, the 5th, at the Fleet Recreation Park. The show would be broadcast nationally over the Blue Network, a division of NBC, and sponsored by Coca-Cola as part of a series called *The Victory Parade of Spotlight Bands*—shortened for radio listings to *Spotlight Bands*. Hampton was the first black bandleader to get the coveted Saturday evening slot, which ran from 9:30 to 10:00.

A milestone for Hampton, the evening was important for Dinah, too—the chance to be heard over the radio and the chance to reach an audience well beyond the theater seats. Dinah's first number, "Shoo Shoo Baby," a boogie-woogie novelty, began with a minute-long instrumental that featured a Hampton vibe solo. When Dinah came in on the vocal, she was assured and at ease, playful, too, as she sang about a woman "off to the seven seas" for a breather from her boyfriend. The lyrics were secondary to the spirit of the moment, which showcased singer and band in sync, note for note.

"Shoo Shoo Baby" was written by Phil Moore, a black writer-arranger in Los Angeles who may have known Hampton from his days with Benny Goodman. Dinah was among the first to sing the song, but it became a hit nine months later for Ella Mae Morse, a white singer from Texas who recorded for Capitol. The Andrews Sisters also made a version that did well commercially at the same time.

Dinah's second number, "Arkansas," another popular tune, was a much briefer turn at the mike—barely a minute of singing about "the promised land" that was squeezed into an instrumental dominated by the horn section. But Dinah made the most of it with another assured presentation.

The band returned to New York to play six nights downtown on Broadway at Loew's State Theater, a distinctly different location and venue from the Apollo. A Loew's audience, even if having a good time, was generally restrained, not given to shouts and ovations. But Hampton and crew had them on their feet as soon as the band finished a version of "Lady Be Good" that featured a trumpet duet and a three-way sax duel between two tenors and an alto.

Dinah sang "Don't Get Around Much Anymore," taking a slow tempo dictated by pianist Milt Buckner's arrangement, and "I've Heard That Song Before." When he reviewed the concert in *Metronome*, Barry Ulanov lamented the fact that Dinah didn't sing any blues numbers. Nonetheless, he wrote, "she sounded better than all but the top three or four [singers]; her phrasing, her beat, the sheer stentor [sic] of her voice were overpowering."

Even better, the magazine ran her picture—that publicity shot taken by Kriegsmann—in the middle of its "Stage Show Review" page. The caption underneath called her "probably the greatest blues-singing discovery of the year."

Variety's reviewer was much less impressed than Ulanov, finding Dinah a mismatch with the material. "Dinah Washington doesn't measure up," he wrote. "Notably she jives one of the top ballads of the year, 'Heard that Song Before,' to completely distort its lyrical and musical potency, being strictly a shouter."

If Dinah saw the review, it was a good lesson: everybody wouldn't love her all of the time—best to develop thick skin early.

From Loew's the Hampton revue returned to the Apollo for five days and then headed west to Cleveland and on to Chicago. On July 30, they played the Oriental Theater, with Dinah featured as the "blues queen." Yvonne Buckner was one of many teenagers in the audience, dancing in the aisles when Hampton raced into "Flying Home," cheering when her classmate took the stage to sing. She only regretted being too timid to go backstage and say hello after the show.

Eight months earlier Ruth Jones was singing in Joe Sherman's Stagebar. Now she had returned to Randolph Street as the up-and-coming Dinah Washington. By one measure she had traveled only one block east to the Oriental, but the literal distance couldn't begin to describe all that had happened to a young woman who would not be nineteen years old for another three weeks.

5.

I Know How to Do It

The Hampton band was moving nonstop now through the Midwest and East. From Chicago the group went to Pittsburgh for six days at the Stanley Theater and then on to Louisville and the aptly named Post and Paddock. Dinah celebrated her nineteenth birthday somewhere between Kentucky and Pennsylvania as the band headed to Philadelphia to play a week at the Earle Theater. *Variety,* which reviewed one evening, gave Dinah another appreciative notice, calling her "an expert song salesman with an innate sense of rhythm which makes her tunes ear-soothing."

Dinah was beginning to understand the rhythm and routine of these road trips: dates at the main big-city theaters—the Apollo, the Earle, the Royal in Baltimore, and the Howard in Washington, D.C., on the East Coast circuit—packaged with dates in between at clubs in smaller towns until the band reached the midwestern cities to fill their theaters—the Paradise in Detroit, the Regal in Chicago. The goal was to have as little downtime as possible, for the simple reason that no one made any money if the band wasn't performing.

As the only woman in the group full-time, Dinah was in an unusual position, inevitably relegated, whether she wanted to be or not, into one of three roles: the mother, the girlfriend, or one of the guys. Dinah was too young for the first and regarded as too unattractive for the second, so she turned into a pal who traded insults and expletives with band members and joined them in their low-stakes card games to pass the highway time. Separated and on the way to ending her marriage with John Young, Dinah looked for her own romantic interludes on the road just as the men did. Slappy White defended her against the raised eyebrows that reflected a double standard, even among musicians who lived fast lives themselves.

"Shucks, every town we go in they had a different girl," he recalled. "Now Dinah Washington, she's with the band, too. So she required the same thing that the band did. It's all right for musicians to do it, but if a girl do it, why is it wrong? And," he pointedly observed, "she was the hit on the show."

Dinah also was making friends on her own. Toni Thompson was a young Philadelphia woman just a couple of years older than she was. Thompson's sister, Dorothy, was married to Cat Anderson, a trumpeter in Duke Ellington's band, so she was used to being around musicians and often came backstage when major acts came to the city. As soon as she met Dinah, Thompson recalled, "We gravitated to one another." On one visit after a show Thompson was wearing the newest-style shoes—stacked platforms that tied in front like Roman sandals—and Dinah admired them so much, she insisted on taking her friend to the dressing rooms so she could show Gladys Hampton Thompson's shoes. Thompson gave Dinah a standing invitation to stay with her whenever she was in Philadelphia. When Dinah took her up on the offer, she happily cooked for the family and once even stepped in to help Thompson's young children at their elementary school when Thompson couldn't make it because of her work schedule. The two young women were close enough in size that Dinah borrowed her clothes—a favorite was a handsome, flared coat with distinctive buttons down the front. Dinah liked it so much she hated to give it back.

Thompson knew Dinah appreciated having a female friend; it could be trying as the only woman among Hampton's band. When the two of them were together, Dinah was funny and polite. Thompson was sure that Dinah had "picked up the bad language as a defense. Those guys were so nasty."

AFTER ANOTHER STOP in Louisville in September 1943—this time at the Club Madrid—and a return trip in October to the Paradise in Detroit, the band came back in mid-November to New York for the rest of the year. Their first stop was the city's jazz haven, 52nd Street, and one of its storied clubs, the Famous Door, in the middle of the block between Fifth and Sixth Avenues. The original Door had opened in 1935 with room for fifty-five patrons, and sold scotch for 55 cents a shot and beer for 35 cents. In 1938 it moved a few doors west to slightly larger quarters (sixty seats) that did little to alleviate crowding. *The New Yorker* dryly observed that "The Famous Door is one of the smallest and smokiest places on 52nd Street. But, then, it's practically impossible to be a devotee of hot music and fresh air at the same time."

It was an unlikely place for a big band, but Count Basie and his troupe had managed to squeeze everybody on the bandstand when they played there—one of the inducements was newly installed air-conditioning. The music didn't suffer; they were a hit. A few years later the club moved again, this time to larger quarters down the street. And once again, nothing was lost musically in the transition to a bigger room with much less intimacy. Hampton and what the *Amsterdam News* reported was his $3,500 gold-plated vibraharp and his seventeen band members gave the club a spirited reopening. When *Variety* reviewed the show, Dinah was given a kind mention. Frank Sinatra and Billy Eckstine dropped by a few days before Thanksgiving to sing a couple of numbers and pronounced Hampton and crew "the greatest new band to hit Broadway in years."

The group closed out the year as the headlining act at the Apollo's annual Christmas show. The theater had been Dinah's entry into New York City ten months earlier, and that first Apollo performance was turning out to be even more important than she could have known. Barry Ulanov was the *Metronome* reviewer who had written those glowing words about her for the March 1943 issue. Sitting with him that night had been Leonard Feather, an urbane twenty-nine-year-old British transplant affiliated with *Down Beat* but already well-known in music circles beyond the magazine.

Feather had come to the subject entirely by accident. He barely paid attention to any kind of music until one of his high school chums persuaded him to buy Louis Armstrong's "West End Blues." It changed everything. Feather immersed himself in Armstrong's music and then branched out to other musicians and other styles. His first writing was a spirited letter to *Melody Maker,* the popular British music magazine, wondering why there were no jazz waltzes. His next was more provocative, asking why there were so few women jazz fans and wondering if any "English girls" could "distinguish Dorsey from Goodman . . . or vintage Armstrong from 1933 Armstrong." The letter prompted immediate and indignant responses from several women readers printed under the banner "Feather and the Fem-Fans." The *Melody Maker* editor was so intrigued by the interchanges that he asked Feather to meet with him. At the end of the conversation, the editor offered Feather a job, and he took it.

On his first trip to New York in 1935 Feather spent eleven days in the city, wangling a guest spot on Willie Bryant's radio show from the Apollo and working out a deal with the *Amsterdam News* to send in reports from London about jazz comings and goings. He was the only white correspondent the newspaper had ever had. Feather moved to the United States permanently in 1939, working at *Down Beat* and expanding his musical horizons as composer, producer, and critic. It was the last of these roles that would bring him the most attention.

Ulanov had written in *Metronome* that Dinah reminded him of Billie Holiday. But that February evening at the Apollo, Feather had heard something different in her "tart, take-me-or-leave-me sound . . . the boldly beautiful echo of her black church background," and he knew right then that he wanted to make a record with her.

The logistics were the easy part. It was no problem to find a studio with suitable equipment, the right material, and good musicians. But there was an insurmountable roadblock to making the record right away: a ban on recording imposed by the American Federation of Musicians that had been in effect since August 1942. The ban was initiated by the union's tough and uncompromising leader, James C. Petrillo, who was convinced that commercial recording cut into the earning power of the union musicians, who made much of their money through live performances. "Nowhere else in this mechanical age does the workman create the machine which destroys him, but that's what happens to the musician when he plays for a recording," Petrillo said whenever he was asked to explain his views. "The iceman didn't create the refrigerator; the coachman didn't build the automobile."

By analogy, Petrillo said, when the musician plays his music for a recording, "the radio station manager comes around and says, 'Sorry, Joe, we've got all your stuff on records, so we don't need you any more.' And Joe is out of a job."

Petrillo ran the union with a heavy hand and by this time was one of the country's most powerful labor leaders. That middle C. stood for Caesar, and both friend and foe thought it appropriate. Committed to protecting his musicians, Petrillo waved off critics who claimed he mischaracterized the recording industry and its impact on union members. He was undeterred by appeals to patriotism, unconcerned that the country was at war. When the Justice Department filed an antitrust suit against the union to end the recording ban, Petrillo fought back, and the suit was quickly thrown out of court. But when a congressional subcommittee summoned him to Washington to address their concerns about the ban's effect on interstate commerce, Petrillo did have to appear. At the hearing, he offered the seeds of what became the compromise that brought musicians back to the studio: recording and transcription companies—firms that made acetate disks from such things as radio programs for later use—would pay fixed royalties to the union for each record and transcription made. These funds were in turn to be used to supply "free, live music to the public." (By 1947, $4.5 million had been collected under the contract, paying for nearly nineteen thousand performances. Petrillo became something of a household word; announcers usually explained at the end of a broadcast that the concert had been provided in cooperation with the musicians union, "James C. Petrillo, president.")

Decca, Hampton's label, was the first major to make a deal with the union, agreeing on terms the last week of September 1943. The label agreed to pay musicians on a graduated scale that ranged from 1/4 cent each on sales of records that sold for 35 cents, which were the "sepia" series that featured "race" artists, and up to 5 cents on records selling for $2, which were opera and symphonic music. By the end of the year nearly one hundred small companies and transcription services had also agreed to terms. RCA Victor and Columbia, the two largest record makers, held off for another year, settling only after President Franklin D. Roosevelt and the War Labor Board interceded.

KEYNOTE RECORDS was one of those small labels that had come to terms with the musicians union. Eric Bernay, the owner of the Music Room, a music store on West 44th Street in New York, also ran the company. His politics were unabashedly left-wing—he had published the premier leftist magazine, *New Masses,* devoted to the causes he championed (one cover story asked, "Should Communists Reveal Themselves?"), and he used Keynote to record such artistic enterprises as the Russian Army Chorus. In 1938 he had backed John Hammond—like Feather, he was another white man devoted to jazz and blues—when Hammond put together a special event at Carnegie Hall, "From Spirituals to Swing." But Hammond made sure that Bernay and *New Masses* were all but invisible in the promotion and advertising for the concert.

Feather approached Bernay about recording Dinah, and Bernay agreed to do the project. During the Christmas week, when the Hampton band was at the Apollo, they booked time at WOR, a prominent radio station in Midtown that routinely made its space available to independent record companies. Feather had already written two blues tunes he wanted to record, "Evil Man," which he recast to "Evil Gal Blues," and "Salty Papa Blues," which he also revised to fit the moment. A third, "I Know How to Do It," needed no alteration. The fourth tune was an impromptu blues given the title "Homeward Bound."

Feather wanted to show Dinah the material they would be recording, so he went to see her at her hotel. After they exchanged greetings, Feather handed her the sheets of music. She looked them over, looked at Feather, and grinned as she delivered her verdict: "Shit, you really think you know me, don't you?"

Feather laughed. All he knew, he told her, was what he had

heard that night eleven months earlier at the Apollo, and he was glad that he had hit it right.

Feather and Bernay picked the early hours of December 29 to record, after Dinah and the musicians were done with the Apollo show. Feather recruited six of Hampton's principals: Arnett Cobb on tenor sax, Joe Morris on trumpet, Rudy Rutherford on clarinet, Milt Buckner on piano, Vernon King on bass, and Fred Radcliffe on drums. To their surprise, Hampton decided to come to the session as well. Whether he had been formally invited or not, it was probably a good thing—he could have barred the other musicians from doing this freelance project, but no doubt sensing a musical adventure, he decided to join in. Though his recording contract was with Decca, Hampton assured Feather there was no problem with the project. Decca wanted big band music, he said, and this was like orchestra members playing chamber music, completely different.

The moment was a first for Dinah. She had never made a recording before. All of her singing had been live, which meant that there was no second chance. You went out onstage, stood before the microphone, and delivered. Feather could see that she carried that sensibility into the studio. The group started with "Evil Gal Blues," and he knew from the first take that he was going to make a splendid record.

The tune followed the format of most vocals with Hampton—a long introduction, here a minute plus of rolling piano chords from Buckner punctuated by Hampton on the drums before Dinah began to sing. She was an "evil gal" who promised rather than threatened to "empty your pockets" and then "fill you with misery." She was direct and clear, buoyant but not brash. Joe Morris shadowed her on a muted trumpet, adding a teasing effect.

Rutherford and Cobb came in on the second verse, staying behind Dinah as the song came to a close.

Hampton also played drums on the second tune, "I Know How to Do It," which seemed appropriate as a title given Dinah's ease in the studio. She was playfully suggestive, trading verses with the soloists, first a freewheeling Rutherford on the clarinet and then Cobb on the saxophone. The third song, "Salty Papa Blues," opened with a long trumpet solo from Morris that fed into a tenor solo from Cobb, each providing variations on the basic blues structure and setting the stage for Dinah to sing the first chorus, a lament that asks

"Papa, why you so salty?" She sounded sweet and unaffected but saucy enough to suit the subject matter.

The final track was the new, up-tempo "Homeward Bound," which was as much instrumental as vocal. It opened with Hampton playing the piano, striking the keys with the same intensity he brought to the vibraharp. Rutherford added a clarinet solo that would have been at home in a Benny Goodman performance. Morris and Cobb got their turns, too. Dinah's spirited vocal fit in like another solo, only this one with words.

The musicians were having such a good time they jammed until 4:30 A.M.

After the session was over and the technical matters taken care of, Bernay, the label owner, pressed twenty thousand copies of the four sides, pairing "Evil Gal Blues" with "I Know How to Do It," and "Salty Papa Blues" with "Homeward Bound." Hoping to capitalize on Hampton's popularity, he styled them "The Lionel Hampton Sextet with Dinah Washington."

In theory a good marketing strategy, in practice it brought only headaches. When Decca learned about the imminent release of the records, label executives threatened Bernay with a lawsuit, insisting that Hampton, with sextet or big band, had an exclusive contract with them. Bernay pointed out that he had already spent a great deal of money on the project and offered to sell the masters to Decca for $10,000. But Decca representatives declined to pay what they considered an outrageous price. The two parties finally reached a deal by March: the record would come out under Keynote as "Sextet with Dinah Washington" and no mention of Hampton.

But Bernay's problems were not over. A printing glitch caused some of the labels to be misnamed, listing "Homeward Bound" on records of "I Know How to Do It."

Right after the records were released there was good news that made the earlier hassles a distant memory. Both Keynote records registered on *Billboard*'s April "Harlem" Hit Parade, "Salty Papa Blues" at number ten for one week and "Evil Gal Blues" at number nine for two weeks. Unfortunately for Dinah, the records were listed as "Lionel Hampton on Keynote" even though Bernay had dropped his name from the labels and only hers was printed. But *Metronome*, which was Dinah's biggest booster, paid attention. The unnamed reviewer rated all four tracks A. Dinah "is a superlative blues singer in

a class with Billie Holiday and Lil Green," he wrote, noting in particular how she "bends and twists her notes and communicates an
exciting, natural feeling for blues."

Dinah was now a recording artist if not a recording star, attract-
ing attention among the music fans—most, if not all, white—who
read *Metronome* and paid attention to the magazine's coverage. In its
year-end poll of various categories of music, published in the January 1944 issue, Dinah made the list of favorite female vocalists, albeit in last place with four votes. (Helen Forrest, a white big band
singer, was first with 166 votes, Billie Holiday was second with
seventy-nine, Peggy Lee third with fifty-eight.)

In a long piece about the Hampton band, which *Metronome*
awarded "Band of the Year" honors, Barry Ulanov compared Dinah
favorably to Hampton's other vocalist, Rubel Blakey, and his "fatu-
ous singing style that should have disappeared long ago." "Fortu-
nately," Ulanov wrote, "there is always Dinah Washington to remind
you how songs should be sung . . . shaping words a little like Billie
Holiday, kicking phrases just the right way, because she knows, because she's got the right feeling, too."

Early in January 1944, after a quick trip to play Passaic, New
Jersey, and then Providence, Rhode Island, the Hampton revue settled into the Capitol Theater at Broadway and 31st—a larger theater
than Loew's and a direct result of their success at the smaller venue.
Every show confirmed the obvious. Hampton was the star, the consummate entertainer, bounding from the vibraharp to the drums
and sometimes the piano. His gifted energetic musicians soloed almost every night, among them tenor saxist Arnett Cobb, Milt Buckner, piano, and Herbie Fields, clarinet. Many nights they didn't just
play but roused the crowd with what a *Down Beat* reviewer called
their "mad antics": throwing their horns in the air, clapping their
hands to the beat, jumping up during a solo, and even marching
across the stage single file for some unannounced purpose.

The *Amsterdam News* noted that "the sensational Dinah Washington" would be part of the Capitol Theater show, but barely. *Variety* lamented that she and Blakey only got "one inning"; Dinah used
hers to sing "Do Nothin' Till You Hear from Me."

. . .

AS A TWENTY-YEAR-OLD black woman, Dinah was not affected by World War II in the same direct and personal way it
touched the young men who were drafted, among them her favorite
cousin, George. But wartime did have a salutary impact on Dinah's
budding career thanks to programs on the Armed Forces Radio Service. Morale was an important consideration, and from the beginning of the war, military and civilian officials sought to boost the
spirits of the service personnel. One way was to present entertainment especially tailored for broadcasts on their bases. The majority
of soldiers, sailors, airmen, and marines were white, but there were
significant numbers of black soldiers—in segregated units—very
often performing the least desirable tasks.

Programs such as *Command Performance* and *Mail Call* were mainstream variety shows geared to the white soldiers. *Spotlight Bands*,
which had included Hampton's live performance June 5, 1943, from
Norfolk, and *One Night Stand* were a mixed bag, though white talent
was featured more than black, no matter how well-known. These
programs had the important if unintentional by-product of filling a
gap during the record ban. The transcriptions made for the armed
services were the only recordings of these musicians allowed until
the labels and the musicians federation reached their agreements.

In 1942, *Jubilee,* the first such program devoted to black jazz,
was put in place by Major Mann Holiner, who had produced the
Blackbird musical revues on Broadway in his civilian life and was
now assigned to the radio section of the army's Special Services Division. The aim was clear: to showcase black talent and to provide
alternatives to the white programs. The format of *Jubilee* was live
shows from rented studios at NBC hosted by Ernie "Bubbles" Whitman, an actor, comedian, and singer, who followed scripts full of jive
talk put together by white civilian Hollywood film writers the army
recruited. The shows were transcribed for later use by the Armed
Forces Radio Service.

From the beginning of 1944, when Hampton was selected to be
on the *One Night Stand* programs, these armed forces radio transcriptions were giving Dinah regular exposure to an overseas military audience but only in the small increments Hampton's program
allowed. Typically she sang one or two songs each performance, and
while she surely expressed opinions about the material, Hampton

had the final say. There was almost no traditional blues in the vein of "Evil Gal" or "Salty Papa." Instead, Dinah was singing popular tunes of the day with big band arrangements: "There'll Be a Jubilee," "No Love No Nothin'," "When They Ask About You."

SEPTEMBER 1944 brought a new adventure for Dinah—her first trip to California, where she and the band would stay almost two months. In the first week of the western swing, the Hampton revue played just outside Hollywood in South Gate at the Trianon Ball Room, a favorite venue for big bands that was owned by white band-leader Horace Heidt. Count Basie had used the ballroom to record his band's part in the film *Reveille with Beverly.* The Hampton show was broadcast to servicemen as an installment of *One Night Stand,* and Dinah sang two new songs. She was relaxed and sassy on "A Slick Chick (on the Mellow Side)," and unlike some of the other tunes, where she barely got equal time with the band, her vocals here were the centerpiece. Though her voice was slightly nasal, it was also crystal-clear, the tart quality that had appealed so much to Leonard Feather obvious to any listener. Like Billie Holiday, Dinah sang just behind the beat. It was a way to make the song her own, and it seemed entirely natural. There was never the sense that she had to rush to keep up with the band.

Dinah followed "Slick Chick" with George and Ira Gershwin's "The Man I Love." The song must have had special poignancy: just twenty years old, Dinah already had a broken marriage and more than one short-term road romance behind her.

On October 9 the Hampton revue was back at the Trianon, a show later broadcast as a *Jubilee* segment.

"It must be recess in heaven," joked Bubbles Whitman, the host, when Dinah came onstage. "Hello, honey—I don't believe I caught your name."

"Oh, I forgot to tell you, I'm Dinah Washington," she said, her speaking voice a chirpy, childlike contrast to her singing.

"You sort of disappoint me," she told Whitman, gamely playing along. "I thought you were a wolf."

"Well, I thought so, too," Whitman replied. "But my howl is now a drool."

"Well, aren't you going to ask me to sing?" Dinah asked. "I'd like to."

"For all you men everywhere," Whitman replied, "Dinah's asking the big question of the hour, 'Is You Is or Is You Ain't My Baby.' "

The band started up, and she delivered a poised and lively performance, the kind that led one of the other announcers who sometimes subbed for Whitman to call her "the young chick with the potent pipes."

A week later, October 16, Dinah and the Hampton band recorded another *Jubilee* broadcast, and Dinah and Whitman engaged in some more flirty banter.

"Say," he asked her, the leer in his voice unmistakable, "what are you doing after the show?"

"You haven't even asked me what I'm going to do *on* the show," she retorted with a bit more conviction than in the previous week's set piece. Then she introduced a new tune Hampton had written, "Million Dollar Smile," with a simple but evocative opening line: "Every time you smile you dim the sunshine." Dinah's no-frills singing had just enough pizzazz to make it swing.

On November 1 the band visited the naval hospital in Oakland, California, to play for the sailors. Their performance was featured on another *Spotlight* band show. Dinah sang "(I Guess) I'm Just the Worrying Kind."

Dinah was coming into her own now, gaining confidence and maturity as a singer and also gaining recognition. She showed up in the year-end polls for 1944 of both *Down Beat* and *Metronome*. In *Down Beat*'s category of "Girl Singer (With Band)," Dinah was fourth with 138 votes. Anita O'Day, a white jazz singer, was the runaway winner with 2,033. *Down Beat*'s categories for men used the somewhat more tasteful "Male Singer (Not Band)" rather than the equivalent "Boy Singer (Not Band)," a small but telling reflection of how women entertainers were perceived.

In *Metronome*'s smaller poll, Dinah placed ninth in the "Female Vocalist" category with twenty votes, just two behind Ella Fitzgerald but well behind Holiday, who was in first place with 225. *Metronome* also gave Dinah another boost, listing her Keynote singles "Homeward Bound" and "Salty Papa Blues" among its records of the year. The magazine called her "an intriguing cross between Bessie Smith and Billie Holiday," the former a reference to the great blues singer who had put an indelible stamp on the genre.

Dinah had come a long way in her one year with Hampton. She was making a bit more money every week, about $100 now. And while that was important, it wasn't the only thing. The larger question was whether she could continue to grow and be satisfied with the current situation. She clearly was an asset to the show, but Hampton and the band were the main attraction. She was just a singer, and not even *the* singer.

DINAH AND THE HAMPTON GROUP ended 1944 with a week in Chicago and then a week in Detroit before heading back to New York for a few days at the Strand. The reviewer in the January 1945 *Down Beat,* who did not care for Hampton's showy band members, lamented that "Dinah Washington, one of the few great jazz vocalists of our day, does almost no singing." She performed only two songs, which had become the standard. Her lack of singing time— not to mention recording time—was beginning to grate. She had been promised the chance to record "Million Dollar Smile," but when she got to the studio for the session, the song "wound up being a vibe solo," she recalled. She never learned whether it was Hampton who cut out the vocals or Decca executives who wanted him as a soloist instead of her. Either way, she was denied the opportunity.

But for the moment dissatisfaction took a back seat to preparations for a special one-night performance on April 15 at Carnegie Hall, Hampton's debut at the preeminent theater on 57th Street. The evening was going to be something different from the usual Hampton fare, with several guest artists featured, including Dizzy Gillespie and winners from *Esquire* magazine's "All-American band contest." Hampton decided to bring in strings on some numbers, and in a nod to Dinah, he asked her gospel forebears to come to New York to join the program. Both *Down Beat* and *Metronome* noted that the "Martins" would appear. It was not clear, though, just who the "Martins" were. Perhaps it was another joint appearance of Roberta and Sallie, the latter by now gaining more recognition in the gospel world. The first half of the show was all instrumental, devoted to Hampton's band and its soloists. In the second half, Rubel Blakey sang first, and he didn't go over well. "Turn on the mike!" audience members shouted during his barely audible version of "Embrace-able You."

Dinah's appearance was scheduled for later. As she waited back-stage, perhaps mingling with her gospel inspirations, her mood was anything but saintly, according to an account in *Metronome*. Miffed that Hampton refused to allow her more than her standard two songs, she threw a fit, demanding more time. He refused. Finally, she relented.

If audience reaction was any gauge, Dinah was gaining the upper hand on Hampton. She took the stage to escalating applause and prepared to sing her trademark "Evil Gal Blues," on this night more than fitting. At Hampton's request, Leonard Feather played the piano on his own composition, opening with a sturdy rendition of the introductory chords and setting a more stately pace than Milt Buckner usually did.

Dinah sidled up to the mike, at once sensual and edgy, and ut-tered the opening words: "I'm an evil gal." The audio problems solved, her voice came through loud and clear—and the audience responded with hoots and howls of recognition. More outbursts greeted her playful talk of the "men in New York" who "love me the best."

If Dinah was nervous about singing at Carnegie Hall and for a raucous crowd at that, it didn't show. And Hampton had no choice but to take notice. The next month he finally agreed to take her into the studio. On May 21 she recorded "Blowtop Blues" for Decca with a sextet from the band. The session went fine—the only disappoint-ment was the company's failure to release the record right away. Hampton said it was because of a misunderstanding over who had the rights to the song. But the episode also illustrated the way Decca and Hampton looked at the music—he and the big band were the focus, not their gifted singer.

Dinah, though, continued to get recognition even if she wasn't the star of the Hampton shows and high on Decca's list of recording priorities. A *Metronome* review of Dinah's early June performance at the Paradise Theater in Detroit positively glowed. Dinah "stopped the show with her own hip interpretation of 'Embraceable You,' " the writer said. The audience wouldn't let her off the stage until she had sung "Evil Gal" and "Salty Papa." When she appeared with Hamp-ton three weeks later at the city's Graystone Gardens ballroom, the *Michigan Chronicle,* which served Detroit's black community, ran Dinah's picture on the entertainment page, announcing to readers, "Here July 3." Dinah's picture showed up in the *Chicago Defender* to advertise Hampton's appearance at an outside festival in Chicago White Sox Park later in July. In Boston at the end of summer, she got billing in a *Boston Globe* ad right under Hampton as the first featured performer.

These were small gestures, but they were important. Dinah could see how valuable she was to Hampton, and week by week she was realizing that if she wanted to sing more and more of what she wanted, she would have to leave, even though Hampton was now paying her $125 a week. Some of that she had to use for expenses. Fortunately a place like the Theresa Hotel in Harlem, right across the street from the Apollo, was not only convenient but also offered rooms with meal plans. Many performers, Dinah now among them, considered it their home away from home. Her rent for the five months between April and September 1945 was $21 and the restaurant tab was $28 (totaling $504 in today's dollars).

As often as she could Dinah sent money back to Chicago to help her mother and her siblings. She was out on her own, to be sure, traveling the country with a busful of men, but her family remained an anchor, even if Alice Jones still disapproved of her daughter's burgeoning career.

The precise details and circumstances of Dinah's departure from the Hampton band are sketchy, but the reason she left is not: she wanted to sing more; Hampton couldn't accommodate her. "I knew I was going to be the best singer in the business," she declared, "but I wasn't getting anywhere at all with Hampton." His recollection of their parting in November while the band was in Los Angeles is matter-of-fact, a conflict of professional goals. An article in the November 1956 issue of *Ebony,* a sort of *Life* magazine geared to the black community, contended that Dinah had pulled a gun on Hampton in her frustration over singing time and song selection. Though the story is a colorful one and took on a life of its own, there is no supporting information to confirm it. Hampton didn't speak of this in his autobiography, and Dinah never made any such claim in interviews about this part of her career. And in the end it really didn't matter, when they parted ways, who said what to whom or how. The important thing was that now Dinah was on her own.

6.

Stairway to a Star

Three weeks after her last appearance with Hampton—a Sunday afternoon jam at the Streets of Paris nightclub—Dinah went to Radio Recorders Studio on Santa Monica Boulevard to record the first of twelve blues sides for Apollo Records, a small independent label in New York City. She was paid $1,800—$150 a side.

In all likelihood Sam Schneider, an Apollo partner cum talent scout, was responsible for the session. His job was to find musicians on the West Coast who could make records for the label. "I wanna record every blues singer in L.A.," he told Jack McVea, a saxophone player who had worked with Lionel Hampton. "Can you help me?"

Schneider's instincts were good, if ambitious. Los Angeles was a city full of young, talented musicians, some just back from the war, willing to play all day in sessions if they could and then work in clubs at night. "We were trying to go from one job to another," recalled drummer Lee Young, the brother of jazz great Lester. Groups formed and re-formed in different combinations, some with visitors from the East, as their schedules, skills, and musical taste dictated.

Most of them were unknowns or barely known; in a short time, a few would be famous: Dizzy Gillespie, trumpet; Charlie Parker, saxophone; Charles Mingus, bass; Milt Jackson, vibraharp.

Though he would not attain their level of celebrity, Lucky Thompson, another saxophone player who had briefly been part of the Hampton band, combined his considerable talent with an entrepreneurial spirit. He used his contacts to put together different groups of "All-Stars," who recorded for Apollo as well as other small independent labels eager to capitalize on all the talent in Los Angeles. Thompson got the nod to recruit musicians for Dinah's sessions, which were scheduled for December 10, 12, and 13. The band was billed as the "Lucky Thompson All-Stars": Thompson, Mingus on bass, Jackson on vibraharp, Young on drums, Jewel Grant on alto sax, Karl George on trumpet, Gene Porter on baritone sax, and Wilbert Baranco at the piano—a stellar lineup to kick off Dinah's solo career.

The recording procedure had a nice symmetry: the musicians union mandated no more than four sides over a three-hour session. Anything longer than that was billed as overtime to the label. On December 10, Dinah and the band cut "Wise Woman Blues," "Walking Blues," "No Voot—No Boot," and "Chewin' Mama Blues." On the 12th, they recorded "My Lovin' Papa," "Rich Man's Blues," "Beggin' Mama Blues," and "All or Nothing Blues," and on the 13th they finished with "Mellow Mama Blues," "My Voot Is Really Vout," "Blues for a Day," and "Pacific Coast Blues." Only the technical matters were left—creating the master discs, pressing the records, and affixing the labels and then officially releasing the record. Dinah knew from her disappointing experience with Hampton and Decca that nothing was guaranteed just because she went into the studio and recorded a song. Now it was up to Apollo.

BY THE FIRST WEEK in January 1946 Dinah was back in Chicago, and while she almost certainly returned to 661 East 37th Street, the family home, this was not a social visit. On the 14th Dinah was in the studio again, but now for a different label. Mercury Records was one of the new independents, formed in Chicago in the fall of 1945 by three young entrepreneurs: Irving Green, who owned a pressing plant but had no records to press; his business partner, Ray

Greenberg; and Berle Adams, who thought he could find the talent to make Green some records. As the manager of Louis Jordan, the popular alto saxophonist and bandleader, Adams had good connections in the music world and a good eye and ear for talent. The men quickly agreed on a structure: Green was chairman of the board and handled production and selected distributors; Adams was the talent coordinator. In the beginning he recommended that Mercury be a specialty label focusing on race, hillbilly, and polka music, and not try to compete with the majors—RCA, Columbia, and Decca. Their first releases featured the Four Jumps of Jive, Bill Samuels and the Cats 'N Jammers Three, their name a takeoff on a popular comic strip, and the piano player Albert Ammons backing Sippie Wallace on "Bedroom Blues." The Samuels record did particularly well, giving the young company confidence and the cash to stay in business.

When Mercury was ready to expand again, Adams signed three white acts with substantial market presence: bandleaders Buddy Morrow and Vincent Lopez, and singer Connie Haines, who had done stints with Harry James and Tommy Dorsey and had been a vocalist on the Abbott and Costello radio show. And he signed Dinah, certain she would be a profitable addition to the race division even if she lacked the visibility of the others.

For Dinah it was a step up—Mercury may have been newer than Apollo, but it was clear the label was going places. On top of that, Adams gave her a multiyear contract. She could see his good faith in the simple fact that she was in the studio for her first Mercury session as soon as the deal was done.

For Dinah's session on January 14, Adams asked Chicago trombonist Gus Chappell to put together a band to record at Universal Studios, which was on the top floor of the Civic Opera Building on Wacker Drive, just a few blocks from Randolph Street where Dinah had gotten her start. The group cut four sides, George Gershwin's "Embraceable You"; "I Can't Get Started with You," a popular ballad written by Ira Gershwin and Vernon Duke that Billie Holiday had recorded; "When a Woman Loves a Man," a jazz standard with lyrics by Johnny Mercer; and "Joy Juice," a conventional blues tune that Dinah had helped write.

Mercury was more than willing to get a little publicity for one of its newest singers, and a few days after the session, *Down Beat* ran a short item noting that Chicago's own Dinah was a new Mercury artist. Unlike Decca, the label was eager to get her records pressed and released. On February 23 a quarter-page ad in the *Chicago Defender* for the Record Haven in Brooklyn, New York, a mail-order house, listed "Joy Juice" backed with "I Can't Get Started" as its top single. The price was 79 cents. And right underneath it was her first Apollo, "No Voot—No Boot" backed with "Wise Woman Blues." This one was more expensive, $1.05, an illustration of the independents' practice of setting their own prices for each record and likely a reflection of Apollo's higher overhead.

The two records offered a chance to hear Dinah doing two different kinds of material backed by two different kinds of groups— straight blues with an intimate sextet like the 1943 Keynote discs and a standard with a bigger band. "No Voot" was a sassy double entendre "about some things you can't buy, some things you won't give away." Dinah's singing was easygoing and supplemented by solos from Mingus on bass and the well-placed notes from Baranco's piano. "Wise Woman Blues" moved at a much slower tempo and featured what was now one of Dinah's stylistic tics, first heard in "Evil Gal Blues"—a triplet trill to accent a particular lyric.

"Don't forget, pretty daddy," she sings, "that the world is full of other men." That triplet fell on "other."

On "Joy Juice," the blues tune on Mercury, Dinah was backed by the much larger Chappell group, but she was unfazed. She had sung comfortably with a much more potent band all those times onstage with Hampton. When she got to the line "take your man down to the nearest juke joint and get him nice and stewed," Dinah used the triplet to emphasize "nice," stretching a one-syllable word into three. Her version of "I Can't Get Started with You" was full of horn solos but noteworthy for her precise diction. In the title lyric she sang "star-ted" rather than a lazier "starded." And she made clear that the year referred to in the song's story was nineteen "twen-tee-nine," not "twenny-nine."

After struggling for two years to make a record and get it released, Dinah now had two that were out on two different labels. And both companies were advertising on her behalf in the two major trades, *Billboard*, which cut a wide swath through the business, and *Cash Box*, which was geared to the jukebox industry. The writers at both were not critics per se. Rather they were reporters who saw their role as informing the readership week by week about activity in the business. They expressed opinions about new records, to be sure, but with an eye toward how a new release would sell. In the Mercury ad in *Billboard* the label called Dinah "the sultry princess of song." Apollo was more straightforward, simply listing the record, "Apollo 368," but running her picture—the same publicity photo that was taken for Hampton nearly two years earlier.

Billboard was the first to review the Mercury record. In its February 23 issue, the magazine said that Dinah "shows plenty of promise" and added that Chappell's "nine-piece Negro crew" compared "favorably" to the Hampton sextet that had backed her on the Keynote records. Two weeks later, Chicago's Wright Music Shoppe, a West Side store, listed "Joy Juice" second on the "Harlem Hit Parade" right behind Louis Jordan's "Reconversion Blues."

Down Beat and *Metronome* also carried reviews of Dinah's first two records. The write-ups were as important for simply appearing as they were for their substance—both magazines liked the Apollo sides better than the Mercury because they thought she fit better with Thompson's group. While a glowing review was nice, it was more significant that Dinah was getting recognition on her own. When the *Defender* published a poll on April 20 of readers' favorite bands and vocalists, Dinah was a respectable fourth behind Ella Fitzgerald, Billie Holiday, and Lena Horne.

DINAH'S MARRIAGE to John Young ended in the late fall of 1942. On the road she liked to have a man around for company, comfort, and fun. In the summer of 1944, she caught the eye of George Jenkins, a drummer Hampton had brought to the Apollo to spell Fred Radcliffe because the band was doing so many shows. Tall and slender, with striking good looks, Jenkins's nickname was "Cochise" because he was part Native American and had the angular cheekbones of many full-blooded Native Americans. He and Dinah dated in the casual way of musicians going from one town to another until he left Hampton for another job. Jenkins returned a year later for steadier work and resumed his relationship with Dinah. At the end of 1945, just as she prepared to leave Hampton, Dinah realized she was pregnant.

George reacted coolly. "I heard from him but sparingly," she said, "and he'd send money home when he felt like it." Dinah had no choice but to persevere with her work, knowing that she would soon have a child to support. She never talked about what her family said when they learned she was expecting a baby. And while it could have been quietly arranged through one connection or another, Dinah chose not to end the pregnancy.

Alice was surely distressed that her daughter would have a child out of wedlock, though she no doubt understood Dinah's conflicting emotions. She herself had become pregnant while seeing Ollie, but the couple did get married and provided a respectable home for their daughter. Alice probably hoped that Dinah would marry George, but she also knew that whether Dinah was married or not, she would have a significant role to play in raising her grandchild.

Five years earlier as sixteen-year-old Ruth Jones, Dinah had a bit part in the revue at Dave's Café on Garfield. Now twenty-one-year-old Dinah Washington was opening April 3, 1946, as the headliner at the same club, renamed the Rhumboogie after a fire had damaged the premises. The opening night extravaganza featured an exotic dancer, a comedy duo that danced while telling jokes, and a choral group. But none could outshine Dinah. Six months pregnant and moving more slowly than usual, she made her way to the stage and delivered a knockout performance. The audience wouldn't let her leave until she sang one encore after another. The *Defender* dubbed her "swing-sational."

Berle Adams wanted to get Dinah back in the studio, and he thought she would work well with a band led by composer-arranger Gerald Wilson. Wilson was in the middle of a ten-week stay at the El Grotto, a supper club in the basement of black Chicago's premier hotel, the Pershing at 64th and Cottage Grove. Wilson had started out as a trumpeter, playing with Chic Carter and then Jimmie Lunceford, where he was first trumpet for five years. After he was drafted into the navy in 1943, Wilson joined the band at the Great Lakes, Illinois, base, and because the base was just an hour train ride from Chicago, he lived in the city. He could absorb its music life during off-duty time and still meet his military obligations. Following his discharge, Wilson went to California, and shortly after his arrival, he created the group that performed under his name.

Dinah had met Wilson in the fall of 1944 in Los Angeles when the bandleader came to the Orpheum to hear the Hampton band and write arrangements for Rubel Blakey, who was still singing in the show. Wilson hadn't seen Dinah for at least a year but the first week in April he received a long-distance call from his booking agent in California telling him to be at Universal Studio on Wacker Drive with his band on the 6th to record with her. (Berle Adams also wanted to sign Wilson to Mercury and book him for a thirteen-week tour with Louis Jordan, and although the paperwork was done, the deal never materialized.)

On the afternoon of the 6th Wilson and nine other musicians gathered in the studio and recorded three tracks: "Oo-wee Walkie Talkie" (a novelty tune as its title suggested and roughly the same melody as Dinah's Keynote disc "I Know How to Do It"), "The Man I Love," which Dinah had sung with Hampton, and "You Didn't Want Me Then." "Everything was smooth," Wilson recalled. "No problems." He liked the fact that Dinah also played the piano, and he considered her a musician, not simply a good singer. "She knew about harmony, she knew about timing."

Dinah, at twenty-one, was younger than most if not all of the band members. But in this setting age didn't really matter. She was the singer, they were there to support her, and she understood her art. She requested—even insisted—that the band be rehearsed when she came to sing. All but a few days of her three-year career had been live dates with Lionel Hampton. In her mind the studio was just another stage except that there was no audience. She made sure she had learned her music so she was ready to sing when the Hampton men hit their first notes. She would be prepared when she came into the studio; she expected the musicians to do the same. "Dinah was a first-take artist," said Snooky Young, Wilson's trumpeter at the time. "She always said that her first try was always her best."

The next several weeks provided more evidence that Dinah had made the right decision to strike out on her own. She got another singing date at the Pershing in early May, and then two more records were released. Apollo issued its second disc, "Mellow Mama Blues" backed by "My Lovin' Papa," and barely a month after it was for sale, Mercury put out a record with "When a Woman Loves a Man" from the Chappell session and "Oo-wee Walkie Talkie" from the Wilson session.

The most interesting thing about this record was the opportunity to hear Dinah with two different big bands behind her—one,

Chappell's, a group put together for a studio date, the other, Wilson's, a cohesive unit that had played together for months. Dinah had no trouble holding her own on either tune, but the Wilson side, even though it was the less substantial "Oo-wee," displayed a more robust sound. The musicians were crisper in their attacks than Chappell's group, the orchestration, with its unusual harmonies, more sophisticated.

As Dinah's pregnancy progressed, George became more attentive and finally moved to Chicago to be with her. Wilson was pleasantly surprised when the two stopped by the El Grotto to see him—Dinah very visibly pregnant. He guessed they weren't married—no wedding ring on either of them. But that was about to change. In mid-April they decided to get married and two months later, on June 11, the simple ceremony was performed by a Chicago minister. The license read "Ruth Jones" even though she had used Dinah Washington as a stage name for more than three years.

Four days after they were formally married, Dinah saw a dark side to her husband. "Who the hell wants a big black bitch like you," he yelled as he slapped her. He probably had been drinking. Sober, George was easygoing; after a drink, friends described him as "ready to fight King Kong." Shocked and frightened, Dinah grabbed a few things and went to her family's apartment on East 37th Street. She tried to work things out with him over the next several days, but on the first of July, barely three weeks after they married, Dinah left George for good after she learned an alarming fact: he had been married before, to a woman named Bertha Henson, and that marriage had not been terminated by divorce or annulment. Adding insult to injury, Dinah learned that beyond his failure to tell her about Bertha Henson, George had been seeing other women even after they agreed to get married.

Though in the midst of personal turmoil and eight months pregnant, too, Dinah needed to fulfill her work obligations and collect her pay, particularly because it was clear she could not count on much, if anything, from George. And she was a trouper: she sang July 13 on the West Side, did a one-nighter at the Pershing July 20 with George Freeman's orchestra, and then joined Freeman again July 27 at the Masonic Temple in Evanston.

The evening of July 29 Dinah went into labor. Around 1:00 A.M. on the 30th the labor pains increased, and ninety minutes later she was on her way to Provident Hospital on East 51st Street, where most of Chicago's black community was treated. She arrived shortly before 3:00 A.M., and at 3:28 her son was born. He was named George Kenneth Jenkins.

However rocky Dinah's relationship with George was, she wanted to be married when the baby arrived, according to her sister Clarissa. When it came time to fill out the birth certificate, question Number 8 asked, "Legitimate?" She had marked the box "yes."

Despite her travails with George, Dinah understood that it was important for her son to have some relationship with his father. Beyond that she could use whatever money George was willing to give her to care for him. Matters between the two apparently improved enough for them to pose for a picture with the baby a few weeks after his birth. Holding a chubby little infant between them, they looked like any proud, young couple. Nothing in the picture betrayed the conflict that lay behind it. But the family photo did show that Dinah had changed from the 1943 publicity picture the newspapers and record companies were still using. Gone was the little girl with the flower in her hair, and in her place was a young woman with a more mature presence and a more stylish, shorter haircut.

That three-year-old picture Apollo, Mercury, and the *Defender* still used was instructive, though: Dinah was not yet a big enough star nor employed by a big enough company to have an up-to-date public relations effort launched on her behalf.

GEORGE KENNETH'S ARRIVAL coincided almost to the day with the release of a third record from Dinah's Apollo sessions, "Walking Blues" and "Rich Man's Blues." A few weeks later, the label took out half-page ads in *Billboard* and *Cash Box*, with Dinah's new release featured prominently at the top. The write-up in *Cash Box* provided a window into the stratified music market and Dinah's place in it. While the reviewer liked the record, he considered it "limited by experience to 'race' locations and spots where her style has a definite demand." *Billboard* took a similar line, complimenting Dinah's "sultry and unforced singing" and adding that " 'Race' locations will mop up 'Rich Man's Blues.' " In other words, Dinah Washington meant black audience only.

By the fall, when young George was barely two months old,

Dinah left him in the care of his grandmother Alice at East 37th Street, and went back to New York to record with a small combo led by Tab Smith. He had played for a short time with Count Basie and then Lucky Millinder before fronting his own group. The session included two traditional blues, "Postman Blues" and "Mean and Evil Blues," the latter of which was a takeoff on Leonard Feather's "Evil Gal Blues," and two others, "A Slick Chick (on the Mellow Side)," which she had sung with the Hampton band, and "That's Why a Woman Loves a Heel." The second week in December "Slick Chick" backed with "Postman Blues" was released, and Mercury included Dinah and the new record in the *Billboard* ad that it was running almost weekly now to publicize the freshest product. The magazine also reviewed the record in the same issue, praising Dinah for an "excellent job" on "Postman" and comparing her easy back-and-forth with the Smith band to the rapport Duke Ellington had with one of his singers, Ivie Anderson.

Back in Chicago for the holidays, Dinah got a taste of how a label treated a major star when Mercury threw a party for Tony Martin in December at Chicago's Shangri-La Restaurant. Eight hundred people attended from radio, television, newspaper, and show business circles. The company spent $7,500 for the evening, bundling it together with a celebration of Mercury's first anniversary.

Down Beat and *Metronome* had paid respectful attention to Dinah when they wrote about the Hampton shows. But at the end of 1946, when they published their reader polls, one effect of Dinah's decision to strike out on her own was evident: reduced visibility. She didn't show up at all in *Down Beat*'s contest. In *Metronome* she tied for twenty-third with Martha Tilton, a white singer formerly with Benny Goodman. Each had nine votes.

These two polls reflected a rather select, mostly white audience, albeit an audience more receptive to black musicians and black culture than the general population. But if the magazine polls reflected one reality, another gave Dinah palpable evidence that she was on the right course: three records on Apollo, three more on Mercury, new sessions in the works for the next year, and steady work in the clubs. Beyond that was the creative satisfaction and release, two things Hampton couldn't give her.

Along with these intangibles was the concrete fact that Dinah was earning good money from her club dates and the recording sessions, and she was probably getting some royalties from the sales of her records, too. Recording contracts provided for such payments, but the amount depended on the cost to make the record and the number sold.

CONFIDENT THAT LITTLE GEORGE was well cared for by his grandmother, Dinah went back to New York early in 1947 to participate in a benefit concert at the Golden Gate, a ballroom and cabaret in Harlem. This event had a certain political tinge to it. The evening's performance was to raise money for the George Washington Carver School, which advertised its purpose as bringing "the Negro people the culture and education from which discrimination ordinarily bars them." The fund-raiser was held in cooperation with Camp Unity, an interracial organization that operated in Wingdale, New York, some seventy miles north of New York City.

After the show Dinah signed autographs, surrounded by giddy young women pressing to get as close to her as they could. She well understood now that a look was important, and she no doubt enjoyed the newfound ablity to dress the part. On this night Dinah couldn't have looked more stylish. She was wearing a dark print dress with a mink-collared jacket over it. Her hair was swept up with curls on the top, and she wore a four-strand pearl necklace.

Dinah was among a dozen or so performers at the benefit, and her willingness to participate brought some unusual attention that she probably never knew about. The Federal Bureau of Investigation, alert to anything that smacked of Communist influence, had clipped an ad for the benefit concert from the *Daily Worker,* the official publication of the Communist Party, USA, underlined her name, and opened a file on her. There was nothing else in her FBI file fifty-five years later.

After a few club dates in Chicago in February, Dinah returned to New York and recorded with a new orchestra, this one led by bass player Chubby Jackson. As before, the session was a mix of blues and ballads: another try at "Mean and Evil Blues," "Stairway to the Stars," which had been popular in the 1930s, and "I Want to Be Loved," a tune recently written and recorded by Savannah Churchill, a New Orleans singer who gained prominence with Benny Carter's band.

Mercury was experimenting with Dinah, trying to find material and musical settings that suited her talents and could take her beyond the blues audience. But it was also true that the songs themselves and the revenue they could generate really drove a project as much as if not more than the individual singer's request or taste. The music trades carried as many ads from publishing companies touting the performers who recorded their tunes as they did from labels pushing a particular disc. And *Billboard* periodically ran a chart, "Music Publishers' Batting Average," listing what company had what songs on the most-played and best-selling lists. The chart reflected label executives' interest in recording songs that had proved successful rather than taking a risk on unknown material, no matter how good the singer. In short it was evidence of the financial dominance of the music publishers.

Dinah came back to Chicago just as Mercury released its fourth single, "Embraceable You" from the Gus Chappell session, backed with "That's Why a Woman Loves a Heel" from the Tab Smith session, which she'd done nearly a year later. No one, label executive or singer, could be sure when a song would catch on or what that song would be. Sometimes just one disc jockey who gave a record a push could get the ball rolling. While Dinah had gotten respectful attention with her Apollo and Mercury releases, she hadn't yet broken through on the popularity charts as measured by *Billboard* and *Cash Box*. All that changed the week of April 7, when "Postman Blues," which had been released the previous November, turned up at number nine in a *Cash Box* column on "race" records: "Burning Up the Jukes in Harlem." (Number one was Savannah Churchill's "I Want to Be Loved," which Dinah had already recorded.) "Postman" remained on the *Cash Box* chart for a month, suggesting that if it took a while for "Postman" to find an audience, once the record made a splash, it had staying power.

Perhaps it was a coincidence, but just as "Postman" was getting notice, Dinah got an offer from booking agent Ben Bart to handle her live dates. Bart had been with the Gale Agency, brothers Moe and Tim, working with such acts as the Jimmie Lunceford Orchestra. He had just started his own company, Universal Attractions, and had already signed the Ravens, a singing quartet that was on the rise, and the Kansas City pianist and bandleader Jay McShann. He was sure Dinah had potential on the club and packaged tour circuit that catered to black audiences.

The first fruit of their association was a weeklong stay at the Regal at the end of May on a bill that included the Ravens and Mc-Shann and his band. When she finished that show, Dinah happily stayed in Chicago, playing a favorite haunt, the Tyree Masonic Hall on the West Side, for a one-night performance and then the next week headlining with singer Tiny Bradshaw and his band at Colosimo's, a club at 2120 South Wabash with a notorious history. It was opened in 1910 by Big Jim Colosimo, an underworld figure who operated a chain of brothels in the city and was known as "the King of Pimps." He was gunned down in May 1920 in a gangland dispute, but the club remained in operation, name unchanged. In 1946, Colosimo's underwent a $30,000 renovation and revamped its talent policy, aiming for big attractions despite a small stage. Billie Holiday had closed an engagement just before Dinah and Bradshaw opened.

The format for their current show was similar to evenings at the Rhumboogie—singers, dancers, and stars woven together by a producer. Some of the dancers from the Club DeLisa were also on the bill; one of them, Eloise Clay, had become one of Dinah's fans, catching a show here and there when Dinah was in town.

With so many different parts, the revues required a few days of rehearsal. Dinah came to the club for one run-through with little George, now nearly eleven months old, in tow. The performers gathered around the toddler, bestowing the customary compliments. Eloise offered young George her finger; he grabbed it and took his first tentative steps to the mutual delight of baby, new friend, and mother.

Decca, Hampton's label, which had been sitting on its one Dinah Washington recording with the Hampton band, chose this moment to release "Blowtop Blues." It immediately went onto *Billboard*'s chart for "Most-Played Juke Box Race Records," but Hampton's name was listed first. "Dinah Washington" was in parentheses. Nonetheless, it was a unique moment: she had records out on three different labels.

Right after the Decca release, Apollo issued a fourth record from the December 1945 Los Angeles sessions, "My Voot Is Really Vout," with "Blues for a Day" on the B side. The label now advertised its singer as "dynamic Dinah Washington." One Apollo ad that ran in the music trades (still using Dinah's early publicity picture) featured an apropos pairing: Dinah's new record listed right next to a new record by the emerging Queen of Gospel, Mahalia Jackson—an illustration of roads taken and not taken.

Early in July, Dinah settled into the Ritz Lounge, a popular South Side nightspot in the Ritz Hotel at the corner of Oakwood and South Park. It was run by Jimmy Cooper, who had worked his way up from hotel doorman (at the nearby DuSable) to club owner and carried himself with a confident—some said pompous—air. The six-piece house band was led by Dave Young, a saxophonist who had honed his craft with the Lucky Millinder Orchestra alongside Dizzy Gillespie and Thelonius Monk. Young put together his band when he returned to Chicago in the mid-1940s after two years in the navy, and he started at the Ritz in February 1947. Blues singer Jo Jo Adams was the main attraction.

When Adams left in late June, Cooper wanted to hire Billie Holiday, but she was not available. Dinah was, and he brought her in for $250 a week (roughly $2,066 in today's dollars). No doubt with prompting from the lounge, the *Defender* took notice, running a two-column picture—that same Kriegsmann photo from the spring of 1943—wrapped around a short item, "Dinah Moves to the Ritz." By now she was so well-known to *Defender* readers that the paper's headline writers knew a first name alone was sufficient.

Word spread fast. A week after opening night, the place was packed for every performance, standing room only. On weekends people stood in lines extending around the corner on Oakwood, sweating in Chicago's summer heat as they waited for the chance to hear Dinah sing. The atmosphere inside wasn't much better—the Ritz was not air-conditioned.

With such good business, an easy relationship between club manager and talent might be expected, with each doing well for the other. But Dinah chafed at Cooper's haughty manner. Her temper and penchant for expletives, sharpened by two years on the road with a group of fast-living men, showed in full force when she and Cooper crossed swords. Because Dave Young knew that Dinah liked him, he wasn't afraid to take her aside and tell her to calm down.

"She'd be cussing Jimmy out, and I'd say, 'Dinah what the hell's wrong with you?' " he recalled.

"Excuse me, but he makes me so goddamned mad," she told him.

"But you can't do that here," Young retorted. "You are a lady."

"Well, I'll be one if he'll let me. The so and so—"

Young cut her off, unwilling to hear any more.

Dinah didn't hesitate to chew out patrons either, most often if they talked while she sang. "She gave Jimmy fits as she swore at the customers and everybody else," recalled Eddie Plique, who announced some of the shows. But that, he said, turned out to be one of the attractions; patrons were curious to see if there might be fireworks from the stage. Plique relied on flattery to stay on Dinah's good side. "Ladies and gentlemen," he would say in his introduction. "Miss Dinah Washington, Queen of the Blues."

Finally at the end of August, nearly two months into her Ritz engagement, Dinah had a new picture taken. Now she wore a braided hairpiece on top of her own swept-up hair, and she looked even more sophisticated than she had in the family portrait taken a year earlier with her baby. Her left hand, which rested just under her chin, showed the dark polish on her nails, accentuating those long, slender fingers.

The photograph coincided with another important personal milestone—Dinah's third marriage. She had been in Chicago for the longest period of time since the beginning of 1943, when she left to sing with Hampton, and she'd reconnected with a high school friend, Robert Grayson, son of the minister at St. Luke Baptist Church. Though Bobby had married after high school, the marriage was over. He and Dinah started to see each other regularly, and on August 15, they were married. The groom's father, who had presided at her first marriage, to John Young, did not perform the ceremony; that duty went to Rev. Joseph H. Henderson.

Thinking Bobby was a musician, one friend asked Dinah what he played. "The jukebox," she retorted.

Her marriage license this time read "Dinah Washington," stage name and legal document now in sync. The license confirmed something else that was much more complex than words on a piece of paper. Two weeks shy of her twenty-third birthday, Dinah was already on her third husband. Clearly she wanted companionship, and just as clearly marriage meant something different to her from settling down in the traditional sense of the word: house, home, and children as the center of the universe. Dinah had no intention of giving up her career. In her case marriage was apparently intended to cement a relationship with the hope that the ceremony itself would insure the expectations of most unions: commitment, support, love, a shared life. Two failures at such a young age did not deter Dinah from trying again. She was also a traditionalist, born of a childhood steeped in the church; if she was going to be with a man, then they should be married.

A picture taken around Dinah and Bobby's wedding day showed a happy couple. Dinah was in a light suit and still wearing the braided hairpiece; Bobby was wearing a coat and tie. She leaned against him, smiling. He smiled, too, his left cheek brushing against her forehead.

Just as George Jenkins may have considered himself divorced from Bertha Henson, Dinah no doubt considered herself divorced from George Jenkins regardless of legal formality. She and George hadn't lived together for months; as far as Dinah knew, he was staying at the Gotham Hotel in Detroit. However, papers to dissolve that marriage were not filed until September 25, 1947, more than a month after she married Bobby. They put into words the reasons she had left George so soon after their marriage: allegations of physical abuse and more than one instance of adultery by Jenkins.

Dinah surely hoped for better with Bobby, and everything pointed in that direction. He was attentive and interested in her work. He took her to the Ritz every night and waited for her after the show to take her home. In a photo of the two celebrating in a club with friends shortly after the wedding, Dinah was kneeling beside Bobby, who was sitting at a table, an adoring gaze on her face.

Though Dinah looked the supplicant in that pose, the reality was something else. She was the breadwinner, proud of the earning power that allowed her to buy what she needed, including, by this time, a car. One evening between shows at the Ritz, she came outside and saw Bobby and a few of his friends in the car smoking cigarettes and visiting. She was livid.

"Get those motherfuckers out of my car," she yelled.

Startled and obedient all at once, they scrambled for the doors at her command.

. . .

WHEN DINAH WENT BACK in the studio on August 5, Mercury paired her with Dave Young's orchestra, a natural fit given their chemistry at the club. Before anything from this session could be released, Mercury reissued one of Dinah's Keynote records, "I Know How to Do It"/"Salty Papa Blues." Keynote had been struggling for months, and Mercury was in the process of buying the company. The Dinah Washington sides were among the first it had purchased. John Hammond, who was now running Keynote, told *Down Beat* that Dinah's blues sides with the Hampton sextet had been the little label's biggest sellers and that its biggest audience was in the "race field." Rereleasing the blues sides now made good sense; Dinah was gaining attention, respect, and fans, and there was every reason to think her earliest sides would do well, too.

Dave Garroway, who hosted a radio show live from Chicago's grand Merchandise Mart, invited Dinah in on September 7. He introduced her with a long monologue about the different kinds of blues—"talking, laughing, crying, philosophical, blowtop, thinking blues"—and the way such material should be sung, with subtlety and sincerity. "Whatever that delicacy is, our girl, Dinah Washington, has it," he said, as he turned the mike over to her. She sang "Since I Fell for You," which she had recorded a few days earlier with three musicians from Dave Young's orchestra who called themselves the Rudy Martin Trio after the piano player.

By mid-September Mercury released a single from the Dave Young session, "Fool That I Am," and the record registered right away on the new *Cash Box* chart "Hot Harlem" top ten. "Fool That I Am" was number seven and stayed on the Harlem tally for several weeks.

"Fool" was Dinah more subdued than she had been, even when she sang ballads with Hampton. Her signature moves were there, but as if in slow motion. *Metronome* didn't like the record, saying the vocals "lacked presence and get no help from weak backgrounds." The reviewer didn't care for Dinah outside of blues settings, declaring that the reissued Keynote sides "remain the best Dinah Washington on record." *Billboard* took a similar view, beginning its write-up of "Mean and Evil" with the statement that "Dinah was miscast as a ballad and standard singer" in several previous records.

Reviewers were expected to give opinions, but something else was likely at work, reflective of more complex matters than simple musical taste. The plain fact was that the reviewers were white men approaching the music from a particular perspective and with certain expectations, whether conscious or not. A black woman singing blues, with all its sass and sensuality, was easy to accept. Hearing her in a different context—a ballad more about romance than sex—was something else, more acceptable from Dinah Shore than Dinah Washington. It was true that some of Dinah's first recordings were less successful than others, but the presentation was not always judged on its own musical merits. Once again, race mattered, not just in marketing but in audience perception. Dinah's singing on these early ballads showed her most appealing characteristics: a straightforward approach to the material and elegant phrasing.

In October Mercury released "Since I Fell for You" with "You Can Depend on Me" from the Rudy Martin session. Now, the label advertised more aggressively on her behalf: big ads in *Billboard* and *Cash Box* with other Mercury stars, her picture (a new one) included.

Dinah was back in the studio in November with the Rudy Martin Trio to record four more songs and then again a few weeks later with Dave Young's larger group. It was the first time since Hampton that she had sung in the studio with the same musicians more than once. There was more recording in New York in December with a band led by trumpeter Cootie Williams and some nice news from *Cash Box*. When the magazine ran its list of best "race records" of 1947, "Fool That I Am" had garnered 1,091 votes—well behind Savannah Churchill and "I Want to Be Loved" with 24,099, but Dinah was gaining ground.

Everything was in place now for the new year—more records in production, an agent to secure bookings, a new husband, and, Dinah learned, she was pregnant again.

7.

Queen of the Juke Boxes

1948 – 1949

inah took a short break from the music business early in 1948, returning to Chicago and some important family business. In February she secured a $6,500 mortgage from a bank and a $2,800 second mortgage from her lawyer and bought a house on the West Side, at 1518 South Trumbull. It would be headquarters for what might be called Dinah Washington Enterprises—Dinah, her mother, her siblings, her own son, and assorted help.

The purchase was her most important move since she had joined Lionel Hampton, and it spoke volumes about her new status— tangible evidence that her growing popularity was bringing financial reward. It was an emblem of membership in two very select groups even though Dinah was only twenty-three years old: the 12 percent of black Chicagoans who owned their own homes and the even more elite number—less than 1 percent—who earned $10,000 a year or more.

The Trumbull house was in Lawndale, a neighborhood that had been almost exclusively Jewish in the 1920s, had shifted to a mix of Italians and Jews by the late 1930s, and was slowly changing once again. The Joneses were the second black family on the block. Their house at 1518 was one of similarly constructed two-story, two-apartment buildings, each with a limestone front, big windows, and a small front porch perfect for an after-dinner chat on a cool evening. In Chicago these two-apartment houses were known as "two flats." Immediately inside the oak front door was a small vestibule with two side-by-side doors. The left entered directly into the first-floor apartment; the right opened to a stairway leading to the second floor. The first- and second-floor apartments were almost identical. Each had three bedrooms, a living room, dining room, bathroom, and a back door that led to the yard. The second-floor apartment actually had an extra small room at the front extending over the staircase and an outdoor stairway at the back that led to the yard.

Dinah bought the house from John and Letitia Salerno and put it in her mother's name. The deed said that Alice was a widow; years later Clarissa joked that the designation described how Alice felt about the state of things with her estranged husband. Ollie was in fact still alive.

There was more than simple generosity behind Dinah's purchase of the house. "She wanted to get her family out of the projects," said Estrellita, who was not yet four when the family left their small apartment at the Ida B. Wells complex on 37th Street. And with a two-year-old son and another child on the way, Dinah continued to need her mother's help so she could pursue her career. As public housing went, Ida B. Wells was among the best, but the family needed a bigger home; Dinah needed a home base, and 1518 South Trumbull suited their needs. Alice and her younger children would be downstairs, and Dinah would have her own apartment upstairs when she came off the road. An added attraction was the backyard, big enough for a swing set and slide and even a wading pool to use when the weather got warm enough.

Dinah's siblings were delighted to have more room and much more space to play, though in the short term Harold and Clarissa had to take the streetcar over to the East Side to finish the school year at Doolittle Elementary.

Dinah had been making money to help the family since she was a thirteen-year-old singing gospel songs with her mother. She loved her father, but she understood as a child that neither she nor her mother could count on Ollie financially. Singing may have been a joy, but it was also a necessity, now even more so. Whether asked by Alice or not, Dinah had assumed responsibility for the family. "Dinah was taking care of us from the time she started making any substantial money," Clarissa said. "She was a major part of our economic situation. She was driven to give us the things she never had."

Purchase of the house on Trumbull coincided with another important musical moment for Dinah. Mercury released a single from the November 1947 session with the Rudy Martin Trio, "Ain't Misbehavin'," a popular Fats Waller tune. In Dinah's hands, "Ain't Misbehavin' " became a ballad, slow and deliberate, with attention given to each word and phrase—quite different from Waller's better-known romp. *Cash Box* liked her version, highlighting it on the record review page March 6 as an example of Dinah's "crystal clear tones." More important, the record made the *Billboard* race record chart the week of March 20 at number six. It was Dinah's first appearance in the magazine under her own name in four years, since the Keynote records with the Hampton sextet. At the same time, Apollo, which still owned those first discs recorded at the end of 1945, released "Pacific Coast Blues" backed with "Chewin' Mama Blues."

THOUGH SHE HAD a new home and was now five months pregnant, Dinah continued to work. She wasn't even in Chicago when Alice signed the final papers for 1518 South Trumbull, having started an eastern swing in Pittsburgh March 2 at Carnegie Music Hall. Bobby was with her and had the chance to meet Viola Battles and her son, William, who had become Dinah's good friends. William Battles, about Dinah's age, loved music and was not shy about going backstage to meet entertainers when they came through town. He tried never to miss Dinah when she was playing, and the two got so friendly that Dinah invited herself to stay with William and his mother. She could have gotten a room at the Bailey, the hotel that most traveling black performers used, but she liked to stay in private homes if she could even if they were in a housing project. Battles gave the couple his bedroom and slept on the couch.

Mrs. Battles was astonished when a maid showed up at the door and said she was there to do Dinah's toenails. "You must be crazy," Mrs. Battles told Dinah.

"No," she replied laughing. "I'm what you call nigger rich, baby."

Though she respected Mrs. Battles, her son recalled that "Dinah didn't bite her tongue." Whatever came up came out.

William Battles was an elevator operator at Kaufmann's Department Store, and he liked to bring Dinah in and introduce her to his friends. When she and Bobby stopped by for a few minutes on one visit, someone found a camera and a quick photograph was taken as a memento. Dinah and Bobby were sitting down; Battles, flanked by two friends, stood behind them. They made a handsome couple, and on this day they looked particularly stylish. Bobby wore a light suit with a buttoned-up sport shirt underneath; Dinah, already exhibiting a bent for furs, had a luxuriant silver-fox jacket over her black satin dress.

When Dinah arrived in Newport News, Virginia, in mid-April to play a week at the Tidewater Athletic Club, she was welcomed back as "a local girl by adoption" by fans who remembered her earlier visits with the Hampton band. In May she joined up with the Ravens again for two shows in Atlanta. One was at the Club Poinciana in the heart of black Atlanta; the other was at the City Auditorium. Promoter B. B. Beamon took out a half-page in the *Atlanta Daily World* that featured big pictures of each of the stars. Dinah's was a recent photo with the same kind of braided hairpiece she had worn in her wedding picture the previous August. She was billed as "Queen of the Juke Box," a nod to her growing popularity with fans who dropped their nickels and dimes in the jukeboxes and played her songs. Though it was a publicity ploy, the moniker stuck.

Dinah caught the attention of some white Atlantans who liked the music so much that they asked her to come back in the fall to entertain their society group. The invitation was unusual; it was rare for a black entertainer in the South to be invited to an exclusively white event, particularly one that wasn't a college fraternity party.

Dinah left the Ravens and headed to Washington for an extended stay—a week at the Howard Theater with saxophonist Eddie "Cleanhead" Vinson and his combo, and the comedian Jackie

"Moms" Mabley, and then an engagement at the Crystal Cavern, which was just a few blocks away.

Since she was in Washington for almost all of May, Dinah took a room at the Dunbar, Washington's most upscale hotel for blacks and frequented by all the major entertainers who passed through town. A few days after the Howard engagement ended, Arthur A. Bowles, the Dunbar's manager, recruited some of Dinah's friends and fellow musicians to throw her a baby shower. A crowd of 150 that included entertainers, disc jockeys, and newspaper reporters gathered in one of the hotel's larger rooms for a buffet-style dinner to honor the mother-to-be.

Dinah told Georgia Mae Scott, a friend and co-host of the party, that she needed some help on the road and back in Chicago when the baby came. Scott said she knew just the right person. Her name was LaRue Manns. She was about Dinah's age, had one year of college behind her but dropped out to move to Washington, where her sister lived. The only job she had been able to find was working as a barmaid in a nightclub. Scott wanted to help her find something better, and as soon as she talked to Dinah, she called LaRue. "I've got just the thing," she said, and explained what Dinah wanted—"companion and friend and sister and helper, you know, everything wrapped up in one."

LaRue didn't pay much attention to show business and had no idea who Dinah was. The first time she saw her was from the audience, when Scott took her to the Crystal Cavern for a quick introduction. By the time they got there, Dinah was already onstage in the middle of a song, but she greeted her friend anyway. "Georgia," she said, speaking in time with the tune, "you made it and you brought the girl along."

LaRue was amazed. "She could be singin'," she marveled later, "and work the words that she wanted to say to people into her song and never lose a beat." Dinah and LaRue met after the show, and Dinah asked her to be at the Dunbar at eleven the next morning.

LaRue got to the hotel, went up to her room, and rapped on the door at the appointed time. "One thing I like about you, you're on time," Dinah said as she invited her in. Over the next few minutes, Dinah laid out her expectations. Would she take the job?

"I'll be glad to," LaRue replied.

"Well, I like you already," Dinah said, and then offered her a two-week trial and told her that if she had any trouble getting a leave from the manager at her current job, "I'll speak to him myself." LaRue got her leave and never went back.

AT THE FIRST of the year, James Petrillo, the head of the musicians union, had declared another record ban, which affected instrumental music made in the studio. But unlike the previous ban in 1942, when recording came to a complete halt, small companies, including Mercury, paid less attention to the directive. Many labels found creative ways to make records. Some used vocal groups— who were not members of the union—to back a lead singer instead of instruments. Some dubbed already recorded band music behind a new vocal or vice versa. It was not a new technique—synchronizing two different kinds of music had already been done for movies. Other companies recorded outside of the U.S. mainland, in Mexico or Puerto Rico, and some ignored the ban altogether.

During the 1942 ban, the record companies had not been able to stockpile much material because it was wartime, and there was a shortage of the shellac necessary to make the discs. This time around the labels were "filling the icebox," as one manufacturer put it, with enough recordings to last several months.

Mercury made use of its own stockpile in June, when the label released "West Side Baby," recorded nearly a year earlier, and "Resolution Blues," which Dinah co-wrote and recorded at her last session before the ban, December 31, 1947, in New York. The song was, appropriately, about New Year's resolutions. Both were on the *Billboard* race chart for most-played jukebox record by the third week of June, just as Dinah returned to Chicago to await the birth of her second child. LaRue, who had accompanied her to New York for a quick recording session, came with her to Chicago as originally planned, settling in on Trumbull to help care for George. LaRue found such quick rapport with Dinah's siblings that years later they couldn't remember exactly when they met. "She was just there," Clarissa said.

Being pregnant with George had not deterred Dinah from performing almost until she went into labor. This pregnancy didn't stop her either. On June 24, billed as the "West Side Baby," she sang for a "graduation ball" at the Savoy ballroom with Illinois Jacquet. *Billboard* reported the next week that "West Side Baby," its staying power intact, still registered on the charts. (The magazine had gotten its Dinahs mixed up one week, crediting Dinah Shore with "West Side Baby." It was likely the only time *that* Dinah showed up on a race chart.)

On July 10 the flip side to "West Side Baby," "Walkin' and Talkin' and Crying My Blues Away," showed up at number fourteen on the best-selling race chart. Two weeks later a fifth tune was on the charts, "I Want to Cry," which debuted at number thirteen on *Billboard*'s retail listing.

This was the kind of moment entertainers strived for, and it would have been the perfect time for a road tour to plug the records in one city after another. But on August 2 Dinah was back at Provident Hospital to give birth to her second child, a son named Robert Grayson, Jr.

The house on Trumbull was bustling now: a new infant, George Jenkins, just two years old, Estrellita, Alice's youngest, not yet four, Clarissa, eight and a half, and Harold, not yet twelve. Bobby Grayson, Dinah's husband, was around and although he was intermittently employed, Dinah was the major source of income, and life revolved around her world. The bulk of the work at Trumbull fell to the women in the house, and their territory was the first floor. Harold, Clarissa recalled, moved upstairs to take one of the rooms in Dinah's apartment. LaRue's main responsibility was helping with George and the new baby.

On August 25, less than a month after Bobby was born, Dinah went back to work, recording in New York with a new producer. Mitch Miller was an arranger and conductor who had just been hired after eleven years with CBS to head Mercury's pop division. He was already recording Frankie Laine, one of the label's most successful stars, and Vic Damone, who appeared to be on the cusp of a big career. Though Miller knew who Dinah was, he had never seen her live, and he was looking forward to the session, even though the record ban put a crimp in what they could do musically. The plan was for two ballads, "I'll Wait" and "It's Too Soon to Know," and both used minimal instrumentation. On "I'll Wait" Dinah hummed a middle chorus and filled out another with a string of la-da-da-dums; on "It's Too Soon to Know," she was surrounded by a vocal group as the song built to its conclusion.

The ban provided one beneficial by-product: these stripped-down arrangements, 180 degrees from singing with the sixteen-piece Hampton band, showcased Dinah's voice. Nothing could obscure her sound or distract from the way she phrased each lyric. A lesser singer might have worried about being so exposed, but there was no trace of anxiety and no holding back in Dinah's presentation.

"She was a natural," Miller recalled. "Bottomless talent." He made sure everything was set before she started to sing, insisting that the engineer work on the right sound balance while the musicians were tuning up. "Many times the first take is the best. I would always work for that—try to capture it on a wing. . . . I would never tell her how to do a phrase," he added. The most he might do was offer a technical suggestion to make her sound better, such as how close to the microphone she should stand. "She was the boss in the studio. She told the band what to do."

While that may have been true, Dinah also maintained a one-of-the-guys attitude. Miller recalled one session in Chicago—he had flown in to record all night after Dinah finished a show—where she catered a middle-of-the-night snack: smoked shrimp from a little restaurant on Grand Avenue near the navy pier. Though he lived in New York City, where anything seemed possible, he was surprised that such a delicacy could be found at two in the morning. Not to worry, Dinah said. She called in the order and in no time at all, the food, still giving off a sweet and spicy aroma, arrived.

With another record on the *Billboard* chart, "Am I Asking Too Much," the sixth since March, Dinah's success since the beginning of 1948 had not gone unnoticed. Record stores and jukebox operators wanted all the Dinah they could get. Mercury received orders for twenty thousand copies of "It's Too Soon to Know" a month before the intended release date even though no one had heard the record.

This good news was coupled with her first Broadway engagement on her own, singing at the Midtown Royal Roost, which billed itself as the "Metropolitan Bopera House," with Count Basie and his orchestra. It was a stellar lineup—in addition to Dinah, Miles Davis, a rising young trumpeter, was on the bill with a combo that featured

another star-in-the-m

just had a baby five w

"an energetic worker,

"I Know How to Do

grinds at strategic mo

and synergy: new re

The week of Oct

Too Much" topped

spectable fifth on t

that fans not only

also buying her r

throne.

(The Royal Ro

and the session v

ing in Atlanta fo

months earlier. She also had to turn down a

refurbished nightclub in Chicago eager to have her name on the

marquee.)

Dinah was back at the Royal Roost on October 17, singing now
with Dizzy Gillespie and his orchestra. This was a "bop concert"
sponsored by one of New York's best-known jazz disc jockeys, Symphony Sid—Sid Torin—who broadcast over WJZ, a prominent station available in many parts of the country. Petrillo's ban had no
effect on live radio shows, and when Dinah sang "It's Too Soon to
Know" in the club it was the kind of full-bodied arrangement that
could have been done had the record ban not been in place—three
trumpets, three trombones, tenor, alto, and baritone sax along with
piano, bass, drums, and guitar. The record had just been released,
but the audience knew the song and singer, erupting in cheers as
she sang the familiar opening line, "Does he love me?"

RIGHT AFTER THANKSGIVING Ben Bart booked Dinah on a
short tour with a six-piece group put together by Joe Thomas, a
tenor saxophonist who had played with the late Jimmie Lunceford.
Lunceford's widow gave Thomas the right to style his new group the
Jimmie Lunceford All-Stars. While the band traveled in a small bus
with a trailer behind for the instruments, Dinah brought her own
car, and no one begrudged her the comfort. "She had no airs about

her," said Richard "Dickie" Ha
Stars. "She liked to gamble
dice, get on the floor with
fanity," Harris added wi
down-to-earth."
Dinah also ha
stop in one Ark
care of lunch
everyone
finished
name
Th

ris, a trombone player in the All-
ith the guys. . . . Dinah would shoot
s and play. . . . She would use a little pro-
h just a hint of understatement. "She was

a playful and generous side. Harris recalled a
nsas town when she told the band she would take
. "We thought this was wonderful," Harris explained,
oking forward to a free meal. After the musicians had
, Dinah took out a pencil and paper and started calling out
s: "Okay, Dick Harris, one order—well, that's five dollars. Joe
omas, five dollars—no, that's double." And so on. "So we paid
er," Harris explained.

A few minutes later Dinah gave all the money back, laughing as she did so.

On December 2 the band pulled into Beaumont, Texas, to play the Harvest Club. That night Dinah got an unexpected visit from a well-known fan, Xavier Cugat, the bandleader and rhumba king, who raced over to the club after his performance at the Beaumont City Auditorium.

The band headed east from Beaumont for dates in Mississippi and then on to Birmingham for a theater engagement right before Christmas. Bobby had joined Dinah for this part of the trip, and he was riding with her in the car along with bandleader Joe Thomas. On the way out of Meridian, Mississippi, the car struck a soft shoulder and careened off the road, rolling over three times before stopping. While the car was damaged beyond repair, miraculously, none of the three was injured beyond bruises, scratches, and some minor burns. Alice and Clarissa shuddered when they saw pictures of the beat-up automobile.

On this same trip, according to the story passed around among musicians, Dinah showed a dangerous bravado. The band had pulled into a gas station in the middle of Mississippi, and Dinah asked to use the ladies' room.

"We ain't got one," the white attendant said.

"What do you mean?" Dinah asked.

"We ain't got none for you."

"You don't have a ladies' room or a toilet I can use?" she asked again.

No response.

"Well, then you take your damn gas out of my tank."

"I'm not going to," the attendant replied.

"Well, I'm not going to pay."

"Yes, you are," the attendant insisted.

Dinah reached into the glove compartment of the car, pulled out a small pistol, and pointed it at the man.

"Am I?"

Dinah and the band must have hustled into the car and roared away from the station, each of them looking back to see if a Mississippi lawman was on their tail. Apparently not, given that there were no reported repercussions from Dinah's impulsive and brazen act. A black woman was not supposed to pull a gun on a white man in Mississippi or anyplace else in the South.

Trumpeter Clark Terry wasn't there, but he was sure the story was true when he heard it. "Dinah was a pretty wild gal in those days," he said.

The unpleasantness in Mississippi was one of the few grim moments in a year that brought a new son, a chart-topping hit, and continued recognition in the industry. Dinah's commercial appeal was evident in two important tallies from *Billboard*. In the year's top twenty-five "Race Record Sellers" Dinah had two, "Am I Asking Too Much" (number fourteen) and "It's Too Soon to Know" (number nineteen). On the other chart, which was for labels with the year's top-selling race records, Mercury was number eight of fourteen, helped by Dinah and the two records that had registered on the race record chart.

Cash Box showed Dinah fifteenth of twenty-one on its race artist list. She was also represented in the smaller music fan magazines. The dividing line in *Down Beat* was still whether a singer was with a band or not; in *Metronome* it was a matter of gender. Neither magazine had a race category. *Down Beat* readers placed Dinah eighteenth of twenty-seven in its listing of "Girl Singer (Not Band)," and she was fifteenth of twenty-eight in *Metronome*'s poll of female vocalists for 1948.

If the world of music was like a solar system, the women singers were among its planets, some larger and brighter than others, each with a distinct sphere of influence. Three of Dinah's contemporaries—Ella Fitzgerald, Billie Holiday, and Sarah Vaughan—reached a white market, particularly the jazz fans. Indeed Vaughan topped the *Down Beat* and *Metronome* polls in 1948, and Fitzgerald and Holiday, in that order, were just a few notches behind her. The rewards for such recognition were clear: the *Chicago Defender* reported that in the new year Vaughan would receive a hefty $4,500 for a week's stay at the Adams Hotel in Newark.

For now, Dinah was still a "race" artist, but she did keep jazz company. While she was in New York the last week in November, Dinah was invited to see Sarah Vaughan, who was opening at a new nightspot, the Club Clique, which had formerly been the Ebony. The *Defender* noted the moment with a five-column picture of Dinah sitting between Vaughan and Jackie Cain, a young white jazz singer. A radiant smile on her face, Dinah was the most elegantly dressed of the three, wearing a scoop-neck dress with a sequined design on the front that was set off by her glittery earrings. With her swept-up hair she looked every bit the sophisticate.

DINAH WAS BARELY HOME long enough for the Christmas holidays to drop off presents for the family and go through her mail. Among the cards and bills was an unexpected letter from Sallie Martin and her singers, by now an established presence on the gospel circuit, offering Dinah the chance to rejoin them. Though "genuinely gratified" she told the *Defender*—and it wasn't clear which side of the exchange alerted the newspaper—she had to decline. She was due in Cleveland January 7, 1949, to play the Café Tijuana, a small club whose name suggested a Mexican ambience but which in fact featured East Indian food. The engagement was to be a limited one, but the draw proved so successful that the club owners wanted Dinah to stay an extra week.

When she returned to New York, Dinah alternated time in the studio with rehearsal for a two-week stay back at the Royal Roost. One ardent fan sent her an orchid corsage every other day.

In the meantime, Mercury had released three more records, and mail-order stores that advertised in the black press now had enough Dinah Washington discs to give her her own section along with such established stars as Louis Jordan and T-Bone Walker and other emerging acts that included the Ravens and Wynonie Harris. Stores that broke out their stock in more general categories invariably put her discs in the "Harlem Hits."

The first week in March Dinah started a major tour as the headliner with the Ravens, who were still riding the wave of two big hits, "Write Me a Letter" and "Ol' Man River," and the Cootie Williams orchestra, which would provide the necessary accompaniment. The plan was to travel to nineteen cities in ten states, from New Jersey south into North Carolina through South Carolina, Alabama into Florida, and back up to West Virginia. Ben Bart's Universal, which put together the tour, would provide the bus to get the group from one place to the next.

The system that made such tours possible—and they were a common means to promote and exploit the artists' success—resembled a pyramid. The talent was at the top. Right underneath was the booking agent. The next layer was the promoters who made deals with the booking agent to secure venues for the talent. The promoters were a diverse group of men, among them Ralph Weinberg, one of the few Jews in the unlikely spot of Bluefield, West Virginia, who handled his own state, Virginia, and the Carolinas; B. B. Beamon, the black Atlanta businessman whose territory covered the deeper South; Don Robey in Texas, another black entrepreneur who was also in the record business; and Teddy Powell, a black businessman who booked shows in New York and New Jersey. The regional promoters in turn dealt with the bottom layer, the club owners and theater managers in each of the towns on a tour, if the promoters didn't own or operate the particular venues themselves.

In Raleigh, Sylvia Weinberg, Ralph's daughter-in-law, recalled that one of their best contacts was a policeman who booked shows on the side. "They put up posters on telephone poles and made contact with radio stations," Weinberg said. It was always a good sign when the tour bus got in town early, she added—a bit of free publicity that let the public know about that evening's show.

The entire enterprise operated by financial rules that carved up the proceeds among all the layers. First to get paid, significantly, was the agent—Ben Bart. The standard was 15 percent of the overall amount that was guaranteed to the artists the agency represented. Fifty percent of what the talent was to make on the entire tour was deposited ahead of time from the promoters (Weinberg,

Beamon, et al.), and Universal took its 15 percent of the total from that amount.

After each date, the musicians got the remaining amount on the deal that had been negotiated, and the promoters and their local contacts, if any, got the rest of the proceeds from the door. Inherent conflicts were obvious. Club owners had incentive to undercount the house; musicians grew used to keeping an eye on the door. But despite the temptations for accounting chicanery, the system for the most part worked.

Though the touring musicians were making money doing what they loved, they were also caught up in the cultural tensions of their time. Traveling through the South in the spring of 1949, they entered a world where change was in the air even as the racial status quo remained firmly in place. Seven months earlier the nation had gone through its most public debate over civil rights, when Hubert Humphrey, the mayor of Minneapolis, electrified the Democratic party convention in Philadelphia with his challenge to "get out of the shadow of states' rights and walk forthrightly into the bright sunshine of human rights." After Democrats adopted the strongest civil rights language to date in the party platform, delegates from Alabama and Mississippi walked out, joining other Southerners in Birmingham, Alabama, to back the states' rights presidential candidacy of South Carolina governor Strom Thurmond. The central tenet of Thurmond's rump "Dixiecrats" was that the states had a right to continue their own "custom and tradition"—the benign euphemism for segregation—without interference from the federal government. In November Thurmond was a distant third to President-elect Harry S. Truman, but the issue of segregation and unequal treatment of America's black population was front and center. In this same year Jackie Robinson had become the first black to play major league baseball, and the Supreme Court had nullified covenants in property deeds that barred sales to anyone but Caucasians.

In the world of entertainment race still operated with striking clarity: white America was more than happy to be entertained by black artists, but when the applause died down, skin color mattered more than talent. It explained why Duke Ellington, Cab Calloway, Ella Fitzgerald, Billie Holiday, and every other major black star still headed from the showrooms of downtown Chicago to the South Side to find lodging for the night. They were still the servant class; their roles just seemed more elegant than cook, gardener, or chauffeur.

A minstrel show by the white Camp Fire Girls of Baltimore in late February 1949 was a vivid reminder of how white appreciation of black culture was infused with racism. These teenagers performed their tap dance routines, "coon songs," and step-'n'-fetchit skits in dialect, wearing bandannas and made up in blackface so the show would seem authentic. They were proud of their talent as mimics, delighting in the appreciative laughter of their white audience.

Traveling in the South, Dinah and the other musicians took nothing for granted, understanding that they had to plan their itineraries according to where they could find the basic amenities of travel—food, lodging, gas. Then when they performed it was both aggravating and demeaning to see how black patrons were often shunted to the least desirable seats in a theater when a performance was in a white venue.

Every now and then a black musician would speak out against the status quo—Lionel Hampton in 1945 refused to play Kansas City's Pla-More Ballroom because of the way the management treated blacks. In December 1948 Louis Jordan made a public protest during a concert in New Orleans after he came out onstage and saw that all the black patrons were seated in the balcony. He announced to the 4,500 assembled that he would not play in the city again unless black patrons were permitted to buy tickets to sit anywhere in the theater. He took the unusual and bold step of urging his fans in the audience to write their congressional representatives to support civil rights legislation that President Truman had proposed.

In Washington, D.C., a few weeks later a group of black city residents donned poster boards and picketed a movie theater to protest the discriminatory way black patrons were treated—either denied the right to buy tickets or relegated to uncomfortable balcony seats with poor views of the stage. The National Theatre, the city's only legitimate theater, closed rather than change its policy on admitting blacks.

These were but snapshots of the contemporary racial landscape, and neither the Jordan protest nor the picketers accomplished any immediate change. Dinah and her traveling companions were under no illusions as their rented tour bus headed into Raleigh, North Carolina, on March 7 for their first southern stop. They knew they would be staying in the black section of town, probably at a room-ing house that served only blacks or they'd be parceled out to pri-vate homes where residents took in traveling musicians.

If this was the reality of offstage life, onstage the transcendent appeal of music was apparent when Dinah and the others looked out into the audience in Memorial Auditorium, Raleigh's largest arena, and saw white faces. The crowd proved that Weinberg was right in thinking that he could tap a market beyond Wake County's black population. He had advertised the show in a two-column ad—"The Greatest 'Triple' Attraction Ever"—in the *News and Observer,* Raleigh's mainstream white newspaper. Tickets were $1.50 in ad-vance. The last line of the ad said, "Reservations for White Specta-tors," the clue that the evening was a concert *and* dance and that it was intended for a black audience. Whites could come, but they couldn't dance. Nor could they mix with the black patrons. In up-scale venues there would be separate seating. But in many there was only a rope that separated the two races. Police officers were stationed in every corner to enforce the required segregation if an exuberant white "spectator" literally crossed the line. It was the in-genious intersection of commerce and ideology, a nonsensical pro-cedure to maximize profits amid an ingrained social caste system.

The setup was the same in Columbia, South Carolina, March 11, where white "spectators" paid $1.30 and blacks paid $1.75. In Chat-tanooga on March 21, the white spectators got in for half-price.

The next night in Asheville, North Carolina, was one of the more unusual stops on the tour. Buncombe County, which was near the Tennessee border in the foothills of the Appalachian Mountains, had roughly 120,000 residents, just 12 percent of them considered "nonwhite." Some were Native Americans, and though the lion's share were blacks, this was still a small number compared to At-lanta, Raleigh, Columbia, or the tour's stops in Tuskegee, Alabama, Jacksonville, Florida, and New Orleans. But Weinberg, the promoter, knew his territory and knew there was an audience in this western North Carolina town. How else to account for Asheville supporting the Harlem Record Shop? Here in Asheville whites paid a dollar to listen, blacks $1.75 to listen and dance.

The shows themselves on this long tour were nightly versions of the Ravens' and Dinah's "greatest hits," and the tour had gotten off to a terrific start. After the first seven dates, the promoters were only too happy to share the news about its success. *Billboard* and the *Chicago Defender* each carried stories trumpeting the audience numbers and cash taken in: $22,596.94 after all taxes were paid; 19,333 patrons in all. The biggest night was March 10 in Atlanta, where 5,788 jammed into City Auditorium for a concert that also benefited the Negro Cultural League.

As Dinah and her tourmates pulled into Fayetteville, North Carolina, April 2 for their performance that night, Mercury had good news about her latest release. "You Satisfy," a typical blues number recorded nearly two years earlier with the Dave Young Orchestra, was number eight on the new *Billboard* jukebox chart and number six in the latest *Cash Box* tally for Los Angeles, "Hot on Central Avenue." L.A. was one of four cities now listed every week in the magazine's race music pages. (The other cities were New York, Chicago, and New Orleans.)

From Fayetteville the group swung north to Roanoke, Virginia, to play Legion Auditorium, where "spectators" were also invited. Then the troupe headed west to Huntington, West Virginia, for their last stop.

On such a long road swing, Dinah called home almost every day. "What are my babies doing?" she wanted to know. Told that Bobby, now seven months old, had started to crawl or was cutting another tooth, she invariably would lament, "Ooh, I missed it."

This was the trade-off, the deal that Dinah struck to have children and a career. Yet it was the success of that career that was enabling her to take care of the entire family. Her income had allowed her to buy the house on Trumbull and now a car for her mother, a black Buick—Dynaflow transmission—that was the envy of the neighborhood.

"We had everything we wanted," Clarissa said. "I went to elementary school wearing cashmere sweaters. The Jewish kids also wore expensive clothes. I was in competition with them."

Clarissa remembered one call from Florida (the tour was in Jacksonville March 14), when Dinah asked what she should bring back. What do they have in Florida? Clarissa wanted to know. When Dinah explained the possibilities, Clarissa recited her requests, and the presents arrived a few days later.

• • •

STARTING IN 1947 the *Pittsburgh Courier,* which rivaled the *Chicago Defender* for influence in black America, conducted a poll among readers to select their musical favorites, a kind of alternate-culture contest to the ones published in *Down Beat* and *Metronome.* Once the winners were decided the *Courier* sponsored a midnight concert at Carnegie Hall that was always a sellout. This year's performance was on April 9, and Dinah was invited to sing as the 1949 winner of the "girl blues singer award."

The evening was a who's who of the top names in black entertainment: Lionel Hampton, winner in the big band category; Ella Fitzgerald, winner as the "girl popular singer"; Billy Eckstine, winner in the same category for men; Illinois Jacquet in the small combo category. Hampton opened the show with a frenetic "The New Look." Fitzgerald came on next to sing "Old Mother Hubbard," Earl Bostic and his group played "Body and Soul," and then Dinah came out and sang "Am I Asking Too Much" to warm and appreciative applause.

Alice Jones was still not happy about her daughter's decision to go into show business despite the benefits that came to the entire family. And she still refused to see Dinah perform in a nightclub. But Carnegie Hall was different, and Alice flew to New York for the event. The *Courier* reported that it was her first trip by plane. She seemed determined to be unsentimental as she watched Dinah being honored. "Coming from the Windy City of Chicago, Dinah's mother denied wiping a tear from her eye, exclaiming 'Nonsense, New York's a windy city, too,' " the *Courier* said.

Dinah was back in Chicago by mid-May to get ready for a week-long stay at the Regal with the Ravens and a band led by trumpeter George Hudson. The engagement gave her the chance to get more settled in her upstairs apartment at South Trumbull and to have some time with George and Bobby. She made her first television appearance on a local NBC show with the Three Flames. And then she was off to Detroit for a July engagement at the popular Flame Show Bar. Club patrons enjoyed laughing about what might have been Dinah's first appearance there when she was still Ruth Jones. Word was that the eighteen-year-old Ruth had come to audition at the club in the fall of 1942, just after she separated from her first husband, John. Whoever was in charge supposedly told her that she would never make it in the music business.

Dinah's Mercury contract was about to expire so it was a propitious time for another of her records to reach the *Billboard* and *Cash Box* charts, the just-released "Baby Get Lost." (In June *Billboard* had jettisoned its "race" category and renamed the genre "rhythm and blues," to be both less obvious in color-coding music and to embrace a wider array of records.) What better selling point for a new deal than another record on the charts? Not surprisingly Mercury included Dinah in its full-page *Billboard* ad August 20, which trumpeted "Mercury's sensational six." She and Patti Page ("I'll Keep the Love Light Burning") were the only women among four of Mercury's male stars: Frankie Laine, Vic Damone, Eddy Howard, and Rex Allen.

Dinah had achieved enough success that rival record companies were taking new interest in her, but when questioned about her plans by a reporter during the Detroit engagement, she said she was flattered by the attention but was staying with Mercury.

"Baby Get Lost," written by Leonard Feather, was a straight blues tune similar to "Evil Gal." "I've got to be the boss," goes the punch line, " 'cause if you can't play it my way, well, now, baby get lost." Popular as "Baby Get Lost" was, the flip side was the more arresting tune, "Long John Blues," and it was by far the most explicit song Dinah had recorded. The lyrics told about a trip to the dentist who is seven feet tall, "Long John," but they were full of sexual allusions about being told "to open wide./He said he wouldn't hurt me but he'd fill my hole inside." Its most recognizable line was probably "You thrill me when you drill me."

The song was recorded during the record ban, and Dinah was accompanied only by a guitar, which playfully followed her through the story. Feather was convinced that Mercury waited a year to release it because company executives were not sure how such a tune would be received. ("Long John Blues" hit the *Billboard* sales and jukebox charts August 20 and stayed there two months.)

When Dinah returned to the Apollo, her name was in big letters overshadowing the others on the bill—the Ravens and Joe Thomas and the All-Stars, which had expanded to thirteen pieces.

She worked a short comedy gag into her singing, asking the audience, "Have you heard the 'Zombie Song'?" Without waiting for an answer, she started to sing "Zombie these days"—a play on words of the standard (and the theme song of Sophie Tucker) "Some of these days . . ."

Dinah ended each show with a steamy rendering of "Long John Blues." The audience loved it, chortling to one another as they left the theater about "the dentist song." She joined the Ravens up in Boston a few days later for a show that was sold out a week in advance.

It was obvious now that Dinah was a singer of note, and within the black community she was evolving into a celebrity. An offhand comment or a rumor about her next project was worthy of repetition in the black press; three- and four-paragraph stories cropped up in such places as the *Chicago Defender*, the *Amsterdam News*, or the *Indianapolis Recorder*. One story September 3 described Dinah's views about the Iron Curtain: During a small gathering at her apartment in the Theresa Hotel, she suggested that a "goodwill" tour of American musicians to the Soviet Union could bring the two countries closer together. The next week there was a story repeating the tantalizing prospect that Dinah might return to gospel music, "Spirituals Seek Dinah." The offer, made backstage at the Apollo from an unnamed group, was "tempting," she said. That same day another story appeared about a possible new tour through the South, retracing the steps of the March–April swing Dinah had just finished.

When *Billboard* published its September 24 issue, the music charts revealed another new high. Dinah had won the rhythm and blues exacta: "Baby Get Lost" was number one on the "best-selling" chart and number one in the "most-played juke box" tally. It was confirmation of the major decisions she had made in the last three years—leaving Hampton, signing with Mercury and with Ben Bart— and affirmation from the public. The issue of *Cash Box* that week carried a small story about Mercury's sales being at an all-time high. One paragraph cited the artists who were responsible for this milestone moment, and Dinah, with "Baby Get Lost," was among them.

Leonard Feather had been hospitalized as his song climbed the chart, and just after he was released, Dinah called to check on him. "Thanks, baby—your timing couldn't have been better," he told her. " 'Baby Get Lost' paid for our hospital bills."

"Fuck the hospital. You didn't break your hand, did you?" Dinah retorted. "Just use it to keep on writing them songs."

Feather appreciated the gruff compliment, but he wondered whether "Baby" sold so many records because customers really wanted the flip side, "Long John," but were embarrassed to ask for it.

DINAH'S CONCERN with her appearance was never far from the surface. Memories of slights from high school and the occasional cruel joke from Hampton band members remained, though she had come a long way from the unsophisticated teenager accepting fashion tips from Gladys Hampton. She dressed with more flair and had changed hairstyles several times. For now the braided hairpiece was gone, and her hair was short, parted on the right and swept over to the left.

Dinah's changing looks did not obscure the fact that she was heavyset—not obese but no sylph either. Reviewers—men, who would never have done so with a male singer—felt free to comment. They didn't go on at length but the adjective or phrase dropped in here or there stung nonetheless: "the buxom" Miss Washington, the "bosomy" singer, "hefty," "plump."

Dinah wanted to be thinner, and now she was willing to try anything that would help her lose weight. The same week she was at the top of the *Billboard* charts, she went on some kind of eight-day reducing plan that left her with bouts of nausea serious enough to require a doctor's attention. She had gone to Bridgeport, Connecticut, for a one-night performance and was so sick that the doctor ordered her to stay there instead of making the short trip back to New York. (Recounting the episode, the *Defender* headlined its story "No More Dieting for Dinah," but it wasn't clear if Dinah had taken pills or was eating particular foods that didn't agree with her.) She recovered in time to get back onstage with Dizzy Gillespie's band for an extended stay at Bop City, a Broadway nightclub that had opened in April. But the Bridgeport episode was nonetheless a troubling one.

AT THE END OF OCTOBER, Dinah and the Ravens teamed up with Joe Thomas and his orchestra to go on the road again. Their first stop was in Philadelphia, to play the Earle Theater for a week. The place was packed every night, and on two of the days, fans had to wait more than an hour in a block-long line to get in.

The group got a similarly rousing reception in Indianapolis, before they headed south for the rest of the tour. They broke a record in Louisville a few days later, with nearly 4,200 fans in the auditorium, and when Dinah and her musicmates played Nashville's storied Ryman Auditorium, city officials closed the doors after more than 1,100 fans jammed their way into the theater, leaving dozens more stranded outside.

Instead of heading home for Christmas, Dinah was back in New York, where she and the Ravens were booked for the holiday show at the Strand, a place she had played a few times with Hampton. She had gotten used to having things the way she wanted them, from food to clothes to cars and even a house. Now she traveled with a dog, named Backstage, and the Strand management balked at letting her keep her pet in the dressing room—even though a dog was in one of the acts.

"If the dog goes, I will follow," she threatened before the first show. But under pressure, probably from Ben Bart, among others, she relented and sent the dog back to the Theresa Hotel, still her temporary home in New York.

The Strand engagement resembled a vaudeville event. Dinah was sandwiched between dancers, the act with the dog tricks, and a comedian. The sound system was not always adjusted to get the best results for a singer, and during one performance, audience members complained that they could barely hear her over the backup band that was blasting away behind her. She fared better when she came out for a couple of turns with the Ravens.

Sound problems aside, Dinah used the engagement to try out new material before heading back into the studio in the new year. One of the numbers she sang was "If I Loved You," from the Rodgers and Hammerstein musical *Carousel*. Dinah sang all the words and followed the same melody the Broadway stars were singing, but she extended a phrase beyond the beat here and there and added jazz inflections where she felt like it. Her version had its own special power, as if to show how Rodgers and Hammerstein might have written the song had they worshiped at St. Luke Baptist. Rather than a musical dialogue between a couple, it was a performance.

The end of the year brought the usual magazine polls, *Billboard* and *Cash Box* measuring the commercial, *Down Beat* and *Metronome,* fan appeal. In the *Cash Box* category of "Best Jazz 'n Blues Artist of 1949," Dinah was ninth of eighteen. Sarah Vaughan was second to last in this category, but in the much broader category of "Best Female Vocalist of 1949," which included the white market, Vaughan was ninth, two slots above Billie Holiday. Doris Day was in first place.

In the *Billboard* tallies for top rhythm and blues artists, which measured the best-selling and most-played jukebox records, Dinah was twelfth of fifteen in both on the strength of "Baby Get Lost" and six other tunes that had been on the charts.

Sarah Vaughan repeated as the winner in the *Down Beat* and *Metronome* fan polls. Dinah was eighteenth out of twenty-seven in *Down Beat* and eighteenth of twenty-three in *Metronome.* She might have wished for better, but her career was unmistakably on the rise. Things on the home front were another matter; the lyrics of all those love songs she was singing now seemed especially poignant.

8.

No Time for Tears

1950–1951

Bobby Grayson had a girlfriend. That was the news from a woman Dinah visited when she came back to Chicago in January 1950. Dinah called her a "fortune-teller," but she was probably a combination of self-styled psychic and neighborhood gossip. "Among other things," Dinah remembered, "she told me that when I found out where the girlfriend lived, I would crack my sides laughing. . . . The fortune-teller wasn't wrong." Bobby had left a phone number lying around, and using an old trick, Dinah confirmed who the woman was and where she lived—right in front of the Reverend and Mrs. S. A. Grayson, Bobby's parents.

It was true that Dinah had been away much of the time since she and Bobby had gotten married, but she was working and making money, and as she saw the situation, Bobby was not interested in keeping a job. That aggravated her. Friends who knew both of them raised an eyebrow when they got married and weren't surprised when the marriage ended. She and Bobby didn't have much in common beyond their connection to St. Luke Baptist and Phillips High School. But it was easy to see why Dinah was attracted to him.

He was good-looking, a sharp dresser, and drove his father's late-model car around, giving the impression that he was prosperous. There was no question he looked good on Dinah's arm, and he enjoyed the benefits that came with her growing celebrity. But he was also a "player," one high school chum remembered, and "Dinah knew that when she married him."

"I'd be waiting for him to drive me to work," Dinah lamented, "and he'd be out someplace having a ball."

Though they had a son, it was not enough to hold the marriage together. Because Bobby Jr. was already living on Trumbull with his grandmother, half-brother, aunts, and uncle, very little, at least on the surface, would change in his young life.

Dinah's marriage to Bobby was the longest of her three, but it had lasted barely two and a half years. Success has a price, and Dinah was no exception when it came time to pay. Her constant absence made any kind of traditional relationship impossible. But at the same time, this very success enabled her to provide for herself and her family. Then, too, there was the plain fact that Dinah loved to work. She was at home with musicians, who were surrogate families to one another on the road, and she was at home onstage in front of an audience that called her "Queen" and begged her to sing some more. To give up that life was unthinkable.

It was crucial to keep up the momentum, and Dinah wouldn't complain to Ben Bart about how and where he booked her. There was new territory to conquer, new markets to reach. Her career was blossoming, and she would serve it regardless of personal cost. So while she ended a marriage, Dinah didn't miss a beat with her schedule. Making use of her brief time in Chicago, she played a week at the Regal with old friends, the Ravens and the Joe Thomas Orchestra, and watched her newest Mercury release, "I Only Know," pick up steam. Dinah headed east again the first week in February, stopping in Washington for several days at Lou and Alex's, a supper club near the Howard Theater. Alex was Alex Underdown, brother of Welker Underdown, the current manager of the Dunbar Hotel; Lou was Louie Murray, a local businessman. It would have been a routine engagement except for one thing: the opening performance was a Sunday evening. Dinah had sung on Sundays with Hampton and again when she went on her own, but she had refused to open on that day of the week. It was a small and private bow to her church and gospel roots. "There was just something in me that rebelled at the thought of a Sunday opening, with all of its attendant thrills," she explained. While she agreed to break her rule for the Washington supper club, she was adamant that "after this, the no-Sunday ban is in effect all over again. I just don't like Sunday openings."

Dinah's decision had nothing to do with the possibility of a small crowd on that day of the week. She claimed not to pay attention to the size of the audience. Entertainers who slack off when the house is half-empty are "way off base," she said. "The best advertising that an artist can get is the word-of-mouth praise of those who have been pleased by a performance. Then it makes sense to give the small crowd everything you've got so they'll go out and tell others to come and see you."

By the time Dinah got to New York she was on the music charts for the first time in the new year. "I Only Know" debuted on the *Billboard* jukebox tally March 4 at number seven—a noteworthy beginning for a Dinah Washington song that was a ballad and not blues. The lyrics were credited only to "Washington," and it was probably Dinah. They seemed to be written by someone who appreciated the mysteries of romantic life. "I only know that I'm in love with you," the song begins, followed by the telling: "I don't know how it happened or how it came to be . . ."

In addition to its regular music listings, the March 4 *Billboard* also included a jukebox supplement. Dinah was the only woman in the "Rhythm and Blues Top Artists" category, twelfth of fifteen, and the only woman on the "Rhythm and Blues Top Records" chart, with "Baby Get Lost," fourteenth of thirty. The listings gave credence to her claim to be Queen of the Juke Boxes, but her sole presence probably also reflected how difficult it was for a host of other black women singers with similar repertoires to get attention.

WHEN THE HAMPTON BAND had played New York City, Dinah took every spare minute to go to Café Society, a small club (seating for two hundred) in Greenwich Village, to listen to pianist Hazel Scott. Next to the music, Dinah's favorite moments were those spent in the dressing room chatting with the star. It was a thrill when Dinah herself was finally booked at Café Society for a two-week stint starting April 6 and given the same dressing room she had visited while still a budding star. On a bill with singer Josh White and comedian George Kirby, Dinah wouldn't do an entire set—just a few songs at each of the three nightly shows. But she was now on the roster of a fabled nightspot, well-known for its top-notch entertainment and its racially mixed clientele, which reflected the club's status as a watering hole for leftist progressives. Billie Holiday had first sung the pointed anti-lynching song "Strange Fruit" on Café Society's stage.

Mercury paid Dinah the ultimate accolade: a full-page ad in the April 8 edition of *Billboard* touting her latest hits, "I Only Know" and "It Isn't Fair," newly entered on the R&B sales chart, and reminding readers they could see her live at Café Society. *Billboard* reviewer Jerry Franken, who caught the April 11 show, was not impressed with that night's performance: "Miss Washington went thru three numbers in quick order and delivered them in so calm and impersonal a manner that results were neglible." The *Chicago Defender*, its reporter apparently more partial to Dinah's style, was enthusiastic and then some in the report filed for the paper's April 15 edition: "Dinah closed the show in traditional headline fashion, with the audience in a state of mild hysteria."

She couldn't spend Easter with her own toddlers, but Dinah, according to press reports, sponsored an egg hunt for Greenwich Village children who lived near the club.

Finished at Café Society, Dinah headed a few miles north to Bop City, where she joined a bill with Nat Cole and Count Basie. Though she wasn't the headliner, it still burnished her credentials to sing every night with two of the biggest names.

The highlight of Dinah's next session, which was the second week of May, was "I Wanna Be Loved." It was already a hit for the Andrews Sisters, with Patty doing the lead vocals and featuring the sisters' trademark harmony, here bolstered by a waterfall of strings.

The title and the lyrics of the song, so obvious in their yearning, seemed a perfect fit given Dinah's domestic travails. Yet her rendition was neither morose nor melodramatic. The Andrews Sisters were polished and smooth. Dinah was hardly ragged, but her version, arranged with horns, was different, everything a Dinah Washington record had come to mean: moving, sassy, and confident, with those distinctive allusions to gospel when she changed the timing of certain phrases and added "baby" when she felt like it. The overall effect suggested that the love Dinah wanted was not just romantic. This kind of singing wasn't a matter of notes on a page or chords on a chart. It couldn't be taught and couldn't be imposed by a producer sitting behind a glass wall in a production booth.

Dinah's fans loved it. "I Wanna Be Loved" would get on the trade charts by mid-June, staying on *Billboard*'s rhythm and blues tallies for nearly three months and registering high on the charts of all the cities that *Cash Box* monitored on its R&B pages. In the larger pop market the Andrews Sisters did even better. By July they were still in first place in the *Cash Box* listing of the nation's top ten juke-box tunes. The two versions of "I Wanna Be Loved," with the same words and the same melody, served as a primer for different musical sensibilities.

It was clear now that Mercury wanted Dinah to record pop songs along with the occasional blues, apparently on the theory that her version of these songs would find a rhythm and blues audience. They were right, and Dinah's success with "I Wanna Be Loved" confirmed a shift in her musical presence. The song was her third consecutive ballad on the charts, a striking contrast to the previous year, when her biggest successes had been all blues tunes. So it was a bittersweet surprise when *Ebony* magazine included a four-page feature in the June issue that portrayed Dinah only as a blues specialist, even if the headline called her "undisputed as nation's top interpreter of blues." Invoking the legend of Bessie Smith, the magazine said most other singers suffered by comparison. "Until the advent of Dinah Washington, a buxom, lusty-voiced young woman with a passion for comic books and tailored suits, no one had come close to making the grade." Dinah, the magazine went on, "is securely on the top of the heap of women blues singers in the U.S."

Dinah's polite response suggested her misgivings about the narrow definition of her talents: "I never knew Bessie but I heard most of her great records and they were simply wonderful," Dinah told the magazine. "She was a tremendous artist, and folks who compare me to her do me a great honor."

Even though Dinah never thought of herself as only a blues singer, recognition from *Ebony* was still important. The magazine, with its mix of news, features, columns, and ads each month, was geared to mostly upscale readers. It conferred a certain status on those it profiled.

The article recounted the basic facts of Dinah's life to date—church beginnings, the Garrick Building, name change, signing on with Hampton. But it also included misinformation about her early years, erroneously telling readers that she and her mother traveled the country as a gospel team and misstating her time with Sallie Martin. Perhaps someone at Ben Bart's Universal Attractions gave the magazine the incorrect history or perhaps Dinah herself embellished here and there.

Ebony offered dramatic figures to illustrate Dinah's earning power. Noting that she started out at $75 a week with Hampton, the magazine explained, "Today she pays her chauffeur more than that." Then the article listed figures it said were Dinah's "grosses" since she left Hampton at the end of 1945: $15,000 in 1946, $45,000 in 1947, $75,000 in 1948. "This year she expects to top her 1949 figure of $100,000 [$760,000 in today's dollars] by at least $50,000." *Ebony* also reported that Dinah traveled with a wardrobe that included fifty gowns, sixty pairs of shoes—which she purportedly changed "10 times daily"—and twenty tailored suits.

The magazine did not say where it obtained the financial numbers nor the wardrobe information, though Dinah or Universal may have been the source. The income levels almost certainly were on the generous side, perhaps reflecting the gross receipts of the tours Dinah was on rather than her particular share.

But the overall presentation, which also boasted that Dinah was a fabulous cook—original meat loaf, macaroni and cheese recipes, "and cakes of all kinds"—was in keeping with the way *Ebony* wrote about entertainment figures, who were among the most important public figures in black America. It was a matter of pride to show how successful they were, financially and artistically. It was not uncommon, as the Dinah piece showed, to note that these stars could have expensive wardrobes, drive big cars, or afford luxurious homes, and the magazine lavished the same attention on them as it did on civil rights activists and the elite of black society. The article even included what it said was Dinah's favorite joke: "Take your girl to Florida so you can Tampa with her. If you don't, Jacksonville. If she goes, she's a Daytona Beach." It had the ring of a crack told on a bus full of men.

Though Dinah performed all over the country, *Ebony*, in keeping with its Bessie Smith theme, emphasized her southern black audience: "Her more excited fans throw dollar bills at her feet," the magazine said. "Others press coins into her hands and whisper 'God Bless you, sister.' " A half-page picture of Dinah in the midst of song let the reader understand how she could elicit such fervor from the stage. Head back, eyes closed, her arms crossed over her chest, she had surrendered to the moment.

Another picture showed Dinah singing along to a recording of "Long John Blues," and while that may have been true, the photo was an inadvertent boost for a competitor: Dinah was holding a record of Mercury's rival Atlantic. *Ebony* claimed that "Long John" sold two million copies, which was highly unlikely in the R&B market. But the claim was typical of wildly inflated sales figures that were common among independents like Mercury, Atlantic, Chess, King, and Savoy, who were competing for the same market.

Positive as such a feature was, some of the writing could only reinforce Dinah's concerns about weight and size. Already described in the opening paragraph as "buxom," Dinah was also labeled "plump." One of the other pictures was particularly unflattering. It was shot while the photographer knelt at her feet and pointed the camera upward. It showed every wrinkle in her skirt and made her appear far bustier than she was. *Ebony* labeled the picture "Sweater girl."

EBONY MADE NO MENTION of Dinah's checkered marital history nor the fact that she had two sons. She had already put Bobby Grayson behind her and was involved with drummer Teddy Stewart, who had played on two February sessions and the May session that produced "I Wanna Be Loved." In fact, Mercury credited the group in the studio as "the Teddy Stewart Orchestra," probably at Dinah's request, because he was the new man in her life, onstage and off-. He was a constant presence in her small cubicle backstage at Bop City, where Dinah kept a collection of trinkets and doodads that she liked to haul from place to place. Stewart had the delicate task of getting rid of what wouldn't fit in the boxes when the date was over, quietly tossing them in the trash or, when possible, giving them to kids who waited at the stage door to get Dinah's autograph.

Stewart was accompanying her now on a trip out to California that Ben Bart had put together. Dinah was on the bill with saxo-

phonist Earl Bostic and his group, also represented by Bart, and together they would make stops in cities along the way until they got
to Los Angeles.

Dinah, Stewart, and Harold Newboldt, a driver she hired, were
traveling in her car, and the Bostic band was in its own caravan.
Everything was going along smoothly, but after the group played St.
Louis the first couple of days in June, something happened between
Dinah and Stewart. Perhaps Dinah got angry when she thought
Stewart looked too long at one of the young women who always
clustered backstage to flirt with the traveling musicians. Maybe they
quarreled over the music or over money. Whatever it was, as they
were heading west for the next job at the Municipal Auditorium in
Junction City, Kansas—it was "Negro Business Week"—Stewart got
so angry he struck Dinah and forced her and Newboldt to get out of
the car. A passerby picked them up, and Dinah got to Junction City
just in time to go on. The Bostic men didn't know what had happened until she arrived wearing dark glasses to cover the bruises on
her face and told them about the incident.

Stewart was from nearby Kansas City, and his family still lived
there. Dinah found her car at the family's home, but Stewart was
gone and was not seen for the rest of the road trip. Dinah must have
been upset and angry about the incident, but whatever she said,
however she calmed herself to perform for the black businessmen,
was lost to history. She went onstage and sang, bruises and all.

At a difficult moment, when life on the road was at its worst, a
local reporter asked Dinah if she would give up popular music and
return to gospel. She was resolute in her answer: a turbulent private
life would not send her back to the church. "I have no intention of
changing to the religious singing field at this time," she said. "I plan
to continue my present pattern of activity for at least two more
years. Thereafter I am not certain what my course will be. I might
add that I have a deep desire to settle down to a domestic life with
my youngsters as soon as it is practical to do so."

For someone who was so earthy and spontaneous, Dinah's comments sounded formal and stiff, as if to define and protect her
image. She not only wanted to appear well dressed but well-spoken
and proper, too. The "deep desire" to settle down may have been
heartfelt, but the divide between Dinah's stated intentions—to be
home with her family—and her behavior, which was defined by

constant work on the road, was too obvious to be bridged by mere assertion.

THE LAST TIME DINAH was in California she had been a supporting player, one of several acts in the Lionel Hampton show. This time, when she drove into Los Angeles for a two-week stay at the Oasis, a storied club "in the better Negro neighborhood" on Western Avenue, according to the black monthly *Sepia*, she was a star. She was welcomed with open arms from her fans and big headlines from the city's black press. It was obvious from stories in the *California Eagle* and the *Los Angeles Sentinel* that the writers at both papers had read *Ebony*. Each perpetuated the myth that Dinah and her mother had traveled around the country as a gospel team, and each repeated the misstatements about her brief time with Sallie Martin. Though inaccurate, they now seemed to be a fixed part of Dinah Washington lore.

Eagle show business columnist Gertrude Gipson also informed readers that Dinah and Teddy Stewart had split up, though she referred to him as Dinah's husband, which he was not.

The Oasis stay was everything Dinah could have hoped for, with sold-out audiences every night still clamoring for more when she finally left the stage. The *Sentinel* (and the story was also picked up back home in the *Defender*) reported that she missed breaking the attendance record set by Billy Eckstine by "exactly twelve admissions." "Yes, La Washington has come to the Coast and captured it—but good," the *Sentinel* gushed. And *Eagle* columnist Gipson said Dinah earned her title as Queen of the Juke Boxes because "she finds out what you like, how you like it and gives it to you (music we mean)."

Ben Bart had put together an ambitious itinerary to make the most of Dinah's seven-week stay in the state. When the Oasis engagement was over, Dinah reunited with Hampton to play the city's "Cavalcade of Jazz," a Sunday afternoon concert then in its sixth year. Sixteen thousand people packed into LA's Wrigley Field for music and a beauty contest to crown Miss Cavalcade of Jazz. The only sour note came at the end, when some rowdy fans started throwing seat cushions and whiskey bottles after Hampton closed the show with his exuberant "Flying Home."

Before leaving for two weeks of club dates in the San Francisco–Oakland area, Dinah sat for an interview with some reporters to talk about the possibility of making movies. She made clear she would not take any "Tom" roles that would cast her in an undignified light. She would sing in a "normally cast role of a Negro" but would not do the eye rolling and grinning that was the stereotype of so many black characters in white-made movies. "Frankly," she said, "I'd like to portray Dinah Washington on the screen. In other words, I'd like to be myself. Come to think of it," she added, a twinkle in her eye, "what's wrong with me?"

Dinah sat down with reporters again in San Francisco while she was playing Longbars Showboat. Now the subject returned to her weight. The writer described her as "corpulent," noting that she had "periodically resorted to various reducing diets etc. to assist her in losing excess avoirdupois, with none giving too successful results." Now, Dinah explained, she was on a fish diet and had lost twenty pounds in fifteen days.

Dinah's willingness to discuss her weight, a subject most individuals considered private, suggested more than a bent for publicity. Constant applause and songs on the charts were apparently not enough to overcome her doubts about her appearance. Dinah wanted to be glamorous, and that meant size six or eight, not twelve or fourteen.

DINAH HAD TO GET BACK to the East Coast for another tour of one-nighters and more recording, but Ben Bart saw to it that both of them could make some money on the way back. She stopped in Denver to play a week at the Rossonian Hotel's lounge, billed alternately as the Queen of the Juke Boxes and as the "famous Mercury and Decca Recording Star from Café Society in New York City." The Decca reference was an unusual addition, though no doubt an effort to add cachet to her appearance; her one record on the label had come out under Hampton's name "with Dinah Washington."

Dinah's stay at the Rossonian was a window into the blurring boundaries of the music market and perhaps into the unregimented atmosphere of a young western city like Denver. It did not have a large black population, yet there was an audience receptive to the rhythm and blues made by black artists. The week before Dinah's appearance at the Rossonian, Julia Lee, a piano player and singer from Kansas City, packed the lounge during her two-week stay, even meriting a long, flattering feature with a picture in the *Denver Post,* the city's main newspaper.

Another window into the stew of race and music was the news Dinah received on the road about her expanding realm as Queen of the Juke Boxes. The Howard Johnson restaurant chain, which had the music machines in so many of its venues, had broken the color line with male singers—Billy Eckstine and the Ink Spots were the most prominent. But it had not put the music of black women singers into its jukeboxes, not Ella Fitzgerald, not Sarah Vaughan, not Billie Holiday. In July, the chain put in its first Dinah Washington records. Told by some fans that they had heard her music while eating at one of the restaurants, Dinah said she was proud of the honor. "Every step ahead that means a fuller realization of the goal of complete recognition is a good one," she said. "The glory that comes to me or any other artist as an individual means little. It is the events that mean something to us all that really count. Howard Johnsons are to be congratulated."

The comment was so formal it didn't sound like Dinah. Perhaps she was trying to sound appropriate to the occasion, perhaps Ben Bart's office had drafted something for her, though it was hard to imagine Dinah letting someone put words in her mouth.

DINAH'S TWENTY-SIXTH BIRTHDAY coincided that year with an engagement in Philadelphia at the Earle Theater. She was once again on a bill with the Ravens and also bands led by two saxophonists, Eddie "Cleanhead" Vinson and Arnett Cobb. Cobb's bass player was Walter "Little Man" Buchanan, Jr., a nickname at odds with the tall, slender man who had a taste for well-cut suits. Dinah was intrigued.

That year she decided to throw herself a birthday party on August 29 and rented a local hall for the event. She told the *Philadelphia Tribune* she had invited four hundred friends and acquaintances and that Earl Bostic and his band were going to provide the music. "Music makes any party, and it's my good luck to have one of the greatest combos in the business to brighten up mine," she said. Ollie came in from Chicago to celebrate with his daughter, and so did

Richard Egan, one of Dinah's favorite actors, who happened to be in the city.

Toni Thompson, Dinah's friend since her Hampton days, who was in charge of the birthday cake, recalled years later that there were nowhere near four hundred guests. The crowd was small enough, she said, that she could chat with Egan all by herself, which thrilled her.

Perhaps Dinah's best birthday present was the chance to spend time with her children. The National Baptist Convention was holding a meeting early in September in New Jersey, and Dinah arranged for her mother, who had just remarried, to bring George and Bobby east with her. She had booked rooms in Pompton Lakes, New Jersey, where boxer Joe Louis trained, and she would join them after she finished a recording session in New York on September 1.

The gathering in New Jersey was going to be a large group: Dinah now had a new chauffeur, a seamstress (who was the chauffeur's wife) and a maid. LaRue Manns still watched after the children, and now Dinah also traveled with her own piano player, twenty-year-old Wynton Kelly, whom she most likely met when he was playing with Eddie "Cleanhead" Vinson, when they were on the same bill.

Wynton was a native of Jamaica who moved to Brooklyn when he was four and immediately began absorbing the music around him. "I didn't have much formal study," he explained, though he was talented enough to go to Music and Art High School and then Metropolitan Vocational. "They wouldn't give us piano, so I fooled around with the bass and studied theory." But the piano was his first love, and he found jobs around Brooklyn. One of the more important was with sax player Ray Abrams and his brother Lee, a drummer. He graduated to work with larger groups headed by Hot Lips Page, Eddie "Lockjaw" Davis, and then Vinson. When Dinah heard him play, she could see how talented he was and appreciated the understated, unobtrusive way he played the piano. "He never let his technical facility, which he had plenty of, dominate," said one admirer. "The swing is the thing with Wynton." It would have surprised audiences to learn that he could make such good music being deaf in one ear.

After her mother and children returned to Chicago, Dinah went back to Philadelphia to play the Club 421 and then headed to New

York for a week at the Apollo. Opening night September 28 was difficult; Dinah apologized to the audience because she said she had a sore throat. A few days later she was back in form, using the show to give a live performance of "Harbor Lights," another ballad, which she had just recorded and which also had been a hit for the Sammy Kaye Orchestra. Dinah finished each show by turning "I Wanna Be Loved" into a duet with singer Herb Lance.

The next week she was on the charts again with "I'll Never Be Free"—the fourth time since March and the fourth ballad. The song was about longing for a past love—"no one can take your place in my embrace. I'll never be free," and it was another cover of a tune that had done well for white singers, Kay Starr in pop and Tennessee Ernie Ford in country. Dinah's presentation was easygoing and assured, enhanced by the solid work of guitarist Freddie Green and bassist Ray Brown.

When *Billboard* published its disc jockey supplement October 7, Dinah captured the number five slot for top rhythm and blues record of the year with "I Wanna Be Loved."

On October 10 Dinah was in Baltimore for a revue at the Royal Theater. Though Arnett Cobb's orchestra kept a different itinerary, Dinah and Walter Buchanan, the bass player, had found a way to keep company. At some point he left Cobb to join her, and their relationship escalated. Before long, Dinah was ready to try marriage again. In a ceremony at a private home in Baltimore Friday, October 13, Walter became Dinah's fourth husband. The Reverend Frederick Jackson, the assistant pastor of the Fulton Avenue Baptist Church, officiated a few days before the state of Maryland gave its sanction to the union by issuing a license on October 17.

At thirty-five, Walter was nine years older than Dinah. He came from a well-established black family. His father, Walter Sr., who attended the wedding, ran a real estate company in Pittsburgh and had been president of Alabama A&M College in Huntsville.

No one beyond family and friends had paid much attention to Dinah's first three weddings. Her fourth, however, prompted a news story in the *Baltimore Afro-American* with all the particulars—Mrs. Ike Salmon was the maid of honor; Walter's brother, Council, was best man. After the ceremony, the bride sported an imposing ring on the fourth finger of her left hand, leaving no doubt about her marital status.

The next day friends threw the newlyweds a breakfast at the Alhambra Grill, just down Pennsylvania Avenue from the Royal Theater. It was a joyous moment, Dinah laughing as she playfully fed Walter a bite of food.

When they left for a honeymoon, the *Afro-American* ran a two-column picture of the couple. Dinah, dressed in a handsome, tailored suit, was waving at the camera, her right arm extended, which kept the fur boa draped over her shoulder in place. Buchanan was smiling at her left. The caption said that the couple planned to live in St. Albans, Long Island, and together with the picture, it projected a normalcy that was not to be.

The honeymoon was short because Dinah was back in Chicago to play the Pershing Hotel Ballroom on October 29. Trumpeter Calvin Boze and his band backed her, though Wynton played the piano on her part of the show. The group played the Roosevelt Theater November 8 and 9 and then went on to Thanksgiving shows in Indianapolis and Gary, which meant another holiday away from the family. In addition to the ads that promoted the still reigning "Queen of the Juke Boxes," Dinah was continuing fodder for the chitchat columns. Now it was that Dinah "seems to be making a bid for the title 'Fashion Queen' if her acquisition of prominent N.Y. fashion designer Vivian Hunter is any indication." Dinah's "entourage now consists of a dressmaker, wardrobe mistress, beautician and personal manager—not forgetting milady's chauffeur," the item said. Though the puff piece was likely exaggerated—Vivian Hunter was Dinah's maid, not a designer—it left a vivid impression: Dinah was making lots of money and living well.

Just before Christmas, another of Dinah's songs hit the charts, the fifth of the year, "Time Out for Tears." It was from the September session that had also included "Harbor Lights," and it was more evidence of her transition from blues to ballads. But most important, the record, like "Harbor Lights," was from Dinah's first session with strings, provided here by the Jimmy Carroll Orchestra. It reflected a decision by Mercury to give its premier race artist the same musical accoutrements other labels gave to their white stars. Beyond the cushion of sound violins and cellos created behind a singer, strings were also a symbol of class, a tip that a particular presentation was going to be high-tone—the very opposite of a suggestive romp like "Long John Blues" or the less explicit "A Slick Chick (on the Mellow

Side)." The session also represented Mercury's investment in Dinah. Strings cost money, and Mercury was willing to spend it on Dinah's behalf. Equally important, the session—and the way the label released the song—was an indication that executives were seeing her, at least in some moments, in a new, more expansive light. "Time Out for Tears," like "Harbor Lights," was released as part of Mercury's pop series rather than its race series, Dinah's customary home even when she sang the earlier ballads. The buying public wouldn't notice the difference. To them a record was a record, but the shift within the company on these tunes showed that Mercury was taking intermittent steps to broaden Dinah's audience.

The year-end tallies in the music magazines continued to highlight the different perspectives within the industry. *Down Beat*'s readers placed Dinah twenty-second of twenty-four in its "Girl Singer (Not Band)" category; in *Cash Box* she made the equivalent list as fourteenth of seventeen. Ella Fitzgerald was the only other black woman mentioned on its overall list of women singers. *Cash Box*, however, broke out a rhythm and blues category, and Dinah was seventh of seventeen on a list that included men and women. Two of her songs were on the list of the twenty "Best Jazz 'n Blues Records of 1950," "It Isn't Fair" at number ten and "I Wanna Be Loved" at number twenty, both closer to jazz than blues.

Though these tallies were arbitrary markers, if Dinah had to choose, most likely she would rather have had the better notices from the industry than from a particular group of music enthusiasts. *Cash Box* was about business—who and what sold yesterday, which was the best guarantor of tomorrow.

Dinah went home to Chicago for the Christmas and New Year holidays and Walter came with her. Clarissa, who had just turned eleven, liked the handsome man her sister had brought to Trumbull. He paid special attention to her, and he gave her a ring as a present.

TWO WEEKS INTO THE NEW YEAR, Dinah's marriage was in trouble. Walter was drinking, and when he had too much, which was often, he swore at Dinah in private and in front of friends. During one angry moment, he threatened to whip her. He embarrassed her and her friends when they were out one evening and he stopped the car, got out, and urinated on the curb.

The handsome, gregarious man Dinah had married disappeared. He drank so much now he couldn't work even if he wanted to—and Dinah had given up asking him to play bass for her.

The afternoon of January 11 Dinah had gone in the basement for something or other.

"Where's Walter?" Dinah asked Bobby, when she came up.

"Walter took the car and left," Bobby told her.

Barely three months after their wedding, Dinah knew the marriage was over. Her first concern was the car. She had to get back to New York to perform and record, so she called Walter's father in Pittsburgh and his aunt in Chicago, hoping to find him. Neither knew where Walter was, and it is not clear when and where she eventually found him and got the car back.

At least there was some good professional news to offset these new personal woes. "Harbor Lights" was on the charts. The Mercury experiment with strings hadn't hurt her standing with her rhythm and blues fans even though she hadn't yet broken through on the pop charts. It was hard to know, however, just how much Mercury pushed the ballads and how hard their distributors worked to find new outlets for a new kind of Dinah.

No doubt Dinah took solace, too, from the warm reception she received in Pittsburgh at the end of January when she played before enthusiastic crowds at Johnny Brown's nightclub. She was so popular that the club added a Saturday afternoon "cocktail matinee" during her run. The *Pittsburgh Courier* was not privy to Dinah's private life, and the January 27 issue promoting her club appearance included a picture of Dinah and Walter right after their wedding, smiling for the photographers.

When Dinah returned to New York it was for a two-week engagement at another storied venue, Birdland, which was right at the intersection of Broadway and the famed 52nd Street. A small and pedestrian basement room, the club was owned by Morris Levy, a tough-talking entrepreneur with connections, legal and otherwise, all through the music business. "When I was fourteen or fifteen, I worked for people that were in the Mob because they were the people that owned the clubs," Levy said. "They liked me because I was smart, I was hardworking, and I was a tough kid."

Levy was candid in explaining that he opened Birdland with his partner, Monte Kay, to compete with Bop City, hoping to force it out of business. Levy had been angered at the Bop City owners because they failed to cut him in when they enlarged their operation even though, Levy contended, he had helped them prosper in a smaller Midtown locale. Rumors constantly swirled through the business that the adult Levy had gotten money to open Birdland from organized crime figures, and federal law officers were constantly watching his activities.

Through an arrangement with WJZ, the Birdland shows were broadcast live late at night and hosted by Symphony Sid. Levy had known Sid from his days at the Royal Roost, when the disc jockey approached the club about hosting a bebop concert. Though Dinah had branched out, Sid still liked to call her Queen of the Blues, sometimes even with an Irish twist—"The Macushla of Blues," which made Dinah giggle.

"Go wail one," Sid said as he opened the January 13 show. Dinah laughed before launching into her October hit, "I'll Never Be Free." She filled out the show with tunes from recent sessions and finally sang "Harbor Lights" after shouted requests from the audience.

In this setting Dinah was backed by a trio, Wynton on piano and a bass player and drummer she would pick up. It was Wynton's job to create the feel of the orchestra that had backed Dinah on these songs in the studio. He provided fill with chords and delicate runs, but it was never fussy. The two were in easy sync. He had an impeccable understanding of her phrasing; she could relax and banter with the audience and with Sid, who encouraged her to "sing all the pretty tunes for the people." She appeared to make a seamless transition from full orchestra with arrangements to improvisation with three other musicians.

The ground rules of a live broadcast were apparent at the January 20 show when the audience yelled out the titles of one song after another. "Ladies and gentlemen," Dinah told them, "anything I sing now was cleared over the air. I have to sing what they tell me." And then without taking a breath or letting even a second pass, she began "I Wanna Be Loved."

When Dinah finally acceded to one boisterous patron's request and sang "Time Out for Tears," she slowed the song down, letting every phrase sink in, both the longing for a departed love and the defiant promise to find someone new after "the time out for tears."

In February Dinah was back in the studio (after a quick trip to Detroit to play the Paradise Theater), and although Mercury apparently planned to let Walter lead the session to please Dinah, it is unlikely he was there. Later discographies nonetheless credited the group as the "Walter Buchanan Orchestra." Mercury probably didn't know how much Dinah's relationship with Walter had deteriorated and didn't change the paperwork after the session was over. Wynton almost surely played the piano along with a gathering of reliable studio musicians whose lot was to remain anonymous.

Even though they didn't become hits, Dinah's versions of "Please Send Me Someone to Love" and "Ain't Nobody's Business" showcased her blending of gospel and rhythm and blues. Dinah sang "Please Send Me" as both prayer and lament, in evocative contrast to the boisterous horns behind her. Her version was tamer than many renditions by blues singers, who turned "Please Send Me" into a torch song, and it more closely resembled the original rendition by Percy Mayfield, who wrote the tune.

"Ain't Nobody's Business" became a sermon in Dinah's hands. In fact she began it by singing, "Lord, lord, lord," and followed with a bar of humming that had the effect of setting a reflective, even intimate, tone. If Dinah seemed so at home with the song, it was probably because its sentiment—"ain't nobody's business what I do"—reflected her outlook.

AS SOON AS the session was over, Dinah got ready for another tour. Ben Bart teamed her again with Earl Bostic's band and Dinah's old friend from Hampton days, comedian Slappy White. He was now a partner with Redd Foxx, whose comedy was a shade more risqué. The group would start at the Apollo, play the Howard in Washington, the Royal in Baltimore, and then work their way west so that Dinah could be in Los Angeles by May for a three-week stay back at the Oasis. She was promised $2,500 a week plus a percentage of the door—at least that was the information that was put out with the tour announcement.

Dinah's second song to hit charts in 1951 was "My Heart Cries for You," another tune that had done well for white pop singers. Dinah's version, with its uncharacteristic "oom pah pah" styling, made only a brief blip on the jukebox tallies.

By the time the tour got to Washington to play the Howard Theater March 20, Walter had come back into Dinah's life, and band
members overheard them fighting all the time. When Walter took
Dinah's car again, she called the police, who put out an all-points
bulletin for him that covered highways, railroad stations, and air-
ports. They found him and her Cadillac the next day in Baltimore.

Walter apparently stuck around, because the other musicians
remembered him staying with Dinah as the group headed west to
Chicago, where they performed at the Pershing Hotel ballroom. By
the time the musicians reached St. Louis April 20 to play two dates
at Masonic Hall, however, things between the couple had reached
the breaking point. Their fights became more ferocious; band members were amazed to see Dinah pull a gun during one altercation.
She carried one now because she usually had a lot of cash on her,
even though she conceded privately that she didn't really know
how to use the weapon. Ben Bart was summoned, and he flew out
to get Buchanan. "We never saw him again," said Keter Betts,
Bostic's bass player.

Dinah admitted later that she hadn't had much hope for the
marriage after the first month or so. "In no time at all I realized the
marriage was doomed," she said, more blasé than sad. "I considered
it a joke when he told me one day that he wanted a new car and he
was going down to pick one out. But I was laughing through my
teeth. 'While you're there,' I said, 'get one for me too.' Of course we
got no car."

Dinah hadn't liked it when Bobby Grayson didn't want to work.
It was a rude awakening when Walter turned out to be the same.
"He said I have enough money to take care of him," she said. In her
mind, Walter's family contributed to the problem. She claimed she
heard someone in the background during a phone conversation
with him say, "You better stay with this woman and get all the
money you can."

DINAH'S NONSTOP SCHEDULE and her emotional armor left
no time for tears over the collapse of her fourth marriage. The
breakup with Walter was also eased by her attraction, mostly musical, to two young musicians with the Bostic band, the bass player
Keter Betts and the even younger drummer he told Bostic to hire,

Jimmy Cobb. She got her first taste of their musicianship when they filled in behind her at a one-night performance in New Jersey in February, just before she and the Bostic group were to leave on their tour.

"If you ever leave Bostic," she told them, "you have a job."

Keter was from Port Chester, New York, twenty-seven miles north of Manhattan. He was full name was William Thomas Betts, but when he was an infant, one of his mother's friends came by and joked that he looked like "a little moskeeter." The moniker got shortened to Sketer and shortened again by kids in the neighborhood to Keter. It stuck.

One day when he was in fifth grade, Keter's mother sent him to the grocery store on a shopping errand, and a parade passed him. He was so intrigued by the sounds and sights, particularly the steady beat of the drums, that he followed the parade all around town. He arrived home four hours later to find his mother furious.

"Mom, I want to play the drums," he told her, explaining where he was and why.

She helped him get a drum kit, and by the time he was a sophomore, he was going into New York for jazz drum lessons every Friday, 12:30 sharp. He would map out his day after checking the papers to see who was performing at the major theaters, the Apollo, the Strand, the Paramount, and then he would see every show he could before the last train back home.

In Port Chester he played at school, evening dances, and neighborhood block parties. The experience tested his energy and commitment because the Betts family lived in a fourth-floor apartment with no elevator, and it took Keter three trips to get his drum kit down and three more trips to get everything back up when he was through.

Keter played the bass a few times in high school but considered it only "fooling around." On one trip into the city, though, a bass player for one of the bands he had seen befriended him. The man later gave Keter the name of a teacher in case he wanted to pursue the instrument. Keter decided to follow through, but the man was too busy and referred him to Arthur Miller, a bass player–teacher in Brooklyn.

At their first meeting, Keter showed off a few things he could do. "I can show you how to do that a bit easier," Miller told him, and

Keter was hooked. His family loaned him the money to buy a bass, and his first break came when tenor saxophonist Carmen Leggio asked him to join his band. Keter jumped at the chance to earn $60 a week. In January 1949 he got an offer to come to Washington, D.C., to play a month at a supper club, and it happened to be when Earl Bostic's group was coming through town. Bostic's regular bass player was leaving, and another band member who had heard Keter told Bostic to hire him, which Bostic did.

Keter had become friendly with Jimmy Cobb, whose love for the drums and jazz was nurtured by those Symphony Sid broadcasts on WJZ. At midnight, when he was lying in bed after a day of school and part-time work, Jimmy always turned on the radio, and though the signal might fade in and out, he still heard enough of Charlie Parker, Dizzy Gillespie, and Thelonious Monk to whet his appetite. When he could afford to buy records, he would play along with them on his drum set, which he bought on time, $20 a week out of the $27.50 paycheck from his part-time job as a busboy. He scrounged up the money to pay for lessons from Jack Dinay, then the youngest member of the Washington Symphony Orchestra.

Jimmy's first performance—not for pay—was providing the music for family gatherings at his grandfather's farm in rural Maryland outside Washington. Paying jobs came along, including one at a small club near the Howard Theater that was a hangout for traveling musicians. Keter occasionally stopped by, and the two became friends. On one of the Bostic band's return trips to Washington, coincidence and friendship combined in Jimmy's favor. Bostic's drummer was leaving and he asked his musicians for any suggestions. Keter told Bostic to hire Jimmy, and the bandleader agreed. It was the summer of 1950, and Bostic told the young drummer to meet the band at 125th Street and St. Nicholas in Harlem. "He picked me up, and we went on the road. Boy, did we ever go on the road—one-nighters forever," Jimmy recalled. There were no rehearsals for the new drummer, but because Keter had once played drums, he was able to tell Jimmy what Bostic wanted.

Jimmy had been intrigued by Dinah's singing after hearing her on that fill-in job with Keter. "I got a feeling from her like I never had from a person singing," he said, " 'cause I was raised in a Catholic school, and I was used to some other kind of sound, you know, like choir sound. You know what I'm sayin'? And she brought a thing to me that I had not experienced." It didn't matter that he couldn't actually see Dinah—he was stationed directly behind her onstage. "I could feel it."

Jimmy's response to the way Dinah sang was at the other end of the spectrum from *Variety*'s review of the Apollo show in March at the beginning of this latest tour. What so touched Jimmy left this reviewer, without doubt a white man, cold. Dinah had built a following, he conceded, then added: "That her rhythm and blues singing style is a strong draw is in the reception afforded her offerings. Miss Washington's styling is more along instrumental than vocal lines. She uses the melodic line as a point of departure for variations and the lyrics as a collection of syllables on which to vocalize. Her singing is moving only in the sense that a hot sax or clarinet is moving. That she has divorced herself from any sense of the words that she is singing is emphasized by a style habit of hers—to go into a falling inflection that ends in a spoken syllable. The impression created by this technique is that Miss Washington is just kidding; and to someone who expects a ballady feeling from 'Harbor Lights' . . . the net effect is disconcerting. However, she gets over solidly."

To criticize Dinah for half-spoken inflections or improvisations that stretched the lyrics was in essence to criticize her for what she was—a singer who took the given material of the song not as fixed boundaries but as the launching pad for her expression of it. The review, though, helped explain why Dinah, even with strings, was having difficulty breaking into a pop market more welcoming of the Andrews Sisters.

The friendship between Dinah and Jimmy Cobb blossomed when he started to ride in her car as the musicians made their way to California, from one city and club to another. The arrangement worked well until Arizona, when the group encountered an obstruction blocking the highway. The Bostic group managed to get to the next venue on time, but Dinah, Wynton, and Jimmy were delayed in the highway backup. Bostic couldn't go on without Jimmy, and when the three finally arrived in the nick of time, Bostic told Jimmy that he either stayed with him for the rest of the trip or he didn't have a job.

When the tour got to Los Angeles, Dinah and Wynton teamed with the Bostic band to play a dance at the Elks Hall May 9. The norm at these one-night events was for the guest artist to drop in and sing two or three numbers at most. But to the delight of the capacity crowd, Dinah sang the entire evening. She opened with an up-tempo tune, "Journey's End," adapting the studio version, where she was backed by a male vocal group, to a solo performance. The audience loved it, and encouraged by the cheers from the crowd, she sang her latest hits.

The Bostic group and Dinah and Wynton went their separate ways after the Elks Club date, Bart, their booking agent, seeking to maximize the earnings for the artists and the agency. A package worked well on tours of smaller towns, but in larger cities like Los Angeles with diverse markets, it was equally lucrative to let the acts separate, play different venues, and reach more people—at least that was the theory. Bostic stayed at the Elks Hall to stage a musical duel with Texas guitarist Clarence "Gatemouth" Brown. Bostic was dubbed "King of the Alto Sax," Brown, "King of the Blues and Guitar." Dinah made a whirlwind round-trip north to Stockton for a one-night performance and then settled in for a two-week stay at the Oasis right as "I Won't Cry Anymore," from a New York session six weeks earlier, went on the charts. It was her third appearance since January.

While Dinah was in Los Angeles Mercury scheduled two days of recording. The afternoons of June 1 and 2 she returned to Radio Recorders on Santa Monica Boulevard, where she had done those 1945 Apollo sessions, for three-hour sessions each day with a studio band led by Ike Carpenter, a piano player and disciple of Duke Ellington. Wynton joined her for the date, though on some tracks Carpenter apparently was at the keyboard. The sessions were important enough to Ben Bart that he was on hand.

All told, Dinah recorded nine songs with the group, a few blues tunes mixed in with pop matter. All the arrangements had that big band horn sound. One of the blues numbers, "Don't Hold It Against me," was full of of double entendres, particularly the last line, "If you hold it against me, I can make it hard for you." A singer who wanted to give the listener a figurative jab in the ribs might have pounced on the obvious wordplay, but Dinah sang with understatement, letting the line play out on its own. Offstage, she was bawdy, earthy, and carnal, but when she sang, those traits were more whispered than shouted.

Mercury released only one record from these sessions in their immediate aftermath, Dinah at her sassiest in "Saturday Night" backed with "Be Fair to Me," a blues tune. The record didn't make any splash. A few other tracks were slated to be put out later in Mercury's pop series.

WHEN SHE FINISHED at the Oasis, Dinah flew back east to make a date at the Earle Theater in Philadelphia with the popular vocal group the Dominoes and Ivory Joe Hunter and his orchestra. She and the Dominoes hooked up again three weeks later, this time with Arnett Cobb's orchestra at Harlem's Renaissance Ballroom. Three thousand fans—a record turnout—jammed the hall, undeterred by pouring rain all evening, which promoter Johnny Jackson feared would keep the patrons at home.

On July 19 Dinah was back at Birdland for two weeks, Wynton with her at the piano along with Percy Heath, whom she had used before on bass, and Al Jones on drums. One advantage of these radio shows was the chance for a larger audience to experience Dinah's playful personality. She was not Moms Mabley or Sophie Tucker, but she could quip.

"Let's have a great big hand for a wonderful young lady, the most talked-about lady in the field," Symphony Sid said as he opened the July 21 show.

"Let's play drums this morning," Sid joked when she came onstage.

"Every morning," Dinah laughed, as Wynton started a riff on the melody of her first song, "It's Too Soon to Know."

Then she sang "Baby Get Lost."

"How many times a year do you say that?" Sid teased her.

"As many times as . . . you know," Dinah replied, laughing before she finished the sentence. "Just like I'm telling you right now—get lost."

Ignoring the good-natured barb, Sid bantered with her about learning the Yiddish word "farblondjet"—to be lost, mixed-up, and wandering around without knowing which way to turn—and then introduced her next song.

"You told me a little while ago that you wanted to dedicate something to somebody," he said.

"I'd like to very much," Dinah replied.

Who is it? Sid wondered. Dinah told him to guess.

"Where does he live?"

"Well, he lives in Washington but he's in Wildwood, New Jersey," she said.

Sid mentioned Slim Gaillard, a jive-talking singer-dancer-guitarist, who was going to Wildwood.

"Heavens, no!" Dinah cried.

"Who's working in Wildwood? Your piano player should know."

"Jimmy Cobb," Wynton yelled from the piano bench, a very public announcement of Dinah's new romantic interest. (*Defender* columnist Ted Yates, who wrote the regular "I've Been Around New York," had breezily noted July 14 that Dinah "shelves former bass player Walter (Little Man) Buchanan.")

Bostic and his band were at the New Jersey resort playing the Surf Club and were staying through Labor Day. Dinah was in close touch with Jimmy, apparently charmed that he had never learned to drive. To remedy the situation she sent a car to Wildwood—a dark blue Buick convertible—so that Keter could teach his friend on the back roads away from the shore.

"You'd like to dedicate this to Jimmy Cobb?" Sid asked.

"Yes," Dinah replied.

"And what is it going to be, dear?"

" 'I Wanna Be Loved.' "

"You say you do," Sid observed, as Wynton struck the opening chords.

Dinah closed her set with a variation on the same theme, "Please Send Me Someone to Love."

"That's for me—or is that for you?" Sid asked.

"I don't need anybody," Dinah shot back. "I have all I want."

It was a telling retort from someone who already had four failed marriages and at least one affair that ended badly. But Dinah seemed to mean it. She passed up the opportunity to comment, even obliquely, on her personal life. She didn't dwell on these past romantic failures, and if they diminished her self-esteem, saddened her in her most private moments, she refused to let them interfere with her ability to make music. If anything, she could use the off-stage turmoil to invest her singing with particular meaning. An audience might not know the details, but they caught the feeling.

With only a trio behind her, Dinah relied on Wynton to do what the horns had done in the studio version of "Please Send Me." His understated piano combined with Heath's quiet, steady bass gave the song a piercing intimacy. Dinah sang the last line unaccompanied, "Please send me someone to love." It was a piquant contrast to her flip retort to Sid, as if in song she had briefly dropped her cover. It was just the kind of moment that enraptured her fans.

DINAH RETURNED TO CHICAGO in time to celebrate her sons' birthdays, albeit a little belatedly—George was five, Bobby three—and to sing at an unusual event. She joined gospel singer Willie Webb and his group August 14 as the guest performer at the Tabernacle Baptist Church, just four blocks south of her childhood church, St. Luke Baptist. It was a chance to reunite with one of her earliest influences, Roberta Martin, who was also performing, and to give nourishment to an element of her life that of necessity had been relegated to the background. The *Defender* once pictured her as a teenage gospel star. Now in every ad they proclaimed her Queen of Juke Boxes, even when she sang at church.

Two days earlier, when the August 8 *Cash Box* was published, Dinah reached another milestone. She was on the magazine's cover in a picture taken during her Los Angeles recording session in June. Dressed in a casual, off-the-shoulder short-sleeved white blouse and a flowered skirt, Dinah was standing and smiling between Ben Bart and Ike Carpenter, the musical director for the session. There was no accompanying story inside; the picture alone was recognition of Dinah's status and also of the magazine's willingness to pay attention to black stars. Ella Fitzgerald had been on the cover; so had such singing groups as the Orioles and the emerging star on Atlantic, Ruth Brown.

It was a nice boost for Dinah as she headed off to Cleveland to play a week at Gleason's, a refurbished nightclub that boasted air-conditioning to ease the heat on late summer nights.

The month of September was shaping up as an important one. Dinah returned to Chicago again to play a new venue, the Hi-Note at 450 North Clark, which sat amid other clubs on a couple of blocks devoted to nightlife. Gus Chappell, who had played on her first Mercury recording, backed her with a quartet. To promote the engagement, the Hi-Note was offering free, signed copies of her latest releases to the first fifty customers who came to the September 27 show.

More significant, Dinah's contract with Mercury was about to expire. Ben Bart was factoring this information into his negotiations with the label on a package deal for the talent he represented as a booking agent and the talent under contract to Mercury to record. Bart, dealing long-distance from New York, was looking for some long-term security for Dinah, not to mention himself.

Dave Young, who had played for Dinah at those hugely successful weeks at the Ritz in 1947, remembered when the Mercury brass—it was probably president Irving Green and vice president Art Talmadge—came to see Dinah as she prepared for a session in Chicago. They walked into the studio carrying a big box. "And they opened it up and there was a full-length mink coat that they gave to her to re-sign."

"What's this?" Dinah asked.

"This is yours, all you have to do is sign," one of the men said.

"Hell, give me the motherfucker!"

"That was her," Young said, laughing at the memory of Dinah caressing her new fur.

Dinah had a practical explanation for the latest gift: "With Frankie Laine gone to Columbia, I guess Mercury was afraid of losing me, too."

Dinah intended this coat as a replacement for one she had had to give back when detectives interrupted an earlier session to repossess the fur. Dinah had paid $700 for the coat, no questions asked. But she hadn't known that the seller was dealing in stolen goods. The coat had been robbed from a furrier's storage room. "It was a beautiful mink," said Mitch Miller, who had been directing the session and stood dumbfounded as the detectives took the coat away.

Dinah's new Mercury contract was for three years, and to cement its commitment to rhythm and blues and its plan to expand in the field, Mercury announced that Bobby Shad, owner of the New York independent Sittin' In label, had been hired to run the R&B division. In its write-up of the deal, *Billboard* noted that Shad would be given a free hand and "a heavy budget set up for promotion." The magazine also noted that Mercury "has had trouble getting an R&B catalogue together, except for Dinah Washington, who has scored consistently." Good publicity for Dinah, it helped explain why Mercury would be reluctant to let its one sure thing in the R&B market, where the label already had several successful white acts, veer off to pop for good.

By the time Dinah got to Detroit to play a week at the Paradise Theater in early October, word was out about her new Mercury deal. Noting Dinah's new mink coat, Ziggy Johnson, a nightclub producer turned columnist, joked in the *Michigan Chronicle* that "I remember her when she didn't have a lumber jacket."

The rumor that Dinah might return to gospel music persisted. Johnson repeated for readers a conversation he had had with her on the subject. "Deanna"—Johnson's nickname for her—"I understand you are going into gospel work à la Sister Thorpe"—a reference to Sister Rosetta Tharpe.

"You say you heard that?"

"Yes, from several people."

"Well, Zigfield"—her nickname for Johnson—"you just throw that idea out of your mind. I have a lifetime contract with Ben Bart, and it says I'm to sing sweet torch songs and the blues . . . and as long as I'm making these four figures, I'm not going to break my contract."

Mercury seemed intent on its promise to spend money on the R&B roster, and on Dinah in particular. The October 13 issue of *Billboard* carried a three-quarter-page ad publicizing her most recent release, "Cold, Cold Heart" and "Mixed Emotions," another ballad.

"Cold, Cold Heart" was Dinah's first venture into country music, which was also known in some quarters—*Cash Box* for one—as "hillbilly" music. The song was written by one of the giants, Hank Williams, whose own version shot to number one on *Billboard*'s country charts and stayed on the charts for seven months.

Dinah's recording of "Cold, Cold Heart" was an afterthought in a Chicago session with Mercury producer Nook Shrier. The musicians, including a backup vocal group used on the ballad "Mixed Emotions," had gone through the numbers planned for the afternoon, but a few minutes still remained on the session. Dinah said she'd been thinking about the Williams song and suggested they give it a try. There was no time to write formal arrangements, so tenor saxist Paul Quinichette improvised an introduction, nodded to trumpeter Clark Terry to think up some fills, and huddled with the backup singers to figure where they should come in. It was one of those magical moments when everything came together, even if country aficionados might have complained that Dinah was too detached in her understated rendering of the song.

"Cold, Cold Heart" became Dinah's fourth hit of 1951, and Shrier admitted he was surprised at Dinah's success with the song. "I didn't think that was going to work out at all. It was strictly a country-western tune." But Dinah was such a fine singer, Shrier said, she could pull it off. "You just to have to spell it out with one word, soul. She just had her own thing." (Tony Bennett also had a hit with a pop version of the song, his laden with strings in a quasi-operatic presentation.)

Dinah was realizing she wanted more control over her music on the live dates, and she could command enough money now to afford the musicians she wanted. She had meant what she told Keter and Jimmy about joining her and Wynton if they left Bostic, and now the moment was right. Keter had left in October and was more than happy to sign on with Dinah. So was Jimmy, because he and Dinah were a couple.

Their first job together would be a late fall tour Ben Bart put together that would team Dinah and the Bostic band again. They would start at the Apollo, play the Howard in Washington and the Earle in Philadelphia. Then the group would head south for seventeen one-nighters arranged by Ralph Weinberg and wind up in Miami on December 16.

This latest tour pointed up an interesting contrast between singers and their audiences. A year earlier, Billie Holiday, after much urging, agreed to do a southern swing in the same locales that Dinah played: Norfolk, Richmond, and Roanoke in Virginia, Charleston, South Carolina, and the like. Gerald Wilson was recruited along with a fourteen-piece group to accompany her. The tour started at the end of June, but by the third week in July, Holiday canceled the rest of the dates because of what the *Amsterdam News* called "a long list of slim crowds."

Revered in certain circles, black and white, Holiday's style and sensibility were not a good fit with southern tastes. One musician likened the situation to different foods for different regions, grits and sausage for breakfast below the Mason-Dixon line, eggs and toast above it. Dinah satisfied the hunger; Billie Holiday apparently did not.

Though Dinah and her trio had each traveled the South before they came together for this tour, the way ideology intruded on entertainment still brought moments of bemused awe among the musicians. When the group played the now familiar Memorial Auditorium in Raleigh—one of Ralph Weinberg's favorite venues—the white "spectators" once again were in the back of the hall. Keter took it as a compliment that social mores gave way to the music. "The band was cookin'," he recalled, and some of the white kids crossed the literal line to start dancing. In a flash, he said, police officers rushed forward. "Get back—get back!" they ordered.

All of the musicians were glad to be busy, even though their schedule meant it was impossible to celebrate Christmas with their families. But they were periodically reminded of the toll such grueling itineraries could take if they failed to proceed with caution. After the Jacksonville date the second week in December, Earl Bostic split off to drive to Alabama. Instead of getting a little sleep and heading out in the morning, he left right from the club, fell asleep at the wheel, and had a head-on collision near Tifton, Georgia. The accident, which was nearly fatal, sidelined him for months.

The tour didn't pause a moment. Burnie Peacock, who had played with Count Basie and Lucky Millinder, was brought in to replace Bostic, and the promoters were emphatic that no dates would be canceled. Dinah was the engine that drove the show. Bostic and Peacock were interchangeable parts.

As was now customary, Dinah was a presence in the year-end music magazine polls. And now she was featured in a new black publication, *Jet*, which premiered November 1, 1951. The cover story of the December 13 issue was the "Ten Best Girl Singers," and Dinah was pictured right below Ella Fitzgerald. "Borrowed from gospel songs to click with the blues," the caption said.

While accurate, the description was one step behind, appropriate for where Dinah had been, not where she wanted to go.

9.

Keter, Wynton, and Jimmy

1952

Though Dinah and the trio had been together only two months, the fit was perfect when they recorded in Los Angeles early in 1952. Bobby Shad, a year into his job as head of Mercury's R&B department, flew out for the session. He was so happy with the results that he had the dubs flown back to New York as soon as the studio work was done. Shad was convinced Dinah had three hits in the making, and he was right. The first two were ballads, "Wheel of Fortune" and "Tell Me Why," but it was the third, "Trouble in Mind," that signaled how at home Dinah was with Jimmy, Keter, and Wynton. In simplest terms "Trouble in Mind" was an uncomplicated well-known blues song that Dinah had probably heard growing up. She brought a piercing elegance to the vocals—"Trouble in mind, I'm blue but I won't be blue always." Wynton was at his best, shadowing her with his feathery touch, bridging one section of the song to another.

To say these young men were starstruck might be overstatement, but it was like going to music school every time they played with Dinah. "She opened up my head about the whole thing," Keter said. "Basically I was just concerned about the changes—melody here, chords here, and changes down here. And then when I was working with Dinah, I saw the whole thing, the whole song. We realized the role we were going to play now. When you back up somebody singing, you're actually like a tailor. Somebody comes into your shop—six foot two—wants a coat with a single vent in the back—if you make the right fit for that person, it makes you a good tailor. With a singer—a singer is buck naked when they come out onstage, and it's your job to clothe that singer and dress that singer with the audience."

During a break at one of their first jobs together, the well-known bassist Oscar Pettiford was in the club, and between sets he told Keter that when Dinah sang, there was a lot of open space. He should show his stuff and fill it.

The man must know what he's talking about, Keter thought. So in the second set, Dinah proceeded as usual, and when there was a pause, Keter added some frills. He noticed a slight twitch of Dinah's shoulder, but she went on. He did it again a few bars later. Same thing. When he started a third time, Dinah held the mike away from her and turned around. "If I want you to have a solo," she hissed, "I'll give you one."

Somewhere in the back Pettiford was laughing. An embarrassed Keter knew he'd been had.

Jimmy became a more versatile drummer in a hurry. "You have to learn to play behind a singer. It's different than playing behind instruments," he said. In the beginning, he used mostly brushes, but as he understood Dinah's vocal power and when the trio was augmented by horns, he played with sticks. "She was a musician," Jimmy added. "She knew where everything was. She can go any-place she wants in the music because she knows exactly what's happening with it."

Keter loved the way the trio worked together, feeding off each other when Dinah wanted to break in a new song. Once they got the melody, Wynton might knock out a riff on the piano, which would prompt Keter to embellish on the bass. Jimmy picked up the beat and added his own touches. Or it might be reversed—Jimmy had an idea, Keter jumped in, and Wynton finished it. "We made up a lot of head arrangements," Keter explained. "Each one had something." They almost never had a formal rehearsal with Dinah.

The camaraderie, musical and otherwise, was evident in a spur-of-the-moment picture of the men standing outside a club in front of Dinah's picture, which was posted in a large frame. All boyishly handsome, the three were dressed in light suits and striped ties, though they weren't matching. It seemed the perfect metaphor for their music making—all on the same team but individuals nonetheless. Dinah's picture was one of the most flattering. Her hair was short now, a mass of curls framing her face and highlighting her cheekbones. She liked the cut because it was "easier to handle. It's also sexier, and it makes a woman look younger. Most important, I find that men respond to the new short styles." Her head tilted down, Dinah beckoned onlookers with a tantalizing half-smile.

"Dinah was like a mother hen to us," Keter recalled. If an admirer came up to her after the show to seek her favors, he might ask, "Queen, can I buy you a drink?" "Yes, I'm drinking champagne," was her standard reply, delivered with just a touch of hauteur. "So is my trio." One well-to-do fan wanted to take her away for a weekend. "Yeah?" Dinah asked. "My trio's got to go with me."

The trio provided some cover for Dinah, to be sure, but she was perfectly capable of handling herself without them. Her gestures to the men reflected genuine feeling that showed when she sought to broaden their musical horizons. On the road she would take them out to catch a set or two of other musicians who were playing the same town they were. "I want to show you something you haven't seen," she explained.

One more sign that Jimmy was Dinah's man offstage had emerged from the Los Angeles session. She insisted that the group be called the "Jimmy Cobb Orchestra," which entitled him to earn double the union scale as the leader of the group. It was an extra dollop that Jimmy hadn't expected, and he professed surprise to see himself listed as the "orchestra" leader.

Though Dinah played several dates in the Los Angeles area, her week at the Club Alabam, on South Central Avenue, the heart of the city's black nightlife, was the most gratifying. She was greeted every night by sold-out audiences who gave her a standing ovation before she sang the first note. Most nights Dinah opened with "Tell Me Why" and then worked backward through her hits. Though Los Angeles in January is plenty warm, she still wore her mink coat, prompting the *Sentinel*'s gossip columnist to chortle that the coat, along with Dinah's "mile long Cadillac . . . will make you flip your wig!"

When Dinah and the trio stopped in Chicago in the middle of March to record again, Jimmy stayed with her on Trumbull and met the family. Alice was civil but cool, no happier now with Dinah's choice of lifestyle than she had been since the beginning. Jimmy seemed to fit right in, soft-spoken and polite but happy to rough-house with Bobby and George, Dinah's sons. A photograph from that moment was a sweet and homey tableau, a portrait of every-thing Dinah said she wanted in her private life. Dinah and Alice were sitting at opposite ends of the living room couch, upholstered with the vivid floral patterns popular at the time. George, in a snappy shirt with matching suspenders, Bobby, equally well turned out with a shirt and sweater vest, stood smiling between them. Jimmy knelt down behind the couch, looking over Dinah's left shoulder.

This Chicago session was devoted to standards, among them Noël Coward's "Mad About the Boy," which Dinah gave a sly, sug-gestive reading, and "I Thought About You," the popular Johnny Mercer–Jimmy Van Heusen song. Her version was a fine illustration of how she made a song her own. Mildred Bailey, one of the great swing singers, who had died three months before this session, set the standard when she'd recorded it. She took the song at a good clip, gliding effortlessly through lyrics in a way that suggested a pleasant, almost matter-of-fact memory.

Dinah slowed everything down, turning the song into a bitter-sweet reminiscence. Even her trademark "hmm" fit. Though Dinah had sung with strings before, this was probably the first time a solo harp was featured in the accompaniment. The arrangement opened with an ascending arpeggio that fed into the violins—by any meas-ure a long distance on the musical spectrum from Lionel Hampton and his horns.

BY THE TIME Dinah and the trio returned to New York in April to play a week at Birdland and another week at the Apollo, the word was out that Dinah and Jimmy were engaged, even though she was not yet legally free from Walter Buchanan. *Cash Box* reported it twice in the March 8 issue. When the couple sat down for dinner with a reporter from the *Amsterdam News,* Dinah showed off her new ring. Along with a new fiancé, she also had a new song on the charts, a revised version of "Blowtop Blues." The biggest difference in this new one was the lively saxophone of Paul Quinichette. When Decca noticed the Mercury disc taking off, the label rereleased its version, which executives had recorded so reluctantly seven years earlier.

While it was always good to be back in New York and at the Apollo, the high point of this return trip was another chance to sing at Carnegie Hall. And once again—the second time since 1949—Dinah was getting an award for winning the *Pittsburgh Courier*'s annual music poll for the best female blues singer. The *Courier* seemed to be wary of typecasting Dinah, though, carefully noting in its profile of her for the April 19 program that "Dinah stands supreme in the field of blues singing, although she sings ballads with equal skill and feeling." Indeed, when she took her turn to perform at the concert, she sang "Wheel of Fortune" instead of one of her well-known blues.

Dinah and the other stars had the added pleasure of reaching a nationwide audience. The Mutual network broadcast from Carnegie Hall for an hour, from midnight to 1:00 A.M., and like previous years it was a showcase of the biggest names: Lionel Hampton, Billy Eckstine, Nat King Cole, Louis Jordan, and from television, Milton Berle. Right before Dinah took her turn, boxing champion Sugar Ray Robinson brought the crowd to its feet when he came out to play drums with the Hampton band.

Dinah may have wanted to get out of the mold of blues singer, but there was no denying the pleasure in recognition. This latest honor came with a three-foot-high trophy engraved with her name that was even bigger than the sizable statue she took home in 1949. It was more tangible evidence of her success, and Alice, who had come to New York for the ceremony, posed with Dinah and the trophy, misgivings about her daughter's career choice temporarily put aside. Dinah was amused at how her mother advertised herself as a music teacher back home in Chicago: the sign on a window on Trumbull said "Alice Jones—mother of Dinah Washington."

A few years earlier Dinah had struggled to look the part of a star. Not anymore. She sauntered out on the Carnegie Hall stage in a sparkling halter top evening gown, stylish and confident. She liked sleeveless gowns, and several she had were strapless. There was no getting around the fact that a full-busted woman in an off-the-shoulder dress was alluring to the men in the audience. One magazine even referred to Dinah as the "bosomy Jukebox Queen." More brazen than flirty, Dinah probably enjoyed that description, despite the double standard. It was hard to imagine *Ebony* or *Jet* using such images to talk about Duke Ellington or Billy Eckstine, even if Eckstine was once promoted as the "Sepia Sinatra."

Dinah knew accessories were important. She often wore a corsage on her gown, and she always dressed up her outfit with jewelry, most often dangling earrings and a bracelet worn on her left wrist. Though the stones might not be gems, she had an eye for designs that would pick up the colors in her outfits and would sparkle when the spotlight hit her. When she went on the road now, the ensembles were carefully coordinated, and she instructed whoever was working for her how to pack, leaving them handwritten notes explaining what went in each suitcase—the green gown with the matching shoes and jewelry in one bag, the blue gown in another, and so on. Dinah wanted to look good, but she didn't want to waste time rummaging around for her performance outfits.

For more casual wear Dinah bought one sweater, probably in her favorite cashmere, and had her name embroidered on the front in the style of a monogram. The middle letter "N" was a good two inches high with the other letters around it somewhat smaller. She wore the sweater to an event where she was photographed smiling on the arm of the actor Robert Mitchum.

Dinah shopped at the best stores—Saks Fifth Avenue and Josephs, the well-known shoe salon in Chicago—but she also shopped through the informal network of "boosters," the show business slang for shoplifters and thieves. Every night they lined up at the back of the Apollo and the other main theaters on the circuit to show their wares for women and men. Some were organized enough to travel so they could take care of their clients on the road.

Jimmy was astonished to learn that in Cleveland you could put in an order, and later, no questions asked, it would be delivered. "You could order mink stoles, you could order anything you wanted," he said. Keter marveled at the fact that a new outfit could be completed in a matter of hours. "You go into a men's store, look around, maybe buy a shirt and sweater. And then at night the suit is here." But his biggest surprise came in Chicago, when a white policeman working the Regal looked at him, sized him up at about 36-long, and told him to come to a side room at the theater. When Keter arrived, the policeman opened up a locked closet and showed him a whole rack of suits. "A cop doing business," he laughed.

"Everybody knew where the goods came from," Jimmy said. "They fell off the back of the lorry."

Dinah prided herself on being ahead of trends, at least in terms of the boosters' collections, and one time when she stopped by the Club DeLisa in Chicago and went backstage, she got into a scrap with one of the showgirls. Dinah called her "a high yellow nigger" among other things before she was not so politely escorted out. Tammy Graves, another showgirl who witnessed the entire fracas, learned later that Dinah got mad because "one of the girls got a 'hot' dress before she did."

If Dinah was poised and confident onstage, offstage she could analyze herself with clinical detachment, confiding her harsh appraisal to LaRue Manns. "She always dreamed of being a glamour girl. But she said she had no shape," LaRue recalled. "She could make her face look pretty. She would buy very expensive clothes and have waist cinchers to give her the shape that she would have. I would always tell her how gorgeous she was and how good she looked, but she didn't like her body."

"Well, I know I got pretty feet and hands and that will take me through," Dinah told LaRue in one of these interchanges. "If I had your body and my voice, I'd be a bitch, wouldn't I?"

Little things here and there reinforced the anxieties. When the *Washington Afro-American* ran a picture of Dinah with a dancer, the caption over the picture said "The Voice and the Body Get Together." Nothing was wrong with anointing Dinah "the voice." It was the combination of the words and the picture that nettled. One of the bartenders at the Club DeLisa who had overheard that dressing room spat thought Dinah's concern about her looks played into the argument. The dancers were uniformly light-skinned and thin; Dinah was much darker and heavier. "She was jealous," the bartender said.

Dinah had been a shoo-in for *Jet* magazine's best women singers poll in the publication's inaugural year, but she was nowhere to be found in its poll the following week of "The World's Sexiest Negro Women." On these pages the reader found Lena Horne, Dorothy

Dandridge, Eartha Kitt, Billie Holiday, and the "exotic shake dancer" Tondelayo.

In mid-May Dinah and the trio were booked on their first inter-racial bill, advertised as the "Caravan of Stars." The group opened in Philadelphia May 18. The "Caravan" was a project of GAC—General Artists Corporation—one of the old, established booking agencies, and Tom Rockwell, who ran the operation, probably approached Ben Bart about including Dinah in the package. The major white act was the Woody Herman band, and instead of the Earle, the Royal, and the Howard, the usual theaters on the black circuit, Dinah and the others were playing bigger venues: the Philadelphia Armory, their first stop May 18, the Baltimore Coliseum, and the Syria Mosque in Pittsburgh.

The show was one of several interracial music packages touring the country, each put together by a different agency. The Gale brothers ran "The Biggest Show of '52," which featured Patti Page, Frankie Lane, and Illinois Jacquet in the spring, and Nat King Cole, Stan Kenton, and Sarah Vaughan in the fall. Impresario Norman Granz was continuing with his interracial jazz concerts styled "Jazz at the Philharmonic," which were held around the country and starting that spring in major European cities. Segregation, whether by law or custom, was still the norm in most facets of American life, but in the music world the boundaries and the barriers continued to be much less rigid.

In some cases, those barriers were broken outright at a concert that featured only black talent. The most recent high-profile episode had been in Miami early in March, when Billy Eckstine and Count Basie performed in auditoriums in Miami and surrounding Dade County. The promoters lost control of the ticket sales because they were offered in so many locations, and ticket sellers ignored local custom and sold the tickets without considering the race of the buy-ers. At the ticket window at Dade County Auditorium, the seller—described in one newspaper account as "a young Jewish sales agent"—issued tickets without regard to race. The management of the arenas had originally protested interracial seating, citing munici-pal regulations and specifications in the auditorium leases, but at the event blacks and whites sat side by side without any interference from the authorities.

The "Caravan of Stars" date May 21 in Baltimore did not go as smoothly. The city already had a reputation for unruly crowds. Most of the time it was white "zoot suiters," as the *Baltimore Afro-American* called them, who disrupted the music with boisterous behavior. During Woody Herman's opening set, one young man caused a disturbance and quieted down only after he was warned by one of the special policemen on duty.

When Dinah came out to sing, she opened with "Wheel of Fortune." Just as she finished, this same young man leaped to his feet and started dancing in a crowded bleacher section, which bothered some of the other patrons. He caused so much ruckus that Dinah and the band came to a stop barely ten bars into the second song.

Police rushed through the crowd to escort the man out of the auditorium, but he lashed back at them, fists flying. Some of his friends tried to jump in to help, but the police were able to hustle them away. Dinah, watching calmly from the stage, signaled the band and picked up exactly where she had left off a few minutes earlier.

The interracial packages and the large venues they commanded had the obvious benefit of allowing the musicians to reach a new audience. But for an artist like Dinah, whose core fans were black even when she recorded pop tunes, such jobs were intermittent, and after this short trip, she and the other black musicians returned to their usual haunts. On Memorial Day Dinah and the trio were back on the circuit, playing the Earle Theater in Philadelphia for the holiday weekend. Ben Bart had booked her again in July at the Royal in Baltimore and the Howard in Washington.

WHEN DINAH BURST on the scene as Lionel Hampton's singer, *Down Beat* and *Metronome* took notice, charting her development as part of the Hampton group with reviews and short articles. But when Dinah left to go out on her own, both magazines had all but ignored her. She showed up in the year-end popularity polls because a few of the readers kept paying attention year after year. Now, after three more songs on the *Billboard* charts—a total of twenty-four since she'd left Hampton—*Down Beat* was taking note once again.

In February the magazine, which caught up with Dinah on one of her California dates, wrote a feature about her contract renewal with Mercury three months earlier. "Now it looks better than ever for me at Mercury—you know, maybe an even better break on songs and publicity," said Dinah, clearly happy. "Not that I've ever had any complaints since I've been there—six years now."

In April the magazine reviewed one of her records, "Trouble in Mind"/"New Blowtop Blues," which it had not done for nearly two years. "After an endless string of musically dog-eared pop songs, Dinah finally gets back to the blues, the style that made her famous," the reviewer wrote. "Dinah is still one of the great blues singers. She should never let her public or herself forget it." Intended or not, the statement seemed the musical equivalent of keeping Dinah in her place.

The cover of the May 7 issue featured a right hand, fingers splayed. Each one was a different kind of music labeled in a different typeface and illustrated with a head shot of a performer: popular— Bing Crosby; rhythm and blues—Dinah; jazz—Louis Armstrong; classical—Arturo Toscanini. Leonard Feather, who had first recorded Dinah on those 1944 Keynote discs and was now a senior writer at *Down Beat,* knew the breadth of her talent and wrote about it in his May 21 "Feather's Nest" column.

"Dinah's stature today bears out our theory that the most successful rhythm-and-blues music can be, and often is, that which qualifies as good jazz," Feather wrote. Though he may have slightly exaggerated her selling power, he made a salient point about her versatility when he described her as "a gal who can sell six figures on 'The Wheel of Fortune' and turn around and make a superb 'Trouble in Mind.' "

Dinah's most recent club date seemed to bear out Feather's assertion. She had been in Chicago a week earlier, to sing at the Blue Note, a small downtown club and the city's premier jazz venue, and on her last night, most of the entertainers who were performing at other theaters came over for Dinah's last set.

THE FIRST FEW MONTHS of 1952 had been so smooth onstage and off. The calendar was full, the music was good, and Jimmy was a sweet companion. No one was prepared for the jolt when Wynton learned that he had been drafted and ordered to report for duty. He and the others were certain the army would not want someone deaf in one ear and with teeth so bad they would have to be fixed, bottom and top. No rhyme or reason was apparent in the army's decision to take him, the men believed, except for race. A black man would be ordered to serve in a situation where they knew no white would be accepted. Keter was amazed that a friend from Port Chester with a glass eye had been drafted. Nothing could be done except to find a new piano player and get ready for the upcoming summer dates.

Beryl Booker, one of the few female jazz instrumentalists, had played with Dinah a few years earlier. Though she didn't read music, Beryl had perfect pitch and the ability to play something back as soon as she heard it. She had started working the club circuit in 1946 when bass player Slam Stewart hired her for his group. By 1949 she was doing dates on her own, billed as a "song and piano stylist." *Down Beat* proclaimed that "properly handled Beryl could be the biggest new piano star since [Errol] Garner." Just before Dinah asked her to join the trio, Beryl was playing cafés in Los Angeles. Though it would be different from having Wynton at the keyboard, Dinah didn't worry, and Keter and Jimmy were confident Beryl would fit.

Dinah and the trio made a long road trip in early June to play the Colonial Tavern in Toronto, and then they were back on 52nd Street in New York to play Birdland for another week. The June 21 evening was another live broadcast over WJZ. Dinah was so comfortable with the material and her trio that she went from song to song without waiting for Beryl to set the key or Jimmy to set the beat on the drums.

After Dinah finished her third song, "Wheel of Fortune," Symphony Sid, who was hosting again, told her the next week at Birdland was going to be even more important. The program would start at 12:00 A.M. instead of the middle of the night as part of WJZ's new six-hour jazz format. Three hours would come live from Birdland, and Dinah could have two of those hours.

"Huh?" Dinah said, obviously surprised. "Now you're being corny."

No, Sid told her. That was no joke.

"A live show, three hours, no kidding . . . Oh, then can I dance?"

"You want to dance?" Sid asked with mock incredulity. "You

think we have television cameras or something. This is radio, Dinah."

"Oh, I'm sorry."

"But you'll be on plenty," Sid promised her. "So be prepared."

"Am I finished?" she asked, ready to pack up for the night.

"No, you got lots of time to go yet—don't run off."

"All right," Dinah said, and sang two more songs.

Birdland itself was an institution. An institution within the institution was Pee Wee Marquette—his legal first name was William Clayton—the diminutive doorman/announcer who acted as though he ran the place. He snapped at musicians and patrons, exercising his self-proclaimed authority to send this person here and that person there. Lester Young called him "half-a-motherfucker" and one disgruntled patron referred to him as the "bellicose dwarf." To some, Pee Wee was of uncertain gender: he dressed like a man, favoring brown pinstripe suits with vests, the pants heavily pleated and tightly cuffed and, one musician joked, "belted at his armpits." But he also wore pancake makeup, several watches, and a bevy of rings. His high-pitched voice added to the mystery, and Keter veered between amusement and irritation at Pee Wee's inability to get his name right. "Skeeter," he would squeal when he saw him, expecting a tip because he called Keter by name.

If Pee Wee liked someone, he was all smiles, even obsequious with some of the stars. Keter saw that side the evening of June 25, in the middle of Dinah's week at the club. He had taken her and Jimmy to Yankee Stadium to watch Sugar Ray Robinson fight Joey Maxim for the light heavyweight title and planned to pick them up afterward so they could all return to 52nd Street to play the midnight show.

After Robinson lost in the fourteenth round on a knockout, thousands streamed out of the stadium, and Keter realized there was no way he and Dinah and Jimmy could find each other. He went back down to Birdland, confident the two would get themselves to the club.

"Skeeter," Pee Wee howled as he looked at one of his watches. "Where's the Queen? Where's the Queen? Mr. Oscar isn't gonna be happy," he said, referring to club manager Oscar Goodstein. "The Queen oughta be here."

"I'm here," Keter told him. "Put on one of the other acts first."

When Dinah finally arrived, Pee Wee was all charm. "Oh, Queen, Queen, I'm so glad you're here," he said, fawning as she came in the door.

"Tell her what you told me," chided Keter, who was standing at the bottom of the stairs watching the scene.

If Pee Wee was an unusual, sometimes aggravating constant at Birdland, others on the staff made the musicians feel welcome, especially regular returnees like Keter and Wynton. They liked rum drinks, helping themselves to the bottle of Three Daggers, 151 proof, that was always behind the bar. When Keter went to get a drink after not being in the club for several months, the bartender cracked that nobody had touched the stuff since the last time he was in.

More was on the agenda of the June 27 show than simply WJZ's expanded live broadcast. Part of the evening was devoted to honoring Dinah as Queen of the Juke Boxes. The designation was based on a poll of weekly ratings in more than 150 black publications around the country, the "Sepia Hit Parade." A representative of *Cash Box* presented Dinah with a specially designed paper scroll. Leonard Feather gave Dinah a trophy from *Down Beat* for her "outstanding performance in the field of entertainment."

Dinah gave the audience, live and on radio, a set that featured more ballads than blues—"It's Too Soon to Know," "Only a Moment," "Make Believe Dreams," and one, she said, that a friend had done. Dinah liked it so much she wanted to sing it, too. "Oh, that friend," Dinah added, pausing just a moment for suspense, "was Sarah Vaughan." The song was "It's Magic."

Up in Boston, George Wein, owner of the small club Storyville, hoped to duplicate Birdland's success in his own place. He had booked Dinah for a week, but he quickly realized that Boston didn't yet have the same jazz crowd as New York. Dinah wasn't the draw he had expected. The place was empty at the first couple of shows. "So after three nights, I asked Dinah if she would agree to cancel the rest of the week," Wein recalled. Dinah agreed—she didn't like singing to an empty club. "She let me out of the deal, and gave seven or eight hundred dollars back. . . . Despite the fact that I was a white club owner in New England, she had empathy for my situation."

The vagaries of opinion and opinion makers were evident in the reaction to Dinah's latest record, "Mad About the Boy." *Cash Box* reviewed the release in its pop section and designated the record the "Sleeper of the Week" June 7, though it did not register in the magazine's tallies or on *Billboard*'s charts, even in the rhythm and blues section. *Down Beat* gave it a nod July 2 as a one of its "five star discs" in the rhythm and blues section. But only among Dinah's black fans was the record a hit, according to the "Sepia Hit Parade." The juxtaposition suggested that Dinah appealed to her black fans regardless of what she sang. They felt a kinship with her music be it blues or ballads. If her white fans lacked the same intuitive connection, over time they would come to appreciate the music for its own sake—the sound, the phrasing, the vitality of the presentation.

IN ITS APRIL STORY about the dinner with Dinah and Jimmy and their engagement, the *Amsterdam News* said Dinah's two sons "are her 'gold bricks.' On tour, when she gets lonesome for the sight of them, she puts in a hurry [sic] phone call to her mother, dashes out to Chicago, packs them up and takes them right back out on the road." George was five, going on six in July, Bobby three, going on four in August. These were whirlwind adventures, Bobby remembered. One night they would be in a fancy hotel, the next sleeping in the car. "Sometimes you didn't know where you were."

Dinah missed her siblings, too. By the summer of 1952 Harold was sixteen and Clarissa would be thirteen in December. Estrellita was eight. Dinah wanted them to spend the summer with her while school was out. Jimmy was from Washington, and it was convenient to have them come because they could stay with his mother and then travel with the trio for nearby dates in the East. She hired someone to pick everybody up in Chicago and bring them back. "We laughingly called her our governess," Clarissa recalled. "We would either take the train or we would fly—we would go on these single-engine props. She just wanted us to be with her and spend time with her and have fun."

If the show was at the Howard or Royal, the kids could either stay backstage in the dressing room or go out front and watch the performance. If Dinah was playing a club, she made sure there was a table near the stage where the children could sit and she could see them. LaRue was on hand to supervise.

One Sunday morning in Washington Estrellita hurt her eye after she fell off a bike. "Ruth"—her family always called her by her given name—"was hysterical," Estrellita remembered, " 'cause she thought my mother was going to get her for letting me get hurt. She personally took me to a doctor on Sunday, and they found an ophthalmologist to look at me. She always treated me like I was her daughter," Estrellita added. "There was a twenty-year difference—she was old enough to be my mother. She wanted my mother to give me to her—she wanted a daughter. So she wanted me." Paraphrasing Alice's sharp retort, Estrellita added, "Hell, no!"

Dinah's August job at the Pershing Ballroom in Chicago turned out to be perfect timing. It allowed her to drop off the children so they could get ready for school. Then she and the trio headed back east the first week in September to do a makeup date for a New Jersey disc jockey. He had booked Dinah for a July 4 dance in Trenton, but there had been a mixup, and she didn't perform. The promoter sued to get a refund on the money he already had paid out, but the dispute was resolved when Dinah headlined a show at the Trenton Arena the first week in September.

THE CARAVAN OF STARS came back together for a swing out west in the fall, with stops in Oakland, Pasadena, Seattle, and Salt Lake City. In one respect this was reminiscent of Dinah's time with Hampton because she generally sang only a couple of songs at each performance. But now she was a star. The *San Francisco Chronicle*'s music critic, Ralph Gleason, devoted his column, "The Rhythm Section," to her just before the Oakland date. He began with a few thoughtful paragraphs about the origins of blues and how it had influenced not only black singers but prominent white artists as well, among them Dinah Shore, Kay Starr, Ella Mae Morse, and Frank Sinatra. Beyond this, Gleason wrote, "the traditions of jazz have always been inextricably tied in with great exponents of the blues." Dinah was the "reigning Queen of the Blues, the Bessie Smith and Ma Rainey of her time." Gleason predicted a long career for her, noting exactly what Ben Bart already knew: "Her records are in great demand, and their popularity in turn makes her wanted by night club and theater operators all over the country."

Though Gleason almost surely meant no harm, Dinah probably flinched at his description of her: "a stocky, round-faced girl."

The Oakland date was another good illustration of why these interracial events drew big audiences—something for everybody. Woody Herman was a well-known bandleader; the mainstream San Francisco disc jockeys eagerly played his records in advance of the event. If Dinah didn't get the same airplay, she was nonetheless a major draw for the Bay Area's large black population.

A staple of road life for entertainers like Dinah was the assistant—a combination of maid, gofer, confidante, and personal shopper. Some, such as Sarah Vaughan and Ella Fitzgerald, used the same individuals for years. Dinah was different, recruiting a succession of assistants to help out, sometimes for only a few weeks or a month, though she generally stayed in touch when the tour was finished. Rose Snow, a young woman from Baltimore, was accompanying Dinah on this trip. She had met her a few years earlier at the Royal, when she was just a teenager but longing to travel. "What are you doing with that young girl?" Alice had asked Dinah when she took Rose home to Chicago.

"Her mother said she could go," Dinah replied.

Even though Dinah could be temperamental and the schedule sometimes made night feel like day and vice versa, Rose loved the excitement of seeing different places and meeting new people. And she took pride in the knowledge that she helped Dinah at the most basic level, literally—packing the suitcases with care to make sure there were enough bras, girdles, and stockings for all the dates, let alone the fancy dresses, or signaling discreetly from the back of the room if Dinah's hair was out of place. So many things were new experiences, even the way dry cleaning was handled at the nicer hotels. She didn't have to call anybody; she simply opened a little door within the door to Dinah's room, hung the soiled clothes on a hook, and shut the door so they could be collected by a bellhop, who opened another door on the hallway side. It was like magic.

Sometimes Dinah had surprises in store. Before they left Pasadena, Dinah summoned Rose to go for a ride, not telling her the destination. After a short while, they came to a large white house. Dinah's driver stopped the car; she got out, Rose behind her, walked to the door, and rang the bell. When the door opened, Rose's jaw dropped. Standing in the doorway was the pioneering black actress Ethel Waters. Waters and Dinah embraced, and they all went inside. "We didn't stay but a few minutes," Rose said.

It was Dinah's way of paying homage to a woman who had opened doors for her and so many other black women entertainers.

As soon as the last California date was over, Dinah and the trio went back east for another swing through the major theaters in November. They were back in Chicago by mid-December, to spend a working holiday. Dinah divided her time between the family at Trumbull and performances at the Regal.

Dinah's presence—and absence—in the year-end polls were the latest reminders of how typecasting and perception, some of it racial, influenced musical tastes. She didn't show up at all in the *Metronome* readers poll of favorite women singers. Rosemary Clooney led the list followed by Sarah Vaughan and Ella Fitzgerald. In *Down Beat,* Dinah was thirteenth of twenty-eight, and with only sixty votes, far behind the first-place Vaughan, who had 1,005. Ella Fitzgerald was second and Rosemary Clooney was third.

Ella, Sarah, and Dinah were all black women, but Ella and Sarah were considered jazz artists and more appealing than a blues singer to the readers of *Metronome* and *Down Beat,* most of them white. But in black America Dinah was a different story. She was named "the outstanding performer on the Sepia Song Hit Parade" for leading the tally seventeen consecutive weeks with "Mad About the Boy," which had failed to reach the mainstream charts, even in the R&B category. Dinah, the *Defender* wrote approvingly, "has moved up the ladder to become a 'pop' singer (joining up with Patti Page, Rosemary Clooney et al.)" Even a black paper considered pop a step up, the bigger market and bigger potential income obvious.

The writers at *Tan,* another black-oriented magazine, gave their own nod to Dinah, asserting that she was "one blues singer whose records have appeal to jazzophiles of all idioms—Dixie, swing and bop." Her emotions were obvious, *Tan* said, "yet they generally come off as controlled and listenable. Her sounds are often amazingly pretty."

10.

Love for Sale

1953

Though Dinah had just been to California in October, she and the trio were on the road west the first week of 1953. They left from Chicago in two cars, one a Cadillac limousine for the musicians and all the luggage, the other a Cadillac sedan for her, her driver, probably Jimmy, and maybe her maid. Keter was in charge of both cars. "I would get a grease job and an oil change, tires—I would fill the gas tank, give her the bills and she would pay them," he explained.

"I became an expert packer," he added, referring to all the suitcases needed to handle Dinah's clothes.

Slappy White, the stand-up comic, was traveling with the group on this trip. Dinah invited him after he split up with Redd Foxx, who was doing so well as a single that he didn't need a partner. Dinah was happy to have Slappy along, never forgetting how he had taken her under his wing.

The group started in Los Angeles at the Elks Hall and then flew to Honolulu, where Ben Bart had booked Dinah and the trio into the Brown Derby for a two-week engagement at the downtown club.

None of the group—and Beryl was still at the keyboard in place of Wynton—had been there before, and no one knew what to expect. They had heard, though, that young Hawaiian women greeted visitors plane-side, put leis around their necks, and gave them a peck on the cheek.

When Keter got off the plane, he could see the surprise on the young women's faces. He had taken up archery, and he carried a small bow and a quiver of arrows with him on the road. He had the bow slung over his shoulder as he came down the stairway and heard one of the young women to say to another, "Here comes a colored Indian!"

He waited for the traditional greeting but didn't get it. A lei was draped over his neck, but, Keter said, "they wouldn't kiss a black person."

At the Brown Derby Dinah and the trio were booked opposite an all-white, all-woman band whose leader was the drummer. Midway through the engagement the woman took a bad spill and hurt her knee. Concerned about her, Dinah went over to see her at her hotel. When she saw the injury, she was aghast. It was a deep cut that needed medical attention, but the woman was adamant against going to the doctor. She told Dinah it was against her religious principles.

"I don't care about your religion," Dinah snapped. "I care about your life." She got on the phone and found a doctor and told him to come in a hurry, not worrying for a moment that she might be interfering in someone else's life, albeit with the best of intentions. Keter and Jimmy were with her, and when the doctor arrived, they had to help restrain the woman so that he could treat her injury.

The group returned to the mainland and a two-week stay at one of San Francisco's premier jazz spots, the Blackhawk Lounge. Buddy Rich preceded Dinah; Illinois Jacquet would follow. Jazz club or not, the Blackhawk billed Dinah as the "Queen of the Blues" when it ran an ad in the *San Francisco Chronicle*. It listed the Jimmy Cobbs [sic] Trio, highlighting Beryl Booker, who was still filling in for Wynton. Only Keter, the linchpin of the group, was not mentioned in the publicity.

The house band was led by bassist Vernon Alley. Because it was his quartet, Alley introduced the special guests, but Dinah could see how awkward this was when her engagement started. "He would have to set the bass down, go to the microphone, introduce her, then go all the way back, pick up the bass, and then start the intro-duction," Slappy explained.

"Slappy," Dinah said, "you bring me on the next show."

It worked so well that Slappy took over as her regular emcee. When she was late, he had to stay at the microphone telling every joke he could remember until she was ready to sing. "I got so good," Slappy recalled, "that I stayed there a month."

Dinah looked her most glamorous opening night, choosing a low-cut black gown and pendant earrings that sparkled under the stage lights. Jimmy and Keter wore dark suits with shirts and ties. Beryl wore an evening gown, too, and if Dinah felt any competition with another woman onstage, particularly one who would be con-sidered attractive by any definition, she could calm herself with the knowledge that Beryl worked for *her*. After all, the marquee said "Dinah Washington," not Beryl Booker.

Dinah's sets were an eclectic mix—ballads, "Dream," "I Can't Get Started," "Make Believe," her hit "Cold, Cold Heart," "Love for Sale," in her hands full of swing, and one or two blues. When she sang "Long John," the risqué tune about the dentist, and got to the line, "he took out his trusty drill and he told me to open wide," now she added "my mouth, that is," which drew a laugh.

The band stayed onstage when Slappy came out to do fifteen minutes of jokes. Every now and then Jimmy punctuated the punch line with a rim shot, and if Dinah stayed to listen, too, she occasion-ally chimed in to banter with the comedian. But as soon as she left the stage, she hurried to the dressing room, got out of her dress, and put on a robe, ready to play a few rounds of gin rummy until the next set.

Dinah and the trio returned to Los Angeles after the Blackhawk job, and while they were playing the 5-4 Ballroom, another popular club, Dinah took time out to appear on a radio show, *Food for Fun,* to talk about recipes. She sat for a charcoal sketch one night during dinner at the Red Hut, which featured a well-known local artist who drew patrons. When he finished, Dinah said the drawing looked like someone else. Her weeklong stay at the Tiffany, another storied Los Angeles club, was sold out every night. Some of the fans egged Dinah on to do her Billie Holiday imitation, shouting, "Sing it, Bil-lie!" Finally she relented and floored the audience with her dead-on take of Holiday's languorous style, in her repertoire since she was a teenager showing off for high school friends at Wendell Phillips.

The end of March brought Dinah the best publicity to date. She was on the cover of *Jet*, now in its second year and gaining popularity. The magazine used an alluring photograph of her, head slightly bent and just a hint of a smile. The cover proclaimed her "Queen of the Juke Boxes." "Anything she sings has almost got to be a hit," said one music man quoted in the story and described only as "the manager of another singer." "She's the poor man's Lena Horne. . . . The *way* she sings a song is her secret. Church folks hear her records and get the idea she's singing a gospel song. The jitterbugs go for her because she puts a terrific beat in what she does. The 'juice-heads' and 'winos' swear she's singing directly to them. How can anybody beat a combination like that?"

One critic told *Jet* the comparisons with Bessie Smith were inapt. Smith, he said, was "a booming contralto." Dinah, on the other hand, "has a tricky tone control that permits her to do things Bessie could never accomplish in this field. Dinah is an unusually clever girl," he added, "and knows how to sing right into a listener's heart, whether on records or on a theater stage."

BACK IN CHICAGO in early spring, Dinah was in the studio with a full complement of horns to surround her and the trio, and there wasn't a straight blues tune among the four songs recorded. Dinah sounded relaxed and free, veering the closest to jazz ornaments in her version of "Don't Get Around Much Anymore," the popular Duke Ellington–Bob Russell song. Instead of the little trills she liked to do on a blues song, here she accented a word—"been invited *on* dates" by going up a third to give the line extra punch. She tipped her hat to Al Hibbler, singing "enty more" instead of "anymore" during one pass. At the very end she let loose, singing the last "don't get around much anymore" a cappella and with a sky-high note, her nod to Ella Fitzgerald.

The opening line of another song, "Ain't Nothin' Good," could have been a slogan for Dinah's turbulent offstage life: "Ain't nothin good about how bad I love you." It was probably why she sang it with such quiet ease, especially the last line, "it's bad but you look good to me." How better to address the mysteries of attraction? It was as good a clue as any to why she married Walter Buchanan, handsome but more than difficult.

When *Cash Box* picked the record for its "award-of-the-week" April 4, the reviewer was prescient in his praise. Dinah, he wrote, "sings to her heart . . . Dinah is soft, tender, caressing and unhappy."

The turmoil of her brief marriage to Walter became apparent May 26 when Dinah went to Cook County Superior Court to testify at her divorce hearing. She had filed the papers fifteen months earlier, in February 1952. Dinah brought two witnesses with her: Vivian Hunter, who had been her maid, and Lela Dudley, a friend who had known Dinah since she was the teenage Ruth Jones living at the Ida B. Wells Homes.

Under questioning from her lawyer with occasional interjections from Judge Donald S. McKinlay, Dinah, whose legal name was "Dinah Buchanan," explained the sudden end to the marriage: "All I know, I came upstairs from the basement and Walter was gone, his clothes and my car."

Had she talked to Walter that day? asked her lawyer, Alexander Ross.

"I asked him to stop drinking so much."

What did Walter say?

"I would not like to say what he said."

Judge McKinlay asked if that meant Walter used obscene language.

"Yes, he cursed me out."

When Ross asked if Walter was working, Dinah said that "two weeks after we were married he quit his job."

Why?

"He said I have enough money to take care of him, too."

How did Walter act toward her? Ross asked.

"He would get drunk and curse me out and abuse me in front of the people."

How often was Walter intoxicated?

"I never seen him sober. . . . He drank from the time he got up until he went to bed . . . whiskey, gin, everything and anything he could get."

Dinah contended that she hadn't done anything to provoke

Walter to leave. His lawyer, Sherwin Willens, asked Dinah why she was away so much—"whenever you felt like it you kept on going."

Dinah explained that she was working, following the instructions of her booking agent. "He makes up contracts and sends my itinerary, where I am supposed to be at such and such a day. . . . My contracts are for my appearances on jobs; if I didn't appear on those jobs, I got sued."

Before she left the stand, Judge McKinlay had one more question. "Did you tell him before you were married about your previous marriages?"

"Sure," Dinah replied.

When she took the stand, Vivian Hunter said she was at 1518 South Trumbull the day Walter left and had heard no cross words between the couple. She testified that Dinah had given him no reason to leave. "She was constant in her attention. She did the things a wife would do. . . . He threatened to whip her," Hunter added. "He was constantly drinking; even when we were traveling from place to place he was drinking in the car. She was constantly trying to keep him from drinking because when he would get that way he was always wanting to be quarrelsome, wanting to fight."

The trouble started the first week of their marriage, when they were all on the road, "and I heard him tell her . . . We had access—we had adjoining rooms and he told her he will beat her this particular time."

What did they fight about?

"Mostly whiskey or money . . . All the money he had would belong to her."

Lela Dudley told much the same story when she testified, recalling in detail that embarrassing moment when Walter got out of the car and urinated in the street. He was "rude and impudent" to Dinah, she said, adding that every time she saw Walter he was intoxicated.

Walter was supposed to have testified the next day, but Willens, his lawyer, explained that although Walter had promised to show up, he was nowhere to be found. After waiting nearly an hour, Judge McKinlay proceeded without him. He called Dinah back to the stand to make sure she understood that she was waiving alimony and any interest in property Walter may have had.

"I don't want anything from him," Dinah said.

The last formalities were taken care of in a few minutes, and Judge McKinlay granted Dinah an uncontested divorce.

IT WAS A RELIEF to be back in New York two weeks later and back in the studio. Music served Dinah well right now as a source of stability, whether a song was a hit or not. This latest session featured lightweight novelty fare, and the trio would be complemented by horns, an organ player, and a highly touted conga drummer, Candido Camero, who had come from Cuba in 1946 and quickly made a name for himself in jazz circles.

Dinah joked that the first song, "Fat Daddy," a fast-moving blues, reminded her of her chubby youngest son, Bobby, while another, "My Lean Baby," was a perfect fit for the wiry George, her older son. But it was the third selection that was the centerpiece of the session, "TV Is the Thing (This Year)," a witty piece of froth about the latest in technology. "Radio is great—but now it's out of date," Dinah sang, and then went up the dial, from channel one to channel eleven, with plenty of double entendres about how the repairman would check her set: "The way he eased into channel five—the man musta had fluid drive. . . ." When he hit channel eleven, "I cried 'Mama, he treats your daughter good,' " a teasing bow to Atlantic singing star Ruth Brown and her hit, "Mama, He Treats Your Daughter Mean." Dinah ended with a suggestive spoken line: "Baby, my TV will need fixin' about this time every night."

An alternate take included slightly different lyrics, two other singers, and some playful business at the end that suggested how much fun the musicians were having. Evoking the popular TV show *Dragnet*, which had been equally popular on radio, the organ player hit the distinctive "Dum da dum dum, dum da dum dum da" that opened the show. Two quick drumbeats from Jimmy finished the song.

Everything felt good in the studio. Now Dinah and Mercury would have to wait and see what the public thought. In the meantime Ben Bart had lined up a busy schedule: another engagement at the Apollo and Birdland, a stop at the popular Carr's Beach Resort in Annapolis, Maryland, and return trips to the Royal in Baltimore, where Mercury was sponsoring a "Lean Baby" contest to help publicize the record, and the Howard in Washington. Taking advantage of Dinah's reputation, Mercury also advertised in *Cash Box*, promoting the record at the top of its list of "hot Rhythm and Blues."

Beryl Booker had taken another job, and Clarence "Sleepy" Anderson, a Chicago musician, was playing the piano for Dinah now. When the trio headed south from Baltimore for two dates at Fort Campbell, Kentucky, Anderson, whose drug use was well-known, was trying to kick his habit. He got so sick in the car, however, that the band stopped along the way so he could buy some paregoric, used to stop babies from crying, in an effort to get temporary relief. But after Dinah and the trio finished a disc jockey's ball at Atlanta's City Auditorium on August 6, Anderson succumbed to his habit. He left his hotel room in the middle of the night, broke into a whites-only clinic in a suburb, and stole a bag of narcotics. He was arrested in the parking lot a few hours later, confessed to police that he was an addict, and admitted he had drug paraphernalia in his motel room.

As soon as she learned what happened, Dinah raced down to the jail to bail him out because she and the band had to leave right away for Detroit. How much is it? she wanted to know.

Five hundred dollars.

No problem. She would pay it.

But there *was* a problem. The sheriff told her Anderson could be released only if he stayed in Atlanta. Dinah didn't know anyone who would take that responsibility, so she had to leave him there.

"The last time I saw Sleepy he was hanging on to the jail bars crying," Keter said. (Anderson's mother eventually came to get him out.)

Dinah's stop at the Graystone Ballroom in Detroit the week after Atlanta was a much happier moment. It coincided with her twenty-ninth birthday, and she threw a party in her suite at the Gotham Hotel, inviting local entertainers and friends to gather for a midnight dinner of fried chicken and trimmings and champagne to toast her birthday. Her father, Ollie, flew in from Chicago. Detroit was in the middle of a heat wave, with the temperature hitting one hundred degrees, and Dinah wanted to make sure the guests knew that her rooms were air-conditioned. "Nothing is going to keep me from having a party on my last birthday in the twenties," she declared.

The party started so late because Dinah and other guests who were performing around town had to finish their jobs. One friend who was the cashier at the Flame Show Bar didn't arrive until 3:00 A.M, and she came away with a photograph of her birthday hug with Dinah. Dinah showed off her present to herself, made-to-order "stocking shoes," which were an addition to her growing collection of real shoes, and she posed for a picture with Jimmy, who planted a kiss on her cheek. (His present was a small portable bar.) In the middle of the night Dinah sang an impromptu version of "TV Is the Thing" a few weeks before its official release.

The August issue of *Our World*, a black magazine that pitched itself as "a picture magazine for the whole family," included a three-page spread on Dinah: "Miss Juke-box—with equal ease this song stylist can sing blues or ballads." The story was full of candid pictures of her on the stage (mugging with Keter's bass, gesturing in mid-song) and offstage (greeting friends in her dressing room, getting a massage, playing the piano, a big smile on her face).

"Her down to earth songs are as homey as ham hocks and greens," the article said. "That accounts for her success in night clubs and theaters, that's why she's 'Queen of the Juke Boxes.' . . . Although Dinah's never sung in the plush bistros of New York's East Side or Chicago's Loop," the piece went on, "every juke box in Chattanooga, Memphis and many other Southern towns boasts five or six of Dinah's records."

Though that paragraph was slightly misleading—Dinah regularly played Birdland and Café Society in New York—it captured Dinah's core audience, the one not measured in *Down Beat* and *Metronome*. The *Our World* article put Dinah's earnings at $150,000 for the year and noted that in addition to her two sons, she was supporting her mother, two sisters, and younger brother with enough left over to "indulge in the expensive clothes, fancy shoes and big cars."

"That's not bad for a 28-year-old girl who started from scratch," Dinah told the magazine.

She could sound cavalier about money, but Dinah kept her eye on business. She had turned down an opportunity to perform in Europe a few months earlier because she didn't like the terms. "The possibility of my having to leave more than half my earnings abroad is out," she said.

The last page of the *Our World* article included another milepost

for Dinah. She was featured in an ad for Perma-Strate hair straight-
ener in grand company: Sarah Vaughan, Louis Jordan, and Count
Basie. The pitch was obvious: "These stars agree! It's always Perma-
Strate." The idea was to get "natural looking straight hair that you
can dress in any style." Left unsaid was the underlying message: the
tightly curled hair common to most blacks was less desirable.

BACK IN CHICAGO, Alice had met a handsome widower at
church, James Kimbrough, who was originally from Mississippi. He
had moved to Chicago to find work and planned to bring his wife
and five children when he got settled. His wife died before the
move, but he brought his children to the city nonetheless. He and
Alice were married July 2. Overnight Dinah had five stepsiblings
and her sons technically had five new aunts and uncles. "It didn't
bother me," Bobby said. He had just turned five, and all those new
faces meant more people to play with. Alice's instructions to her oldest daughter were clear: "When you come home, I want you to be
good to them."

Dinah and the trio came to Chicago at the end of the summer to
record and to play a big dance at a West Side skating rink. It was
quite a scene at 1518 South Trumbull when Dinah's two-car caravan pulled up to the house, each one laden with suitcases and instruments. George and Bobby, her siblings, and James's children
were waiting on the front steps to greet them. Farris Kimbrough, fifteen and already chummy with Clarissa, who was almost the same
age, could barely contain her excitement.

"She got out of the car—she had on white shorts and a red top
with a boat neck," Farris recalled. "The first thing I wanted to do—
my heart flipped—I wanted to run and hug her. I got halfway down
the steps but nobody was moving but me. I said, 'Well, maybe I'm
out of order.' I stopped and didn't do that."

The pause was only momentary. Dinah came up the steps to
greet everyone. She introduced herself as Ruth, and Farris got over
her shyness. "I did hug her," she said. Those first awkward hellos
dispensed with, George, Bobby, Estrellita, and three of James's children gathered for a picture in front of the station wagon, a suitcase
still resting on top of the metal luggage rack.

Dinah was immediately taken with James's youngest daughter, Alfred, who was named for her mother's beloved brother. "That's no name for a little girl," Dinah said, and promptly renamed her Alfreda. Dinah was so used to being in charge now that she thought nothing of intruding on matters that were none of her business. But everyone accepted the name change, and Dinah couldn't wait to go shopping for Alfreda to buy the pretty little dresses she couldn't buy for her sons.

Her first full day home, Dinah took her sisters and stepsisters to get their hair done and then gathered everyone up to go to an amusement park. It took three cars to carry all the children and adults and the food Dinah and her mother had cooked for a picnic dinner. Jimmy was in charge of the novelty rides. "We would go to a booth and buy a long row of tickets," Farris recalled, "and he wrapped it around his arm until all the tickets were gone." It was another of those moments Dinah said she dreamed of—a day at home with family, doing typical things.

But business, of necessity, intruded, first the West Side dance and then another session. An eclectic group of songs had been selected for the record date, several of them using the conga and organ that had been featured on "TV Is the Thing." One of the tracks, "Since My Man Has Gone and Went," was a calypso number, and Dinah had fun with the West Indian idiom. She affected a slight accent—"mahn" for "man"—and clipped off the end of each word. Though it was not her usual material, she sang with gusto. Record producer Milt Gabler loved to explain how Ella Fitzgerald mastered her accent for "Stone Cold Dead in the Market," his successful calypso production with her and Louis Jordan. Ella told him she picked up the accent from her West Indian hairdresser. Dinah probably heard the same patois in Chicago or New York, which had sizable Caribbean populations, and like Ella, her good ear made her a good mimic.

Two other numbers were in anticipation of the upcoming Christmas holiday, "Silent Night" and "The Lord's Prayer," and an opportunity for Dinah to record the music of her church origins. Though the producers surrounded her with an uninspiring vocal group, Dinah's deeply felt singing rose above her surroundings. The stylistic tics that were now her trademarks—the triplet trills and the "hmms"—were left at the door. Though Dinah did not have Mahalia Jackson's singular power, her treatment was in the same vein as Jackson's majestic presentation.

Cash Box predicted that the record would "certainly garner its share of holiday disc sales."

THE RELATIONSHIP BETWEEN Dinah and Jimmy was souring by the time they returned to New York in mid-September. Perhaps it was doomed from the start, given the reversal of convention. Dinah was always in charge, not her husband or boyfriend. They lived in her place. Jimmy worked for her. She paid the bills, set the schedule, made the rules. And she operated with a double standard. When they were out on the road, she could have a roving eye for as many men as she wanted. Her liaison with Harlem Globetrotter Ducky Moore was obvious enough that *Jet* wrote about it twice, putting Dinah at the center of delicious gossip: "Ducky Moore (Harlem Globetrotter) and drummerman Jimmy Cobbs [sic] almost came to blows over who loved her the most."

But Dinah considered Jimmy off-limits for any other woman and made that clear to any potential admirers. Jimmy was perplexed for a while when he got such cold shoulders from women who normally paid him lots of attention. He was tall and handsome; his carefully trimmed goatee gave him a continental look. When he learned about Dinah's directives, he was irritated and resolved to do as he pleased. He renewed his friendship with a woman in Arnett Cobb's band, and at the end of the summer, she told him she was pregnant.

Jimmy decided honesty was the best policy. One evening when he and Dinah were back in New York, he told her his situation. "She just went off," Jimmy said. "She jumped out of bed and went down to Minton's," a popular restaurant-bar in Harlem. "I took all my stuff and walked it up to the Theresa."

Hurt and angry, Dinah nonetheless realized she had to be practical. She would have to figure out a way to work with Jimmy, even if they weren't together offstage. He and Keter and the piano players who cycled in to replace Wynton were so good behind her that if she and Jimmy couldn't figure something out, the music would suffer. Perhaps some time had to pass, but maybe they could reach an accommodation. At least, she reasoned, he had been honest with her about what happened, had told her himself.

Dinah found a momentary diversion when she went down to Philadelphia September 25 for a gala evening at the Academy of Music. The event was to honor the year's winners in the *Pittsburgh Courier* theatrical poll. Ruth Brown won in the blues category; Dinah was second. (In the *Cash Box* disc jockey poll in July, Dinah had been third in the most programmed female vocalist behind Willie Mae Thornton and Brown.) The paper had departed from its traditional Carnegie Hall event in April, but like other *Courier* concerts, the lineup was full of stars.

The concert had special resonance for the performers because that year's proceeds were going to the NAACP Legal Defense Fund. The organization's lawyers, led by Thurgood Marshall, were in the midst of a protracted struggle before the Supreme Court to end racial segregation in public schools. These entertainers might not know the intricacies of the legal arguments Marshall and his staff were making, but each of them knew firsthand how segregation defined their careers and regulated their public lives. Making music for an organization that could improve their world only added to the gala's appeal.

Back in New York Dinah assumed a new role, social director for Keter's upcoming marriage to Mildred Grady, nicknamed Pinky by childhood friends who made a play on words from "Mild—red." Dinah could be opinionated about other people's choices—though often joking, she might greet someone's girlfriend with "This the bitch you told me about?" But not with Keter. "She's a nice girl," Dinah told him. "You should get married."

Keter and Pinky had been introduced by a friend of Keter's, and the timing was right. Keter was tired of "rippin' and runnin' " on the road, he admitted, and his friend told Pinky, who was from Durham, North Carolina, to write Keter a letter. "It was such a nice letter," Keter recalled, that he wrote back and suggested they meet when he got back east. Pinky came up to Washington, and a few months and many letters later, they were engaged.

Dinah recruited her doctor for the couple's blood tests, secured the church, found the pastor, arranged the catering, and took Pinky to Saks to buy her a wedding dress, a light-colored short-sleeved

chiffon gown with a ruffled skirt just above the ankle. Dinah made
sure Pinky had the right shoes to complete the outfit, and on her
wedding day, she also wore a large orchid corsage. Dinah had chosen a velvet dress with appliquéd shoulder trim and topped it off, literally, with a small hat that featured a trailing feather. She had
wanted the Reverend Adam Clayton Powell Jr. to perform the ceremony, but he was away. An assistant married the couple, and just
before the ceremony in a small room off the sanctuary of Abyssinian
Baptist Church, Dinah carefully pinned a boutonniere on Keter's
tuxedo.

As the couple took their vows, she stood right next to Pinky, and
Jimmy, the best man, stood next to Keter. After the ceremony,
Dinah arranged for the reception at Birdland.

"She gave us the wedding," Keter said, though he chuckled that
she declined to pay for the post-wedding pictures at the club because they were too expensive.

One of the guests was Larry Wrice, a drummer from Chicago
who was friendly with piano player Sleepy Anderson. Larry had
come to a show at Birdland the last week in September just after
Dinah and Jimmy had their blowup. Bobby Shad, the Mercury producer, was on hand, and when he learned about the Chicago connections, he asked Larry to take Dinah to a suite at the Theresa he
had booked for her because she didn't want to go back to the apartment where she and Jimmy broke up. "They pushed us into a cab,"
Larry recalled, and one thing quickly led to another. "It started automatically. I started living with her in New York."

(By the time *Our World* got around to publishing a story on
Dinah's August birthday party, the pictures of Dinah and Jimmy together were already out-of-date.)

The first week in October Mercury released "TV Is the Thing
(This Year)," backed with "Fat Daddy." Dinah and the label didn't
have long to wait to see the response. "TV" shot to the top of the
charts by the end of the month, reaching third place on the *Billboard*
jukebox chart and number five on the sales chart and staying there
until December. It was an equally strong entry in the *Cash Box*
listings, rising to number four on its rhythm and blues top ten
and landing in the top ten of the half-dozen cities the magazine
monitored.

Bobby Shad had never heard the final pressed record, though he was involved in the recording session. To help Dinah learn the song quickly, he had asked the writers to come into the studio and go through a take with her. "So we're running it down on tape and playing it back to her," Shad recalled. "You hear the two songwriters and Dinah's mumbling with them." Dinah did a second take without the writers, then everyone went on to other things, and the record was eventually released.

Driving with the car radio on one early November day, Shad could hardly wait to hear the first notes after the deejay said "Now, ladies and gentlemen, number seven on the charts, Dinah Washington—'TV Is the Thing.' "

Dinah started singing and then he heard those two other voices. "They put out the wrong take," an astonished Shad blurted out loud. "Worst record I ever heard," he said laughing when telling the story decades later.

DINAH'S ROMANTIC ADVENTURE with Larry Wrice intensified while she made a late fall swing through Florida. As the new drummer he fit right in with the group, which now included Dinah's new assistant, Ann Littles, who had first met Dinah when she was fourteen-year-old Ruth Jones singing gospel songs on a visit to Ann's church in Newark. They had reconnected a year earlier when Ann came backstage at the Apollo to see Dinah. She didn't remember Ann at first, but as the two kept talking, memories of their few days together at Ann's church came back. Ann was now working in a beauty shop as a hairdresser, and as a sideline hobby she made small beaded handbags. Dinah admired the one Ann had with her and bought it on sight, for $65. She sensed in Ann a kindred, nononsense spirit with a vocabulary that matched her own. They made a striking pair standing next to each other—Dinah barely five feet, Ann a good ten inches taller.

Dinah asked Ann to come to work for her, offering her $65 a week to take care of the apartment she was renting on 116th Street and to cook when Dinah didn't feel like it. "I did her hair. I paid attention to her clothing," Ann said, adding that the arrangement was easy because Ann still lived in New Jersey and it was just a short trip across the river to get to Dinah's apartment. Before too long Ben Bart was teaching her the business so she could go out on the road and run interference for Dinah with club owners. "You could wait on her hand and foot 'cause she was a lazy motherfucker," Ann recalled with a laugh. "She didn't want to get up to do nothin'."

Slappy always chuckled when sparks flew between the two women. "She'd fire Ann every twenty minutes," he said, "and I'd say, 'Aw, Dinah, when are you going to bring her back?' " And she always did—even when Ann would tell Dinah she couldn't fire her because she quit.

Beyond her other duties Ann was also a spare driver, able to spell Keter on the long road trips between jobs. Perhaps more important, Ann acted as Dinah's informal press agent. Ben Bart had given her a stack of discs and either he or the local promoter also gave her a list of radio stations, shop owners, and jukebox operators to contact in each town to get Dinah's music played and sold. With Larry along, she could get a little more rest between stops, too, because he was able to take her shift at the wheel of the band's car.

Larry was having a grand time. It was good to be Dinah's man, which conferred a certain status and brought many tangibles, even if there were drawbacks. Dinah liked her man to look good and was willing to buy him the clothes to fit the part. Larry was a dazzled beneficiary. "She's the only woman in the world who could wake up and sing and have a clear voice," he said, remembering times when she would stretch out in the back seat to sleep as they traveled from one date to another.

"She had a heart as big as gold. Birthdays? She would give you a gift on Lincoln's birthday," he added, though he was surprised to see his pay docked for a couple of outfits he thought were gifts.

Larry knew Dinah was sensitive about her looks and size, and occasionally they would argue when she thought he was daydreaming about an old girlfriend who was, Larry admitted, "very gorgeous." He always insisted that wasn't so, and the moments passed.

Perhaps it was the beautiful setting in Miami—the ocean, the palm trees, the beach, one sunny day after another—that made Dinah and Larry think they were right for each other. They decided on a Friday to get married and went to the courthouse to take the appropriate steps. They got there too late, Larry said, but they decided to tell everyone that they'd gotten married anyway. Friends threw them a reception at the hotel. The next day they headed back to New York as word spread. The December 10 *Jet* announced that

Dinah had taken her fifth husband and that friends there threw them a party at Café Society. The magazine ran a picture of Dinah, a corsage pinned to her left shoulder, resting her head against Larry, both of them smiling.

Like the photographs with Bobby Grayson and Walter Buchanan, this one, too, was the picture of contentment.

IT DIDN'T MATTER that Dinah had fallen off the year-end popularity charts in *Down Beat* and *Metronome*. Novelties like "Fat Daddy" and "TV Is the Thing (This Year)" held little appeal for their readers or critics. But at the end of 1953 Dinah, still Queen of the Juke Boxes, continued to reach diverse audiences. She was a regular now at Birdland, and Café Society had invited her twice in three months. And in Chicago, she had been welcomed warmly at the Blue Note. Just as important was the invitation for her and the trio to play the Graystone Ballroom in Detroit on December 28 with Dizzy Gillespie and Gene Ammons, the saxophone player. It didn't matter that the date cut into her holiday time in Chicago, and even if Dinah chafed at being listed third on the bill, this was another chance to break the mold. Gillespie and Ammons were jazz musicians, and in their company Dinah could claim those credentials, too. She knew she was a jazz musician, and now a new audience would, too.

11.

Dinah Jams

1954

Dinah's evolving musical presence and the material Mercury had her record were not always in sync—either she didn't have the clout to name her own tunes or she didn't mind doing what the label wanted. When she was in the studio, it was their time. Onstage in the clubs it was hers. She controlled everything from the opening note to the encores. Then, too, were the different sides of Dinah's personality. She liked to be the sophisticate, but she loved to be earthy. No one sang double entendres any better than she did.

Her first 1954 session captured these disparate elements, a mix of novelty tunes and standards. "Short John" was a takeoff on "Long John," and though it was about going to the doctor rather than the dentist, it had the same kind of suggestive lyrics, if slightly less explicit: "He examines me carefully and he takes care of my ills./Well, he checks me all over and he gives me the right size pills."

"Old Man's Darlin' " was an acerbic piece about a young woman who marries an older man for his money. Dinah provided a witty punch line by tossing in the Gershwin standard—"Our love is here to stay"—but with a personal twist: " 'Cause he made out his will to Miss D." She sang it with perfect mock sweetness.

Prominent on both recordings was a guitar, played not with the brashness of Muddy Waters, the popular blues man, but with the crisp, sure strut of a Charlie Christian. It gave the songs a light, almost jazzy feel even though they were standard blues. The guitar player was probably Bryce Robertson, one of the few white musicians who regularly played with Larry.

Dinah also recorded Cole Porter's "Love for Sale," which she was singing on most of her club dates. This studio version, with more instruments involved, had a different feel from the live performance. Onstage, she had only her trio and dispensed with any kind of introduction. In this studio version, supplemented with organ, guitar, and saxophone, she started out slowly, singing the first two verses as a contemplation, wondering, with an edge, "Who will buy, who would like to sample my supply?" Then with a little growl she changed stride, picking up the tempo and letting the rest of the song fly. The lyrics must have hit home when Dinah sang about going through "the mill of love . . . every love but true love. . . ."

Larry Wrice remembered the recording date as a makeup session that Dinah owed Mercury. She loved to play cards and didn't mind doing so for money. She had gotten in a fast game some weeks earlier on one of their road stops—Larry thought it was in Cleveland—and lost so much she had to call Bobby Shad to wire the cash so she could pay her bills and leave town. The session, according to Larry, was to cover the loan.

By the time Dinah and the trio got to Baltimore February 5 to play a week at the Royal, Dinah was unhappy about the way Larry fit in with the trio. She accused him of "hogging the show." When the group went on to Chicago for a February 19 date at the Regal with Cootie Williams, she and Larry got into an argument. Larry couldn't remember what started it, but in a flash the tense moment exploded into a full-scale fight. When they calmed down, they agreed to call it quits. "She was a very beautiful person to be with," Larry said, even if he had to give back most of those natty clothes she had bought him. He considered it an honor that his name had been woven into one of Dinah's blues tunes, "My Man's an Undertaker," whose lyrics describe how the singer will deal with unwanted attention. Her new man, the undertaker, has a coffin "just your size." The line that made Larry chuckle was "Down in the cellar where it used to be bare,/Now Mr. Wrice keeps his coffin there."

Dinah got back at Larry by putting the name of a new man in the song when she performed it at the Regal. Now instead of "Mr. Wrice," she talked about "Mr. Johnson"—Harold "Killer" Johnson, who owned the Archway Bar and Grill in Chicago. "I intend to let the world know I'm through with Wrice and that I'm now on the trail of Killer Johnson, sweetest man in the world," Dinah proclaimed. Implicit was the assumption that her fans were trying to keep up with her romantic life, too. After she ran up a $75 wine and food tab at the grill, Dinah nonchalantly told the waiter to give the check to "my man," referring to Johnson.

Dinah had to use a pickup drummer for the Regal date, but she wanted a permanent replacement. Ed Thigpen, the son of Ben Thigpen, Andy Kirk's drummer, had played for the Cootie Williams band before he was drafted into the army in the winter of 1952. He had been on a number of dates when Dinah and her trio were on the same bill and was impressed. "I had never heard a trio like that," Ed said. "Jimmy floored me as a drummer, and everybody was so nice."

He had been a fan of Dinah's since high school, and he never forgot the first time he heard her voice, walking down the street in Los Angeles as the sound of one of her records was coming out through the windows of a house. He had to stop and listen. "I was struck by her diction, the clarity of her words, plus the feel, everything about her," Ed recalled. "That was the beginning of my infatuation with this wonderful voice and expression and the English language."

When Ed came back to Chicago just before his official discharge, he noticed that Dinah was at the Regal. He called Keter at his South Side hotel to say hello.

"The Queen is without a drummer," Keter explained, and he told Ed to come by the Regal to talk to Dinah.

Ed followed through, explaining to the "Duchess," which was his nickname for her, that he would be out of the army in a matter of days. Dinah told him the upcoming schedule, offered him the job, and Ed accepted.

The entire Regal show—Dinah, her trio, the Cootie Williams band—was onstage together in Detroit the first week in March at the Broadway Capitol. The promoter billed the package as "modern jazz," though it also included Peg Leg Bates, a one-legged dancer. He made the biggest impression on *Detroit Free Press* reviewer Helen Bower. Dinah was the star, she wrote, "but 'Peg Leg' Bates steals the show." Nonetheless, Bower added, Dinah was in good voice. "Numbers like 'Love for Sale' are her speciality, sung in trumpet tones but quietly mannered."

One of the more flamboyant personalities in Detroit's black community was Bishop James Jones, the self-styled Prophet Jones of the Church of the Triumph Dominion of God. He claimed to have a following of six million, and two of the more ardent followers, sisters from Chicago, gave him a white mink coat valued at nearly $13,000. He lived in a fifty-four-room mansion that he had converted from a gambling casino. Jones invited Dinah to dinner one evening, and she accepted, decked out in her best gown and wrapped in mink. Her friend Bea Buck came with her, and when the two arrived, they were formally announced and told to wait in an anteroom. "We waited and waited and waited," Bea said. After nearly two hours, Dinah had had enough. "She told his little servant that he was the king. She was the queen, and she never had known a queen to wait on a king. And we left."

Though Dinah didn't put on airs, she did enjoy the perquisites of stardom. It was not exactly a sense of entitlement, but Dinah liked the attention, was used to it by now, and certainly in public venues she insisted on being treated with respect. Callers were never quite sure if she was joking when she answered the phone, "Hello, this is Dinah Washington, Queen of the Juke Boxes." Or she might use the other title, pausing a moment after she picked up the phone to say, "Queen of the Blues speaking." "It was like she was always making a grand entrance, even on the telephone," said Eddie Plique, who had introduced her so many nights at the Ritz Lounge. The one time Plique brought Dinah on as "that mean and evil woman," a take on "Evil Gal Blues," "she jumped all over me. I never did it again."

One night in St. Louis, Dinah had stopped into a club run by the "glamorous Ruby Hines," as the papers called her. Dinah didn't know Hines, but "there was a woman standing there scowling at me and God knows I hadn't done anything to her," Dinah recalled. "I invited her to join us, have some fun. I wasn't mad at anyone. But she turned to the waiter and said: 'Give her a drink so she'll know how it feels to drink with a lady.' It was a cruel thing to say, and it hurt," Dinah continued. "So when the drink came, I conked her on the head with it. She was no lady."

EVEN THOUGH DINAH was at home with the blues and had demonstrated success with pop ballads, she was shifting her musical profile to jazz. Propelling the transition was the creation in March of a new label within Mercury called EmArcy to focus on jazz. Bobby Shad, who had briefly left the company, was returning to head the enterprise. EmArcy was a variation on the initials M.R.C., short for Mercury Record Corporation. The plan was to release singles, extended plays or EPs, which looked like 45s but included more music, and LPs, long-playing records.

In Shad's embracing philosophy jazz included rhythm and blues. "So you can say in general that what I dig first about any performance—jazz or the blues—is the beat," he explained. "Whether it's a ballad or up-tempo, if it doesn't swing, it doesn't make it." The observation was a perfect explanation of why Shad loved Dinah's music.

Appearing on a network radio show with Mercury vice president Art Talmadge, Shad promised that EmArcy records would be "uninhibited," so that the artists could bring their own interpretations to the music without worrying about "commercialism." But it remained to be seen how far the musicians could go. Records did have to sell.

One of the first EmArcy singles was Dinah's "Pennies from Heaven" with "Love for Sale" on the B side. *Metronome* paid attention, which was good for Dinah's profile, but the reviewer didn't care for the record. The organ and sax "keep Dinah on the beat" in "Pennies," he wrote, and "after a soft, almost tender start in 'Love,' Dinah goes her shouting way and the record goes with her."

Well before the EmArcy division was created, Mercury had been repackaging material by its singers, including Dinah. To broaden the market, they released the songs in different formats to take advantage of the changing technology. As early as 1951, Dinah's recordings, like those of pop singers Patti Page and Vic Damone, were assembled on 78s and 45s, and then repackaged once again as LPs to play at 33¹/₃ rpm. Dinah's earliest record in this LP format was released in October 1951 as part of the label's "long playing microgroove" series, and included eight ballads, among them "I Want to Cry," "It Isn't Fair," and "I Wanna Be Loved."

In spite of the material she was recording, Dinah's identification with rhythm and blues remained strong, and of all the singers that *Ebony* could have used to illustrate a March essay about R&B, "Juke Box Sociology," the magazine chose to run a full-page picture of Dinah. "So popular have become these lyrical epics of Negro life that R and B is today a $50 million industry featuring well known singers like Dinah Washington," the article said. The picture *Ebony* chose was hardly flattering. It was at least five years old and was taken when Dinah looked like she was in a housedress, hardly the well-turned-out woman who now appeared onstage.

Intended or not, the magazine made a telling point about the commercial disadvantages of being labeled rhythm and blues. "Occasionally rhythm and blues become so popular that they spill over into the general market, but for the most part, these probing songs escape non-elevated riding whites"—a reference to Chicago's El train. "They are confined to Negro juke boxes, cabarets and radio programs heard only from small stations at the extreme ends of the dial. . . . Rhythm and blues serve the Negro well," the essay concluded. "If others wish to know his full life story, they might do well to listen to his song."

Dinah fit in a session at the end of March in Chicago that once again featured a vocal group. And once again the results were dubious. Fans could wonder why the producer thought she needed such uninspired singing behind her. On "Such a Night," with its Latin feel, Dinah sounded like she was enjoying herself, singing about a wonderful evening with a wonderful kiss. But the backup singers dampened the fun. It was only when she sang the song live, without the fussiness, that she could soar. Clyde McPhatter and the Drifters had had a hit with the song, and Mercury probably felt it needed to replicate the arrangement.

The next song, "Until Sunrise," featured Hawaiian guitar effects, and the third, "One Arabian Night," was a silly piece of fluff about one Arabian night when a handsome sheik will "kiss my cheek and he'll wear a turban hat."

Dinah sang gamely, but it remained a mystery why Mercury picked these songs for her with these kinds of arrangements and why she agreed. Perhaps someone at the label knew the writer and wanted to do a favor or take care of a debt. Perhaps this was another makeup session, and it wasn't worth the energy to argue. Besides, Dinah knew she had a full plate of live dates ahead of her when *she* made the set list.

LEONARD FEATHER had created a niche for himself in the world of music criticism. He not only reviewed records and performances, he also liked to hear what musicians thought about other musicians—how they listened, what they liked and didn't like. For his "Blindfold Test," a regular *Down Beat* feature, he picked a musician and several songs by an eclectic group of performers and played them without identifying the personnel. He ran a tape recorder and later published the musician's comments verbatim after a brief introduction. *Down Beat* ran the story whenever he had completed his test.

The May issue featured a listening session with Dinah, which presented her opinions and offered clues about her personal tastes. "Because Dinah has manipulated her eminent tonsils both in the rhythm and blues field and in the pop music market, the records selected for her reaction represented a variety of styles in both these areas," Leonard wrote in his introduction. "And because before she became Queen of the Blues, Dinah had acquired a substantial background as a religious singer, I played her 'Do Lord,' confident I'd get some kind of definite reaction."

Of Charlie Ventura with Jackie Cain singing "They Can't Take That Away from Me," Dinah correctly identified the musicians, and said, "Sounds good." She asked for a second listen. "I'd say it's soothing; nothing exciting. Just pleasant listening, but I didn't get anything out of the ordinary. I'd say two stars."

She had a much stronger opinion about the Treniers with the Gene Gilbreau Quartet, Don Hill on the alto sax, doing "Rock-a-Beatin' Boogie." "That's just a lot of loud noises. . . . Nothing happening; just the same thing over and over, loud," she said. "The drums are too loud, too. Lyrically and musically there's nothing here. And that one horn—they need something to back that one horn up! That sounds terrible. Who is it? It sounds like the Treniers."

While she praised Billie Holiday's "Autumn in New York" with Oscar Peterson at the piano, she said, "Lady could do a better job on it," instantly recognizing Holiday and referring to her nickname, Lady Day, "But she has an awful lot of soul, and she's one of my favorite singers. . . . The piano is terrific. I'll give it three stars." She loved Frank Sinatra on "Violets for Your Furs": "Well, that's just superb; the band is terrific, the bass player is the end, and of course Sinatra's just singing like crazy now. . . . I would rate it the highest. Five."

Dinah was less enthusiastic about Ivory Joe Hunter and "I Feel So Good." "It's all right; didn't have too much feeling. The band's loud and I don't like loud bands. Just fair—two." But she loved Sarah Vaughan and "Come Along with Me." "Of course that was Miss Divine herself. I think it's a very good recording; the music's pretty, and it's something different. I would give that an excellent rating; five."

Leonard then played the rendition of "Do Lord" by four women with no gospel experience, Jane Russell, Connie Haines, Beryl Davis, and Della Russell. The beat was fast, the harmonies tight, but Dinah didn't like it. "I don't care for that at all because they seem to be playing with a sacred song. That *really* didn't kill me. It's in *very* bad taste. When I do a sacred song, I do it with sacredness. I think that's terrible. I don't give that *no* rating. And I don't know who it is. But they should all be punched in the face."

Dinah's strong reaction helped explain why her versions of "Silent Night" and "The Lord's Prayer" a few months earlier had been sung with such solemn restraint.

"Of course, I'd have liked anything you played me by Nat King Cole, too. Sinatra kills me," Dinah said after Leonard had finished playing all of his selections.

Dinah probably surprised readers when she said she also liked Jackie Gleason, particularly his album *Music to Make You Misty*, which was instrumental mood music. Perhaps it appealed to her sentimental side, and she surely appreciated the featured soloists, Bobby Hackett on trumpet and Toots Mondello on alto saxophone, and found kindred spirits in the way they phrased their solos amid the overly lush orchestra. "That's all you hear at my house," Dinah said. Her favorite number was "Say It Isn't So." She played it so often that whenever Keter came over, he stood at the door and said, "It isn't so! It isn't so!" The album was played so often, Keter joked, "the record got hoarse."

Dinah herself had been included in a blindfold test administered to Nat King Cole in March 1948, when the feature had been in *Metronome*. Talking about one of her Apollo records, "Mellow Mama Blues," Cole thought Dinah was singing too high, which "gives her a metallic sound—but I always did like the way Dinah sings the blues."

The third week in May Dinah and the trio played a week in a most unlikely venue, Club 86 in Geneva, New York, in the state's beautiful Finger Lakes region. The club, named for its address, 86 Avenue E in Geneva, had originally been a restaurant built by Nicholas Legott in 1933 in the Italian-Irish section of town. After World War II Legott's son James, a veteran with a love of music and a feel for business, expanded the building and turned it into a night-club. Two military bases were in nearby Sampson, which meant fifty thousand servicemen could easily get on buses and come over to Geneva for some recreation. Louis Armstrong had played eight shows over a week in 1952 for $3,500. Jane Russell did a week of shows for roughly the same amount and even helped Legott's wife, Eileen, watch the couple's six children during the day. Stan Kenton had recorded a live album in the showroom Legott had built with such care.

Nearly a thousand miles from the South, race was still a factor. Legott could not put up his black talent in Geneva's main hotels, which were located in the old-line part of town. But the Mulvey family ran a boarding house a few blocks from Club 86 at the informal border between the city's Italian and Irish neighborhoods, and all were welcome there.

Sixteen-year-old Al Colizzi, who lived in that "butt end of town," as he called it, had the heady experience of chauffeuring Dinah around during her week at the club. "She was very personable," he remembered. Dinah still liked to get the trio together every day when she was playing live dates, if only for a half-hour to run over the tunes, and Colizzi was responsible for making sure she was on schedule. By now the musicians knew Dinah's signals if she tossed a new tune into the set—a curved hand meant the key of C, one finger up was F, two was B-flat. They would adjust accordingly.

"You run over the melodies together and how you're going to treat the little arrangements," said drummer Ed Thigpen.

They weren't terribly complicated. "You need good ears and good fantasy—imagination. A lot of the stuff, they orchestrate themselves. Our gift as jazz musicians, which I think is unique, is to be able to interpret on the spot, a combination of interpretation and improvisation. We had a role—the rhythm section. The drummer is keeping good time, the groove is right, the bass player has good bass lines, so the trio becomes a little orchestra. A good singer like Dinah sort of leads you. You didn't play forever on one tune. The way she phrases would almost dictate the way you phrase."

Keter enjoyed watching how a song changed over time, he and his colleagues adding a little something with almost every performance as they got more and more comfortable with the material.

Dinah liked to eat in the Club 86 kitchen before her shows, which endeared her to the staff. "She loved Italian food," Colizzi said, and the contrast between the woman eating pasta with the help and the elegant singer onstage was striking. Colizzi was smitten with how Dinah looked in her white silk evening gown. Though he loved her music, as did owner Legott, both were surprised that she proved to be a bigger draw than Sarah Vaughan, even though Sarah was more well-known at the time. "You know," Legott confided, "I think I like her better than Ella Fitzgerald. I like her style—a lot of class."

On one of the days in Geneva, Dinah wanted to take advantage of her surroundings and go fishing. She and Colizzi decided to go early in the morning—about five—without going to bed the night before. "She loved it," he said, and was tickled to catch a fish, "the first fish she ever caught." Dinah wanted to take it home and eat it until Colizzi explained how much time would be needed to clean and prepare it. So they threw the fish back in the lake.

Keter was still bringing his bow and arrow with him on the road, and because Club 86 was on the edge of the woods, it was easy for Colizzi to take Keter out for target practice. "We had a good time," Colizzi recalled, chuckling at the memory of Dinah reeling in her catch and Keter tromping through underbrush, bow slung over his shoulder.

From this small venue in upstate New York, Dinah and the trio turned around and headed back to the city, Philadelphia, and its well-known nightclub Pep's, which was one of the few places that featured a Monday matinee. "We get there about ten, eleven in the morning," Keter said, "get in a little bit of sleep and hit it at four in the afternoon."

EARLY IN JUNE Mercury booked new sessions for Dinah, and this time the jazz influence promised by EmArcy was unmistakable. She was reunited with trumpeter Clark Terry, who had been signed to the label; Gus Chappell on trombone, who had arranged Dinah's very first Mercury recording eight years earlier; and Ed Thigpen on drums; now on the piano was Junior Mance, another Chicago native who had started his professional career with Gene Ammons's band. After he was drafted, Junior played in the 36th Army Band at Fort Knox, and when he returned home after his discharge, he was immediately hired as part of the house rhythm section at the Bee Hive, a jazz club on East 55th Street near Lake Michigan. Dinah had asked Junior to come for a session earlier in the year, "and after the record date, she offered me the job."

The material for this latest session featured songs by Duke Ellington, George and Ira Gershwin, and Irving Berlin, and the format resembled a nightclub setting with a group of jazz musicians. Dinah sang and then solos were passed around to the sidemen. In Ellington's "I Let a Song Go Out of My Heart," Dinah was relaxed and easy from the first note, her voice another instrument that alternated with the musicians. The tenor saxophonist for the session was Eddie "Lockjaw" Davis, who took the first solo turn and then handed off to Terry on the trumpet. Junior took the next solo, and after another turn from the saxophone, Dinah finished the song.

She started "A Foggy Day" almost as a spoken monologue, setting the scene of a woman alone in London, feeling sad on a gloomy day. Then she picked up the beat to sing about how a chance meeting turned the fog into sunshine, aided by Candido Camero on the conga drums, Keter, and Junior.

"Bye Bye Blues" started out with a blistering solo from Terry at a pace that would fluster many singers, but Dinah had no trouble keeping up. The rest of the song was filled with more alternating solos, almost as if it were a friendly competition between bandmates. When Dinah came back for the final chorus, she was undaunted, singing her lines with the usual crispness and then slowing everything down for a dramatic finish. "I'd like to hear another singer attempt this tempo and swing as hard as Dinah did," one admiring reviewer wrote. "She more than held her own."

Beyond the innate talent and an understanding of how to shape the song was the fact that all the musicians fed off one another. They kept order but with obvious inspiration.

The last song on the session was "Blue Skies." Once again Dinah started out slowly but with a deliberateness to each of the words— "Blue skies smiling at me"—before she picked up the beat. In the middle of the song, Keter and Junior traded solos, and Dinah came back with a flourish at the end.

A second session in June featured more blues-oriented material, and one of them, "Big Long Slidin' Thing," had the same sexual innuendo as "Long John." Ostensibly the song was about hearing the trombone for the first time, and Dinah asked how it was done: "I slide it right up, then I slide it back down again."

She sang those lyrics the same way she sang conventional ballads. That was part of the fun—to be earthy *and* elegant at the same time.

THE MAIN EVENT on the summer schedule was Dinah's first trip to Las Vegas to be followed by six weeks of dates in California. As usual, the plan was to play stops along the way. Ben Bart had lined up a package with Earl Bostic, and the date in Chicago at the Trianon on South Cottage Grove offered Dinah a brief chance to see her children and the rest of the family. The group also played St. Louis, where they performed for a sold-out Kiel Opera House. A large crowd was turned away at the box office just before showtime. In his review, *St. Louis Argus* columnist Chick Finney said Dinah was "magnificent, just like her records." The audience clamored for more, Finney wrote, and Dinah obliged with a medley of "old favorites."

Slappy White was on the bill, too, and he loved the way Dinah worked him into shows in such big theaters. He came on after Dinah had sung her first set, the audience all revved up. She would tell them Slappy was on the way, but first, they had to settle down. "No, ladies and gentlemen," she told them. "When y'all get quiet I'll bring my comedian out."

"See," Slappy explained, "she got them quiet, that's how I could work in those kinds of rooms because she got them quiet for me."

Junior learned quickly that when the official job was over, it didn't mean he was done for the night. "Dinah knew every after-hour joint in the country," he said. "She always took me with her. Most after-hours places have a small group, some just a piano player. . . . Sure enough," he went on, "she always wanted to sing. 'All right, Junior, I feel like singing.' Sometimes she would sing for an hour. I remember coming out [of one place] and the sun was up, high in the sky. I knew that the hanging out was part of it," he added. "I used to have to hang if I wanted to keep the job."

All the singing could take its toll on Dinah, and the next day, at the job they were booked to play, Dinah might have new instructions: "All right, Junior, drop everything a half-tone." Still hoarse, she had to sing in a lower key, never doubting that her musicians could make the instant transition.

Junior was intrigued by Keter's fascination with archery. He tried to practice every chance he got, using time on breaks during long stretches of travel to improve his marksmanship. One day on the way out west, the cars stopped, and everyone got out to buy some fruit at a roadside stand. Keter bought a watermelon, and Junior, thinking what a kind gesture this was, eagerly awaited a slice. Keter duly took out a knife and cut off some wedges, but he didn't offer any of them to his bandmates. Instead he walked away from the cars onto some vacant land, bow and arrows in hand, set the wedges on the ground, and started shooting arrows at them.

Junior watched in amazement, but still hoped for a piece of melon when Keter retrieved the wedges, now broken into smaller pieces. Finally, he thought, they were going to have a snack. But instead, Keter took the smaller pieces, tossed them in the air, and tried to hit each piece before it landed on the ground.

"This dude is weird," Junior said to himself, and walked back to the car without getting a taste of what had looked like a delicious melon.

Dinah and trio were due in Las Vegas June 29 to play at the Patio, a club that had opened recently at one end of the city's burgeoning main street known as the Strip. Las Vegas had been a gamblers' mecca for little more than a decade, and it was growing at a frenetic pace month by month. New and ever larger casinos were being built, creating hundreds if not thousands of new jobs. But for all of its relentless glitter, this self-styled new town was as old as an antebellum plantation when it came to race, as segregated as any town Dinah and her fellow artists had played in the Deep South.

Instead of a north–south divide, Las Vegas was segregated east–west, with the west side home to its black residents. Lacking the amenities of the east side, west Las Vegas was derisively called "the Dust Bowl." But even with its rigid segregation, the city had captured the attention of black America just as it had the white tourists who filled the hotels and casinos. The black population was now roughly fifteen thousand, a nearly hundredfold increase since 1940. In April 1953, *Sepia* correspondent Roy Rainger published an account of his few days of "Jim Crow gambling," as he called it. His adventure began at the Cotton Club, the main attraction for blacks on the west side, where the only games were cards and dice and the highest stake was $10 (across town it was $200). Rainger wanted to see what the big clubs on the Strip were like even though the natives warned him he would not be welcome. Undaunted, he and two friends got inside the door without a problem, and one of the men put down $2 at the dice table to start playing. Before he could place another bet, a white uniformed guard stopped him.

"I'm sorry, fella, but the table's too crowded."

"It's not too crowded," he retorted, though with no belligerence in his voice. "I have a place here; it's comfortable."

"I'm sorry," the guard answered. "We're permitted to let so many play at a table, and you're just one too many."

The message delivered, the men left without incident.

Ebony, too, took its turn on Las Vegas in an unsparing account it headlined "Negroes Can't Win in Las Vegas." The opening paragraph lamented that the city was "like some place in Mississippi— downright prejudiced and really rough on colored people. It's worse than any place in Mississippi."

Major black stars were not exempt from discrimination. Lena Horne had been the first black entertainer to play a major hotel, headlining in January 1947 at the new Flamingo and billed as "MGM's Exotic Singing Star Sensation" because of her affiliation with the MGM studio. She was treated rudely by the white musicians hired to play for her, and conditions improved only when she complained and hotel owner Bugsy Siegel, the notorious mobster, intervened.

If the artists were given rooms in the hotels where they performed, they were barred from mingling with the guests and gambling in the casinos. "A Negro can entertain on The Strip but not be entertained there," was *Ebony*'s acerbic observation. Away from the Strip things were no better. The singer Nellie Lutcher was refused service at a drive-in, *Ebony* said, and other entertainers suffered insults when they tried to eat at some of the city's restaurants.

But playing Las Vegas still had its advantages. Tourists were dropping $200 million a year (roughly $1.3 billion in today's dollars) in the hotels, casinos, and clubs, and that translated into hefty contracts for the talent hired to entertain them. Then, too, there was simple geography. R&B stars like Dinah regularly played the West Coast and always worked their way there and back from the eastern circuit. Las Vegas was a convenient stopping place. A tight-knit local black community operated like an informal chamber of commerce, providing visiting entertainers with leads about accommodations and the like.

Compared to the big hotels with their glittery casinos, the Patio, which had opened May 27, was a modest establishment, though it had the distinction of being the only club that offered dancing between shows. The owners also prided themselves on the food, which was Chinese, cooked and served by a large kitchen staff. As important, the club was able to command well-known talent. Helen Forrest, who had sung with the Artie Shaw, Benny Goodman, and Harry James bands, closed the night before Dinah and the trio opened. And the owner was willing to advertise. The day before Dinah's engagement, a half-page ad appeared in the city's main paper, the *Las Vegas Review Journal,* announcing "The Incomparable Dinah Washington—Queen of the Juke Boxes."

Opening night went smoothly, though it was a night that went into morning. Dinah and the trio were booked to play three shows every day—10:30 P.M., 1:30 A.M., and 3:30 A.M. The second night the singer Kay Starr, who was also performing in town, came by to hear Dinah and so did Sunny Gale—a coincidence because both of them had also recorded "Wheel of Fortune" and done well with their records. Dinah invited them to come up onstage, and all three sang the song together.

When they came to work Friday evening, July 2, Dinah and the trio were stunned to see a padlock on the door and a sign announcing that the Patio was closed. The owners had piled up $180,000 in unpaid bills in the club's one month of operation, and one of the creditors, who was owed $3,500 for the liquor he delivered, was not content to wait any longer to be paid. The sheriff's office served an attachment on the Patio after the liquor distributor went to court to get his money.

Not only were Dinah and the trio out of work, but Ed's drums were locked up inside and so was Slappy White's favorite onstage suit. He was traveling again with Dinah, as was Ann Littles, who was handling her wardrobe and other personal needs. Gus Chappell, Dinah's latest boyfriend, was also along, though he wasn't performing in the band every night.

They were stranded, wondering where and how they would find money to make it through the week and get to Los Angeles. Keter was distraught. He had a new wife and other family members to care for, and they were used to his sending money home every week from the road. Now he had nothing, and it wasn't even his fault. One way to get funds, albeit risky, was to gamble in the few clubs open to blacks in the Dust Bowl and hope to make a killing. Dinah gave it a try, but with poor results. "She gambled away our money," Keter said. He had better luck. One night he won $300 shooting dice, all paid in silver dollars. He stuffed them in his pocket, and walked from the Dust Bowl to the Western Union office downtown to wire the money to his wife—slightly off-kilter from all that extra weight, the coins clanking every step of the way.

With no work Keter had plenty of time to practice his archery skills, and just as he had amazed Junior with the watermelon, he amazed Ed one afternoon by shooting a catfish in a creek that ran through the country outside the city. Ed didn't have family obligations, so he was enjoying this time off more than Keter. He had saved up some money from the army, and a local woman who had taken a liking to him gave him a place to stay at her house. "I was having a good time out there," he said.

Ben Bart couldn't get Dinah any other booking in town, and

years later those still living could not recall why Dinah simply didn't have money wired to help them out. Whatever the reason, it didn't happen, but a black businessman with connections all around town—Keter remembered him as Oscar—came up with a plan. He got Dinah and the trio a job playing in the banquet room at the municipal golf club after seven days of no work. When they got paid, they finally had enough money to leave Las Vegas for Los Angeles, where Dinah was booked for five days at the Trocadero, a Sunset Boulevard club, and then for a week back at the Oasis on Western Avenue.

Although Dinah wasn't scheduled to open at the Oasis until July 16, she and the trio went in one evening ahead of time after they finished at the Trocadero. They were invited up onstage and started to perform when they were interrupted by a loud voice: "If you don't get off the stage, I'm fining everyone $300." It was a union official who happened to be in the Oasis, and he knew who was supposed to play and when. This was not Dinah's night, and that was that. Facing $1,200 out-of-pocket, she and the trio left immediately.

Both the *California Eagle* and the *Los Angeles Sentinel* carried articles about "Dee Nite," which was to honor Dinah on opening night. And both ran identical stories, probably based on press releases, bubbling enthusiastically but incorrectly that she was "one of the highest paid singing stars in the entertainment field." The claim was particularly ironic given Dinah's trouble getting from Las Vegas to Los Angeles. The *Sentinel* and *Eagle* stories were also examples of how press releases got ahead of the facts. They claimed that Dinah had played every large city in the United States and Canada "and is booked for a tour of Europe, London and Paris after filling night club, ballroom, theatre, radio and TV engagements already contracted for."

The ambitious itinerary might have been a booking agent's plan, but those dates never materialized.

Gus Chappell was slated to play the L.A. club dates, backing Dinah on trombone and the vibraharp. When the couple got to the Watkins Hotel, guests in adjacent rooms could hear them arguing, though exactly what set them off was unclear. During one fight two days into their Oasis job, Chappell was so mad that he smacked Dinah in the head with his trombone stand. Her cheek was cut, and she had a black eye, and this time sunglasses could not hide the injury.

"There was blood all over the room," said Clark Terry, who had come to Los Angeles with Duke Ellington's band and had heard what happened.

Slappy White had an ingenious idea. "Go get a white mink patch, put a mink patch on your eye," he told her. "Be different." Dinah liked the suggestion, but the club owner would have none of it. He told her she could not get onstage with a misshapen face, so ten days after the disappointment in Las Vegas, Dinah and the trio were out of work again until she healed.

"That's two jobs in a row messed up," Slappy lamented.

The band members wanted to avoid further trouble, knowing how angry Dinah was. "She was gonna finish him off," Ed recalled. "We had to get him out of town." Indeed, Chappell confided to a friend that during the altercation in the room, "I had to get between Dinah and the gun" so she wouldn't shoot him. After Chappell fled the premises Dinah called the police and told them to check the airport, and the railroad and bus stations. She wanted Chappell arrested for assault. His musician friends smuggled him out of town, hiding him in the back of the Ellington band's bus as the musicians headed for their next job.

The timing of a short feature on Dinah in *Hue*, the *Jet* look-alike, seemed perfect. The magazine called her "the bad girl of show business," and admitted she was "good copy" because of her "countless escapades." The magazine recounted her spats with Prophet Jones and Ruby Hines and repeated the rumor that she had pulled a gun on Lionel Hampton (though they put the moment in the wrong California city). Where *Ebony* had called her "bosomy," *Hue* said she was "buxom" and emphasized the point by running a waist-up picture of Dinah in a dress with its buttons straining across the chest. The magazine added in its caption that Dinah "fairly 'lives' each word of her songs."

Not the most flattering story, it was publicity nonetheless.

On August 4 Dinah went into the studio to record four songs with a new producer, Hal Mooney, Mercury's musical director who'd been hired by Bobby Shad. He had been married to Kay Starr and two years earlier produced her hit version of "Wheel of Fortune." Mooney brought in horns and a guitar player to supplement the rhythm section and wrote smooth arrangements designed for mass appeal—nothing edgy, no odd syncopations or jarring harmonies. The session opened with the ballad "Dream," with a baritone sax providing nice counterpoint to Dinah.

The next song, "I Don't Hurt Anymore," gave Dinah a chance to let loose. Country singer Hank Snow had recorded the song, and it was an instant hit on the country charts. His version was the epitome of the genre, with fiddles and guitars and a laconic pace. Snow also sang "It don't hurt anymore" rather than the more personal "I."

Dinah remade the tune, blending the pain of a torch song with the redemption of gospel. She sang with passion and purpose, and the musicians seemed to respond, particularly Ed. Dinah was just a few weeks shy of her thirtieth birthday. She had been through four husbands and at least three failed affairs, two of them with ugly endings. So it was easy to imagine how certain lyrics would resonate. Why not proclaim with satisfaction, "Yes, it's wonderful now that I don't hurt anymore"?

The version eventually released included backup singers—Keter said they were added later because only the musicians were in the studio. But even a lame chorus by the add-on group couldn't detract from Dinah's singing.

Slappy knew "I Don't Hurt Anymore" was a hit when he watched Dinah sing the tune live. "Everybody in the audience just screamed," he said. "They would not let her off the stage." One time, he added, "she had to go back and do it again. . . . Boy, she just upset the whole auditorium."

The other two songs recorded that day were "Soft Winds" and another ballad, "If It's the Last Thing I Do." A mellow trombone solo was featured, though not from erstwhile boyfriend Gus Chappell.

As soon as the session was over, Dinah and the trio left for a weeklong swing through Northern California. When she returned to Los Angeles on August 13, she had to get ready for another session the next day. Bobby Shad was in town and had rented the Capitol Studio at 5515 Melrose Avenue in Hollywood for a jam with Dinah and her friends. She wanted it to be a party with food and drink available and invited friends to sit offstage and watch.

The previous week in L.A. Shad had recorded with drummer Max Roach and his group and apparently asked the group to stay in the city for the jam. The Ellington band was gone, but trumpeter Clark Terry remained. Shad may have recruited him, too, but Terry said his participation was at Dinah's bidding. As he was coming into the Watkins Hotel on the 14th, the day of the session, he heard Dinah shouting from her window to a friend on the street. "Hey, Queen," he hollered, "what are you doing?"

"I'm recording today," she answered.

"Who's on the date?"

"You are," she shot back. So Terry said he got the details and showed up to find a stellar cast at the studio: Roach, Junior, Keter, two other trumpeters, Clifford Brown and Maynard Ferguson, Herb Geller, an alto saxophonist, Harold Land, who played tenor, and Richie Powell, who played the piano for Roach, and George Morrow, his bass player.

Because there were at least two musicians for each instrument except drums, the idea was to have them alternate on the tunes.

Ed Thigpen was matter-of-fact when he learned he would not be playing on the session. "Max was hot. Clifford was hot. She wanted to use them," he said. Not only that, now that Gus Chappell was gone, Dinah had taken up with Roach, at least for the moment, and she bestowed on him the gift she usually gave her boyfriend-husband if he was a musician: she designated Roach the session leader. (It entitled him to $82.50 for the afternoon—twice what the other sidemen were paid.)

The session was called for 4:00 P.M. on August 14 and was to last three hours. Dinah had invited most of the guests, many of them friends from the Watkins Hotel—her hairdresser, the manicurist, and so forth. She also booked the catering company—she knew the spots that made the best home-cooked food, and she had been to Los Angeles enough times that the restaurants would take good care of her. Sometimes she had them cook for her and deliver the meals to the Watkins.

"The session was the first of its kind, with an audience," Terry insisted. And it was going to be impromptu. "We hadn't had a rehearsal for nothing—not anything," Junior said. He was impressed with the setup—a spacious studio with its adjustable draped walls and plethora of microphones. And he and Richie Powell played on a grand piano. "It was very upscale. They had the best equipment, the best," Junior added.

The casualness of the session was apparent in the way the musicians dressed. The men wore short-sleeved sport shirts and pants; Dinah wore a shirtwaist dress with a full skirt. The white collar and white cuffs on the elbow-length sleeves, though, gave her a proper look, as though she were going to lunch with the ladies instead of tearing it up with her musician friends.

Dinah, Keter, and Junior knew each other's styles and musical habits; Terry had been on other sessions; and Shad had already recorded with the quintet of Roach, Morrow, Powell, Brown, and Land. So while the musicians had not all played together, common ground existed. Even if it hadn't, the craftsmanship was so high, the concept was bound to work.

Dinah was not a jazz singer the way Ella Fitzgerald was with her scat singing, and she didn't improvise around the lyrics and melody with the same panache as Sarah Vaughan, but she had much the same sensibility. She felt the rhythm and found the beat and made her hallmark diction a counterpoint to the music that pulsed behind her.

Bobby Shad introduced the proceedings. "We got a lot of people here," he said. "So let me introduce them to you. So let's open up the curtain and let me tell you who's here."

He announced Dinah first. She stood onstage in front of a music stand that had been placed near some card-table chairs, the mike hanging over her tilted at just the right angle to pick up her voice. Then Shad nodded to "a pretty fab drummer called Max Roach," and finally the rest of the group. When he got to the bass players, he noted that there were two of them, Morrow, "and when he gets tired, there's an archer here, Keter Betts."

The jam opened with Roach setting a fast Latin beat that Dinah joined a cappella on Cole Porter's "I've Got You Under My Skin." Her intonation was perfect, her timing precise. After a few bars the other musicians joined in, the three trumpeters alternating solos. Dinah came back with a flourish, slowing down a few phrases and then picking up the tempo to clip off the lines "use your mentality, wake up to reality" before the final fanfare. The guests loved it.

"Lover Come Back" raced from the start, opening with a bass solo and then the piano. Dinah, at ease, joined right in, singing about a blue sky, a blue moon, and memories. Few other singers could have been so clear at that tempo on the line "I remember every little thing we used to do." "Lit*t*le," not "liddle," she sang, determined not to sacrifice clarity for speed. After a few more bars, Dinah gave way to nearly eight minutes of solos on the trumpet, sax, bass, and drums—each accompanied by applause from the guests.

The session slowed with "Come Rain or Come Shine," with Dinah accompanied by Roach and Morrow on bass and Powell on the piano. She sang it like a blues number, but this time only hinting at those trills she had used so effectively years earlier on "Evil Gal Blues" and "Blowtop Blues." The guests burst into applause when she cranked it up a notch to sing, "Days may be cloudy or sunny, we're in or we're out of the money."

Dinah tossed in her prized Billie Holiday impression on "Crazy He Calls Me," copying Holiday's insouciant phrasing and shaky vibrato. "I'll goof if you cut it," she said, stopping after some giggles, an indication that Dinah may have intended the takeoff to remain in the studio. Dinah's version wasn't a caricature, but it wasn't an homage to Holiday either. She was just having a good time, demonstrating the command she had over her instrument.

"I know a good one," Dinah said after the applause died down. " 'No Greater Love.' I'll do that. That's real bad. Come on, Junior Mance," she said, signaling her piano player to start the next song.

Clark Terry loved every minute of the jam. "You don't forget her—her tonality. She had pitch. Her intonation was fantastic. Her diction was impeccable. There is never a question about what did she say. You knew right away," he said. He didn't mind when Dinah called him on something musical—"Clark Terry, your treble is flat," she said during one session, stopping in mid-song to correct him. "She had confidence. She wasn't overconfident. She had grace and style, but she was still one of the gang."

Junior was ecstatic. "It was the greatest record date I ever made—the camaraderie—we all knew each other, respected and loved each other. I consider the whole record date one of the highlights of my career." When he left the Bee Hive to join Dinah, one of Junior's bandmates had told him, "You'll be the best blues player in the world." A few dates into this trip west, he knew it was true. "I learned a lot about phrasing from Dinah," Junior said, "just the whole entire scope of interpreting music. . . . With Dinah I really learned how to get a tune across."

This recorded live jam wasn't the only unusual twist to the California trip. Dinah and the trio were hired to be part of a thirteen-segment television series, *Showtime at the Apollo*, hosted by Willie Bryant, now known as the "Mayor of Harlem," and organized and written by Dinah's old friend from Chicago Leonard Reed. The programs featured prominent jazz and R&B talents—Duke Ellington, Nat King Cole, Count Basie, Ruth Brown—and though Dinah's production and some of the others were recorded in Los Angeles, all were made to appear as though they had been filmed at the Apollo. Each episode began with shots of the theater, nearby clubs—Small's Paradise, Ray Robinson's—and the Theresa Hotel, their signs lit up in neon. The performers' names for each segment exploded on the screen like fireworks.

Dinah and the trio were joined by the Hucklebuckers, a group of horn players led by Paul Williams and named for his 1949 hit on Savoy, "The Hucklebuck." One of Dinah's selections was "I Don't Hurt Anymore," and this time with no vocal group to intrude. Audiences all over the country would finally be able to see—not just hear—how Dinah could inspire her fans to leap to their feet and cheer when she sang.

Dinah impishly indulged her yen for mink by wearing an off-the-shoulder fitted dress, the elbow-length sleeves trimmed with so much billowing white fur that it looked like she had on skating muffs. She sang with power and emotion but with an economy of movement. She barely moved off center stage, but she could swing standing still—with the tilt of her head, a raised eyebrow, a knowing smile, or a brief gesture—until the end, when she extended her arms wide. She smiled and threw her head back on the final note, at home onstage and having a ball.

PERHAPS IT WAS FITTING that Dinah turned thirty on the road, with no time for a big celebration. August 29, 1954, was a moment in transit, Dinah probably napping in the back seat of the car as her caravan made its way from the West Coast to the East. She had wanted to be a star, and now she was. This was what it took, and more of the same lay ahead. A busy schedule awaited her in New York, including another engagement at Birdland, now one of her favorite places and the scene of an informal, belated birthday celebration. Two of the performances with the trio, on September 3 and September 10, were broadcast live as part of the NBC program *Hear America Swingin'—Stars in Jazz*. The first half of the show was live from nearby Basin Street with Louis Armstrong, and the second part was from Birdland, hosted by Fred Collins.

"This portion of the show is starring the one and only Dinah Washington and the Keter Betts Trio behind us. Keter Betts on bass, Julian Mance at the piano, and Edmund Thigpen—that's T-H-I-G-P-E-N—on drums," Collins said as Junior played softly up-tempo behind him. (Julian was Junior's given name.) "It's time to get on with Dinah and 'Pennies from Heaven.'" Junior paused barely a second to give Dinah the perfect introduction to "Pennies." (She had done an impromptu version a week or so earlier from her table at Basin Street, when she stopped in to see her old boss, Lionel Hampton, on his opening night.)

Dinah slowed things down with "Dream," which Mercury had just released. She sang it with a reverence that made it a hymn to the imagination.

"That was just lovely," Collins said when she finished.

The pace picked up with "I Don't Hurt Anymore," and then "Such a Night." The crowd was enchanted, prompting Collins to joke, "Such enthusiasm for this time of night."

The last number was another mellow tune, "If It's the Last Thing I Do."

"Thank you, Dinah," Collins said before signing off. "Bless your heart."

Keter was thrilled that Dinah had named the trio for him. "When I looked at the marquee, I said, 'Whew. I made it on Broadway.'"

Collins was back as emcee the next week, this time introducing Dinah by her well-known moniker Queen of the Juke Boxes and making sure to introduce the Keter Betts Trio, too. Once again she sang "Pennies from Heaven" and "I Don't Hurt Anymore," which Collins plugged as Dinah's very latest release. Then she sang "Until Sunrise," which she had recorded in March, but this time with the sophisticated playing of the trio and no Hawaiian guitars. A spirited "My Lean Baby" gave Junior another chance to shine.

"We have time for one more song, Dinah," Collins said.

"Okay," she replied. "We'll do 'A Foggy Day.'" Dinah's trademark diction was on display when she sang the opening line about a stranger "in the city" and then followed up with another line about "self-pity." The t's were wonderfully clear—no "ciddy" or "piddy." Junior was a perfect complement on the piano—light, fluttery notes in the introduction that turned to heavier minor chords when she sang about walking "the dreary street alone."

"Dinah," Collins asked when she finished, "what do we do when we have a minute left?"

"We sing one chorus of my new release 'Dream,' " she answered and started to sing.

The minute up, her voice faded as Collins signed off with the music in the background.

Shortly after her birthday, Dinah mused with a reporter about her bad luck with husbands. She would probably not marry again, she said. "I just can't find anyone who is really in my corner. Companionship is the greatest thing in the world. That's what I'm looking for," she continued. "I don't expect a fellow to make as much as I do. The money's there; that shouldn't be any worry, but it's awfully hard to find someone who doesn't make a problem of finances."

That was Dinah's not-so-subtle reference to previous husbands, Walter Buchanan in particular, who expected her to take care of them. For now her companionship came largely from the trio.

Ed was having a grand time. He loved the music, enjoyed Dinah, and appreciated the lessons learned from Keter about how to drive in all kinds of terrain. "He taught me to be a road driver, how to hug the road in tight curves," he said. He marveled at the way Keter could pack the cars and how much luggage came with Dinah. "She had one big suitcase with nothing but shoes in it," he said. He didn't mind the constant travel either—right after Birdland, Dinah and the trio were at the Howard in Washington, New York again at the Apollo, Philadelphia, and then Pittsburgh. But he was not at all prepared for the brief conversation with Keter just before they all left for the Pittsburgh date, a one-nighter at the Diamond Skating Rink.

"I'm sorry, man," Keter said as he handed Ed a pink slip. "I've got to give you this." Ed knew Dinah didn't have anything against him. He just figured it was "one of those things." A bit later he learned that Jimmy had come back into Dinah's orbit and she wanted him on drums. "Her love life got me the gig. Her love life got me out of it," he recalled with a laugh.

Though Ed's last date with Dinah was in Pittsburgh, he found new work in a hurry. The informal network of musicians, especially those with good reputations, operated like an employment service. Backstage, Ed learned that saxophonist Johnny Hodges needed a drummer. He called Hodges's wife to confirm, and as soon as he packed up his drums at the ice rink, Ed was on the train to Philadelphia to start his new job.

By the time Dinah got to Flint, Michigan, in October for one of her more unusual dates—headlining the "Queen Contest and Coronation Ball" at the Flint Armory—"I Don't Hurt Anymore" had reached the *Billboard* rhythm and blues charts. (Hank Snow's version was in its fifth month at or near the top of the country charts.) This was Dinah's first appearance in eleven months on the *Billboard* tallies—since "Fat Daddy"—but lack of hits, as the magazine measured them, did not reflect her continued popularity among her fans. Two weeks later, "Dream," from that same August session in Los Angeles, also reached the *Billboard* charts. And both songs were beginning their climb on *Cash Box*'s tally of the nation's top fifteen rhythm and blues records.

At the same time, Mercury released another four-song EP compilation, styling this one *Blues in Fashion* and featuring a drawing of Dinah in a sleeveless evening gown on the cover.

A date in Chicago at the Trianon October 15 with James Moody allowed Dinah another brief visit with her sons and family. Bobby and George were always delighted to see her and sad when she left. They were well cared for on Trumbull, surrounded by aunts and an uncle not much older than they were, as well as by the Kimbrough steprelatives. But amid all that activity, it could be hard to get attention. Alice may have been in charge of the household and even called "Mama." But to George and Bobby, Dinah was always "Mother," and they missed her. "You know, if you had a bad day," Bobby said, "you wanted your mother." When they told Dinah they missed her, sometimes through tears, she hugged them and said she was sorry she had to be away. It was understood, if not explicitly promised, that as soon as she could manage the how and the where, the boys would move to New York so they could be with her more often.

The goodbyes were always difficult, reminders of what were in truth the choices Dinah made even if they felt like necessities. It wasn't just the need to make money to support her children and help the family but also that undeniable need to sing and to entertain. It was hard to leave her sons, yet impossible to imagine a life without the music. Returning to a city like Baltimore, where the audience included friends as well as fans, boosted the spirit. Rose Snow, her occasional travel assistant, and her family still lived there, and that meant a home-cooked meal and a chance to relax away from the hotel.

Dinah and the trio were booked into the Comedy Club, which was right across the street from the Royal Theater, and one of the most popular black nightspots. Whites with a taste for rhythm and blues also were welcome, and they were among Dinah's Baltimore fans. Unlike the DeLisa in Chicago and some of the famed Harlem clubs of an earlier era, which reserved the best seats for the white clientele, the smallish Comedy Club put guests wherever there were tables. Whites were scattered among the crowd.

Dinah's sets depended on her moods—of course she would do her latest hits and was conscious of the time—five, six tunes and then a break. But if the spirit moved her, she might sing a little more. On opening night at the Comedy Club—it was November 1— she sat down at the bar for a drink between sets. She was in the mood to sing, and a few notes into a song, one of the patrons grabbed a microphone, sat down beside her, and held it in place. Rose, who was Dinah's guest that night, was sitting next to her, enthralled like the other patrons, their eyes fixed on Dinah and her impromptu performance.

Another time, this one at the Regal, she strode away from the spotlight without saying a word, sat down on a step at the side of the stage, and sang a quiet blues, the audience hanging on every word: "Nobody knows the way I feel this morning./If I had my way, don't you know the graveyard is where my man would lay." The emotion was raw, a moment when Dinah let the audience know how she was feeling—a reminder, too, that the lyrics she sang with such feeling were not simply a story but the truth about her life.

MERCURY CONTINUED to have Dinah record pop material at her next session. The label picked "Teach Me Tonight" as the best bet to break out. It was a love song, lyrics by Sammy Cahn, music by

Gene DePaul. The song built wittily on the teacher-student motif: "Let's start with the ABC of it/Let's roll right down to the XYZ of it." "Teach" had already been a hit for the DeCastro Sisters, a trio from Cuba that struggled to find an audience in the United States until the women clicked with the song on the small independent Abbott label. Jo Stafford also had a good-selling version on Columbia. Dinah gave it a relaxed but earnest reading, sounding as if she really did want to learn "the mystery of it," and the arrangement provided for her was similar to Jo Stafford's.

Record producers continued to find material and then look for a singer to record it rather than vice versa, though that was changing somewhat. And the success of "Teach Me Tonight" showed that the voice that gave life to the words could be as important as—perhaps more important than—the words themselves. Gene DePaul told *Down Beat* that he and Sammy Cahn had first given the song to Decca, which recorded it with a little-known singer named Janet Brace. "It sank at launching, with barely a ripple," DePaul said.

When he played it for the DeCastro Sisters, they loved it. Their version took off and spawned the others.

"I Just Couldn't Stand It No More" and "Remember Me" were upbeat blues romps. On the first, Dinah's precise diction and the down-home feel of the song created an amusing tension. She dropped a consonant here and there—"sittin' ", "missin' "—but she couldn't get rid of her good singing manners. In one chorus, her enunciation was perfect: "My heart is aching, my heart is breaking." But then she seemed to remember that the mood was casual and reverted to slang—"he don't know how much it is a breakin'."

Mercury wasted no time getting "Teach Me Tonight" pressed, re-leased, and in the hands of the music writers, but the label was cal-culated in the way it spent its advertising dollars. When it placed a full-page ad in *Billboard* December 4, Dinah was not mentioned, though the magazine gave the record some free advertising when it designated "Teach Me Tonight" one of the week's best buys on the strength of its sales in a half-dozen big cities. But Mercury bought a half-page ad devoted to Dinah and "Teach Me" in the November 20 *Cash Box*, the magazine geared to jukebox operators and smaller in-dependent labels whose bread-and-butter was R&B. The *Cash Box* buy doubtless made advertising sense for a singer still considered Queen of the Juke Boxes.

Dinah prided herself on her eye and ear for talent, and earlier in the fall she heard a female quartet called the Honeytones and was impressed. She liked their singing but saw room for improvement in the intangibles—stage presence and, as she told them, "how to sell a song." The young women were so thrilled with Dinah's attention that they asked her to be their manager. She invited them to go along on her end-of-the year tour, a Ben Bart package that included Cootie Williams, the singer Danny Overbea, and the Checkers, a male vocal group.

The itinerary for this one, booked for mid-November through the third week in December, was unusually ambitious—a swing south then out to the Pacific Northwest and then back so that Dinah would be in Chicago for Christmas. Very little fazed Keter on the road now, but even he was taken aback in Seattle when the group had to wait a couple of extra days before heading east to Spokane because there was so much snow in the mountain passes that they were closed. Dinah picked up some extra dates when she was asked to cover for an ailing Ruth Brown, and Brown later insisted it was true that when the announcer said that the "Queen of the Blues, Miss Dinah Washington" was going to sing, one irritated patron shouted, "I don't give a damn *what* she's queen of. I paid to see Ruth Brown."

Brown enjoyed twitting Dinah in a bit of friendly competition, reminding her about how she stole the show one night at Birdland when Dinah invited her up onstage to sing one song. Dinah told the audience she was going to take "a breather" and turned the stage over to Brown, who sang her big hit, "Mama He Treats Your Daughter Mean." The audience loved it, chanting, "Mama, Mama," and, Brown said, Dinah came rushing back out and told her, "Hey, I didn't invite you up here to give a whole goddamn show!" Brown left immediately, conceding that "nobody, not even little spitfire Ruth Brown, argued with the Queen."

LIFE AT 1518 SOUTH TRUMBULL was bustling during Christmas. The informal census, not including Dinah and any boyfriend, was twelve: her mother and James Kimbrough, three siblings, two sons, and James's five children. Alice kept order with military precision—Bobby thought of her as the general, marching the children through their daily routines with special attention to Sundays, when they were in church all morning, came home to eat, and then went back to church again. "Sometimes," he said, "we didn't get home until 10:30 at night."

On weekday mornings, each of the children had an assigned task. Clarissa and Farris and maybe one of the older children got up and made breakfast, scrambling the eggs while someone else made the toast, "stacks and stacks," Alfreda Kimbrough remembered. Because she was the youngest girl, her job was to butter all that toast and set it out.

Alice did not tolerate misbehaving. One time when Clarissa had crossed her, Alice got a switch to mete out the discipline. Clarissa tried to hide, running into the bathroom and locking the door, ignoring the fact that her younger sister, Estrellita, was taking a bath. Undeterred, Alice followed, lowered her shoulder against the door, pushed it open, and delivered the punishment.

The careful routine on Trumbull was usually disrupted when Dinah came in from the road. Alfreda was wide-eyed at first to see this glamorous older stepsister sweep in with an entourage. "There were certain parts of the house—upstairs—we weren't allowed to go up in," she added. "And they always slept all day. We had to be quiet." Clarissa and stepsister Farris never told Dinah that while she was gone they would sneak into her apartment and try on her furs. "Oh, she had stuff," Farris said, remembering the luxuriant feel of a Persian lamb stole with a fox collar. She and Clarissa were only teenagers, but wrapping themselves in Dinah's clothes, they could be stars onstage, too.

Dinah's time at home was precious, and asked by sympathetic reporters about her days off the road, she always had a compelling answer. One writer enthusiastically described Dinah's appreciation for "simple pleasures," which included going to the movies as often as possible or staying home to "look at teevee and play her vast record collection. She likes to have a few friends in for a card game, while a picnic or a trip to an amusement park are all delights to her." But the list was more fantasy than fact because Dinah had almost no time to do any of these things.

But she could indulge her domestic side during the Thanksgiving and Christmas holidays. She and Alice loved to cook, so the family meal was always special—turkey with side dishes, especially greens cooked southern-style, homemade biscuits, and everyone seated around the table. Alice was at her most commanding during grace before meal and brooked no interruptions, even if she tried the family's patience. Much was to be thankful for, and it was important to be thorough in counting the blessings. Guests learned to stifle yawns, laughter, and sweaty palms holding hands through Alice's long recitation. Slappy White couldn't help himself during one of Alice's perorations when she went down her list and said, "Lord . . ."

"Is he here, too?" Slappy asked aloud before she could say the next word.

Everyone wanted to laugh. Alice's stern look meant no one dared.

Keter rescued the main dish at another of these bountiful gatherings when a crash resounded from the kitchen before Alice had finished the prayer. Keter excused himself and went to take a look. The big turkey, all cooked and ready to be carved, was resting on a platter near the edge of the kitchen table. The family dog had jumped up, grabbed it in his jaws, and pulled it to the floor. Keter yanked the turkey away but not before the dog had pulled off a huge chunk.

Like so many before, the Christmas of 1954 would be a working one. Dinah and the trio were booked at the Trianon for a holiday show. And as soon as that was finished, they were off to Louisville to play a New Year's Eve dance at the armory. Dinah brought the Honeytones with her, and the group was getting its own publicity. The *Louisville Defender* ran their picture and a story, dubbing the ladies "Dinah's Discoveries."

One of the benefits of playing Louisville beyond a decent place to stay—Brown's Guest House, which catered to musicians—was its proximity to Fort Knox. Dinah had many fans among the black soldiers, and when they knew she was coming to town, they invited her to the base for a party, working inside deals to get food catered and gathering up their Dinah Washington records to play while she was with them. Eloise Clay, the dancer from Chicago and one of Dinah's friends, happened to be in Louisville for one of these events and went with her to Fort Knox. The party was delightful but the biggest surprise was a surreptitious visit to the supply room filled with all kinds of outdoor clothing and all manner of bedding. Eloise loved to fish and always packed her rod and reel on road trips with her dancing troupe. She made a beeline for the rain slickers, hats, and boots. Dinah loaded up on sheets, pillowcases, and blankets, stuffing them into the big duffel bag the soldiers had given her.

"Girl, you know one thing," Eloise said, laughing, "if they catch us going out, we're going to be in the brig." But nobody did.

Fans gave Dinah their own holiday gift—her third song on the R&B charts since October, "Teach Me Tonight," which was going strong as 1954 came to a close. And in *Down Beat*, Ruth Cage, one of the magazine's new columnists, predicted good things to come. Dinah was "too long underrated," Cage wrote. "She has, however, so consistently delivered wonderful performances that today some measure of the acclaim due her is on the way."

12.

Much More Than a Blues Singer

1955

Billboard's December 18, 1954, issue included a short paragraph about Dinah that was the kind of mention she and Bobby Shad hoped for. EmArcy had just released her first album on the new subsidiary, *After Hours with Miss D*. It was a ten-inch LP with four songs: "Blue Skies," "Bye Bye Blues," "A Foggy Day," and "I Let a Song Go Out of My Heart." Reviewing the record in its jazz column, the magazine noted that to many people the album "will come as no surprise. These people have always known that Dinah Washington was much more than a blues singer. Here's the proof." The reviewer called the sidemen "a near-fabulous jazz combo. The tunes, performances and arrangements (?) are just wonderful."

That question mark was probably inserted to suggest that much of the music making was improvisation rather than written musical notation. And the notes on the back promised as much. A couple of the songs apparently were recorded after the regular session was over and the musicians just wanted to "have a ball."

Two weeks into the new year the jazz literati paid attention, too, though not with *Billboard's* enthusiasm. *Down Beat's* January 12 issue gave the record three stars out of a possible five. The reviewer liked Dinah's singing but not her backup. "Had there been more of the excitingly direct Miss D on this date and less of her spotty accompaniment, this could have been a much better set. Dinah deserves better support than this, but the album is worth hearing for her ringing clarion calls."

Metronome weighed in the first week in February with a B– and seemingly contradictory observations. "Fairly violent versions of four standards by Dinah and a free-swinging band," the reviewer wrote. But then he added, "Dinah now and then reminds one of her softer efforts a decade or so ago with Lionel Hampton, and she never becomes raucous."

Even though neither review was a rave, recognition in the two jazz-oriented magazines was still an important step, helping confirm the shift in Dinah's profile and encouraging Bobby Shad to keep going in the same direction. (To boost the record EmArcy also released an EP it called *5 A.M. with Dinah* that included "A Foggy Day" and "I Let a Song Go Out of My Heart.")

Shad loved working with Dinah and didn't mind the testy give-and-take if their ideas were different. Most of the time she listened to him, even when she didn't want to do a second take, and he thought she should. "How come you're such an evil bitch with everybody? How come you listen to me all the time?" Shad asked her one day, expecting some kind words about his talent.

Well, Dinah told him, she believed in psychics, and one she trusted in Chicago—she called her a "Gypsy fortune-teller"—told her that a man fitting Shad's description "is going to come into your life, and whatever he tells you, listen to him." Dinah and Shad both had a good laugh—but Dinah meant it.

Dinah may have been moving to jazz in the studio, but when she returned to the Apollo on January 24, she was wearing her familiar crowns, Queen of the Blues and Queen of the Juke Boxes. (The *Amsterdam News* used both titles on the same entertainment page.) The Honeytones were still with her, and she had gotten them signed to Mercury. Dinah had top billing in the eight-act show, singing the closing set every night as well as a few tunes with the Honeytones. To publicize the Apollo show, the four young women and their mentor happily posed for the *Amsterdam News*, Dinah sitting in the middle, smiling and hands outstretched, the four women looking down with appreciative gazes. Dinah's fashion sense was on display, a mix of the demure and the provocative. She wore a tasteful hat and single strand of pearls around her neck, but the curvy neckline of her dress took a revealing plunge. Writers had already called her buxom and bosomy. She seemed to be saying, "Okay, here I am."

Ben Bart had been Dinah's booking agent for nine years, and there was no question that he had helped make her a star and helped her make enough money to live as comfortably as any successful black American could. All that said, the whole business of bookings, contracts, fees, and advances could be mysterious. How much was the deal really for? What was a fair share for Ben Bart to take? Was Dinah getting all the information she needed and jobs equal to her stature? Suspicions ebbed and flowed, tinged by their own stereotypes. The major booking agents and theater managers were white, and most of them were Jewish. They had reputations among performers as sharp businessmen, shrewd and maybe dishonest, too.

By early 1955, when Dinah played the Apollo, her latest contract with Universal was expiring and her uneasiness with Ben Bart was at its peak, Dinah had made another visit to the fortune-teller in Chicago, Ann Littles in tow, "and the fortune-teller told her Ben was robbing her," Ann said. Dinah put stock in such things now. Hadn't a fortune-teller been right about Bobby Grayson's girlfriend and about paying attention to Bobby Shad?

Perhaps word leaked out in entertainment circles that Dinah was dissatisfied with Bart, because after one of the Apollo shows, Joe Glaser, the head of Associated Booking Corporation—ABC—came to see her. Glaser was one of the titans in theatrical circles. He knew Dinah from her years with Lionel Hampton, and he was still Louis Armstrong's manager along with handling other major talent. Keter took Glaser to Dinah's dressing room, and the two had a lengthy closed-door meeting. Glaser left without ceremony, and when Ben Bart came by a little later to see Dinah, it was clear that something was up. Keter and Ann were nearby, and they heard Dinah and Ben yelling at each other. She accused him of cheating her, each charge peppered with a favorite expletive. Ben protested that it wasn't so, insisting he had taken good care of her from the beginning. When the door opened, Ben stormed out, red-faced and teary-eyed. "His beard grew in five minutes," Ann said.

Dinah would not renew her contract. She was signing with Glaser and ABC, convinced he would make good on his promise that she would bring in $250,000 in the first year. Beyond the money, joining ABC was a step up, a sign of Dinah's status in the entertainment world. Ben Bart kept his clients busy, but Joe Glaser represented the cream of black talent, and now Dinah was among them.

Fortune-tellers or not, Shad took credit for instigating the change. Reminiscing years later, he said that when he looked at Dinah's contract with Ben Bart, he saw that Bart was taking not only his booking agent's fee but also a percentage of Dinah's record royalties, an arrangement approved by Mercury when Dinah's contract had been renewed. Shad thought that was wrong. "You're not allowed to manage an act and book an act at the same time," he said.

Shad gave Dinah a new contract that provided her with the full record royalty, cutting Bart out. He told her to sign with Joe Glaser.

Bart was furious. He called Mercury president Irv Green to complain, and Green in turn chewed out Shad for upsetting Bart. "Do you want to keep Ben Bart happy or do you want to keep Dinah Washington happy? You can't keep them both happy," Shad told Green, who reluctantly agreed.

Like Ben Bart, Joe Glaser had the rough-hewn manner of a self-made man. He could cajole with the best of them when the situation demanded, but he had little patience with small talk and foot dragging. He prided himself on his reputation for loyalty to his clients and the way he did his job. "You don't know me," he would say to a new acquaintance, "but you know two things about me: I have a terrible temper and I always keep my word."

Ann knew two things, too. "He was a Jewish man, a very stern businessman." That boded well for Dinah.

Around the same time Dinah moved to Glaser and ABC, Mercury released a new single, "That's All I Want from You," backed by "You Stay on My Mind." The record repeated the strategy of having Dinah put her stamp on songs already successfully recorded by white singers—Jaye P. Morgan's version of "That's All I Want" was number three on the *Billboard* pop charts. On February 19 Dinah's version entered the magazine's R&B tally and eventually got to number eight.

Morgan's recording was cut with the Hugo Winterhalter Orchestra and Chorus. Swooning violins and cellos and "oohs" and "ahhs"

from the choir rose up behind her—all in all much busier than anything created for Dinah. Where violins introduced the Morgan version, Dinah's began with a resonant baritone sax solo, and then the
other horns filled out the bridge between choruses. Not surprisingly,
Dinah found a place to insert that "mmm" she liked so much, and it
seemed nothing but natural, coming between two phrases: "When
dreamers dream too late . . . mmmm—a little love that slowly grows
and grows."

THOUGH PIANIST Junior Mance had clicked with Dinah and the
trio, his personal life was getting in the way of the music. "I was in a
bad marriage. My wife gave me an ultimatum—stay home or we're
going to split up." One solution would have been to let Junior's wife
travel, "but she and Dinah had a falling-out," Junior explained.
"Dinah said, 'I'm sorry but your wife can't come out anymore.' " So
Junior left. "I'm sorry it's like this," he told her.

"One day," Dinah said, "you're gonna wake up."

"And I did, too," Junior said. His marriage broke up shortly after
he returned to Chicago, and he and Dinah remained good friends,
amiably spending time together when they found themselves in the
same city on the road.

Junior's departure coincided nicely with Wynton Kelly's return
from the army. The fact that Jimmy Cobb had come back to play
drums made the music even better. Dinah honed her jazz skills at
Detroit's Crystal Lounge the week of February 5, a setting that allowed trio and singer to be at their best. To watch them together
from the audience was to witness the special communication among
musicians who knew one another so well. No words were needed.
Keter was the anchor, the one who never missed a day and broke in
new drummers and piano players as the situation required. Dinah
could count on him offstage as well as on. In performance she
couldn't see him but she knew he was behind her, in the literal and
musical sense. And Keter knew from a feint this way, a shrug that
way, how to make sure the sound fit the singer.

If she was hoarse one night, Dinah knew she could send a cue to
Wynton in mid-song. He would pick it up and signal Keter: "Now
you're wondering why I switched that key, my love, come on and
teach me tonight."

The Detroit stop was bittersweet for Keter. He was loving his work, playing the best he ever had and getting attention. In fact, Clark Terry wanted him to go around the corner, where Duke Ellington was performing, to audition for an opening in Ellington's band. He planned to do that, though he had mixed feelings about leaving Dinah. His mind, however, was more on his wife than his music. Pinky was expected to give birth to their first child at any moment, and he was half a continent away.

Early in the evening of February 8, he got a call from Washington that Pinky had delivered a boy. His name would be William.

"I ran out telling everybody," Keter said. "I felt like of all the kings of the world, I was the biggest."

Dinah was tickled. After all, she had encouraged the couple to get married. She insisted they have a party to celebrate and invited everyone to the bar at the Gotham Hotel, where they were staying.

"She got me pie-eyed drunk," Keter recalled. "She was buying rounds for everybody." He never made the audition for Ellington.

He had told Dinah about the opening, and while he knew she was genuinely happy about the birth of his son, Keter thought later that maybe the party was her way of making sure he didn't leave the trio.

Dinah Jams, recorded the previous August in Los Angeles, was released in mid-February to enthusiastic nods from the trades. *Billboard* called it "some of the finest jammin' heard on wax in a long time." *Cash Box* bubbled that Dinah was "definitely one of jazzdom's top songstresses and Queen of the Blues."

Down Beat was more discerning, giving the album three out of five stars. It was a good effort, the reviewer said, but in his view Dinah suffered by comparison to the bigger names: "She shows here (as on her other recordings) one limiting characteristic—she lacks diversity of approach and feeling for some (not all) lyrics. Her tendency is to hit each song hard on the head; with some songs it works well; with others this relentless approach by Dinah illustrates why Ella, Billie, and Sarah are greater because they know when and how to be subtle." Yet the reviewer recognized other Dinah attributes, what he called "that fine, hard Dinah clarity and impact of sound"— the same qualities that had drawn Leonard Feather to her when she was barely eighteen years old.

Along with a new album Dinah made her first appearance on

one of the national television variety shows February 15, *The Tonight Show* hosted by Steve Allen broadcast at 11:30 P.M. on NBC, a mix of conversation, entertainment, and sketches. She sang "A Foggy Day," "That's All I Want from You," and "Teach Me Tonight." It was noteworthy that none was a blues song. Ella Fitzgerald and Sarah Vaughan had been doing these shows regularly, and it was most likely Glaser who engineered the booking.

Mercury scheduled another session in New York for mid-March and a new arranger was on hand, twenty-two-year-old Quincy Jones. Like Dinah, he was a Chicago native, but the two didn't know each other from there. They had met backstage at the Apollo on one of her many appearances. Quincy had also done some arranging for Lionel Hampton and James Moody. Dinah liked what she heard, and while Quincy was working for Moody, she asked him to write arrangements with the same instrumentation she could use on the road when she had horn players. Quincy had also helped out on the risqué "Big Long Slidin' Thing" and a couple of other tunes.

Dinah liked more than the music. "Excuse me," she said when first introduced to the cherubic young man. "Is your wife married?" Dinah didn't care that the answer was yes (Quincy was married and had a child). "If she saw somebody she wanted, she was gonna getch-ya," Ann said. "She gave some to Quincy and brought him on the road."

Quincy conceded that his "tryst," as he called it, with Dinah led to the breakup of his marriage to Jeri Caldwell Jones. "I seemed to amuse Dinah because of my age. She used to call me 'grasshopper kid' because I was young and green, and we used to drink grasshoppers together," he recalled. After one all-night party, Quincy finally struggled home and fell asleep. A few hours later the phone rang. His wife answered before he could and was on the line to hear Dinah: "You know what, Mr. Green-ass Grasshopper? In case you forgot, I got your li'l ass drunk last night and we did the doogie three times."

Their intimate moments "never got in the way of the music," Quincy said. "You can't let it." Regardless of what went on between them, he loved Dinah's singing. "She had a voice that was like the pipes of life," he said. "She could take the melody in her hand, hold it like an egg, crack it open, fry it, let it sizzle, reconstruct it, put the egg back in the box and back in the refrigerator, and you would've still understood every single syllable of every single word she sang. Every single melody she sang she made hers. Once she put her soulful trademark on a song, she owned it and it was never the same."

Quincy loved to tell the story of how he was hired to arrange songs for her. Mercury told Dinah they wanted "a name" to work on her next record, probably to make her more appealing to pop radio programmers.

"Here's a name for your ass," she retorted. "Dinah Washington, and Quincy Jones is my arranger."

"She started me in the professional record business," Quincy said. "I'm very grateful for that."

Their first session together, which lasted all night, featured Dinah singing standards, among them Rodgers and Hart's "I Could Write a Book" and "This Can't Be Love," Cole Porter's "I Get a Kick Out of You," "Make the Man Love Me," and "Blue Gardenia." Dinah was surrounded by her own rhythm section—Keter, Jimmy, and Wynton—supplemented by Barry Galbraith on guitar and old friend Clark Terry on trumpet and Paul Quinichette on sax. Jimmy Cleveland played trombone, and Cecil Payne was on baritone sax.

Quincy liked to pass particular lines in his arrangements through all the instruments and liked to put the instruments together in interesting combinations—say a piano and a muted trumpet—to get the effect of another instrument. He blended the horns in unusual ways so that to him "it almost sounded like an organ at times." But Quincy's artful arrangements left plenty of room for solos and plenty of room for Dinah. A case in point was "Make the Man Love Me." When the spirit moved, Dinah liked to interact lyrics from one song into another. Midway through this one, she twice wove in a deeply felt lament from "I Got It Bad and That Ain't Good." The fit was seamless. "My poor heart is sentimental and lord"—that "lord" was Dinah's addition—"Why can't he see it this way? I got it bad and that ain't good."

The difference between a Hal Mooney arrangement and one by Quincy Jones was evident right from the start on "I Get a Kick Out of You." The interplay of instruments and the chord structure in the introduction were edgier than Mooney's easy-listening approach. Dinah gave the lyrics a wry and knowing reading, just short of world-weary until the end, when she gave it one of her Ella Fitzgerald upper-register flourishes.

Given her past, it was no surprise that Dinah gave such a solemn cast to the opening line of the last song in the session—"This can't be love because I feel so well." But after that slow and sober moment, the tune took off into an improvisational Latin beat that started with Dinah's vocal twists and went through solos by all of the horn players. Payne, on the baritone sax, did his in double time.

Making space for all these solos endeared Dinah to the musicians. "A tune might be three minutes, but she'd figure out a way to open it up where she could hear all of her favorite people on her records," said tenor saxist Buddy Collette. "Most artists wouldn't do that. They would be too self-centered or selfish or something. But she would surround herself with all-star people, and she'd sing and then she'd stand back and sort of let everybody play. . . . She had a big love for her musicians."

AFTER SEEING HER FAMILY in Chicago over Easter and playing a holiday show at the Trianon, Dinah returned to Los Angeles with the trio for an extended stay at the Tiffany Club, which was not far from the Oasis. Slappy White and Ann Littles were along, as well as Dinah's new boyfriend–road manager, David Heard, a drummer she had met in Detroit and the brother of another well-known drummer, J. C. Heard.

Their relationship started slowly, first as a business arrangement. Heard was flattered that Dinah trusted him with the money—when he went with her from Detroit to New York and then out to California, he paid the trio, and nobody had any problem with the arrangement. He and Dinah had shared a sad moment in March, when Morris Levy came to find them during Dinah's week at Birdland to tell them Charlie Parker had died. And Heard had been in the wings April 2 when Dinah joined an all-star lineup for a midnight tribute to Parker at Carnegie Hall.

Heard loved Dinah's music and the company she kept. "Slappy made me laugh all the time." But when the couple "got intimate—you know, those man-and-women things," trouble started. Dinah was "highly jealous" and she was suspicious if Heard seemed too friendly with women in a club or even women they both knew. Ella Fitzgerald was staying at the Watkins while they were in California, and she had a birthday party in her suite to celebrate. Dinah didn't go, but Heard did. "She was pissed."

Jimmy Cobb had seen that side of her; so had LaRue Manns. "If she had a young man with her, she would declare that some other woman—he was liking some other woman while being with her 'cause I saw him looking at her,' " LaRue said. "Then she would say, 'Hey, that's who you want? Well, you go over there and be with her 'cause I thought you were with me.' She wanted that man to pay strictly attention to her and not look at no one else, not talk to no one else unless she told him, 'You can talk to so-and-so. That's a friend of mine.'

"But they couldn't talk too long 'cause she come back and say, 'What you talkin' about? Me?' " It was "that inferiority complex," according to LaRue. "She was very insecure with herself."

On April 18 Dinah made her second national television appearance, going to the NBC studio in Hollywood to appear on Tennessee Ernie Ford's midday show. She sang "A Foggy Day" and the calypso-like "I Diddle," which she had recorded a month earlier with Quincy. Mercury scheduled another session on the 28th with Hal Mooney and a dozen other musicians to complement the trio—eleven men on horns and a guitar player. It was not the best session—two of the songs were uninspiring pop tunes and Dinah forgot the lyrics on the third. The most successful song was "The Cheat," a kind of elegant blues about saying one thing and doing another. It was released after the session as a single backed with "I Hear Those Bells," an overproduced number with a vocal group added and Dinah's own voice overdubbed to make the sound of pealing bells.

As usual, Dinah was staying at the Watkins Hotel and doing some of her own cooking in the suite. Her specialty was still the southern dishes she had learned to make from her mother. After Quincy and his brother Lloyd were treated to chitterlings (the small intestines of a pig, commonly called chitlins) at one meal, Lloyd would never eat them again unless Dinah was cooking.

One evening Dinah had prepared an especially ambitious dinner—chicken, ham, collard greens, sweet potatoes, black-eyed peas—"all the soul stuff," according to Jimmy. Toots Thielemans, the Belgian harmonica and guitar player, happened to be in Los Angeles. Taken under the wing of the jazz musicians, he stayed at the

Watkins—one of the few whites at the hotel. "They thought I was a nice little cat from Belgium," Thielemans remembered with a chuckle.

A couple of the musicians invited him to join Dinah, the trio, and a few other friends, perhaps ten in all, for dinner in her suite. He was wide-eyed as the steaming plates were passed around the long table. It was obvious how much he was enjoying the food and just as obvious that he had never seen some of the dishes before. In whispered tones he asked Keter, dish by dish, what he was eating. When Dinah noticed his plate was empty, she asked if he would like seconds.

"Yes, Miss Washington," he said in his French-accented English. "Can I have a little more of the green things?" Jimmy howled with laughter. He realized Thielemans didn't know a cabbage from a collard green, and from then on, whenever he saw Thielemans, he would greet him the same way: "Toots, give me some of them green things."

Thielemans laughed, too. "I was soul brother ever since," he said.

The problems that could develop when artists changed booking agencies emerged during Dinah's quick swing to Northern California after the L.A. engagement. Ben Bart's associate had booked her earlier in the year to play a community concert in Berkeley, May 8, but ABC, thinking she was free, booked a date at Slim Jenkins in Oakland. The short distance between the cities made a Solomon-like solution possible: Dinah split her time between the two places.

THE NOMENCLATURE of music was of interest to more than label owners, their producers, and music writers. What something was called—blues, ballads, pop, rhythm and blues—influenced who heard it and how it was heard. Terms carried unspoken racial cues: pop was white, ballads could be white or black, blues and rhythm and blues were black. But lines were blurring now between categories and within them. *Billboard*, which paid close attention to such matters, noted two simultaneous trends: pop musicians were recording R&B tunes, notably Patti Page using an orchestra to record "Piddly Patter Patter," which had originally been done by Nappy Brown on the independent Savoy label, and black musicians were doing well in the pop field. Nat King Cole had been the most successful, the magazine noted, but others had been drawing attention. Among them, *Billboard* said, was Dinah.

But a transition was under way within rhythm and blues itself. A new crop of musicians was emerging who loved heavy beats, electric guitars, harmonicas, and songs about fast cars and teenage romance. Drummers rarely if ever used brushes. The music was more visceral than cerebral, and the musicians who made it found homes at the smaller, scrappier independent labels—Atlantic, Chess, King, Modern, and Savoy. Compared to them, black singers like Dinah and Nat King Cole had more in common musically with singers like Patti Page and Frank Sinatra, given their taste in material and the more elaborate arrangements created for them.

Alan Freed, a white disc jockey from Cleveland, championed this newer R&B sound, styling the music "rock 'n' roll." He plugged it constantly on his shows, and by 1955 he had become so successful that WINS, a major station in New York City, hired him. The move not only gave Freed a larger audience but also enhanced his ability to put on big live shows that mixed and matched musical styles under his "rock 'n' roll" banner.

Dinah was invited into the mix when she and the trio went to Boston May 20 for a weeklong "Rock 'N' Roll Revue" at the big Loew's Theater. Freed and Dinah's friend from Birdland, Symphony Sid Torin, were co-hosts. They packed the bill with talent that represented the many facets of R&B. Dinah was joined by Buddy Johnson and his orchestra, the singer Dakota Staton, the harmonica wizard Little Walter, who was a blues staple on Chess Records, the Chicago independent, and Bo Diddley, an emerging Chess star who played his homemade guitars like percussion instruments and was the newer face of R&B.

Dinah held her own among the electric guitars and the heavy beat. *Boston Globe* reviewer Leonard Lerner apparently considered her an elder statesman, though he praised her performance, and more than many other writers, he recognized her versatility: "Dinah Washington, the girl who has been around the blues and jazz for as long as anyone can remember, sang two slow numbers in her inimitable fashion and then rocked the place with 'Such a Night.' "

Dinah had the added satisfaction of seeing both sides of her newest single reach the *Billboard* chart a few days after the Boston performance, when the revue played Providence, Rhode Island. "If It's the Last Thing I Do" was a ballad from the August 1954 L.A. session with Hal Mooney, and the fast-paced "I Diddle" was from Dinah's first session with Quincy Jones. Her tally thus far: four songs on the charts in the last five months.

Though she regularly played Birdland, Dinah was welcomed at another New York venue, Basin Street East, the second week in July. The city was in the midst of such a hot spell that the emcee took a moment during one show to commend management for keeping the place cool. "Of all of the clubs we've visited in the last weekend, the highest rating for air-conditioning goes to Basin Street," he said, "including the Starlight room at the Waldorf."

"You can say that again," Dinah said with a laugh.

In a nod to Keter's continuing importance to her, the trio was still named for him. And her pleasure at having Wynton back was apparent when she introduced the band members between numbers— "We have Keter Betts on bass fiddle, we have Jimmy Cobb on drums, and Mr. Piano himself, Wynton Kelly."

Dinah had almost ten years of material to draw on for her club dates, and invariably she mixed new material with songs she had recorded years earlier. "New York, Chicago and Los Angeles" was recorded in 1949 but Dinah gave it a fresh and peppy read, helped by a witty introduction from Wynton that mimicked the unmistakable opening bars of "Take the A Train," the Ellington–Billy Strayhorn hit. When Dinah sang "Mixed Emotions," she made sure to tell the audience the song was available on Mercury. As she had done in so many performances, she started singing in the very next breath, no pause between the last word spoken and the first word of the song. While an audience might have expected a momentary transition, if for no other reason than to signal the trio, Dinah showed her absolute comfort onstage and with the band. Four individuals, musically they were one.

"I think we've got time for one more number now, Dinah," the announcer said near the end of the set. "What have you got in the way of an up-tempo?"

"In an up-tempo?" she asked.

"Anything you want to do. I don't care."

"All right," Dinah said, ready to announce the tune when someone hollered a request from the audience.

"That's not up-tempo," she retorted, and then launched into "I Diddle."

As the applause died down, the emcee's sign-off captured Dinah in two of her worlds: "Dinah Washington, Queen of the Juke Box . . . we're at Basin Street, home of fine jazz." Dinah's companions on the bill confirmed that claim: trumpeter Chet Baker's quartet and another quartet fronted by vibraharpist Terry Gibbs.

A few days later, on July 16, Dinah was even more firmly in the jazz world when she went to Newport, Rhode Island, to play with Max Roach at the Newport Jazz Festival. This was the second year that businessman and jazz enthusiast George Wein had gathered the premier jazz musicians to perform outdoors over two days. When Dinah's turn came, announcer John McLellan gave a brief recap of her career: "raised in the tradition of church music," first recorded by Leonard Feather, now with Mercury's EmArcy. Then he introduced her—"Queen of the Blues—Dinah Washington."

She walked out onstage to loud applause accompanied by Richie Powell, Roach's piano player, and a fast-paced "Dinah Is There Anyone Finer?" She opened with "Pennies from Heaven." Her next song, she told the audience, was "the first song I cut with strings. I hope you like it, and I hope you remember." And then she sang "I Won't Cry Anymore." She went right into "Teach Me Tonight." After the applause died down, Dinah introduced her fourth number and gave a gentle plug to EmArcy. "Not too long ago, I made an album, *After Hours with Miss D,"* she said, "and from that album, I hope you like . . ." In the next breath she began "A Foggy Day," her fingers snapping to the beat. When she sang "Such a Night," Roach played his snare with a military precision that gave the tune a lift.

This was supposed to be Dinah's last number, and she walked offstage amid cheers and another few bars of Richie Powell playing "Dinah." Introduced as "Queen of the Blues," she hadn't sung one blues tune. When the audience shouted for more, Dinah came back and sang a lusty "Birth of the Blues," not a traditional blues but certainly a nod to the subject. She was slightly hoarse by the end, but it seemed the perfect touch.

"Dinah, take a bow," McLellan said, the cheering unabated. "Dinah Washington, take a bow."

When the audience quieted down, one fan shouted, "TV," apparently wanting to hear "TV Is the Thing (This Year)."

"No TV. We're on the radio," Dinah admonished. She ended her set with the ballad "If It's the Last Thing I Do."

To *Billboard*'s Gary Kramer, Dinah had scored a "personal hit." *Variety* said she "sent the congregation like no other vocalist except possibly Jimmy Rushing on Sunday night." Writing in *Down Beat*, Jack Tracy called her set the high point of the evening on the 16th. "She took two encores and could have stayed on all night had there been time." Even *Metronome* gave her a nod, though not without a little jab: "Dinah Washington broke up the audience: in fine voice and really wailing, despite the affectations."

All in all it was a triumph. People could tie her to blues or the jukeboxes. Critics could carp about her style. It didn't matter. Dinah was singing what she wanted, the way she wanted to sing it. Best of all she was finding her audience.

The one-night live jam with Roach's group was just one example of the camaraderie that existed among musicians. When Dinah was playing at Week's, a popular club in Atlantic City, Sarah Vaughan came in toward the end of the show. Dinah invited her onstage, and the two sang together, loving every minute. When they finished, a man in the audience offered to open up a small club he owned on the outskirts of town so the women and the musicians could continue. Dinah and the trio and Sarah and her driver got in their cars and started all over again in this little out-of-the way place. First Keter, Jimmy, and Wynton played and Dinah sang. Then they played for Sarah. "Wynton played for Dinah, and Sarah sang a couple," Keter said. "Then Sarah sat down and played for Dinah. And Dinah sat down and she played." Musicians, especially singers, could be competitive, but not on this night, even though Dinah had told Bobby Shad she didn't want Sarah to have the same arrangers at EmArcy that she did. "This was no cuttin' contest," Keter added, referring to the friendly rivalries among musicians that were legend in Harlem. "I wish I had had a tape."

The same sort of impromptu performance happened with Big Maybelle—Maybelle Louise Smith—when Dinah had played a Sunday afternoon show in Columbus, Ohio. She didn't even know Maybelle was in town until she spotted her in the audience inside the steaming tent. Dinah told her to come onstage, handed her the microphone, and took a seat near the bandstand.

Though Maybelle had never sung with the trio before, it was

easy enough to play some blues, so the band wasn't worried and looked forward to the fun.

Maybelle kicked off her shoes, as was her custom, grabbed hold of the mike, raised her left hand for the downbeat, and started singing. The crowd shouted with delight.

"Sing another one, bitch," Dinah hollered when Maybelle had finished.

Maybelle obliged, tearing into "Candy," one of her favorites. The floorboards were vibrating so much Keter could barely hold on to his bass. Sweating and smiling at the same time, he hung on for dear life.

The audience hollered for more, but Dinah had seen enough. Like that moment with Ruth Brown, she apparently felt threatened. She jumped up from her seat, rushed to the stage, and grabbed the mike. "Let's take a break," she told the audience.

But Dinah herself could niggle another performer, sometimes surreptitiously. When she ran into Billie Holiday at Jimbo's, an after-hours club in San Francisco, they decided to sing for each other. Dinah had the trio with her; Holiday was traveling with only her piano player, Carl Drinkard. Keter and Jimmy played a few numbers with Holiday, but Wynton was left out. When they took a break, Dinah chatted with Drinkard at the bar, buying him one drink after another, knowing that he would get too high to play the way Holiday liked. Indeed, when he went back to the piano, Holiday could tell something was wrong and told him to leave. She invited Wynton up, and Dinah, a knowing smile on her face, watched her trio play with Holiday.

DINAH'S THIRD EMARCY ALBUM, *For Those in Love*, was released in June. The unsigned liner notes, perhaps written by Bobby Shad or Leonard Feather, made clear that the label was trying to position Dinah in the jazz world just as she was securing a foothold with this audience in her live dates. "Simultaneous with the continuance of her work in the pop and blues fields, Dinah is now engaged in the fourth phase of her career, represented by the singing of memorable standard tunes which she selects herself, accompanied by an all-star line up of great jazz musicians." Quincy was quoted in praise of Dinah's skills. "And, of course, the fact Dinah is a musician herself made things that much easier. We had just asked her for keys on these tunes, and when we ran down the arrangements, she read the music almost at sight."

For Those in Love was a full twelve-inch LP from that first session with Quincy in March. The cover featured an evocative picture of Dinah in profile, looking to the right, set against a blue-gray background. Though she was smiling, it was a pensive smile that seemed to capture both the complexities of her own life and the subject of the album.

Billboard and *Cash Box* offered their usual praise. More important, *Down Beat* gave the record its highest rating yet, four stars. The reviewer complimented the "tasty" arrangements and the soloists, calling the whole album a "thoughtful framework" for Dinah. But he couldn't seem to make up his mind about her. Some things he liked—"She sang with her characteristic strength and sharp-edged warmth," he wrote, an apt description of the tartness that kept even the sad songs from being mawkish. Still he found her wanting. "Dinah doesn't have the phrasing flexibility, command of sound shadings or overall inventiveness of conception of Fitzgerald or Holiday, but," he admitted, "she's always vigorous kicks to hear."

While *Metronome* said the record was "much better than Dinah's recent things," its reviewer, too, expressed mixed feelings about her: "The only qualification is that you have to dig Miss W. and her particular groove, which tends to make everything the same texture regardless of musical or lyrical intent."

Reviews by nature are subjective, often revealing as much about the listener as the music under discussion. Both *Down Beat* and *Metronome*, like some earlier reviews in *Variety,* suggested that some critics still had trouble appreciating Dinah's distinctive style, even if they were correct in the way they compared her to Ella Fitzgerald and Billie Holiday. But Dinah was a blend of her past: gospel, blues, big band. Perhaps because she defied categories—she wasn't "pure" anything—and because of that tart, direct delivery, some found her an acquired taste.

It was almost as if parallel worlds existed—the white critics in one place and the public, black and white, in another, and among them jazz aficionados. Her success at Birdland and Basin Street, her triumph at Newport, were proof that they not only took Dinah as she came. They loved her.

. . .

IT WASN'T ALWAYS POSSIBLE for Dinah to celebrate her sons' birthdays in person. But this year, because she was back at the Crystal Lounge in Detroit the first week in August, George (July 30) and Bobby (August 2) could make the short trip to spend time with her. She took them on a picnic at Belle Isle, one of Detroit's popular parks. David Heard came along, though their relationship was winding down—no fireworks, just a recognition that things had ground to a halt. Other friends and their children came along, too.

George and Bobby cherished these celebrations and so did Dinah. When they were with her during another birthday, this one celebrated in Washington, Georgia Mae Scott, who had brought LaRue Manns and Dinah together, organized the party. Georgia's sister Marva, younger than Dinah but older than her sons, remembered that the party was held at the home of a minister. The family had a piano in the parlor, and when Dinah came in with the boys, she sat down and played them "Happy Birthday." Barely pausing, she sang them a gospel tune, "Let Us Cheer the Weary Traveler Along His Heavenly Way."

Though Marva was just a teenager, she knew who Dinah was and knew about her music. It impressed her that the song Dinah chose to sing was "where her roots are, the church." Dinah's own birthday—her thirty-first on August 29, 1955—was just a couple of weeks away, and midway through her stay at the Crystal Lounge, the management threw her a party, albeit a little ahead of schedule. The event was announced in the *Michigan Chronicle*, which almost always gave Dinah free publicity when she was in town courtesy of Ziggy Johnson's *Michigan Chronicle* column, "Zagging with Ziggy." "Received a call last Thursday morning," he wrote Saturday, August 6, "and the voice on the other end said, 'Hello, this is the Queen,' and it certainly was. That is the way Dinah Washington lets me know she has hit town."

A few weeks earlier Johnson informed readers that Dinah had not forgotten that Gus Chappell had banged her up with his trombone stand. Now she was suing him. "Gee the kid can take it, but not as much as her many husbands," he wrote. "But that's our girl, eh?"

One of the other benefits of playing Detroit was the chance to spend days off, generally Mondays, at Idlewild, a resort for blacks on

the edge of the Manistee National Forest 180 miles northwest of Detroit. One of Dinah's favorite restaurants there was the Fiesta, run
by Arthur Braggs, and he enjoyed recounting how he took orders
from Dinah when she wanted to dine.

"Hey, Arthur, get me reservations for ten—we'll be coming with
my kids, my trio, and my new love."

"Okay, anything the Queen wants she can have."

"I went to Idlewild with her, and we had a ball," Dinah's friend
Bea Buck recalled. They were walking around, taking in the sights,
and getting hungrier by the minute. "People were barbecuing everywhere. And here comes Dinah walking down the street. 'Ooh, that
food smells so good,' " she told Bea.

"Yes, it does," Bea agreed. "Makes you hungry."

"We got to get something to eat," Dinah said.

Bea had noticed a woman making ribs at her stand, "and they
looked so pretty. Dinah walked up to the lady—and gave her the
nicest smile."

"How are you," Dinah said.

"I'm fine."

"My name is Dinah Washington. I'm Queen of the Blues. Would
you mind giving us some ribs?"

"And she did," Bea said.

THE ARTICLES IN *Ebony, Jet, Our World,* and the countless newspaper pieces confirmed that Dinah was one of black America's
celebrities. She and all the other prominent black entertainers—
Ellington, Armstrong, Fitzgerald, Holiday, Vaughan, Eckstine among
them—constantly came up against racial boundary lines that black
citizens who led more traditional lives could avoid. Segregation had
created independent, contained communities, however much they
might suffer by comparison to the comforts and amenities in white
areas. And in these neighborhoods blacks could keep their distance
from whites and the indignities that went along with their second-
class status, though if they ventured out, they, too, felt the sting of
racism. One young woman had sued Greyhound in February after a
white policeman, gun drawn, forced her stand in the back of a Greyhound bus from Clarksdale, Mississippi, to New Orleans, at least a
seven-hour trip.

Entertainers, whether consciously or not, lived the business part of their lives negotiating the spotlight, facing the contradiction of being idolized and demeaned at the same moment. They were welcomed onstage and applauded for their talent, but unwelcome after the lights went up and the show was over. A five-day trip to New Orleans August 19–24 was another reminder. Dinah and the trio would perform two shows a night for three evenings at Lincoln Beach, the amusement park for the city's black citizens. It had opened amid much fanfare in May, promising patrons "luxurious white sands" that extended to the famed Lake Pontchartrain, a promenade lined with flowers and shrubs, and a "California styled bath house" with two thousand lockers. With its resonant name, Lincoln Beach was the city's recreational "separate but equal," intended to give black families a chance to frolic at the lake the way white families did at Pontchartrain Beach.

Dinah and the trio arrived just as special festivities for "Dixie Day" had concluded at the white park. "Dixie" was a popular adjective that gave businesses or holidays a certain local feel—Dixie Motors, Dixie Hardware, and the like. It was also a synonym for the Confederate South and evoked among whites memories of a heroic struggle for the homeland. For blacks "Dixie" meant slavery and then the Jim Crow laws that kept them in their place.

Such unpleasant notions could be kept at bay onstage, when the music was good and the audience responsive. Lincoln Beach management did its best to take care of Dinah, meeting her and Keter at the airport with an air-conditioned Cadillac. It was one of the few times she stayed behind with Keter while Jimmy and Wynton drove to the job.

Dinah and the band were amazed to have two white visitors after one of their performances. "We were in the black section," Jimmy said, "and Rosemary Clooney—she was married to José Ferrer—they came through all of this, you know all of these neighborhoods and stuff to see Dinah."

The day after the Lincoln Beach job was finished, Dinah and the trio started a three-day engagement at a new club, Curley's Neutral Corner, near the French Quarter and just two blocks from Rampart Street, which had been the center of New Orleans jazz. Alphonse Gagliano had opened the Neutral Corner the first week in July with an associate, Blaise Dantoni. Gagliano also operated Curley's Gym in the same building and hosted boxing matches upstairs. Dinah was the first black act that management had brought to the new enterprise, but they apparently were interested in drawing black clientele, because in the club's first week of operation, Gagliano had taken out an ad for Curley's in the *Louisiana Weekly*, the paper for black New Orleans.

Dantoni couldn't have been nicer to Dinah and the trio. As soon as they got to the club, he told them they had the run of the place. He didn't care a bit about the law that said blacks could be hired to perform but could not mingle with white customers or use the same facilities they did. "I'm going to set up a long table here," Dantoni said, motioning to the main room. "Come and sit at that table. If you want to go into the bathroom, it's no problem, 'cause it's my damn club, and I own it and I do what the hell I want to do." He told them they could order anything they wanted to eat, and he made sure their table was stocked with whatever kind of liquor they wanted to drink.

"The next night," Jimmy recalled, "a detective came in and said, 'They can't stay in the club. They can't stay inside the club when they're not on the bandstand.' So now this is the stuff that we're going through all our lives, you know, so we expect that. But Dantoni said, 'That's bullshit. This is my club, and if I say they're going to stay, they're going to stay in it.' "

Dinah and the band didn't budge.

Though the name Curley's Neutral Corner was a play on boxing terminology, Dantoni's actions resonated across the racial divide as well.

"It was beautiful," Keter said.

Two weeks after finishing their job in New Orleans, Dinah and the trio were back in Las Vegas, memories of the previous disastrous trip still fresh. This one, though, promised to be different. Dinah was booked into a new hotel built on the west side that catered to black patrons. Joe Louis was one of the partners. It was called the Moulin Rouge, and evoked notions of Paris nightlife with the curvy lettering of its sign and neon Eiffel Tower. One of the murals on the wall showed long-limbed cancan dancers but with black faces. The decor and architecture of the low-slung building, however, were modern— a glass-enclosed dining room, pink pastel paint on the walls, thick carpeting in the hallways, and soft, plush lounging chairs.

While it might to be flip to suggest that "separate but equal" had come to Las Vegas gambling, that notion was not far off the mark. Black entertainers, black residents, and black tourists continued to chafe at the discrimination and second-class treatment they received in the city. The Moulin Rouge gave them something of their own, and it was first-class, too. The price tag for building it, *Sepia* reported, was $3 million. That covered two hundred well-appointed rooms, a state-of-the-art casino, bars, lounges, cafés, a showroom, a pool, access to a dude ranch, a golf course, and private boat rides on nearby Lake Mead.

When the first notices for jobs at the casino were posted, black residents swarmed into the employment office. Topflight producers were hired to supervise the hiring of dancers and singers who would put on floor shows every bit as dazzling as the creations found on the other side of town on the famous Las Vegas Strip.

The *Defender* reported in March that the producers were scouring the country looking for "good looking, fast stepping dancers." Already, the paper said, Clarence Robinson, well-known in black entertainment circles for his productions, had "come up with some of the best dancers and most shapely to be found from New York to California."

When the hotel officially opened May 24, the major black newspapers sent their correspondents out to cover the event. The bubbling enthusiasm of the *Defender*'s Al Monroe was tempered by an undercurrent of sobering reality. "Bias, long an important part of things here," he wrote June 4, "was completely erased when the Moulin Rouge opened. Something had arrived to revolutionize the whites' way of thinking and acting at the sight of black faces. For the first time in the long history of this town of dollars, dice and cards, dominoes were rolling as profitably for Negroes as for whites. And there was no bias as in who picked up the winnings or frowned at their losses. Everyone was the same. . . .

"Actually there is nothing in Las Vegas for Sepians after the Moulin Rouge," Monroe went on. "The rest is a story of sand, rocks, heat and the lingering sameness in discrimination that maintains along the old Strip." But the Moulin Rouge was big enough that black patrons would have plenty to entertain themselves.

Amsterdam News columnist Alvin "Chick" Webb reported that the casino took in $20,000 in gambling receipts the night before its official opening (roughly $132,000 in today's dollars). He noted that besides Joe Louis, the lineup of all-black management included Sonny Boswell, an ex–Harlem Globetrotter, who was the general manager, and Benny Carter, the saxophone and trumpet player, who was the music director.

Down Beat covered the Moulin's opening, its correspondent inadvertently exposing the racial divide that existed even among whites who paid close attention to black music. "One facet of Las Vegas has received little publicity—it is almost 100 percent Jim Crow," he wrote. To blacks that was a given, well discussed in long articles in such magazines as *Sepia* and *Ebony*. "When our party was whisked from the airport to the Moulin Rouge," he continued, "I discovered that fancy as it is, its owner had to build it on 'the other side of town' in what some cities still call the 'colored district.' "

In addition to the big floor shows with bejeweled dancers and a bevy of singers, the Moulin Rouge also had smaller rooms for the kind of music Dinah made. Ahmad Jamal, a young, exciting jazz pianist, and his trio played the opening week, as did jazz organist Wild Bill Davis. Lionel Hampton was booked for August, just before Dinah, and played in the Café Rouge.

Dinah's entourage was larger than usual for this trip. Keter wanted his wife, Pinky, and their six-month-old son to be with him. He and Jimmy and Wynton rented a three-bedroom house in the Dust Bowl, as Keter still called it. Slappy White was along because he was part of the act. And Ann Littles and LaRue Manns had come, too. Dinah had also picked up a new man, Joe Davis, a policeman she had met in Miami who was so smitten that he left his wife and children and came out to be with her. It hadn't bothered Dinah that Quincy Jones was married, and absorbed in the moment by what felt good to her, she was apparently unconcerned that Davis was married and had children, too. Dinah's celebrity brought her attention, power, and control. She played the part of Queen with gusto, even if she attracted hangers-on who hoped to gain by their mere association with her.

In private Keter told Davis not to come, told him to think about his own family, warned him that this was a fling for Dinah that would never last. But it did no good.

Dinah and the trio were greeted at Café Rouge opening night

with a packed house filled with celebrities, among them the white bandleader Spike Jones, the mayor and police commissioner of Las Vegas, Billy Eckstine, and Billy Daniels. Jones's attendance was part of a trend that had started as soon as the Moulin Rouge opened. White entertainers, if not overt allies of their black counterparts, let their feelings be known about the city's racial divide by taking every opportunity to fraternize on the other side of town. Within its first month of operation, the hotel had become a favorite after-hours hangout for the performers on the Strip. Jam sessions could erupt and go on all night.

It was apparent that the Moulin Rouge was trying to attract white gamblers, too. They advertised not only in the *Los Angeles Sentinel* and the *California Eagle*, aiming at the large black population in the L.A. area, but also in the *Las Vegas Review Journal.* In one publicity shot, Dinah posed with emcee Bob Bailey and his wife and a few of the dancers. Dinah stood next to Bailey, who towered over her; she was dressed demurely in a black dress with matching sweater, white pearls around her neck. Jimmy was there, too, kneeling down in front of her.

He and Keter and Wynton were enjoying themselves in their time off, even going horseback riding one day. Davis came with them, and when he tried to show off, his horse threw him. "It scarred up the whole right side of his face and arm and everything. We took him to the hospital and got him bandaged up," Keter said. What made matters worse was that Dinah had lost interest in Davis, and Keter was left to clean up the mess with an angry and now former boyfriend.

"He talked about killin' Dinah. So I went by the room, Big Ann went by the room," Keter recalled, referring to Ann Littles. "I'm the peacemaker. I started talking to him, and he's crying." Davis realized that he had left his wife and children and now, it appeared, for nothing. "I said go ahead and kill her—go ahead, but the only problem you got, if you kill her, your whole life is gone—you got kids, I got my wife out here," Keter went on, reminding him of how many people depended on Dinah.

By the most extraordinary coincidence some friends of Davis's from Miami happened to be in San Diego and had heard a broadcast of Dinah from the Moulin Rouge. They knew he was with her, so they made a long detour in their car on the way back to Miami and came to Las Vegas. They found Davis in a terrible state, calmed him down, packed him up, and took him back to Florida.

Dinah was as cavalier about the consequences of leaving Davis as she had been when she allowed—perhaps encouraged—him to leave Miami with her. Her callous behavior certainly showed a self-ishness, but it was also probably an act of self-protection, however unconscious. When it came to men, Dinah was determined to do the leaving, never wanting to risk being left.

FINISHED AT THE Moulin Rouge at the end of September, Dinah and the trio went back in the studio, most likely in Los Angeles. Four more ballads were recorded, this time with a complement of strings. The best part of the session was a moment between songs when Dinah told a joke. It was about a performer who desperately needed a job and went to a booking agent to get work with his talk-ing dog. A few words into the story a man—probably producer Bobby Shad—interrupted. "Excuse me, you pay the overtime," he joked, reminding her that the clock was running.

"You got to give me some kind of gig here," Dinah continued, playing the part of the needy performer. "I don't know what's hap-pening. I got to have me some kind of money. See my dog here, ask him anything.

"So the booking agent said, 'How was your trip coming from Eu-rope?' The dog says 'Ruff.' " Dinah stopped to laugh.

" 'How was things in Europe?' The dog said 'Ruff.'

" 'Hey, what was the headlines in the newspaper this morning ?'

"The dog didn't say nothin'," Dinah went on.

"I said, 'What was the headlines in the newspaper this morning?'

"The dog didn't say nothin'.

"The booking agent was annoyed. 'You must think I'm crazy— you get this dog outta here. Are you kidding?'

"This cat got the dog back home," Dinah continued, "and started whipping him." Dinah clapped her hand on the table for emphasis. " 'How come you didn't tell that booking agent what the headlines was in the newspaper this morning?'

"And the dog got on his knees and looked at him and said, 'You know damn well I can't read.' "

The room broke up in laughter. "All righty, we'll pay the overtime," Shad joked.

"Pretty good, huh?" Dinah chuckled.

She and the trio opened at the Mocambo on Sunset Boulevard the first week in October. It was the most upscale venue she had played in Los Angeles and quite a contrast to the smaller Tiffany, which could seat only eighty-six people. The Mocambo meant more money and prestige and felt like another dividend from signing with Joe Glaser. *Variety* sent a reviewer to Dinah's show, and he observed smartly that she had moved from "smoky den to the satin drape circuit." He wondered in print how good the fit would be and answered his own question: "With only slight changes in routine, she's a ready candidate for the swankier boites." Indeed, Dinah, dressed in her favorite halter-top gown, received a thunderous reception. Her music and her highly personal way with songs, particularly the standards the audience might know, provided a change of pace for patrons. She gave them her custom versions of "All of Me," "Love for Sale," and brought down the house with "TV Is the Thing (This Year)."

Stars had come out for the occasion—Zsa Zsa Gabor, the actor James Mason and his wife, Pamela, Billy Daniels, who had just seen Dinah at the Moulin Rouge, and tough-guy actor Broderick Crawford. The trio tried to take all of the hoopla in stride, but at times it was hard to concentrate. "Hello, dahling," could be heard as Dinah was singing, Gabor more interested in greeting friends than the show.

"Loud? Jeez, it was worse than loud," Keter said, further distracted by the heavy-drinking Crawford making noise at the back of the house.

It must have been a disconcerting moment—finally playing a fancy Los Angeles club only to have the stars drunk and rude.

Jet covered Dinah's Mocambo appearance and tried to suggest her career trajectory in the few words of its headline: "Hollywood Gets the Blues; Dinah Lands on Sunset Strip." "Hefty blues chirper, Dinah Washington . . ." the article began—just the kind of description that made Dinah cringe, this one on two counts. *Jet* gave a rundown of Dinah's numbers, and among them, only "Fat Daddy" could be called blues. Taking the long view of such things was the best strategy: it was good to be noticed, even if the notice wasn't perfect, and the article, which included four pictures, did end with praise: "Dinah in white tulle served up the blues and Hollywood loved it."

Dinah and the trio returned to the Blackhawk in San Francisco in mid-October for a two-week stay. Opening night she drew one of the biggest audiences of the year, according to *San Francisco Chronicle* entertainment columnist Hal (the Owl) Schaefer. *Jet* called Dinah "hefty," but Schaefer saw something else: "She's slimmed down since her last appearance here and she has never looked—or sung— better in her life." Though it was churlish to complain about such a nice notice, Schaefer made one glaring error. He said Dinah had sold "a lot of *Decca* records," forgetting for the moment that she recorded for Mercury.

Blackhawk co-owner Helen Noga had taken a liking to a hand- some young singer who was a student at San Francisco State College and making local headlines not for his pleasing voice but his athletic feats as a high jumper. His name was Johnny Mathis. Noga often asked the stars who were performing to listen to him. "We let him sit in—he brought his family in—and we played for him," Keter said. Dinah even asked Slappy, whom she had brought along, to make a formal introduction. "And I'd say, 'Ladies and gentlemen, Johnny Mathis.' I didn't know who Johnny Mathis was," Slappy recalled. "Nobody knew Johnny Mathis."

From a jazz club in San Francisco Dinah and the trio had to change hats on their return to Los Angeles, this time for a week on a new rock 'n' roll show at the downtown Paramount Theater and tai- lored for the city's market. The host was popular disc jockey Hunter Hancock, one of several white deejays in the country who had long programmed black music. Dinah shared the bill during the four daily shows with saxophonist Big Jay McNeely and his orchestra, and the singing group the Penguins, who had had a hit with "Earth Angel."

She was getting even more exposure in the genre courtesy of Studio Films, which had repackaged its television productions, *Showtime at the Apollo,* into a feature-length film that the company called *Rock 'n' Roll Revue.* So at the same time that Dinah wore her blues and jukebox crowns and was burnishing her jazz credentials, she was labeled a rock 'n' roll star in movie theaters nationwide. The movie title was an obvious effort to latch on to this newest thing in music, even if Dinah, Nat King Cole, Lionel Hampton, and Duke Ellington, who were also in the film, hardly thought of themselves as rock 'n' rollers. That was beside the point. What mattered was the movie producers' belief that they could market these performers as rock 'n' roll, synonymous with black music, regardless of style.

And now another of Dinah's songs—the fourth since February— went on the charts. It was the Cole Porter tune "I Concentrate on You." Dinah had recorded the song in January with Hal Mooney, and it bore the smooth Mooney sound. But her trademarks were evident—emphasizing a particular lyric, nonchalantly working in "mmm" before the signature phrase, "I concentrate on you."

When Dinah went back in the studio for three days after the Paramount show, she and the trio were backed up by strings, a guitar player, and a dozen horn players. They cut a mix of standards and ballads, among them "Smoke Gets in Your Eyes," "The Show Must Go On," "What Is This Thing Called Love," and "Birth of the Blues," Dinah's encore at Newport. In the meantime, Mercury had released a single from the September session, "I'm Lost Without You Tonight" backed with "You Might Have Told Me," and both sides were on the charts when Dinah and the trio returned to Las Vegas at the end of November.

The Moulin Rouge, which had opened with such promise and fanfare, closed after barely four months, falling victim to a shortage of cash, poor management, and the inability to find solutions to these problems. *Jet* summarized the problems in a comprehensive account. "The real reasons the world's largest and plushest interracial hotel flopped are economically simple and sociologically uncomplicated," wrote correspondent Vincent Tubbs. "Costing over $4 million to build, furnish and open, the original owners and stockholders somehow made the error of capitalizing the project for only $1 million. They left themselves with a $3 million 'nut' of short term loans, apparently expecting to rake it in over the gambling tables." The big debt helped explain why that promising first night of $20,000 taken at the tables, even if matched most nights, was not enough. When notes came due, there was not enough money and not enough "friends" to cover the payments.

Tubbs believed that race was not a factor. "Significantly, despite the fact that Las Vegas is a notoriously Jim Crow town and the Moulin Rouge was an interracial oasis in Nevada, race matters had nothing to do with its failure. Not a single racial incident had ever occurred," though one could wonder if that was the truest test in the complex dynamic of black and white.

Joe Glaser had booked Dinah into one of the premier hotels on the Strip, the Sahara, which had opened five years earlier with Ray Bolger, the scarecrow in the famed *Wizard of Oz*, as the headliner. Owner Milton Prell wanted to capture the flavor of Africa and named the various rooms in the hotel to evoke that theme—the Congo Room, the Casbar Lounge, and the Caravan Room, which was the main restaurant where Caesar salad was mixed tableside and every dish was cooked to order. Life-size models of African warriors, their spears held high, stood outside the Congo Room, and outside the hotel was a nomadic caravan scene that included a large Saharan camel.

Dinah and the trio were booked to play twelve days in the Casbar Lounge. But neither she nor the trio nor Ann and LaRue could stay at the hotel. "They had a trailer outside the kitchen," LaRue said, "equipped with a bedroom, living room, all the trimmings, everything we wanted to eat or drink. That's where we had to stay. We could not even go into the casino to play, you know, where she was working. Now if I went in with one of the white musicians, it would have been all right, but I could not go in there on my own with another black guy."

To get to the Casbar stage to perform, Dinah had to come out of the trailer, and go up a path and through the kitchen. She was not permitted to come in the casino's main entrance. Nobody liked the situation, but no one had the power to change it, and the obvious question was never asked: if Dinah was good enough to work and perform for a Las Vegas audience, why couldn't she go into the casino through the front door?

The singer Kaye Ballard was also playing at the hotel, and LaRue remembered that she was upset about the hotel's policy. "Between shows she would come out and stay in the trailer with us. And we'd eat, play cards, and have cocktails, whatever," LaRue said.

Dinah vented her feelings to Bob Bailey, who had been the emcee at the Moulin Rouge and hosted a local radio show that featured backstage interviews. "Dinah used so much bad language talking about the conditions that existed, staying in a trailer—even to change clothes or dress," Bailey recalled, laughing, that he could barely find enough tape to air on his show.

Dinah promised herself she would never play the Sahara again.

IT WOULD BE GOOD to be home in Chicago for Christmas, and because of the light schedule, Dinah gave the trio time off, too. But before saying a temporary goodbye to everyone, she asked Keter to go shopping with her. She wanted some advice on buying a new television—how big, what kind of console, what brand? So Keter went along, going from store to store until Dinah figured out what she wanted—a black-and-white Zenith, eighteen-inch screen. Then they had to drive it back to Trumbull and take it to the basement. Dinah wanted to hide it as a surprise for the family. The next day Keter stopped by to say so long before going back to Washington, D.C., to be with Pinky and their son. Dinah told him to take one of the cars. As he was leaving, Dinah asked him to go down in the basement with her. She motioned to the television still in its box. "That's yours," she told him. Asking for his advice had been a ruse. She wanted to be sure she bought Keter the kind of set he wanted.

It was easy for Dinah to feel magnanimous at the end of this year: six records on the charts, exposure to a new jazz audience, playing the upscale Mocambo and the Las Vegas Strip, even with the racial indignities. EmArcy had just celebrated its first anniversary and was now considered a major jazz label. Dinah could share in that achievement. When Bobby Shad started the imprint, *Billboard* noted in an anniversary piece, "all he had to start with were two vocalists—Sarah Vaughan and Dinah Washington. Even the latter was considered more a blues than a jazz artist."

No one should say that anymore.

13.

"Hot, Fresh and Invigorating"

1956

Jazz is a touchy subject," Bobby Shad conceded. "There are too many people who consider themselves experts. . . . We live in a glass house, and the rocks thrown come fast. No matter what you do, you will find dissenters as well as those who think you can do no wrong."

The challenge—or perhaps it was more a conundrum—was constant: defining who and what was jazz and finding the proper audience, especially for someone like Dinah, who seemed to be caught in the middle. Detroit promoter Frank Brown considered Dinah a jazz presence, giving her star billing on his first "Big Show of 1956" on January 16 at the Graystone along with Count Basie and established jazz instrumentalists Charlie Ventura and Sonny Stitt.

When she left the Big Show to play a week at the Howard in Washington, D.C., at the end of January, Dinah was again paired with a jazz musician she'd known since her Hampton days, saxophonist Illinois Jacquet. Her performance coincided with the release of a single on the Mercury imprint, but it was the bluesy "I Just Couldn't Stand It No More" on the A side, with a ballad on the other,

"The Show Must Go On." Like other companies, Mercury wanted to exploit its catalogue, and its choice of material revealed a strategy common to many of the labels—singles aimed at one audience and albums—for Dinah, the EmArcy music—aimed at another.

On the surface, not much had changed in the eleven months that Dinah had been with Joe Glaser and Associated Booking. She was still playing the same venues in the same cities, though Glaser may have been getting her more lucrative deals. But Dinah was satisfied: "He drives me hard and gets results," she said. That was evident in New Orleans, where Glaser seemed to have better connections than Ben Bart. Dinah and the trio had enjoyed playing Lincoln Beach and then Curley's the previous summer. Now Glaser got her a weeklong booking at the Safari Room, a nightclub on the New Orleans outskirts that welcomed black talent for a white audience.

The club management thought enough of Dinah's draw that ads were placed in both the city's mainstream papers, the *Times-Picayune* and the *Item.* The latter's ad featured a provocative three-quarter-length shot of Dinah that was just shy of a Mae West come-hither pose. She was in a strapless gown, left hand on her hip, head cocked slightly to the right, a knowing look on her face.

In the South, race was ever present, if unmentioned in daily conversation. In the midst of a song or in the sweet waves of applause that came after, it was possible to forget about skin color and its consequences. But sometimes the coincidence of events raised the antennae and sharpened the moment. Five days before Dinah and the trio arrived in New Orleans, a special three-judge federal court told state education officials that the city's system of segregated schools was invalid, another aftershock from the United States Supreme Court *Brown v. Board of Education* decision two years earlier, which had declared segregated schools unconstitutional.

Louisiana officials were livid and promised an appeal to avoid any mixing of the races in the classroom. An editorial in the *Times-Picayune* noted with approval an argument made in the *News and Courier* of Charleston, South Carolina, another southern city facing its own racial tension. "The Southern pattern of segregation, subject to changes from time to time, has preserved order," the editorial said. "Use of force, even with court sanction, to upset the pattern, will produce disorder." This comforting and comfortable notion of "order" meant that the same whites who nodded in agreement over the morning paper and enjoyed Dinah at the Safari at night would keep their children from going to school with hers had she lived in New Orleans.

Barring supreme indignity, Dinah and her musicians paid no attention to the situation, putting on blinders as a matter of habit and reminding themselves, as Keter told himself on every southern trip, "I came to play, not to stay."

Dinah hadn't expected to run into Bea Buck, her Detroit friend, in New Orleans, but Bea had signed on to assist the Reverend C. L. Franklin of the New Bethel Baptist Church on his trip through the South with the Clara Ward Singers. And they were all in town during Dinah's engagement at the Safari. Dinah invited Bea to come to the show.

"What do I do? Do I ask for you?" Bea wanted to know, sensitive to her surroundings and quite aware that the Safari was a white club. "Do I come through the back door?"

No, no, Dinah assured her. Just come in through the front door.

Bea didn't argue. The next evening she made her way to the club and was escorted inside. "They were very nice," she said, adding that she was given a good seat for the show. "To my dismay," Bea recalled, "I had to go to the bathroom." Dinah hadn't started her set yet, and she asked her what to do.

Use the bathroom, Dinah told her.

But there was only one, and Bea was concerned: a young black woman using the only bathroom in a white club in New Orleans felt like a recipe for trouble.

Bea's solution was to find Jimmy Cobb and insist that he stand outside the ladies' room door. If she didn't come out in five minutes, she told him, he should check on her. "I was scared to death."

Dinah's next big job was back in Detroit—though Bea, still with Rev. Franklin, would miss it. Frank Brown had recruited her for another of his Monday night shows at the Graystone, the timing a constant reminder that race intruded in northern venues, too. Brown's shows could take place only on Monday, the day set aside for blacks. Whites were free to come to those performances and on any other night when white acts played, but the reverse wasn't true. The March 12 show had a new gimmick. Brown billed the package as "Jazz vs. Rock 'n Roll." In addition to Dinah the lineup featured top talent: Thelonious Monk, Miles Davis, Terry Gibbs, T-Bone Walker,

Little Willie John, and the Clovers. The concept reinforced how in this moment musicians with seemingly disparate styles could be packaged and sold to the public.

"Week by week it becomes harder and harder to differentiate between the various categories of the music business," *Cash Box* mused in one of its regular weekly editorials, this one titled "What Is Pop?" "There was a time when a record automatically fell into either the pop, rhythm and blues or country field. Today no such easy distinction is possible." From an industry perspective this was all to the good. "With no more physical frontiers left to conquer, it almost seems as though we have to set out to conquer our regional frontiers and make the advantages of each part of our country available to all others. This can only mean a greater appreciation of music and songs on the part of all our people and wider, expanding horizons for the music business as a whole."

Some jazz musicians objected to the conglomerations that were showing up on theater stages. Pianist Billy Taylor found the rhythm and blues–rock 'n' roll music "trite." "It's obviously gimmicked up with old boogie-woogie phrases, pseudo-Spanish rhythms, recurring triplets, et cetera, ad nauseam." But he recognized that this newer music was pulling jazz along, not the reverse. "The promotion and exposure of rhythm and blues is like nothing this side of pop music. I can't go into a radio station and not find at least five rhythm and blues records to one record of *any* style of jazz," Taylor lamented. "The tenacity of the guys who promote rhythm and blues is fantastic—they'll tie the disc jockey's shoelaces, shave him, baby-sit for him. They don't do that for jazz."

DINAH MADE HER SECOND APPEARANCE on *The Tonight Show* in New York on April 12. She sang the B side of her January release, "The Show Must Go On," and "Let's Get Busy Too," which had been recorded a year earlier but just released. Though this was late night TV with a smaller audience than daytime shows, the exposure was still important, introducing Dinah to listeners unlikely to see her on the road or in the big-city clubs. There was also a certain cachet to being part of a hip, cutting-edge show, thanks to host Steve Allen, even if Dinah just sang in street clothes in front of a simple drape set.

She made a quick trip to Chicago a week later to do a benefit for the American Boys Commonwealth Club. The event, which included a fashion show, was at the Herzl Auditorium on the city's West Side, and because it wasn't in a nightclub or a downtown theater, it was one of the few times that Alice Jones would come to hear her daughter perform. Not only that, Alice had been invited to open the late afternoon event with her solo version of "Bless This House." It had been years since mother and daughter were on the same stage, even if they didn't sing together, and though she didn't speak of it often, Dinah treasured those times when her mother was in the audience.

When she returned to New York, Dinah went right into the studio for two days of recording with Hal Mooney. The plan was to put together another album, but two of the tunes recorded were put out quickly as a single, "Cat on a Hot Tin Roof," the title coming from the 1955 Pulitzer prize–winning Tennessee Williams play, backed with "The First Time." Both tunes were as much an example of Mercury trying to fit Dinah into the changing world of music as they were of Dinah's singing ability. "Cat" seemed like a blues, but it wasn't in the classic form. Dinah gave some of the lyrics an exaggerated growl but the more interesting feature of the song was a mournful harmonica that opened the tune and then provided haunting accents that occasionally were crowded by the backup singers.

"The First Time" was Mercury's effort to put Dinah in a modern doo-wop setting, complete with the "bump bump bump bah" of a vocal chorus and a honking saxophone. The combination of these elements and Dinah's clear diction and tone was interesting if not entirely successful. (As measured by the *Billboard* and *Cash Box* tallies, the record didn't make much of a splash, though *Billboard* gave it brief praise in the May 12 issue.)

Recording during the day, Dinah and the trio went over to Brooklyn in the evening to play the Baby Grand, filling time until they returned to the Apollo to headline a new show that started May 4. One of the continuing pleasures of playing the storied Harlem theater was the backstage ambience, where performers could relax together and greet their friends. Every week was like an informal music convention—entertainers who were playing other venues in New York would come up to 125th Street, see the show, and then go backstage to visit with friends who were performing.

Dinah had run into jazz trombonist Gordon Austin years earlier when she was with Lionel Hampton, and Austin never forgot their introduction. "We met at the Braddock Hotel in New York, on the way to the bathroom," he said. "I had on a short robe, and she came passing by and said, 'Ummm, you sure got some pretty legs.' From then on she called me 'Pretty Legs.' "

Dinah and Austin hadn't seen each other for some time. In the interim he had married a second time and had a young daughter named Patti, who would be eight in August. The family now lived on Long Island, and Austin brought his wife, Edna, and Patti backstage after one of Dinah's performances.

"This is my little girl," Austin said, introducing her to Patti.

"Hi, I'm Dinah Washington, and I'm a singer," Dinah said, shaking Patti's hand, giving her a kiss on the cheek and a wink at the formal introduction.

"Well, I'm Patti Austin, and I'm a singer, too," Patti said with utter seriousness. In her mind it was true, too. She was used to drawing crowds at the Woolworth's near her home when she sang along to whatever was on the store's sound system while waiting for her mother to finish her errands.

Dinah blanched for a moment, but then she burst out laughing, charmed by Patti's precociousness.

"Well, if you're a singer you're going to go out onstage tonight," Dinah told her. What did she want to sing?

"I'll sing 'Teach Me Tonight' in B-flat."

Everyone in the dressing room cracked up. Dinah took her to the piano player—most likely Wynton—and they had a brief rehearsal. But no one had told Keter and the Apollo band that Patti was going to sing "Teach Me" in a different key than Dinah.

Patti came out onstage later, and the band started the song. But she knew something was wrong. As soon as the introduction was over, she stopped the musicians. "You're playing in the wrong key," she told them.

The audience rocked with laughter.

The band made the adjustment, and Patti did her number. Dinah came out, gave her a hug, and escorted her back to her parents. "Never follow children or animals," Dinah cracked before finishing the rest of her show.

Dinah loved the moment, though. "Well, that's it," she said at

the end of the evening, "I'm your godmother," and promised her a
spot in the May show at the Apollo. She even had the gimmick—
"Queen of the Blues and the Princess," which is the way the Apollo
advertised the May 4–11 revue. Not only that, Dinah wanted to
make sure that Patti had the tools to keep going. She found her a
manager and took her to James Kriegsmann, the well-known entertainment photographer who had taken several of Dinah's shots, to
get a formal picture. Dinah also wanted Quincy Jones to write
arrangements for them.

"Go and sing for this man so he can get your keys and everything," she told her.

Quincy was smitten, too. "That's it. I'm your godfather," Patti remembered him saying. "So in the course of about a week," she
added, "I got all these godparents, and all I had to do was sing—it
was a good deal."

The only disappointment was not actually getting to do the
Apollo show with Dinah. The Children's Aid Society heard about
the plan to have Patti sing and put a stop to it because she was underage. It was only a momentary setback, though. Within weeks
RCA signed Patti to a record deal, the youngest singer on the label's
roster.

The night she met Dinah, Patti recalled, "my whole career
started. She was just very loving. She showed me great kindness. It
was a maternal kind of relationship that my parents allowed." Patti
went on to success in the pop and R&B world with numerous well-
received albums to her credit.

DINAH HAD NOT HAD a legal husband since Walter Buchanan,
but she was rarely without a man. Late in 1955 Sugar Ray Robinson
had introduced her to the Reverend Russell Roberts of Atlantic
City's Shiloh Baptist Church, dubbed the "Playboy Preacher" by
Sepia because of his athletic good looks and his taste for nightclubs,
new Cadillacs, and women entertainers. Roberts had called Dinah
every day while she was in Las Vegas and certainly left the impression that he was serious about her. Dinah reciprocated. Syndicated
columnist Dorothy Kilgallen reported early in 1956 that Roberts
asked Dinah to marry him. The minister denied he had done any
such thing and called the report "preposterous."

"He's the one who's preposterous," Dinah retorted, obviously hurt. "Yes the Reverend Russell Roberts and I were going to be married," she insisted. "However, he and his members don't think I'm good enough. Some of them, I hear, nearly fainted when they heard about it. . . . I didn't ask him to marry—he asked me. In fact he wanted to know how long it would take for us to get hitched. You can get married at any time out there. Those church sisters are really the cause of our troubles," Dinah continued. "They just didn't like the idea of him marrying a person who works in the theater. One of them broke all of my recordings when she heard I was engaged to the reverend."

"I'm just as much a churchgoer as anyone else," Dinah declared, even if memories of childhood days at St. Luke Baptist overshadowed the sporadic church attendance of the previous decade. "And just because I sing, I don't think it should be held against me." Hazel Scott, the popular piano player, had married the Reverend Adam Clayton Powell Jr., and Powell, she said with a well-placed dig, "is a much bigger man in the ministry than Roberts and yet he married Hazel."

Any reconciliation with Roberts was out of the question. "I'm not interested in that man any more."

Dinah wasted little time worrying about the reverend. By early spring she was keeping company with Pete Buck, who worked for a furrier headquartered at the Waldorf-Astoria, the upscale hotel on the city's East Side. Dinah threw Buck a birthday party in April, serving up pigs' feet and other soul food for the guests. The party was at least partially integrated, racially and musically. One visitor was a white opera singer named Lillian Rappola, who made herself right at home, according to *Jet*. She arrived in an expensive mink coat, which she threw on the floor, and then took off her shoes before sitting down to dinner.

Ann Littles, a veteran of Dinah's romantic entanglements, knew that Pete Buck would never last. "He was a street hustler," she sniffed. The only question was when and where this liaison would end.

The answer turned out to be Detroit. Dinah played a return engagement at the Flame Show Bar for two weeks starting May 18— an opening night that found fans lined up for a block waiting to get in. In the hotel one evening Dinah and Buck had a huge fight, loud enough for guests in nearby rooms to hear the fracas. Unlike the hotel room scrap with Gus Chappell in Los Angeles, this one ended without any injury to Dinah. However, the door at their Gotham Hotel room took a beating when Buck kicked it. Dinah told Ann to pack up Buck's clothes and "get him out of the room."

"I'm through with violent, jealous men," Dinah declared.

During one of her sets after the breakup she found catharsis in song with improvised lyrics to "Baby Get Lost": "Don't come kickin' in my door. Baby can't you see I just can't use you no more."

Tan, the black monthly feature magazine, came up with the idea of asking Dinah to talk about men in spite of—or perhaps because of—her romantic travails. In May the magazine published "My Dream Man," Dinah's answers to the question of who was an "ideal man for a happy and successful marriage? . . . After four marriages and the same number of divorces, I may not be considered an authority on that subject," she conceded, "but I have ideas and ideals."

Dinah's fourteen examples were as telling as the descriptions, which purported to be her own words but almost surely were helped along by a ghostwriter who talked to Dinah and then shaped the prose to fit the magazine's style. Dinah's first selection was her father, Ollie. "Like many fathers, he did not fully understand me, his daughter, and made a few mistakes which he has since striven to correct," she said. "He has shown himself to be a big-hearted, generous, and affectionate father whom I will always love and admire."

Next was her brother, Harold, a student at Crane Junior College in Chicago. "His heart and spirit are in the right place. Well-behaved and courteous," she added, "he has never given our family any trouble and he has been a model son all of his life."

Slappy White—"he deserves a whole chapter in my admiration book"—and Quincy Jones—"one of the most brilliant musical arrangers"—made the list. So did Joe Glaser and Birdland owner Morris Levy. "I like a man who keeps his balance and modesty and feet on the ground despite success," she said of Levy. "Morris and I are old friends who know what it's like to be poor. Years ago we used to share our wealth to buy sandwiches, things were that tough. The years have changed all that, but Morris has remained the same, a smiling, generous easygoing guy who doesn't take advantage of people and is never happier than when he's helping."

Loyalty and support were important to Dinah, and Levy provided that. Her observations about eating sandwiches with him were renewed evidence that her memories of early struggles never faded completely. Dinah's gauzy comments reflected the Levy she knew, and her impression was decidedly different from those who had much less pleasant moments with him.

Dinah's musician choices were illuminating. Like Leonard Feather's blindfold tests, they were a window into what she prized in an artist, and the men she selected shared her sophisticated approach to music. Frank Sinatra: "he moves me" because of his "voice and courage." Duke Ellington: "he breathes romance through his music and his very being. Such a man is rare indeed." Lionel Hampton: "a spectacular man . . . When he travels abroad he is a wonderful ambassador for the United States as well as the Negro." Perry Como: "because he's sincere and sweet and sings like an angel." Sammy Davis, Jr.: "a great talent . . . a great performer and a kid with an extremely bright future . . . I love and admire the guy, but I do wish he would pay me that $485 he owes me." Dinah declined to elaborate on the cryptic remark.

Her last three choices were Ethiopian emperor Haile Selassie— "a man of courage and dignity"—John White, operator of the Gotham Hotel in Detroit—"a superb host who always makes me feel at home"—and the actor Richard Egan, who had attended Dinah's Philadelphia birthday party in 1950 (her twenty-sixth). "He is a rugged masculine type," she said, "who can also be soft and gentle, and I just love that type."

Though some of the comments in *Tan* sounded too formal for Dinah, something in the overall tone matched her occasionally haughty attitude, whether she was deflecting a request from the audience—"No TV. We're on the radio."—or chiding her father about his parenting duties. The effect in the article was to put some distance between Dinah Washington, the performer and the Queen, and the individual offstage who still would answer to Ruth.

PLAYING CLEVELAND felt a lot like playing Detroit. Dinah had been there enough times to have friends in the community. One of them, Olivia Foreman, invited her to a late night dinner after she finished one of her shows at the Loop Lounge, where Dinah and the trio were booked for a week at the end of May. Mrs. Foreman had made lamb with lima beans and fresh, hot buttered rolls, and Dinah was loving every bite until a loud knock at the door stopped every-one cold. Two policemen, the brothers Leon and Delwood Jackson, stormed in and broke up a spirited poker game going on in another room. The officers ignored the fact that Dinah was eating, not play-ing, and she was arrested and ushered into a paddy wagon for the ride to the police station along with everyone else. In an hour or so Dinah was released, but Mrs. Foreman was charged with running a gambling house, and the players charged with visiting a gambling establishment.

Dinah joked to friends that her post-performance dinner was the first "square meal" she had had in some time. In the previous several weeks, she had been dieting anew, this time with noticeable results. Jackie Gleason, who had long struggled with his own weight problems, sent Dinah to his doctor—the same one, Ann said, that Frank Sinatra used, Dr. Harry Stone, whose office was in a fashion-able Midtown Manhattan neighborhood. LaRue Manns, Dinah's girl Friday, remembered that bandleader Paul Whiteman, who was friendly with Dinah, also recommended Dr. Stone.

"He gave her diet pills, a pill to get up, a pill to go to sleep so she could lose weight," Ann recalled. More than once she had watched Dinah enjoy a middle-of-the-night breakfast at Count Basie's near the Apollo, loving every bite of the chicken-and-waffles combina-tion, and then go right into a dieting routine. "I got sick and tired of that stuff," Ann said with a gruffness that masked concern about Dinah's health.

One of Dinah's favorite dress shops in New York was Wilma's Gowns on West 57th Street. When Dinah wanted to shop there for new clothes, Ann would call the owner ahead of time with specific instructions: "Dinah has not lost a fuckin' pound, but you go in the back and you get those tags and put a twelve tag on a fourteen, and it will work. . . . Do like I tell you if you want to sell some dresses." Ann knew Dinah shopped by size, especially when she was in the middle of a diet craze.

This time, though, it was more than a craze. The pounds were coming off, and it was showing, enough so that before the Apollo revue in May Dinah had a new publicity picture taken in a manner reminiscent of Billie Holiday. She was wearing an off-the-shoulder satin dress with poofy sleeves and cinched waist. Around her neck was a beaded choker with a long beaded pendant attached. She also sported a new haircut: short bangs in front, the rest pulled back. She posed hands on hips, head tilted slightly to the right, but she was looking straight at the camera. The look on her face seemed to say, "How about this?"

As if to answer, the *Amsterdam News* ran the picture with the caption "New Glamour" and pronounced Dinah "slimmer and prettier than ever."

By the time Dinah reached Cleveland, the weight-loss tally was twenty-five pounds, duly noted in a *Cleveland Call and Post* story about Dinah's week at the Loop Lounge. It was ironic that in this moment of attention for her new, slimmer look, *Sepia* featured Dinah in an article about buxom black celebrities: "Bosom Secrets of Women." In *Life* or *Look,* which catered to white readers, Jayne Mansfield and Dagmar were the bosomy favorites. In the pop culture version of "separate but equal," *Sepia* offered Dinah, Ruth Brown, Ella Fitzgerald, and LaVern Baker. In a picture caption, Dinah was dubbed "King size Queen." Such articles, whether the women were white or black, also sent another message: their bodies were fair game for scrutiny in and of themselves, reinforcing the notion that for female entertainers looks were as important in getting attention as talent.

DINAH WAS A LOYAL FRIEND. Those in her inner circle quickly learned to take her salty language and outbursts in stride. Being called "a bitch," even a "big black bitch," was, coming from Dinah, a term of endearment. "Motherfucker" was a special category, too, though Dinah tried to be careful around children, her own and others. It amused the young singer Leslie Uggams, who was sometimes on the same Apollo bill with Dinah, that she would warn Uggams's mother when she was about to explode.

"Okay, Juanita," she would say, "take baby into the dressing room. I got some strong cuss words I gotta use." Mother and daughter would dutifully go down the hall and close the door, "but Dinah's voice carried everywhere," Uggams recalled. "It wasn't like you couldn't hear it. Dinah could cuss better than anybody I ever heard in my life."

Dinah might snap at Ann and argue with her over the small matters of daily living, but none of that diminished her feelings of friendship. So it was no surprise when she threw Ann a party for her thirtieth birthday in June in one of the Theresa Hotel's party rooms. The guest of honor was given a corsage and two-tiered birthday cake, and among the guests were Ann's mother, Anna Mae, who had come over from Newark, Dizzy Gillespie, Quincy Jones, Jimmy Cobb, Junior Mance, and LaRue Manns. Patti Austin was invited, too, and nearly stole the limelight from the guest of honor when she sang "Teach Me Tonight" and then "Some of These Days" like a pint-sized Sophie Tucker. When everyone posed for a picture, Dinah, who was standing next to Ann, barely reached her shoulder, even wearing a favorite pair of open-toed high heels.

After Ann's birthday party, Dinah and the trio went to Chicago, where they were booked into Budland at 64th and Cottage Grove, a bistro with an interesting history. Located in the basement of the Pershing Hotel, the club was first known as the El Grotto, then re-named the Beige Room, and then renamed again as Birdland, hoping to capitalize on the popularity of the New York club. But when the Birdland management learned about the new name and threatened legal action, "Bird" became "Bud" to avoid litigation. Budland modeled itself on other clubs, presenting several acts on a bill along with the headliner, in this case Dinah. One of the supporting bands, which had been playing at the club since January, was led by pianist Sun Ra (born Herman Sonny Blount), who took credit for suggesting the slight name change that avoided a court fight.

Delighted with her new figure, Dinah was happy to show it off. Her favorite outfit was a tight-fitting black lace cocktail dress with spaghetti straps. Always concerned that shoes match the dress, she wore black high-heeled mules and still liked those dangling beaded earrings that swayed back and forth as she sang.

Dinah thought it would be fun to have her sister and stepsister come see her perform one evening—Clarissa was sixteen and Farris was almost eighteen. She had a table set aside for them, and made sure the bartenders and waiters took good care of them. They had a wonderful time, but when they all got home, Alice had a fit.

"Nothing was gonna happen," Dinah told her. "They were with me."

"But what if something did happen," Alice insisted. "How am I going to explain to the church that my children got killed in a nightclub?"

Dinah's new look made even more of an impression on the West Coast when she opened August 7 at the Blackhawk in San Francisco. In his column right after opening night, the *San Francisco Chronicle*'s Hal Schaefer proclaimed "a new Dinah Washington." Though she was "slim, trim," Schaefer hastened to add that the weight loss had not diminished her singing.

Even the *Los Angeles Sentinel* paid attention to Dinah's San Francisco engagement, writing about her return to the coast in language that must have thrilled her. "A new small sized Dinah Washington, complete with glamorous petite figure, pony tail and the same great vocal styles" was how one piece began. Dinah worked at her glamorous image and was surely gratified to have confirmation in print that others noticed. She didn't mind divulging specifics—she had lost forty pounds—and couldn't complain later if stories discussed how she looked with as much detail as how she sang. Rather than talk about new tunes in her repertoire, writers now were likely to comment on her new wardrobe of "svelte sheaths."

Dinah had also bought new evening gowns and chose one of them for an updated publicity shot that was both evocative and provocative. The gown was another off-the-shoulder dress, this one with a beaded top that flowed into a satin skirt and was cut low enough to reveal the kind of cleavage celebrated a few months earlier in *Sepia*. Dinah's confidence in her appearance was apparent not only in the dress but in her pose: she was leaning slightly against a curved chaise, left hand—adorned with a wide beaded bracelet—resting on the top. Her back was arched ever so slightly, and she cocked her head to the left, a half-smile on her face.

The *L.A. Sentinel* and the *California Eagle* ran the picture on the front of their entertainment sections as a preview to Dinah's two-week stay at Zardi's Jazz Club in the high-traffic location of Hollywood and Vine. The *Sentinel* could barely contain itself in a description of Dinah onstage: "spectacularly trim in a wardrobe designed to draw gasps from the ladies for the high fashion displayed, and similar gasps from the men for the curves even more vitally displayed." Almost as an afterthought, the paper noted that Dinah sang "generously a program from early Washingtonian such as 'Long John Blues' to her latest, 'Soft Winds.'" The latter, recorded nearly two years earlier, was about to come out as a Mercury single, and that was probably why Dinah was including it now in her live shows.

During Dinah's second week at Zardi's the *Sentinel* and the *Eagle* still wanted to talk about her weight loss. Both papers carried identical articles reminding readers of her new look. "A Dinah Washington three sizes smaller, but amply curved nevertheless," was how the writer put it, calling her weight loss "spectacular." She had an amusing take on all the attention. "I just got all jazzed up," she said. "Fat singers went out with Tristan and Isolde." Her allusion to opera took close friends by surprise; they had never known her to be an opera buff. Still, everyone had to chuckle, even if Dinah may have had some prompting.

Dinah was so tickled with her new look that she happily posed in a bathing suit for *Jet*, which pronounced her "streamlined Dinah."

August 29 was Dinah's thirty-second birthday. She didn't have anything special planned except the evening performance, which was the day before she and the trio closed at Zardi's. She would sing her usual set, maybe have a glass of champagne and collect greetings from whoever remembered that the date was special.

The evening got under way uneventfully, and Dinah's set was proceeding smoothly. A few bars into "There'll Be Some Changes Made," the lights dimmed and then went out. Her voice trailed off; the trio stopped playing, and the crowd got quiet. No one knew what had happened.

Suddenly a man jumped up from his seat. "Ladies and gentlemen," he said, "we interrupt this program with an important news bulletin. Tonight is Miss Dinah Washington's birthday." The audience was already applauding when he asked them to "Please help us celebrate." At the same time a giant cake, courtesy of Mercury, was wheeled out from the kitchen, thirty-two candles blazing. Led by Keter, Wynton, and Jimmy, the audience serenaded Dinah with "Happy Birthday." Usually ready with a quip when she was onstage, Dinah was at a loss for words as she cut the cake and drank the first glass of celebratory champagne.

What made this birthday even more special was the fact that Dinah's sons were with her. George had just turned ten, and Bobby had just turned eight. They accompanied her on the trip out from Chicago along with the trio, Slappy, LaRue, Ann, and Ann's much younger brother, Ronald, who was about the same age as George. Disneyland in nearby Anaheim had opened a year earlier and was now a popular attraction for families with children. Dinah decided her sons should have no less, so one day she packed everybody up— the musicians, the helpers, the kids—and took them all to Disneyland to spend the day.

Keter was tickled when Walt Disney himself found the group and said hello. Dinah was having the time of her life. She dressed casually for the occasion—button-down blouse and matching bermuda shorts and big wraparound sunglasses that were not only functional but added a touch of glamour. She didn't want to miss a thing with her children. When they got to Frontierland, she climbed up on the top of the Disneyland stagecoach and sat with George and Bobby as though they were guiding the horses across the prairie. She shrieked with delight and grabbed on to the boys as they spun around and around in the giant Alice in Wonderland teacups that were a favorite among the thousands of daily visitors.

The day at Disneyland was not only a respite from the club work but also a rare opportunity to spend the whole day with George and Bobby before LaRue had to take them back east. Dinah and the trio still had other Los Angeles dates, including a starring role in the twelfth annual Los Angeles Cavalcade of Jazz. As in past years, the Sunday afternoon event would be outdoors at the city's Wrigley Field, and in keeping with the mélange of styles that now were mixed and matched on music bills, the lineup was hardly straight jazz. Headlining with Dinah was a new rock 'n' roll sensation, Little Richard, who sang and played the piano with a flamboyant fervor that matched his fanciful stage outfits. His "Tutti-Frutti" and "Long Tall Sally" had gone to the top of the *Billboard* and *Cash Box* rhythm and blues charts earlier in the year. The rest of the bill was made up of local acts, and beyond the music, a highlight of the afternoon festival remained the finals of the Miss Cavalcade Bathing Beauty Contest.

Dinah and the trio wound up their trip to Los Angeles with two nights at the Savoy Ballroom on South Central Avenue. Dinah's appearance was now so much a part of the public conversation about her that just before this last performance the *L.A. Sentinel* felt free to comment one last time: "The new look Dinah having lost forty pounds had to have all new gowns made and looks great. Here's hoping that when she comes back she will not have gained a single pound."

One couldn't be sure if the paper was suggesting that its readers liked the trimmer Dinah best or if they wanted her to stay slim because it meant so much to her. Left unmentioned, though, was what the weight loss might be doing to Dinah's health, given that she was apparently relying on pills, which were probably dexedrine or "speed" that revved up her metabolism and then required another pill to help her slow down and sleep.

A few weeks later, when Dinah and the trio played eight days at the Club Riviera in St. Louis, the weight loss attracted attention once again. "Her new figure, she lost 40 pounds or more, makes a beautiful stage appearance," wrote Chick Finney in the *St. Louis Argus*. The *Kansas City Call* commented, too, in advance of Dinah's week at the Orchid Room in October: "Losing 40 pounds cost blues singer Dinah Washington a tidy sum in replacing the dresses and gowns in her wardrobe which she can no longer wear."

Dinah's engagement there was interrupted by an unwelcome couple of hours at the local magistrate's court. One of her former maids, Flora Wilhite, contended that Dinah owed her $50 in back wages from the end of 1953, which Dinah denied. Dinah had hired Wilhite, then a waitress at the Orchid Room, after the young woman told her she wanted to change jobs. Dinah needed a maid and agreed to pay Wilhite $50 a week plus expenses. Dinah sent Wilhite a ticket to join her in Chicago the week of Christmas 1953. Dinah testified that she also sent Wilhite $10 in spending money and that the two agreed on $25 for the first week because Dinah was taking a short break from work.

Wilhite denied there was any such arrangement and argued that she was owed the full $50. But both women said the relationship was short-lived. Dinah claimed that she left the house on Trumbull to go to a party and that when she returned Wilhite had gone "bag and baggage." Dinah said she had paid the young woman all that she was owed beforehand, which Wilhite denied.

Asked why she waited three years to bring charges, Wilhite testified that it had been difficult to "catch up" with Dinah. When Dinah's two lawyers pointed out that she had played Kansas City three times since 1953, Wilhite replied that by the time she learned Dinah was in town she had already left.

The magistrate awarded Wilhite $50 and ordered Dinah to pay the court costs.

NO DOUBT SPENDING more time with George and Bobby during the summer helped convince Dinah that she wanted them to be with her more often, and that meant bringing them to New York. For a time the boys were with her in a suite she rented at the Theresa Hotel, but Dinah wanted more space and a more permanent place in a city so important to the business. Over the summer she had rented a large apartment in Harlem that was a mile or so north of the Theresa. The apartment was in the new Bowery Bank Building at 145th and St. Nicholas, so named because the bank occupied the ground floor with three residence towers above it. Even while the building was under construction there was competition for the apartments on the upper floors. One of Dinah's friends, a restaurant owner named Jennie Lou, who owned a café at 135th Street and Seventh Avenue, put in an application for her, and Dinah was given a lease for Apartment 14A-3, one of the largest in the building, with windows overlooking St. Nicholas Avenue and 145th Street and handsome parquet floors in every room. The $225-a-month rent reflected the building's status as a high-end residence.

With three bedrooms, one full bath, and a half-bath attached to the master bedroom, 14A-3 was big enough for Dinah and the children with an extra room for LaRue. The view from the master bedroom was to the south, and in the middle of the night, when Dinah returned from playing the Apollo or Birdland, she could see the lights of the Empire State Building 111 blocks away as she drifted off to sleep. The kitchen was small but it extended into a dining area and living room that provided enough space for informal rehearsals and entertaining. The western exposure allowed the sun to pour in by the time Dinah woke up in the early afternoon. The view here was dramatic, too, looking out on the sturdy elegance of the George Washington Bridge. Amenities and entertainment were nearby. Right next to the bank was Landera's Beauty Shop, and Joe Louis's club, the Brown Bomber, was a few doors up. Just around the corner on 145th Street, next to the residents' entrance, was a dry cleaners.

LaRue recalled that she helped Dinah move from the Theresa on

July 15, which probably occurred during Dinah's short break between engagements in Chicago at Budland. Whatever the precise
date, Dinah's plan was clear: she wanted George and Bobby packed
up and ready to move so that they could enroll in school in New
York in the fall. Alice was unhappy that Dinah was taking the boys
with her, convinced she could provide a more appropriate atmosphere for two young children. Alice was also surprised at how fast
things happened, LaRue said, "because she didn't know I did all this,
but I did most of it while she was at church. So we sort of eased out,
and that's how we got back to New York. And I don't think the
mother ever forgave me for not telling her," LaRue added. "She
thought I should tell her everything. But Dinah was my boss and
was the one who was sending me my salary."

   LaRue said Dinah put her in charge of decorating the place, and
Dinah, according to *Jet,* was helped by a "new boyfriend"—
unnamed—who owned a furniture store and sent her $1,500 worth
of furniture for the apartment.

WHILE DINAH WAS ON the West Coast, Mercury had released
another album on the EmArcy imprint and a new single. The album,
Dinah, was filled with a dozen songs pulled from the two sessions the
previous November in Los Angeles with Hal Mooney and was largely
devoted to standards and ballads. The cover was simple but inviting, a close-up of Dinah in the studio, eyes closed, her right hand—
perfectly polished nails evident—cradling the microphone. Next to
her was a single word in white capital letters, "DINAH." This time
EmArcy listed the featured musicians: Keter, Wynton, and Jimmy
along with Georgie Auld on tenor sax and Herb Geller on alto sax.
The liner notes explained that these five men were supplemented
on several tunes with nine string players and four trombones. In
other words, this was a serious production for an EmArcy star.

   On "More Than You Know," which had been a hit for Mildred
Bailey, Wynton started out with soft piano chords, and when Dinah
joined him, it was as though they were in their own intimate musical world, so much so that the addition of the horns was jarring, and
Dinah had to work to keep the mood.

   It was almost impossible now to separate Dinah's turbulent romantic life from some of the material she recorded. So simply

singing "Sunday Kind of Love" with a line like "I want a love that's on the square—I can't seem to find somebody to care" was freighted with meaning even in her restrained presentation. If other singers turned "All of Me" into a lament of self-pity, Dinah sang it like Frank Sinatra, whom she admired, as a challenge—"I suggest, baby, that you come and get the rest of me." Left unsaid but implied was "if you can."

Enough *Down Beat* readers bought the record to keep it on the magazine's Jazz Best-Seller list for a month, though never higher than seventeen of twenty. (The survey was conducted every two weeks among 150 retail record outlets.)

The new single—just her third of the year—was "Soft Winds," which Dinah was performing on her live dates, backed with "Tears to Burn" from a session with Quincy Jones in June. It was "Soft Winds," though, that briefly captured the public's attention. Detroit disc jockey Frantic Ernie Durham of WJLB listed it as one of his top ten plays in the magazine's survey of R&B jockeys, and that no doubt helped it register in the *Cash Box* regional R&B charts. The song had been an instrumental, a favorite of the Benny Goodman Sextet with guitarist Charlie Christian, to which lyrics had been added. Dinah's version was a bit gimmicky, opening with a vocal group's "ooooo-eeee" ascending a scale. After she started singing, the group hummed behind her the entire time, and at the end, Dinah's voice was put through an echo chamber as her sound got softer and softer.

"Soft Winds" was Dinah's first appearance on the singles charts in 1956 and her first in ten months. But it didn't mean her career was languishing. Quite the opposite. She was no longer a typical R&B star dependent on turning out one hit single after another to keep working but an entertainer whose popularity transcended any weekly or monthly tally. Recognition in *Billboard* and *Cash Box* was always helpful, but it was almost beside the point.

Though Jimmy and Wynton had left Dinah intermittently since 1951, Keter had been her one constant—five years of keeping the beat in more ways than one. It was a mutually beneficial arrangement—he was making good music for Dinah, and she was helping him make a name for himself. Life offstage was more complicated. Keter already had a year-old son, and he and Pinky wanted to have more. "Are you going to be a husband and a father?" Pinky asked him at more regular intervals.

"That was hard to do when you're traveling all the time," Keter acknowledged. All during the California trip and in the days working their way back east, he compiled a ledger sheet in his head. On the plus side he loved the music, loved the job, enjoyed seeing his reputation grow, and enjoyed the ambience. The more successful Dinah was the better she and the trio could travel. He had never had a car before, and now he was in charge of two of them, late models and top-of-the-line.

On the minus side were those deeply personal issues—as Pinky told him, the difficulty of being a husband and father, not just a long-distance provider. She was serious and already had talked about a separation. Even Keter's mother told him he couldn't fulfill his family obligations if he was traveling all the time. Wasn't there other work he could find that would allow him to stay home?

Dinah inadvertently helped Keter make his decision. As usual, he was doing all the driving on the California swing, getting the group to the Blackhawk in San Francisco and then down to Los Angeles for their month of dates there. In all the road trips they'd been on, Keter had never had an accident, but in L.A. one day, he had momentarily taken his eyes off the road and hit something. He damaged one side of the car, and it cost $500 to fix. Dinah told him to take care of the repair, and she would take it out of his salary.

"I've been driving all these years—through ice and snow, everything, never had an accident, and now one time, you're going to charge me?" an incredulous Keter asked.

Dinah didn't budge even when Keter reminded her that she hadn't docked Jimmy's pay after he had an accident on a highway in Pennsylvania. And his was much worse—he had driven the car too close to the shoulder, and it slid down a hill.

Keter didn't quit on the spot, but it proved to be a crystallizing moment. When they all got back to New York, Keter told her he was leaving.

"Oh, it was emotional," he remembered. He was crying and so was Dinah. "I really didn't want to leave," he added. "But I was being pressured from the other side." He and Dinah "barked at each other," Keter said, over whether he quit or she would fire him. She did make it official on paper, and Keter was struck by the disconnect between those hard words of departure and Dinah's beautiful handwriting. Somehow something so difficult shouldn't have looked so pretty.

Keter's leaving had a domino effect. Within the month, Wynton and Jimmy went their separate ways as well. Having built their reputations in music circles through their association with Dinah, they were confident they could easily get other jobs. (Keter found work with jazz guitarist Charlie Byrd and then Ella Fitzgerald. Wynton had his own trio for a time with Kenny Burrell on guitar and Paul Chambers on bass, but by early 1959 he had rejoined Jimmy Cobb in Miles Davis's band, where Jimmy had been the drummer since the summer of 1958.)

In the space of a few weeks, Dinah's most intimate musical world was turned upside down. Whatever she thought of this seismic change, she didn't say publicly. When she went back in the studio November 21, the three men she was most used to seeing were gone. Now the most familiar faces were the producers, Quincy and Hal Mooney, and a few sidemen—trumpeter Clark Terry and two musicians from much earlier days, saxophonist Lucky Thompson and pianist Sleepy Anderson, his narcotics arrest in Atlanta now an old story. Mercury had recruited two other top session men for the rhythm section, Milt Hinton on bass and Jimmy Crawford on drums.

Dinah was an optimist at heart and so experienced by now that she could make a smooth transition with the many good musicians who were available. Singing with Keter, Jimmy, and Wynton had been the hand in the glove. With other musicians, the fit would still be there, just not as perfect and not quite as comfortable. But then there was always the possibility that new blood might give her new ideas and new energy.

Dinah's transition into this new phase of music making was probably made easier by her keeping busy. On November 13 she got national exposure on both radio and television, appearing at 8:00 P.M. on the Robert Q. Lewis radio show on CBS and then going over to the NBC television studio to sing two songs on *The Tonight Show*, this time hosted by jazz fan Ernie Kovacs. More attention came in print. *Ebony* published another long feature on Dinah in its November issue, this one titled "Darling of the Hi-Fi Set," in a nod to Mercury's recent strategy of tapping into the new audio technology with albums styled "in the land of Hi-Fi." Dinah's—*Dinah Washington in the Land of Hi-Fi*—was set for release in December. Several were already for sale, among them *"Patti Page in the Land of Hi-Fi, Cannonball Adderley in the Land of Hi-Fi,* and *Dancing in the Land of Hi Fi* with Georgie Auld.

This most recent *Ebony* article focused as much on Dinah's off-stage life as her music, calling her in one breathless summary "a four time loser in marriage" who had "parlayed a sultry voice, numerous headlines of coast-to-coast brawls and a reputation for eccentricity into a $100,000-a-year personality."

"Honey, I'm just trying to get along and sing the songs that make the people happy and get them to buy my records," Dinah said with determined understatement. "I haven't done bad at it so far, have I?"

She was more pointed about her romantic adventures. "With me it was 'Blowtop Blues' each and every time," she said of her marriages. "When I try to be nice to men, they don't appreciate it. When I marry them they think that's a signal to sit down and let me take care of them. I ain't going to hold still for that no more, either. All I want is a man to love me." Among the photos illustrating the story were ones with Larry Wrice, Joe Davis, the policeman, and Jimmy Cobb.

Even in a branch of entertainment where appearance would seem secondary to sound, *Ebony*, while it didn't go as far as *Sepia*, couldn't resist commenting on Dinah's shape, calling her "buxom" in one sentence and the odd "deep-bosomed" in another. They made no mention, though, of her weight loss.

Dinah returned to Boston to play a week at Storyville, the club operated by George Wein, the Newport Jazz Festival impresario, and there were few if any empty seats when she played this time. One of her sets the evening of November 24 was part of the Mutual Broadcasting System's *Bandstand U.S.A,* a program that was gaining listeners and attention by hooking up to jazz clubs on weekend nights to broadcast musicians live. *Variety* reported the week after Dinah was on one of the shows that 350 stations in the Mutual system were picking up the program even though they had no special sponsorship to help pay for it.

Early in December Mercury repeated the strategy it used in late summer, releasing an album on EmArcy and a single on Mercury.

The album was the one mentioned in *Ebony, Dinah Washington in the Land of Hi-Fi,* and the single was "All Because of You" with "To Love and Be Loved."

Not surprisingly, the album's jacket copy pushed the jazz connection and the new audio technology. "There aren't many more versatile singers, who still remain jazz singers, than Dinah," the notes said. "Who belongs in The Land Of Hi-Fi more than the lady with the hi-fi voice? Long before the advances in recorded sound, Dinah had a wonderful resonant quality. In the land of hi-fi, a good thing gets better."

Dinah gave a slow, saucy reading to Cole Porter's already suggestive "Let's Do It." A listener could almost hear her good-natured wink at "Birds do it, bees do it." She updated "There'll Be a Jubilee," which she had sung a decade earlier with Lionel Hampton. Her voice had deepened since then, but she gave it the same infectious swing that was second nature to her, even as a teenager. This new version included a sizzling solo from Cannonball Adderley.

Dinah's treatment of the oft-recorded "Sunny Side of the Street" was another example of how she put her stamp on a song. She altered the melody line, stayed in the lower register, and saved the upper for the climax of the song. And while the tune bubbled with optimism, Dinah stayed far from sentimentality, even tossing in a little joke—"If I never had a cent, I'd be rich as Rockefeller—and that's what he is."

She charged into "If I Were a Bell," taking it at a fast and buoyant clip but never sacrificing her diction, especially on tongue-twisting lines about salad dressing and quacking ducks. George and Ira Gershwin's "Our Love Is Here to Stay" was another one of those songs that took on a certain resonance when Dinah sang it. It was easy to imagine how many times she had expressed that very same sentiment in her offstage life.

The new album immediately registered on *Down Beat*'s Jazz Best-Sellers page, although it was in last place. A review in the December 12 issue was another that stroked with one hand and spanked with the other. *In the Land of Hi-Fi* was "a 100-proof bonded antidote to the affected line of pink gin, female quasi jazz singers of the past couple of years," the reviewer wrote. But he still considered Dinah "a shouter with a beat that can shake bridges." Nonetheless, he continued, "in everything she sings there is the earthy honesty of the blues and gospel singing." Next came another little whack: "Admittedly, Dinah is not the subtlest nor most supple phraser of lyrics." And then some praise for the finish: "but she is becoming more and more effective on standards; invariably her interpretation, while it may be debatable, is certainly hot, fresh and invigorating."

Dinah must have liked that—"hot, fresh and invigorating." She probably took it as a badge of honor, too, that some listeners, at least among the critics, couldn't get comfortable with her style. If nothing else, it was proof again that she was in control of how she made the music, even if she didn't always pick the tunes or the musicians. (When *Down Beat* ran its year-end readers poll December 26, Dinah was thirteenth out of thirty-one in the female singer category. Ella Fitzgerald was in first place and had twice as many as votes as the second-place finisher, the white singer June Christy.)

THOUGH SHE HAD a new apartment in New York and George and Bobby were with her, Dinah and the children went to Chicago for the year-end holidays. Following her usual practice, Dinah earned a little money on the way out, stopping for a weeklong engagement at Cleveland's Chatterbox Cafe. Chicago would be a working visit, too. Dinah was booked into Budland starting Christmas Eve. Albert Anderson, writing for the Associated Negro Press, the news service for black newspapers, was more appreciative—perhaps accepting—of Dinah's sound than critics in *Down Beat, Metronome,* and *Variety,* reflecting a continued racial divide in the response to her work. Asserting that Dinah had "won the rights to the title 'Queen of Hi-Fi' to go along with her blues and jukebox crowns," Anderson lavished praise on her. "Today her style is a wondrous blend of her many splendored vocal talents—combining the sure showmanship of a pop singer with the earthy forthrightness of the blues and the tasteful subtlety of a truly great jazz artist."

The house at 1518 South Trumbull was always full of activity, even with George and Bobby gone, and although Dinah had her own rooms on the top floor, she wanted something she could call her own in Chicago. With Joe Glaser's assistance on a $35,000 loan, she acquired a small building at 8125 South Vernon in the city's Chatham neighborhood, which was filling up with successful blacks able to afford better housing on the South Side. The paperwork was completed December 20—Glaser bought the building and put it in an anonymous trust with Dinah as the beneficiary. Dinah gave an apartment to her father, Ollie, and planned to stay there whenever she was in Chicago. In addition Ollie was hired as the janitor and paid $77 a month. One of his neighbors was the Chess Records harmonica star Little Walter Jacobs.

For Dinah and for Glaser this new building was at once a recognition of a thriving present and their collective investment in the future.

14.

"You've Got to Lay It on Charisma"

1957

By the time he was a senior at Phillips High School in 1941, Eddie Chamblee was performing around Chicago. Phillips and its South Side neighbor, DuSable High School, together had enough teenage talent for bands to play in different combinations almost every night. Eddie played the saxophone, and though he was on the varsity football team, he wrote in the yearbook under his senior picture that he was going to be a musician. Dinah—then still Ruth Jones—was a year behind Eddie, and while they shared the same love of music, they didn't travel in the same circles. Dinah actually liked his younger brother Roland better.

Over the years it was easier for Eddie to know what Dinah was doing than vice versa. He was making a living, but he didn't have a national reputation. He joined Lionel Hampton's band in 1955, and the next year he and Dinah crossed paths in Los Angeles during Dinah's monthlong western swing. Eddie admitted there was an attraction, but he told European friend Kurt Mohr that while he thought about marrying her, he decided "she's just too much. She'll drive any man crazy, and I won't get hooked, oh no." But then they ran into each other again, and something clicked.

"You've got to lay it on charisma," Eddie said. "People fell in love with her voice. And she had her womanly wiles."

Dinah's busy schedule at the beginning of 1957 kept the couple from being together, at least temporarily. She opened at the Apollo January 11 for a week with Cannonball Adderley's band, a show that featured one innovation—a portable mike that allowed her to move around the stage and engage the audience even more directly. From the Apollo Dinah went to Philadelphia for a return trip to Pep's and then made a quick stop in Detroit to play another of Frank Brown's Monday night shows at the Graystone. This one, on January 28, was the first "Big Show of '57" and featured another bill that crossed back and forth over musical boundary lines: Dinah, Ray Charles, Charlie Ventura, and tenor saxophonist Sil Austin, whose "Slow Walk" was climbing the rhythm and blues charts.

When Dinah and Eddie got together at the end of January, Dinah spoke first: "Let's get married."

She enjoyed embellishing the scene in the retelling. "He told me he wouldn't marry me until I asked him," she insisted. "I waited and then we both laughed. I thought he was joking, but he wasn't . . . so you guessed it, I asked."

"Well, not so strange," Eddie explained. "We'd kind of got together, and she was just the one who first said it."

Neither of them wanted to wait, but Dinah had to fulfill a February 4 commitment in New York, where she had agreed to head a fund drive and sing at a benefit concert for the Powell Community Center at the Abyssinian Baptist Church, whose pastor was the outspoken Reverend Adam Clayton Powell Jr. The fact that she stayed in New York proved to be a help for an ailing Ella Fitzgerald. The jazz star was booked at the Paramount Theatre but suddenly took sick and was rushed to the hospital for emergency surgery. Dinah performed four shows over three days along with Ruth Brown and the Mills Brothers.

These pinch hitters earned generous praise in the music trades for helping the Paramount pull in big crowds despite the missing star. Alluding to some recent public embarrassments by rhythm and blues entertainers, *Billboard* gave Dinah an extra nod for the benefit appearance at Abyssinian, citing her as a "refreshing" example of an R&B performer doing something "to help the community." *Tan* reported that Dinah "raised a lot of loot for the fight against juvenile delinquency."

Dinah and Eddie decided to combine the personal with the professional at Dinah's next job. They would get married in Washington, D.C., at the Casino Royale, a nightclub two blocks east of the White House, where Dinah was booked for a week starting Monday, February 18. Even though little time remained to plan her wedding, Dinah insisted on three things: she wanted her sons to be there, she wanted a real ceremony, and she wanted a new dress. The event was set for 7:00 P.M. Saturday, February 23.

Dinah wanted Bobby Shad and his wife, Molly, to be there, too. The relationship between them was not just musical now. Dinah considered them her friends and vice versa. Molly loved it when Slappy White would drive Dinah out to the house on Long Island to spend the day. They would cook and visit, and sometimes Dinah would sing if she felt like it. There was always plenty of laughter. When Dinah invited Molly to lunch at 145th Street, she also took her to the Apollo, but not before they stopped at the barbershop near the Bowery Bank Building so Dinah could play the numbers.

Though Dinah had been married four times before, she was still a bit nervous on the evening of the 23rd as she put on her wedding outfit, a new pale blue, short-sleeved, V-neck dress with a matching hat that reportedly cost $750. Bobby, so used to keeping Dinah calm in the studio, provided the steady hand to give her away as a local band played the wedding march.

Eddie, dressed in a dark suit and dark tie, waited for her at the makeshift altar with the Reverend Browning J. Peyton of the Goodwill Baptist Church, who officiated. LaRue Manns was the maid of honor, and Molly Shad the matron of honor at Dinah's insistence. Shouldn't one of the family members have that designation? Molly asked. Dinah was insistent, but she chided Molly for wearing a tasteful black dress instead of something more colorful. Slappy was the best man. Though this was Dinah *and* Eddie's wedding, the attendants were from Dinah's orbit, a quiet reminder that he was marrying into her life, not the other way around. (The District of Columbia's marriage license asked about the marital histories of the bride and groom. Perhaps to avoid any difficulties, Dinah answered "none" to the question about previous marriages.)

She carried a white orchid bouquet; her two attendants carried purple orchids. Patti Austin, who came with her family from New York, was the ring bearer.

The simple ceremony didn't take long, and afterward, Dinah and Eddie cut their wedding cake and posed for a few pictures. Dinah's good friend Georgia Mae Scott, who had introduced her to LaRue, was honored with a corsage even though she was not an official member of the wedding party. Dinah's son Bobby, as elegantly dressed as the groom, kept his eyes on the cake, eager for his mother and Eddie to finish the formalities so he could share in the dessert. While he was waiting, Bobby gulped down a glass of champagne, claiming he thought it was water. The drink made him a bit tipsy, and he broke up the wedding guests when he ran around the room giggling.

Eddie gave Dinah a $2,000 mink stole; she gave him a new $600 saxophone. Slappy gave the couple five crisp, new $100 bills. Then it was time for work—the newlyweds had to go on for the late show.

Dinah was now a full-fledged celebrity in black America. Her wedding was big news, the papers and magazines making much of the fact that this was her fifth though only Eddie's second. The Associated Negro Press sent out a story that was picked up in several papers across the country, but Dinah was irritated that the piece got her age wrong: she was thirty-two, not thirty-six. Equally striking was the attention to her size and shape, a continuation of the public conversation she herself had started years ago with all the talk about her diets. The *Washington Afro-American* story was likely the only time the paper began a marriage notice by citing the bride's weight: "A demure Dinah Washington—tipping the scales currently at 140 pounds . . ." The story added that Dinah intended to lose another five pounds within a week.

Dinah was fast with a quip and wasn't above embroidering the facts to make a good story. Several publications reported that after the ceremony she waved four telegrams around, insisting that they were good-natured regrets from her four ex-husbands, who had been invited to the wedding. It made for amusing repartee even if it wasn't true. No one had seen or heard of Walter Buchanan, number four, since he and Dinah split up six years earlier.

Sparring amiably with Eddie, she promised this marriage would be her last.

"But Dinah," Eddie interjected with a smile, "you've said that four other times."

According to the bridegroom, the couple's wedding night was unusual. "When we got back to the hotel room, there was a girl in the bed," Eddie recalled in a published interview thirty years later. "We knew her. I didn't care. Men were attracted to Dinah. Women were attracted to her, too. . . . A girl one night in a club was sticking her tongue out at Dinah and me. She wanted to go home with Dinah. It wasn't anything much. People in show business lived like that."

Eddie did not elaborate, and if his comments suggested that Dinah may have had intimate relationships with women, those liaisons remained hidden from public view and never discussed with or by those closest to her. Farris Kimbrough recalled seeing a woman come out of Dinah and Eddie's hotel room one morning on the road, but, she quickly added, "I didn't see anything, I didn't hear anything." And she asked no questions.

Dorothy Anderson, trumpeter Cat Anderson's wife, shared a bed with Dinah every now and then when Dinah was still with Lionel Hampton and stayed with Dorothy's family when she played Philadelphia. "Have you ever fucked a woman?" Dinah asked Dorothy one night.

"No," Dorothy said sternly. "And you better turn over and go to sleep."

When Dorothy told the story to her sister, Toni, they both decided Dinah was just being provocative, maybe a little curious.

"Dinah liked men," said Ruth Bowen, one of Dinah's closest friends. Dinah and women? "I can't see that. If she had any relationship with any woman, she kept it to herself."

EDDIE AND DINAH planned what Dinah called a "working honeymoon." They left Washington with Slappy for Los Angeles and Dinah's return engagement to Zardi's. The *Sentinel* and the *Eagle* once again welcomed her in print, each noting that she appeared to be even thinner than she was six months earlier, "three dress sizes smaller, but nicely curved." Dinah encouraged the focus on her looks by changing her gowns during the sets, enough so that the *Eagle* could describe a night at Zardi's as part music and part fashion show.

It was not unusual for fans to send Dinah cards and small gifts at the clubs she was playing, so no one paid attention to the pound-and-a-half box of chocolates that showed up at Zardi's March 5, on opening night. The greeting card inside was odd, though: a drawing of a bobtailed lamb and a typewritten note: "My tail is short as you can see, goodbye to you from me." It was signed "Yasha."

Dinah offered the candy to band members and friends back-stage, declining any herself because of her constant dieting. No one wanted any, so Dinah sent the candy home with a Los Angeles friend, Ann Moore, to share with her family. "I was just a little hungry when I got home so I bit into a piece of the candy and got a mouthful of glass," a shaken Moore told Dinah after she returned the box to her. "I opened three other pieces. They all had glass. I was terrified."

Dinah immediately called the police. An Associated Press photographer was on hand when an officer interviewed her, and the picture that went out over the wires was a different Dinah Washington than the one her fans saw onstage. Though she was not very tall, Dinah was a huge presence when she performed. She filled the stage. This Dinah looked understandably concerned and vulnerable. She had a shawl pulled tightly around her shoulders and only her hands were visible. Her right hand clasped the left so firmly that the veins protruded, as though she were hanging on to herself for comfort and strength.

Jack Gordon, the manager of Zardi's, asked Dinah if the candy might have been sent by an old boyfriend out to settle a score. Dinah acknowledged that she had seen two or three men before marrying Eddie, but none of them was known as Yasha.

In size and substance the headlines in the *Eagle* and the *Sentinel* were the kind reserved for serious matters: "DINAH WASHINGTON CHEATS MURDERER" in the *Eagle*, "MISS DEE DODGES DEATH" in the *Sentinel*.

Dinah was determined not to miss a performance, and *Billboard* reviewer Bob Spielman complimented her on the "best 'show must go on' tradition." "It's true the blues did not seem quite as blue as they have sometimes been in the past," he wrote of the first show after the candy incident, "but then it probably was great just to be alive." Even he couldn't resist commenting on Dinah's appearance: "Trimmed down to about one-hundred-fifty pounds, Miss Washington presented a chic appearance. Although perhaps not quite as strong as it used to be," Spielman added, "her voice still remains tops and caught just the right inflections for each song."

A dollop of good news came in the midst of this troubling episode—Dinah's most recent album, *In the Land of Hi-Fi*, was still on the *Down Beat* Jazz Best-Sellers chart, renewed confirmation that she had cemented her foothold with the jazz audience.

Dinah and Eddie made a surprise visit to the Oasis one night, where Slappy was performing. They delighted the audience with an impromptu duet, "The More I See You," and when they finished, Dinah gave Eddie a kiss.

After Zardi's, Dinah, Eddie, the band, and Slappy went up to San Francisco for seventeen days at the Blackhawk. Between sets one night, she talked to *Oakland Tribune* writer Russ Wilson and made the most of the occasion. She already controlled what she sang on-stage and how she sang it. Now she sought to shape how she and her music were received. "I'm not a one-style singer," Dinah said. "Whatever comes from my heart I want to go on and sing: blues, pops, jazz, jump tunes, spirituals. I try to tell what I feel. Every song I sing has a message, and I try to get it across."

Though not quite as critical of rock 'n' roll as some of her fellow entertainers, Dinah didn't think much of the music. "It's based on the blues and on jazz, but Elvis Presley has done something to it. The big audience for it is kids, and when they grow enough to understand what it is, they won't like it," she said. "It'll die out. After a while, even the FBI won't be able to find Elvis Presley."

Metronome had barely paid attention to Dinah in the eleven-plus years since she left Lionel Hampton. But now that she was an established presence with a large and loyal following, they were making up for lost time. The magazine put her on the cover of the April 1957 issue—the picture was from the album *Dinah*. The headline on the front—"Dinah Washington: Queen of the Blues"—and the headline on the story inside—"I'm No Blues Singer"—captured the contradiction between the public perception of Dinah and how she saw herself.

"I sing everything, anything at all. I sing blues, pops, and if I have to I can *go to church*," she said, striking the theme she had in

Oakland. She'd even tried a little classical music and opera. "I like to sing," she explained. "I like to get inside of a tune and make it mean something to the people that listen. Something more than just a set of lyrics and a familiar tune."

Why did so many want to stamp her as only a blues singer? "The critics and people that call me a blues singer hear a sort of blues quality in my singing—so they call me a blues singer. Actually, though, if they really felt what I was doing, here inside, they'd know that there's more to it than just putting a title on me. Getting inside of a tune is so important," Dinah continued, "and when you do, there's a feeling—a strong feeling—that comes out. When you get inside of a tune, the soul in you should come out. You should just be able to step back and let that soul come right out. It should flow out of you. That's what I feel I do. That's what I want and try to do. It seems that if you try to sing the way you know you must, with soul," Dinah added with some irritation, "that people continually call it blues singing.

"You know who my favorite singers are today, really the top two?" she went on. "Frank Sinatra and Nat Cole. They get inside of a tune, and yet no one calls them blues singers. Frank and Nat use words and tunes so wonderfully that they make you know what they mean. They just don't move through a tune mouthing the words, they use the words to tell the way they feel. This is *real* singing. On records Jeri Southern gets this kind of feeling too—she makes me move inside. Della Reese does it, too. That record she's just done, 'If I Could Tell You,' it's the same one that Dick Haymes sang the hell out of sometime back, is wonderful."

When the record came out, Dinah added, "people were pouring quarters into the juke box to hear it. I was, too."

Metronome found its own way to link Dinah's observations and examples. "If you were to look for a common trait among all these people, regardless of their particular styles the answer you invariably come up with is the single word: conviction," the magazine said. "The quality of conviction that Dinah likes in these others is just as applicable to herself. It is an at-homeness, a solidity of feeling and a deep-seated completeness." *Metronome* couldn't resist a bit of carping, though, observing that if "affectations" sometimes "creep into her performances" they "never completely cover the conviction and the indomitable will that projects from her singing."

. . .

WHEN DINAH GOT BACK to Chicago in May, she and the group
were booked into Mister Kelly's, a well-known club on the city's famous Rush Street. Rush had replaced Randolph Street, where
Dinah got her start fifteen years earlier at the Garrick, as the city's
main entertainment venue for white patrons. Though she had
played clubs that catered to whites in New York, San Francisco, New
Orleans, and Los Angeles, this was the first time Dinah, as a star, was
booked in her hometown outside of black Chicago.

Slappy was keenly aware of the different atmosphere.

"Mister Kelly's is kind of a classy spot, you know, sophisticated,"
he explained. "So where I've been used to working, these jobs
where it's like the jazz joints . . . all the jokes I was tellin' were like
called bebop jokes," his shorthand reference to comic stories about
drugs and troubles with wives and girlfriends. He was used to one
laugh after another in the "jazz joints." At Mister Kelly's he came to
a sobering realization halfway through his routine: "I ain't getting
no laughs."

He was so disgusted that he left the club without telling anyone,
went back to his hotel, bought a fifth of whiskey, and drank himself
to sleep. When a friend came to see him between shows, all Dinah
could say was, "I don't know where he is."

Dinah also understood that Mister Kelly's was not Birdland or
even Budland, and she acknowledged that while the money was
good and a certain cachet came with the booking, the audiences had
their drawbacks. "I don't even like to sing for them," she said. "They
come in and talk loud while you're trying to sing and think they've
got the right to get familiar and push you around. . . . I don't like
them because most of them are a bunch of phonies."

Onstage Dinah pushed those thoughts aside and found a way to
connect to patrons, who, after all, paid to see her. "All the big society
people, they got Dinah Washington records," Slappy noted. "They
were still her fans." They wouldn't go to many of the places she
played, but they would turn out in a club like Mister Kelly's. Before
an all-black audience, or even at Birdland or Basin Street, where her
white fans came time after time, Dinah would hear whoops and
hollers of recognition when she sang the first words of her hits. But
the white patrons who came to Mister Kelly's were more restrained.

She could hit that piercing "I don't hurt anymore," "and not a soul would react," Slappy said. "That worked on her mind, too, because she was used to hearing those screams."

It was noteworthy, though not surprising, that Mister Kelly's advertised Dinah's engagement in the *Chicago Sun Times,* one of the mainstream white dailies, but not in the *Defender.*

For five years Dinah had traveled with a trio, picking up horn players only occasionally. Now, because Eddie was a saxophone player, she changed her sound and show for live dates, expanding to six or seven pieces—the rhythm section, Eddie, a baritone sax, a trumpet player or a trombonist, maybe both. Several of the men had gone to Phillips's rival, DuSable. They were well trained, students of the legendary Captain Walter Dyett, head of the DuSable Music Department and a man known for his knowledge, discipline, and faith in the belief that hard work applied to talent would yield success: Charles Davis, baritone sax, Julian Priester, trombone, Richard Evans, bass.

These musicians were five to ten years younger than Dinah and Eddie, but each of them knew her by reputation, and Evans, who took Keter's place, always remembered the first time he saw her with the trio, at Budland in the Pershing Hotel. "She was a cutie-pie. Pleasant, nice brown skin, big eyes—she was dressed to the nines." He could hardly take his eyes off her, and when he did, Evans was looking at Keter, watching how he played for Dinah and *with* her. "I not only marveled at her ability to sing, but I also said, 'Man, if I could swing like that.' "

After a few days behind Dinah, Evans realized he could. "What I didn't know was that she made you swing like that—that wasn't something you came with yourself. If you hear her sing, and you couldn't swing, then you need to give up your horn."

Dinah, Eddie, and the other musicians—now seven people—went to Philadelphia to start a week at Pep's. Dinah liked her musicians to look good. She dressed up to be onstage and wanted them to as well. Krass Brothers department store was not far from the hotel they were all staying at, and she told the men to go down and get fitted for new suits. They started out walking and hadn't gone very far when Dinah and Eddie in her new white Chrysler came by.

"Get in," Dinah told them. She would drive them the rest of the way.

The group proceeded down South Street, one of the main thoroughfares in downtown Philadelphia, on their way to the 900 block where the department store was. They came up behind an older car with paint scratches on the side and two scruffily dressed white men in the front. The car seemed to be stalled. The men got out and walked to the rear as though they were going to get a tire jack or some other piece of equipment from the trunk to fix the problem. Suddenly they turned and headed straight for the Chrysler.

"Police," they yelled. "Open up."

Dinah and the band were flabbergasted. What was going on? Dinah showed them her identification and told them the Chrysler was hers.

"They wanted us up against the wall," said Charles Davis, the baritone player. They told the group they were under arrest.

Under arrest? For what? Dinah demanded.

The plainclothesmen wouldn't give a straight answer, and Dinah insisted that they go immediately to the police station.

Richard Evans, the bass player, was incensed to be asked whether he had ever been arrested or used drugs. "No, I have not," he snapped. "I don't use drugs."

Dinah was fuming. She didn't buy the story the police were telling: they had gotten word that a white car had been stolen.

"Well, when you stopped me and asked me for my license, I gave you my picture and everything on it. You could see it was my car," she told them. "You arrested me because I'm a black woman in a white car."

The band members didn't buy the other story—that they were looking for drugs. "Nobody had any," Davis said. "After Dinah got through insulting them in her famous dialect, the police were totally embarrassed," Davis added.

Dinah and the band were released, and for the moment she put the distasteful episode behind her.

ROBERTS SHOW LOUNGE at 6622 South Parkway in Chicago aspired to be a nightclub in the mold of the DeLisa and the Cotton Club in Harlem. It had a large raised stage, tables with cloths and individual place settings, and a full-fledged revue to go with the headliner. The club was named for owner Herman Roberts, who also operated a hotel across the street, which made him one of the more successful entrepreneurs on the South Side. The club opened in February 1955 and was featured in *Ebony* fifteen months later as one of Chicago's nightlife successes. Count Basie and Louis Jordan and his Tympany Five had performed there, and finally in 1957 Roberts was able to book Dinah for a three-week stint to run from June 12 through July 2.

He and Jimmy Caruth, who had just taken over a small South Side club, got together for some publicity by honoring Dinah at Caruth's place. It had been Ada's, but he renamed it the Comeback Trail. On June 10, Caruth invited Dinah and Eddie to come by so that she could be given an honorary scroll of appreciation. She didn't mind doing these sorts of things; they were mutually beneficial. She kept her name before the public and the club owners could trade on her celebrity. The *Defender* wrote about it and published a picture of Dinah shaking hands with Caruth to announce the event. *Jet* magazine included a picture from the evening in the magazine's June 27 entertainment section showing Dinah and Eddie admiring the scroll with Herman Roberts looking on.

Dinah also agreed to do another benefit performance, this one at the Cook County Jail and the first of what Sheriff Joseph D. Lohman considered "rehabilitative measures" for the 750 inmates. Doing such things was part of the landscape—entertainers often gave of their time to help others when the only payoff was the joy and appreciation of the audience. The Cook County event was no slapdash affair. Popular Chicago disc jockey Sam Evans of WGES hosted the show in the jail's large courtyard, and joining Dinah were the Dells, a singing group still riding the wave of their hit, "Oh, What a Nite," harmonica star Sonny Boy Williamson, and blues guitarist Jimmy Rogers. The performers got a treat of their own, listening to the Cook County Jail band, which was made up of a group of inmates who played under the direction of jail chaplain Rev. James Jones.

Dinah was at home right away at Roberts. It was her kind of place, her kind of audience, and just a few miles from her new Chicago apartment on South Vernon. Working with a portable mike, she moved around the stage and threw in a few dance steps when she felt like it. Her new wardrobe featured dresses with a fitted bodice and full skirt that twirled when she danced. The *Defender*, which captured one sequence in pictures, called it a "Harry Richman strut," referring to the vaudeville star of the 1930s.

Dinah got a kick out of teasing Herman Roberts and thought nothing of going after an audience member either. "I'd be walking across the floor, going to the table or something, and she might right out holler, 'Herman Roberts, you better have my money when I get off a here—oh, yeah, you better have my money,' " Roberts recalled with a laugh. "She wouldn't bite her tongue about nothin'."

Always attentive to her stage appearance, Dinah occasionally wore a wig now and not just a hairpiece attached to her own short cut. The most striking was the blond one, which stood out against her dark skin. "She was the first one . . . nobody would hardly wear a wig. If a woman wore a wig, she wouldn't want nobody to know it—that would mean all her hair was fallin' out," Roberts explained. "But Dinah knew the wig would attract attention." One night a woman in the audience made a remark that Dinah didn't like.

"Listen, bitch, you better get you a wig," she snapped.

Roberts winced. The customer had paid to see a show, not to be insulted. Would she and her party get up and leave? But then, he reminded himself, "They knew Dinah in the first place. Some people," he added, "like to be abused by the stars."

No one could remember who suggested it or why—perhaps it was the giddy feeling that comes at the end of a run. But on her last night at Roberts, Dinah and the other performers decided to change places for part of the night, donning one another's clothes and doing one another's act. Dinah came out for one number and did an impromptu striptease that left her looking like she was ready for the beach—in a halter top and short-shorts and barefoot. Someone took a picture, and two weeks later the photo was in *Jet*.

Roberts was so pleased with Dinah's run that he threw a party for her after the last show and couldn't wait to sign her up for another engagement.

DINAH, EDDIE, AND THE BAND packed up and headed east when the Roberts job was over. On July 23 they settled in for a week at the Club Tijuana on Baltimore's busy Pennsylvania Avenue. The audience for the shows was decidedly more mixed than those that had come to see Dinah at the nearby Comedy Club a couple of years earlier. The Tijuana focused more on jazz and booked white acts along with black jazz performers—Gene Krupa had preceded Dinah. Oscar Pettiford would follow. The booking was also another illustration of Dinah's ability to draw blues, R&B, *and* jazz fans.

Dinah stayed in the jazz mode when she returned to New York. She was invited to be one of the headliners at the city-sponsored "Jazz Under the Stars" program, which ran for two weeks in Central Park. Dinah played the second week along with Kai Winding and his sextet, the Modern Jazz Quartet, Stan Getz, Gerry Mulligan, one of the premier baritone sax men, two well-known drummers, Buddy Rich and Philly Joe Jones, and Billie Holiday. Even if many fans still called her Queen of the Blues, this was as serious jazz company as any performer could want.

Dinah's latest album, *The Swingin' Miss D,* was released early in September. The tunes had been recorded at the end of 1956 in New York with Quincy Jones arranging and conducting an eighteen-piece orchestra that featured some of Dinah's old friends—Clark Terry playing one of the trumpets, Lucky Thompson on saxophone, and Sleepy Anderson back on the piano. Milt Hinton came in to play bass and Jimmy Crawford played drums. The eclectic album featured two Duke Ellington tunes, "Perdido" and "Caravan," and a wistful reading of Quincy's own "You're Crying," which he wrote as an instrumental. Leonard Feather added the lyrics. Dinah had fun with "Makin' Whoopee," which was enjoying a revival after three decades. She sang it crisply and even spoke a couple of lines for added emphasis.

Her live versions of "Is You Is or Is You Ain't My Baby" with Lionel Hampton never failed to grab an audience. She was just twenty when she first sang the tune, and for all its energy, there was a kind of innocence to the presentation. This newer version arranged by Quincy was no less spirited but different in its own way—there were no flute solos in the Hampton arrangement. Quincy joked that since he was eighteen, "I was always writing in the flute." And where Hampton was buoyant, Quincy was edgy. It was also a different Dinah. Her voice had deepened, and the tune was in a lower key. Lines like "a man is a creature that has always been strange—just when you're sure of one you'll find he's gone and made a change" resonated with all that Dinah had packed into the twelve years since she had left Hampton.

The release of *The Swingin' Miss D* coincided with Dinah's return to the Apollo, this time with Eddie's band backing her. Though they didn't do it at every performance, Dinah and Eddie sang "The More I See You." Eddie told her he was more comfortable in the background just playing his saxophone, but the two of them together out front gave the sets a more intimate flavor, even if it was the intimacy of the stage.

Dinah was a fine piano player, though she rarely played in public. But one night the mood struck her, so she sat down at the keyboard and played an instrumental accompanied only by Eddie on the sax. The audience was enraptured.

BEYOND HER LIVE PERFORMANCES Dinah remained a captivating personality to black America. Sixteen months after it featured her talking about "my dream man," *Tan* published another long piece about Dinah in its September issue. The story was titled "I Know I'm No Angel" and the hook was Dinah's supposed reputation as an "Evil Gal." "It was right after I recorded 'Evil Gal Blues' with Lionel Hampton," Dinah said. "I remember a man coming to me after he had heard that record. After we chatted awhile he told me he was surprised to find me a nice person because he said, 'Nobody could sing that song with that much soul unless they were that evil.' I was typed from then on. But don't get me wrong. I know I'm no angel—I know I'm no angel."

The article chronicled some of Dinah's past contretemps—the Ruby Hines incident in St. Louis and flouncing out of Prophet Jones's mansion in Detroit—and reminded readers that she was on her fifth husband with some messy breakups along the way. Dinah conceded that she had had a tough time or two with club owners "I've had to straighten out. This hasn't been an easy life," she added, "and more than once, I've had to tell them I was paid to sing and not to serve their other ideas."

She wasn't bitter, "but I wish people would let me alone. I don't bother anybody, and I'm no different from the rest of the people, and I don't do any more wrong than they do. . . . Once someone asked me if the reason I sang with so much feeling was because I was so unhappy. But I don't think that is so," Dinah went on. "I am happy, very happy, now with my husband, Eddie Chamblee, and because I'm happy, I don't think I have lost any soul, if that's what you want to call it. I think happiness has helped me. But I don't think I've had any more unhappiness than most people . . . there have been good times and bad times and I've met good people to whom I'll always be grateful."

Though she played the upscale Mocambo in Los Angeles and Mister Kelly's in Chicago, Dinah preferred the smaller no-name clubs on the national circuit. "I'm happiest when I'm singing for people who pay $1.25 in hard earned nickels and dimes and quarters tied at the end of a dirty handkerchief because I feel these people want to hear me sing," she said. "These people," she added with emphasis, "I never want to let down, because they appreciate the things I'm singing."

Dinah's observation pointed up one of the contradictions of success: the greater the star, the more removed they became from the fans who loved them most intensely. The fans Dinah described were not likely to turn up at Birdland, the Blackhawk, or even Roberts.

As if to enhance Dinah's comments with a picture, one of the photos accompanying the article portrayed a down-home Dinah bent over an ironing board pressing one of her gowns backstage. Another showed her in the midst of a spirited card game on a makeshift table in the dressing room of a nondescript club. The big picture at the front of the article showed Dinah lounging barefoot in bed in a lace-trimmed nightgown. There was a bit of glamour in the fashion, but for the *Tan* readers it still showed that Dinah was down-to-earth.

Ollie Jones enjoyed his daughter's success. Where she played and what she sang made no difference. "My father is a sweetheart. When I was singing in clubs at fifteen and sixteen, he would take me and bring me home. He has always been for me." Alice, Dinah's mother, was a different matter. Though she continued to accept the fruits of her daughter's work, she was still disapproving. Dinah didn't speak of it often, but when she did, however briefly, the disappointment was evident. "My mother has only seen me perform once," Dinah said. "She's very religious."

Estrellita, Dinah's youngest sister, insisted that even though mother and daughter would "fuss and fight, the love was still there. There is no way in the world Ruth would have left her children with someone she didn't respect," Estrellita added.

The dilemma of work and family that Dinah had spoken of when George and Bobby were toddlers remained, expressed most often in her fantasy of what life offstage could be. "I want to be a mother and a housewife and cook all the dishes for my family that they like," she said. "I don't think that's too much to ask from life."

Right now Dinah presented herself as living as close to that fantasy as her work permitted. She loved the apartment in New York, especially the spacious master bedroom with its own bath. She decorated it with a mixture of the modern and exotic. The furniture was smoke-gray with black trim. Ebony lamps hand-carved in Africa were on each side of the bed. A radio shaped like a telephone—a wedding gift—was at the head of the bed, and a large television was at the foot.

When she was working in New York, Dinah didn't get home until the middle of the night. She generally slept until about 2:00 P.M., "Then I lie around the house, make a few business calls on the telephone, spend time with Bobby and George, cook dinner, take a nap, then it's off to work." She really did cook her own meals, she insisted, and her specialities remained collard greens, macaroni and cheese, and chicken.

Dinah was pleased that George and Bobby had made a good adjustment to living in New York. In addition to LaRue, Dinah had a housekeeper whose name was Esther Epps, whom everyone called Epsy. The boys liked her even though Bobby thought she was "old-fashioned"—but not old-fashioned enough not to play the numbers, which she did every day without fail at one of the neighborhood stores. Epsy was a member of a black Jewish sect and on occasion brought some traditional food with her to the apartment. One day Bobby noticed her eating something that looked like a large cracker, and he badgered her to try a piece. It was matzoh, the unleavened bread for Passover, and he quickly realized it was an acquired taste, made more palatable with a little butter and jam.

Whenever the boys went to the Apollo, George looked for a spare drum set to practice. He had inherited his father's talent—one of the first pictures of him as a toddler was leaning on one of his father's drums—and every now and then the musicians would let him play with them. Bobby always headed for the street out back where some kind of ball game was in process. Even if he was the smallest one, he raced to join in.

The boys got along so well with Eddie that they called him "Pop" and loved watching TV westerns with him, all three sprawled out on the double bed in the master bedroom. Taking their cue from the screen, they challenged him to "put 'em up and fight." "Of all the fathers, he was the most fun," Bobby remembered.

The boys attended PS 90 a few blocks away, and LaRue supervised their daily routine. Bobby often gave LaRue "fits," and he was grateful for the wonderful view out his bedroom window because the preferred punishment for his misdeeds was to be sent to his room. It wasn't so bad when he could gaze down St. Nicholas Avenue and make up stories about playing in the grand Empire State Building.

Every time she looked at her sons, Dinah saw herself. Each had her sparkling eyes and distinctive cheekbones, and it took little prompting for her to pull out a picture from her wallet and show them off. Earlier in the year, Dinah, George, and Bobby had posed for an impromptu publicity shot touting the boys' talent. Just eight and ten, they claimed to want to start their own band to play rock 'n' roll, the music *they* liked. But in a nod to their mother, they would call themselves the Chryslers after Dinah's favorite car model.

It was no secret that Dinah liked to shop, and when she sat for an interview with Elizabeth Oliver, a reporter for the *Baltimore Afro-American*, she wasn't shy about giving the inventory of her own wardrobe: three hundred pairs of shoes—the newest, at $150, were silver mesh with long pointed toes, 150 gowns, and ten fur coats, among them a black diamond full-length mink, a stole, a breath-of-spring mink jacket, a silver blue mink jacket, and a white mink scarf. She also had two Persian lamb coats and one vicuña sports jacket. Her jewelry was custom-designed. Not all of the clothes were in New York. Some she kept in the custom-made closets she installed in the basement of the apartment building on South Vernon in Chicago.

Dinah also told Oliver that she liked to drink only champagne— her favorite was Cordon Rouge, 1949. (She admitted to superstitions, too: "When my left eye jumps, I know something will happen to make me angry. When my right hand itches, I always get

money, and if it's my left, I know I'll get a letter." And she was afraid
of lightning—during a thunderstorm on the road, Dinah would
cower on the floor of the car until it was over.)

Dinah also shopped for Eddie. "He never picks out anything he
wears," she told Oliver. "I do all the shopping from top to bottom
without his being along with me." During one outing for new shirts
the clerk rang up the bill as $69. Dinah pointed out that the total
should be $73.

"If you'd kept your mouth shut, you would have saved yourself
some money," the woman snapped.

"Honey," Dinah retorted, "a few dollars doesn't mean anything
to me. I handle thousands regularly." Seeing the sneer of disbelief
on the clerk's face, Dinah opened up her purse, pulled out a wad of
cash, and let her see $100 and $50 bills riffling through her fingers.
Point made, Dinah, shirts in hand, put the money away, closed her
purse, and walked out.

Eddie seemed content, too. He dismissed the canard that "married show people were almost always on the rocks." He said, "There's
no trouble here; we're a happy family. To us marriage is a sacred
thing. When you have a wife in public life, you have to take a lot. Of
course I draw a line. It's only when someone tries to cross the line do
I get fighting mad. No, we're a happy couple. The only problem is
the outsiders." In their spare time, Eddie said he was teaching Dinah
to play golf, "and she's always loved to cook."

When the *Baltimore Afro-American* published Oliver's interview
with Dinah, the caption under her smiling picture said, "Now a con-
tented housewife."

Dinah's celebrity occasionally spilled over to Eddie's pre-Dinah
life. Even his troubles were defined by her. Earlier in the year Eddie's
former wife, who divorced him in 1952, sought to have him arrested
for failing to pay more than $2,500 in child support for their eight-
year-old daughter. Eddie denied that he owed that much, and his attorney produced money order receipts made out to his former wife
that came close to the alleged amount in arrears. When the *Defender*
wrote about the matter, the headline said: "Dinah's Mate Denies He
Owes Ex-Wife $2,535." "Dinah's Hubby in Court Feud with Ex-
Wife," was how *Jet* described the matter.

. . .

THE *TAN* ARTICLE had given Dinah exposure to black America beyond her live performances and records. On September 29 a large, predominantly white audience saw her via television. For the first time Dinah was among the stars, white and black, who performed in prime time on the *DuPont Show of the Month* on CBS. It was another mark of her stature as an entertainer who had appeal across the racial divide. The September 29 show was one of several in a series, and on this one the English actor Rex Harrison, star of the Broadway hit *My Fair Lady,* was tapped to connect each of the acts to the other. He was cast as a visiting Englishman who took a dim view of American culture. During the ninety-minute show he was introduced to a variety of musical styles to overcome his skepticism. Dinah was the blues, and she sang "Birth of the Blues" in a setting apparently meant to evoke the rural South. She sat in a rocking chair on a small platform with two pillars meant to symbolize a front porch. But she didn't look anything like a country wife tending the house. She wore a low-cut, strapless dress with a short skirt. Women clad in tight knit tops and long sheaths surrounded her, waving palm-shaped fans as she sang. Perhaps meant to suggest New Orleans ladies of the night cooling themselves in the heat of that fabled city, they looked uncomfortably like slaves at the plantation. The setting, the song, Dinah's outfit and theirs seemed television's allusion to the combustible mix of sex and race.

The contrast between Dinah's appearances for the *Showtime at the Apollo* movies three years earlier and the CBS show was striking. She looked tiny sitting in her chair. But if she was much thinner now, she had the same dynamic Dinah Washington voice. Her hands had always been expressive. Now, because she had lost weight, they seemed even more so, and she used them to great effect. When she got to the line, "From a whip-poor-will high on a hill"—she spread her arms and opened her hands as if in explanation for what came next, "they took a blue note." Then she snapped her fingers to accentuate the beat.

Toward the end Dinah used a favorite gimmick, weaving the lyric of one song into another: "This is how the blues began. I hope you understand that I don't hurt anymore."

There were no recorded accounts of what Dinah thought of the *DuPont* production; even if she had objected, she likely had little choice. She could sing her song or bow out. Dinah wasn't shy in expressing her views on the way television worked, however. "Rehearse and rehearse and rehearse over and over until you couldn't care less if you sing or stand on your head," she complained. "Sure the pay is big. But there's three weeks of work in a couple of days of rehearsal. . . . I had to stand on a white line all one day, and then on the day of the show I just had to sit waiting. That's not for me."

THE INCIDENT in Philadelphia with the white policemen still festered. As reported in the September 26 *Jet*, Dinah instructed a lawyer to file suit against the Philadelphia police department for false arrest. She didn't take the action lightly. A calculation always had to be made when black entertainers spoke out about race: Was the benefit—the personal satisfaction of righting a wrong—worth the very real cost of being labeled a troublemaker and then possibly losing work?

A year earlier Nat King Cole had been attacked by three men on the stage of the Birmingham Municipal Auditorium, where he was performing for a white audience. He was criticized by some in the black community for not responding more strongly, in racial terms, but he defended his right to handle the incident in his own way. Since then racial issues had become part of the national debate because of the efforts by Arkansas Governor Orval Faubus to stop nine black teenagers from integrating Central High School in Little Rock. The robust discussion may have prompted Dinah to act, particularly after Louis Armstrong spoke out to criticize what he and civil rights activists felt was the federal government's tepid response to Faubus.

"The way they are treating my people in the South," he said, "the government can go to hell." He called President Dwight D. Eisenhower "two-faced" and said he had "no guts."

Armstrong was the last person expected to speak publicly in such sharp fashion, despite what he may have thought privately. He was known as "the ambassador of goodwill," and his reputation on matters of race, whether deserved or not, was just short of the unflattering Uncle Tom. But Armstrong refused to back down despite persistent questions from reporters: "I said what somebody should have said a long time ago."

When *Jet* asked for comment from well-known blacks, their

mental calculations about the cost of a hasty response were almost as audible as the words themselves. "One has feelings," the contralto Marian Anderson said, "but now is not the time to say something. He [Armstrong] is a great artist. I could say something." Baseball star Jackie Robinson, now a business executive, said Armstrong was correct "in principle . . . I think the government and President Eisenhower have failed miserably in the Arkansas situation. I can't agree with Louis on his 'to hell with the government' statement because this is a wonderful country." Nat Cole acknowledged that "it came as a surprise naturally. Louis usually goes along and doesn't say too much. All of a sudden he just probably felt the pains. We all agree with him morally."

Dinah must have been heartened by the strong support from Joe Glaser, who had represented Armstrong for years: "I'm proud of him. He has demonstrated that he has class and guts, and is a real spokesman for his people."

The national turmoil over Little Rock seemed to have heightened racial awareness in the entertainment world. Norman Granz canceled a "Jazz at the Philharmonic" concert in Dallas in September. Dave Brubeck and his quartet also canceled when the city's promoters refused to desegregate the audiences. Leonard Feather canceled the southern leg of his "Encyclopedia of Jazz" tour in the early fall rather than play for any segregated audiences. And Morris Levy and his partner, Al Wilde, insisted that their "Birdland Stars" tour of 1957 play only desegregated theaters. Promoters were on notice that they would have to forfeit a pre-show bond if the tickets were sold based on the race of the buyers.

The Feld brothers, who operated "The Biggest Show of Stars," reacted differently to the swirling racial pressures. They dropped Paul Anka and the Crickets, their white acts, for a southern swing in the fall. *Amsterdam News* entertainment writer Jesse H. Walker lambasted the Felds *and* the black talent who remained in the show. The promoters had "cleaned up in Canada and other Northern states and didn't even need to take this show south," he wrote. Walker pointedly mentioned how Granz, Feather, and Levy took a stand against segregation.

"But also due their share of criticism," Walker continued, "are the Negro acts who continue to go along with this type of thing when other performers are against it—such topnotch artists as

Fats Domino, LaVern Baker, Clyde McPhatter, Frankie Lymon and Chuck Berry. Especially one of such stature as Fats Domino. When are they going to wake up?"

Walker thought it was unacceptable for black artists to work in any kind of segregated conditions. Reality on the ground, however, was more complicated. A few months earlier, when Frankie Lymon had danced with a young white girl on disc jockey Alan Freed's television show, the program was canceled by virtually every southern station. And Fats Domino had been threatened by police when he played integrated venues in the South.

Nothing that dramatic had happened to Dinah, though she had absorbed the same indignities as every other black performer. Even though the lawsuit against the Philadelphia police went nowhere, she didn't dwell on the matter. And she wasn't traveling the South right now, so segregated audiences and second-class hotels were not on her mind. Dinah was staying put in New York. Three sessions were called for October 1, 2, and 4 to record songs either written by Fats Waller or made famous by him, something of a two-for-one concept. Dinah, an acclaimed interpreter of songs, was paired with a well-known composer and stylist. The final product would reflect glory on both of them.

Bobby Shad was on hand, but this time the arranger-conductor was Ernie Wilkins, who had made a name in music circles arranging for Count Basie's band and the singer Joe Williams. Wilkins had been friends since childhood with trumpeter Clark Terry, who returned for these sessions, and musical ability aside, that made the transition into Dinah's sessions all the easier.

There seemed to be easy camaraderie as Dinah and the band went over the arrangements. Though everyone was casual, the men all in open-necked sport shirts and pants, Dinah was dressed up. On the first day she wore a gray tweed dress with a matching cape and accented it with a darker gray turban on her head. The usual assortment of musicians was on hand, trumpeters, trombone players (five), a half-dozen sax players including Eddie, two piano players, and guitar player Freddie Green, a longtime member of the Count Basie rhythm section. It was noteworthy that two of the musicians were women. Melba Liston played the trombone. Patti Bown was one of the piano players. Dinah was particularly interested in Freddie Green's work. When the group took a break around 4:00 P.M. on the first day, Dinah went over to Green and watched as he picked a few bars on his guitar.

She also wanted to work in Jack Wilson, the piano player she had just hired to go on her live dates. The two met in Atlantic City a few weeks earlier, where Wilson was working with the American Jazz Quartet. Dinah and the band were at the Cotton Club, and she fired the piano player she had been using after he got drunk and couldn't play, according to Wilson. Dinah needed somebody new, and another musician recommended him.

He was enthralled to be at the record session with so many topflight musicians. "Baby, I was so . . . when I walked in the record date I was so knocked off my feet by all these cats I had been reading about all my life and a lot them were my heroes." Though some of the older musicians "had some smoke" and went to a bathroom near the studio to light up, Wilson and a couple of his bandmates were afraid to use the restroom on that floor for fear of getting "a contact high." "We were worried about reading that music," he said, and in fact one of the drummers "messed up and couldn't play his part," Wilson recalled, so a fifteen-minute break was ordered, a new drummer recruited, and the session resumed. "They weren't messing around. When we saw that we had our noses so far into that music you would have thought something was in it."

"The musical standards were just the highest," added Julian Priester, one of the trombone players. "Dinah was impeccable."

Wilson was surprised Dinah didn't play the piano more. Sometimes at rehearsals, if he made a mistake, she would sit down on the piano bench, scoot him over, and play herself. Ernie Wilkins had stopped to see Dinah at the Bowery Building and came into the apartment while Dinah was accompanying herself on "Honeysuckle Rose." "What chord are you playing?" he asked her. "I don't know," she replied, lost in the moment. Later at the studio Wilkins told band members how impressed he was "by the musicality of her arrangement."

In the version eventually recorded, "Honeysuckle Rose" was a duet with Eddie. Where some singers milked the song for all its sexual innuendo, Dinah's reading was for the most part sweet and straightforward, with a few playful moments about honey in the cup.

She sang "Ain't Misbehavin'," one of Waller's best-known tunes, at a languorous pace, emphasizing every word. Her deliberate tempo and Wilkins's arrangement, which used horn flourishes as accents to Dinah's phrasing, made the overall effect more blues than swing.

In the evenings, Dinah, Eddie, and the band were playing in Brooklyn at Town Hill, though one night, according to the *Amsterdam News,* Dinah was under the weather and Billie Holiday came over to sing in her place. The good-hearted gesture prompted a police inquiry because Holiday had been denied a cabaret card, a requirement for singing in New York City clubs. (Hers had been revoked after scrapes with the law over drugs.)

Dinah was in an expansive mood the night David Potter, a writer for the *New York Age,* stopped in between shows to visit with her and Eddie. It had been barely two years since the Empire Room, the main venue at the stylish Waldorf-Astoria hotel on New York's East Side, started booking black talent. Dorothy Dandridge was the first, followed by Lena Horne, Harry Belafonte, and then Sarah Vaughan. The first three entertainers had two important things in common—light skin and sophisticated profiles. Sarah Vaughan was a jazz darling to audiences *Hue* described as "the mink and white tie set." No less talented, Dinah cut an earthier swath through the music world, so it was not surprising that she was not high on the Empire Room's list of potential entertainers. She professed not to care.

"No, I'm not the highest paid female Negro singer," she said with her customary directness, "but I do make more money than the other top three vocalists because I don't play prestige houses like the Empire Room over at the Waldorf-Astoria. You can't eat prestige, you know. I play smaller places and draw bigger crowds, so they tell me."

Dinah had just finished a set when Potter first came backstage, and her face was still moist from singing under the lights. She was wearing a tailored gray dress but she explained that she would be putting on a new outfit, a navy blue cocktail dress, for the later show. Dinah was used to backstage visitors and undid the buttons and snaps of the gray gown in front of Potter. But as a stagehand yelled "five minutes," she rushed past him to a private dressing room to finish getting ready for the next show. When she returned and headed for the stage, Dinah told Potter, "I'm a lucky girl. I'm booked solidly into different clubs for many weeks." She reminded him that her new EmArcy album, *The Swingin' Miss D*, had been well received, and on top of that, Mercury had just released a new album that repackaged some of her earlier blues tunes, *Dinah Washington Sings the Best in Blues*.

DINAH, EDDIE, AND THE BAND returned to Chicago October 16 for a ten-day engagement at Roberts. Chicago club owners always advertised Dinah's engagements in the *Defender*, but the paper rarely wrote separate stories about her shows. This time, though, the *Defender* carried a long piece that was part review and part profile, mentioning, as articles in other cities had, Dinah's new appearance. The headline October 22 trumpeted, "Slimmer Dinah Exciting in New Show at Roberts." The story also commented on the "besequined" sheath gown she wore one evening that was cut "about as devastating as one would have it be."

As usual, Dinah mixed her sets with old material and new songs she had just recorded. Sometimes tunes rejected for an album worked well live. One of them was the frothy Latin number "Boom Boom"—"Can I come over and visit in your front room./Well, when your voice says 'please do,' then again my heart goes boom boom." It had been recorded in March but never released. In a live show, the tune was an upbeat change of pace, and Dinah could do a lot with gestures and well-timed facial expressions to make the song fun. She and Eddie did at least one number together every night to the crowd's delight, and it was usually "The More I See You."

After the Roberts job, Dinah and the group headed back east. The first stop was in Baltimore for another week at the Club Tijuana. From there they were booked to play Pep's in Philadelphia starting Monday, November 18. Dinah was never fond of the Monday matinee requirement. She claimed she told owner Bill Gerson that she had to return to New York because one of her sons was ill. But Gerson claimed he had never been informed, and the way *Variety* reported it, Dinah was expected for the matinee.

When she showed up Tuesday evening ready to go onstage, Gerson told Dinah he was going to cut her salary for the missed performance. Pat Peterson, the representative of the local union representing entertainers, the American Guild of Variety Artists, was on hand, and Gerson gave him the $3,000 Dinah was owed for the week to hold in escrow. Peterson advised Dinah to finish out the engagement.

Dinah would have none of it. The band was onstage ready to go; the house was full, but Dinah came out and told them to leave.

"The joint was packed, and we packed up and left," Jack Wilson recalled. "She wasn't going to work for this cat."

According to *Variety*, AGVA disciplined Dinah two weeks later, reporting that she was "brought up on charges" for failing to complete the booking. The punishment was not disclosed but probably involved some kind of fine beyond the forfeiture of her salary.

Dinah was unfazed by the flap. Back in New York she went into the studio with Bobby Shad and Ernie Wilkins to do another session of Fats Waller material. They had assembled a terrific group of musicians. In addition to Eddie and his regulars, the orchestra included trumpeters Charlie Shavers, who had played with the Dorsey brothers, and Doc Severinsen, who played for TV personality Steve Allen, and saxophonist Benny Golson, from Dizzy Gillespie's group. Mac Ceppos, a violinist with Perry Como's orchestra, booked the strings.

The expansive Waller could be joyful and satiric; if Dinah was less so, she could be saucy even when giving a song a straight-ahead reading. When she slowed the tempos and tossed in a "lord, lord, lord," or a couple of bars of humming, it transformed a tune from a caper to small drama. On "Tain't Nobody's Biz-ness if I Do," Dinah once again tailored the lyrics to make the song more personal. "If Eddie and I fuss and fight all night then tomorrow we wake up and we're all right, well it ain't nobody's business if we do." Dinah ad-libbed another line when she and Eddie sang "The More I See You."

"I know the only one for me can only be you," Eddie sang.

"And you better mean it, baby," Dinah retorted.

(A few days after the session, Eddie was the subject of his own profile in the *Baltimore Afro-American*. The story carried a piquant headline: "Dinah's Last Man.")

It had been several years since Dinah had played Milwaukee, but she was booked for a week starting November 25 at one of the city's premier jazz clubs, the Brass Rail. The *Milwaukee Journal*'s novelty section, "The Green Sheet," welcomed Dinah with her latest publicity picture and an admiring caption that called her "a top flight singer working in nightclubs, television and other mediums."

Dinah packed the Brass Rail with a largely black audience every night, but the owner, who was white, complained privately that he wasn't making any money even though every seat was filled. Unlike the fans of other blacks who had played the club—Earl Bostic came to mind—Dinah's fans didn't buy drinks from the bar, where most of the nightly income came from. Instead they brought their own liquor and slipped into the bathroom to drink.

AN EXTENDED STAY at Roberts allowed Dinah to spend the Christmas holidays in Chicago. Herman Roberts had made improvements in the club, and now it featured a revolving stage to enhance the glittery shows. Some of the band members had left the group in the East, among them the drummer Dinah and Eddie had been using. One of the other musicians, trumpeter Fip Ricard, had recommended James Slaughter, a jazz drummer who had played for other Roberts shows. He knew the music that accompanied the dancers' routines and could play for those numbers as well as Dinah's sets. Slaughter auditioned for Eddie and got the job even though he didn't know any of Dinah's music.

The transition proved easy enough, and before long, Slaughter was as caught up in her music as the other musicians. "I grew quickly to respect her because whatever she had it really came through," he said. "In fact she spoiled a lot of stage singers for me 'cause to me they seemed phony."

Slaughter understood that Dinah was an exacting musician who heard everything. Whether or not she would call out a band member who made a mistake depended on her mood. Slaughter knew that he couldn't get the introduction to one song quite right, but Dinah never chewed him out. One night, when he finally got the beat just so, she simply turned around away from the mike and said, "You finally got it, huh?"

If Dinah would overlook an occasional mistake from the band, she had no patience with an inattentive audience. The crowd could get loud at Roberts, and by now she had different strategies for quieting them down. The most obvious was direct confrontation—stopping the show and singling out the noisy patrons. One evening during the Christmas run she used a different tactic. From his stool behind the drums Slaughter saw Dinah step away from the microphone, still singing, walk slowly to the edge of the stage, and then sit down, her legs swung over the edge. She continued to sing, and because it was hard to hear her without amplification, the audience, table by table, quieted down until everyone was focused on her. The audience properly attentive, she waited for Eddie to help her back up and together they returned to center stage and the microphone.

Mercury had scheduled another session while Dinah and the band were in Chicago, and this one was devoted to the music of Bessie Smith. Dinah had long been mentioned in the same breath as Smith even as she sought to emphasize that she was more than a blues singer. Shad probably suggested the concept, and Dinah did not object. Beyond the different instrumental arrangements, and there was a decidedly Dixieland flavor to these, she would put her own stamp on the songs. The acerbic "Send Me to the 'Lectric Chair" was a confessional about a woman who murders a cheating man and asks no mercy from the judge: "I done killed my man—I want to reap just what I sow."

Smith's was a robust and straightforward telling of the tale; she seemed a supplicant before the court. Dinah turned hers into an ironic conversation with the judge, adjusting the beat and accents to give the tune a saucy feel.

Normally the sessions were roughly three hours. If they went over, the musicians were entitled to overtime pay. On one of the days the session was set for three o'clock, Slaughter remembered, "so Dinah, she was over an hour late getting there—and we were just sitting around having a good time. And she comes in and she says, 'I'm hungry. I want some Chinese food.' So they went out for some Chinese food—whatever she ordered. And around the corner was a liquor store—got her a bottle of Courvoisier. . . . She ate some, drank some, killed some more time, which really meant that we weren't really going to get very much done that day so we had to come back."

Slaughter finally realized what was going on: the band had some downtime before the Roberts engagement, and stretching out the studio time was Dinah's gift, a way to get them some extra money. She didn't worry about the other side of the ledger—that Mercury would charge these expenses against her next album, recouping the additional money before paying her any royalties on the sale.

Though the holiday season was always busy, it was important to make time for charitable endeavors, and Dinah willingly headlined the annual Christmas benefit at the veterans hospital in Hines, which was a few miles west of Chicago. Another of her disc jockey pals, Daddy-O Daylie, emceed the event, and the two of them stayed around after her performance to visit with the veterans.

On the surface life was good. She and Eddie professed to be happy together, the boys were settled in New York, and the rest of the family was taken care of. The couple even posed for *Jet* with one of Dinah's Christmas presents, a negligee that she said cost $250. But private distress no doubt compounded by fatigue caught up with Dinah during the New Year's show at Roberts, and she nearly had to cancel after collapsing at the club. "It took four people to hold me down for the shots necessary to calm my nerves that night," Dinah remembered.

Slaughter knew that despite their sunny appearance onstage she and Eddie were having problems. The audience couldn't hear any of the snappish asides, but the band members could. "They used to have words between each other from time to time," Slaughter said. "You know, man-and-woman problems."

15.

"Ah, I Got You"

1958

Dinah and Eddie stayed in Chicago to start the new year, continuing on for another week at Roberts. For the time being they papered over their differences. The publicity shot that Joe Glaser's Associated Booking put out showed a happy, smiling couple, Dinah even willing to accept billing—at least in the picture— as "The Chamblees—Eddie and Dinah (Washington)." The bandstands for the musicians were a variation on that theme, "Chamblee" written across the top, "Dinah" going down the left side, "Eddie" going down the right. A sketch of a saxophone was in between.

By the time the Roberts run ended the second week in January Dinah was happy enough to engage in what was now an end-of-the-run tradition, adopting an entirely new stage presence for the final act. This time Dinah put on one of the dancer's outfits—a brightly colored swimsuit with a flared skirt attached—kicked off her shoes, and became a shake dancer. She appeared to love every moment, smiling as she wriggled through the routine.

On the tenth of January Dinah and Eddie moved uptown to the

Black Orchid—like Mister Kelly's, another Rush Street club. Though Dinah preferred less formal settings, the booking reflected her continuing ability to capture a predominantly white jazz audience. The *Down Beat* readers poll at the end of 1957 had placed Dinah at the high end of its female singer poll, behind Ella Fitzgerald, Sarah Vaughan, and Billie Holiday but ahead of Lena Horne, Patti Page, and the other Dinah, Dinah Shore.

Not only was the Black Orchid a different kind of audience from Roberts, but it was also a smaller venue. *Variety*'s reviewer had seen Dinah at Roberts, and when he compared the show there to the Black Orchid, he found her wanting. "The sudden switch from bigness to smallness may have something to do with why she failed to ignite the opening crowd," he wrote. "It was clear that she did not have the feeling of the room and her twenty minutes on stage never jelled."

Unlike some of the other *Variety* reviewers, however, this one showed a greater appreciation for Dinah's talent. "Miss Washington's attractive vocal apparatus is distinguished by a sensuous trill, and she has a sharp sense of rhythm, but for some reason she used these pluses to the full on only a couple of occasions." Dinah and Eddie continued to perform their onstage duets, which the reviewer found "moderately charming."

His observations were a reminder nonetheless that even the most experienced entertainers have to adjust from one performance to another. An added but unspoken element was race. Black Orchid patrons were almost all, if not exclusively, white. Had Dinah gone from Roberts to a small black club, the transition would have been easier, the show not that different from the one in the larger venue, and the reviewer would likely have noticed that Dinah seemed more at home.

Dinah's return to Detroit the first week in February put her in that kind of venue, the Frolic Club, which was a few blocks away from the better-known Flame Show Bar on John R Street, one of the city's black entertainment hubs. Like the Flame, the Frolic was run by a white businessman, and on opening night, as was usually the case when Dinah was in town, the show was a sellout. Morris Baker, the owner, smiling at his good fortune, had to go outside to tell waiting fans that he couldn't let any more of them inside. Because the engagement coincided with Dinah and Eddie's first anniversary, they threw a party at the club. (*Michigan Chronicle* columnist Ziggy Johnson dubbed Eddie "King Eddie the 5th," in honor of his place in Dinah's matrimonial pantheon.)

The Detroit guests included personal friends like Bea Buck and disc jockeys Frantic Ernie Durham from WJLB and Marcellus Wilson, who worked out of Flint but had a following in Detroit. Several guests came in from out of town to give the event the same national flavor as some of Dinah's past birthday parties. Ollie Jones, Dinah's father, came from Chicago. Mabel Page, one of her dress designers, arrived from Kansas City with a satchel of new clothes. Though Dinah's wardrobe was large, she wanted new pieces for this event. Page was known for an innovative use of flaps, buttons, and snaps that could make three outfits out of one by moving a piece of fabric this way or that. Dinah had summoned her to Detroit once before, when she was singing at the Flame for her usual crowd of black Detroit fans. "Page, you have to come here," Dinah told her. "They don't believe a black woman did these designs."

Dinah appreciated that Page would not make clothes for any of Dinah's friends. She wanted her look to be unique, even though Page was also making clothes for LaVern Baker and Sarah Vaughan. One of the dresses Dinah wore during the evening was a "sack dress," which was then in fashion. Sleeveless, it billowed out to the knees where the material was gathered into a six-inch border that fit tightly against the legs. *Jet* considered Dinah onstage in that dress its best photo of the week March 13, and gave the picture an amusingly suggestive caption: "Dinah Hits the Sack."

Ruth Bowen, who was now working as Dinah's press agent, came from New York. She was married to Billy Bowen, formerly one of the Ink Spots and nicknamed "Butterball" by Dinah. She and Dinah had met fourteen years earlier, just after the Bowens got married, when the Ink Spots happened to be in Pittsburgh at the same time that Lionel Hampton and his group were in town. Bowen spotted the Hampton bus outside a hotel; he and Ruth stopped for some sausage and grits with the musicians, and then went up to see Dinah in her room.

"I want you to meet my wife," Bowen said as Dinah eyed the petite young woman.

"I heard you robbed the cradle," she joked to Bowen, and then invited Ruth to come over and sit at the edge of the bed. "Come here and let me brush that hair," Dinah told Ruth, who was a bit taken aback but obliged nonetheless.

"Butterball, I like this girl," Dinah said.

"We clicked right away," Ruth recalled, noting that Dinah called her not long after that first meeting and told her, "we must stay in touch." Over the years Ruth taught herself the offstage side of show business, learning some of her craft from Joe Glaser, whom she had gotten to know through her show business connections. "He had a habit of sitting down in his office by himself on a Saturday to sign his mail, and I'd go down and I'd sit with him and just sort of talk to him," Ruth said. "And then one day he decided, 'You're picking my brain. That's why you come down here. You don't come to visit me.' So he gave me a lot of good pointers, and he admired my spunk and everything."

The anniversary evening at the Frolic lasted four hours—starting with a buffet supper and then a performance from Dinah, Eddie, and the band. Rather than sing new numbers, Dinah turned it into a night of nostalgia, running through a bevy of hits. Marcellus Wilson, the disc jockey, presided as master of ceremonies, stopping midway through the evening when a giant anniversary cake was wheeled out. Everyone watched and then applauded as Dinah and Eddie shared the ceremonial first piece. While the rest of the cake was cut, Wilson introduced some of the guests, and a few of them who were entertainers serenaded Dinah and Eddie. When the evening was over, guests were invited to an after-party in the Holiday Room of the Gotham Hotel.

On the surface the evening was lighthearted fun. But the relentless celebration suggested a darker undertone, as if Dinah told herself she had to mark this moment and mark it well because another like it, an anniversary of a marriage, might not come along again.

A few nights after the party, Dinah's mood changed. She came onstage and told the sold-out Frolic crowd she wasn't going to sing. Clearly angry, she said Baker, the owner, owed her $900 from the previous week. She wanted her back pay and to be paid for the current week, too. If anyone wanted to hear her sing anymore, they could find her at the Detroit office of AGVA, the American Guild of Variety Artists.

For his part Baker claimed that Dinah had failed to live up to the terms of their deal.

Dinah hired a local attorney to prepare a formal lawsuit, but the matter was settled after Baker deposited $2,000 with AGVA, which guaranteed her salary.

DINAH, EDDIE, AND THE BAND played two shows in Atlanta at the Magnolia Ballroom April 3, headlining a bill that also featured Huey Smith and his Clowns. Smith's music was flavored with New Orleans rhythms, and he and his band had scored a hit a few months earlier with "Rockin' Pneumonia and the Boogie Woogie Flu." As Eddie and Farris Kimbrough, Dinah's stepsister, who was now traveling with her, remembered it, Dinah wanted to go back to New York before starting an engagement in Florida on April 7. So the band went on and the three of them went to New York for a brief stay before driving straight through to Miami to start the new job, which was at the Palms in nearby Hallandale.

In the past year, a few hotels here and there had eased their prohibition against black guests, spurred in part by Harry Belafonte, who had threatened a lawsuit when he was denied a room at Baltimore's Stafford Hotel. Finally the city's hotel owners agreed to admit black guests, albeit in limited numbers. The first were baseball players from the American League teams in town to play the Orioles.

The major cities still had hotels that catered to blacks, and in Miami the most upscale was the Sir John. Along with its spacious rooms, the hotel had a formal patio, a swimming pool, and a lounge that served as an after-hours gathering place for the musicians who played in the area. It advertised itself in black newspapers as "the resort of stars . . . the most luxurious hotel in America where everyone is welcome." Sir John manager Bud Ward was an enterprising young businessman who was the first black graduate of Cornell University's School of Hotel Management. He knew his Sir John clientele and took pains to make all of the entertainers comfortable. He got to know who wanted what in his or her room and what their habits were. As important as anything was keeping control of the lounge, where the musicians liked to jam when they got back from their clubs. Other guests and local residents knew that there would be wonderful music after hours, and Ward needed a way to keep order. The place was supposed to close at 2:00 A.M., so he adopted a rule: whoever was in the Sir John lounge by that time could stay. Then he would lock the door and draw the curtains.

"The next time the doors got opened, the sun was shining," he explained. "The entertainers liked that. They loved that. They did all kinds of things in there. They like to do what they don't do onstage or sing what they don't sing onstage or play whatever instrument other than what they play onstage."

Ward had known Dinah when he managed the Booker, a smaller hotel in the area where she had stayed a few times. He found her delightful, kindhearted, and generous. The only time they even mildly clashed was over the handling of her money. Entertainers often deposited their cash with the hotel for safekeeping. Dinah dispensed gifts here and there and didn't like to be bothered with paperwork when withdrawing $25 or $50.

"Miss Washington, you're going to have sign this receipt," Ward would tell her.

"Just give 'em the money," Dinah replied, waving him off.

"No, no, no, no," Ward politely insisted. "You have to sign the receipt."

Ward was also used to taking care of her jewelry. "She had some that looked damn good," he recalled, not always sure what was real and what were high-end costume pieces.

Dinah cursed when she felt like it, sometimes out of anger, sometimes for effect, especially when she knew it made the listener uncomfortable. That only encouraged her, and Ward was an easy target.

"You don't like the way I talk, do you?" she teased.

"No, ma'am," he admitted.

"You're one of those educated niggers."

"Yes, ma'am," Ward replied.

While it was true that he blushed when Dinah swore, Ward knew it wasn't aimed at him. "We got along very well. . . . She covered a lot of inferiority complexes with gross language. It's a tactic I have used myself some time—go into a meeting with a white person, you just want to know up front—what do you think about black people. . . . So it kind of puts them on the defensive right away. She would kind of do those things. Any moment she is going to bust out with all this foul language—I think it was mostly to cover up."

Her high school friend Vera Hamb had thought the same when the teenage Ruth used profanity to negotiate the tricky social scene at Wendell Phillips. And Toni Thompson, Dinah's friend in Philadelphia, saw one person in private, kind and funny, and the rougher version in front of Lionel Hampton's band members.

Ward cherished a compliment Dinah gave him one day at the hotel.

"You're the only one who makes sense around here," she said.

"Well, we try."

One of Dinah's friends threw an impromptu party for her at the Sir John lounge before the official opening at the Palms. Though she was the guest of honor, Dinah ended up singing, "and the whole place just rocked," according to the *Miami Times*, the city's black newspaper.

Farris, Dinah's stepsister, had been traveling with Dinah since the fall of 1957. She had graduated from high school the previous year and jumped at the chance to come to New York to help out at the apartment on 145th Street and then go on the road. She had done a few short trips with the group but this one to Miami was the longest. Farris was a budding clothes designer—Clarissa had been the guinea pig in high school—and Farris's interests made her especially careful with Dinah's wardrobe. No one had ever taken such good care of the clothes, right down to scrubbing Dinah's black lace Lily of France bras with a fingernail brush after each wearing.

"I used to meet her at the stage door or in the dressing room—most of the time by the time she got to the dressing room she had her dress unzipped—and put on something else to go out and mingle," Farris explained. That way it was easier to keep her clothes clean. "Her clothes were never put away dirty," Farris added, "and her shoes were never put away dirty."

Dinah loved Farris, but she could be thoughtless in the way she expressed her affection and sometimes couldn't keep herself from stepping into other people's lives. She could be shockingly crude, too. Farris had not been feeling well before they left for the Florida trip and told Dinah she had been having dizzy spells. Concerned, Dinah took her to her doctor for some tests. The doctor called back, and, Farris recalled, gave Dinah an unusual diagnosis: "This girl just needs to be married."

"You mean I spend money to send her to you, and all she needs to do is fuck?" Dinah blurted.

Without consulting Farris, Dinah was determined to get her a man, and said so right in front of her. The singer Austin Cromer happened to be there. Featured with Dizzy Gillespie's band, he had turned "Somewhere Over the Rainbow" into his signature song. "There's a whole band here," Dinah told Cromer, "and I don't understand it—Farris ain't sleepin' with none of them. Austin, why don't you?"

Cromer demurred. Farris was so mortified she didn't know which way to turn. But it only got worse. Dinah saw King Coleman, a disc jockey at Miami's WMBM who was going to emcee the show at the Palms.

"Listen," Dinah told him. "That's my sister. I'm introducing you to her—she hasn't had any sex in over a year. I want you to do it."

"I wanted to crawl under a chair," Farris said. "I could have crawled under the floor." But before she could move, Coleman came over, put his hands on her face, and pronounced her "kind of cute." He made a date to pick her up in his baby-blue Cadillac after the show.

Farris and Coleman in fact had a few dates, but after the first one, Dinah jumped in again, having second thoughts about her matchmaking. She wouldn't let the two of them be alone. When Coleman came to get Farris to go for a ride, Dinah got in the car with them. If Farris tried to say no to Dinah, it did no good.

The first few performances at the Palms had gone wonderfully well. The house was full and the audience enthusiastic. But things were tense again between Dinah and Eddie. The problems started early in the new year, when Dinah complained about Eddie's musicianship. "Night after night he would deliberately play my music bad and just do silly things to upset me and distract me while singing," she said. "It made me a nervous wreck because I am awfully sensitive about my singing, and when I am not doing my best I become irritated."

Farris thought the problems might have something to do with Eddie's drinking—sometimes a fifth of gin a day. She was used to his routine in New York: he came out of the master bedroom after he got up, naked but holding a newspaper strategically in front of him, walked down the hallway to the dining area, poured himself a drink, shifted the newspaper to his backside, and then went back into the bedroom. The drinking left an indelible impression on Bobby, not because he saw Eddie drunk but because of Eddie's favorite brand, Gordon's. The bottle had a distinctive boar's head on the label that piqued Bobby's imagination.

Julian Priester, the trombone player, also thought something was amiss between the couple because Dinah started to pay attention to him "in sort of a romantic way. I was uncomfortable," Priester said. Dinah knew he was married but said she didn't care. When Priester told his wife what happened, "she got on the next plane" to join him.

On April 10 the first set went as smoothly as the previous days' shows had gone. Dinah and the band received hearty applause for each number. By the time the second set was under way, Eddie seemed out of sorts. He had left the stage a couple of times in the middle of the numbers, and when he was onstage, he turned his back to the audience and to Dinah. During one song, he went offstage again, and when he returned he didn't pick up his saxophone. He just stood there, hands jammed in his pockets, a cigarette dangling from his mouth. Dinah was irked.

When a member of the audience requested a favorite song, Dinah said she would like to oblige but was not getting cooperation from Eddie. "This same thing happens from coast to coast," she declared, her voice rising with anger. "I'm getting sick and tired of that man always embarrassing me and trying to hurt my living. I won't stand for it."

The crowd applauded, but that was not the end of it. She picked up Eddie's saxophone and smashed it to the floor.

Aghast at the spectacle, King Coleman tried to make peace, but Jack Wilson, who was playing the piano, got up and hollered that Coleman had no business interfering with a man and his wife. He stormed over to Coleman, fists raised, ready for a fight. The police were called and arrived in time to separate the men. One of the cops told Coleman to get Dinah out of the club and take her back to the Sir John.

Jody Williams, a guitar player from Chicago who was performing nearby with Memphis Slim, had come into the Palms to catch the second show. He couldn't believe what he had seen and heard. "She was cussin' him out," he said, "talkin' about him like a dog."

When Dinah returned to their room, she called Ruth Bowen in New York.

"I just wrapped Eddie's saxophone around his head," she said.

"Calm down and call me in the morning," Ruth said, not sure what had happened and wondering if Dinah was exaggerating.

Farris had come back to the room, too, and Dinah told her not to let Eddie in. Dinah hustled out the back door of the suite as Eddie banged on the front door demanding to see her. Farris told him she wasn't there, which was true. She told Eddie she couldn't get the door open, which was not true. As Dinah instructed, she was determined not to let him in, determined not to disobey her stepsister.

By late morning, the fracas was over, and Eddie was on his way out of town. He took time, though, to give his version of the breakup to *Miami Times* columnist Dave Bondu, known in the paper as Mr. Swing. "It started when Dinah was calling out her number to the piano player and when I told her to tell me what the tune was going to be, she just ignored me," Eddie said. "Now I'm the band leader, and I have the right to know what the next song is going to be. That's when the argument started. If King Coleman didn't butt in, this thing would never had started. I told him that I was talking to my wife."

When the cops came, Eddie went on, one of them "told me to keep my mouth shut or he'd knock my choppers out after we got outside. I tried to get my car started and found that somebody had pulled the distributor cap." He said the police told him and the other band members they'd give them a ride back to the hotel. "Yeah, man," Eddie said. "My wife tried to have me done in, but that's all right. I'm cuttin' out for Chicago." He added that he had to borrow train fare from Dinah to leave town.

Rumors flew the next day, picked up by out-of-town newspapers, that Eddie had chased Dinah around the Sir John in her underwear. Eddie told Bondu that was absolutely not true. Farris concurred.

In the first day post-Eddie, Dinah called LaRue in New York and told her to get his clothes out of the closet. Even though she knew that George and Bobby had formed a bond with Eddie, she did not tell them directly that he was not coming back. Dinah either didn't think about the effect of the breakup on the boys or perhaps she assumed the impact would be minimal because their daily routine would not be disrupted, and while that may have been true, Eddie's absence meant there would be no more watching television with Pop, no more playing cowboys with him on the big bed.

Dinah asked her father to come to Miami, and the next night she introduced Ollie to the Palms audience as the man, the *Miami Times* said, who arrived "pronto to 'save his baby' from further humiliation."

Dinah and Eddie's breakup mirrored the marriage—a spur-of-the-moment explosion of emotion and, on Dinah's side at least, little apparent thought for the consequences. The soap-opera quality of Dinah's personal life lent itself to catchy newspaper headlines and dishy stories. "Dinah Dumps Her Fifth Husband," said the *Amsterdam News*. The *Jet* headline boiled the brouhaha down to a few words: "Dinah Washington Fights, Fires Hubby in Miami." "Five Down for the Queen" was the *Michigan Chronicle*'s take.

Dinah called her friends in the press, telling them that she wanted to set the record straight before the gossip got out of hand. She wanted to control the story if she could, but Ruth Bowen worried about these impromptu chats. She reminded Dinah, even though she knew it did little good, to watch her tongue lest she go too far and slander someone. Dinah reiterated her complaints about Eddie's playing and behavior onstage. "After I see my darling boys," she told the *Chicago Defender*, "I'll decide what I am going to do. Perhaps I may wait until school is out and take my boys on a nice trip to South America."

The plan was appealing, but Dinah probably knew as soon as she said it that a trip like that was next to impossible because of commitments she had already made to perform and record.

For his part, Eddie swung between remorse and matter-of-factness. He blamed his behavior the night of the blowup on fatigue. "I was just exhausted," he recalled years later, remembering the twenty-four-hour drive from New York down to the Palms, "and I just walked off. If I'd waited just two more minutes it never would have happened." Yet Eddie admitted that in the fourteen months he was married to Dinah, he had never given up his own apartment in New York. "That was one of my little shenanigans." He didn't elaborate on whether he had a girlfriend or two, or whether the apartment was a safety valve and a sign that he was skeptical from the beginning about the marriage.

Paul West had replaced Richard Evans on bass early in the year. Dinah had heard him play when he was with Dizzy Gillespie and the two were on the same bill. Even before he started to play for Dinah, West was impressed with the way she held an audience. He thought it was because of "her sincerity, her believability." He felt it every night he was onstage with her, and was moved to tears the first time he heard her sing "I Thought About You. " 'I took a trip on a train . . .' I don't know what it is about that song," West said, "but it moved me so. And she turned around, and she saw me. 'Ah, I got you,' " she said. "The next three or four times it affected me the same way," West continued. "She turned around and said, 'I got you again.' "

A day or so after Eddie left, West was heading to his hotel room when the show was over, and Dinah saw him. She wanted to talk. "She breaks down," West recalled, "comes in my arms like a little girl—'Paul, I'm so alone.' " West wondered for a moment if this was a come-on, but he decided she was sincere. "I found out she is a very lonesome person, afraid to be alone, almost like a little country girl, a little girl caught in a storm, can't find shelter. That's when I realized how vulnerable she was, as opposed to this image she presents onstage, an image offering her protection."

Dinah didn't show that side very often, even to family and her closest friends. What they saw was the Queen, even if the crown was occasionally askew. She finished the Palms engagement, found another saxophone player, and headed to Jacksonville, where she was booked for a "Barn Dance" benefit for the local union of cabdrivers. The promoter was unable to keep up with Dinah's offstage life, so the billing still advertised her with the Eddie Chamblee Orchestra.

Like Miami, Jacksonville afforded successful black performers decent accommodations—spacious individual cabins behind a popular venue that until a few months earlier was known as the Two Spot. The only drawback to the club and the cabins was the city's water supply. When Keter had come with Dinah a few years earlier, he was sure the bartender had given him bad scotch. Only later, when he was brushing his teeth, did he realize it was Jacksonville's sulfuric water.

When the original Two Spot owner, a successful black entrepreneur, died late in 1957, Ben Bart, Dinah's old booking agent, and a partner bought the club and renamed it the Palms. It was one of the city's largest venues, holding two thousand on the dance floor and another one thousand in a horseshoe mezzanine.

Among Dinah's good friends in Jacksonville was Dr. Warren Schell, a prominent surgeon who would later become the first black doctor permitted to practice at one of the city's white hospitals. Schell and his wife, Venoria, loved music. Their large Spanish-style home on Jefferson Street, the best address in black Jacksonville, became the site of nightly jams for local musicians and the stars who came through town. Dinah was introduced to the couple by Teddy Washington, a trumpeter who played in local clubs before joining James Brown. "They fell in love with her," Washington said, and told her she had a standing invitation to come by whenever she was in Jacksonville.

"The Queen is here," Dinah announced every time she arrived at the house.

On this trip she took Farris and another young woman who did her nails over to see the Schells. While the two of them and some of the Schells' friends were chatting in the backyard, Dinah grabbed a camera and took an impromptu photo of the group. She was so cheerful and smiling during the outing that no one would have guessed she had just separated from her husband. Teddy Washington wasn't surprised. He and Dinah had had a fling a few years earlier when she came through Jacksonville and had parted amicably. "This was an outgoing lady," he explained, accepting the way Dinah presented herself in public. "Life is just a bowl of cherries. . . . You know how the Queen can be."

HUE MAGAZINE gave Dinah some publicity in its April issue, having nothing to do with her marital troubles. She was included in a three-page feature—"Will Women Rule Jazz?"—that also mentioned Ella Fitzgerald, Sarah Vaughan, Carmen McRae, and Billie Holiday. The magazine used an old picture of Dinah standing next to Duke Ellington, who was at the piano. The caption called her "a jazz world giant."

Farris chuckled when she saw the picture because she remembered the dress Dinah was wearing when it was taken, a white off-the-shoulder gown with fringe at the sleeves, from one of Dinah's heavier periods. She had since given the dress to her mother. One of Dinah's trips back to Chicago with Farris coincided with a rummage sale Alice Jones was having at the house, and there was the dress on a makeshift rack in the yard in front of 1518 South Trumbull.

Dinah was annoyed. "I send her enough money to take care of everything," she told Farris. "She has no business having a rummage sale."

When she returned for a week at the Apollo May 16, Dinah was backed by saxophonist Willis Jackson and his quartet. She mixed genres in each set, singing a few straight blues, tunes that veered toward rock 'n' roll, and ballads. One night Dinah made a particularly dramatic entrance. Comedian Nipsey Russell, her friend who was an Apollo regular, had just bought a new Vespa motor scooter. He had taken Dinah for a spin behind the theater, outfitting her with the same kind of goggles he wore. Later, he took the Vespa inside and drove Dinah right onstage, dropping her off at the microphone.

Dinah treated the Apollo like a second home; she was relaxed when she played there and turned her dressing room, when she was in the mood, into her personal salon. One day during the engagement, she invited *Amsterdam News* reporter George Barner for a visit while she was getting a massage, interrupting their conversation with an occasional groan when a particularly sensitive spot was touched. "I hate men," she declared. "I was married to the first one for three months. I don't know what was wrong; he was a mechanic and didn't want me to sing. He wanted me to stay home and cook. Hell, I got married to keep from cooking.

"The others," Dinah went on, "more or less followed suit. We had our good times, but something or other would come up lacking and that would be that."

Though not yet divorced from Eddie, she was asked if she would marry again. "Who knows?" Dinah said, eager to change the subject and not interested in discussing whether her own choices or her behavior might have contributed to all the breakups. She wanted to talk about music, specifically singers who move from popular genres to religion with "a flourish of publicity." "A bunch of 'em are just shuckin' and jivin'," she said, smiling as she delivered the jab. "But for those who are sincere, it's good. I think it's swell. . . . I acknowledge a debt to Bessie Smith," she went on. "I like her for the same reason I go for Frank Sinatra and Ray Charles. They've got soul, baby. If you've got soul, you've got everything."

She got up and went to the turntable in her dressing room and played four recordings, pairing Bessie Smith's "Trombone Butter" and "Send Me to the 'Lectric Chair" with her own versions. "I just love blues," Dinah said, putting on a Ray Charles record as her last selection for Barner. She also wanted to talk about clothes and showed Barner the twenty-five gowns and thirty pairs of shoes she had brought down to the Apollo from 145th Street. Barner described them to readers as "chemises and flapper styles."

When he asked her whether she considered Chicago home, Dinah joked that she was from Tuscaloosa, "but I don't know nothin' about it. I just learned how to spell it recently."

Although LaRue had primary responsibility for George and Bobby, when Farris was back in New York with Dinah, she helped out. One of Farris's favorite times was Sunday, when she and the boys would get up in time to go to the 11:00 A.M. service at Abyssinian Baptist. Afterward, they would have lunch at Jennie Lou's, a favorite restaurant nearby on Seventh Avenue, and take the subway to 42nd Street for a movie and pizza. By the time they got back up to the Bowery Building in the late afternoon, Dinah would be up.

The boys came to the Apollo whenever they wanted, and every now and then Bobby, who was the more mischievous of the two, had to be tracked down and picked up because he was running up and down the aisles when he wasn't out back playing ball.

Ray Charles was booked at the theater right after Dinah. He called the apartment one day, hoping to charm her into making him some of those southern dishes he'd heard so much about. Dinah was just getting ready to leave for a business appointment, she explained. "But my sister is here. She can cook as well as I can."

Ray seemed satisfied, and Farris got right to work. She made collard greens, candied sweet potatoes, macaroni and cheese, and cornbread, and Charles arranged to have it sent over to the Apollo. Dinah planned to stop by the theater later, and Farris eagerly awaited her return to find out how everything went.

"Did he like it?" she wanted to know.

Oh, yes, Dinah told her. "He was eatin' and rockin' just like at the piano."

"I never got a chance to meet him," Farris recalled later. "But he was eating my cooking."

Like most of the other black stars, Dinah rarely spoke publicly about racial matters, but when asked to perform at events intended to help a cause or a group working to improve conditions for black Americans, she did so. She made a quick trip to Chicago May 31 to sing at a special midnight benefit on the West Side for the Negro Labor Relations League. The theme of the show was "the crusade for freedom."

An upcoming television performance by Mahalia Jackson was a reminder about the progress already made and the distance yet to go. While Dinah was in Chicago, Jackson was getting ready to appear on Dinah Shore's evening show on NBC. She would be the first black entertainer to perform on the popular program. Earlier in the year Jackson had pointedly noted the lack of black faces on television as a whole. "If folks on the moon came down here and looked at television, they wouldn't even know Negroes are on earth," she said.

The *Chicago Defender* reported that Jackson's booking was partly the result of pressure from Chevrolet, Dinah Shore's sponsor, on the network. Although other programs, notably those hosted by Steve Allen and Ed Sullivan, had featured black performers, Shore's had not, and the *Defender* was in the forefront of newspapers pushing for change. "Frankly it is hard to imagine Chevrolet motors sponsoring a program that offered no employment to the Negroes at a time when so many sponsors and stars are trying to do at least something in television for Sepians," said one *Defender* article. "Certainly most any salesman for the Chevy could tell the 'brass' that countless thousands of Negroes own or are 'promising to pay' for one of their cars."

No one directly blamed Shore for the absence of black talent on her show. She had already taken a stand on another racial matter, omitting the word "darky" whenever she sang Stephen Foster's "My Old Kentucky Home." Representative Frank Chelf, a Democrat of Kentucky, objected to Shore's alteration and told her to sing it the way Foster wrote it or not at all. Shore refused.

In June Dinah went out on the road again with musicians who had been part of Eddie's band: James Slaughter on drums, Charles Davis on baritone sax, Jack Wilson on piano, and Paul West on bass.

Their itinerary took them to Oklahoma, south to Houston, and then to Mississippi.

The jobs in Houston were spread over four days, June 14–18. Dinah played three evenings at the Eldorado Ballroom and then did another performance at Sylvan Beach on the 18th. The *Houston Informer*, which covered the black community, welcomed Dinah with two stories. One of them slightly exaggerated her real estate holdings, referring to the ten-room house at 1518 South Trumbull as "a 15-room house." The article also included a new version of Dinah's domestic dreams: "The singing star's real ambition is 'to buy that hotel in Chicago some day and settle down.' "

Dinah, the band, and Farris, who was also along, went from Houston straight to Laurel, Mississippi. "The gig was in an old corrugated steel barn," Wilson remembered, "and the piano strings were sticking out of the piano." The club owner also owned a small hotel, the only place blacks could stay, but there was only one room. The men said Dinah should use it. "We decided to go to the gig, unload the instruments, and try to find a place to wash up," Wilson said. "It was hot and sticky, and we had to put on these white shirts and clean suits over all this grime."

Dinah didn't want to stay in Laurel any longer than necessary. "We checked into the hotel, took a bath, and went to the club," Farris said. Dinah instructed her to go back to the hotel before the show ended and pack up the few things that had been unpacked to get ready. "When I get off and I get paid," Dinah told her, "I'm not sleepin' in this town. I'm gettin' out." She may have been the Queen, but in Mississippi, skin color trumped musical royalty.

The job in Biloxi was memorable to Paul West, the bass player, because it was the first time he had met the popular black singer Al Hibbler. He was playing just down the street from the club Dinah was at and came by to visit. The performers had a small room behind the stage where they could stay between shows. White patrons or fans could come back to visit if they wished, but the performers were not permitted to go out and fraternize with the customers, nor could they go to the bar and get a drink. A couple of days into the engagement, Dinah had had enough. Hibbler and some white guests happened to be visiting backstage. "I'm going to buy you a drink at the bar," Dinah told Hibbler. So the two of them and the white patrons walked out of the back room toward the bar. One of the managers came over and stopped them.

"Dinah, come on. You know better than that. Go back to the room or I'll call the police."

Not in the mood for confrontation, Dinah relented.

"That was normal, commonplace procedure," West said of the incident. "You can think about it beforehand or contemplate it after, express disgust. But while's you're in that situation, it's just a normal everyday function. You don't look to analyze."

Wilson, though, remembered a time when Dinah was bolder, albeit in the North. A policeman, obviously drunk, harassed the band members as they were loading instruments after a show. "One thing led to another and he arrested everybody in the band. Dinah came down and bailed us out and cursed the whole police force out."

Slaughter, the drummer, and Davis, the saxophonist, were looking forward to the next job, back in New York at Birdland. When they went to the Bowery Building on 145th Street for what they thought was rehearsal, the doorman stopped them. Dinah had sent instructions: They were not allowed up to the apartment. She had fired them, though they didn't know why, and she never said.

Slaughter took a philosophical view of his change in status. "There are certain things in the music business that I have always accepted," he said. "One of them being when you go on a job you're going to leave it at some point. If you're fired, man, you don't have any control over that." He had enjoyed the seven months with Dinah and the camaraderie of the band. "We were very tight from the beginning. We were like brothers." Dinah was generous with the car, and someone always had her gas credit card so the men could take a little side trip when they wanted. Things were easy with Dinah, too. Sometimes the band would be back in one of the rooms at the hotel, "and there would be a knock on the door, and it would be Dinah," Slaughter said. "She would come in, sit down and just hang out with us for a couple of hours or so."

DINAH WAS EAGER to get to Birdland. "I'm going to give the Broadway and Harlem scribes something to write home about, I don't mean maybe," she declared to one reporter. Part of her enthusiasm likely stemmed from two album releases within a month of each other, first *Dinah Sings Fats Waller* and then *Dinah Sings Bessie Smith*. (Bessie Smith tributes were in vogue. At the same time Dinah's record came out, Atlantic released an album of LaVern Baker doing Smith's tunes, and RCA put out a collection with vocals by Ronnie Gilbert, a white folk singer. Both followed the reissue of Smith's music on LP, which made many of her songs available for the first time in this format.)

According to the *Defender*, Dinah planned a new look to go along with the new music. "The Queen of the Blues has two dressmakers busy night and day on her new wardrobe, and plus that she has ordered ten new sack creations from Wilma's, famous Broadway designer," where she had shopped before. To go along with the new dresses Dinah reportedly bought "fifteen pairs of shoes from her bootery and some extra accessories."

Though Dinah's penchant for talking about her wardrobe might look like bragging, she didn't care. She had worked hard to be able to afford nice things, and talking about the new clothes was almost as much fun as buying them. And Dinah didn't buy only for herself. Her sisters still went to school in cashmere sweaters and shoes from Joseph's, the fancy Chicago shoe salon. Her sons played in $75 sweaters, and when they dressed up, they wore cuff links with tiny diamonds and sapphires and custom-fit overcoats.

"Honey, you're ruining the boys," LaRue would tell Dinah.

"Well," she always replied, "I want them to look like Dinah Washington's kids, not the average kids."

Dinah returned to the Newport Jazz Festival in July, scheduled to sing Sunday, July 6, along with Anita O'Day, the white jazz singer. Portions of their performances would be broadcast live on CBS radio, which was beaming an hour-long show from the festival every night. Because she was in the middle of a Birdland engagement, Dinah chartered a plane to take her to the Rhode Island festival so that she could fly back in time to sing the late night show in New York.

Beyond the music making, these festivals offered the entertainers a chance to see one another in a relaxed atmosphere and a beautiful setting. "This festival is better than Jesus Christ," O'Day told one friend backstage. Dinah was reunited with Max Roach and Wynton Kelly, the piano player she loved so much. Jimmy Cobb was also there but playing with Miles Davis. Dinah and Davis chatted a few minutes before their sets, and at one point, Davis laughed so hard at something that was said—perhaps one of Dinah's new jokes—that he had to bury his head on her shoulder for support.

Dinah had dressed up for the occasion. She wrapped herself in a cerulean mink stole, wore elbow-length gloves, and carried a purse with beaded trim. The crocheted hat on her head was apparently intended to keep her hair in place until it was time to sing. Big tents had been set up as dressing rooms, and Dinah was sitting down in one of them when she noticed a young man walking toward her whom she had not met before. He introduced himself.

"Miss Washington, I'm Jack Tracy, and I'm going to be your new A&R man at Mercury." Tracy had been the editor of *Down Beat* for nine years. A month or so before the festival, Mercury vice president Art Talmadge told him that Bobby Shad was moving into the pop area, and the label had to decide how to run the jazz and R&B division. Tracy wrote Talmadge a memo with his thoughts. Talmadge read it, liked Tracy's ideas, and offered him the job. Tracy accepted and was immediately sent to Newport to supervise the recording of all the Mercury artists who were on the bill, among them Dinah, Roach, and Terry Gibbs, the vibraharp star.

Dinah could sense that Tracy was uneasy.

"Are you scared of me?" she asked, aware of her reputation as the "Evil Gal."

"To be truthful, yes."

"Why?" Dinah wanted to know.

"Because I have heard so much about you."

"Well, you don't have to be," Dinah replied.

Tracy relaxed, charmed by the ease of the encounter. A little later he chuckled when he saw Dinah, who had been complaining loudly that her feet hurt, take off her shoes and walk barefoot across the festival grounds.

Dinah took the stage in the middle of the evening July 6 with a seven-piece band behind her that mixed the old and the new—Wynton Kelly and Max Roach from the past, Paul West from her current band. They were supplemented by three horn players. After two pop tunes, "Lover Come Back to Me" and "Crazy Love," Dinah launched into a determined "Send Me to the 'Lectric Chair," barely a hint of remorse in telling the tale of killing her wandering man.

"Still with Bessie Smith," she said as the applause died down and the band started the introduction to "Me and My Gin," another Smith classic.

"Thank you, ladies and gentlemen. We're on this Bessie Smith series," she said when she finished the song, Wynton playing softly in the background. "I'd like to do one of Bessie's most soulful tunes. It's called the 'Backwater Blues.'" This time Dinah was accompanied only by Roach, Wynton, and Paul West, and she introduced them one by one.

A slight rasp crept into Dinah's singing, but it took nothing away from the clarity of her presentation—the phrasing, the diction, the tempo all working together.

When Dinah had sung at Newport with Max Roach two years earlier, she was introduced as the "Queen of the Blues" but didn't sing one blues number. By coincidence Jack Tracy had reviewed her performance and noted that very fact. This year, more firmly recognized by jazz enthusiasts, she made Bessie Smith the centerpiece of her set, no doubt to promote her latest album. (When *Down Beat* ran its annual jazz critics poll in the summer, Dinah made the list, tied for last place out of ten with Eydie Gorme. Ella Fitzgerald was first, with four times as many votes as second-place Billie Holiday.)

Dinah left the stage while Roach and several of the other musicians stayed and were joined by Terry Gibbs. She came back out to do one number with the group, a spirited "All of Me." She was wearing one of her more eye-catching stage gowns—a gold satin sleeveless sack dress that featured a big bow and a rhinestone bauble in the middle, just below the waist where the dress hugged her legs.

Dinah's live "All of Me" was still a challenge and not a lament. She threw her head back and smiled as she sang, her earrings swinging with every beat. When Gibbs took his solo, Dinah walked away from the mike, went behind the vibraharp, picked up a pair of mallets, a wicked grin on her face, and played a few bars with him. The band members hooted with delight behind her. "Come on, hit it, Dinah," one of them hollered as she edged Gibbs out of the way to strike a few notes. It was true that Dinah cut in on his solo, but she was having such a good time, Gibbs didn't seem to mind.

She came back to the microphone and ended with a flourish, a satisfied smile on her face.

. . .

DINAH ASKED WYNTON to stay on for a few dates after the festival. Later in July the two of them along with bassist Paul West and saxophonist Harold Ousley and a drummer went to Bermuda. They played a week at the Clayhouse Inn, a well-known nightspot on the island. Ousley, another Chicagoan taught by Captain Walter Dyett at DuSable High, had come to Dinah's attention through his high school friends Charles Davis and Julian Priester. Ousley loved the job in part for its exacting nature. "You had to know your part. The music had to be correct," he said.

Ousley thought Dinah's reputation for bombast was overblown. "She was very soulful. This is the thing people loved about her," he said. When an audience was louder than Dinah wanted, he added, "she didn't always curse." Instead, she would take a direct approach. "I'm doing a show. You have to stop talking. If people keep talking, I'm not going to sing." At one club in Baltimore Dinah instructed the bartender not to ring the cash register while she was singing. She expected the waitresses to remember the customers' tabs until her set was over. Once she had finished her business, they could then get on with theirs.

Dinah's most recent trip to Baltimore had been a week at the Club Tijuana. In August she returned but this time to play again at the Comedy Club, whose owner, Howard Dixon, seemed to be taking a leaf out of the Tijuana book and moving toward jazz. Miles Davis and his quintet had preceded her.

Unbeknownst to Dinah, Dixon was apparently on the outs with local authorities, and she got caught up in his problems. She played the usual full house Tuesday, August 20. John Robinson, a young lawyer from New York who was doing some work for her, had come down for the show, and after the last set, Dinah, Robinson, club owner Dixon, and some of the help were visiting around a table. At 4:00 A.M. on August 21, police officers burst in and arrested the group. They were charged with disorderly conduct and taken to a police station in northwest Baltimore. Dixon posted the $51.45 as collateral for later bail for each person arrested, except Robinson. Dinah, Dixon, and the others left the jail about 7:00 A.M. Robinson posted his bail a little later.

Dinah was supposed to be back in court around 10:00 A.M., but Robinson told her to skip the proceeding and get some rest. A "technical warrant" for her arrest was issued, but she showed up on her own for an afternoon bail hearing. By that time, the police had leveled another charge against her and three others, "unlawful consumption of alcohol." In other words, someone was drinking after the club was supposed to have closed.

Dinah came to court looking stylish, wearing an off-the-shoulder tan chemise and black slip-on shoes. She expressed surprise when she was asked to take off her shoes and then was patted down by a policewoman. She cooperated in silence. Dinah and the others were then taken to an upstairs hearing room, and she had to stand against a railing sandwiched between Dixon and Robinson for nearly an hour until a seat became available.

"Are you a singer or dancer?" an officer asked when Dinah was called forward to address the bail issue.

Dinah smiled. "I'm a singer."

"She's a singer of renown, famous the world over," the magistrate broke in.

He approved $250 bail for Dinah and the others and set a hearing on the charges for Friday, August 23.

Outside the courtroom, Dinah let everyone know she was furious about the "police comedy," as she called it, and incredulous at a policeman's testimony that he heard "drums and piano playing and the voice of a man singing at 4 A.M.," according to the *Baltimore Afro-American*.

"If it was a party, where were the people?" Dinah asked. "They're ridiculous. I called the NAACP to look into the matter because it's prejudice." Though she didn't say so specifically, apparently the police officers were white men. Dixon, the club owner, and his mother, Evelyn, the holder of the official club license, were black. "We were sitting here just talking business," Dinah went on. "If you can't sit and talk with your manager after a night's performance, if that's disorderly, I was disorderly."

"I'm a bundle of nerves," Dinah added. "My throat is giving me fits. I don't know if I'll be able to sing tonight or not. I never ran into anything like this in Baltimore before or any place else."

Dinah said she had summoned Allen Saunders, another New

York lawyer, to represent her at the Friday proceeding on the actual charges.

Robinson was as angry as Dinah. "We're being taken as a result of something they're doing to Mr. Dixon," he asserted. "I've been in Baltimore eighteen hours, and I've been in jail ten of them, all because I'm working. We were discussing business, contract terms and whatnot. . . . And I don't drink," he added.

During the hearing on the 23rd, Saunders told the judge that Dinah and Robinson were getting ready to go to a restaurant when the police broke down the door to the Comedy Club. One officer grabbed a sealed champagne bottle and another grabbed two glasses as "evidence that several patrons were drinking in violation of the 2 A.M. curfew." The judge seemed sympathetic. He dismissed the charges against Dinah and Robinson, fined the club's head waitress and doorman $25 each for disorderly conduct, and sent the charges against Dixon and his mother to a grand jury.

The *New York Amsterdam News* minced no words in its coverage of the episode. Dinah had gotten caught up in the arrest "by accident." The real target was Dixon "because he assertedly refused to pay off."

ON THE SURFACE the small town of Newport, Kentucky, was an unusual stop on the R&B–jazz circuit, but its location, just across the river from Cincinnati, made it a convenient place to break up a trip from the major eastern cities to Detroit and Chicago and earn some money while doing so. Without the dazzle of Las Vegas, Newport had turned into a hub of gambling and nightlife run by organized crime figures who unabashedly went about their business free of local interference. One of the popular jazz spots was called simply the Copa, no doubt to evoke New York's famous club. Dinah played there the weekend of October 3, just after Carmen McRae.

Dinah went on to Chicago for two extended engagements at Roberts, bringing Slappy White along with her and recruiting drummer Red Saunders, a longtime Chicago favorite, and his band to back her. Eddie was back in town and keeping busy with jobs at various South Side clubs. He and Dinah apparently had gotten over any bitterness since their breakup, and he made it a point to come by Roberts one evening. Dinah even invited him to attend a session that Jack Tracy had put together at the Chess Records studio on Michigan Avenue because the usual Mercury spot, Universal, was not available. When Dinah was asked if this meant the couple would reconcile, she gave a resolute "No."

The session at Chess got off to a rocky start because Dinah didn't like the way the drummer played. "She looked up at me in the control booth and gave me the most pained look, a real pained look," Tracy said, and pointed her thumb in the direction of the drummer. "She couldn't stand the way he was playing." She finished the song but then told Tracy she wouldn't work with that drummer again. He found another one, and while Dinah came back for a second try, nothing was ever released.

Even though Dinah and Eddie had separated, EmArcy was still trading off the marriage. A Chamblee instrumental album that was released later in the fall, *Doodlin'*, showed her on the cover, dancing while Eddie played. Though the title said "Eddie Chamblee and friend," Dinah didn't sing on any of the tunes. *Down Beat*, which called the album a "bewildering mixture of crass rock and roll and some fair jazz," was incensed. "Dinah Washington fans—beware of that cover. The color photo is crazy, but the message is a lie."

Though Dinah and Mabel Page had done business long-distance— Dinah would call and ask for a gown; Page would send something along—it was always easier when the two could meet face-to-face. Dinah could pick out the material she wanted and Page could get more exact measurements. Page had moved to Chicago and opened a dress shop at 64th and Cottage Grove, Page Creations, and because Dinah was in Chicago for an extended stay, they could work together in person. Page had seen Dinah near size eighteen and then several sizes smaller, as she still was, and prided herself on the ability to make instant judgments. "I could look at her and tell," Page said. "I told her I could keep her looking better than anybody else."

Ollie's apartment on South Vernon, with its big front room, spacious kitchen, and back porch, was large enough for parties when Dinah wanted to entertain. There was plenty of food and conversation, and Dinah Washington was usually on the turntable. But nobody minded. Those who attended were invited because they liked Dinah and loved her music.

Dinah had a whirlwind late fall—a short stay in New Orleans at

Ciro's on Bourbon Street doing three shows a night, on to Los Angeles to play the Elks Club, and then back across the country for five days over Thanksgiving at the Showboat in Philadelphia, which was a friendly competitor of Pep's.

On the brief trip west Dinah apparently developed a new romantic interest in a prizefighter, undeterred by the fact that he was married. It didn't sound very promising, though. "San Francisco heavyweight is having wife troubles over the blues queen," said a cryptic mention in *Jet*.

Dinah liked to spend the holidays in Chicago, and Herman Roberts was happy to have her back because she was one of his biggest draws. For this holiday season Dinah's major acquisitions were a full-length mink coat and a new pink Chrysler, the 1959 model, which had just come out. She loved the coat so much that she wore it indoors. Slappy White was engaged to LaVern Baker and had given her a new mink. So one evening the two singers teamed up for a number at Roberts, each wrapped in her Christmas fur. *Jet* estimated that $15,000 worth of mink was at the microphone.

16.

What a Diff'rence a Day Maker

1959

Dinah was so busy with live dates in 1958 that she had done only two sessions, the fewest in a decade. Mercury was eager to have her return to the studio early in 1959, but first she had to finish her run at Roberts. Then she played another week at the Apollo starting January 23, this time headlining a bill that was unmistakably geared to a jazz audience. Joining her were the baritone sax star Gerry Mulligan, who had riveted the crowd during his set a few months earlier at Newport, and Maynard Ferguson, who had played on *Dinah Jams,* and, like Mulligan, was a white musician.

Dinah rarely missed a performance for any reason. But when she came down with a sore throat in the middle of the Apollo week, she asked Ernestine Anderson, a young singer whom the *New York Age* called "the new darling of the café society," to fill in. Dinah may have feigned illness, though, to give her friend a boost. She told Ruth Bowen to tell Anderson to be at the theater and then call Bobby Schiffman, whose family ran the Apollo, at the last minute to explain that Dinah couldn't perform but that Anderson would. "It worked," Ruth said, though Schiffman "hit the ceiling" when he learned Dinah wasn't coming.

"Ernestine broke up the first show," Ruth added, and Dinah's friends joked that she would get well quickly when she realized how well Anderson had gone over. Dinah's ploy apparently helped, though, because the Schiffmans invited Anderson back on her own in February, and even though she didn't do much box office on her own, Schiffman noted in the theater's private scorecard—index cards on most of the performers—that Anderson was a "fine singer" and "bears watching."

Dinah had more jobs in early February—a week at the Flame in Detroit, a performance at Boston Symphony Hall, a concert in Newark, and then one at Carnegie Hall. Finally the second week in February she was free to concentrate on recording. Much had changed at Mercury since her last session ten months earlier. After taking a new position within the company in the summer of 1958, Bobby Shad had left for good a couple of months later to join a new venture involving international music production and distribution. The label replaced him with a groundbreaking hire. Clyde Otis, a tall, gregarious songwriter and freelance producer, was brought in to be the main artist and repertoire man for East Coast productions. (Jack Tracy remained in the Chicago office.) Otis was the first black to be given a senior position at a major label. He had produced hit records with the Diamonds and Rusty Draper and had written them as well, including "The Stroll" and "Looking Back," with co-writer Brook Benton. By replacing Shad, who was more jazz-oriented, with Otis, Mercury was looking to put more of its artists on the pop charts, and that included Dinah.

Otis had been a fan of Dinah's for years. He was well aware of her popularity as a blues singer, but with the right material, he thought she could reach well beyond her loyal black fans and the whites with a jazz bent who knew her music. Otis set up a meeting to discuss his ideas with her before they were in the studio in front of musicians.

"You deserve a broader image and audience," he told her.

"Well, I'm pretty good right now," Dinah retorted.

Agreed. "But I still think there's an even greater audience for you."

"What have you got in mind?" Dinah wanted to know.

Recording with strings, Otis told her.

"Nah, I don't cut with no strings. I'm a horn person," Dinah shot back, even though she had recorded with strings several times before to good effect in productions handled by Hal Mooney.

Otis was undeterred. "One song I'd love to have you do to see what happens—do you know 'What a Diff'rence a Day Makes'?" The Dorsey brothers had recorded it in 1934, and it was a hit.

Dinah said she knew the tune, though not well.

"Would you record that with strings?" Otis asked.

"I'll think about it," Dinah replied.

"Well, how soon would you let me know?"

"Oh," Dinah said, "pretty soon."

Otis thought the meeting was over, rueful about the future of their relationship. He got up to leave.

"I'll give you one take on that," Dinah said.

"One take?" Otis stopped. One take meant everything had to be just right. What were the chances Dinah and the musicians could pull it off? He made himself think about it for a moment before answering.

"All right."

Otis had asked Belford Hendricks to write the charts. One of the few black arrangers, Hendricks had started out as a piano player and was already arranging by the time he and Otis met on what Otis jokingly called "a songwriting expedition." Otis liked what he heard in Hendricks's work and brought him to Mercury, no questions asked. "He went with the traffic, which was me," Otis explained.

Given that Otis had agreed to Dinah's stipulation of one take, he gave Hendricks specific instructions to make the most of it. "Work out all the kinks in the orchestration. . . . If she's gonna give you one take, that's what you're gonna get."

When Dinah came into the studio on February 19, she recognized a couple of faces among the assembled musicians—Charles Davis on baritone sax and Milt Hinton on bass. "Good to see you motherfuckers," she said. They took it with good cheer, knowing it was Dinah's term of endearment. A moment or so later she stepped before the microphone and turned to Otis.

"Ready?"

He nodded. The strings played the introduction, the backup

singers hit their notes, and Dinah sang the first words with her perfect diction, each one precise but still connected to the longer phrase.
Two minutes and twenty-five seconds later it was over. As Otis
hoped, the strings had given the arrangement a softer feel, and they
complemented Hinton's strong and jazzy bass. It all sounded good
now, but only after the song was released on a record would Otis
know if he was right—that Dinah, placed in a new setting, gospel
and blues touches intact, could reach a new audience.

Otis told Dinah he wanted to record a few other songs because
he needed something for the flip side of "What a Diff'rence."

Dinah looked at him for a moment. "Okay," she said.

It was her understated sign of approval. He had passed her test.
Over the next couple of hours, she recorded several songs, among
them a new version of "I Won't Cry Anymore" and "Time After
Time," the Sammy Cahn–Jules Styne song.

MERCURY RELEASED a compilation from the 1958 Newport
Jazz Festival, *Newport '58,* at the end of February, which featured
Dinah, Max Roach, and Terry Gibbs. It was great timing for Dinah—
she was making her debut March 3 at the Village Vanguard just as
the storied jazz club in Greenwich Village was getting ready to celebrate its twenty-fifth anniversary. Beryl Booker had come back at
the piano to anchor Dinah's trio. The opening-night audience included Dinah's friends in the business and members of her offstage
circle, among them Otis, Ruth Bowen, and her husband, Billy, representatives from Associated Booking, one of her dressmakers, and
her dentist.

Dinah devoted the first set to a mix of her past hits—"Evil Gal
Blues, "Fool That I Am," "I Won't Cry Anymore"—and a few numbers from the Bessie Smith album. The crowd was enthusiastic and
appreciative. After the usual break, Dinah started the second show
just after midnight with a bawdy reading of "Long John Blues." The
song, the circumstances, the friends in the audience all seemed to
put her in a flippant mood. Instead of packing the set with one tune
after another, Dinah began to interrupt herself to introduce everyone who was in the audience, including a man from New Orleans
who had given her "the loveliest necklace I have ever received," she
told the crowd.

She went back to singing, but after one number she stopped again and asked Ernestine Anderson, who was at one of the tables, to come onstage and sing. When Anderson finished, Dinah sang another song and then invited Slappy White, who was also there, to take a bow. He grabbed the microphone and didn't let go until he had done nearly fifteen minutes' worth of jokes that proved to be a mismatch for the Vanguard audience. It was a carbon copy of the near-silence that had greeted him two years earlier at Mister Kelly's in Chicago.

Dinah finally took the stage again to sing another song. Finished, she announced that it was the last amid protestations to do at least one more number. No, Dinah said, that was it.

Billboard reviewer Howard Cook attended both shows. He praised the first, but the second, he said, "deteriorated into a complete shambles . . . In fact there was much more clowning than singing. Late-comers were definitely cheated from what had promised to be a knockout performance."

The *Variety* reviewer didn't arrive until midnight and was sorely disappointed. He chided Dinah for "turning opening night into a private party . . . She acted up, throwing all pro rules out the window." But he gave her the benefit of the doubt for being careless with her audience, even cavalier. "It's probably safe to assume that once she got the opening night frivolities out of her system that she was able to turn in a good show because when she belts she definitely hits a striking note."

Word of the opening-night fiasco traveled, however, and *Jet* observed in one of its gossip columns March 26 that Dinah "annoyed paying customers when she kept interrupting her song act." The *Variety* reviewer was right about one thing. Dinah settled down and broke the Vanguard attendance record. The *Chicago Defender* reported that the club management rewarded her with a mink stole, which Dinah happily modeled for photographers. Owner Max Gordon brought Dinah back for another two weeks at the end of April by popular demand "following so many requests for the famous blues chanteuse by letter and by telegram from jazz and blues fans," according to the *Amsterdam News*.

Dinah had already given a boost to Ernestine Anderson, and one evening at the Vanguard she gave another to the young singer Gloria Lynne. Beforehand Dinah told Lynne to come up to the apartment at 145th Street and pick out some clothes. Lynne was dumbfounded, but she went up to 14A-3, had to wait about an hour while Dinah was doing other things, but then she was escorted into the master bedroom. Dinah opened the closet doors: "Go ahead and pick out a couple of gowns. I want you to look nice tonight."

Dinah could be equally generous with young women she didn't know—if she liked them. Darcy DeMille was a young writer for *Sepia*, who caught one of Dinah's shows in a small Midwest club. Uninvited, DeMille went back to Dinah's dressing room to wait for her. "And just who are you?" Dinah asked when she came in, pointing one of her well-manicured fingers at the momentarily frightened young woman. DeMille gathered herself together to say her name, and when she told Dinah she had come from Chicago, the ice melted. They chatted like long-lost friends, discovering that they had both gone to Wendell Phillips and under the same principal.

DeMille had admired a pair of Dinah's shoes as the maid was packing them. When she got up to say goodbye and headed for the door, Dinah stopped her, slipped off the shoes she was wearing, and gave them to DeMille. They were more to be admired by DeMille than worn; Dinah's feet were tiny, and the shoes were two sizes too small.

When she finished the Village Vanguard engagement, Dinah went immediately to Toronto to play a week at the Queen Street E. Tavern, one of the city's popular jazz clubs. During her stay, she appeared on Jack Duff's late night television show, *Here's Duffy*. She sang a spirited "Lover Come Back to Me" and then after a stagehand brought out a stool, Dinah sat down to tell the audience about her next number. "I imagine back in 1927 you could hear Bessie Smith singing something like this," she said, and then began "Send Me to the 'Lectric Chair."

A day or so later Dinah talked to a *Toronto Daily Star* reporter about doing TV shows and the current state of music. Of course the exposure of television was important, but, Dinah said, she didn't like the process, especially when she had to lip-sync one of her records. "I hate mouthing, and I do it very badly," she admitted. "I never sing a song the same way twice. The lyrics always change a bit. There's always fluff."

She found television jazz shows boring. "All I know is they were terrible. I turned them off. They didn't gas me at all." The only singers she liked to watch on TV were Frank Sinatra and Nat King Cole; otherwise she loved westerns and cop shows.

Dinah was regularly asked what she thought of rock 'n' roll, and she hadn't changed her opinion. Yes, it was an outgrowth of rhythm and blues, but, she quickly added, "There's no similarity at all between the two. One is good music. The other is just noise with a lot of guitars twanging."

More of Dinah's musical opinions were on display in another of Leonard Feather's "Blindfold Test" features in *Down Beat*, and like her turn five years earlier, she was direct and blunt when she felt the music didn't measure up. Leonard introduced her this time as "an honest and competent listener."

The first tune featured vocalist Annie Ross backed by Art Farmer and Gerry Mulligan, and Dinah gave the record four out of five stars. "It's an enjoyable thing. . . . I caught myself kicking my leg with the beat, so it was swingin'."

She didn't like Eugenie Baird's version of "I Let a Song Go Out of My Heart," by Duke Ellington. "I won't give that *any* stars." Max Roach and his group received three stars for "Deeds Not Words." "I like that sound—soft, pretty, and not too much going-off-the-melody." But she wouldn't give any rating to the one gospel record Feather played, Ernestine Washington with the congregation of the Washington Temple Church of God in Christ. "Well, there was a time when I was really up on this kind of thing. It didn't sound like that when *I* was going to church," Dinah said. "This performance didn't kill me. . . . In the first part of the song they were lingering too long, and they weren't together. At one point somebody really had left the tune. . . . It sounded like it was recorded in a church."

She was critical of Chris Connor singing "Something to Live For." "When I'm hoarse I sound bad enough . . . but this!" Dinah liked the introduction and the arrangement, but that was all. "I'm very sorry, Chris, you didn't do that justice. . . . I'll give the background five stars, but I can't rate that."

Dinah gave two stars to an instrumental version of "The Man I Love" featuring Bill Holman, calling it "nothing out of the ordinary." She had no trouble recognizing Ella Fitzgerald and gave her five stars doing "What's Your Story, Morning Glory." "That was the First Lady, and I must say she sounded like her old self—that pure soul."

Dinah remembered that Ella had given her a dress when she started out with Lionel Hampton in 1943. "Bless her heart, I sure needed it, too. Incidentally I didn't give her five stars because she gave me the dress."

Dinah gave no stars to the last two selections. The first was Chet Baker singing "Old Devil Moon." "Who the heck is that? Is that a singer or someone just kidding. I don't know who it is, but the diction is terrible. At the end it sounded like he said 'That old bubble moon' and I thought the words were 'old devil moon.' It sounds like he had a mouthful of mush. I thought it was the Velvet Fog for a minute," a nickname for Mel Tormé, "but I can't imagine who it was, unless it was Chet Baker," and indeed Dinah was correct.

The last selection was Joni James and "Hey Good Lookin'." "Has she got a cold? I want to know, who could sound that bad? It's a movie star. . . . She's not a singer, because singers don't sound like that. When she says, 'Say, what-cha-got cookin' ' it should have been *her* that was cookin'. She sings out of her nose. Well, I'd like to compliment her on nothing."

DINAH WAS BACK in the studio April 7 for her second session under Otis's direction with Belford Hendricks arranging and conducting again. They had picked an interesting mix of songs, among them another try at "Time After Time," a second Cahn-Styne tune, "It's Magic," and "Cry Me a River," a song by Arthur Hamilton with stirring imagery and resonant lyrics about romantic longing.

Dinah took her place at the mike for "River."

"Do you want me to sound like Julie London?" she asked, a bit of the coquette in her voice. Julie London's original version had been a pop hit in 1955.

"No. Sound like Dinah Washington," Otis said from the control room.

"Would you rather me sound like Lady?"—meaning Billie Holiday, Lady Day.

"No, I'd like you to sound like Dinah Washington."

"I could sound like Spokane Washington."

"I'd like you to sound like Dinah Washington," Otis said again, this time more firmly, amid chuckles from the engineers.

The playfulness out of the way, Dinah was ready to record. Otis's instructions to the contrary, Billie Holiday fans would hear a bit of their idol in the opening bars, Dinah mimicking ever so slightly that languorous phrasing and Holiday's much more casual diction.

Five days after the session, Dinah left for a few dates on the East Coast with Maynard Ferguson's group. He was happy to be on the same bill with her and thought she brought a particularly light touch to their performances. "She had a great way with audiences," Ferguson said. "It's so important . . . that fun type of rapport." He loved the way she treated musicians, too. On one California session, Ferguson raced into the studio straight from the golf course wearing bright red pants and what he admitted was a "white lacy golf shirt," hardly the standard wear in the studio. Dinah was in a playful mood, and he was tickled that she "flirted with the only white boy to the amusement of everybody."

Dinah's short tour was a perfect boost for her latest release, "What a Diff'rence a Day Makes." Beyond introducing live audiences to the tune, Dinah had the enthusiastic support of Arnold Shaw, who worked for the Edward B. Marks Music Corporation, which published the song. Like Otis, Shaw was certain that Dinah could reach a larger market. He recalled that it was he who suggested "What a Diff'rence a Day Makes" for Dinah, though Otis insisted he was the one who brought the tune to her.

But Otis agreed that Shaw was an indispensable ally. After Otis had taken the finished product to label executives, "I hadn't gotten the interest that I expected from Mercury," he said, "and Arnold said to me, 'Look, I believe in this so much, I will go out and promote it.'"

True to his word, Shaw took the record to white disc jockeys around the country whom Mercury tended to ignore, its marketers satisfied to keep promoting Dinah to a largely black audience and content with the 25,000 records she could sell with every release. On May 9 "What a Diff'rence a Day Makes" debuted on the *Cash Box* pop singles charts. Two weeks later Dinah was on the *Billboard* pop chart—a first in sixteen years of recording. By early June she recorded another first, landing on *Variety*'s weekly disc jockey poll. By that time the song was also on the *Billboard* R&B chart, Dinah's usual territory. It was almost always a mystery why one record took off and another didn't, and this was no exception. But Otis and Shaw had been proved right: if given the chance, and that meant good marketing to go along with good music, Dinah could capture a new audience.

Still, the success of "What a Diff'rence a Day Makes" was unusual. It was not rhythm and blues by any conventional definition. And it certainly wasn't rock 'n' roll. Nor was it the usual kind of blues. It had nothing in common with most of the songs that were on the same pop charts: Johnny Horton singing "The Battle of New Orleans," Fabian, the heartthrob of Philadelphia, and "Turn Me Loose," or Edd Byrnes and Connie Stevens, from the television show *77 Sunset Strip*, singing "Kookie, Kookie," which was about an infatuation with a hairdo and a comb.

But Dinah's version of "What a Diff'rence" was accessible and pleasing the way a painting by Renoir or Monet was. The sound and the texture were welcoming and easy on the ears. Yet it was still Dinah Washington with her favorite stylistic tics, that well-placed "hmmm" and an interjected "lord" to emphasize a lyric. Underneath Dinah's vocals and the lush arrangement was Hinton's distinctive bass, which would have been at home in any jazz club. Piece by piece, the parts didn't seem to make sense; packaged together they turned into an intriguing whole.

It was a singular recipe: strings from the mainstream, a beat from rhythm and blues, leavened with Dinah's soul.

GEORGE, DINAH'S OLDER SON, was going to be thirteen in July, and Bobby eleven in August. She didn't push them into show business, but she thought they had some talent. George was taking drum lessons, and he was also taking judo lessons, which came in handy when a couple of toughs from the neighborhood started a fight. Bobby thought it was over a leather jacket, but whatever the cause, George held his own, calling on all that he had learned to get the boys literally off his back.

Dinah wanted her sons to be good dancers. She signed them up for lessons with one of the best, Cholly Atkins, one half of the superlative duo Coles and Atkins and a choreographer at the Apollo. Atkins taught in a studio in the CBS Building in Midtown Manhattan, and one of Farris's first duties when she came to live with Dinah at the Bowery Bank Building was to pick up the boys from their lessons. Even though it took her a while to master the subway, with its multiple exits and transfer points at so many stations, Farris didn't mind this chore because she was starstruck around Atkins. "He's so fine," she giggled to friends.

The boys had made enough progress in their dance lessons to work up a little routine as part of their mother's act. When Dinah opened again at the Apollo June 5, the boys made their debut billed as the "Queen's Jesters." Dressed in matching dark suits, white shirts, and boaters, they did a soft-shoe to "Tea for Two." The *New York Age* ran a picture of Dinah and her sons with a caption alluding to another entertainer who performed with his boys: "If Bing Can Do It—So Can Dinah." In Dinah's view, the boys stole the show. On top of that they each were paid $125.

George and Bobby didn't worry about forgetting their steps; the biggest problem was keeping their mind on the routine. George was prone to the giggles, and when he tried to stifle them, he would emit a series of grunts. Pretty soon he couldn't contain himself, and that could incite Bobby, setting the two of them off into peals of laughter.

Given the success of "What a Diff'rence a Day Makes," Ruth Bowen, who was becoming increasingly involved in Dinah's business affairs, didn't think Associated Booking was working hard enough on Dinah's behalf. Granted she had just done another week at Pep's in Philadelphia—the tiff with owner Bill Gerson now a thing of the past. But Ruth thought Dinah should be even busier.

"I went down and spoke to Joe Glaser about it," Ruth recalled. "I said, 'What is this? You can't get any work for this girl? She's hot as hell.' He had a meeting with his agents to fire them up, and I said, 'Well, if you people can't get it done, I'll just have to do it.' "

Dinah loved that can-do attitude. She called Ruth "Dinah Jr." and joked, "Next to me, you're the evilest bitch I ever knew."

Ella Fitzgerald and Sarah Vaughan had played Europe several times. Billie Holiday had been there, too, and Dinah wanted to go. "I was very fortunate because in traveling with my husband, I'd made a lot of friends throughout the world, promoters," Ruth explained. So she picked up the phone and went to work.

On June 10 Dinah flew to London for two weeks of dates to be followed by engagements in Stockholm. She took LaRue Manns, still her faithful assistant, and Beryl Booker, who would play the piano. Before boarding the Pan American World Airways jet clipper at New York's international airport, Dinah posed for photographers.

She dressed to travel as if she were going out to an elegant dinner, a tasteful black sleeveless dress, high-heeled shoes, jewels on the front, a mink stole over her shoulders, and a sailor hat set at a rakish angle over her platinum wig. Though her own hair was short now, Dinah was wearing wigs in public, and the platinum one was her favorite, at least since the performance at the Village Vanguard.

Someone asked her why she wore the blond wig. "Because I can," Dinah replied.

Max Jones, a writer for the popular British weekly *Melody Maker,* arranged to interview Dinah at her hotel on Oxford Street in the city's West End right after she arrived. He was eager to meet her though anxious about how everything would go. "I had heard Dinah was on the fiery side," he said, and he was familiar with the tart assessments she had made about music in Leonard Feather's "Blindfold Test."

But Jones found a charming if voluble woman who took a liking to him right away. Though Beryl and LaRue excused themselves, tired after their long trip, Dinah was full of energy. She did a few dance steps to prove it, ordered some brandy and glasses, poured drinks for Jones and the photographer he had brought along, and then, as Jones recalled, "swung around the smallish room pulling faces for the photographer's benefit and suggesting various robust poses."

She talked for a few minutes about her offstage life, listing one husband after another and then talking animatedly about Bobby and George. The thought of her boys prompted her to pick up the phone and call them in New York, where Epsy was taking care of them while she and LaRue were gone. Dinah explained to Jones as she dialed that the boys had just made their Apollo debut with her.

Like several writers in the United States, Jones wanted to know what musical category Dinah put herself in. "I don't think of myself as anything except a singer. I like to sing," she said, "and I'll sing ballads, church songs, blues, anything. I'll sing 'Eli Eli' if you hang around," referring to the oft-recorded Hebrew song. "To me the important things are soul and conviction. You've got to have a feeling. That 'Backwater Blues' of Bessie's that I did," she went on, recalling a performance. "I had tears in my eyes. Someone came up to me right after I'd finished, and I had to say, 'Sorry, I'll see you later.' Whenever I sing 'Backwater' my friends practically have to carry me off the stage. Rock-and-Roll you can have, but I like real blues. You can break loose on that."

Aware of Dinah's gospel background, Jones asked Dinah about mixing the two genres. "I don't know about the mixture as a general thing. But it sounds all right when Ray Charles sings," she said. "So far as I'm concerned it's a source of feeling. It doesn't matter too much what the emotion is if you've got any kind of feeling, you know, soul—it'll do. I'll tell you what it's like," she continued. "The Negro has been downtrodden in America for a long time, as you know. Maybe when you're singing a certain song you think of things that happened to you years ago. I've done that, and there's guys in the audience who couldn't guess at what you're feeling—that have jumped up in their chairs. What I'm saying," Dinah added for emphasis, "you might not understand the exact emotion but you can feel something—right? Spiritual, blues, ballad, it doesn't matter."

Dinah tossed off her opinions on a few other matters: Female pianists—"There's only four women that I say can really play piano, Beryl Booker, Martha Davis, Terry Pollard and Mary Lou," Dinah's shorthand reference to Mary Lou Williams. "They used to try to get me to play in my act," she added, "but I prefer to stand and pick the customers out." Male singers—"I'll tell you what I like in one sentence: Ray Charles, Frank Sinatra, and Nat Cole."

Ray Charles was in Dinah's special category. "He and I sit up and sing together," she said. "You ought to hear us in 'Drown in My Own Tears.' "

Jones and his wife, Betsy, were recruited to take Dinah to her first engagement in London, recording a three-song performance for *The Variety Show,* a new television program of Granada Productions. Then they took her to an impromptu session for the BBC radio's *Jazz Club* that was organized by Leonard Feather, who was vacationing in London. The program was featuring a number of his compositions, and he had booked the American jazz singer Helen Merrill for the program. But there was a misunderstanding, and she wasn't available to do the show. By chance Leonard had run into Dinah and Beryl Booker on the street, explained the situation, and asked Dinah if she could fill in.

Dinah agreed to do so, and for free as a favor to Leonard. She sang "Evil Gal Blues," "no preparation or anything," Leonard said, and the show went off beautifully.

Helen Merrill was singing at the Lagoon, one of London's jazz clubs. Dinah, the Joneses and Beryl in tow, decided to stop in for a set. Merrill was already onstage, sitting on a stool and singing "in her quiet, sensitive fashion," as Jones put it. She spotted Dinah in the back of the room, and in between songs she told the audience that "America's Queen is in the house." She invited Dinah to sing a number. Dinah agreed and brought Beryl to the stage with her. She sang a few songs, playfully competed with Beryl at the keyboard, and took a few turns on the bass—as she used to do with Keter Betts—and on the vibraharp in an amusing reprise of Newport the previous year.

The audience was delighted, and all Merrill could do was wait until it was over.

Jones thought Dinah had been out of order in upstaging the headliner, and after they left the club, he screwed up his courage to say so.

"Shit, the broad invited me up there and got what she asked for," Dinah retorted, forgetting for the moment how angry *she* was when Ruth Brown and Big Maybelle threatened to derail her performances by staying onstage too long.

Ruth Bowen, who was keeping tabs on Dinah's first overseas trip through regular phone calls from LaRue, had told Dinah to stay clear of any remarks about England's own Queen. "They don't take kindly to that," she warned her.

"Well, she did it," LaRue reported during one call.

Did what? Ruth asked.

"She walked out onstage, got a standing ovation, and when the audience quieted down, she said, 'Ladies and Gentlemen, I'm happy to be here, but just remember. There's one heaven, one earth, and one Queen. Elizabeth is an impostor.'

"I wanted to die," LaRue told Ruth, "but they loved it."

Neither Max Jones nor others in the British press apparently considered Dinah's amusing jab to be newsworthy. It was not mentioned in articles about her stay in London. But the story traveled widely among Dinah's friends in the United States, one passing it on to the other with great delight in each retelling.

The Joneses learned quickly that if Dinah liked you, she wanted you to be around, on her terms and her schedule. One evening, perhaps about ten, their phone rang. It was Dinah from her hotel. She wasn't feeling well and was unhappy with the hotel medical staff. "That doctor's a prejudiced motherfucker," she told Betsy Jones. Would she please come over? Betsy agreed to come and see what was the matter. By the time she got there, Dinah was feeling better, the doctor had come, and she was calmed down. Outside the room, the doctor told Betsy he couldn't find anything wrong with her.

By the time she got back home, Betsy told her husband what probably had happened. Beryl and LaRue had gone out for the evening, leaving her alone. "Dinah disliked solitude," Max observed, and the medical alert had brought her company and attention.

At 5:30 A.M. another day, Max Jones was awakened by the phone. Dinah was on the line. Could he come over right away? She was upset with the hotel help. She claimed the night porter, who had delivered a bottle of brandy to the room, had insulted her by offering her sex. Max awakened his wife and the two of them drove to Oxford Street. Upon their arrival at Dinah's room, she gave them the details. Indeed she had ordered a bottle of liquor, and when she answered the door in a short nightgown, the night porter drew the wrong conclusion. Her pride was injured.

Max went downstairs to speak to the night porter, who, according to Max, agreed that "he might have been out of order while tired and rushed." Dinah was barely mollified by this quasi-apology, but she let it go for the moment. Max learned a few days later that she apparently had gotten the man fired.

If Dinah could be demanding, the Joneses also saw her generous side. She insisted on cooking them dinner, promising that she knew her way around the kitchen. "I'll give you something to write about. I love to cook, and I really can burn," she said. So Max and Betsy took her marketing for chicken, pork chops, various vegetables, and, at Dinah's insistence, a large oval frying pan. She said was it was impossible to do good work in the kitchen without the right utensils.

Everything purchased, they returned to the Joneses' flat so that Dinah could prepare the dinner. Music accompanied the chopping, cutting, basting, and baking—Louis Jordan, Lionel Hampton, and Dinah herself. A couple of times she emerged from the kitchen, an apron covering her dress, and demanded, "How about another brandy for the cook." Getting her glass refilled she might, Jones said, offer "a ribald remark or a coarse gesture."

The food was delicious, and the Joneses considered themselves lucky to have a few more meals cooked by Dinah, these with other guests including Beryl, and the singer Abbey Lincoln, who was also in London.

During another meal at the Joneses', this one a late lunch, Dinah was in a gospel mood. She talked about Thomas Dorsey, Sallie Martin, Roberta Martin, and Sister Rosetta Tharpe and then sat down at the piano to accompany herself on a few spirituals. "That was better than Rosetta Tharpe," she declared when she finished one song. None of the listeners dared contradict her. She and Beryl then traded places and jokes at the piano, and Jones thought they had the makings of a jazz-comedy act that could rival Fats Waller.

Dinah struck up a friendship with the British singer Beryl Bryden and was invited to make dinner at Bryden's flat. The most memorable part of the day was not the meal itself but the shopping beforehand. Max Jones accompanied Dinah, Beryl Booker, and Bryden, and they finished just in time to visit a few clubs in the late afternoon. One of their stops was at a Greek café, which happened to have a piano in the corner. Beryl Booker sat down at the keyboard "and Dinah was soon attacking another of her Bessie Smith favorites, 'Send Me to the 'Lectric Chair.' "

Finished at that club, the group proceeded along Oxford Street heading to the hotel when they came upon an amateur band, the Happy Wanderers, busking in the roadway. Dinah burst into a smile. "I've got to sing with them," she said, and led the group up the street past Selfridges, the famous department store, singing "I Can't Give You Anything but Love."

The Wanderers had been a bit hesitant to accept a parade leader, but Beryl Bryden straightened them out. "I explained she was a very famous singer from the United States." Maybe she wasn't a jazz singer, Bryden added, "but she was a jazz person, that's for sure."

Before Dinah left London for Sweden, she wanted to have another night out with the Joneses. Max told her he was too tired, but Betsy was available. They went first to the Palladium to catch the act there and then went to an after-hours club. Betsy was flagging a bit, but Dinah told her not to worry. She opened her purse, took out a bottle of prescription pills, and gave one to Betsy, probably dexedrine.

They worked, but Betsy was unable to get a good night's sleep for another two days. Though she didn't say anything to Dinah, Betsy told her husband that it worried her to see Dinah taking so many of those pills to keep going.

DINAH AND EDDIE were divorced in the spring—he had filed the papers and had since remarried—and Dinah had been linked to a few other men the previous months. *Jet* reported in January that she had her eye on Paul Wilson, a member of the Flamingos sextet, and was vying for his affections with Valerie Carr, another singer. And then, according to Ruth, she developed a crush on George Treadwell, Sarah Vaughan's former husband and manager, and even agreed to let him be her manager. "It lasted about a week and then it fizzled," Ruth said.

The more serious boyfriend was a twenty-seven-year-old cab-driver from the Bronx, Horatio Maillard, known as "Rusty" and seven years younger than Dinah. They had met at the Brown Bomber, Joe Louis's club a block north of the Bowery Building. "He says he was surprised that I talked to him. After that we started dating," Dinah explained. By the time she got to Sweden at the beginning of July, she was lonesome and called Ruth Bowen.

"What is my marital status?" she asked, only partly in jest. She was legally single, Ruth said.

Well, then, send Rusty over. Dinah would pay his airfare once he arrived, a boyfriend sent COD, she joked.

Ruth managed to convince an airline to let Maillard fly to Sweden, where Dinah met him. Under Swedish law, couples had to abide by certain waiting periods after filing the required papers. Dinah was impatient, so she hired a boat to sail beyond Sweden's three-mile boundary and had a minister conduct a ceremony. LaRue and Stefan Landeroff, a Swedish bass player, were the attendants.

"I wanted to get King Gustav to perform the wedding," Dinah said afterward, "but he was away on a gig. . . . Who knows if it'll last, but we both hope so." While the couple said they were husband and wife, privately Dinah and her friends thought the ceremony might not have been a legal marriage recognized in the United States.

Dinah wanted Max Jones to hear the good news about Rusty directly from her. A few days after she had left London, his phone rang at 5:00 A.M. Dinah was calling to say hello and wanted Jones to greet Rusty. "Hey, what's the matter with you? You asleep?" she asked, seemingly surprised that at that hour he sounded groggy.

Dagens Nyheter, a large daily newspaper in Stockholm, was on hand when Dinah performed one weekday evening at Grona Lund, a popular amusement park. In a review after the show, printed under a picture of Dinah, still wearing that platinum wig, the paper noted her blues origins. "No one can be mistaken by the spiritual guidance from Bessie Smith or why not Fats Waller?" Dinah wore a bright red dress and matching bejeweled pumps, and, the paper added, "the greatness she showed during her performance . . . leads your thoughts straight to the 'red hot mamas.' But it doesn't mean she's old-fashioned. She's the total opposite, alive, fresh, and, well, she is simply a thoroughly honest and real jazz singer."

The *Michigan Chronicle* reported that Dinah had played to "more than 250,000 fans" while she was gone, though that was probably an overstatement. "It was the greatest thrill of my life playing to my first European audiences," she told the paper. A sidelight in Stockholm was lunch with heavyweight boxing champion Ingmar Johansson and his fiancée, Birgit Lundgren.

DINAH RETURNED to New York at the end of July to more good news about "What a Diff'rence a Day Makes." Nearly three months after its release the record was still climbing the charts in the major music trades. By the end of August the record would reach number one in *Variety*'s disc jockey poll, number one in the ten most-played records on jukeboxes, and number four in the *Cash Box* and *Billboard* pop charts. It also spent a month on a chart in the *Amsterdam News* that listed its top ten songs.

"I finally got a hit, but I practically had to whip those disc jockeys to get it," Dinah declared to Jones. She had indeed delivered in the studio, but it was Arnold Shaw who had done that important promotional work once the record came out.

Dinah was in New York barely long enough to unpack her suitcases and repack to go on the road. She and Rusty did make time, however, for a small party at Randolph's Shalimar, a local club, where Dinah happily showed off the latest ring on her left hand. On July 31, Rusty in tow, she arrived in Atlanta with Beryl Booker to play four days at the Auburn Casino. The promoters made much of her recent success, one ad trumpeting "The Queen Is Coming—(Just Returned from Europe)" and promising that she would sing "What a Diff'rence a Day Makes."

From Atlanta Dinah went straight to Detroit for a week back at one of her favorite spots, the Flame Show Bar. Though it rained opening night, August 7, her fans were not deterred. According to *Chronicle* columnist Ziggy Johnson, she broke the attendance record that Sam Cooke had held. Sammy Davis, Jr., happened to be playing in Detroit during Dinah's week, and told Bea Buck, their mutual friend, that he had to drop by the club to see her. So on Sunday, the 9th, he picked Bea up, and they went down for the evening. When Dinah saw Davis in the audience, she stopped the show and insisted that he come up onstage. Though rarely willing to cede her place in the spotlight, Dinah stepped aside for Davis and watched in admiration as he worked his magic.

Dinah joined Dizzy Gillespie and Dorothy Donegan for a week at the Regal after Detroit. This jazz bill was paired with *Warlock*, a new Hollywood western starring Richard Widmark, Henry Fonda, and Anthony Quinn. The mixture of genres seemed to highlight the difference between stage and screen, black stars on one, white on the other.

Clyde Otis had been eager to get back in the studio with Dinah. Finally at the end of August, she was back in New York so they could record. Nat Cole had had a big hit with "Unforgettable" in 1952, and Otis thought that Dinah was the perfect singer to revive it. He had Belford Hendricks write the arrangements along with remakes of "I Thought About You," which bassist Paul West had loved so much, "A Sunday Kind of Love," and a few other ballads.

Hendricks used the same elements in "Unforgettable" that he had for "What a Diff'rence a Day Makes" but in different combination— here the backup vocals started off the song instead of the strings, and then everything came together. All those layers of sounds were what Otis wanted, but the chord structure and musical ideas were not complicated, and Dinah refused to let them get in her way. She presented the song with unmistakable conviction, putting her stamp on it from the first word: "Unforgettable," perfectly enunciated, and then "mmmm" as a lead-in to "that's what you are."

The smile on Otis's face as they talked between songs was evidence of his pleasure with the session. Dinah, holding the music in one hand, the other nonchalantly on her hip, was smiling, too. The chemistry between them was still working.

Mercury planned to get the record out as soon as possible, hoping to ride the wave of "What a Diff'rence a Day Makes." Dinah was riding that wave in her club dates. She was paid $5,000 for a six-day booking at the Rip Tide in Coney Island, which started August 31. The *New York Age* reported that this was the highest amount management had ever paid an entertainer, no doubt one of the benefits of having a hit record.

Dinah returned to Philadelphia to sing at Pep's over the Labor Day holiday, but her singing was temporarily overshadowed by some offstage comments. When she was last in Philadelphia, some friends had thrown a pigs'-foot dinner in her honor at the home of an attorney in nearby Germantown. Among the guests were Lois Green, a dress designer of some note, and the Reverend Samuel Shepherd.

Green contended that Shepherd had assaulted her after she had had too much to drink, that Dinah had witnessed the attack and had told her about it. Green brought charges against the reverend but explained at a hearing in July that Dinah could not corroborate her story because she was still in Sweden.

"I'm certainly available now if she wants to repeat that lie," Dinah told a reporter, sharply disputing Green's version of events and demonstrating anew the effort to shape her own press. "It's a lie if she says I told her anything. And she wasn't drugged either. She acted like she knew exactly what she was doing." For all her romantic escapades, Dinah could sound like a prude, certainly judgmental. "Some undressing went on," she said, "and both of them carried on so that I just looked on in amazement. . . . That behavior was awful. I told them I thought I had gone there to eat dinner. I didn't think it was going to turn out to be a freak party."

Onstage at Pep's, Dinah was in a somber mood one evening. Billie Holiday, both inspiration and friend, had died July 17, and Dinah used some of her time to remember the singer. Dinah's tribute came in the form of "I'm a Fool to Want You," which she sang in Holiday's style.

A more private remembrance came with her friend George Wein, who had booked her at his Boston club, Storyville, and the

Newport Jazz Festival. When she saw Wein not long after Holiday's death, she walked up behind him quietly and sang a verse in his ear—"I say I'll move a mountain, I'll move the mountain. . . ." "A shiver went up the back of my neck," Wein said. "It sounded exactly like the ghost of Billie Holiday."

"I know you love the Lady," Dinah told him. "I just wanted you to know that there are others of us who loved her, too."

DINAH WAS BACK in New York by late September to record again and for a more official celebration with Rusty. This one was hosted by Morris Levy at his new club, the Round Table, which was on East 50th Street. James Moody and his group and the singer Austin Powell entertained the guests. They included friends from several of Dinah's circles, including musicians and politicians, most prominently Adam Clayton Powell, Jr., her friend from Abyssinian Baptist Church who was now a Democratic member of Congress. "Just for the record and scoreboard," Ziggy Johnson wrote in his column, "this makes number six. 'What a difference a husband makes.' " A few days later, Dinah and Rusty partied at Birdland with Levy and visiting club owner Tommy Tucker, who operated the Playroom Café in Los Angeles.

Mercury released "Unforgettable" in mid-September, and by the first week in October, the single was on all the pop music charts and moving up steadily. (It would eventually go to number two in *Cash Box*, the top ten on two of *Variety*'s tallies, and number seventeen on *Billboard*'s pop chart.) The label also released a new album under the Mercury imprint, *The Queen*, which was a mixture of blues and ballads. Some were remakes of songs she had previously recorded, including a more fully orchestrated "Trouble in Mind" and "Backwater Blues."

Liner notes were often intended to help a label position an artist. The notes for *The Queen*, written by Martin Williams, co-editor of the new publication *The Jazz Review*, suggested that Dinah was a seasoned veteran, even if she had just turned thirty-five. He commended her to young listeners embarking on jazz with praise for her versatility and the way she wove her church origins into a song so that nothing she did was a sterile musical exercise. "People are talking about how all these young rhythm and blues singers are now using a churchy style," Williams wrote, quoting one of Dinah's fans. "Why Dinah Washington has always used one. She's more sophisticated, sure, but sometimes I think she sounds like she just walked out of a Baptist church, stopped by the Brill Building"—the legendary home of songwriters—"just long enough to pick up a copy of a tune, and started to wail."

The month of October was shaping up to be one of the most noteworthy in Dinah's career, the attention from the different segments of the music world proof of her claim that "I sing everything, anything at all." The success of "What a Diff'rence a Day Makes" and now "Unforgettable" in the pop community demonstrated her appeal to a more mainstream audience, and the first week in October, when the two-year-old National Academy of Recording Arts and Sciences announced its nominations for the year's music awards— the Grammy—Dinah was nominated for "What a Diff'rence a Day Makes." Despite the record's success in the pop category, though, she was nominated for best rhythm and blues performance. (NARAS had been formed in mid-1957 by a group of executives from the largest record labels looking for a way to honor artistic creativity and at the same time promote the industry.)

Ten days after the Grammy nomination, Dinah made her second appearance on the cover of *Cash Box*. She was shown in mid-song from one of the sessions for *The Queen*. The caption neatly summarized her musical trajectory: "Mercury's fabulous 'Miss D,' long a favorite of blues and jazz enthusiasts, this year developed into a tremendous pop favorite with her smash waxing of 'What a Diff'rence a Day Makes.'"

WHILE WORKING SHOWS with Maynard Ferguson's band, Dinah had been impressed with Ferguson's piano player, Joe Zawinul, a young white man from Vienna who had gotten a scholarship to the Berklee College of Music in Boston but left the classroom for an on-the-job apprenticeship onstage. During a break on one of the dates in Atlanta Dinah came up to Zawinul at the bar. "I sure like the way you play," she told him. "Please call me." And she grabbed a bar napkin to write down her New York number.

Zawinul was flattered, but he was happy with the Ferguson band, and never called Dinah after he returned to New York. A few months later, Ferguson made changes in his band, and Zawinul was fired. One evening he decided to go to Birdland, and as he was going down the stairs to go in, Dinah was on the other side of the door ready to go upstairs. They nearly knocked each other over, standing nose-to-nose in the stairwell.

"Aren't you the guy who plays the piano?" Dinah asked. Zawinul nodded. She invited him to come down to the Village Vanguard, where she was performing. The next night Zawinul went to the club, and when Dinah saw him, she invited him to sit in. After a couple of numbers, Dinah was sold.

"You want to be the piano player?" she whispered, away from the mike. "You got the job."

"She hired me in front of the audience," Zawinul said. "It was so strange." But he loved the way Dinah introduced him to their audiences: "The touch of George Shearing, the soul of Ray Charles." (Dinah was probably using a pickup piano player at the Vanguard—after Junior Mance left in 1955, she had used an assortment of musicians.)

When Zawinul went up to the Bowery Building for a rehearsal the next day, he brought her a new bass player, too, Jimmy Rowser, who had also been with Ferguson's band.

New players in place, Dinah headed out for a tour that would take her to the Midwest and then the South. One of the first stops was back at the Copa Club in Newport, Kentucky, October 23 through November 1. Since the last time she had played the nightspot, the Copa had instituted the added attraction of Wednesday nights with popular local disc jockey Dick Pike of WNOP. At six foot seven he was an imposing figure at the turntable, and his entrepreneurial instincts seemed to match his physical stature. Not only did he work the Copa, but his deal also included the right to have the weekly entertainment drop by his Sunday afternoon dances in nearby Covington. The fall was providing a stellar lineup—Sam Cooke and Al Hibbler right before Dinah, LaVern Baker and Jackie Wilson among those who were coming after her.

Dinah spent a week at Roberts in Chicago, did a one-nighter in Detroit, and then headed south. She and the trio were booked into a club in Odessa, Texas, owned by a black man. It was a large place, but had such slapdash accommodations for the performers they had to dress in the kitchen. The place also didn't serve liquor, just the food and the setup for drinks—glasses, saucers, cocktail stirrers. Dinah had been to the state several times before, but not with a white band member. She and the other musicians were getting ready to go onstage, and Zawinul had gone to another part of the club. He came back and started for the bandstand. A white woman, holstered gun at her hip, stopped him. "Where you going, boy?" she asked, declaring herself the local sheriff.

Zawinul told her he was the piano player and that he was going onstage. No, you're not, she told him. Zawinul went to tell Dinah, who was in the back with the owner, what had happened.

"He don't play," Dinah said, "I don't sing."

The club owner pleaded with her to work out some arrangement—couldn't she just play the piano herself this one time? The place was packed, he pointed out, and the patrons were getting restless. They could hear them tapping the cocktail sticks on the table, a sure sign of their impatience.

Dinah refused. "Open the window," she said to Zawinul, realizing that she couldn't march out through the packed house. He obeyed her command, "and we went out the back window, and we got in our cars and we left."

DINAH RETURNED to a busy couple of weeks in New York at the end of November. She played Basin Street with Dizzy Gillespie, appeared Thanksgiving eve at Carnegie Hall in a concert to benefit the Roy Campanella Foundation, which was set up in honor of the Brooklyn Dodgers catcher who was paralyzed in an automobile accident, and then played the Mosque in Newark on a bill with Al Hibbler. The Campanella benefit was another of the many Dinah did over the years. *Tan* reported in June that she and her driver had been picked up for speeding on her way home from a show to raise money for a police organization. "When she explained the gig," *Tan* said, "they let her go." Dinah had also performed at her sister Clarissa's high school a year or so earlier, wowing the kids and the white teacher in charge, who didn't know who Dinah was and didn't believe that his student had a famous singer in the family.

Basin Street East had been going through something of an identity crisis, according to the *Amsterdam News*. The usual jazz crowd, many if not most of them black patrons, had stopped coming while the Trenier Twins, high-energy singers backed by a quartet, were performing their blend of jump blues and rock 'n' roll. The place was still packed, the paper said, "since the Las Vegas–Miami Beach crowd goes for the wild and furious Treniers. Few Negroes seen." With Dinah and Dizzy Gillespie the makeup of the audiences was expected to change.

NARAS held its second annual awards ceremony in Beverly Hills November 29. The winners received a small award shaped like a gramophone. Dinah, still performing in the East, had to learn the results secondhand. She had won a Grammy. "What a Diff'rence a Day Makes" was judged the best rhythm and blues record of 1959.

Dinah had long had the recognition of fans who packed clubs and theaters to hear her play. The music trade papers paid attention to her as a salable product, but this was something new—an honor from other music makers applauding her art. It was a moment to savor.

Clyde Otis was a beneficiary, too. The production of "What a Diff'rence a Day Makes" had been his idea, though it was Dinah who carried it off. *Jet* called him "one of the hot names in show business" and credited him with "reviving Dinah Washington's record popularity." (While some of the record companies took out *Billboard* ads trumpeting their Grammy winners, for some reason Mercury did not do so for Dinah. Perhaps they worried about sending the wrong signal—she had won a Grammy for "best R&B" and the label was pushing her as a pop star.)

On the heels of the Grammy win, Mercury put out an album with the same title as the song. The dozen tunes were all ballads and included "A Sunday Kind of Love," "It's Magic," "Time After Time," and the bluesy "Cry Me a River." The liner notes came from Otis himself. "Here's the new Dinah Washington!" he said. "New in the sense that for the first time in her 15 years of vocalizing for the wax works she finally made it big with a pop-styled singles release. . . . *What a Diff'rence a Day Made*," he wrote, had "projected her past the thousands who dug her the most as a jazz ambassador and 'Queen of the Blues.' Past the thousands of jazz afficionadoes to the millions who now join her legion.

"Dinah's the peak of emotions," Otis added.

Dinah seemed to see herself that way, too. "Maybe I'm too impulsive and too vulnerable. I don't know. I lead with my heart all the time. . . . That's why on the stage I sing in every show as if it were my last."

The album jacket had an unusual producer's note about the title song and album title. The tune originally had been published as "What a Diff'rence a Day Made," which is how it was listed on the back of the album. Dinah sang "makes," as many singers had done in the years since the tune had been introduced. "Actually, Dinah's forging the song into a current hit was responsible for the research" into the song's history, Mercury said. "We didn't want anyone to think that either our researchers or Dinah had goofed!"

Dinah had been featured in *Ebony, Sepia, Tan,* and *Hue,* and had been on the cover of *Jet* once. In December *Sepia* put her on its cover with an "as told to" story about her offstage life. Her co-writer was Dave Hepburn, a journalist well-known in the black press. The title of the article was "Me and My Six Husbands." "Applause is nice but a husband is much better," said one of the subheads.

"Like most women," Dinah said in the opening paragraph, " 'I wanna be loved,' and despite what my critics may say, I see nothing wrong in that. Mine has been a never-ending search for love and affection, but for some reason, without success.

"I have been hurt, humiliated, kicked around, robbed, maligned by lies. Name it, it has happened to me, but I refuse to give up. Sure I'm a success in my chosen field," she continued, "and the warm applause of the people who listen to me sing is music to my ears, but even Madame Dubarry couldn't take applause to bed with her. . . . Sometimes I have found I give too much to the wrong people," she went on, "but I'm too old to change now. I'll go on giving, loving and searching for the happiness I want. And if everything fails, as that famous song said, 'I'll give my heart to the junkman.' "

Dinah had high hopes with Rusty. "He is kind, thoughtful and gentle," she told Hepburn. Though she said Rusty was free to keep driving a cab, Dinah didn't really mean it. "I need business help and I want him near me. I pay him a salary, and he handles my affairs with intelligence and thoroughness. . . . Some people have wondered whether I dominate my man," she added. "I don't think I do. I give a man his due." It was Dinah, though, who decided what and how much was due.

Dinah's fantasy of the perfect life had taken on new details. "I have certain ideas about happiness: a ranch style house with plenty of acres around it, a couple of horses for my boys, a man that loves me and a perfect understanding between us. I don't think that's asking too much," she added, "and I'm sure I'll get it."

Dinah said her parents and siblings remained important to her. She was especially proud of her brother, Harold, who was now in the air force. "I do all I can for them, which is as it should be. . . . I love all of them, but I also want a life for myself and my husband and children."

The pictures that accompanied the *Sepia* story showed Dinah, still wearing that favorite platinum wig, at her most domestic. An apron over her dress, she posed in one photo standing at the stove, ladle in hand. In another, she and Rusty were sharing a bite of one of her dishes. In a third picture Rusty was sitting with her at the piano, Ollie, George, and Bobby looking on.

Dinah made a point of noting that Rusty "showed a great love for my kids. He took them out, saw that they attended school and did a lot of little things for me."

The boys didn't argue when their mother wanted them to participate in such things. Bobby, though, already had an instinct about the men in his mother's life. He didn't think Rusty was going to last very long. Some of that might have been wishful thinking. When Dinah wasn't around, Rusty told the boys things were going to change now that he was in charge. Bobby didn't like the sound of that.

Given everything that already happened that year—two pop hits, a Grammy award, success in Europe—the year-end polls in the music trades were the cherry on top of the sundae. "What a Diff'rence a Day Makes" made the *Billboard* and *Variety* lists of top fifty songs of the year and made the *Cash Box* tallies for "Best Pop Record" and "Best R&B Record." Music writers promoted it as a Christmas gift. *Cash Box* also named Dinah the "Best R&B Female Vocalist," and she was number two—behind Connie Francis—for "Best Pop Female Vocalist." Jazz fans still liked her, too; she made another appearance on *Down Beat*'s list of top female singers, and the International Fan Club of America, made up of 3,500 jazz fans, according to its president, named Dinah their top female singer for 1959.

Dinah threw a party in Apartment 14A-3 a few days before Christmas to celebrate the holidays and the banner year she'd had. Who wouldn't raise a glass to the achievements and hope for more of the same in the 1960s?

17.

Baby, You've Got What It Takes

1960

Dinah celebrated the beginning of 1960 in Los Angeles, head-lining a New Year's Eve show at the Cloister, an upscale club on Sunset Strip. Patrons decked out in their best gowns and described by one wag as "quasi-hip" paid $30 per person for a seven-course dinner, drinks, party favors, and the entertainment. The rest of Dinah's two-week engagement was less formal as she alternated sets with drummer Chico Hamilton and his quartet.

Like other reviewers over the years, *Down Beat*'s John Tynan, who caught one of the shows, talked about Dinah's wardrobe as well as her singing. "Washington is as flamboyant a showman as she is distinctive vocalist," he wrote. "Strolling on stage in a full-length termaline mink coat and sporting a glittering $200 pair of shoes, she delivered a good set composed mostly of her recordings."

If Tynan knew how much Dinah's shoes cost, most likely she told him and the rest of the audience, proudly showing them off as the spotlight hit her feet.

Most of the Cloister shows were standing room only and ran longer than planned because of repeated requests for encores. Every now and then if the mood struck her, Dinah sang a Billie Holiday song, captivating the audience with her spot-on impression. Her musical references to Holiday were probably related to rumors swirling through Hollywood that a movie about the late singer's life was in the works, with Dinah handling the vocals and Dorothy Dandridge playing Holiday. (The film was never made.)

Rusty had accompanied Dinah to Los Angeles, and while plenty of social and monetary benefits came with being "Mr. Dinah Washington," the notoriety had its downside, too. One early January evening as the couple headed into their hotel after the Cloister performance, policemen stopped them. The officers said they were investigating reports of drug sales in the area and became suspicious when individuals started running after police cars pulled up. Dinah was taken to a nearby police station and then to the city narcotics bureau after an officer found several bottles of pills in her purse.

Rusty was handcuffed and taken into custody.

Dinah told the police that the bottles were filled with prescription diet pills. But there were so many of them that the police were suspicious and confiscated the bottles until they could call her doctor in New York. Dinah was allowed to return to her hotel in a matter of hours, and a short time later Rusty was let go, too.

Allen Saunders, Dinah's lawyer, wouldn't let her speak to reporters eager to hear her version of events. "I'm talking for her," he said. "She was not arrested. She was not booked. She's committed no crime. It was a misunderstanding. There's no story."

The police later returned Dinah's diet pills after the doctor confirmed that they were not narcotics. He explained that he had given her a month's supply because she was on the road.

At first Dinah was upset about a headline that ran over her picture on page one of the *California Eagle*: "No Dope." But then she joked to the paper's entertainment writer that the entire episode had been "a press agent's dream" because of all the publicity.

Less flattering was a front-page headline in the *Sentinel* January 21 about some unhappy business from the previous September: "Dinah Faces $60,000 Contract Suit." The story said that promoters in Memphis had filed an action against Dinah because she failed to appear at a concert September 20, 1959, in Memphis to benefit the St. Jude Foundation Fund. The suit also named Joe Glaser's Associated Booking Corporation in the action. Dinah was to have been paid $1,500 for the performance, but the promoter contended that he lost $60,000 in the transaction.

Dinah had no comment on the allegation and refused to let such things interfere with her daily activities onstage or off-. The evening of January 11 she had performed at a gala formal for black socialites from Los Angeles and New York. The hosts were the Rinkydinks, a social club first formed in New York by the wives of prominent men in the entertainment field. The reason for the ball, held at the swank Beverly Hilton, was to welcome the new Los Angeles chapter, and several of the New York Rinkydinks flew out for the event. Among them were Ruth Bowen, president of the chapter, and the wives of Count Basie, saxophonist Illinois Jacquet, and Milt Hinton, the bass player. All of the women were in specially designed gowns and swathed in their best furs. Before leaving for California, the New York Rinkydinks had posed in theirs for the *Amsterdam News*.

Dinah chose her white full-length coat for the event, wearing it over a yellow silk, floor-length ball gown with matching shoes that were studded with rhinestones. She was a study in contrast as she stood in such formal wear nonchalantly holding the microphone while Earl Bostic played the saxophone behind her and Ray Charles, who was also performing, accompanied her at the piano.

A few days later Dinah was a special guest at another reception for the Rinkydinks, this one hosted by Betty Clark, whose husband owned the Clark Hotel on Central Avenue. Ann Littles was accompanying Dinah on this trip, and when the three women stood together, their full-length fur coats ran the palette: Dinah in the middle in white and holding a bouquet of flowers, Betty Clark on her right wearing a tan mink, and Ann on Dinah's left in an equally luxuriant black mink. It was the first gift Dinah had given Ann, though Dinah hadn't paid full price. Ann knew she had gotten it from one of her favorite boosters.

Dinah stayed in the jazz mode after finishing the Cloister job. She was paired with the popular Dave Brubeck Quartet for a jazz concert January 22 at the nearby Pasadena Civic Auditorium. Despite the lineup and considerable advance publicity—Dinah was billed as "the Unforgettable Queen of Song"—the promoter said he didn't make a profit. Jazz critic Ralph Gleason noted later that, economics aside, there was still talk of holding a two-day jazz festival in San Francisco.

. . .

CLYDE OTIS HAD already produced Dinah's two biggest hits, so she was more than willing to listen when he had suggested pairing her with his occasional writing partner and Mercury star Brook Benton, who was on an even hotter streak than Dinah. Benton was born Benjamin Peay and had been a truck driver in South Carolina, but he loved to write songs and sing. He had raced up the charts in 1959 with "It's Just a Matter of Time." Tall and handsome with a smooth, easygoing style, he was the epitome of a star. Otis thought that Dinah and Benton together would be an inviting mix—her tart swing, his sweet cool. "Baby (You've Got What It Takes)" seemed like the right vehicle.

Otis called on Belford Hendricks to write another of his string arrangements. This time the violins and cellos were more in the background than on "What a Diff'rence a Day Makes" and "Unforgettable." A guitar was prominent as a counterpoint to Dinah's and Benton's alternating vocals.

The two seemed to be having a good time, each ad-libbing a phrase here and there. But the playfulness belied occasional tension in the studio because Dinah didn't like Benton. She conceded he was a good singer, but she didn't think he was very smart. In subtle ways, with well-timed digs, she let him know that. They hadn't had much time to rehearse "Baby," and there was a certain intricacy to getting the duets right. Because no one was ever sure when a take might work, the engineers kept the tape running so that nothing would be lost. On one try, everything was going beautifully, Benton coming in with the first vocals after a breezy string introduction, Dinah following him with her lines. They went on back and forth for another few bars before giving way to an instrumental passage.

Then Benton started to sing just as Dinah struck her note. "You're back in my spot again, honey," she chided.

"I like that spot," he retorted before backing off.

"Now it's you," Dinah said when she finished her lines.

Otis and the engineers didn't interrupt, and when the session was over, they decided the take with the flub was the one to release. This bit of inside business would lend the record cachet, as though each listener had been privy to the session.

Publicly Benton laughed off Dinah's snappishness. "She could be difficult," he said, but insisted they got along "very well in the studio . . . The goof wasn't intentional," he went on. "We were playing around really, you know, testing as we went along. Frankly, some of the time we didn't even know they were taping. We were like having a dry run."

"Baby (You've Got What It Takes)" was released early in January, and it took off right away. (The flip side, "I Do," was a sugary ballad about marriage vows, which seemed a strange selection given Dinah's tempestuous and very public marital history. The opening bars were a variation on Mendelssohn's wedding march, which the strings reprised later in the tune.)

"Baby" was a confirmed hit. It was on *Billboard*'s pop and R&B charts by the end of January, registered immediately in *Cash Box* and *Variety*, and was also a hit in the tallies kept by some of the black newspapers. According to the *Michigan Chronicle*, "Baby" charged to the top of Detroit's top ten. Mercury had to make one adjustment with the record, however, agreeing to let the song be known for chart purposes simply as "Baby." A few weeks before the release United Artists had put out a record by Marv Johnson, "You Got What It Takes," which was a completely different tune. The two labels agreed that Mercury would use the short name.

The success of "Baby" had proved Otis right once again. On top of that it was renewed confirmation of Dinah's ability to cross musical boundary lines. She had just finished a successful club date at the Cloister, where some nights she was Queen of the Blues. She had headlined a jazz bill with Dave Brubeck, and now she was on the pop charts with Brook Benton—but not so pop that she didn't draw her faithful rhythm and blues fans, too. Ella Fitzgerald and Sarah Vaughan may have been bigger stars, but neither, in part by their choice of material and where they put their energies, commanded such sustained attention across the musical spectrum.

With strings or with horns, upbeat or ballad, Dinah continued to put her stamp on anything she sang. The penetrating timbre and the incisive phrasing that captured Leonard Feather's attention seventeen years earlier had only gained in power.

DINAH HEADED to San Francisco the first of February to play Facks II, a new venue for her and a club that was known as much for featuring young folksingers as it was musicians in Dinah's mold. The reviewer *Variety* sent one night got his arms around the essence of her art. "Her voice is not a great instrument," he wrote. "She has to strain for some notes. But her use of it, her inflections, phrasing, diction, are sufficiently stylized to compensate for whatever defects her voice may have. She has a vivid, outspokenly honest personality. . . . She's always in command, so that she can fill in between songs with bright and candid remarks while she readies her next number. This, the fact that it's evident she likes her work, and the fact that she's got a fine feeling for the blues, sets her aside from most singers."

Musical observations aside, the reviewer seemed to be saying that an evening with Dinah was, simply put, a lot of fun.

Dinah's puckish nature was on display after one show early in the morning when she bantered with club owner George Andros. He admired one of her diamond rings, which Dinah claimed was from a "late husband." So was the mink she was wearing. "Are they all dead?" Andros wondered.

"No, honey. But after I leave 'em, they're just too late, that's all."

When the Facks II engagement was finished Dinah returned to Los Angeles for a recording session. Clyde Otis had flown out to supervise. Belford Hendricks was on hand to arrange for a full orchestra—twenty-two musicians, including eight violins and four violas. The plan was to record eight songs the evening of February 16, but Dinah got sick, and the session was over after three songs.

Dorothy Kilgallen had reported in one of her "Voice of Broadway" columns that Dinah had a throat ailment that was "causing her great concern." Privately friends blamed Dinah's dieting for her illness. *Jet* published one such report after the shortened session, but Dinah insisted it wasn't true. "I never diet," she claimed, and then, as if to prove her point, gave an exaggerated account of her next meal. "Why I'm about to have my breakfast now of roast beef, green beans and corn bread. I have lost weight, yes, but not by dieting." She made no mention of the bountiful supply of pills she kept at the ready. "I have a special method I use which I won't tell any one. And," she added defiantly, "I'm not near collapse and never have been."

Less than a year after they met, Dinah and Rusty appeared to be finished. He had gone back to New York, uncomfortable in the role

of the unemployed "Mr. Dinah Washington." He was reportedly trying to line up a job in sales for Gladys Hampton's record label. Bobby
had been proved right in his assessment that Rusty wouldn't last,
Dinah's protestations and all those homey pictures in *Sepia* to the
contrary. She made an announcement about their split to the *Chicago
Defender* when she returned to the city in March to get ready for a
week at the Regal Theater. In the meantime, she told *Jet* that her
"number one fan and admirer on the West Coast is Mickey Cohen."
The magazine described him as "the widely known gambling figure
who's been a constant ringside visitor." Dinah was coy when asked if
he was her new boyfriend.

"Let's just say he likes my down home cooking, greens and
cornbread."

For his part, Rusty told *Tan* that he "would welcome the opportunity to become known as Dinah Washington's ex-husband No. 6."
He told *Jet* that he had moved his clothes out of the apartment at the
Bowery Building and was going back home. Dinah told the magazine he packed up on her orders, but she deflected questions about
any divorce, probably because she knew the "marriage" off the coast
of Stockholm wasn't really legal. Dinah instructed the maintenance
staff at the Bowery Building that under no circumstances was Rusty
to be given the keys to her new Thunderbird. George Dixon, one of
the building engineers, made sure to keep the car in the back of the
garage and boxed in by other vehicles so that Rusty couldn't get
to it.

Dinah's romantic life was so public now, at least in black
America, that nothing was off-limits nor considered in bad taste. As
soon as singer Larry Darnell heard that Dinah and Rusty were
through, he wooed her by telegram: "You've tried the rest, now wed
the best." She apparently passed up the offer.

Dinah was on national television again when NBC broadcast
one segment in a series re-creating the big band era, *The Swingin'
Singin' Years*. The program, which aired March 8, was sponsored by
Ford Motors and hosted by Ronald Reagan. Among those working
on the show was Berle Adams, the co-founder of Mercury who had
signed Dinah in 1946 to her first major record contract. Though he
left the label in 1950 and moved to California, he still worked in the
entertainment industry and had suggested that Dinah be on one of
the Ford shows. Initially Adams got a cold shoulder from the pro-

ducer, who pronounced Dinah "too much trouble, and I don't really need her."

"She's such a great singer," Adams persisted, promising Dinah would behave.

The day of rehearsal Adams was working in his office when the phone rang. The producer was on the line. "Berle, I think you better get over here. Miss Washington refuses to rehearse. She's in her dressing room, and she will not come out." She apparently told the crew that she would do the show but nothing else.

Adams hung up, went to his car, drove the few miles to the studio in Burbank, and was ushered to Dinah's dressing room. "Miss Washington," he said through the door, "my name is Berle Adams." She jumped up and opened the door, he recalled. " 'That's my father, that's my father,' and she ran over to me, kissing me. I said, 'Dinah'—she said, 'Oh, no, no, no—my father tells me what to do. I'll do it. I'll do it.' They never had a problem with her after that," Adams said.

Dinah's segment was introduced by some banter between Louis Jordan, who was leading the band, and Reagan, the host, about how hectic it was to play the Apollo Theater—though the show was filmed in Burbank, they spoke as if they were at the Harlem theater. "Excuse me, Ronnie, I'm up," Jordan finally said, as the camera followed him onto the stage.

"And now it's star time at the Apollo Theater, and what could be finer than my Dinah. Here she is, 'Queen of the Blues,' Dinah Washington."

Dinah went right into "What a Diff'rence a Day Makes," giving it a slightly more bluesy cast than the studio recording. When she got to the line, "Oh, yeah, one thrilling kiss," she bent down slightly, leaned toward the microphone, and shook her head for emphasis. As the song neared the end, she segued into a spirited "Makin' Whoopee," bowed briefly when she finished, and then left the stage to the sound of applause.

Dinah opened at the Regal on Friday, March 11. The first one hundred patrons were given free copies of her most recent hit records. Depending on their place in line they received either "What a Diff'rence a Day Makes," "Unforgettable," "Baby," or the newest release, "It Could Happen to You," which was already moving up the music charts. A ballad from an old Dorothy Lamour movie, the song was a revival of a Jo Stafford hit from 1944 but revived Dinah's way. The repetitions of some phrases and the delicate crescendo on others were reminiscent of those first blues tunes recorded with Leonard Feather. Mercury was so pleased with the single that the label took out a full-page ad in *Billboard* March 7 to promote it. Suprisingly, the company used a two-year-old picture of Dinah, a wide-eyed, smiling photo taken during her brief marriage to Eddie Chamblee.

But it was "Baby (You've Got What It Takes)" that was the biggest hit by far for her, and for Benton, too. The disc was sitting at number one on *Billboard*'s R&B chart, it was near the top on the magazine's pop chart, and in a similar spot on the tallies in *Variety* and *Cash Box*. Not only that, the record also placed high on the music poll published by United Press International and carried in the mainstream white press, whose music columnists also took note.

Dinah often spoke about "soul" when she talked about singing, but she used the word to describe a feeling, not a musical category defined by a beat or style. Now some promoters were using the term as a catchall for their multiact concert bills. One of the first, touted as "Soul 60," featured Dinah, Ray Charles and his orchestra, the Horace Silver Quintette, and Art Blakey's Jazz Messengers. The promoters booked the group for two performances at the posh Civic Opera House Friday, March 25, and then the next night in Detroit at the Broadway Capitol Theater. This was the kind of bill that could draw an integrated audience, and in both cities the promoters advertised in the mainstream white papers—the *Chicago Tribune* and the *Detroit Free Press.*

It was noteworthy that on a program brimming with talent, Dinah was singled out in the *Free Press* to advertise the concert. Her picture was the one used on the entertainment page, the caption a reminder of her broad appeal: "Blues stylist Dinah Washington highlights the jazz concert."

GIVEN THE SUCCESS of "Baby (You've Got What It Takes)," it was natural to assume that Dinah and Brook Benton would work well together onstage. "They sounded so good, people thought they were lovers," remembered Dinah's son Bobby, although that was not the case. Dinah and Benton teamed up for a ten-day Easter holiday show at the Paramount in Brooklyn, but most nights they only sang "Baby" together. Bobby and George were in the show, too, though they were not announced ahead of time. Their short dance routine came in between Dinah's numbers, when the announcer introduced the "Dinah-mites," who, *Variety* wrote, "come across as amiable tapsters."

Before Dinah agreed to do the show, she insisted on getting the same as Benton—$7,500 for the run. "I make hit records, too," she declared.

Clyde Otis had wanted to do an entire album of duets with Dinah and Benton, and he even invited photographer Chuck Stewart to be present for the session to get some good shots of the two singers working together. But according to Otis the plans had to be scrapped after four tunes because Dinah was carping at Benton for making mistakes. Though Benton's later accounts of the session were benign—he always spoke gently about Dinah—Otis remembered the tension. "She had no respect for him, no respect for him personally," Otis said. "She kept saying, 'You're a dumb so-and-so' . . . and he didn't like having her chastise him."

According to Shelby Singleton, another Mercury executive, Dinah told Benton she was "tired of making you a star" and didn't want to make any more records with him.

Otis finally sent Dinah home and had Benton record as solos the remaining songs they had planned as duets. Otis cobbled an album together from the four duets the singers had finished, Benton's solos, and some of Dinah's previously recorded tunes. Otis called the album *The Two of Us,* and Stewart's amiable pictures of Dinah and Benton sitting on the floor together looking over the music gave no hint of the scrapping that Otis remembered so vividly.

Dinah's behavior toward Benton was perplexing. It would have made good sense for them to record again together. They fit so well musically and had found an audience—her fans and his, potentially bigger than either alone. But Dinah's reluctance to let this collaboration work suggested that she didn't want to share the spotlight—at least not for very long. She would do an award show, like the events the *Pittsburgh Courier* had sponsored at Carnegie Hall, or the television specials. But if she was going to be onstage or cut a record, then she wanted all eyes and ears on her.

Sometimes, too, Dinah couldn't resist being part of someone else's act. During a Redd Foxx show at the Apollo, Dinah and an entourage trooped in and sat down near the front. Jazz critic Dan Morgenstern was nearby and was convulsed with laughter as he listened to Dinah trade jokes with Foxx. "It was a wonderful series of repartee," he recalled, which apparently overshadowed any impropriety in Dinah's stealing another entertainer's thunder, if only for a moment.

Mercury released a single from *The Two of Us* in early May, "A Rockin' Good Way (To Mess Around and Fall in Love)." The tune, which was first recorded in 1958 by Priscilla Bowman with backing by the Spaniels, had the same infectious beat and spirit of "Baby (You've Got What It Takes)," and some playful interjections by each of the singers. At the end, Dinah gave Benton a little jab—"Baby, you got what it takes—stay outta my spot."

"Oh, yeah," Benton retorted, "I like that spot."

By mid-May the song was a hit, climbing up the charts of all the music magazines and getting to number one on *Billboard*'s R&B tally. At the same time Mercury had released a solo album for Dinah titled after her most recent solo hit, *Unforgettable*. While *Cash Box* didn't employ reviewers with the kind of critical eye found in *Down Beat* or *Metronome*, the short item about the new album in the May 4 issue noted how the label capitalized on Dinah's "new-found pop acceptance." And it nicely summarized the way the arrangements and Dinah's voice fit together: "The string and chorus accompaniment contrast and therefore point up the singer's vinegary, earthy qualities." *Variety* singled out Dinah's "instinct for lyric and phrasing," a constant since she first took the stage with Lionel Hampton.

When Dinah returned to Birdland in early May, it was clear how comfortable she was with her latest trio—Joe Zawinul still on piano and Jimmy Rowser still on bass joined now by Al Jones on drums. Symphony Sid Torin was back hosting one of the shows broadcast live on the radio and gave Dinah his customary welcome as "Queen of the Blues." When the applause died down, Dinah opened the show with an upbeat version of "Soft Winds." Midway through Zawinul took a solo, with Dinah's encouragement. "Go, Joe," she said.

"Sit down, baby, and have a ball," Sid interjected.

"Thank you, darling."

"That's Joe Zawinul on the piano," Dinah said when he had finished.

Every audience now expected to hear Dinah sing "What a

Diff'rence a Day Makes," and she obliged by making it part of a medley, as she had done on the March television special. The studio
recording had strings and backup vocals. The live version was
stripped down but no less interesting. The trio played sparely, providing small accents to Dinah's telling the story about a new and
hopeful romance. The sidemen followed her seamlessly when she
went into "I Thought About You," came back briefly to "What a
Diff'rence," and then changed tempos for a fast-paced "Our Love Is
Here to Stay."

"Play, Joe Zawinul!" she exclaimed as he took another solo.

Dinah didn't write many songs, but she had formed a publishing
company for her latest compositions—DeLaru Music, her partnership with LaRue Manns. The lyrics to "Somewhere Along the Line,"
which she co-wrote, seemed to come right out of her offstage life. It
was about a man who touched her heart "and won it, now you
would shun it / Over a glass of wine." When Dinah sang it at Birdland, she drew out every line as if to make sure the audience understood exactly what she was talking about.

On May 11 Dinah flew to North Carolina for what was supposed
to be three shows, Charleston, Winston-Salem on the 13th, and then
Charlotte on the 14th. The contract called for her to get $3,000. The
show in Charleston, which was a dance and not a concert as Dinah
had expected, took place without any problems, but something
went haywire in Winston-Salem. She was booked to play the Coliseum, which held nine thousand, but only about 350 were in the
audience. The show was scheduled to start at 9:00 P.M., but Dinah
was nowhere to be found. To keep the small audience satisfied, promoters Benny Fowler and Bob Friedman sent the warm-up band
out onstage to play. The audience was receptive for fifteen or twenty
minutes, but by 9:30, they were restive. Dinah finally arrived, went
to the stage area, looked out at the small crowd, and then turned
around and left.

According to Roy Thompson's account the next day in the *Winston-Salem Journal,* she called a cab, and "She didn't even say 'goodbye' to her promoters. They didn't know she was gone until they
were asked for comment on why she left."

Dinah had spoken briefly to a reporter on her way out of the
Coliseum. She said Fowler and Friedman had bawled her out for
getting to the Coliseum late. "They're not pulling any techs on me,"

she said as she got in the cab, using the shorthand term for "contract technicalities."

By 10:45 P.M. the promoters told the weary band to stop playing and announced that refunds would be provided at the box office. One of the men told Thompson that Dinah was "always temperamental." He added that the concert set for Saturday the 14th in Charlotte had been canceled.

A few days later Fowler and Friedman filed formal charges with the American Guild of Variety Artists, accusing Dinah of arriving late and then walking out on the performance. The promoters were seeking not only the $3,000 for the concert but also damages for the salaries they had to pay other musicians who were waiting to play. Dinah's contract, though, stipulated that under the "play or pay" provision, she was liable only for the amount of her agreement.

Allen Saunders, Dinah's New York lawyer, was again called into service. He had a different version of events. He said the promoters had failed to keep their end of the bargain, that Dinah had chartered a plane to make the Winston-Salem date but was told that because she arrived shortly after their deadline, she would not go on until 11:30 P.M. Saunders also said that there had been problems with the portion of the contract paid in advance. One check had bounced, though it was later made good. And another $1,000, which was to have been deposited with AGVA for later payment, had been held up by the attorney representing Fowler and Friedman.

Variety wrote about the dispute in its May 18 issue, though it was not clear how the matter was ultimately resolved. The publicity, however, was not the sort to burnish Dinah's reputation. It was one thing to be in the gossip columns over this man or that, but quite another to be presented in an unprofessional light, especially because live performances were the foundation of her career. And this was the second incident of bad publicity since the January story about the missed performance in Memphis.

BY THE TIME Dinah returned to New York, her offstage life was on display once again. Separated three months from Rusty, the dalliance with Mickey Cohen behind her, she announced that she had a new boyfriend and intended to get married again. He was Jackie Hayes, a model with movie-star looks who also worked in public relations. Dinah introduced him to her friends at a party thrown for her by Al Duckett, who managed the Wells Restaurant and regularly sponsored a "cabaret" night to honor performers working in the New York area. The couple posed for photographers, Dinah wearing a fashionable broad-brimmed hat, a white fur stole around her shoulders, Hayes in a dark suit and silver tie, accepting honorary membership in a newly integrated golf club outside New York City. During the evening Dinah sang a few numbers and according to the *Amsterdam News* even played the organ.

Rumors of grandiose wedding presents swirled about. The *Chicago Defender* reported that the golf club planned to give the couple a ten-thousand-square-foot home site as a wedding present. The *Amsterdam News* said that "if and when Dinah weds Jackie Hayes, the couple have been promised a gift of Chicago's Grand Terrace Ballroom by Joe Glaser." And *Jet* ran a picture of the couple, Dinah sporting an engagement ring reportedly worth $4,500.

Friends mindful of Dinah's impulsive nature about men wondered privately if Hayes would be around for a wedding, let alone the building of a new house.

The rest of May and early June were typical for Dinah—a big concert in Baltimore with Bull Moose Jackson May 28, followed by a week back at Pep's in Philadelphia. The highlight during this job at Pep's was meeting a millionaire fan. "Man, that cat's so fabulous, he's got wall to wall *walls*," Dinah chortled.

There was also the release of another single, "This Bitter Earth," written by Clyde Otis and arranged by Hendricks with full strings and a chorus. It was a somber tune—"This bitter earth, what fruit it bears" was the opening line. Dinah gave it punch by pausing after the first phrase and inserting "well," before the next line. She inserted "lord" before another phrase, and it seemed so natural because Dinah sounded as though she was preaching a sermon about hope. "I'm sure someone will answer my call," she sang at the end "and this bitter earth may not"—and Dinah paused again—"be so bitter after all."

By the middle of June "This Bitter Earth" was on the pop music charts, Dinah's fourth hit since January, including the two with Brook Benton. All of them were produced by Otis, and now when Dinah said, "Clyde, you motherfucker," he knew for certain that it was a compliment.

It may have been a self-administered reward or perhaps a bit of indulgence for this recent success that prompted Dinah to buy a mink-trimmed sofa bed reportedly costing $3,500. The sofa was too big to fit into the Bowery Building's elevator so the deliverymen had to carry it up the stairwell, negotiating each landing until they eased it through the door of 14A-3 and set it down in the living room.

Since March, Ruth Bowen had effectively become Dinah's business manager. One of her duties was looking over the contracts sent by Associated Booking for each of Dinah's dates, though the flap in Winston-Salem was evidence that no deal was immune from problems. By June Dinah and Ruth agreed that Ruth would open a personal management office with Dinah as her first client. They called it Queen Artists, and took space in a theater building on Broadway in Midtown.

"I understood that she wasn't the easiest person to get along with," Ruth said, "and I told her when she asked me to start handling her business, giving her advice as a manager and so forth, I told her, 'If you trust me enough to ask me to do this, then you must respect me when I give you this advice or whatever I might say,' and if we have to argue, we don't need each other." They never had a formal contract. "If you're unhappy, and I'm unhappy, let's just 'c'est la vie.' "

Public denials to the contrary, Dinah was still trying to lose weight and regularly took her reducing pills, as she called them, and then tranquilizers if she was having trouble getting to sleep. The combination apparently caught up with her during an engagement at George Wein's Storyville club in Boston in mid-June. She collapsed and had to be rushed to Massachusetts General Hospital. She rebounded in time to open June 24 for a week at the Flame Show Bar in Detroit. Though Dinah and Eddie Chamblee were through as a couple, she brought him back in her act to help coordinate a revue that featured talent she had discovered while on the road: an organ trio led by Perri Lee, dancer Ray Snead, and a female singer named Del St. John. Dinah performed with her own trio led by Joe Zawinul.

Dinah got sick again early in July—it wasn't clear if the illness was related to the Boston collapse—and she had to cancel her performance on the 13th at the Berkshire Jazz Festival in Lenox, Massachusetts. She was supposed to have played the Newport Jazz

Festival the week before, but that performance was canceled when the festival closed early because drunk and disorderly fans—most of them college age—rampaged through Newport.

Dinah and Jackie Hayes made it through the spring as a couple, amusing guests during a visit to Philadelphia when they demonstrated the Madison, a dance then in fashion, for guests at the Chesterfield Hotel. Dinah's svelte look was apparent in pictures of the couple that appeared in the *Defender* and the *Los Angeles Sentinel*, which referred to Hayes as "the leading candidate" to be Dinah's new husband. But the paper added that "according to some gossip columnists Jackie is getting 'cold feet' about the marriage." The rift between the two apparently widened for good a short time later when Hayes took Dinah's car to Chicago while she was at the Flame in Detroit. She hired local lawyer Lawrence Massey to seize the car and remove all of Hayes's personal belongings. According to *Jet*, he caught a bus back to New York.

Hayes was the latest in the stream of men in Dinah's life who usually arrived and left at her bidding. Clark Terry was at one party at the Bowery Building—it was shortly after the mink-trimmed couch had arrived—and she was "shopping for a mate," as he put it. "We were having a great time, and all of sudden she found the mate," Terry remembered. "All right," she told the group. "The party's over. All you motherfuckers go home."

Dinah liked to have a man on her arm for a night out, and when the bill came, she took out some money and pressed it into the man's hand so he could pay. On the surface convention was preserved, but the private gesture told an entirely different story. Dinah was determined to get the change back, too, said Ruth Bowen, who sometimes went along. "When the cash register started going, Dinah was counting—a human calculator to keep up with her money."

One of those young men was Joe Stone, a handsome young employee at the Bowery Building. When Dinah invited him to go nightclubbing, he quietly protested that he had to work during the day and needed to get some sleep. Don't worry, she told him, grabbing a bottle of her prescription pills. Take one of these. Stone did and later confided to his friend George Dixon that he couldn't get to sleep for a day—the same thing that had happened to Betsy Jones after her night out in London with Dinah.

At the moment at least Dinah was not interested in getting married again. In the past, she said, "my men didn't want to pitch in and make our affair a swinging thing . . . they just wanted to set back." Then, too, Dinah conceded with more introspection than usual, "it ain't easy to be married to a star. You're in the limelight all the time, and it's easy for your man to get jealous."

WHEN THE TWO OF US was released, fans and reviewers had no idea that Dinah and Benton didn't like each other. Nor did they know that Otis had planned for the entire record to be duets. *Cash Box* used one of the pictures from the session on its cover July 9, describing the photo as a moment when the singers "relax between takes." Dinah and Benton, each dressed in casual clothes, were sitting on the floor going over the music. Milt Hinton, arm around his bass, was standing a few feet away in the background, all of it the picture of serenity.

"This is a pop album all the way around," *Down Beat* said in its review. The writer predicted the record would do well, even though he was somewhat dismissive of the music. He liked Dinah, but he seemed to like her best as a blues singer. "Her saving grace amidst the pop pap is her refusal to shake loose the earthiness that so distinguishes her singing style," he wrote. "But it's a poor substitute for the genuine musical worth within her. Dinah can cut it with the best of the jazz singers. Presumably material of this caliber sells better than the blues, which, when all is said and done, is more than somewhat of a pity."

(Dinah had tied with Mary Ann McCall for last place in *Down Beat*'s midsummer poll of jazz critics. Ella Fitzgerald was first, with nearly three times as many votes as Sarah Vaughan.)

By coincidence Benton and Clyde Otis happened to be in Chicago when Dinah returned August 3 for a week at Roberts. They went to one of the shows, and among those in the audience that night was a group of women from a South Side church who had been given tickets by Herman Roberts. Carrie Taylor had enjoyed the first half and was looking forward to the second, when Dinah would sing some more. Roberts came out before Dinah started her set and announced that Benton was in the house and that he hoped he could persuade him to come up and sing with Dinah.

He hadn't asked Dinah about this ahead of time. "She started swearing," Taylor recalled, "and said Brook Benton was so dumb he couldn't read music."

An angry Benton got out of his seat and started yelling at Dinah. "She walked off the stage leaving Herman all alone," Taylor explained. Everyone in the showroom was stunned, not knowing quite what to do. To ease the tension the band played a song, and then Dinah came back onstage, wearing a different gown. She cued the musicians and started to sing "like nothing happened," Taylor said.

The outburst, however brief, confirmed that there would be no sequel to *The Two of Us.*

One of the summer traditions on Chicago's South Side was the Bud Billiken Festival, named for a fictional character and started decades earlier by Robert S. Abbott, the founder of the *Chicago Defender,* to foster community spirit and help the underprivileged. The highlight was a parade that wove a mile or so through the South Side, followed by a picnic and concert in Washington Park. This year's event was emceed by popular disc jockey Daddy-O Daylie, and Dinah was invited to perform along with Big Maybelle and the Oscar Peterson Trio. Dressed in dark slacks, a loose-fitting white blouse, and a wide-brimmed hat to shield her from the sun, Dinah sang a half-dozen songs that were all requests from her fans in the audience. The *Defender* estimated that 35,000 had gathered for the show.

Though Dinah was supposed to return to New York for some club dates, she instead was held over for a second week at Roberts. She agreed to be part of a new feature that debuted Monday, August 16, at 7:00 A.M.—a "gala" breakfast show at Roberts, free of charge and with no cover. According to management, "the morning show will enable performers and musicians working in Chicago to come out and enjoy themselves and meet their fellow workers," most of whom would come straight from their sets, usually in the middle of the night. Breakfast was served until noon, and the music was impromptu, whatever the performers felt like doing.

After Dinah's final show Herman Roberts was happy to pose for a picture, planting an appreciative kiss on her cheek. He told the *Defender* that only Sammy Davis, Jr., had drawn more customers than she did. The club apparently had been in the red, and Dinah's strong showing got Roberts back on track.

Dinah was featured at a jazz festival August 19 on Randall's Island in New York that was noteworthy for the inclement weather and the interracial audience. Promoter Franklin Geltman went ahead even though it was raining because he had already postponed the previous day's concert. Undeterred by the drizzle, Dinah put together a well-received set that mixed recent releases with some older blues. George Hoofer used his full-page review in *Down Beat* to comment about the music and the festival in general. Geltman, who said he lost nearly $30,000 on the event, told Hoofer that he planned to do it again. The promoter added that the police, mindful of the riot that had occurred in Newport, complimented him on the crowd's good behavior.

"Not only was Randall's Island an example of a festival without trouble," Hoofer wrote, "but it was even more, an example of smooth racial relations. Here in America's largest metropolitan area, 26,000 persons—about equally divided between Negroes and whites—sat down to hear music together, and this writer did not see a ripple of friction. It was an achievement that should not be overlooked."

The *Amsterdam News* saw it the same way. Underneath a half-page collage of pictures, the editors noted that the musicians "played to thousands of interracial jazz buffs with nothing in evidence but harmony." It might have been a cliché to reflect on the transcendent power of music, but Randall's Island proved the point.

The *Amsterdam News* gave Dinah a breathless welcome-back when she returned to the Apollo for a week starting September 9. She had always been one of the most talented singers with "moderate success in the recording field," the paper said, "but Dinah in the last 18 months has suddenly blasted out of the pack like an echo satellite going into orbit, and smash hit records have come off the presses one after the other until she is now one of the most prolific recording stars."

Dinah and Frank Schiffman and his sons, Bobby and Jack, who ran the theater, were like family now. Bobby never forgot Dinah's irritation when she realized before one engagement that Eartha Kitt had a better dressing room than she did. "She came up to the office and cussed me out," he recalled with a laugh. "Her favorite expression was j.a.m.f.—jive-ass motherfucker. She cussed me out something awful," yet, he said, her bark was much worse than her bite.

The Schiffmans also knew that Dinah was a good draw. Jack remembered going outside one day while Dinah was rehearsing in the cramped smoky hall underneath the lobby. He could hear her from the street, as could passersby. Two of them stopped for a moment as they reached the Apollo's main entrance.

"Ain't that Dinah Washington?" one of them said.

"Sure sounds like Dinah, don't it?" the other replied.

"Yeah, man. Guess there ain't anybody can wail the blues like her."

Dinah often asked the Schiffmans for an advance, which sometimes surprised Jack because he knew she was getting paid well—at least $2,500 for a week, sometimes more, and was earning money from Mercury and regular live dates in other venues. Often her pay envelope included more "draw slips"—reflecting what she had already received—than actual money. But every now and then he understood that it was Dinah's generosity that left her short of money. He knew that when she heard about a fellow performer's sick mother, she visited the woman at a nearby Harlem hospital and was so distressed by the poor conditions that she arranged to have the woman transferred to another hospital, hired an ambulance to take her there, and went along in the ambulance to keep her company. "The tab for the transfer and extra expenses was quietly picked up by Dinah," Jack Schiffman said.

Another apparent expense was ironing out a dispute with George Treadwell, whom Dinah had hired briefly to handle some of her business affairs. An ad for Dinah in the March 14 *Billboard* listed Associated Booking as her agent and Treadwell as "personal management." Dinah apparently defined "personal" more broadly than Treadwell, and when he rebuffed her advances, she told him their deal was off. Treadwell told her she would still have to pay him. *Defender* columnist Al Monroe reported September 17 that Dinah paid Treadwell $15,000 to settle the matter, though Ruth Bowen, recalling the dispute years later, said that figure was high.

Because "This Bitter Earth" was such a hit, Dinah told Bobby Schiffman that she wanted new staging for the show and outlined her idea. A stage carpenter built a huge sphere that looked like the Earth, Schiffman recalled. "It was a big damn thing, and Dinah was to be discovered seated in the middle of it. Holding a hand mike, she would sing her hit song. Just to make the whole thing more effective, we rented two smoke machines and put one in each wing. Man! When we turned those things on, the stage looked like the cover of a gothic novel, with eerie wisps of smoke curling around. . . . And when you hit all that smoke with reds and blues from the overhead spots, it looked like the world was coming to an end."

Dinah came in the night before the show was to open to inspect the set. "Proudly I took her into the theater to show her how magnificently we had translated her idea into scenic design," he went on. "I turned on the smoke machine and had the Earth lowered from overhead. It hung about six feet above the stage and swung back and forth."

Dinah's eyes widened as she absorbed the full effect of the swinging perch.

"Well, what do you think?" Schiffman asked.

"Sheeeit," was all Dinah could muster.

DINAH'S CONSIDERABLE SUCCESS in the last year was masking some disturbing moments, nothing that couldn't be overcome but troubling nonetheless. She wanted to be thin but was relying on medication rather than changing her diet to stay slender. She sloughed off two bouts of illness, one requiring hospitalization, that must have only increased the pressure she felt to rally quickly and keep going. But there seemed to be periodic breaking points: that missed date in Memphis, flouncing out of the Coliseum in Winston-Salem, and then showing up so late for a performance in Battle Creek, Michigan, that promoter Robert Montgomery filed an action to recoup what he said were significant losses. The matter was settled through arbitration, and the American Guild of Variety Artists fined Dinah $1,500.

But even with a judgment against her, Dinah was having trouble keeping accounts up-to-date. According to Montgomery she was so behind in her payments that he filed the required papers to have the Wayne County sheriff seize some of her assets just as she was settling into a two-week run at at the Flame Show Bar in Detroit. On September 21 two deputies stopped Dinah in her 1960 Chrysler, impounded the car, and grabbed the mink stole—rudely, she said—that was wrapped around her shoulders.

The stole was returned to her a short time later at the Flame, and not long after, her Detroit lawyer, Lawrence Massey, was able to retrieve her car. Dinah's troubles were not over, though. The car she had been riding in after deputies took the Chrysler was struck by another. She was shaken up in the accident though not seriously hurt. When she got to the Flame, she was still seething about the way she had been treated and recounted her story from the stage to sympathetic fans.

Dinah's latest show featured the same revue she had brought at the end of June. Typically she opened each performance with one song and then told the audience, "I'll be back shortly after you hear from my protégés."

One evening Paul R. Adams, a *Michigan Chronicle* reporter, chatted with her over a cocktail between the other numbers. She described Queen Artists as a "corporation of friends. That's my ex-boyfriend." Dinah nodded, probably in the direction of Jackie Hayes. "My ex-maid is the vice president," evidently a reference to LaRue Manns. Dinah found the new acts, which were in addition to her backup musicians, and, she boasted, "I have each of these performers under a five-year contract. Incidentally, I have an exclusive agreement with Count Basie in New York. . . . You know the Count has his own room now," Dinah went on. "Well, any act I discover will be placed in Basie's room for its debut if I so choose." Why Basie's room? "Because it swings," Dinah said, "and they get good exposure there."

Ruth Bowen said there indeed was a deal with Basie, though not as ironclad as Dinah claimed.

Dinah closed the show every night, singing the final songs sitting on a red-cushioned stool placed midway between the red velvet curtains on the stage. If she was occasionally hoarse and half spoke a line, no one seemed to mind. When she sang "This Bitter Earth" those closest to the stage could see tears in her eyes, which sometimes rolled down and streaked her makeup.

Dinah was in a more whimsical mood on the last night at the Flame, forsaking her usual evening dress for a ballet costume—a fitted bodice with spaghetti straps and tutu. The only thing missing was the ballet slippers.

Sometimes Dinah put on the costume back home in New York. One day she greeted a surprised George Dixon when she opened the door in the ballet getup as he was sweeping the hall in front of 14A-3. He burst out laughing. "She gave me a look—like 'What are you looking at?' " he said, as though it were normal to see a ballerina in the hallway. The moment was in keeping with her personality— at least around the building. She never put on airs, Dixon said, and was friendly to the staff, often inviting them to her parties. At Christmas one year, she gave the building employees alpaca sweaters. Joe Zawinul received shirts and ties and a fancy pen-and-pencil set. "There was nothing cheap about Dinah," Dixon said.

DINAH RETURNED to Las Vegas in mid-October for the first time in five years. This time she was booked at the Flamingo, where Lena Horne had played in 1947 right after the hotel opened. It was the first on the Strip to institute a "kings row" of VIP tables for specially favored guests who stayed at the hotel for weeks at a time. And where other hotels used stainless-steel flatware, sterling silver graced the tables at the Flamingo's high-end restaurant. When Dinah opened at the Driftwood Lounge, the Flamingo had just been bought by two Miami men with long experience in the hotel business.

Race remained a divisive force in the city's daily rhythms, though things were changing. In March, the NAACP had threatened mass demonstrations against the main establishments to protest their segregationist practices. Just before the threatened deadline, black leaders and civic officials reached an agreement to relax the rules that had prevented stars from staying in the hotels in which they performed and had limited blacks' access to many of the major gambling rooms and restaurants. The improvements were taking time, but enough progress had been made to prompt *Sepia* to declare in a long feature about Las Vegas that "any Negro, properly heeled, can visit the city with assurances of being treated decently and of enjoying himself."

Despite the changing atmosphere, Dinah decided to stay with friends, a black doctor and his family who lived on the west side not far from the defunct Moulin Rouge. Her trio stayed in other private lodgings.

Joe Zawinul was having the time of his life. "We rehearsed every day, we played every day. We were in super shape," he said. The musicians were well paid, he added, and he got extra because he wrote the arrangements for the live shows. Like other musicians before him who had played with Dinah, Zawinul looked at the job as a tutorial. "I learned a lot about phraseology, using the lyrics," he said. "There was always a lyricism in her phrasing." He knew, too, that he and bassist Jimmy Rowser had to be ready for on-the-spot changes if Dinah was feeling tired or hoarse. "We could drop it down a third with no problem," he explained. "We were so in tune with each other.

"I really liked her," Zawinul added. "She was not a meek person, very volatile," but if they had a fight, it was never about the music. "Every time we had a fight," he recalled, chuckling, "my salary went up." Though Zawinul and Dinah never had an affair despite an obvious attraction, "there were," he admitted, "a couple of close calls."

Dinah's romantic attention in Las Vegas was fixed instead on a young Egyptian captain, S. Ares Omah, who had served as a technical adviser to Cecil B. DeMille for *The Ten Commandments* and was now assisting on the movie *Cleopatra*. "I guess I just flipped him," Dinah explained. "He lost $8,000 gambling, and I told him if he felt like gambling any more, he could gamble on some dresses and furs and things. . . . He sent me a bouquet of flowers every day—at $100 a bunch—and he gave me a ruby necklace. The card on each said 'from your Egyptian servant.' And every time nobody could find me, they claimed I must have been in that Egyptian's harem. I don't know what's gonna happen," Dinah added, "but I'm gonna be here and see."

Eddie Chamblee was still traveling with Dinah and playing the saxophone in the show, "but it don't mean a thing," she insisted. They were not getting back together.

Dinah went to Hollywood November 13 to attend the wedding of Sammy Davis, Jr., and Mai Britt, the Swedish actress. When she arrived at Davis's large home in the hills above Sunset Boulevard, she was stopped by security guards who wouldn't let her in. Dressed to the nines, a black mink draped around her shoulders, and waving the invitation in her hand, she stormed to a bank of microphones set up by waiting reporters to deliver a tirade about the treatment she had received.

A short time later the mystery was solved. Dinah had an invitation for the reception, not the actual ceremony. "The office sent me a telegram telling me to go to Sammy Davis's wedding," she told *Jet* later, "and when I got there they told me to go around to the back door. I guess you know I told them where they could go."

Dinah hustled up to Portland, Oregon, for a two-week stay at the Bali Hai, which billed itself as Portland's "Finest Supper Club." "Families welcome," the weekly ads promised, which might have put a crimp in Dinah's style. She liked to be irreverent from the stage and wasn't shy about swearing if she felt like it—or if she thought the situation demanded it. She had recently stopped a show, stared at a noisy patron, and said, "Please, mister, don't make me call you no motherfucker."

From Portland Dinah went back to Los Angeles for the rest of the year. First came a concert December 3 at the Pasadena Civic Auditorium, where Dinah performed along with a "New York style revue" that included the Perri Lee Trio, dancers, a calypso singer, and a female saxophone player known as "Lady Bird." The audience roared with appreciation when Dinah joined the chorus line for a couple of numbers and didn't miss a step in the intricate routines. The *California Eagle* reported that she didn't disappoint in her stage outfits, noting with its customary hyperbole that Dinah "displayed one of the most fabulous wardrobes in show business."

Mercury had released another album from the Clyde Otis sessions, *I Concentrate on You,* which was a mixture of blues and ballads. The songs, which included "Crazy Love," "Good Morning Heartache," and "I Got It Bad and That Ain't Good," suggested that Dinah was now such an established presence that she could record what she wanted, and Mercury could market the music however it wanted. *Down Beat* listed *I Concentrate on You* in a December list of "recent jazz releases." *Cash Box* declared that Dinah now had "permanent pop stature" that enabled her to "return more and more to the blues."

On December 5 Dinah settled into Ciro's, the famous nightclub in Hollywood. Frank Sennes, the new owner, dubbed the room where Dinah was playing "the Queen's Quarters" and in honor of her recent hit promoted her show, which featured her "protégés," as "the Bitter Earth Revue." George and Bobby had come out to join her, and they expected to do their dance routine during some of the shows. Bobby was tickled the day they all ran into Elvis Presley, recently back from the army, who seemed to know something about his mother's music. "You're in my spot," he teased when he saw her.

Though black entertainers regularly confronted racial barriers, few, including Dinah, were visible participants in the burgeoning civil rights movement. Lawyers and community activists were wag-ing those battles with lawsuits and demonstrations. But in recent months some black stars were stepping forward to help. Jazz musicians led by Miles Davis, Art Blakey, Kenny Burrell, and Dakota Staton held a "Jazz for Civil Rights" benefit at New York's Hunter College to raise money for the NAACP. And in Chicago Sarah Vaughan donated her first night's proceeds at Roberts to the organization. In Atlanta, Clyde McPhatter joined a picket line to protest segregation at one of the city's department stores, wearing a sign that said, "The presence of segregation is the absence of Democracy. Jim Crow Must Go!" Harry Belafonte, one of the most outspoken, made a dramatic and pointed gesture early in December when he refused to appear as the guest star at a $1,000-a-couple dinner in Chicago honoring former president Harry Truman. Belafonte rejected the invitation "as a matter of principle because of Truman's statements earlier this year denouncing Negro sit-ins." Belafonte was referring to groups of students in the South who would not get up from segregated lunch counters when they were refused service.

One of the discomfiting by-products of the heightened racial tensions was the loss of work for black musicians whose staple was the southern rhythm and blues circuit. Booking agents, following the Feld brothers' decision a year earlier, jettisoned the black acts and instead put together all-white packages for the region. The black talent was diverted to northern venues. The only exceptions were such rock 'n' rollers as Chuck Berry, who were hired to perform at fraternity parties at some of the all-white state universities.

Dinah had performed a number of benefits to aid black causes—the most recent was in May to raise money for African students studying in New York—and watching television in Los Angeles on an early December morning, she was moved to do more. Incensed by the conflict in New Orleans over integration of the city schools, she stopped a rehearsal of fifty people at Ciro's and called a news conference at the club. Newspaper, radio, and television reporters arrived in short order. Sitting before a microphone, hands folded, a scarf around her head, and wearing no makeup, Dinah said she had wired Mercury president Irving Green to take all of her records out of New Orleans shops. "I just couldn't take what the South is putting down," she said. "I was watching TV when suddenly I saw grown men and women chasing little children and screaming like cannibals in front of a New Orleans school. I have two children of my own, and it brought tears to my eyes to think what was happening to these children could happen to mine. Someone had to start this crusade," she went on, "so here I am."

One of the reporters asked what the next step should be. "Well, the first thing I am suggesting is that other top Negro entertainers do likewise," Dinah replied. "I would like to invite Lena Horne, Ray Charles, Nat Cole, Billy Eckstine and other recording artists to join me in a 'record boycott.' " Anyone interested, she added, could contact her at Ciro's.

The club manager blanched; he had told Dinah not to mention the club's name over the air.

Dinah also issued a direct appeal to the "good Southern people" who sat and drank at her table when she performed in their clubs, urging them to dissociate themselves from the whites who were harassing the black students.

The *Los Angeles Sentinel* noted that Dinah asked some of the white musicians who performed with her to comment. "They made it clear that Dinah believes integration works both ways and that she shows no discrimination in casting her acts," the paper said.

Dinah apparently had no second thoughts about her news conference. "As long as the poor whites in the South do comedy and don't want to socialize with Negroes," she later told *Jet*, "I demand that they stop selling records in those parts of the country because I don't need it [their money]."

Dinah had every reason to feel confident. She was finishing another successful year, her credentials as a pop presence now beyond question. The songs on the charts—solos, duets, albums, and even a spot on the list of top female jazz singers in *Down Beat*'s first ever Japanese poll—provided confirmation. The difficult moments had all passed. So had the new boyfriends. But Dinah seemed to want it that way.

18.

September in the Rain

1961

During her run at Ciro's, Dinah noticed a handsome, slender young man coming to every show and watching her with rapt attention. His name was Rafael Campos. He was a twenty-five-year-old actor who had made a splash in *Blackboard Jungle*. He was also the son of a Dominican Republic diplomat, and had met Dinah a year earlier in Los Angeles when she was playing the Cloister.

"I was going into the Interlude"—which was nearby—"when I heard this lady call out to me, 'I know you,' " Campos explained. "I turned to a friend and said, 'I don't know her'—because I didn't know her. But to Dinah, I said, 'Hi.' "

"I'm Dinah," she replied.

Campos didn't say anything. Her name didn't register.

"Dinah Washington," she said.

"I'd never heard of her," Campos admitted. They chatted amiably for a few minutes and went their separate ways. A few months later Campos connected the name and the face with the voice when "This Bitter Earth" became a hit.

The two met again at a party in Los Angeles in December 1960, and when Campos learned that Dinah was playing at Ciro's, he came to see the show. He was smitten. He started calling her all the time and sending her gifts—Dinah had an inkling he was serious when he gave her a white sable jacket for Christmas. George and Bobby were spending the holiday weeks with their mother, and the way Dinah told it, "the boys were the first to realize that we were deeply in love."

A few days into the new year, Campos called Dinah at home at 1:00 A.M. as she was watching television to wind down.

"Will you marry me?"

Dinah didn't say anything for a few moments, half asleep and ready to go to bed.

"When?"

"This morning," Campos said. "We can go now."

By now Dinah was fully awake, but she told him no. "I'm looking at TV. I don't have any clothes on."

The next afternoon Campos came to the apartment. He asked her again to marry him.

"Okay," Dinah said.

Campos immediately reached for the telephone and called his secretary, Mike Cantoni, to make arrangements for a quick wedding ceremony in Tijuana, Mexico. The logistics were complicated: Dinah and Rafael would fly to San Diego; Cantoni and LaRue Manns, who was with Dinah in California, Curley Symes, Dinah's current road manager, and Lady Bird, the saxophone player in Dinah's revue, would drive to San Diego to meet the couple and then take them by car the rest of the way to Tijuana.

At the airport Dinah wanted to get on the plane quickly, without being recognized and having to stop for explanations. "We kept ducking and dodging," she recalled. "But the word was out, and we ran into some people we knew."

"What are you two doing out here?" one of them asked the couple.

"Oh," Dinah said, "we just came for a drink."

"You mean to tell me you two came all the way out to the airport just to get a drink?" the friend replied in disbelief.

"Uh-huh."

Dinah had wanted a photographer to come along to take pictures of the ceremony. But when she and Rafael got ready to board the plane, the ticket agent said that the three standby reservations available hours earlier had dwindled to two. The photographer couldn't go.

Connecting with Cantoni and the others in San Diego went smoothly, and the group arrived in Tijuana the afternoon of January 6, 1961, for the ceremony. They made their way to the chapel serenaded by a mariachi band that Rafael had hired. López Castro, a local official, was waiting for them and performed the ceremony in Spanish.

"Are you sure we're married?" Dinah asked when Castro finished.

"You're married," Castro replied in English.

Right at that moment, a large mirror on one of the chapel walls fell to the floor. Dinah held her breath, thinking that broken mirror could be a curse, seven years of bad luck. Miraculously, the glass didn't shatter; Dinah considered it a good omen.

The bride and groom had dressed in business attire for the ceremony. Dinah wore a blue wool dress with a pleated satin trim and navy blue shoes. As she frequently did for serious occasions, Dinah wore a single strand of pearls around her neck. She also had on small pearl earrings set with diamonds, simple but elegant. Rafael wore a brown business suit, white shirt, and, though he hated them, a tie.

After the wedding, the couple and their attendants celebrated at a nightclub. The mariachi band returned, and Dinah liked their sound so much that she ended up singing a Latin version of "What a Diff'rence a Day Makes." She told the band she wanted to make an album with them.

A fan of champagne and Courvoisier, Dinah was not prepared for a wedding toast with Mexico's traditional drink. "I don't want any more tequila ever again," she said.

"You're not getting married again so you won't need any," Rafael told her with a confidence undiminished by Dinah's history.

The only thing that dimmed the happy day was the news from Chicago that a fire had broken out in the apartment building at 8125 South Vernon and caused $10,000 worth of damage.

By the time Dinah and Rafael returned to Los Angeles, the news about their marriage was out, stories running on the entertainment pages of several of the black weeklies. In a cheeky observation, the *Defender* noted that Dinah was "familiar with both trips to the altar and across theatre stages." Dinah was miffed that several articles put her age at forty-two; she was thirty-six. Some played up the racial angle, asserting that each had married out of the race, though *Sepia* noted that Campos was no lighter or darker than "millions of American Negroes. But as a native of the Dominican Republic, he has not been recognized, or described as a Negro in this country."

Campos told *Jet*, which published a four-page feature about the newlyweds, that "if interracial marriage hurts my career, I couldn't care less. Besides I'm just as colored as she is because we both belong to the human race."

"You're not colored either," Dinah interjected, "but I didn't marry out of the race. I married the man I loved—a human being. The race thing never entered my mind."

The couple presented themselves to reporters as the picture of happiness, holding hands and giggling, sometimes both talking at once, and during a visit at the home of Dinah's friend, the actor Troy Donahue, they sat, arms around each other, on top of Donahue's stuffed tiger. Dinah was already signing her checks "Dinah W. Campos."

Dinah and Rafael planned a honeymoon in the Los Angeles area with a few days in Las Vegas. But Dinah had to be back by January 21, when four days of recording were scheduled. Clyde Otis put together the sessions, with Belford Hendricks arranging again. This time he wanted to record Dinah doing songs from motion pictures.

When Otis arrived in Los Angeles, he went straight to United Recording on Sunset Boulevard, where eighteen musicians had assembled—a rhythm section and a dozen or so strings. He waited and waited but Dinah didn't show up. He called Ruth Bowen, who had also come out to Los Angeles.

"Where's Dinah?" he asked.

"I don't know, Clyde."

A little later, Ruth called back and told him that Dinah was staying at a motel operated by Earl Bostic, though she wasn't sure why. Ruth suggested that Otis go and talk to her. He caught a cab, gave the driver the address he got from Ruth, and went to Dinah's room. When he knocked on the door, Dinah asked who was there.

"This is Clyde."

"Oh, okay," she said. "Come on in."

Otis was astounded to find Dinah standing in front of the bed wearing only a sheer negligee. Though Dinah had married Rafael in Tijuana two weeks earlier, he was nowhere around.

"You know we're supposed to be in the studio," Otis said. "What are you going to do?"

"Motherfucker, I need some Jones," Dinah said. Otis knew exactly what she meant.

"Wait a minute. You and I, we don't do that." He reminded her of all the musicians who had been hired and were waiting to do an album.

"I don't give a shit what you're planning."

Otis didn't know what to worry about first—losing the session because he thought Dinah was leaving the next day or getting out of this sticky predicament. He decided that making a quick exit was the best solution. Dinah was standing in such a way that Otis didn't have a clear path to the door. But with a couple of quick moves, he got by her and out of the room. As he was running down the hallway all he heard was her voice: "You damn nigger."

Back at the studio Otis announced that Dinah wouldn't be doing any vocals that day. Dinah did show up the next day, January 22, when twelve tunes were scheduled over two three-hour sessions, though according to Otis, Dinah, still peeved, agreed to give him only one hour of vocals.

"She walked in and looked at me and said something like, 'You're the dirtiest black motherfucker I ever saw in my life,' but she cut all the tunes in one take during that hour. She was a consummate musician." She might be temperamental, but Otis was impressed every session by the way she could revamp a melody on the spot so it fit more comfortably in her range.

Typical of the session, which one critic later referred to as "forgettable schmaltz," was "Love Is a Many Splendored Thing," which Dinah sang at a such lugubrious pace the song seemed labored. A more riveting moment came in the middle of "Without a Song," when the strings backed off and Dinah was on her own. She slowed the tempo, broke up the rhythm, and let loose with a bluesy flourish on the climactic line "I'll get along as long as a song is strong in my soul," taking extra time on those resonant final words.

For all the melodrama surrounding the session, Mercury put

half of the tunes on the shelf and didn't release them for several years.

THE CLYDE OTIS MOMENT aside, Dinah and Rafael seemed like a normal married couple. She took him back to Chicago for her upcoming jobs and happily introduced him to her mother and siblings. Her sisters thought he was cute; privately they expressed surprise not that he was so young but that he was not black. "Dinah always said she would not marry out of her race," said Clarissa, now nearly twenty-one and engaged to be married. Alice, Dinah's mother, didn't say much. According to Clarissa "she was immune" to Dinah's behavior. "It was like 'oh, yeah, she got married again.' "

Still finding Dinah good copy, *Jet* came to do a story about the newlyweds, filling its pages with family photos of Rafael hugging his new mother-in-law and standing arm in arm with Clarissa and Estrellita. "I not only got a wife, but two lovely children, George and Bobby. One of them is taller than me," Rafael told the magazine. He said he wanted two more, a boy and a girl.

While they were chatting, Dinah admitted to the *Jet* reporter that she had gained five pounds. As she munched on a chocolate bar, Rafael, who was rail-thin, shot her a disapproving look.

"Well, I'm hungry," Dinah retorted.

The boys liked Rafael. He was fun and treated them "with respect," according to Bobby. But neither he nor his brother paid much attention to their mother's romantic life. Now fourteen and twelve, they were caught up in their own activities, which served as protective armor against the dramas that played out around them. They might not be able to ignore what was going on, but they didn't have to dwell on it. Bobby, in particular, immersed himself in sports, playing every kind of ball and starting to run track.

Dinah and her revue opened at the Tivoli Theater on 63rd Street January 27; the ads boasted of a "Cast of 40." Rafael was listed as a special guest with a reminder that he had been in *Blackboard Jungle* opposite Sidney Poitier. He said he didn't even mind that husband number five, Eddie Chamblee, was directing the band. The two of them playfully posed for *Jet*, Dinah between them, as though they were fighting for her favors.

Since the last time she had played Roberts, club owner Herman

Roberts had been having trouble keeping the operation afloat. For a time, C. B. Atkins, Sarah Vaughan's husband, and Charles Margerum, a Chicago businessman, took over the club. Although they were running the place, Herman Roberts was still out front meeting and greeting, and as far as the patrons knew, he was still the boss. Though it was never clear who came up with the idea and put together the deal, at some point during the Tivoli engagement, Dinah accepted an offer to take over Roberts for the foreseeable future. She dubbed it Dinahland, and planned to make her show the centerpiece of the entertainment. Opening night was scheduled for February 15 with the same acts that had appeared at the Tivoli along with comedian George Kirby. Instead of being a special guest, Rafael would be the host.

On Sunday, February 12, three days before opening night, Dinah woke up feeling so sick she was rushed to Provident Hospital. Doctors diagnosed appendicitis and performed an emergency appendectomy. While the procedure went smoothly, Dinah was told she would not recover quickly enough to open the show at Dinahland on the 15th. Rafael was the dutiful husband visiting her every day in the hospital, posing for photographers as he spoon-fed Dinah a dish of ice cream.

On the 15th the show went on without Dinah, and according to the *Defender,* the other entertainers "appeared to be giving that something extra to make certain the opening was a huge success. They sang, danced and pranced about the place in Broadway fashion while giving out with the latest steps and the tops in hit parade material."

Dinah returned to Roberts on February 22 to start another week of the revue, which ran Wednesday through Saturday evenings. An added attraction was Will Hutchins, the star of the television show *Sugarfoot* and a friend of Rafael's. Dinah made the most of her new status as operator of the club, not only singing onstage but walking among the tables to greet patrons. "Hello, Dinah" was often heard as she ambled around the floor. She accommodated fans who wanted to take her picture, grabbing her friend, the dancer Eloise Clay, who had known Dinah since George was a toddler, for one impromptu photograph sitting at the bar.

In a March 4 story the *Defender* credited Dinah with giving a stalled Chicago nightclub scene new life. "Chicago like most other cities about the nation has seen its night club business tumbling for the past several months. Many major spots like the Blue Note, Chez Paree and others have gone by the wayside." Other clubs had opened up to take their places but certainly were not doing the business those places enjoyed in the past. Before Dinah, Roberts had "slowed down to a walk." But since her show started, the place was bustling.

Joe Zawinul, the piano player, and bassist Jimmy Rowser had not played on the record sessions in Los Angeles in January, but they reunited with Dinah for the week at the Tivoli and started with her at Roberts. Within a few days the two reached the same conclusion simultaneously: it was time to move on. They weren't enjoying playing backup for a show business revue; it was too far from their jazz roots. "I'm getting tired of this shit. I came to America to play jazz," Zawinul confided to Rowser. One evening a fellow jazz musician came by the club and spoke bluntly. "Joe, you got to get off that."

"I don't mean that I don't love what you're doing," Zawinul told Dinah when he gave notice the same time Rowser did.

"Okay," Dinah replied, barely raising an eyebrow. Then she called him "an ungrateful motherfucker."

Zawinul knew she was joking. And she knew he was more than grateful. "I left in a good way," he said.

Dinah understood that she was the major draw at Roberts, but she realized she needed help to keep the customers coming. She inaugurated "Celebrity Night" one evening a week, and in March she brought in comedian Dick Gregory and the singers Arthur Prysock, Etta James, the new star at Chess Records, and Etta Jones, the jazz singer. Louis Armstrong stopped in one evening for a jam, and Dinah sang with him to her left and Eddie, still directing the music, playing the saxophone on her right.

Etta James had long been a fan of Dinah's and had often been compared to her, a comparison she found flattering. But she had learned firsthand that Dinah was very proprietary about her image and her music. "I was playing a small club in Providence, Rhode Island, while Dinah was working at the Loew's State Theater [in Boston]," James recalled. "My show didn't start till midnight, and when someone came 'round to say Dinah was in the house, my heart started doing flips. . . . When I hit the stage, instead of doing my regular show, I decided to open with 'Unforgettable.' Well, right in the middle of the song," James went on, "I heard this crash. *Boom!* Someone swept the glasses off a table. I looked in the audience and saw it was Dinah."

"Girl," she screamed—and James was sure Dinah was pointing at her head—"don't you ever sing the Queen's songs."

James ran off the stage in tears and slammed the door to her dressing room. But before the road manager could stop her, Dinah came in, dressed to the nines in one of her minks. "Don't ever pull shit like that," she told James, "not when I'm around."

James burst into tears again. A moment later Dinah was at her side to give her a hug. Dinah's cutting a new version of an old song was one thing. But someone else singing what was now a Dinah Washington hit was another. "I'm sorry, baby. I lost my temper," she said, "but you had to learn a lesson: Never sing another artist's song if she's in the house. Never."

All James could say was "Yes, ma'am."

Dinah kissed James on the cheek and invited her to come to Loew's the next night. James did, and had a grand time, amused as she watched Dinah's snippy reaction to a fan who sought an autograph but forgot a pen. "Am I supposed to sign this thing with my finger?" she asked, and then turned her back.

"Dinah took no shit," James said.

One night Dinah had gone to the Club DeLisa with some friends to see comedian George Kirby, whose specialty was impressions. He decided to do his version of Dinah, which according to Kirby, "the crowd loved. But she got all pissed off and told me, and I'll never forget what she said—'Don't ever try to imitate the Queen again.' "

Kirby was flabbergasted. He had done Sarah Vaughan when Vaughan was in the audience, "and afterward she told me I sounded better than her." Besides, Kirby said, Dinah did imitations, especially of Billie Holiday. Indeed that was true, but by now Dinah had drawn a line around herself. The persona she had created was every bit as important to her as the music, serious business not to be trifled with.

Farris Kimbrough, Dinah's stepsister, had moved back to Chicago at the end of 1959. She had become pregnant and wanted to have the baby there. She gave birth to a son, James, and was still living in the city, but now that the boy was eighteen months old, she was helping Dinah again—and finally getting paid. Farris had been surprised when Dinah married Rafael—he was cute, there was no denying that, but it was hard to imagine what they had in common. Farris didn't think it would last very long, and after spending some time around the couple, she surmised that it was an unconventional union. Farris had come down to the Roberts Motel, which was across the street from the club, where Dinah and Rafael were staying in the Georgia Suite. She happened to be there when Rafael came into the bedroom and Dinah was nearly naked. After having lost weight, she had folds of skin around her midsection, Farris said, and Rafael apparently had never seen Dinah without clothes on.

It was a bizarre scene. "Rafael went berserk. He had an epileptic fit. He fell on the floor. Dinah was trying to keep him from swallowing his tongue." Dinah was embarrassed. Farris was astounded. "I had never seen anything like that," she said. She was surprised, too, because the two put up such a good front, exhibiting the comfortable intimacy in public of so many married couples.

A short time later, Dinah decided the marriage was over. "I get the message before God. That's why I had his bags packed the day he came home to leave," she declared. "He sure was surprised to find his clothes already packed, and you should have seen the expression on his face. I've been in this game a long time, and you've got to stay up late and get up early to get the jump on the Queen."

When the first rumors flew around the South Side that Dinah and Rafael had split up, *Defender* columnist Al Monroe tried to squelch them in the March 22 edition. He checked with Dinah, he said, and "this check brought information that Campos and Miss Washington had been talking on the phone (both here in Chicago) a few moments before our call." One week later Monroe recanted. He announced that Dinah couldn't find Rafael or her Cadillac and had called the Chicago police to look for both.

Like the breakup with Eddie, Dinah was determined to control this story, too. She summoned reporters to her dressing room at Roberts at the end of the month to present her version. "Sure I hated to have it come, but I had known several days before the actual breakup what to expect. Tried to do everything possible . . . to make a go of this one but bad advice received from others was too much for the wedlock. Sure I opened this club for us and at a cost of several thousand dollars in bookings, but why worry about that?"

When *Jet* came for an exclusive, Dinah spiced up the story. "I know what you're looking for. You're looking for some gossip, and you have come to the right place. Tell your readers that Rafael has split the scene. The 'Queen' showed him a taste of high life and it went to his head. . . . He's out of sight and out of mind. I was hurt when he left me. . . . I tried to make a marriage for us. He had wrong advice and wouldn't listen to me," she added, sounding like a parent discussing a wayward child. Dinah ended the interview when it was time for her set, the *Jet* reporter behind her as she walked away. "The 'Queen' strode onto the stage," he wrote, "and eased into a familiar refrain: 'Trouble in Mind, I'm blue. . . . ' "

Speculation was wild about where Rafael went and with whom. One rumor was that he left with the actor Will Hutchins. Not so, went another. Rafael had left with a male member of the band. The *Pittsburgh Courier* reported that Dinah had dumped Rafael because he spent too much time "lounging around Dinah's Chicago apartment during the day and cruising about the city streets at night in her pink Cadillac."

Confirming her change in status, Dinah was back to signing her checks "Dinah Washington."

So often the stuff of soap opera, her offstage life now descended to opéra bouffe. The crowning moment was the arrival of the April issue of *Sepia,* which featured a four-page spread on the couple professing their love for each other. The magazine's lead time proved to be longer than the marriage.

LaRue, who had been one of the handful of individuals at the wedding ceremony, was dubious about the relationship from the beginning given the age difference. "He was so much younger than she was, and she began to feel self-conscious. George and Bobby would tease that 'he ain't much bigger than I am. I can wear his clothes,' " LaRue said. Dinah "began to get jealous because he was so friendly."

Barely three months after they played the part of happy newlyweds, Dinah suggested that she didn't think much of Rafael's acting ability either. "He couldn't even pretend he loved me," she complained.

Dinah was not yet thirty-seven but had already had six legal husbands, one quasi-husband—Rusty Maillard—and a handful of reported fiancés. It was a stunning scorecard by any measure, reflecting a woman, for all her complexities, with a basic and intense desire not to be alone, in a profession that served to undermine the very thing she said she wanted. By choice Dinah was always on the go, and the men she met were those she saw on the job—other musicians or fans. When they were together, the world revolved around her, and there was little time to spend away from the spotlight in the day-to-day routines that most couples share.

At times it seemed as though Dinah sought companionship for its own sake, and when a relationship went sour, or when those deepest fears abated and she lost interest, she turned the page and claimed, at least in public, to have no regrets.

DINAH TOLD JET that she had lost $60,000 in her own engagements to take over Roberts. "I had to pay fifty people out of my purse for four weeks. Why am I doing this? Chicago is my hometown and show business was dead. I want to bring it back," she said. To keep the Dinahland show fresh, Dinah continued the practice of inviting special guests to perform, and by early April she had revamped the lineup to include a set with strings. *Down Beat* praised the move as "imaginative programming." The *Defender* advertisements boasted of the "$50,000 Mink-Clad Chorus," which apparently referred to the stoles, jackets, and coats the young women wore from Dinah's personal collection.

According to *Jet* Dinah made a permanent gift of one of them to Gerri Spencer, a dancer and the wife of another dancer, Prince Spencer. The couple had volunteered their services to rehearse the Dinahettes for the stage show, and the stole, the color of gold dust, was Dinah's thank-you.

"Dinah thought everybody should have a little mink," joked Ruth Bowen.

Most of Dinah's assistants over the years were women, but there was a coterie of gay men who floated in and out of her world. Some were hair specialists; others took care of clothes as Farris used to do, though none cleaned those underwire bras as meticulously as she did with a fingernail brush. Drake Tolbert, who called himself "Dinah's valet," was certain she liked to have a man around because of the furs. "Dinah has eleven mink coats," he explained. "If a woman tried to lift eleven mink coats in and out of packing trunks, her arms would fall off from fatigue."

· · ·

THREE MONTHS in Chicago was the longest Dinah had been in her hometown since she was a teenager. The first week in May she packed up the revue and returned to New York to play a week at the Apollo. The show in Dinahland went on without her, billed as "The Parade of Stars," featuring singers Arthur Prysock and Del St. John and a second chorus line advertised as the Dinahettes No. 2.

In what was surely a publicity stunt to boost the interest in the Apollo show, Dinah, the harsh comments of a month earlier either ignored or forgotten, let it be known that she and Rafael were speaking again, and that he might come to New York to appear with her onstage at the Apollo. The management was so sure he would be there that the advertisements promised "duets."

Rafael in fact came back to New York and was onstage the evening that *Variety* sent a reviewer. "Apollo's management should be chided for billing Rafael Campos as a special guest star. All Campos did," the reviewer wrote, "was stand around and nibble at his frau's ear. If that's what the Apollo calls a 'duet,' then the theatre works from an unfamiliar showbiz lexicon."

Apart from Rafael's appearance, an added fillip was Eddie Chamblee's presence as the bandleader. The tableau on the Apollo stage was as strange as it was titillating. There was Dinah with one ex-husband behind her and the estranged one by her side, listening as she teased him with "Our Love Is Here to Stay." Such was the roller coaster of Dinah's romantic life that a new boyfriend was probably in the dressing room waiting for her.

Dinah and Eddie were apparently experimenting with a new sound onstage. The band included seven violins, according to *Variety,* and the musicians didn't seem to understand how to modulate their sound to show off the music to best effect. Seven violins were too many, the reviewer, said, "almost as out of place in the history of the Apollo as a Dixiecrat senator."

Farris was sure Rafael's appearance was only for show and had nothing to do with any reconciliation. *Amsterdam News* columnist Jesse H. Walker reported in his regular "Theatricals" feature a few weeks later that Rafael in fact had gotten a divorce from Dinah in Mexico and "is now wed to a young Hollywood starlet. Dinah's not too unhappy. Didn't cost her a cent."

Dinah told *Jet* that she was was working on a book with her friend Dave Hepburn with the tentative title *Husbands I've Known*.

Given the breakup of this most recent marriage, Dinah's re-recording "Our Love Is Here to Stay" had a certain irony. Mercury released the disc the first week in May, and it went right on the music charts, though staying in the bottom half. This latest version was entirely different from the first, which had been recorded in 1956 under Hal Mooney with horns and a swinging beat. Now it was a ballad, with the strings shadowing Dinah phrase by phrase. Her reading was contemplative, as though she knew the sentiment might feel exactly right at the moment it was uttered. But the truth was something different—love didn't stay.

One of the new acts in Dinah's revue was the singing quintet the Dells, who had had a big hit in 1956 with "Oh What a Nite," on Vee-Jay, like Chess another of the Chicago independents. Two years later, still doing well, the group had been in a bad car accident, and shortly afterward they disbanded. They got back together by early 1961 with slightly different personnel and found small jobs around Chicago. According to bassist Chuck Barksdale, when they learned that Dinah was auditioning acts for her revue at Dinahland, they decided to try out.

"Dinah liked you for a lot of reasons—you looked good, you're young men, and you could sing. You had all those combined, you got a gig," Barksdale said. "We had all of that."

Dinah took them on in Chicago and then brought them with her to the Apollo. Barksdale said it was one of the best things that happened to the group. "She taught us stage deportment, about being on time, spending her own money that she didn't have to do to take us under her wings. Oh, she was a bee, the big bee," Barksdale added. "She could really put it on your tail, pal. . . . She tightened our lids up, made us understand this business here is nothing to play with, and she did it with great charm. Sometimes you were ready to choke her," Barksdale went on. "Sometimes you just wanted to love her. . . . She gave us that respect and some things we needed in order to sustain in this business."

Mickey McGill, another Dell, loved the shopping trips with Dinah. "She would take us downtown, show us what to wear—you don't wear this with this, the best type of cologne," he explained. But she was "ornery," said Marvin Junior, the group's lead singer. Like

McGill, he liked the shopping trips, but the next day, he said, "she'd tell you you're fired. Oh, she was evil."

Dinah was the same way with some of her household help. Drake Tolbert, "Dinah's valet," loved to tell friends how many times he had been hired and fired, sometimes in the same day or week. He often was the first to see Dinah when she got up in her New York apartment, knocking on her door with a glass of orange juice and "a pep pill," the household's euphemism for Dinah's medication. He didn't know what kind of mood she was in until she spoke. "You happen to be fired today," she might say, which was his cue that she would be on the warpath for the next several hours. The others in the household awaited Tolbert's report when he came back to the kitchen. "Don't ask me," he would tell them. "I'm fired again."

At the beginning of July Dinah took the revue to Detroit for a two-week run back at the Flame Show Bar. Mickey McGill remembered what a taskmaster Dinah could be. She hadn't been happy with one night's show, and even though the Dells' wives and girlfriends had come over from Chicago to see the group, she wouldn't let them leave. Somebody was flat in the background, she told them. Stay and rehearse. "And we did," McGill said.

He and Junior felt that all her unpredictability and idiosyncracies were worth it. "You learned from watching her," Junior said. "She had perfect pitch . . . her timing, her stage manner, she was just a pro." McGill wasn't joking when he told friends that Dinah could be in front of a big band, stop, and turn to tell the trombone, "You hit a bad note. You should have hit a B-flat."

Her ear was so good, she joked, she could hear grass grow.

While Dinah was at the Flame she decided to relinquish her role as manager of Roberts/Dinahland. Opinions differed about what happened. She said she gave it up. Herman Roberts said she lost it "by default." The club had done well while Dinah was performing, but attendance suffered when less-well-known acts were booked. Roberts said he was trying to get big names back on the stage and planned to reopen with the Count Basie Orchestra for four days followed by Brook Benton and then singer Nina Simone.

The *Defender*'s Al Monroe said in his July 10 column that Dinah gave up the club "because she could not pass up some of her previous commitments."

Dinah was still mad about the way Wayne County sheriff's

deputies impounded her car and took her mink stole the previous September because she was behind in paying off the fine. She decided to sue the sheriff and two deputies in federal court for $1 million and again hired her Detroit lawyer, Lawrence Massey, to draw up the papers. In the complaint filed July 3, Dinah alleged that the deputies used an invalid "writ of attachment" to impound her car for three days, and that she was humiliated when they took her mink, assuming it was stolen. Dinah also claimed that the deputies had told others ahead of time what they were going to do so that there would be an audience when they took her car away. Their actions, she asserted, were malicious and calculated to damage her reputation.

In addition to the "humiliation and mental stress" Dinah also claimed that she lost $3,500 in wages and had to spend $1,000 to pay her lawyer and another $1,500 for "physician and psychiatrist fees." "The thoughts of this occurrence," she said in the complaint, bothered her every night she had to go into the Flame to perform.

So much of Dinah's private life was public that now when newspapers talked about her, they did so with a certain irreverence. Under the headline "The 'Queen' Sues the Law," the *Detroit Courier* said, "Men have always been a headache (and a source of pleasure) to blues Queen Dinah Washington. She has sued six husbands (she's shedding the seventh). Last week she came up with a new angle; she sued the Sheriff of Wayne County and two of his deputies for $1 million."

Even Dinah's good friend Slappy White now worked a joke about her private life into his routine: "I have a profitable sideline job selling wedding rings to Dinah Washington."

On August 28 attorneys for Sheriff Andrew Baird filed a motion to dismiss the suit against him, and two weeks later, a judge threw out the claim. The claims against the two deputies remained for further proceedings. In their response, the deputies contended that their writ was valid, that they did not make slanderous remarks about Dinah, and that if she was "experiencing a nervous state" it was not their fault. On September 18, Dinah formally asked for a jury trial, which was to be scheduled sometime in 1962. (U.S. District Judge Wade H. McCree, Jr., eventually dismissed the lawsuit when Dinah failed to show up for a deposition.)

.   .   .

MERCURY HAD CHANGED again since Dinah was last in a studio in January. Most significantly, Clyde Otis, who had presided over her most successful records, abruptly resigned at the end of April. He and Mercury president Irving Green disagreed over how the publishing rights to Otis's songs should be handled. Ten days later Otis joined Liberty Records as the head of the New York office and director of artist and repertoire for the East Coast. Whatever concern Dinah may have felt about losing Otis was probably eased by the announcement early in July that her friend Quincy Jones, whom she had brought to the label as her arranger in 1955, would be musical director for Mercury's New York office. Though she hadn't known Jack Tracy well, he, too, was returning to Mercury after a two-year stint running Argo, the jazz subsidiary of Chess Records.

Since Dinah and Quincy had worked together in 1955, he had gone on to great success composing and arranging and putting together an eighteen-piece band that toured Europe. Cannonball Adderley had joked in his weekly *Amsterdam News* column that at twenty-seven, Quincy "is already an old man in the music business." His most recent big project, though, orchestrating music written by Harold Arlen for the play *Free and Easy*, had not gone well. The play opened in Europe but closed quickly. He kept his band together to tour but came back to the United States in the spring. The group had played at Pep's in Philadelphia at the end of May. Quincy remembered Dinah coming to a show and later helping him write checks for the band because he didn't have a manager.

Dinah and Quincy reunited in the studio the second week in August to start working on new material. The Dells came along to do some of the backup vocals. Also present were Dinah's horn-playing friends, trumpeter Clark Terry and trombone player Jimmy Cleveland, who had been on a number of earlier sessions. Terry was always happy to work with Dinah and appreciated how she looked out for her musician friends. Dinah may not have walked a picket line or sat in at a restaurant, but she was willing to exercise power where she could: in the studio. Terry recalled one session when Dinah walked in, saw mostly white men with their instruments, and turned to the producers. "Wait a minute. Is this Sophie Tucker's date? I'm the Queen. This is my date. Where's Clark Terry, Snooky Young, and Ernie Royal?" she asked, referring to other black musicians.

The next day, Terry said, they were all called in to record.

Dinah had done the same thing on a date that included Joe Wilder, whom she had met in 1943 when they were both with Lionel Hampton. "Racism in the country was so pervasive that Dinah determined that she had every right to stand up and use Afro-Americans on her date," Wilder said.

Like Clyde Otis, Quincy wanted to record Dinah with strings. Hal Mooney and Ernie Wilkins were brought back in to arrange, though the presence of Terry and Cleveland also meant that Dinah was back to singing with horns, too, which she loved. They were featured on "Wake the Town and Tell the People," and Dinah sang it with gospel fervor. It was about announcing a new romance, but with the change of a word here or there, it could just as easily have been sung in church to herald a new revelation. Dinah was playfully at ease sauntering through Cole Porter's "You Do Something to Me." Her singing and the arrangement put it somewhere between jazz and the Broadway stage.

The highlight of these August sessions, however, was a nine-minute blues, apparently extemporaneous, which Mercury called "Trouble in the Lowlands." Introduced by a spare guitar solo, Dinah began the lyrics to her favorite Bessie Smith tune, "Backwater Blues." Singing about a tough time in a tough spot, she improvised a line to make it personal—"I packed all my minks and jewelry, and then they rolled me back home." She repeated a phrase several times as she often liked to do, and then she did another of her favorite things, segued into another tune, here when she got to the line "If I ever get my nerves settled down." And then she started into the blues standard "Trouble in Mind."

Her first version, recorded a decade earlier, was a model of simplicity and quiet intensity. The music now was equally spare, but Dinah gave a bold, bravura performance, the kind of moment in the studio that so many fans had witnessed live on the stage of a small club, when Dinah lost herself in a melody. It was as if she was exorcising demons in the safest way she knew how and in the safest place, in song surrounded by friends to support her. The musicians seemed mesmerized, too, the ragged ending evidence of an unexpected though glorious moment.

Dinah's remake of Percy Mayfield's "Please Send Me Someone to Love," featuring solos from saxophone and flute—which Quincy had used on those 1955 sessions—was also more muscular than her haunting version from the early 1950s. Dinah's voice had deepened, and a rasp was more evident, and more frequent. And if she didn't fly over the notes the way she did at twenty, Dinah, about to turn thirty-seven, used those qualities to get deeper meaning from a song that seemed to express the flamboyant complications of her personal life. (The male singer who interjected a couple of lines was probably one of the Dells.)

As soon as the sessions were over, Dinah and the revue left for a week of dates in the Miami area. The first job was at the Cat and the Fiddle in a big show hosted by *Miami Times* columnist Dave Bondu, who had given readers that minute-by-minute account of Dinah's onstage breakup with Eddie Chamblee. Then the revue moved over to the Knight Beat. The *Times* entertainment column gave readers an unusual heads-up about the seating arrangements. "Because of the heavy demand for tickets and tables for the Dinah Washington shows, chiefly from members of the other race," the column said, "[the manager] announces this week that he is forced to use a special policy for these shows, in order to accommodate all of the people who want to see and hear Dinah."

The special policy was not spelled out, but it almost certainly had to do with how the club owner could accommodate a mixed-race audience and not run afoul of Florida's segregation laws.

Given that school was out for the summer, George and Bobby were with Dinah and the revue. The boys enjoyed jousting around with the Dells, and one day George teased that "Mama's gonna leave you all tonight." The group was staying at the Sir John, and not entirely sure if George was making up a story, the Dells went to the hallway in front of her hotel room to plead their case. "We're poor little lambs who have lost our way," they sang in their perfect harmony. It cracked Dinah up; she didn't strand them in Miami.

Dinah had hoped to be in Chicago for her sister Clarissa's wedding, but the Miami bookings prevented her from attending. She did, however, give the couple a handsome wedding gift, an entire bedroom suite, and some other furniture for their home. Her celebrity prompted *Jet* to send a photographer to the ceremony. The August 31 issue included a picture of Clarissa, identified as Dinah's sister, and her husband, Eugene Smith, being congratulated by the minister at Shiloh Baptist Church, where the family had worshiped for years.

. . .

THERE HADN'T BEEN any obvious repercussions for Dinah after her news conference eleven months earlier protesting the racial situation in New Orleans. It was not clear if Mercury actually pulled her records from the stores, and it was doubtful that other stars followed her lead. Dinah hadn't said anything else publicly about racial matters since then. But as the civil rights movement continued to gather momentum, other entertainers were speaking out either to raise money or stage their own individual protest. Sammy Davis, Jr., had put together a Carnegie Hall benefit for the Reverend Dr. Martin Luther King, Jr., in January. Ray Charles canceled a date in Augusta, Georgia, in late March when he learned that the seating would be segregated. Even white performers got involved later in the spring and summer after headlines blared from Alabama and Mississippi about the beatings and arrests of "freedom riders," young men and women, most of them black, who went into southern states by bus to integrate the bus stations.

Charlton Heston, who had won an Oscar in 1960 for the title role in *Ben-Hur,* was among the white artists who decided to speak out. He went to Oklahoma City to join a march for integration of the city's businesses, prompted in part by his friendship with a prominent white doctor there who was active in civil rights matters. "I think every man should express his feelings at least once on a controversial matter," Heston told *Sepia,* which covered the protest. "It's time that I do a bit more concerning racial freedom than merely give it lip service at cocktail parties."

Though in more modest ways, Dinah helped, too. From Miami, she and the revue went north to Jacksonville for two performances, one at the Palms Saturday, September 2, and the next night at the Duval Armory, which was a benefit for the NAACP Youth Council. Before the Palms engagement, Azzie McFarland, one of the city's well-to-do black society matrons, hosted a reception for Dinah and "her entourage," as the *Florida Star* called it, at her spacious home. Dinah brought along LaRue and Buzz Pridgeon, who had worked as her road manager off and on since the 1950s. Dinah had taken a particular liking to Chuck Barksdale, and she made sure he was sitting next to her at the reception. She had had her eye on Dells tenor Vern Allison, Farris said, "but he wouldn't play."

"Well, we went out to sing," Allison recalled. "I didn't mix business with no employer of mine—I didn't want any jeopardy with the group because of some personal affair with me and the boss. I wasn't interested in her in that way."

At the benefit the next night at the Duval Armory, Dr. Warren Schell and his wife, who had hosted Dinah at their home on previous visits, had a full bar set up at one end of the room. At the other end a group of patrons brought in an extravagant buffet that included caviar and borscht. When the show was over the Schells treated Dinah and the rest of the cast to breakfast, and then the group hustled up to Philadelphia, where Dinah was booked for a week at Pep's starting Labor Day.

Because she played Philadelphia so often, Dinah had made many friends in the city, among them Bertha and James Foreman. She had actually met them in 1949 in Washington, when they were engaged to be married. She took an instant liking to the couple and, when she learned they wanted to get married as soon as possible, she sent her driver to their hotel to take them to a church in Rockville, Maryland, where she knew the pastor. Then she threw the couple a surprise reception after the ceremony.

The Foremans now had a daughter, Marsha, who was a year younger than Bobby. She had just celebrated her twelfth birthday, and when her parents took her down to one of the Pep's matinees Dinah surprised Marsha with a little fox terrier. "If she liked you, she went all the way," James Foreman said, though he admitted that if you rubbed Dinah the wrong way, "she would show you the other side."

Dinah also made public some dramatic news: she was leaving Mercury for Roulette, operated by her good friend Morris Levy, who also ran Birdland and the Roundtable. Mercury label mates Billy Eckstine and Sarah Vaughan had already made the switch. According to Ruth Bowen it was a matter of economics—Roulette offered Dinah a better deal—more money and the promise of better promotion. Jack Tracy wondered if it was something that had to do with Levy's alleged associations in the entertainment world, though he couldn't pinpoint it. "A number of the black artists left Mercury and other labels to go to Roulette—why they went, I don't know," Tracy said. "But somebody knows something. . . . There were no big screams of protest that I heard from anyone. They just accepted that they went to Roulette because of Morris Levy. All I can say, Roulette all of a sudden assembled a big roster of black artists."

Levy's acquisition of the talent put him in the enviable position to cross-promote, featuring stars at Birdland who made records for his company. It was also true that Levy, whatever his reputation, was devoted to jazz.

By the time Dinah returned to New York in mid-September, her latest Mercury single, "September in the Rain," from an Otis-Hendricks session in October 1960, was climbing the charts, those Hendricks strings once again cushioning Dinah's still tart delivery.

Dinah was scheduled to return to the Apollo October 13. She hadn't been feeling well during the Pep's run, and according to Ruth Bowen, Dinah's doctor was at every show in case she got sick. The problem seemed to be some kind of stomach virus, and one day early in October Dinah was sick enough to be hospitalized. Ruth told reporters it was probably an ulcer and didn't have anything to do with the fact that Dinah was as thin as she had ever been. The *Pittsburgh Courier* reported that she weighed 125 pounds now, down from 170 a year or so earlier.

Dinah made the Apollo opening as planned on the 13th and finished out the week.

After the final show Thursday the 19th, she was paid and in turn paid the cast. She tossed her envelope to Farris, who had accompanied her to the theater, and told Farris to count what was left. Only $39. It had been one of those weeks when Dinah had taken a lot of "draws." She still had to pay the dress designer Lois Green, who had been visiting from Harrisburg, Pennsylvania, and staying at the Bowery Building apartment to work on some new clothes for Dinah. The two had apparently resolved their differences from a year ago over what Dinah did or did not see at that party in Philadelphia.

Green was due $700, and Dinah told Farris to pay her after the first performance the next night at the 5000 Club in Brooklyn. Dinah, though, apparently didn't tell Green about the delay.

Dinah invited the Apollo cast to Apartment 14A-3 for a party as she often did. But Farris remembered this one was "a dud." Not very many people came and Dinah was not in much of a party mood. By midday Friday, the 20th, she wanted to get some rest so she could get to Brooklyn for the show. Sometime in the early evening, Green knocked on the door to Dinah's bedroom. Dinah told her to go away and let her rest, but Green, according to Farris, persisted, and chided Dinah for "sleeping your life away" while the people who were supposed to be running the apartment were not doing their jobs.

Dinah again told Green to leave her alone, but Green reminded her that she was still owed $700. Irritated and exasperated, Dinah yelled to Farris to "get me my gun." Recalling the evening years later, Farris said that instead of answering Dinah, she ran into the bathroom at the end of the hall and locked the door. She didn't see what happened next.

In the meantime, the owner of the 5000 Club had called the apartment and wanted to know where Dinah was. The place was packed, the audience restive waiting for her. It was either Farris or LaRue who said that Dinah didn't feel well and couldn't perform. Irwin Steinhauser, the brother of the owner, was dispatched to the Bowery Building with a doctor and two police officers because Steinhauser wanted to determine for himself if Dinah was really ill.

In the apartment Dinah and Lois Green were arguing face-to-face while Dinah's latest boyfriend, an aspiring heavyweight boxer from Canada, was asleep in the master bedroom. Green claimed that Dinah reached into her purse and pulled out what Green thought was a gun. She ran into another room and tried to call the police but the line was tied up. She finally left the apartment and went to the police station a few blocks away to ask for help.

It was probably LaRue who called Ruth Bowen and told her about the chaos in 14A-3. Ruth sped down to the apartment from her house on 168th Street to smooth things over with Steinhauser from the 5000 Club. He and the doctor and the policemen were leaving—without Dinah and without any examination being performed—as Green returned accompanied by two Manhattan detectives. They came inside and placed Dinah under arrest, charging her with felonious assault. The officers told her she would have to be taken to the station seven blocks away at 152nd Street. She insisted on getting properly dressed before leaving. According to the *New York Post* the detectives waited until she put on "a shimmering gold house dress."

"What will my neighbors think if they see me going out with this small army of the law?" Dinah asked the policemen, only partly in jest.

"Just tell them you're on your way to play a cops' benefit dance," one of the arresting officers suggested.

Dinah was booked at the station under her real name, Ruth Jones. She remembered that her friend, Major Robinson, the *Jet* correspondent, had told her about a young lawyer named David Dinkins, and Dinah insisted that he be called. When Dinkins, who would go on to become mayor of New York City, answered the phone about 2:00 A.M., he tried to explain that he didn't do criminal work. No matter. Dinah wanted him. "I got dressed and went up to the precinct," Dinkins said. "She was already booked, but at least I could see that they brought her downtown"—to headquarters—"in a car, not in a paddy wagon."

Dinah had also called Farris and told her to bring some money to the station. As she was walking the seven blocks north on St. Nicholas, Farris could hear "September in the Rain," Dinah's latest hit, coming out of every bar.

By the time Dinah got back to the apartment, the boyfriend was gone. Dinah also noticed some jewelry was missing, and she chastised Farris for pointing out the obvious. "Are you trying to say the man I'm sleeping with is stealing from me?" Farris didn't say a word; later Dinah conceded that she was probably right: the boxer had taken some jewelry. The boyfriend was "just a filler" anyway, Farris said. "Dinah just hated to be alone."

As a thank-you for her coming up to the jail, Dinah intended to give Farris a new suit she knew Farris wanted. But when Dinah learned that Farris had won the numbers the next day, betting on a combination that was related to "September in the Rain," Dinah changed her mind. Farris could buy the suit on her own now.

Dinah appeared in New York City's Felony Court on Monday, October 23, before Magistrate David Malbin. Determined to look every inch the star, Dinah wore a green beaver coat over a two-piece white suit and a white mink fezlike hat over a new wig, this one reddish brown. She was also wearing a canary-yellow diamond ring with ten baguettes. Dinkins and another lawyer, Emil Ellis, were there with her.

Under questioning, Magistrate Malbin asked Green what exactly she saw in Dinah's hand. "It was a blackish, bluish, grayish object which might have been a gun," she said. Green, the only individual to testify, said the dispute started when Dinah asked her why she was telling people she hadn't been paid. "She then asked me if I would lend her my car." Green refused because she hadn't even been paid enough to get back to her home in Harrisburg. That's when Dinah took out an item from her handbag, waved it around and said, "I'll blow your brains out."

Under cross-examination, Green conceded she might have called Dinah "a dumb and stupid moron."

At the end of the session Malbin reduced the felonious assault charge to third-degree assault and let Dinah remain free on $500 bail.

Later Dinah's lawyers said that because the gun charge had been dropped, she was in no danger of losing her cabaret card, which allowed her to sing at New York clubs. Beyond that, Dinah was getting ready to leave for engagements elsewhere and was not expected to return to New York until sometime early in 1962.

After the court session, Ruth Bowen told the *Amsterdam News* that the dispute had not started over money but because Dinah was still recovering from a virus and ulcers and "was trying to get some rest." Remembering the incident years later, Ruth said "the girl was totally wrong" and should have left Dinah alone when she told her to "get out and don't bother about the money." But Farris conceded that Dinah should have told Green directly that her pay would be delayed.

Publicly Dinah brushed off the incident as she prepared to leave town October 25 for a nine-day job at the Cave in Vancouver, Canada. "It's just a damn shame this thing had to happen," Dinah said. Asked by a reporter if Lois Green and she were still friends, Dinah replied, "I guess as of last weekend, she never was a friend of mine."

Dinah didn't have much of a sense of humor about what had happened. She demanded that a club owner remove a sign he had put up advertising her as "a Pistol Packin' Mama."

WHEN DINAH RETURNED to Chicago in November, she played a week at the Birdhouse, a new venue for her north of the Loop on Dearborn. The club was known for modern jazz acts, but owner Art Sheridan was changing the policy to bring in such names as Dinah, Sarah Vaughan, and Carmen McRae. Sheridan had worn many hats in the Chicago music business—record presser, distributor, label executive, and now club operator. He also ran Basin Street and had just taken over the lease at the popular lounge in the Sutherland

Hotel on the South Side. He announced that he was going to set up a shuttle bus service for patrons who would pay one cover charge a night and then go from club to club via his bus service. Dave Turner, who had joined Dinah's show a month or so earlier, was taking Slappy White's place as the evening's comic.

Sheridan was startled when Dinah showed up opening night accompanied by two off-duty policemen acting as her bodyguards. He introduced himself and asked if she was worried about the facility. Oh, no, Dinah told him. As of the last few months, this was standard procedure.

MERCURY WAS ACUTELY AWARE that Dinah was leaving shortly for Roulette, and management was determined to have her recut some of her past hits with stereo sound. Irving Green was convinced that as soon as Dinah got to Roulette, the label would have her re-record a lot of the songs she had done so they could offer their own catalogue. "To intercept that we went in to re-record those ourselves," explained Jack Tracy, Mercury's Chicago recording director.

A few sessions were set up with Quincy directing full arrangements, including strings, on some of the songs. Dinah had grown fond of Boris Zlatich, an accomplished violinist Eddie Chamblee had recruited to provide string players at the Tivoli earlier in the year and then at Roberts in the Dinahland months. She told Zlatich she wanted him to organize the strings for these Mercury sessions even though Zlatich told her the major labels had their own "clique," as he called it, of musicians they liked to use. Dinah told him not to worry. She'd take care of it.

On the day of the first session, Dinah came in the studio, looked around, and didn't see Zlatich or any of his string players. She asked where Zlatich was and was told that he hadn't been available on that date. Okay, Dinah said. "We'll cancel the session and pick a date when Boris is able to make it." And she walked out.

Dinah invited Zlatich and his wife, Dee, who had been an informal hostess for Dinah down at Roberts, to see a show at the Birdhouse. In between sets someone came to get Zlatich, told him that Dinah wanted to see him, and escorted him upstairs to her dressing room. "I want you to meet someone," Dinah said after they exchanged greetings. She introduced him to one of the Mercury producers. "This is Boris Zlatich. Let's pick a date so you can do that album."

When all the musicians finally gathered, Jack Tracy remembered a festive air, especially when Irving Green and his wife, Irma, were there. Mrs. Green and Dinah were friendly, and both liked nice clothes and furs. "She was there to keep Dinah happy," Tracy said. Dinah admired the mink Irma Green was wearing, so she took it off and let Dinah put it on. "Dinah was so excited," Quincy recalled, "she came in the men's room to show me."

Dinah liked to have "good booze" around, Tracy added. She would have a sip or a small glass of brandy to "refresh herself," but years later he scoffed at the notion that she drank excessively at a session. "My impression is she valued her talent too much to be drunk on record. She would walk away rather than do that. She was too good for that."

Patti Austin, now a young teenager, had been part of Quincy's cast in *Free and Easy* and happened to be in New York earlier in the fall when Dinah was recording. She stopped by to surprise Dinah and recalled seeing her drinking pink champagne between takes, demanding, "Where's my pink champagne?" "And Quincy would say, 'Oh, no problem. Pink champagne coming up. You want a buzz-on? If that's what's gonna get this performance out of you, great.'

"Of course, drunk, sober, upside down, right side up, she sang her ass off," Austin said.

Since losing Joe Zawinul, Dinah had picked up Patti Bown, a piano player from Seattle who had joined Quincy's big band. Bown periodically needled Dinah about their rocky start together. When Dinah first called and asked her to play, Bown picked up the phone to be greeted by "Bitch?" "I hung up. She called back and said, 'This is Dinah Washington, Queen of the Blues,' and the conversation went on from there." Bown said her first job was in New Jersey "and rehearsal took place in the car on our way to Asbury Park. She told me the keys and the songs she wanted to sing. That was the whole rehearsal." Onstage, though, Dinah jumped around "from key to key," but Bown, who had perfect pitch, followed her easily.

One evening Dinah called a tune, and Bown didn't catch it. "Excuse me, Miss Washington," she said, and asked to hear the title again.

"Bitch," Dinah said before repeating the title.

"I'm still trying to be a lady," Bown said.

"Bitch," Dinah repeated.

Bown stood up, apologized to the audience, and said, "Play it yourself, bitch. You're supposed to be a piano player."

So Dinah played and Bown, still standing, sang. "The audience loved it," she recalled. "They thought it was part of the act!"

Not many people talked back to Dinah, especially onstage. She liked Bown's sass and asked her to stay on for the upcoming jobs. "Dinah called me a two-bit piano player," Bown recalled, laughing. "I called her a two-bit singer."

Bown was on hand for the Chicago sessions and so was pianist Jack Wilson, who had played with Dinah when she was married to Eddie. He had gone into the army but had just gotten out and was in Chicago. When Dinah learned that he was in town, she invited him to come to the session. According to Wilson, trombonist Billy Byers, who was doing some of the arranging, liked the way Bown played and expected her to handle all the tunes on the session.

Wilson was sitting to the side, expecting only to watch and listen. "And the next thing that I know Dinah comes over to me and says, 'You play on the next number.' "

Wilson was surprised and a little embarrassed. But as gracefully as he could, he walked over and told Bown that Dinah wanted him to play.

"Okay," she said, and got up.

But Byers told her to go back and sit down. Bown dutifully returned and explained the situation to Wilson. So he got up and went back to his chair by the side of the room. Dinah had been watching the musical chairs from the vocal booth and came out into the studio. "What are you doing sitting there?" she asked Wilson. "I told you to go play."

Wilson explained what had just happened. Dinah turned around, went into the control room, and turned on the microphone. "Billy Byers and Quincy Jones, I want you to know one thing. This is my record date, and if I want John the Baptist to play, that is who is going to play."

After that outburst, Wilson recalled, "Quincy and Billy didn't say anything. They were sort of looking like little kids that had been reprimanded." Wilson went back to the piano and the session re-

sumed with a remake of "I Want to Be Loved." Ten years after the
original and with a lush orchestration, Dinah sang with knowing
conviction, that occasional rasp suggesting all that had occurred in
the intervening decade.

Musicians changed positions on another tune when the drummer couldn't get the ending of "Teach Me Tonight" right. "They
must have tried that ending four or five times and the drummer
simply could not play it," Tracy said. So Joe Newman, the trumpet
player, put his trumpet down, walked over to the drums, said,
"Move over," and played it exactly right and with a flourish. "The
place totally broke up laughing," Tracy said. "Here's the trumpet
player showing the drummer how to play."

Zlatich liked the way Dinah handled sessions with a large orchestra. He never minded that she came late and thought it was on
purpose—not to waste time but to give the orchestra a chance to rehearse. She hadn't wavered in her view since her earliest days in the
studio that her first take was the best, and she wanted the musicians
ready. Jack Tracy had to stifle a laugh when he watched Dinah walk
out of one session even though someone wanted to do another take.
"It's not going to get any better," she said on her way out the door.
"You fix it."

Zlatich and his wife, Dee, were flattered to be part of Dinah's entourage when she was in Chicago, even if their time with her could
feel more like a command performance than an invitation. Like others recruited into Dinah's circle, they sometimes found it hard to say
yes and nearly impossible to say no. One winter Sunday afternoon
Dinah insisted that the couple go along with her to a party her sister
Clarissa and her husband were hosting in their apartment in a new
housing project south of the Loop. Dinah had agreed to go to "razzle
dazzle the attendees," as Zlatich put it, "and Dee and I were brought
along because we were kind of glamorous, both being very good-
looking as well as white."

Zlatich had a nice car, and Dinah particularly liked it when he
drove her around. On this chilly afternoon, Dinah was wearing one
of her minks with a matching mink muff to keep her hands warm.
Dee wore her mink, too. As the three got into the elevator to head
up to Clarissa's, three young toughs forced their way in just as the
doors were closing. "What are you doing with these white people?"
one of them sneered at Dinah, seemingly unaware of who she was.

"Why are you wearing that rag on your head?" she retorted. At the same time she was maneuvering inside her muff to slip Zlatich a small .38 caliber pistol. Zlatich was momentarily surprised—he didn't know Dinah carried a gun—but he understood what was happening and smoothly took the weapon with one hand while with the other he abruptly stopped the elevator at the next floor. He pulled out the gun and orderd the three young men out. He, Dinah, and Dee went on to Clarissa's apartment and called the police.

"What a brain in that woman's head to act so quickly and so daringly and to trust me, a white musician five years her junior," Zlatich marveled years later, recalling the event.

MERCURY RELEASED another album, *September in the Rain*, after Thanksgiving and by mid-December it was on the charts. Like the April *Sepia* article, Dinah's latest record failed to keep up with her personal life. On Irving Berlin's "I've Got My Love to Keep Me Warm," she substituted "Rafael" in one line—"What do I care, I've got Rafael to keep me warm." And in another pass, she tossed in the Spanish diminutive *"papasita"* instead of his name. Though the reference had been apt during the January recording session, Rafael was gone by early April, well before the record was released.

The liner notes, signed by Clyde Otis, were effusive yet pointed. "She revels in the title of 'The Queen' (bestowed upon her by her fellow singers, musicians and recording people) and assumes a regal air when voicing her opinion of bad tunes, rock and roll, and long rehearsals. She loves good songs and music, and is just as vociferous in her praise for the good as she is in condemning the bad." Otis said the tunes were chosen on purpose "for their ability to create a mood and for their capability of being sung by Dinah with the utmost of feeling and expression."

The hallmarks of Dinah's singing were still present—thoughtful phrasing and palpable feeling—but her voice was often husky. At times she sounded weary, half speaking the lines to make her point. Dinah was tired, but she had to keep going.

19.

Roulette Wheel

1962

Dinah opened 1962 in Miami Beach, playing to a standing-room-only crowd at the Singapore Hotel. She and her piano player, Jack Wilson, however, still had to stay at the Sir John in Miami proper. Dinah brought out the platinum blond wig again, explaining that "it changes my personality," though she didn't say what that change was. On her way to Roulette, Dinah was nonetheless welcomed by Mercury's Miami representative, Steve Brookmire. The label had hustled her final album, *Tears and Laughter*, into stores right after the new year, and perhaps in recognition of the kind treatment from *Cash Box*, the two posed smiling for the magazine at the hotel. *Tears and Laughter* was made up of tunes from the final sessions with Quincy Jones and included one track, "Jeepers Creepers," where only the Dells sang.

Dinah had let Patti Bown go after the Chicago date in December, and according to Bown she was more than happy to give Wilson the job. The offstage business was wearing her out. Dinah still had trouble sleeping, and everyone who had spent time with her—LaRue, Farris, Ann Littles, the Joneses in London—knew that she didn't like to be up and around alone. While Bown was with her, she felt as though she was on call all the time. Dinah would convince a hotel clerk to give her a passkey to get into Bown's room and then expect her to get up and accompany her on middle-of-the-night or early morning jaunts.

Dinah insisted on being paid promptly, sometimes in advance if she was running short of cash. But as Lois Green had learned, Dinah could be late paying *her* bills. Bown learned that, too, and it was a contributing factor in her decision to leave. It also stung that Dinah would not acknowledge Bown onstage, even when someone complimented her. Maybe it was because of the praise for another woman. Asked who was at the keyboard, Dinah might say, "Oh, that's Stella Dallas."

"She wouldn't say my name," Bown said. "I loved her, but I'd had enough."

Farris had had enough, too. She had moved out of 14A-3 a few months earlier after another of Dinah's impromptu firings. She didn't even know what had set Dinah off that day, and while they patched things up, Farris decided that it was time to find her own place and to get other work. Drake Tolbert, the "valet," also decided to leave, and afterward he regaled readers of the *National Enquirer* with his tales of working for Dinah. "I've seen her act as sweet as a person could . . . and as mean," he wrote. "She's a mixture of tyrant, angel, full-grown woman and little girl. She's mean, moody and magnificent. . . . Dinah sometimes forgets that other people have feelings," he added, "and she rides right over them and pushes them around."

In one of the accompanying pictures Tolbert was caught in a show business act of fealty: Dinah was sitting on a stool in an evening dress, microphone in hand, a tiara on her head. Tolbert was on his knees, changing one of Dinah's bejewled high heels.

He explained in the *Enquirer* article that he got tired of the repeated firings and hirings, but he admitted that while he wanted to strike out on his own as an interior decorator or beautician, he might go back to work for Dinah. It was hard to resist when the phone rang and that familiar voice more commanded than cajoled, "You better get over here and take care of me."

Dinah had even fired LaRue, and the one time she had actually left—they were in Kansas City—Dinah was begging her to come back by the time LaRue reached Chicago. Dinah was angry that LaRue had gone out for the evening without telling her. LaRue thought Dinah was in for the night, but she had gotten out of bed, put on her robe, and gone down the hall to play cards with the band. LaRue never forgot the scene outside their hotel as she was returning: Dinah out on the street, a mink coat over her robe, screaming, "Why didn't you tell me?"

"And I told her I was grown," LaRue recalled. "I didn't think I had to tell her."

Jack Wilson was happy to be back playing with Dinah despite her idiosyncrasies, confident their relationship would be strictly musical. One time earlier when he'd backed her, Wilson was resting at his hotel in Midtown Manhattan when he heard a knock at the door. It was Dinah. Surprised to see her, Wilson invited her in. He couldn't figure out why she was there and worried silently that she had come to give him his notice in person. Dinah sat down on the edge of the bed, crossed her legs, and, Wilson thought, looked invitingly at him as she made small talk. "I dig that she is there for some other reason," he said. "She's hitting on me—what's this all about?" Wilson was momentarily flummoxed. Though he was "swept up in her musicality," as he put it, he wasn't physically attracted to Dinah and didn't think he had done anything to lead her on. So he pretended as though nothing was going on. "I just, as it were, pooh-poohed it." Dinah left a few minutes later.

Right after the Miami Beach job Dinah took Wilson along for her second trip to Europe, this one to play armed services bases in Italy and Germany. She planned to pick up other musicians when she arrived. The stop in Naples included three nights at the United States Naval Base playing the ballroom at the Bluebird Club January 16, 17, and 18. The final night was the most formal; the navy men in attendance were required to wear jacket, buttoned-up shirt collar, or military uniform.

Dinah and Wilson were staying at one of the nicer hotels in Naples, and Italy's reputation for fine fashion was not lost on her. "She saw this shop," Wilson explained, "and had the driver stop." The place was closed, but Dinah got out of the car, knocked on the window, and woke up the proprietor. He opened up the shop, "and Dinah bought, I think, at least $2,000 worth of clothing, maybe more."

Before she left for Europe Dinah had hired a new backing trio for all the dates on her return. The men called themselves the Allegros, Jimmy Sigler on organ, Earl Edwards on sax, and Jimmy Thomas on drums. Dinah had first heard them at the Shalimar, which was around the corner from the Apollo. She would come in now and then when she was in New York and sit in. One evening she asked the musicians if they knew "I Understand," which she had recorded for Clyde Otis. "We didn't tell her we had an arrangement," Jimmy said. "So she started to sing and the Allegros started to harmonize. It knocked her out. She bought out our contract that night. We were booked for four weeks and only had done two."

Jimmy was thrilled. He had first seen Dinah when she was with Lionel Hampton and they played the Earle Theater in his hometown of Philadelphia. "I started liking her singing right after that. When we met her, I knew everything she was doing. That's how long I had been following her."

The Allegros' first big job with Dinah was in Las Vegas, but before they headed out west, Dinah did an afternoon show at the Baltimore Civic Center with Quincy Jones's band and Tony Bennett on the bill. It had apparently been booked while she was still at Mercury. Dinah was a little surprised to see more black faces than white in the audience. "Where are all your folks?" Dinah teased Bennett, who was about to have a huge hit with "I Left My Heart in San Francisco."

Dinah started a monthlong engagement in Las Vegas February 3 at the Thunderbird, another of the city's fabled hotel-casinos. It had opened in 1948, the fourth on the Strip. Dinah was paid $6,000 per week (the equivalent of $36,000 in today's dollars), but that amount covered the entire revue she had brought with her, which included Wilson, the Allegros, a new vocal group that included Chuck Barksdale and Johnny Carter, who had temporarily left the Dells, Cornelius Gunter, who had been with the Coasters, and another singer, Richard Williams. They were known as "Dee's Gents." Dave Turner, the comic, was also on the bill, along with a young dancer, Lola Falana. Dinah's share of the weekly $6,000 from the Thunderbird was probably between $2,500 and $3,000. Sigler remembered that the Allegros were each paid $125 a week.

Sigler was surprised to find that Las Vegas was still segregated. None of the musicians could stay at the Thunderbird. They stayed instead at Mr. B's, a hotel on Jackson Street on the west side. "It was decent, and they had nice furniture," Jimmy said, and it was affordable. A band member's $125 per week had to cover expenses.

Buddy Rich happened to be performing in town; he knew Dinah and liked the sound of the Allegros. "Jazz organ was new to the Strip," Jimmy explained, and Rich sat in with them perhaps five or six times when they played a few instrumentals before Dinah came on to sing. Jimmy Thomas wasn't upset that he had to give up his chair to Rich. "He was honored," Jimmy Sigler said. Besides, Jimmy Thomas was a singer who had learned to play drums and did far less complicated things behind Dinah than the virtuoso Rich could do when he picked up the sticks.

Billy Eckstine came by for a show or two as well. Though he and Dinah apparently had feuded, according to Patti Austin—Eckstine once sent Dinah chitterlings through the mail, which created quite a stench when they arrived—Dinah never mentioned it. She talked instead about Eckstine's natty appearance. "Cleaner than the board of health," she joked.

When Dinah was between marriages, she was never without a man—sometimes more than one caught her fancy. She had her eye on Dave Turner, the comic, but she also flirted with Earl Edwards, the sax player in the Allegros. He was thrilled to have the star's attention, and when Dinah wanted to "hang out" one night, of course he said yes. The next day Dinah was distant. It was no big thing to her, but Edwards was devastated. "He couldn't handle it," Jimmy Sigler said. He thought he was going to be Dinah's new man, though if confronted, she would swear she made no such promise.

Edwards was so out of sorts that when the Allegros flew to San Francisco for a job at the nearby Richmond Auditorium, Edwards forgot his sax at Mr. B's. He realized it on the plane, and the pilot radioed back to Las Vegas so that Dinah, who was coming in later, could bring it. (The Allegros subsequently replaced Edwards with John Payne, who had such a slow-moving manner offstage that Dinah called him "Old Folks.")

After a couple of other one-nighters in the area, Dinah and the revue flew back east to open March 9 at the Town Hill in Brooklyn. As she had done in Las Vegas, Dinah did three shows a day, but the difference between playing a hotel-casino with all the gambling revenue to sweeten the pot was evident in her paycheck: $3,000 for the week—half of what she commanded in Las Vegas.

Dinah's first session for Roulette was probably right after she returned from the Thunderbird. She asked Jimmy Sigler to play on the date and wanted to use his arrangement for one of the songs, "Where Are You," which had been a hit for Mildred Bailey a quarter-century earlier. Though he was a good musician, Jimmy couldn't read; he did everything in his head, so he had to dictate the music, and conductor Fred Norman had it transcribed. Dinah normally had little patience with musicians who couldn't read music. But she liked Jimmy and appreciated that he knew what she wanted.

"Dinah fought for me with the arrangers," he said.

After a week at Pep's in Philadelphia that started March 19, the group went to Revere Beach, a few miles northeast of Boston, to play a return engagement at the popular Frolic Club. Opening night March 31 a line snaked down the block with patrons trying to get into the sold-out show. "Dinah commanded the stage whether singing perched on a stool, behind the orchestra or on stage," the *Variety* reviewer wrote. Her demand for complete attention had not abated. "Nobody fools with her when she's singing," the reviewer said, admiring her ability "to insert a tart phrase like 'shut up' to noisy ones without missing a beat in rhythm."

The reviewer also gave a nod to the Allegros, calling their backing arrangements "superb" and their vocals "effective choruses."

Masco Young, who wrote entertainment pieces that appeared in the black press, said in one column that Milt Buckner, who had played with Hampton and on Dinah's first recordings, dropped by one evening and that Dinah joined him for a crowd-pleasing spur-of-the-moment organ duet. Young had managed the Allegros when they first got started in the late 1950s, and Jimmy chuckled years later that Young was fabricating. "Milt Buckner was my idol. If he was there, I would have remembered."

THE FIRST WEEK in April Dinah was the subject of a flattering feature written by Young, this one focused on her burgeoning enterprise with Ruth Bowen, Queen Artists, which still represented the Perri Lee organ trio, the singer Del St. John, and now the New Allegros and Dave Turner. Dinah turned on the charm, self-deprecating if occasionally self-serving. "I'm anxious to help struggling and talented young people get the breaks they deserve," she said. "There are too many of our folks who have the talent but no place to use it. For years I found myself helping many people get ahead in the entertainment field, but I asked nothing for myself but that they do their best to succeed and help others as I have done. Then one day," she continued, "I got the idea that if I organized my own talent agency I might be able to offer even more help to many more people. So here we are."

Ruth Bowen, who had just gotten her booking license, had printed up a brochure with a letterhead listing the address—1697 Broadway, Suite 1209 in Manhattan. This information was set inside a little flag, a small crown on top of the staff. "If it's talent you're after sit back and leave the thinking to us," was the legend, all in capital letters, under the flag. The agency described itself as "a young, vibrant newcomer in the theatrical booking field, but we have the zest, energy and drive to make money for our clients and clubowners and promoters with whom we do business."

Dinah was listed first and pronounced the "greatest voice of the century." Though Ruth was handling much of her business through Queen Artists, Dinah still maintained her relationship with Associated Booking. The brochure noted that Dinah was available through either organization.

Dinah also now had two labels handling her music. Mercury still had new material from the late 1961 sessions and fifteen years of recordings in the catalogue. Early in April the label released a new single, her remakes with Quincy Jones of "Such a Night" and "Dream." Within a week Roulette released its first album called *Dinah '62* and a single, "Where Are You," backed with "You're Nobody 'Til Somebody Loves You." "Where Are You," with Jimmy's transcribed arrangement, was the side that got the most attention. Compared to many of her previous recordings, this one was sedate if not spare, even though there were strings. At the end the backup vocals dropped off, and Dinah gave the last "where are you" her best bluesy flourish. Though "You're Nobody" was a well-known, much recorded song, Dinah set a different tone right at the start simply by changing "'til" to a determined "until."

There was nothing particularly different to distinguish the Roulette arrangements from Dinah's earlier Mercury sides. All these new songs, whether ballads or upbeat numbers, had more strings than horns, though the Roulette strings were not as prominent as the ones Hendricks had used. But with all this going on, it was harder now to grasp Dinah's intuitive feel for the beat and the phrase that were so apparent in her earlier years.

"Won't somebody—please—put a small swinging band behind this wonderful singer—and restore her crown and throne to Queen D?" lamented *Down Beat* in its review of *Dinah '62*. "Big, bruising bands are fine and dandy; but for a singer such as Miss Washington, there seems little point in cluttering up the date with arrangements that do little or nothing to enhance her performance." Some of the settings, the reviewer asserted, were "out of character" for her, including a "creamy organ—and a vocal group, yet." But Dinah obviously liked this, perhaps because it was a throwback to the church and the sound and feel of all those Thomas Dorsey songs.

Arrangements aside, the reviewer pointed up what was now more obvious: this was a different Dinah. "The fact of the matter here is that she is not in top shape. She sounds tired. There is too little evidence of that wondrous electric vitality that established her as a peerless singer."

If the Mercury and Roulette arrangements were similar, one readily apparent difference between the labels was promotion. More than Mercury had when she was on the label, Roulette treated Dinah like a star. They took out full-page ads in the music trades and in *Down Beat*. In a couple of issues they even bought the back cover. Bud Katzel, Roulette's general sales manager, insisted to *Cash Box* in early May that orders for Dinah's album had exceeded "all of the label's expectations." (By the third week in June *Dinah '62* was on the *Billboard* LP chart; it went on the *Cash Box* album chart a few weeks later, and showed steady sales according to both magazines well into the fall.)

Dinah and the revue had been held over at the Frolic for an extra week, playing into mid-April. Then the group left for a ten-day engagement in Flint, Michigan, at the Major Key. Ann Littles was back working for Dinah and signed on to drive one of the cars for the month's engagements. Although Dinah made all the performances at the club and squeezed in a benefit for the Genesee County Cancer Crusade, she was not feeling well, more tired than usual and more often unable to sleep without the aid of her prescription sleeping pills. On top of that Dinah was irritated because club owner Melba Earhart hadn't paid her all of her salary. At the end of the job, Dinah checked into the Flint Osteopathic Hospital for five days, telling *Jet* she needed to rest because "that place caused me so much aggravation."

Jimmy, the Allegros' organist, recalled that the musicians and Ann, also functioning as road manager, gave themselves two days to get from Flint to Houston, where they were booked May 5–7 at the Palladium. Dinah flew down after she was discharged from the hospital. The Palladium proved to be "a bad booking," Jimmy said, because James Brown and Ray Charles were in town at the same time and cut into Dinah's draw.

Dinah was aggravated enough about the problem with the Flint club that while she was in Houston, she instructed her lawyer to file an action against Melba Earhart for $9,000 to get her back pay. "She didn't give me my money so I had to close her," Dinah said, another example of her double standard when it came to paying bills.

The next engagement for Dinah and the revue was a two-and-a-half-week job at a new club in Oakland, California, the Flamingo. The Allegros and Ann were driving the cars west; Dinah flew on a commercial flight, but she had started to lease small planes for some of the other musicians. Though she hadn't told Ruth Bowen, who tried to keep Dinah on a $500-a-week budget, Dinah wanted to get her own plane. Dee's Gents and one or two others in the party were put on a small private plane to get to Oakland, according to Sigler, but something happened at one of the refueling stops—perhaps in Amarillo or farther north in Kansas City. When the plane started down the runway to resume the flight, it never got liftoff and skidded to a stop, damaging the underbelly. Fortunately no one was hurt, and everyone made it for opening night May 11.

By the time Dinah and the revue finished their first week at the club, Dinah's first two Roulette singles were on the charts, "Where Are You" registering in both *Billboard* and *Cash Box* (pop and R&B), "You're Nobody 'Til Somebody Loves You" spending one week on the *Billboard* pop chart. The *Chicago Defender* reported in mid-May that 150,000 copies of "Where Are You" had sold "in less than ten days"; *Jet* called it "a smash hit" and "rated by disc jockeys as her best." "Dream," the April Mercury release, also registered in both music trades, though only for a short time.

Dinah was still unusually tired during the Oakland run, and after she complained to a doctor about not feeling well, he put her in the hospital—the second time in three weeks she had fallen ill. But she was determined not to miss an engagement in Washington, D.C., and she insisted on being released to travel back east. She was among the performers booked to open the first International Jazz Festival at Constitution Hall May 31, an event sponsored by President John F. Kennedy's Music Committee, which was part of a larger outreach program to citizens around the country. Over three days other stars, including Duke Ellington and Benny Goodman and their orchestras and Cannonball Adderley, would perform. Dinah was scheduled to sing with the National Symphony on opening night and then play the next day with the Allegros.

With the symphony behind her the evening of May 31, Dinah did an abbreviated version of "Summertime" that was unmistakably hers. "Summertime and the *living* is easy," she sang. There would be no dropped g's on her Catfish Row. And if George Gershwin failed to write a "lord" or a "but" to introduce a line, that didn't stop Dinah.

"Thank you," Dinah said to loud applause when she finished. "Thank you," she repeated as the applause went on.

"There's been a little change in the program," she continued when the audience quieted down. "On the greatest moment of my life, I'm gonna have the great Duke Ellington accompany me on 'Do Nothin' Till You Hear from Me.' " Dinah made that substitution after an afternoon rehearsal when she quarreled with symphony conductor Howard Mitchell about what she should sing. The program called for her to do another Gershwin number from *Porgy and Bess*, "My Man's Gone Now," but she didn't think it was right, and she didn't have confidence that Mitchell would handle "Do Nothin' " properly either. Ellington was greeted with an ovation as he came onstage and then played a nifty solo introduction for Dinah. Five minutes later when they were done, the song filled out by trumpet and trombone solos, the crowd applauded for three minutes.

When the announcer came back out to introduce the next part

of the show, he delivered a message from Dinah. "Miss Washington wants you to know that she loves you madly," he said to chuckles and more applause from the audience.

Washington Post music reviewer Paul Hume was privy to some of the back-and-forth about the opening festivities, and his June 1 account included a pointed paragraph about Dinah's moment. "Dinah Washington may be a singing star," he wrote, "but she is out of place singing 'Summertime,' and she wisely changed the program from 'My Man's Gone Now' to 'Do Nothin' Till You Hear from Me.' " Referring to her argument with Mitchell, Hume added that she could have no argument with Ellington's work, "since it was tremendous."

The next day Dinah and the New Allegros were part of the program in the Washington Coliseum; it proved to be a disastrous setting, the stifling heat combining with a terrible sound system. The *Down Beat* reviewer complained that some of the singers couldn't be heard and that the "desultorily turning" ceiling fans were so ineffective that many in the audience left early. Dinah persevered, singing three short numbers, but in his account of the second day's events, The *Washington Post*'s Tony Gleske wrote that she and most of the other musicians "were lost in the noise."

Despite the many technical problems, the hosts of the festival considered it a success, if for no other reason than the attention it drew to the performers and their music. One disappointment, though, was the failure of President Kennedy to attend any sessions. Jouett Shouse, a prominent Washingtonian who headed the president's music committee, chided him in public. "It's a shame he couldn't go two blocks to hear a concert although Khrushchev went to hear Benny Goodman," she said, a reference to Goodman's recent trip to Moscow.

Dinah was on a tight schedule; she and the Allegros had to be in Philadelphia to open later in the evening June 1 at the Erie Social Club. The festival organizers hired a limousine for them and arranged a police escort to the Washington airport so they could catch the short Eastern Air Lines flight to Philadelphia.

By the Sunday evening performance Dinah wasn't feeling well again, but she came onstage determined to complete the engagement. She finished two sets, but as she was getting ready for the last show, she collapsed. The Allegros didn't know what happened until they were told she had been rushed to St. Joseph's Hospital. Doctors quickly diagnosed her with acute anemia and began giving her the first of what turned out to be four blood transfusions, according to the *Philadelphia Tribune*. Later in the day her doctor put out a request for blood donors. "We all went to the hospital and gave blood," Jimmy said.

By Monday evening Dinah felt well enough to talk to *Tribune* reporter William J. Daniels. Dinah was booked to open at Pep's on June 11, and she intended to make that date. "The doctors tell me I'll be well enough to begin my week," she said, "but they have told me I'll have to stay in bed until then."

Dinah was discharged on Tuesday, June 6. Associated Booking had lined up a one-nighter for her at the Mosque in Newark on the 9th, and though she had been out of St. Joseph's barely two days, Dinah and the Allegros made the date, which also featured the Jimmy Smith Trio.

Dinah was going to be thirty-eight on August 29; she had worked nonstop even through her pregnancies. She performed right up to her due dates and was back onstage within a month after both boys were born. Those closest to her knew she relied on "pep pills" and sleeping pills, and more than once, LaRue had to take care of her when she took too many of one or the other. "I'd have to walk her and pour black coffee down her and walk her and walk her," LaRue explained.

Dinah had even tried more dubious measures to lose weight, taking mercury injections that were supposed to draw the water out of her body in a matter of hours so she could drop a pound or two to fit into a dress. If Dinah was determined to wear a size eight, LaRue explained, "she'd take her own shot, and she stayed by that bathroom because it made her to go the bathroom. And if she took that shot by like nine or ten o'clock in the morning, when she got ready to go out at nine or ten o'clock at night, she was wearing an eight."

Keter Betts hadn't seen Dinah in three or four years, and when he and his wife went backstage after a show in Washington, he was amazed at how thin she was. Dinah was so tickled, proudly showing off her new slender figure. Keter smiled politely; later he told his wife how dismayed he was. She might have been thin, he told Pinky, but she didn't look well to him, and he thought her voice suffered, too.

Three hospitalizations in six weeks for fatigue were a warning sign. But Dinah was nonchalant about her health problems, and if Ruth or LaRue or Ann Littles or anyone at Associated Booking told her to stop or slow down, it apparently did no good. Such conversations were difficult in the best of circumstances. And for someone like Dinah—her sharp tongue and quick temper were the least of it—the situation was double-edged. Yes, she might be harming her health. But she not only loved to perform, she needed to. She was the marquee name, the one who earned money for herself and her children, the driving force behind Queen Artists, and she couldn't afford not to work. Besides, "Where Are You" was a hit, and it was important to be out there live, boosting the product while the public was paying attention.

After Pep's Dinah and the revue flew to Atlanta to play three days at the Royal Peacock. That job ended early in the morning of June 26, and on June 28 Dinah was back in New York to open at Birdland for two weeks, her first stint there since signing with owner Morris Levy's Roulette. It may have been a sign of how Levy did business that Dinah was paid only $2,500 for the week when her usual price was $3,000 for such engagements. Perhaps it was a discount Roulette artists were required to give Levy in exchange for some provision more favorable to them in their recording contracts, or the differential could have reflected the fact that because Dinah lived in New York, she didn't have the hotel expenses she had on the road.

Dinah's Birdland contract included the usual provisions—that she was to perform four shows Friday and Saturday night with Monday off, that $500 for each week would be sent directly to Associated Booking, and finally that Dinah, like other stars, was to receive "100 percent star billing." The others who performed at each show were the Allegros behind her, the Perri Lee organ trio, and Dave Turner. The Horace Silver Quintette was also on the bill.

Backstage before opening night, Dinah told visitors she was still "extremely tired," but she went on with the show anyway. On opening night she alternated past Mercury hits—"Unforgettable" and "Dream"—with new material with from Roulette including "You're Nobody 'Til Somebody Loves You." The sound and feel were different now, not simply because Dinah's voice had changed, but because Jimmy's organ dominated rather than the jazz pianists who had so often accompanied her—Wynton Kelly, Beryl Booker, Junior

Mance, Joe Zawinul, Jack Wilson, Patti Bown. The Allegros harmonized behind her on many of the tunes, and now Dinah peppered each set with medleys to work in crowd favorites, singing a few bars of one song and then picking a note or a lyric as the transitional moment to the next. The Allegros had to pay attention so they could follow her, which they were able to do with ease.

Dinah also bantered back and forth with audience members. These weren't hecklers. Dinah was such a regular at Birdland that some fans treated her like a friend, so it was more good-natured ribbing from the stage to the tables and back. She ended the set with "Where Are You" and then came back for seven encores, according to the *Amsterdam News*.

Jet reported that Dinah was so pleased with the Allegros that she gave each of them a new $2,800 Chevrolet. It was a good piece of gossip, but it wasn't true, though Dinah's reputation for the grand gesture made it plausible.

Dinah had worked out an arrangement to have her own small plane at her beck and call. In short order she "drove the pilot crazy," Ruth said, when she called him for impromptu trips or told him to make a landing one place or another because she wanted to drop in and visit a friend. One of Dinah's favorite things, Ruth added, was to buzz the Bowens' house at 168th Street.

Dinah decided to use the plane to get from New York to Carr's Beach in Annapolis, Maryland, for a one-day performance Sunday, July 15. It was another tight day because she and the revue had just finished at Birdland the night before. The flight to Annapolis was uneventful, but Jimmy was uneasy as he watched the pilot "enjoying himself tremendously" with afternoon drinks while he waited for Dinah and the musicians and their return trip.

DINAH'S SECOND ROULETTE ALBUM, *Drinking Again*, was released in July; this time Don Costa directed the session. The title came from the Johnny Mercer–Doris Tauber song. After several Mercury album covers that featured atmospheric scenes apparently intended to convey a mood rather than Dinah's particular look, Roulette put out its second album with a picture of Dinah on the front. *Dinah '62* had shown her standing in an evening gown at the microphone, shot as though fans in the audience were looking up from their seats. *Drinking Again* was a darkly lit three-quarter head shot, and the jacket featured an unusual credit. Ann Littles, who was a hairdresser by profession, was given credit for Dinah's up-swept hairstyle, a wig with affecting gray highlights.

Ann remembered that Dinah argued with Costa over the arrangements, an argument that Ann thought was silly. Costa was a talented man, and "Dinah was just acting like a fool, trying to tell Don Costa what to do." Finally, she said, Costa gave up, telling her, "We won't argue about this."

Because he had to master everything by ear, Jimmy was having some trouble getting the music down for *Drinking Again*. The cello player was chiding him about his difficulties, and finally Costa had enough. "Do you want to play this job?" he asked the cellist. That was all he had to say, Jimmy remembered. Knowing that Dinah wanted him on the job, "Don defended me." But Dinah was losing patience. "Jimmy Sigler, you better learn something," she told him. And he did.

"I didn't get a formal music education till Dinah got on my butt about it," Jimmy admitted.

Just as *Drinking Again* went on sale Mercury released another single, her remake of "I Wanna Be Loved" backed with "Am I Blue," and an album also called *I Wanna Be Loved*. Both were the latest ex-amples of Dinah in a pop idiom, though one track of *Drinking Again*, "I Don't Know You Anymore," was a blues with no strings, the sparest of the twelve tracks.

Down Beat's reaction to this latest music was both barometer and synthesis, a reflection of Dinah's evolving career and the musical choices made to stay current. The magazine, which reviewed both albums together, didn't care for either, observing what reviewer John Tynan called "an alarming decline in the quality of Dinah Washington record releases." "Though it is possible the vocal equip-ment no longer is what it used to be," he wrote, "one might expect that more experience in the art of living would have compensated and added depth to her performance. . . . Dinah is still DINAH," Tynan added, "and it would be difficult for her to produce a com-pletely bad album."

The Mercury album, he went on, sounded like leftovers from several sessions; the Roulette was better, and while there were mo-ments of "great Dinah, even here, she is hardly at her peak." (*Bill-*

board and *Cash Box,* which took a less critical approach, were much more complimentary. In fact *Billboard* proclaimed Dinah "at the top of her form," and both albums sold enough to get on the magazine's charts; *Drinking Again* stayed there for two months.)

Even if Dinah's fans disagreed with Tynan, the *Down Beat* review was another warning—not as dramatic as collapsing backstage, but a hint from outside the inner circle that all the hard living was taking a toll where it counted most, on Dinah's voice.

AFTER ANOTHER WEEK at the Frolic in Revere Beach in August, Dinah had planned to have a lucrative rest of the month centered around a two-week $10,000 engagement on a Caribbean cruise. But the trip was canceled and a planned stop at the King O'Hearts in Miami apparently also fell by the wayside. The cancellations meant that Dinah would be in New York for her birthday, and friends threw a surprise party for her at Sardi's. It turned into a combined celebration for Dinah and her boys, since their birthdays were all within a month of one another; George was turning sixteen, Bobby fourteen. He had gone from her chubby "Fat Daddy" to a long, lean teenager who towered over his mother when they posed for a celebratory picture, Dinah with a corsage pinned to her dress, a smiling Bobby in a trim-fitting suit with a Nehru collar, the latest fashion. She posed for another photo clinking her champagne glass with another guest, fellow singer Damito Jo.

Though Dinah could claim pop credentials and remained an R&B presence, albeit modest, she still registered in *Down Beat*'s annual August jazz critics' poll. She was eighth of ten, though well behind regular first-place winner Ella Fitzgerald. Dinah also notched her sixth record on the *Billboard* pop chart, her remake of the 1934 Hal Kemp hit "For All We Know" from *Drinking Again.* Her seventh came a week later with the flip side, "I Wouldn't Know," though their short stay on the tally would not qualify them as hits.

In the middle of Dinah's early September engagement back at Birdland, the gossip columns were buzzing with news that she was ready to get married again. Not so, Dinah protested. She didn't even know the presumed groom-to-be, a rock 'n' roll songwriter named Jay Ferguson. She dispatched Ruth Bowen to squelch the rumors. Dinah was "too busy raising her two sons and concentrating on her career to worry about marriage at the moment," Ruth said. "Not now or later . . . She has lost all confidence in men—for the time being. We don't even know the man. As far as we are concerned," she added, "he is some press agent's dream. It's simply not true." Dinah told *Jet* she wanted a formal retraction.

On September 14 Dinah opened another month run at the Thunderbird in Las Vegas. She played a late night, early morning schedule, with shows at midnight, 3:00 A.M., and 5:15 A.M. Opposite her in the larger Thunderbird theater was a Las Vegas production of *Flower Drum Song*, the Rodgers and Hammerstein hit. Dinah's audience was particularly star-studded her second week, with Lucille Ball, Carol Burnett, Ray Bolger, and Nat Cole stopping by.

By now the three Allegros understood Dinah's music, the pacing of her sets, and how to adjust musically to her moods even though they almost never rehearsed with her, just among themselves. They were all good enough musicians to turn on a dime, and equally important, they knew the way Dinah signaled a key. Whatever she gave them—C, F, B-flat—Jimmy would give her an arpeggio in the dominant chord of that particular key, and then they'd wait for Dinah to begin the song she had picked.

Typically, a Thunderbird show would start with a few instrumentals from the trio. Then Jimmy would announce, "Ladies and gentlemen, the Thunderbird proudly presents the dynamic queen of song," and the trio started to sing "Dinah, is there anyone finah?"— but the words were stretched out for effect: "Di . . . NAH, is there anyone Fi . . . NAH?" as she came out onstage.

The trio never knew what Dinah's first song would be, probably because she was making up her mind as she approached the microphone. But as she walked on from stage right, she would signal the key. And from the simple gesture of her hand, they knew what the tempo would be—though they still didn't know the song. It might be "Wake the Town and Tell the People," "A Foggy Day," or "September in the Rain."

Whatever she sang, she would always raise the last verse a half-step. "It was her view that if the audiential ear is allowed to hear the same thing too long it stops listening," Jimmy recalled. "I had to learn to keep my eye on her," he added, especially when Dinah went to the front of the stage and sat down, her legs crossed demurely over the apron. It meant that she was going to take the women to school, as she put it. She would ask a waiter to bring her a glass of Courvoisier and then tell the women to "listen up" as she gave her instructions about dealing with men.

She would stop singing, crack a joke, and talk a little, and then when she was ready to sing, she would motion to Jimmy what key she wanted. "I would give her an arpeggio still not knowing what was coming." For this portion of the show, Dinah generally sang some combination of "Nobody Knows the Way I Feel This Morning," "Mean Old Man's World," "Long John," "You've Been a Good Old Wagon," and "This Bitter Earth."

"It goes without saying that she had to trust her backups," Jimmy said, "and she did. She was such a great musician that she could give us tempos by voice inflections."

Dinah finished her sets back at center stage. If she sang "Don't Go to Strangers," the trio would chime in on the line "I've been through it all" with "You can say that again." Dinah feigned consternation, and the audience ate it up. She usually ended each show with either "You're Nobody Til Somebody Loves You" or "Baby, Won't You Please Come Home."

Dinah was back at Birdland for a week at the end of October, and some nights the midnight show was broadcast over WJZ. On October 19 host Symphony Sid gave Dinah one of his usual effusive introductions, calling her "the most talked about young lady of song, ladies and gentlemen, the Queen, Dinah Washington."

Dinah used the occasion to talk about her third album from Roulette, *In Love*, which had just been released, and a new single from it, "In the Evening." Don Costa again arranged and conducted, with full strings that included timpani and French horn on some tracks. *Billboard* called it a "dreamy, warm album," though it would disappoint those who preferred Dinah in a simpler mode. She told the Birdland audience that her favorite track was "Fly Me to the Moon," and her live version, much pared down from the recording, as well as the live "In the Evening," was full of the ad libs, repetitions, and little embellishments that she loved so much. In a way it was call-and-response, though in this case between Dinah and herself.

Roulette scheduled more recording in November around another week at Pep's in Philadelphia that started November 19. While Jimmy had been the only one of the Allegros to work on Dinah's previous Roulette albums, the other two were also scheduled to work on this new one, which was planned to be a return to the blues. "We were supposed to show up for rehearsal," Jimmy recalled. "And we forgot. We overslept." Dinah was angry. "She swore a blue streak, and we deserved it. We were sorry." Their punishment was being knocked off the album; at Dinah's instruction Roulette found other musicians.

Dinah registered her eighth and ninth records on the *Billboard* pop chart in mid-November, a remake of "Cold, Cold Heart" on Mercury and "You're a Sweetheart" on Roulette—neither of them hits. This new "Cold, Cold Heart," with a Belford Hendricks strings arrangement, was markedly different from the 1950 version. That one, which began with Paul Quinichette's light but dynamic sax solo and featured Clark Terry on trumpet, was closer to jazz than anything else. While Dinah's singing was crisp and clear in this later version, it was aimed at the same pop audience that liked violins and cellos behind her on ballads.

On December 2, Dinah returned to the Pittsburgh area for the first time in a few years to play a new venue for her, the Holiday House, which was on the outskirts of town in Monroeville. The club was on Route 13 not far from Pittsburgh's famed steel mills and drew a largely white audience. Dinah flew to the job from New York, posing for photographers just before she boarded her TWA flight, smiling and waving. Looking ready for an evening out, she wore a short silver mink jacket over a dark dress and had on a large black hat with the brim turned back. Perhaps TWA had arranged for the picture. Resting on the floor next to Dinah was a small carry-on bag with the airline's letters prominently displayed.

The Holiday House management was supposed to have installed an organ for Jimmy; instead they had an imitation instrument called an "organo." The sound wasn't quite right, so Dinah requested that the local musicians union send over a bass player. As they ran down the tunes for the first evening, Dinah wasn't happy; she didn't think the bass player, who came from the black local, was very good. This was not the way she liked to start a job, and it probably put her in a bad mood. She didn't like a noisy crowd in the best of times. When she was cranky, she was even less forgiving.

Some of the patrons who had come to the show December 3 seemed to treat Dinah as background music for their partying. "If

LEFT: Fifteen-year-old Ruth Jones in a publicity picture for gospel recitals in Chicago, April 28 and May 10, 1940. Her mother, Alice Jones, was the accompanist.

BELOW: Ruth, now eighteen, with her first husband, John Young, twenty-four, after their wedding, June 24, 1942. The photo was taken outside of the Jones family home at 661 East 37th Street in Chicago. *Courtesy of Berna Dean Brown*

ABOVE: The last week in December 1942, Lionel Hampton hired Ruth, who
had recently changed her name to Dinah Washington, to tour with his band.
This 1945 document shows a portion of her expenses and where she stayed
when the band was in the New York area. *Author's collection*
BELOW: Dinah onstage with Hampton at the Strand Theater in New York,
January 1945. *Frank Driggs Collection*

ABOVE: Dinah and her second husband, George Jenkins, a drummer who occasionally played in the Hampton band, with their son, George Kenneth. Dinah and George were married on June 11, 1946, and separated within a few months. *Courtesy of Clarissa Smith*

BELOW: Dinah signing autographs after a show in New York in 1947. *Vivian G. Harsh Collection, Ben Burns File, Chicago Public Library*

RIGHT: Dinah seated next to Robert Grayson, her third husband, whom she married in August 1947, with Dinah's friend William Battles and two of his friends. Battles was an elevator operator at Kaufmann's Department store in Pittsbugh, and Dinah often stayed at his house when she was in town.
Courtesy of William Battles

BELOW: Dinah in performance, circa 1947.
Dave E. Dexter Jr. Collection, Department of Special Collections, University of Missouri, Kansas City

ABOVE: Dinah with Beryl Booker, one of her piano players (seated at her left); LaRue Manns, her personal assistant (standing, center); and other family members on the Jones side. *Seated, left to right:* Margaret Jones, Evelyn Jones, Bertha Jones Layton, Sam Jones, Dinah, and Beryl. *Standing, left to right:* Robert Grayson, Dinah's husband; Ollie Jones, Dinah's father; LaRue; and McKinley Layton, Bertha's husband. Late 1948–early 1949. *Courtesy of Sam Jones*

BELOW LEFT: Dinah and Walter Buchanan, her fourth husband, shortly after they got married in Baltimore on October 13, 1950.

BELOW RIGHT: A sign of Dinah's growing success was her picture on the front of the music magazine *The Cash Box* on August 18, 1951. The picture was taken during a Los Angeles recording session. With Dinah are her agent, Ben Bart (right) and musical director Ike Carpenter. *Courtesy of Edna Albert*

ABOVE: Dinah (at back) in the vocal booth during a Mercury Recording session in New York, probably during the fall of 1951. Nook Shrier, who also went by the name of Walter Rodell and later David Carroll, was conducting. The musical demarcation of the time is clear: members of the rhythm section were black; the rest of the orchestra was white. *Courtesy of Tami and Molly Shad*

LEFT: Dinah with her mother, Alice, photographed at the Theresa Hotel in New York after Dinah won the 1952 *Pittsburgh Courier* poll as the female blues singer. *Courtesy of Clarissa Smith*

BELOW: Dinah's trio, circa 1952, outside of a club. *Left to right:* Keter Betts, Wynton Kelly, and Jimmy Cobb. *Courtesy of Ann Littles*

ABOVE: Dinah with her sons, George and
Bobby (whose father was Robert Grayson);
her mother, Alice; and Jimmy Cobb (behind
the couch) at 1518 South Trumbull in
Chicago, the home Dinah bought for her
family. The photo is circa 1953. *Courtesy of
Clarissa Smith*
RIGHT: Dinah with Lionel Hampton and
Sammy Davis Jr. in the dressing room at
Basin Street in New York, 1953. *Frank Driggs
Collection*
BELOW: A ticket for a May 1953 perform-
ance. *Author's collection*

DINAH WASHINGTON
and
ORCHESTRA
Thursday, May 7, 1953
War Memorial Building

ADMISSION $2.00
9 P.M. -:- 1 A.M. № 106

ABOVE: Dinah's two sons, sister, and stepsisters in front of the station wagon her trio used on road trips, just after Dinah and the group arrived at 1518 South Trumbull in Chicago, August 1953. In June, Alice had married James Kimbrough, who had five children. *Front row, left to right:* George and Bobby, Dinah's sons, with Alfreda Kimbrough. *Back row, left to right:* Sunny Kimbrough; Estrellita Jones, Dinah's sister; and Pat Kimbrough. *Courtesy of Farris Kimbrough*

RIGHT: Dinah pinning a boutonniere on Keter Betts before his wedding, which she sponsored at Abyssinian Baptist Church in New York, October 1953. *Courtesy of Keter Betts*

BELOW: Dinah singing in an impromptu moment at the Comedy Club in Baltimore, November 1, 1954. Rose Snow, her onetime assistant, is to her left. *Courtesy of Rose Snow*

LEFT: Dinah with Larry Wrice, November 23, 1953, at Cafe Society in New York. They told friends they had gotten married in Miami a few days earlier, although they had not, and the gathering was to celebrate the "marriage." *Copyright © Bettman/CORBIS*

BELOW: Dinah lost in thought during a March 1955 recording session in New York. *Copyright © Herman Leonard*

BOTTOM: Dinah in performance at a club, Keter Betts behind her, mid-1950s. *Courtesy of Keter Betts*

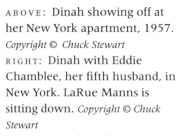

ABOVE: Dinah showing off at her New York apartment, 1957. *Copyright © Chuck Stewart*
RIGHT: Dinah with Eddie Chamblee, her fifth husband, in New York. LaRue Manns is sitting down. *Copyright © Chuck Stewart*
BELOW: Dinah with LaVern Baker backstage at the Regal Theater in Chicago, December 1957. *Copyright © Ted Williams*

ABOVE: Dinah, mid-song at the Newport Jazz Festival, July 6, 1958. *Copyright © Ted Williams*

LEFT: Dinah killing time while she waited for drummer Max Roach to join a rehearsal at the 1958 Newport Jazz Festival. *Copyright © Ted Williams*

BELOW: Dinah at Roberts Show Lounge in Chicago with her friend Eloise Clay and three other patrons who posed for the picture, circa 1958. *Courtesy of the late Eloise Clay Hughes and Leon Hughes*

ABOVE: Dinah with producer Clyde Otis and one of Otis's favorite arrangers, Belford Hendricks, August 1959. Among other things Otis produced and Hendricks arranged was Dinah's Grammy-winning record, "What a Diff'rence a Day Makes." *Copyright © Chuck Stewart*

RIGHT: Dinah and Rusty Maillard, whom she claimed to have married on a boat offshore in Stockholm, Sweden, at her apartment in New York, August 1959. *Copyright © Chuck Stewart*

BELOW: Dinah in the mood to sing at her apartment, December 1959. A framed copy of the *Dinah Sings Fats Waller* album cover is on the wall. *Copyright © Chuck Stewart*

LEFT: Three of Dinah's closest friends and confidants. *Left to right:* LaRue Manns, Ruth Bowen, and Ann Littles, January 1960, in Los Angeles. *Courtesy of Ann Littles*

BELOW: Dinah with her sons, Bobby on her right, George on her left, April 1960, at the Paramount Theater in Brooklyn. *Copyright © Chuck Stewart*

BOTTOM: Dinah and Rafael Campos, her sixth husband, January 1961, in Los Angeles. *MichaelOchsArchive.com*

ABOVE: Dinah (center) in a mink jacket, and members of her "mink-clad" chorus at a fashion show in Chicago in the spring of 1961. *Copyright* © Chicago Defender
LEFT: Dinah and Quincy Jones at a Mercury session, August 1961, which was one of Dinah's last before she left for Roulette Records. *Copyright* © *Chuck Stewart*
BELOW: Clarissa Jones, Dinah's sister (at the piano); Alice Jones, Dinah's mother (standing behind her); and Dinah in July 1962, when they came to New York for a gospel concert. *Copyright* © *Chuck Stewart*

RIGHT: Dinah with the Allegros, the trio that backed her 1962–63. From left to right, they are Jimmy Thomas, Earl Edwards, and Jimmy Sigler. Shortly after this picture was taken, Dinah bought the group new uniforms because they joked about the sweat stains that wouldn't come out despite repeated cleanings. *Courtesy of Jimmy Sigler*
BELOW: Dinah in the studio for a Roulette session with Don Costa (left) and Henry Glover, May 1962. *Copyright © Chuck Stewart*
BOTTOM: Dinah and Richard "Night Train" Lane, her seventh husband, walking out of the Little Chapel of the West in Las Vegas after their wedding, July 2, 1963. *Courtesy of Boris Zlatich*

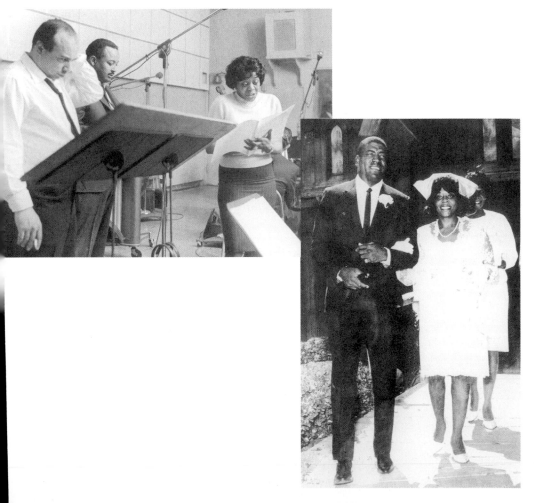

BELOW: Dinah's funeral at St. Luke Baptist in Chicago, December 18, 1963. *From left:* LaRue Manns; Richard "Night Train" Lane; Alice Jones, Dinah's mother; an unidentified family friend; Ollie Jones, Dinah's father; Harold Jones, Dinah's brother; Bobby Grayson, Dinah's son; Ruth Bowen (in white hat); and George Jenkins, Dinah's other son. Eugene Smith, the husband of Dinah's sister, Clarissa, is behind Ollie. Clarissa, with glasses, is next to him, and next to her (in hat) is Estrellita, Dinah's other sister. The man behind Ruth Bowen, hand to his mouth, is Isaac Sutton, one of a Dinah's good friends, who sometimes photographed for *Jet.*
AP/Wideworld Photos

ABOVE: Dinah in the studio during a Roule session, October 1963 wearing two of her favorite things, a min and a wig. The sheet music she is holding i for "The Good Life." I was released posthumously. *Copyright © Ch. Stewart*

you shut your mouth, do you think it would hurt your sex life?" she asked at one point, aiming her remark at three boisterous men and their escorts, each of them drinking heavily. When the noise continued, Dinah tried another line: "People pay to come here and see me. Shut up."

The six seemed unfazed and continued their loud merrymaking. Finally a large, bald-headed man came over to the group from a nearby table and confronted the men. "Listen, I came to hear the singing. I'm enjoying it. Either shut up these drunken broads or I will." The men got up, but before they started throwing punches, management separated the potential combatants and ushered the six drinkers out of the club.

Dinah's penchant for changing clothes between sets had not diminished, and she had brought so many evening dresses, offstage sports outfits, shoes, and accessories that there was barely room to move around in her quarters. The audience loved to see each new outfit, and while most were attentive at each show, almost every night there were noisy patrons who bothered Dinah onstage. She refused to ignore them and berated those who continued to carry on. One evening she was so miffed, she walked offstage until the crowd got quiet.

Club owner John Bertera was upset. His patrons were not used to being lectured from the stage. He told *Billboard* he had received two hundred letters of protest; worse, he was forced to refund $1,300 to dissatisfied patrons. When he told Dinah he was going to dock her salary by one day because she hadn't shown up, Dinah protested that she didn't come on December 6 because snow blanketed Pittsburgh, and roads were closed.

Bertera refused to back down. He detailed his concerns in a formal letter to Nat Nazzaro, AGVA's representative in Pittsburgh. "For reasons unknown to me, Miss Washington behaved in a thoroughly unprofessional manner. She continuously harassed patrons in the audience for fancied wrongs, chided and embarrassed valued customers who were trying to enjoy the show, was thoroughly insulting and generally out of order."

Dinah had agreed to meet the press for a few minutes after one show, he said. "After an hour's wait, it became apparent to them she was not coming." She was called at her hotel, he went on, and the response was "that she was resting and a cavalier refusal to talk to anyone." Dinah had also agreed to do a television spot arranged by the *Pittsburgh Courier,* Bertera added, "then simply did not appear."

Already tired after a long year and now in a new place that wasn't comfortable, Dinah seemed unable to tamp down the edginess that dissipated more quickly when she was in familiar surroundings. Then, too, it could have been the discomfort itself, which started with the subpar equipment and fill-in musician, that set her off. Whatever the case, more than on any other occasion she seemed to embody the nickname she claimed to detest, "Evil Gal." When Dinah returned to New York in mid-December, her dispute with Bertera was still unresolved.

A THREE-WEEK STAY at Birdland that would carry Dinah into the new year was a welcome change from Pittsburgh. Her contract specified that while she would sing New Year's Eve, she would have New Year's Day off. Dizzy Gillespie was also on the bill and sometimes played on one of Dinah's sets, all of the musicians performing under a "Merry Christmas" banner strung over the Birdland stage.

Once again Dinah showed up in *Jet'*s assemblage of interesting Christmas gifts, this time showing her latest mink to Ruth Bowen. It was a lush fur toilet seat cover. "Dinah had every other kind of mink," Ruth joked. "Why not this?" The *Defender* teased in one of its year-end stories that Dinah did not find a new husband in 1962.

Dinah registered in two year-end music tallies, as a top-fifteen female jazz singer in *Down Beat,* in the top ten for rhythm and blues in *Cash Box,* as a singer and for album sales. By now, though, these kinds of designations didn't mean much for a performer of Dinah's stature. Her presence was so established that she still filled clubs and sold records regardless of how they were marketed even if she didn't sing with the same "electric vitality" she had ten, even five years earlier.

Dinah had bounced back from three hospitalizations, but there were more times now when she was unpredictable and erratic, the delicate balance of life onstage and off- going askew.

20.

For All We Know

January–November 1963

Roulette released Dinah's fourth album, *Back to the Blues,* early in 1963. For the first time in nearly five years, she was singing without strings, back not only to blues but to the kind of arrangements that had brought her so much success at Mercury. Saxophones and trumpets, with an occasional guitar, replaced the violins and cellos.

Fred Norman, who wrote most of the arrangements, understood how at home Dinah was with blues, particularly when they got to "You've Been a Good Old Wagon." "Oh, she was going, singing like crazy," he recalled, "and it was getting so long. 'Jeez,' I said to myself, 'there's got to be an end.' And I cut the board."

Dinah exploded. How could Norman cut her off in midstream? But he did. "The final version was five minutes long anyway," he said, chuckling at the memory.

Another track ran even longer, Dinah's eight-and-a-half-minute version of "Nobody Knows the Way I Feel This Morning." She sang verse after verse with understated intensity, neither belting nor shouting. Her vocals were accented by two different trumpets, a baritone sax, piano, and a guitar, each of the musicians playing so carefully that it seemed as though they were in awe of the masterful performance unfolding before them. Dinah's favorite stylistic tics were still there—interjecting "lord, lord, lord" as the spirit moved her, using a crescendo to highlight a particular word, tossing in the well-placed "hmmm."

It was another moment of release, just like "Trouble in the Low-lands" from the Mercury session, and Jimmy found the song an apt metaphor. "We'd say 'Good morning,' some days and she'd say 'That's a matter of opinion.' We knew we were in for a bad time till her mood changed. Change it did . . . sometimes for the better."

The opening track on the new album was another of those songs that resonated in Dinah's hands, "The Blues Ain't Nothin' but a Woman Cryin' for Her Man," and she sang it as if she were delivering a primer on romance. "Many who profess an understanding of the blues really don't know what the blues is all about," Dinah had told a *Defender* interviewer not long before the album was cut. "The blues is something you've got to know and feel—in every muscle and nerve of your body, and from experience that comes from the hard knocks of the world."

The cover on *Back to the Blues* had an eerie cast, Dinah in the shadows, her hair flecked with the same gray highlights used on *Drinking Again*. It made her look older than her thirty-eight years.

In mid-January Dinah went to Puerto Rico with Dave Turner, the comedian who seemed to be her current boyfriend. The *Defender* speculated that he was going to be her next husband, but when they got back, Dinah squelched such talk. Once again she was determined to be the one who shaped the story. "When we came from Puerto Rico, he tried to play cat and mouse and I found out what he really was," she told *Jet*. "I figured he used me, so I said, 'later.' . . . I showed him the world, and he lived in the best hotels and always had maid service," she went on, "but that's just like a—you can't ever educate them away from a cold water flat mentality. I don't know whether it was good while it lasted because it might have been a joke on me. Ha, ha, ha. But I've got the last laugh because now he's got to figure out a way to get his rent paid, and he will find this very unfunny, too."

Dinah professed bewilderment about her failed romances. "I just don't understand Negro men. They don't want to stay with the

Queen. They prefer to act like commoners." But she was determined to take this latest blowup in stride, quoting a line from "No Hard Feelings," her latest single: "Just kiss me goodbye and blow."

Comedian Nipsey Russell, appearing at a Friars Club roast for Sammy Davis, Jr., at the end of the month, offered his own take on Dinah's offstage life. She's been married so many times, he said, "they don't issue her a new license. They just punch her old one and give her a transfer."

THE FIRST WEEK in February Dinah celebrated twenty years in show business. She rounded up members of the Lionel Hampton band who had worked with her—her first appearance on the stage of the Apollo had been February 12, 1943—and went over to the Kriegsmann Photo Studios on 46th Street to take pictures, a choice both sentimental and symbolic, since James Kriegsmann had taken her first formal publicity shot. Then she threw a party for everyone at Town Hill in Brooklyn. The three Allegros were still backing her, and each received monogrammed cigarette lighters, though Jimmy, the organ player, was the only one who smoked. How fitting that *Back to the Blues* went on the *Billboard* pop album chart within a week or so of its release.

Bad publicity from the flap at the Holiday House near Pittsburgh had continued intermittently through January. AGVA, the artists organization, was still negotiating with John Bertera, the club owner, trying to get Dinah's back pay. Bertera insisted that he had grounds to withhold money because of Dinah's behavior, which he now alleged included anti-Semitic remarks, though he did not specify what she said, and a bounced check. The opposing lawyers were not making much progress until AGVA threatened to place the Holiday House on the organization's "unfair list." This amounted to black-balling the club, which meant that artists would refuse to work there. Bertera's attorneys obtained a temporary restraining order in federal court in Pittsburgh on January 23 to prevent AGVA from going forward. A judge dismissed the stay on technical grounds three days later. But the club's action proved to be the catalyst. The two sides quickly reached an agreement, and Bertera sent Dinah a certified check for $1,200, roughly the amount she was owed less the amount of her bounced check.

Dinah and the Allegros were scheduled to perform an afternoon benefit concert in Norfolk, Virginia, on February 10 to raise scholarship money for the Norfolk State College chapter of Delta Sigma Theta, the black sorority. The scholarship concert, now in its fourth year, had brought other major stars in the past, including Duke Ellington, Dizzy Gillespie, Lionel Hampton, and Dave Brubeck. Delta Sigma Theta took out newspaper ads during the three weeks before the event, and the *Norfolk Journal and Guide,* a black paper, suggested that prospective patrons buy their tickets promptly because it was sure to be a sellout and to arrive early to get a good seat.

On February 10 Dinah and the Allegros arrived separately at La-Guardia Airport in New York for their chartered flights to Norfolk. They were ready to leave, but the airport imposed a delay. President Kennedy had been in New York City the day before on a "private social visit," the White House said, and was flying back to Washington. No planes could land or take off within a half-hour or so of the president's arrival and his departure.

Dinah and the Allegros subsequently were airborne but much later than planned. Dinah arrived first in Norfolk. By the time the trio landed and got to the terminal, they received a terse message from her with no elaboration: Stay at the airport.

The Norfolk Arena was packed by 5:00 P.M. The crowd grew restless, and local musicians started to play on the instruments set up for the Allegros. More than an hour later, a sorority representative announced that Dinah would not be coming, blaming her failure to show up on the delay at LaGuardia. Delta sisters frantically worked the phones, calling airlines in New York and hotels in Norfolk in a futile attempt to find her.

Around 9:00 P.M. Stan Allen, an agent who had arranged the date, called Hilary Jones, the Deltas' lawyer, and told him Dinah would be willing to play the next day, Monday, February 11. Jones said this was impossible and impractical. Many patrons had come from long distances, he explained, and could not be expected to have an unplanned layover in Norfolk. Back at the airport, the Allegros, who had been waiting for hours, were finally instructed to get back on the plane and return to New York. "I don't know who told who what," Jimmy recalled. "All I know is we didn't do the job."

Beyond the disappointment of the canceled concert, sorority

members were upset about the lost money. Dinah had been paid half of her $3,500 fee beforehand, and the group had spent roughly $1,000 promoting the event. They promised ticket holders a refund, and within two days, they had given back $4,500 of an anticipated $8,000 in ticket sales. One patron gave $2 back to the Deltas as his contribution to the benefit fund, and some declined to accept a refund so that the ticket money could still be used for scholarships.

Jones, the sorority's lawyer, said the group hoped to recover the advance it had given Dinah and "some consideration" toward to the $1,000 it had spent to promote the event.

The *Chicago Defender* pilloried Dinah. "Dinah Stands Up 3500 at Norfolk Concert," said a headline on the paper's story about the event. "Dinah Washington did it again!" read the first line. The *Pittsburgh Courier* wrapped together this latest flare-up with the problems that had erupted at the Holiday House. And the *Carolinian* in eastern North Carolina reported that in addition to these disputes, Dinah had to settle threatened legal action over an unpaid bill for her set design two years earlier at Ciro's in Los Angeles.

Though Dinah had been in public disputes before, this latest episode with the sorority smacked of an unbecoming cavalier attitude. As was the case with the missed date in Winston-Salem two years earlier, she acted as though she owed no one an explanation for her behavior, and beyond the offer to reschedule, she did nothing, at least publicly, to help Delta Sigma Theta raise scholarship money.

Dinah returned to familiar territory March 1, playing a week at the Apollo. The new comedian on the bill was Don Sherman, who billed himself as "the Soul of Laughter." Dinah had seen Sherman in Puerto Rico on the trip with Turner when he opened for Juliet Prowse at the Carib Hilton. She invited him to join her revue on the spot.

A month after Turner was shown the door, Dinah announced in a long interview with the *Chicago Defender* that her attentions were now focused on Bill Jackson, a patrolman in the Chicago police department. Dinah had met him in the summer of 1960 when she performed at the Bud Billiken concert, and he was on the security detail. "I don't know what's on his mind," Dinah told the *Defender*. "All I know is that we're two people who don't let nothin' bother us.

We make a perfect match. . . . We speak our minds fast, and we don't go in for the worrying, holding things back. Once the storm's over, it's done."

The fact that Jackson was in Chicago and Dinah was in New York was no problem. "He comes to see me about three days a week," she said. "I send my plane for him." This was Dinah's newest acquisition, a De Havilland Dove that seated eleven. She had put $5,000 down by check to Decker Airways early in March, but the check bounced. On March 27, Dinah paid the company $2,000 in cash and worked out an arrangement to pay the remaining $3,000.

When Dinah and Jackson were apart, Jackson sent her an orchid every day, the flower matching her favorite color and the color of the newest television set in 14A-3. (Because it sat on a high shelf, rabbit ears extended, George and Bobby dubbed it Sputnik in honor of the Soviet Union's first space satellite.) Fans surmised that every time Dinah sang "So Nice to Come Home To," it was dedicated to Jackson.

Dinah was hospitalized unexpectedly shortly after the Apollo show—the fourth time since the previous April. She ended up undergoing a fairly routine procedure to take care of a gynecological problem and was determined to be ready for a benefit performance at the Waldorf-Astoria on March 31 to raise money to send six hundred children with troubled lives, white and black, to summer camp. Patrons paid $100 a plate to attend; Governor Nelson Rockefeller was expected to be on the dais. "Me," Dinah joked, "I'll be on a diet."

The cause seemed to strike her in a personal way. "I can see how important a thing like this is," she told the *Defender*. "I have two boys of my own. They're good boys, but they have love and security in their lives. What about the kids who don't?"

George and Bobby had performed with Dinah when the revue played a week at the Galaxy on Long Island, and they were going to do a number with her at the Waldorf. "Why they get paid in Mutual Funds," she said when asked if her sons received a salary. Bobby's pants split during their Dinah-mites routine, leaving him alternately mortified and convulsed with laughter. Neither he nor anyone else had checked to see if he had outgrown his tuxedo pants.

Dinah had been the subject of harsh publicity in February and March. In April Jackie Robinson gave her a belated Valentine, using his regular column in the *Washington Afro-American* to praise her. Recent articles left the impression that "Dinah is constantly getting engaged, married, getting divorced; that Dinah is constantly getting into hassles like lawsuits, arguments with club owners and promoters over contracts, checks she was given which bounced and et cetera." Maybe, he went on, "you have the picture that Dinah is fickle, that she is a character and that she is evil. People talk about her behind her back and say she has the vocabulary of a longshoreman and about as much diplomacy as a midtown Manhattan cabdriver."

But that wasn't the whole story. Robinson said Dinah had a generous nature, and he repeated the story from the Apollo's Jack Schiffman about her taking care of all the medical bills for another performer's ill mother. There were other such gestures, too. "She has heart—this lady who sings the blues—to do good things and the good taste and unselfishness to do these things expecting nothing in return."

This was the Dinah many of her friends saw—especially those not in show business, Toni Thompson, the Foremans, William Battles, Georgia Mae Scott. Their Dinah was the woman who cooked in their kitchens, played with their children, and slept in the extra bed when she came through town.

DINAH'S NEWEST AIRPLANE was not immune from problems. On the way to Las Vegas, where Dinah was to open at the Thunderbird April 5, the De Havilland had to make a forced landing in New Mexico. Though the plane was damaged no one was injured, and Dinah apparently didn't worry about flying these small aircraft. But Ruth, who had to handle all the paperwork, wished Dinah would go back to regularly scheduled commercial flights, and it was at times like these that she felt she earned every penny of the $125 a week Dinah paid her.

When Jimmy and the other Allegros arrived in Las Vegas, they realized the city's strict segregation had eased. They were able to stay at the El Rancho Vegas Hotel across the street from the Thunderbird instead of being exiled to the Dust Bowl, as the west side was still known. The changes were the result of concerted action by black activists in Las Vegas, but the lore among visiting musicians gave credit to Frank Sinatra. In this version, Sinatra was furious when he couldn't find Sammy Davis, Jr., one day, only to learn that Davis was not staying on the Strip but over in the Dust Bowl with all the other black performers. "So he went to Giancana," Jimmy said, referring to the notorious gangster Sam Giancana, "who owns Las Vegas, and said, 'We can't have this.' "

Bill Jackson was Dinah's man's back east, but she was on the road now and pursued Chuck Barksdale, still one of Dee's Gents, to keep her company. Something or other went awry between them one day, however, and Dinah was angry enough to call security at the El Rancho Vegas. Barksdale raced into Jimmy's room and hid under the bed. When the police came to ask questions, Jimmy feigned ignorance. Can't help you, he told them. Haven't seen Barksdale all day.

Dinah was not staying at the El Rancho Vegas. Instead she was at the Thunderbird, but segregation had not eased so much that she was allowed to stay in the hotel itself. Instead, she was given a spacious and well-appointed bungalow on the hotel grounds. Because this engagement coincided with spring break at her sons' school in New York, George and Bobby came out shortly after Dinah arrived.

Bobby was amazed at what good service the hotel provided. Whatever they wanted—soft drinks, more food, more towels—the hotel staff was there in a minute. Only later did he realize that the attention was intended to make sure Dinah was content to stay at the bungalow and not come in the hotel. The boys were upset, however, when they were told they could not swim in the hotel's pool. Bobby, the more mischievous of the two, paid no attention on one hot day, playing in the cool clear water until he was ordered out by hotel personnel.

There was no question that the Las Vegas version of separate-but-equal was demeaning, but the pay was good and the audiences receptive, so Dinah put up with it.

Though the Thunderbird had its racial restrictions, the adults in Dinah's party were allowed to gamble. Casino manager Dave Victorson explained "the parameters" to the Allegros, Jimmy said, pointing out a buffet that was available to them and a separate table where they could sit down and eat near the bandstand. Bobby sneaked into the casino one evening to play a slot machine over in the corner. But before he could drop in too many coins, a guard spotted him and hustled the fourteen-year-old out, not because he was black but because he was underage.

By coincidence George Jenkins, Dinah's second husband and the father of her older son, was in town with one of the show bands. While it was nice for George Kenneth to see his father, Dinah and George did not get along well even after so many years. "Every time she saw him, she would grit her teeth," Bobby remembered. And when Jimmy Sigler happened to see them together, he heard the sparks fly. When they spoke to each other, though it seemed more like *at* each other, "there was nothing printable," he said.

Dinah remained unforgiving of noisy patrons and was never reluctant to quiet them. One evening a man sitting a few tables from the stage started to chatter. At first Dinah tried to ignore him, but he got louder. Finally in mid-song, she reached into a glass of water onstage, took out an ice cube, and threw it right at him. She made her point and didn't miss a beat.

She wasn't cowed by celebrity or status either. When California governor Pat Brown and his wife, Bernice, came to the show, Mrs. Brown talked too much for Dinah's liking. She asked her to be quiet, but Mrs. Brown persisted. So Dinah stopped the show and began an extemporaneous discussion about good furs and bad. Bernice Brown's coat, she said, was an example of the "raggedy." Sitting at the organ, Jimmy stifled a laugh; he had never seen *this* tactic before. Then Dinah turned to the side of the stage and told a maid, who was always nearby, to bring one of her coats to the lounge. Dinah would show Bernice Brown what a real fur looked like.

Dinah had even chewed out Mercury president Irving Green when he was too noisy for her liking at a Chicago nightclub. "You big SOB, if you don't shut up and get out of here . . ." she declared, stopping the show cold. "You—Irv—you know who I'm talking to."

Dinah wouldn't hesitate to speak her mind to the casino operators, either, according to Joe Delaney, a Las Vegas transplant from the East who had befriended Dinah. Among other things the pit bosses were supposed to keep the gamblers happy, especially the high rollers. "If the sound was too loud and would aggravate a gambler, the pit boss could turn it down," Delaney explained. "There was a gambler from somewhere in the South," he went on. "He didn't like Dinah, and all of a sudden she noticed a significant drop in her volume onstage." She stopped, politely said, "Excuse me," to the audience, and "walked through the casino slowly up to the pit boss," Delaney recalled.

"Motherfucker, I'm going to turn that back where it belongs," she said evenly, "and if you touch it I am going to break your fuckin' ass."

The head of the casino happened to be nearby, and he took Dinah's side. "Don't go near that button," he told the pit boss.

"Everybody in the casino heard what Dinah had to say," Delaney remembered. "As long as you treated her with respect she loved you. If you were going to make her a secondary citizen, you had a tigress on your hands."

Clara Ward, the gospel singer, and her troupe were on a long engagement at the lounge of the New Frontier. She had come in the previous October expecting to stay a few weeks but was such a hit that her booking was repeatedly extended. Dinah went over one night to sing with her, and Jimmy thought it was Dinah's quiet way of lending support. Some of the more religious blacks on the city's west side had been upset with Ward for taking the New Frontier job, insisting that gospel and gambling didn't go together.

Sarah Vaughan was also in town at the Riviera, and she was a particular favorite of the Allegros. One evening, with Dinah's blessing, they went to the hotel to catch Vaughan's early show but got stuck in traffic and were ten minutes late for Dinah's set. They came into the Thunderbird Lounge and found Dinah singing and playing the piano. When she saw the trio, she got up to great applause, told the audience that the piano had once been her "shtick," and finished the set.

Afterward, Jimmy Sigler said, "She gave us both barrels. We had it coming, but she sent us."

For all her impatience with noisy audience members, Dinah herself could be just as bad. Those moments seemed to occur when she didn't like someone—perhaps it was competition or maybe some inexplicable grudge. Dinah didn't care for Nina Simone and had even made unkind remarks about her appearance. Boris Zlatich was surprised to hear Dinah being so catty when they dropped in on one of Simone's shows while the singer was in Chicago.

Bud Katzel, the Roulette sales representative from New York, had come out to Cleveland one weekend to help promote Dinah's latest album. Simone was playing at one of the city's clubs, and he and Dinah went to see her. They sat down at a table and had a couple of drinks. Katzel thought Dinah was a little high.

"Throw her a fish," she suddenly shouted while Simone was singing.

An embarrassed Katzel told Dinah to be quiet.

"Oh, throw her a fish," Dinah repeated.

That's it, Katzel said, taking Dinah by the arm and walking her out of the club.

"We got back to the hotel, and that was the end of it," Katzel said. He thought the outburst was as much related to the liquor as anything else. "I didn't find she drank a lot. It just happened to be this time."

That evening, though, showed Dinah's unappealing side, when she was ornery and self-absorbed, haughty and even unkind. She was the opposite of the woman who could bring an audience to tears and to their feet when she sang with such feeling.

But even when she was haughty, Dinah could be fun. When another singer dropped in to see her at a San Francisco club, eager to show off her new fur, the woman hollered, "Hey, Dinah, have you seen my new white mink coat?"

"Come on outside," Dinah retorted, "and see my new white chauffeur."

ART SHERIDAN AND EWART ABNER, who operated the Sutherland Lounge back in Chicago, had been working hard since January to make the club, at 47th and Drexel Boulevard, a major jazz venue. Miles Davis, Simone, Count Basie, and Cannonball Adderley were among the stars who had performed there in recent weeks. Dinah was booked from May 8–19. "On opening night you couldn't move," recalled Artie Frazier, Jr., one of the bartenders—"mixologist" in the club scene vernacular—and a sharp-looking man with his own following. The 250 or so patrons took every seat and every inch of standing room.

Frazier's station at the bar was right in front of the bandstand, so he could feel Dinah's presence onstage and at the same time see how she captured an audience. "Dinah had a special crowd," he said. "They would kill for her." One night one of her fans gave him a corsage for her, and when he motioned that he had the flowers, she bent over so that he could pin it to one of the spaghetti straps on her evening gown. Frazier was trying to get in the right position to put it on, reaching over his head and extending his hands, corsage in one, pin in the other. He didn't have the angles exactly right, and he stuck Dinah.

Surprised, she screamed a curse over the microphone to chortles all around until Frazier finally got the flowers properly attached. To make sure he knew there were no hard feelings, Dinah "tipped me gorgeously," Frazier said, handing him a twenty-dollar bill. She liked to tease him, though, and when there was chatter about the club being for sale, Dinah piped up that she'd like to buy it and turned to Frazier. "You're the first motherfucker I would fire," she said, trying to keep a straight face.

Charles Walton was the drummer with the Bill Henderson Trio, who played an opening set during Dinah's first week. On the trio's last night, which happened to draw a heavily black crowd, Walton was riveted by Dinah's blues selections. "She was so soulful," he said. "She was in tears."

Jimmy knew it was so. "Every time she sang 'For All We Know,' she cried. If she sang it three times a night, she cried three times. It set up certain feelings in her."

Just before Dinah was getting ready for her last performance at the Sutherland, the manager told her he was going to garnishee her draw because she owed a store some money, and the owners wanted the money taken from her pay. Upset, Dinah went onstage and told the audience that she wanted to sing for them, but she couldn't because the Sutherland wouldn't pay her. She hoped they didn't tear up the place, but what could she do?

"The crowd began to knock on the tables," Frazier said, "so the man agreed to give her her money."

Dinah was earning a lot of it—$149,700 in 1962 (about $910,000 today), according to one account, and was on track to make that much in the new year. She was also spending it as fast as it came in, and if she wasn't paying some of her personal bills, she apparently wasn't paying her taxes in a timely fashion either. The Internal Revenue Service had taken note, and David Dinkins was called in to help. For a time, he said, IRS agents "practically camped in my office" while they tried to work out an arrangement for Dinah to pay down her tax bill and still earn money. If the IRS garnisheed all of Dinah's earnings from every job, he told the agents, he knew what she would say: "Okay, I won't work."

At the same time someone—and it might have been her new accountants—told Dinah that she may not have been getting all she was due from Mercury. They had been paying royalties over the years under her successive contracts, but she had no idea if the label was paying all it was required to. The lawyer handling this piece of business, Martin J. Machat, filed suit against Mercury on Dinah's behalf May 13, asking for an accounting of the sales and royalties due Dinah since 1951. Mercury immediately sought to dismiss the suit. The label's motion was denied, Mercury appealed that denial, and both parties now had to wait until the appeals court ruled. No one expected a decision until sometime in 1964.

LIKE MOST OF the well-known black entertainers, Dinah continued to remain in the background of the civil rights movement even as it was gaining strength month by month. She was playing the Thunderbird in Las Vegas on September 30, 1962, when James Meredith was finally admitted to the University of Mississippi after a protracted legal battle, a thousand miles away literally and figuratively from the riot that subsequently engulfed the Ole Miss campus. She had just opened at the Sutherland on May 8 as hundreds of school-age protesters in Birmingham were beaten down by high-pressure fire hoses and jailed in their orchestrated effort to desegregate the city. A few were set upon by police dogs, one teenager severely bitten in the stomach in a moment captured by a news photographer and sent around the country for all America to see. Upset by the events and wanting to help, Dinah announced one evening that she would give all the proceeds of a night's work to the civil rights protesters and asked patrons to make individual contributions as well.

She wasn't the only performer to make such a gesture: Eartha Kitt told a Harlem rally that, after watching the news from Birmingham, she was giving her week's salary of $5,000 from the Apollo to movement leader Martin Luther King. Helpful as these contributions were, the *Chicago Defender* criticized them as too little. "Do Top Entertainers Dodge Peace Parades, Integration Protests?" asked a headline atop one story in mid-April.

"For a long time now Negro entertainers have contributed to the fight for integration," reporter Bob Hunter wrote. "But the truth is— not many have participated in actual demonstrations that require personal physical action. . . . Most of the stars give lip service—and very often money, but as far as facing jail for equal rights—never. . . . How long will it be before they cast off their makeup and mascara and take to the battle fields in both the North and the South? Where are you—Eartha Kitt, Harry Belafonte, Nat Cole, Ossie Davis, Miles Davis, Count Basie, Billy Eckstine, Dinah Washington, Chubby Checker, Fats Domino and Mahalia Jackson?"

Despite the *Defender*'s call for more direct action from entertainers, King seemed willing to accept their names and talent to raise much-needed funds. On May 27 he came to Chicago for a huge benefit at McCormick Place. In the early evening more than five thousand individuals jammed into the Arie Crown Theater while hundreds who could not get inside milled around the lobby and applauded the performers one by one as they entered the building— Dinah, Mahalia Jackson, Eartha Kitt, Al Hibbler, Gloria Lynne, Dick Gregory, and the Chad Mitchell Trio, a white act. Beyond the talent, organizers received many in-kind contributions, among them a pit band led by Red Saunders made up of performers from the black musicians union and ushers who worked for nothing. Even Mayor Richard Daley stopped by. The event was important enough to Dinah that she paid for the Allegros, who were supposed to be off for two weeks, to come back to the city and play behind her, even though they had a small part of the program.

The atmosphere was electric inside as the throng waited for King and his two associates, Rev. Ralph Abernathy and Rev. Wyatt Tee Walker. Bob Hunter noted in the *Defender* that the three leaders appeared together for only the most important meetings "for fear of being wiped out by some insane bigot." Mahalia Jackson, one of the sponsors, brought the crowd to its feet when she sang a new anthem dedicated to freedom. Dinah, the Allegros behind her, sang two of her biggest hits, "What a Diff'rence a Day Makes" and "Where Are You." King's message to the huge crowd was simple: "We have heard the words, 'Slow up—and cool off.' Our answer is that the motor is cranked up, and we're moving up the highway of freedom. We shall overcome."

. . .

DINAH, THE ALLEGROS, AND DON SHERMAN left for Detroit right after the performance. Dinah was booked at Ford Auditorium May 31 for another benefit to raise money for a small black college. The program started at 8:30 P.M., and Dinah was supposed to come on about an hour later. But stagehands were slow changing the set and getting the organ for Jimmy in place. So Dinah came out onstage alone before the roughly one thousand in the audience and apologized for the delay. Then she sat down at the baby grand piano to sing a few numbers, playing the piano the way Roberta Martin had taught her so long ago and bringing a gospel touch to her pop tunes. Dinah told a couple of jokes but turned serious to quiet a noisy audience member. "I'd hate to have to put you out," she said. "You know I'm so bad I have been known to fire club owners."

Shortly after ten the real program got under way. A new group of Dee's Gents led by the Dells' Johnny Carter sang a few numbers, and then Dinah, backed by the Allegros, came out for twenty-five minutes. She did the same music in a big auditorium that she did in a small club, on this night singing "Unforgettable," "Blowtop Blues," "This Bitter Earth," and the song she had to sing every night, "What a Diff'rence a Day Makes."

Dinah's spur-of-the-moment solo earlier was evidence that she was in a good mood, and her later request for quiet was gentler than usual. But Dinah's typical fire returned when one patron kept snapping pictures. Please stop, she admonished. "Mr. Ford has a nice place here, and I'd hate to close it up over a few pictures."

All during May in Chicago, Dinah partied with Bill Jackson in her offstage time. *Jet* caught up with them at one where they tried their hand at the Twist, the new dance craze. She told the magazine that Jackson had given her a Thunderbird as an engagement gift, "and that's no joke." But it was. Jackson could never have afforded such an expensive car, and, he said, it was actually the other way around—Dinah wanted to give him a car, but he wouldn't take it.

Now in Detroit to play the Flame Show Bar again, Dinah rekindled her friendship with the Detroit Lions' star defensive halfback, Dick "Night Train" Lane. "Is Dinah Washington already planning to marry for the eighth time?" Ziggy Johnson wondered in his *Michigan*

Chronicle column without naming the potential groom. (Johnson apparently counted Rusty Maillard as one of Dinah's husbands, though the ceremony at sea off the shore of Stockholm was not considered a legal marriage.)

Dick's nickname came from the famous Jimmy Forrest instrumental, which was a hit in 1952, his rookie season with the Los Angeles Rams. His teammates gave him the moniker while he was making a splash in that first year. He set a season record of fourteen pass interceptions. His brutal tackling style—taking down a receiver at full speed by thrusting an arm around his neck—became known as the "Night Train Necktie."

Dick first met Dinah years earlier in Los Angeles when she was playing the Tiffany. He told her frankly that he didn't know a thing about her music, but his wife did. "She don't do nothin' but sit in the corner and play your records all day long. I don't know what she hears in them," he said, "but they gotta be something."

After the Rams traded Dick to the Chicago football Cardinals in 1954, he ran into Dinah now and then. When they happened to be at the same party one evening, he chastised her for being too loud and bossy. "Girl, you know what, if I was your old man, I'd put half my fist down your throat, talking like that."

Dinah threw her drink at him. So he picked her up, walked toward a window, and pretended he was going to throw her out. He put her down and gave her another short lecture before walking out the door: "You oughta try and clean up your mouth."

No one, man or woman—except perhaps Alice Jones, Dinah's mother—talked to Dinah that way. It made an impression.

The two didn't see each other again until 1956, when Dick was playing an exhibition game in Cleveland, and he and some other players went to hear Dinah's first set at the Loop Lounge. She had just been arrested the night before when police raided the house where she was eating dinner because it was also an illegal gambling club.

"I guess everybody heard about me going to jail last night," Dinah had said as she opened the show. "These cats were just shooting craps, and I was having a little fun with my fans and whatnot. . . . Yeah," she went on, looking in Dick's direction, "I think there's one of them standing over by that post."

Dick took a step or two forward. "Oh, no," Dinah laughed. "It's the football player."

From then on, according to Dick, the two kept in touch and had friendly chats whenever they found themselves in the same city.

When Dick was traded to the Detroit Lions in 1960, he usually saw Dinah whenever she came to perform. He had opened a small restaurant called the El Taco, which he ran in the off-season, and Dinah made it a point to order food from there. By the time she returned to Detroit for this latest Flame engagement, Dick had fathered a son with another woman who lived in Detroit. But their relationship was over. He and Dinah started to see each other, and it was getting serious. After the last show on June 17, he gave her a ring. "Dick didn't propose exactly, not in the traditional manner," Dinah explained. "He just bought a ring and said I knew what it was for. He shocked me speechless—the first time in my life I was ever speechless." Dinah added that she couldn't pinpoint the moment she realized she loved Lane. "I don't know. It sneaked up on me."

Dick joked that he would be Dinah's "lucky seventh."

He accompanied Dinah to a big benefit for the Southern Christian Leadership Council June 23 at Cobo Hall, and when Dinah finally caught up with her longtime Detroit friend Bea Buck, she was eager to tell her the news. "Where have you been?" she asked Bea, who was running late. "I want you to see my new husband." And Dinah nodded toward Dick a few feet away.

When the news about the couple became widely known, the *Chronicle* put the story on the front page. "Has Dinah Taken Our Night Train?" the paper asked. A front-page picture a few days later confirmed that she had. Dinah was sitting down; Dick was standing on her right, an arm on her shoulder, a huge grin on his face. The caption reported that Lane flew to Los Angeles, where Dinah had just opened at Basin Street West, and from there the two would go to Las Vegas to be married.

Dinah had summoned Ruth Bowen from New York to help her make the arrangements, though it took several entreaties. "Frankly I didn't pay too much attention to her," Ruth said. "But she kept on calling and saying, I want to get married. So finally I flew out." Dinah also called her friend at the Thunderbird, administrative director Vince Anselm, and asked him to find a place for the ceremony and a person to perform it.

"Do you want a minister or a justice of the peace?" he asked.

"I don't care, honey, as long as it's legal," Dinah told him.

The afternoon of July 2, Dinah, Dick, and a small wedding party gathered at the Little Church of the West where Justice of the Peace Tom Pursel married the couple. Ruth was the maid of honor, and Dinah's friend Ishmael "Ish" Evans, co-owner of Basin Street West, was the best man. Dick's friends from his days on the Rams, Ollie Matson and Dick Bass, were relegated to informal groomsmen.

The pictures of the smiling couple walking arm in arm out of the chapel had the look of a storybook romance. Dinah, at her thinnest, wore a short white appliquéd dress with a lace-trimmed jacket, a single strand of pearls around her neck, and a white bow in her hair, this time a black wig just short of shoulder-length. She carried a bouquet of flowers. Lane, at six foot two and two hundred pounds, was the most physically imposing of all her husbands, and he looked dashing in a well-cut black suit, a boutonniere in the left lapel. Unlike her other husbands and boyfriends, he had a career in his own right, was as famous in his world as Dinah was in hers. Perhaps it was a sign of his independence that Lane wore no wedding band. His only jewelry was a large pinkie ring. Dinah had asked Ruth to make a booklet with the story of the couple's relationship, and when they posed for photographers, they made sure the first page was visible, "How We Met."

Dinah promised she would find a new use for mink at the Lions' late fall football games; this time instead of wearing a coat she would keep warm with a mink blanket.

After the ceremony and brief reception at the Thunderbird, Dinah and Dick hurried back to California, and Dinah was onstage that night. Patrons who had been at the club just a week earlier professed surprise at their marriage. Rafael Campos, the husband before Night Train, had been at Basin Street one evening, and another guest described him as sticking to Dinah "closer than white on rice." That fueled speculation that they might get back together until the news was out on the West Coast that Dinah had married Night Train. And three weeks before the wedding Dinah had to tamp down a rumor that she was reuniting with Eddie Chamblee, husband number five, because she planned to fly to New York when he opened at a new nightclub.

This latest marriage was much noted in the black press and mentioned in mainstream white papers, too. The stories were respectful, though some headline writers couldn't resist weaving sports metaphors into the couple's marital past. " 'Night Train' Lane falls behind in marriage score 7–2, but both sides win," was the way *Sepia* put it, agreeing with other Dinah-watchers that Rusty Maillard didn't count. One New York paper wrote that Dick was Dinah's tenth husband. "It's only seven," she seethed, "and they have to produce the other three or come up with a million dollars apiece for them."

Dinah and Dick stopped in Chicago on their way back east so that Dinah and the Allegros could play a pop-jazz program July 19 at Ravinia, the outdoor ampitheater in suburban Highland Park that usually hosted classical fare. Hugh Hefner, publisher of *Playboy* and owner of the Playboy Club, threw a party for the couple while they were in the city. On August 22 Dinah was honored again, this time in Atlantic City at an early celebration of her thirty-ninth birthday at the Club Harlem. She was a guest artist in Larry Steele's *Smart Affairs* revue and gave the audience an extensive set that included "Love Walked In," "Baby (You've Got What It Takes)"—without Brook Benton—and "Everybody Loves My Baby."

"I am happy to be thirty-nine because I have at long last caught up with my good friend Jack Benny," Dinah joked.

Dick, George, and Bobby were with her in Atlantic City, and as was their custom, mother and sons celebrated their birthdays together. The boys usually received cash gifts from relatives and some of Dinah's friends; she liked to put the money in the bank for them. But now that they were teenagers, they were allowed to roam around on their own. When Dinah asked for their birthday gifts so she could deposit the money, Bobby told her he and George had spent it all. She picked up one of the golf clubs Dick had brought in anticipation of a playing a few holes and rapped Bobby across the back of his legs. He momentarily blanched; Dinah burst out crying, aghast that she had struck her child. Bobby laughed. He wasn't hurt and found the moment hilarious.

AFTER THE EARLY BIRTHDAY celebration, Dinah returned to Detroit to settle in with Dick in the large second-story apartment he had rented at 4002 Buena Vista, just a few miles from the El Taco.

She had some of her favorite things sent from the Bowery Bank Building in New York and directed Ruth and LaRue to put other furnishings in storage. Apartment 14A-3 was rented to a new family.

Dinah was eager to get involved with Night Train's restaurant and brought Ethel Harrison, a woman who had cooked for her in Los Angeles, to work in the kitchen. Dinah herself came in most days, and when word got out that she was at the restaurant, it brought the El Taco a certain cachet and more customers. After work, Bea Buck came over and voluntarily typed up the next day's menu, which included tacos, enchiladas, tamales, "Texas steaks," and "Mexican cornbread." " 'Mama' Ethel Harrison is your cook when Dinah is 'On the Road,' " the menu said.

Publicity flyers for the restaurant featured Lane wearing his distinctive number 81 Lions uniform—most defensive backs wore numbers in the twenties or forties—and an old publicity picture of Dinah sitting on a stool in a bathing suit, mink stole around her shoulders. Dinah now referred to herself as "Dinah Washington Lane."

Ziggy Johnson told *Chronicle* readers that Dinah had made the El Taco "a place that a gentleman can bring his lady friend, and the 'Queen' is there to serve you."

Dinah's routine was interrupted by another brief hospital stay. Rumors swirled that she had suffered a miscarriage.

"What baby?" she told an inquiring *Chronicle* reporter, declining any further comment.

Dinah was well enough to play the Michigan State Fair August 26, where she performed with the Allegros and sang "Do Nothing Till You Hear from Me" with Duke Ellington's band. Nate Holloway, who knew Dinah from Chicago, happened to be in the area visiting a girlfriend in Flint. He took her to see Dinah, though the young woman didn't know who she was, and, Holloway remembered, wasn't much impressed later. After the performance Dinah and Dick were supposed to sign autographs for an hour. Holloway and his friend were in line, but Dinah and Dick left before they got up to the table, leaving them and several others waiting in vain.

Fans still mingling at the fairgrounds whispered that Dinah was annoyed "that more people were asking for Night Train's autograph than hers," Holloway said. As he watched them get into a car, Holloway was struck by what an unusual couple they made. Dinah had on a big floppy hat that made her face look very small; Dick wore a handsome suit and a fedora, and Holloway said, "He looked like he was double her size."

Dinah officially turned thirty-nine on August 29, and perhaps as a birthday present to herself, she took nearly a month off, the longest respite she had had in years. She spent much of her time at the El Taco, supervising the kitchen and the wait staff, though to some of them it felt more like Dinah was riding herd. Roulette released her fifth album, *Dinah '63*, which was arranged by Fred Norman. Henry Glover, another of the few blacks with important jobs at the major record companies, was the producer. The album included Dinah's take on pop tunes, including "I Left My Heart in San Francisco" and "What Kind of Fool Am I?," a remake of the bluesy "Drown in My Own Tears," which Glover had written and Dinah first recorded in 1956, and a swing version, even with strings, of the Jerome Kern–Oscar Hammerstein "Why Was I Born" reminiscent of Dinah ten years earlier, without strings.

While she had performed at benefits for the Rinkydinks, the high-toned social club, Dinah had never been asked to be a member. Now that she was establishing herself in Detroit, Dinah decided she wanted to have her own club that would do good works. Her first idea was to raise money to give out scholarships to young people interested in the arts. So she gathered some friends she had made over the years, recruited Bea Buck to be the secretary, and was installed as president of the Ballantine Belles. Ballantine was the name of a liquor company—Dick had an endorsement deal with Ballantine Scotch, and he and Dinah had appeared together in some newspaper promotions. Dinah reasoned that beyond the nice alliteration, the Ballantine company, because of the chance to get publicity, would help the fledgling organization.

Some of the Belles were "prostitutes, ladies of the night," Dick said; Bea knew this, too, though none of the women walked the streets. They were really call girls who worked by appointment; a few were boosters. But they were Dinah's friends nonetheless, and she wanted them in her club. Before Dinah left Detroit for her fall engagements she and the other Belles had already started planning their first benefit, a New Year's Eve ball at Detroit's Statler Hilton. Dinah contacted one of her dressmakers, who was going to make special mink-trimmed pink gowns for each of the women. She told the staff at the El Taco that she would be back in six weeks and warned that "things better be running just like I left them."

ON HER WAY to Las Vegas, Dinah, with the Allegros in tow, stopped in Cleveland on October 10 for ten days at the Jazz Temple, a small club that had just reopened after a mysterious bombing in August. The bad publicity for missing the Norfolk, Virginia, date in February seemed to weigh on Dinah because she vented her irritation at reports that she had failed to show up on the tenth for a benefit to aid victims of an automobile accident.

"I wasn't there because I didn't know anything about it," Dinah told the *Cleveland Press*. "I don't sing anywhere unless I have a contract or unless somebody asks me to. This thing is a big drag for me. Somebody is going to get sued."

Dinah's bark was worse than her bite in this instance, and after the Jazz Temple job was over, she and the Allegros headed to Las Vegas to open at the Thunderbird. Dinah was making $7,500 at the hotel (roughly $45,000 in today's dollars), and on top of that were advances from Roulette for recording sessions and royalties from sales of Roulette and Mercury discs. Tax problems notwithstanding, Dinah bought what she wanted when she wanted—dresses, shoes, furniture, the plane—much of it on credit. There was no reason for shop owners to think she was an unusually high risk; they knew she was working constantly, and they had every reason to believe they would get paid, if later than they wished.

Some creditors were impatient, however. During the summer, General Dealers Services, Inc., which was handling Dinah's installment purchase of the De Havilland airplane, filed a suit against Dinah and Regina Productions, Inc., an arm of Queen Artists, because she had failed to keep up the payments. On September 5, a judge in Berks County, Pennsylvania, where the plane was held, issued a judgment against her and in favor of General Dealers, which intended to repossess the aircraft.

"We set up Regina Productions to handle all of her income from stage, night clubs, royalties, record sales, and acts," Ruth Bowen explained, and then she tried to keep Dinah on her $500-a-week allowance. But it never seemed to work. "She would run up bills as high as $6,000 at a time buying things for her herself and her friends," Ruth said. "We also had an order to provide anything her family asked for. We never really knew what she was going to do."

When she was strapped for cash, Dinah sometimes asked the labels for an advance. She asked Bobby Shad for $10,000 on one occasion, and he gave it to her, though he was a bit taken aback at the size of the request. A few days later, Mercury got a call from a department store. "There's a lovely lady by the name of Dinah Washington," the woman on the other end said. "Did you give her a check to buy a fur coat?"

Shad got on the line. Yes, the check is good, he said. Later he told his wife, Molly, he had no idea Dinah wanted the advance to buy another mink.

It was still important to Dinah not just to look good onstage, but to look great, to have her appearance command comment as well as her singing. She usually wore wigs now, preferring to change styles and colors to suit her mood. She periodically had them refurbished, and on this trip she sent them over to Continental Coiffures, a two-year-old salon operated by Isadore Marion. She was not happy with the result. When she came on to do the last show at 5:00 A.M. November 3, she decided to talk about it.

"I very rarely have anything interesting to tell," Dinah told the audience, "but something happened to me the other day. I took my wigs to Izzy's Continental Coiffures—or whatever the hell the name is—and they came back looking like two wet rats, and when I wore it that's exactly what I looked like—a wet rat. So naturally, I had to find someone to fix them over and took them to David at the Stardust. Now this is the way it looks," she said, pointing to the wig.

"A nice hand for David. It looks so much better. So all you girls be sure and take your wigs to David and not to Izzy. Shall we sing something now that isn't Izzyish?" she asked, turning to the Allegros.

When Marion heard what Dinah had said about his beauty shop, he was so furious he filed a $70,000 lawsuit against Dinah in Clark County District Court. Dinah was not only wrong, he claimed, but she slandered him and the shop, causing damage to his reputation and loss of business.

While Dinah was plenty feisty the night she talked about "Izzy," she hadn't been feeling well during the run. She was sick enough one evening that she couldn't sing. Diahann Carroll and Belle Barth, who were performing in town, came by and filled in with the Allegros.

Marion's lawsuit was still pending when Dinah and the trio left the Thunderbird for a return visit to Basin Street West in Los Angeles that started November 15. The first week of the run had gone well, the usual appreciative fans filling the club. Sam Cooke and Nat Cole were in town and had come by to see the show. Cooke and Dinah even sang a couple of numbers together, reaching back to their gospel roots. Ish Evans promptly extended her run a few days until December 1.

Dinah made regular calls to Bea Buck back in Detroit to check on the Ballantine Belles plans. During one conversation, she could tell that Bea was distracted. What's going on? Dinah asked. Because of the time difference it was evening in Detroit, and Bea explained that she was watching Lou Rawls on television. "I'm calling my girlfriend in Detroit," she could hear Dinah say to whoever was in the room, "and she's such a damn fool, she's talking to the Queen and she's looking at some Lou Rawls on television."

Properly chastened, Bea told Dinah she had her full attention.

When Dinah got to Basin Street West the evening of November 22, she was out of sorts. The entire country was in shock over the terrible news that President Kennedy had been assassinated earlier in the day in Dallas. Dinah and the Allegros came out onstage, but when she got to the microphone, she told the audience how upset she was. "How could they kill that pretty man," she said. "I bought a gun cause I'm gonna protect myself. Anybody who would kill a pretty man like that doesn't have any respect." Then she apologized. "I can't sing tonight. I'm all messed up. The only thing I can give you is 'What a Friend We Have in Jesus.' "

Dinah hadn't told the Allegros ahead of time what she was going to do, but it didn't matter. They knew the song. Dinah was crying when she finished. Then she left the stage to a standing ovation.

"We had never seen her like that," Jimmy said. "We had never played a hymn with her."

Five days later Dinah and the Allegros went to a studio in Hollywood to tape a segment of the Steve Allen television show. "She's made history in our business," Allen said in his introduction, propping up *Dinah '63*, the latest Roulette, on his desk so the cameraman could get a good shot. He told the audience she'd just finished "a wonderfully successful engagement at Basin Street West. I don't know if you know, but Dinah is married to famous Detroit Lion football star Night Train Lane. . . . The one and only, the wonderful Dinah Washington."

The camera switched to Dinah, standing in front of the Allegros, Jimmy to her right on the organ, John Payne next to him on sax, and drummer Jimmy Thomas on a small riser. (She had worked mink into her outfit this evening; the collar on her jacket was fur, and so was the trim on her skirt. The heart-shaped diamond necklace she wore was a wedding present from Dick.)

"HEY!" Dinah shouted as though back in church.

"Hey," the Allegros answered.

"I said, 'Hey, hey, hey, hey—show me the way to go to Soulville,' " she sang, tearing into a tune she co-wrote with Titus Turner. Though it was about a place with good folks, good food, and good dancing, it was as close to gospel as anything Dinah sang, a return to her true roots in a moment of undisputed pop success.

The song was an unusual choice for a white audience, many of them probably unfamiliar with Dinah and with the kind of "Soulville" joint she was talking about. But Jimmy knew Dinah wasn't really concerned about the reaction. "Dinah was Dinah," he said. "She was going to sing what she wanted and make you like it."

The audience seemed to catch Dinah's feeling even if few of them nodded their heads to the beat. When the applause died down, Dinah said she would do a number from *Dinah '63*. "And that's not my age either," she joked. It was an absorbing version of "Make Someone Happy," and in one pass she made it personal: "Make someone happy. . . . You see I've made Night Train Lane happy."

The audience clapped so long when she was done that Dinah seemed a bit embarrassed. She blew them a kiss to say thank-you. Jimmy Sigler was sure there were tears in her eyes.

The only thing that diminished the moment was Dinah's disappointment at not being able to have a short on-camera visit with Allen over at his desk.

21.

"Move Me a Little Higher"

December 1963

Dinah returned to Detroit the first week in December, another legal hassle trailing her. According to the *Los Angeles Sentinel*, she had rented the home of well-known golfer Maggie Hathaway for a month but left after only one night and failed to pay the rest of the rent.

Dinah sang at a benefit concert for Dick's alma mater, Prairie View College in Texas, at the 20 Grand's Oak Room. It was one of the opening celebrations in a week that would culminate in honors for Dick at halftime Sunday, December 8, when the Lions played the Cleveland Browns.

Dick seemed especially tickled that William Clay Ford, the owner of the Lions, and his wife liked Dinah so much. Whenever they went to hear her, they stayed for all the sets and then came backstage to visit. "Unbelievable, in the ghetto," Dick said. "I'm sitting there looking at that man, he is worth $650 million—just goes to show you. . . . It was unbelievable how Dinah could take kings and bring them under her spell. And she could take the tramp out there on the street, the prostitute and do the same thing."

The benefit performance had gone particularly well, and later Dinah joked to some visitors that "the Queen is really cooking tonight." She added that she was tired. Even though she didn't have to do those killing one-nighters anymore, and she hadn't traveled through the South with all its attendant indignities in eighteen months, she planned to "settle down" in Detroit and get some rest. She and Dick finally left about 2:00 A.M.

Dinah didn't plan to perform any more until the new year, so the Allegros went back home to Philadelphia. She was looking forward to the Ballantine Belles ball on New Year's Eve, and before that a family reunion, first in Detroit and then in Chicago. The Lions were playing the Bears there December 15 in a tight division race, so Dinah's world and Dick's dovetailed perfectly for the Christmas holidays.

George and Bobby were due home for Christmas. In September Dinah had enrolled them in the pricey Windsor Mountain School in Lenox, Massachussetts. Tuition, including fees, for each was $2,600, which Dinah was paying on the installment plan. They were not the only black students at the school, but they were in a distinct minority. The boys were among the best athletes, though, and Bobby loved being something of a star on the sports teams, those dance lessons burnishing his natural athletic gifts.

The boys were expected at the airport the afternoon of Friday, December 13. Dinah had been busy all day shopping for Christmas presents, had most of them bought and wrapped, and had decorated the apartment. She talked on the phone with Ann Littles, telling her about the New Year's Eve ball, and about her latest single due to come out, "Stranger on Earth." Dinah was sure it was going to be as big as "What a Diff'rence a Day Makes" or "This Bitter Earth." She called Ruth in New York to check in and catch up. When Ruth reminded Dinah that she owed her some money, Dinah chortled that "If I owe you money, you'll never be poor." And then she hung up. Dinah called LaRue, too, bubbling about all of her Christmas shopping.

Though it got colder and colder as late afternoon turned into evening, Dinah wanted Bea Buck, who lived just a couple of blocks away, to come over and wait with her until Dick got back from the airport with the boys. She told Bea that she had some dishes to give her, and she wanted to show her a new mink-trimmed couch that had just arrived.

Bea admitted she had never seen a couch with fur, and cold or not, she bundled up and hustled over. After Bea arrived, she and Dinah went to the back of the house for something or other, and all of a sudden Dinah stopped.

"They're here," she said.

"How do you know?" Bea asked.

"I just know they're here."

At that moment they heard footsteps on the stairs. And then George, Bobby, and Dick were at the door. After they exchanged hugs, Dinah stepped back to look at her sons.

"Don't they have no people up there that know how to do nappy hair?" she asked. "You get haircuts first thing in the morning."

George, Bobby, and Dick went off to do other things; Dinah and Bea sat down in the living room because Dinah wanted Bea to take some notes for her. She was starting to gather information to write her own book, but she realized that she didn't have a complete list of her recordings, and she wanted to get all the information from Mercury, fifteen years' worth. She told Bea whom to call Monday morning. Dinah also invited Bea to come to Chicago for the week-end, but Bea demurred.

"Miss Dee, I can't go to Chicago 'cause I haven't made any arrangements." She reminded Dinah that she had just become a su-pervisor in her job with the city of Detroit, and she didn't want to be late, let alone miss a day.

Dinah told Bea the same thing she had told Ann, that "Stranger on Earth" was going to be her biggest record yet. "The story of my life," she said. Bea didn't take that as a complaint from Dinah, and she hadn't said it morosely. More that she found truth in those lines about people who have it easy and people who have to struggle.

The two women decided to have some tea with lemon while they chatted. Dinah talked about a house she liked nearby with a pool *and* pool house. Bea fretted that she might not be able to fit into the specially made ball gown for the Ballantine Belles' affair, but there was no way she was going to let Dinah give her another one of those weight-loss injections. She knew she'd been a damn fool to let Dinah give her even one.

Around 11:00 P.M. Bea got up to get her coat and go home.

Dinah wanted her to stay and watch a movie on the big television set in the bedroom.

"I haven't got any business sitting in a bedroom with a husband and wife," Bea said.

"Oh, don't worry," Dinah said, laughing. "We're not fucking tonight so you can come."

Bea laughed, too. Dinah could be blunt about anything. She volunteered to the Allegros that Dick was "hung like a stallion—damn near killed me." None of the men was surprised or shocked; they just chuckled along with her.

Bea told Dinah she really did have to go home, and as they hugged good night, Dinah couldn't resist a little jibe—Bea didn't know how to drive and Dinah had no sympathy for her going out in the cold. "If you could drive, you could drive yourself home," she said. But she was joshing, and she summoned Shirley Couch, who was working for her as a secretary and still at the apartment, and told Couch to take Bea home.

Dick and Dinah went to bed about 1:00 A.M. Around 3:45 he woke up and heard the television buzzing—the station they were watching had gone off the air. He didn't see Dinah, and when he looked around, he found her slumped on the floor. He reached down to pick her up and heard a little moan, and then silence.

Frantic, Dick tried to wake her up but to no avail. He called the doctor, and while he waited, Ethel Harrison, the cook and housekeeper who was staying at the house, awoke and came to the bedroom. Fearing the worst, she gently stroked Dinah's hand and noticed a bottle of blue-and-orange prescription pills on the nightstand—some fifty still in the bottle, newly prescribed.

George and Bobby were awake now. They stood in the hallway, looking into the master bedroom. Bobby saw his mother lying on the floor. He didn't move an inch, but an eerie feeling washed over him just as Dick came out.

"She's gone," he told the boys. Bobby already knew.

Dr. B. C. Ross arrived around 5:00 A.M. on December 14 and pronounced Dinah dead. The police arrived a half-hour later. By 6:00 her body was on the way to the city morgue.

When the telephone rang at Bea Buck's house, she couldn't understand what a reporter was telling her. She had told Dinah to give her name to the press for the New Year's Eve benefit. Her first thought was that Dinah had gone too far this time, staging this death thing and then coming back to life so she would get publicity. "Dinah ought to be ashamed of herself," Bea murmured as she headed to the house. "This is really too much."

By the time Bea arrived there was near pandemonium. She couldn't believe the news was true. She had just been drinking tea with Dinah a few hours earlier. The little china cups were still in the sink. So was the piece of lemon Dinah had put in hers. No one had thrown it away. Dinah had once told Bea that she would never leave New York except for heaven. It had seemed like a throwaway line. Not now.

Dick called his mother-in-law, Alice Jones, in Chicago, where it was barely 4:00 A.M. Estrellita still lived at 1518 South Trumbull with her mother in the house that Dinah had bought them. She heard the phone ring, knew it couldn't be good news this time of night, and then she heard her mother say, "Dead? Dead?" Estrellita was bereft. Her big sister had treated her like a daughter, even wanting to adopt her.

Dick had also awakened Ruth in New York. She was numb like everyone else, but she had the presence of mind to call a neighbor of LaRue's, who had just had surgery and was recovering at home, to go to her apartment. Ruth didn't want LaRue to hear such terrible news by herself. She also called Morris Levy and the three Allegros and told them to head to Chicago, where everyone agreed the funeral would be. Though Dinah wasn't there very much, Chicago was still her hometown, and there was only one place that was fitting for the service, St. Luke Baptist Church at 37th and Indiana, the church of her childhood.

Saturday night in Chicago, WVON, the station operated since March by Leonard and Phil Chess, who owned Chess Records, interrupted its regular lineup to play Dinah's music.

Family, friends, and fans were uncomprehending. It was as though Dinah had been snatched from them literally in the fullness of life. It was true she said she was tired and looking forward to a rest, but she was still Dinah, still the Queen, ordering people around, laughing and joking, making plans for the next day, the next week, the next year. She had even persuaded Boris Zlatich, the violinist whom she liked so much, to move to the East so that he could do the string work on her upcoming sessions. She told him Morris Levy wanted her to do all her recording in New York now.

Even before she married Dick, Dinah had embraced and been embraced by Detroit, and her friends and fans there didn't want to let her go without paying their proper and formal respects. On a blustery, freezing Sunday afternoon more than seven hundred mourners shivered outside the Thompson Funeral Home waiting their turn to file past her open casket. Dinah's family made sure she had on her best clothes. She wore a yellow chiffon dress with a soft white jacket, a ribbon just below the left shoulder, elbow-length white kid gloves with twelve buttons each, and slippers decorated with jewels. Her hair was tinted red, a tiara resting on the top of her head.

Dick was supposed to have started for the Lions in their crucial game against the Bears Sunday afternoon, but he didn't play. The Lions were vying with the Green Bay Packers for the conference lead. The Lions lost 24–14. Two of the Bears' touchdowns were on passes over Dick's replacement.

The question on many people's minds was whether Dinah had committed suicide. Impossible, said her family and friends. She was happy now, and beyond that, Dinah would never go so quietly on purpose. On the morning of Monday, December 16, Wayne County medical examiner Dr. Edward J. Zawadzki released his report. Nothing was out of the ordinary except for excess barbiturates in her blood. His official conclusion: "May have taken barbiturates by mistake because of misidentification." The autopsy showed a combination of amobarbitol and secobarbital, the latter sold as Tuinal.

Zawadzki told *Jet* Dinah's body contained more than twice the normal dose of the medication, which made the dosage lethal. She had two types of sedatives, "and she may have taken an overdose of the wrong ones," he said.

LaRue was convinced that Dinah had weakened her system from all the pills. "She was almost living on borrowed time because her resistance is so gone," she said. There was gossip that Dinah was taking street drugs. "But it was legit," LaRue added. That's what made her death all the more distressing. Every single bottle of pills had been prescribed by a doctor.

On Monday afternoon Detroit bade Dinah farewell in a memorial service at the New Bethel Baptist Church. The Reverend C. L. Franklin handled the religious duties; Ziggy Johnson, who had known Dinah when she was still the aspiring singer Ruth Jones, handled the secular. "You don't discover a talent like hers," he said, choking back tears. "I just happened to be around when she burst upon the entertainment field. . . . They needed another songbird in heaven. That's why our Dinah is gone."

Though she hadn't attended church every Sunday she was in Detroit, Dinah and Franklin were good friends, and she often stopped by his house when she was in town. She enjoyed his daughters and had told Ruth some time ago to keep an eye on Aretha, who by now was making a name for herself as a noted singer. Aretha sang a solo before her father delivered a eulogy. While he was speaking, Lovi Mann, the house organist at the 20 Grand who had accompanied Dinah many times, softly played her hits.

After the service, Dick, George and Bobby, and Ruth Bowen, who had come directly to Detroit, boarded a plane to accompany Dinah's body to Chicago. When they arrived at the United Funeral Home on Sacramento Boulevard not far from 1518 South Trumbull, three hundred people were already packed in the chapel to pay their respects. Within an hour another two hundred filed by the casket.

In Los Angeles, Ish Evans announced that Basin Street would close for five days in memory of Dinah. In Tuscaloosa, the *News,* the city's main newspaper, ran an Associated Press story on the front page December 14 noting the death of its native daughter. "Both Miss Washington and Lane are Negroes," the last paragraph noted.

By Tuesday evening, friends and associates in the entertainment world were gathering in Chicago—Joe Glaser, head of Associated Booking, LaRue Manns, Ann Littles, Ella Fitzgerald, Clara Ward, Redd Foxx, Slappy White, Dick Gregory, Gladys Hampton. Though Dinah and Brook Benton had a famously testy relationship, he flew in from California and was designated an honorary pallbearer.

The funeral program had one of Dinah's late 1950s publicity photos on the front. On the top was her real name, Ruth Lee Jones. On the back was a drawing of a crown, underneath it "Dinah Washington." The legend at the bottom read, "No more stranger on this earth."

The service was scheduled to begin at 2:00 P.M. Wednesday, December 18. By that time nearly a thousand mourners had crammed into a sanctuary built for six hundred. Church officials had to escort some of them out of the balcony for fear it would collapse, and the service didn't get under way until well after 2:30. Police were outside redirecting traffic away from an estimated additional thousand who wanted to pay their respects. Mahalia Jackson had been offered a seat in front, but she chose to sit in the choir loft in tribute to Dinah's beginnings. She sang an affecting "Move Me a Little Higher" that prompted sniffles and sobs in the audience. Sallie Martin sang, too, as did the Roberta Martin Singers, taking the assembled crowd back to Dinah's gospel days as Ruth Jones.

Years earlier Dinah had said that whenever she died, she wanted the Reverend Eugene Ward, whom she got to know in Cleveland, to conduct the service. He came to Chicago to honor her wish. Indeed he had known Dinah a long time, he said, "as a friend, Christian and fine gospel singer. Ruth has done what few other people could do. She brought many of you to church today." He moved back and forth across St. Luke's large stage, his voice rising and falling with a well-schooled cadence, talking to Dinah, about her, and finally urging God to accept her soul.

Several times Clara Ward leaped up from her seat to offer "amen." One woman fainted and was quickly attended to by a nurse stationed nearby. Robert Grayson, Dinah's third husband and father of her second son, sat quietly in the back. Eddie Chamblee, her fifth husband, sent a telegram. So did Dave Turner.

When the service was finally over some three hours later, the family and close friends filed by the casket one last time. One of the two policemen standing watch was Bill Jackson, trying to keep his composure. Dick bowed his head tearfully one last time. "I'll miss you, baby," he said. He had admitted to friends that he didn't think the marriage would last "five minutes." But things had gotten better and better. "We couldn't believe we'd made it this far." Ruth Bowen, dressed as elegantly as Dinah always dressed, could barely contain her sadness. When she got to the open casket, surrounded by an array of flowers, she reached down and stroked Dinah's face, murmuring, "She's really dead." That same impulse came over Brook Benton, who stopped for a silent prayer and then caressed Dinah's cheek.

By the time the pallbearers were ready to escort the casket into the hearse, the sun had gone down and the usual bitter Chicago wind whipped through the street. The steps of St. Luke were icy now, and Redd Foxx, one of the pallbearers, slipped, leaving the other men to hold up the casket until he could regain his footing. No one wanted to drop the Queen. The family and dozens accompanying them got in their limousines for the thirty-minute drive to Burr Oak Cemetery on the city's southwest side. Someone had broached the idea of taking the casket to the cemetery by helicopter so that little girls could drop rose petals along the way, but the family said no. Dinah loved a good show, but that would be too much.

When everyone assembled again at the grave site, it was dark, well past Burr Oak's 5:00 P.M. closing time. Mourners huddled around the open grave, which was illuminated by only a few flashlights and the headlights of the nearby automobiles, snowflakes swirling in their beams. The pallbearers brought the casket to its resting spot, but this December night was so cold—fourteen degrees below zero—that the winch that lowered the casket into the grave was frozen. The cemetery workers tried again and again, but it wouldn't budge.

Those closest to Dinah smiled through their tears. She often said, only half in jest, that no one would ever see her buried in the ground, and just two weeks earlier she had commented on how hard it was to watch John Kennedy's casket lowered into his grave at Arlington Cemetery. No one would be around when her time came, she promised. The mourners filed back to their cars, leaving this last chore to the attendants who came in the next day. Most everyone had the same thought: it was Dinah saying, "What'd I tell you?"

22.

Long Live the Queen

Dinah was as complicated in death as she was in life.

There wasn't even agreement among her closest friends and confidants about her marriage to Dick. The romantics believed that Dinah had met her true love, a successful man who didn't need her and could take care of, finally, so many things *she* always had to handle, a man who could make her happy.

But those closest to Dinah—Ruth, LaRue, Bea—said things were not so rosy. While it was true that Dinah occasionally looked at real estate in Detroit, the sure sign of a readiness to resettle and put down new roots, she confided to Bea that Dick might be seeing an old girlfriend, a Detroit schoolteacher. When Bea made a little joke about Dinah's own checkered marital history, she snapped back: it didn't matter how many damn times she'd said "I do," cheating was unacceptable.

"I had my instructions," Ruth recalled, to get Dinah's furniture out of storage and make arrangements for her to move back to New York. Bill Jackson, the policeman who had stood such solemn guard at her bier, believed she was coming to Chicago to be with him. He said Dinah had called and told him to pick her up at the airport. She was going to tell Dick it was over.

In the immediate aftermath of Dinah's sudden death, everyone kept quiet about the state of their relationship, still grieving and consumed with the daily tasks of going on and bringing a formal close to a life and a career.

Tributes to Dinah poured in from the music world in the United States and in Europe, where magazines in England, France, and Sweden published obituaries. The major black publications, which had paid so much attention to Dinah when she was alive, did not disappoint at her death. *Ebony, Sepia,* and *Tan* ran long stories leavened with personal reminiscences. *Jet* filled two issues with features and pictures, putting her on the cover of the magazine January 9, 1964. It was a sweet picture of Dinah with her sons, Bobby resting his head on her shoulder, George standing behind them.

Leonard Feather wrote affecting columns in *Down Beat* and in London's *Melody Maker,* recalling for readers the first time he heard Dinah's distinctive voice and how their work together propelled each of them on their way in the music world. "Dinah sang and phrased like nobody I had ever heard," he said. He noted with pride that nineteen years after she first recorded his song "Evil Gal Blues," she was still singing it. Feather had been at one of the last performances at Basin Street West three weeks before she died and reveled anew in "that earthy intensity."

Ralph Gleason, music critic for the *San Francisco Chronicle,* had seen many of Dinah's shows at the Blackhawk. "When the news came in that Dinah was dead," he wrote in one of his columns, "it was doubly shocking because she herself had been such a vibrant, real and salty personality." How she would have enjoyed the fact that this critic, a white man whom she didn't really know, so appreciated her music, seemed to understand it and accept who she was offstage. "Lord knows she was easy to talk to if you didn't panic," Gleason said. One could almost hear Dinah chuckling in agreement.

"Dinah was one of the jazz people other jazz people constantly talked about yet her biggest financial successes came from singing pop tunes with a jazz flavor." He was thinking specifically of "What a Diff'rence a Day Makes." Gleason insisted, though, that Dinah's songs "were pure jazz any way she chose to sing them."

Down Beat had released its year-end poll just after Dinah died, and Gleason was bemused, as he usually was, at Dinah's place, "number eleven behind better than a half dozen singers who aren't worthy to be mentioned in the same breath with her." Dinah "had a full, sophisticated attitude towards life that was reflected in the way she sang," he added. "Many singers on stage are merely little girls singing romantic songs. Dinah, like Carmen McRae and Billie Holiday and Bessie Smith, was a woman singing about life. And she made you believe."

Half a continent away, in Gary, Indiana, Doris Johnson felt the same thing. "We will miss the way she had of bringing the blues right home to you, making them hit you right where you live," Johnson wrote to the *Defender* two weeks after Dinah's death. "You got the feeling when she sang that she had been given the special privilege of singing and that she lived with them to produce the 'live' effect." Joey Livingston, a fan in Brooklyn, felt it, too. "Dinah always put so much soul into everything," he wrote *Sepia*. "She was effervescent and lived with a daring that was unusual in our society."

AT BEA BUCK'S INSISTENCE the Ballantine Belles went ahead with their New Year's Eve benefit, the "Pink Champagne Ball." Each of the club members came into the ballroom of the Statler Hilton dressed exactly as Dinah had wished: in those pink gowns trimmed with black mink. Clarissa, Dinah's sister, came from Chicago. Dick told her to go in the basement at Buena Vista, where almost all of Dinah's clothing was stored, and take whatever she wanted. Dinah had been several sizes over the years, and although Clarissa was nearly six inches taller than her sister and built differently, she found a dress that she could wear. It was orange with a beaded top, long skirt, and spaghetti straps. Something of a seamstress, Clarissa found a needle and thread and hastily took in a couple of seams so it would fit. Later at the party, she sang a few songs in memory of her sister—a poignant reminiscence of when she last had sung for Dinah—in the summer of 1962, when she and Estrellita and their mother came to New York and sang gospel with Dinah at Abyssinian Baptist Church.

The Belles had invited Gloria Lynne to be the main entertainment for the evening, but when travel problems prevented her from arriving on time, Freda Payne, a young singer from Detroit who was home on vacation, stepped in.

Payne had an indirect connection to Dinah, even if she didn't know it. Quincy Jones had written an arrangement for her of "Secret Love," one of Dinah's songs. Dinah happened to be in the audience at the Apollo when Payne sang it. Later Dinah told Quincy, "If I didn't have such a tight dress on, I would have run up onstage and taken my music back." They both had a good laugh, though Dinah was only half-joking.

Early in January 1964 George and Bobby returned to Windsor Mountain to finish out the school year.

To the executives at Mercury and Roulette it was as though Dinah were not really gone. *This Is My Story*, a two-volume compilation from Mercury released in 1963, was still selling. At the end of March, Roulette released two compilations, *A Stranger on Earth* and *In Tribute*. (The liner notes for the latter must have been written in a hurry; they put Dinah's age at thirty-seven and the place of death as Chicago.) Dinah was featured on a third album, *We Three*, with Sarah Vaughan and Joe Williams.

Over at Columbia, Leonard Feather wrote the liner notes for a novel tribute, Aretha Franklin recording ten of Dinah's tunes her way. The album, called *Unforgettable*, leaned more to church than nightclub. "I didn't try to do the songs the same way she did them, necessarily—just the way they felt best, whether they happened to be similar or different," Franklin said. "The idea of doing a tribute to her grew out of the way I've always felt about her."

ON JANUARY 6, 1964, the first notice was published in Detroit newspapers informing any creditors who believed Dinah owed them money to file their claims with the Wayne County Probate Court by March 19. Dick was named acting administrator of the estate.

Dinah had executed a will December 29, 1949, in the office of Jack Pearl, a New York City lawyer. She had signed it "Ruth Grayson," and a copy had been filed in Cook County. Alice Jones, her mother, was named executrix and the guardian of George and Bobby. She gave a specific bequest of $200 to her father, Ollie, and directed that whatever was left should be divided among her sons and three siblings, Harold, Clarissa, and Estrellita. The will was sent to the Wayne County Probate Court January 7, 1964, but questions were raised immediately about the will's validity given the passage of time since it had been executed and the many significant changes in Dinah's life that had taken place.

In the meantime more than two dozen claims were filed by individuals or companies alleging unpaid bills, each one adding new details about Dinah's penchant for clothes, nice furniture, jewelry, and gifts for the men in her life. One claim that covered 1960 and 1961— when Dinah was between marriages—showed charges for three suits, one tuxedo shirt, an assortment of other shirts, cuff links, handkerchiefs, and shoes, a reminder that whoever was on Dinah's arm had to look good.

The claim from the furrier, dein-bacher at the Waldorf-Astoria, was an inventory of Dinah's fur collection. Sixteen pieces were stored there, including four mink coats, two stoles, a jacket, and two black Persian coats, one with a white mink collar. The storage bill was $640. Photographer James Kriegsmann claimed he was owed $400 for photo shoots from 1962 and the winter of 1963. And Lois Green filed a statement for the $700 she had tried to collect in 1961 on that raucous evening in Apartment 14A-3 when the police were called and Dinah was arrested.

Dinah also still owed Decker Airways $4,153 for the De Havilland Dove and for several charter flights; and there was an outstanding bill of $1,154 for furniture Dinah bought to decorate the apartment at 8125 South Vernon in Chicago. Two funeral homes also submitted bills, $2,747 from Thompson Funeral Home in Detroit and $4,651 from United in Chicago.

But the claim that overshadowed all others both in size and priority came from the Internal Revenue Service. The IRS asserted in its initial filing February 13 that Dinah owed $92,117.17 in back taxes, which covered income tax owed in 1960, 1961, and 1962 plus penalties and interest. The agency filed a lien against any royalties the estate might collect from Mercury.

Apart from the IRS, the outstanding claims totaled $72,000, and they confirmed that Dinah lived ahead of her means, if not beyond them. With a few exceptions, she always paid her musicians. She didn't owe the Allegros a dime when she died, and she never missed a payment to David Dinkins, the lawyer. But with others, she operated by a double standard, willing to be tardy with her payments when she wouldn't tolerate anyone being late with her money.

Yet there was no reason to think Dinah couldn't eventually pay her debts given that she was already booked months ahead for 1964. The previous three years showed how much she could bring in from bookings alone—$135,700 in 1961, $149,700 in 1962, and $147,951 in 1963 (an average of about $870,000 per year in today's dollars). And that didn't take into account money coming in from record sales at Mercury and Roulette and royalties from the performance of her songs on the radio and television. Her accountant in New York at Waldbaum, Siegel and Dubi knew that she was not up-to-date with the IRS, and the firm had been working along with David Dinkins on her behalf right up until she died. Its claim was for $13,836 for all the tax work that had been done to straighten out the problems.

In Chicago, Joe Glaser, who had put the building at 8125 South Vernon in trust for Dinah, and held the mortgage for the purchase price, took steps to protect his interests. He learned that under Dinah's ownership, property taxes had not been paid regularly, and the building was in danger of being sold for the amount of the back taxes. Glaser settled the tax bill and initiated proceedings, completed in 1966, to take the building back for the amount of the unpaid mortgage loan.

Despite various court proceedings through 1964, at the end of the year nothing had been settled.

After the spring semester at Windsor Mountain ended, George and Bobby returned to Detroit. They would not go back to Windsor Mountain in the fall given the high tuition and the unsettled financial situation. The plan was for the boys to continue their education in Detroit, but George and Dick did not get along so George went to Chicago to move back in with his grandmother at 1518 South Trumbull. Bobby stayed in Detroit with Dick. Nine months after Dinah died Dick married the schoolteacher who had been a former girlfriend. But the marriage didn't last very long. "She could never forget Dinah," Dick said.

INTERMITTENT PROCEEDINGS in Wayne County Probate Court continued through 1965. Finally on January 17, 1966, a

Wayne County probate judge ruled that the will was valid, though Dick—not Alice—was formally declared the administrator of the estate. The assets were listed as $6,439—the appraised value of Dinah's jewelry, including a platinum and diamond dinner ring, and a $1,704 death benefit from the America Federation of Television and Radio Artists. The house in Chicago on Trumbull was in Alice's name, and the building on South Vernon was in a hidden trust, so neither was listed as an asset. Likewise there was no mention of Dinah's furs or clothing, perhaps because of the confusion for so many months over how the probate of the estate would be handled.

On November 30, 1966, the IRS filed a revised claim, this time contending that Dinah now owed the government an astounding amount—$405,600, which covered taxes not paid starting in 1960 and the accrued interest and penalties.

In the meantime the lawsuit against Mercury over Dinah's royalties had proceeded through the New York court system. Mercury lost another appeal of its motion to dismiss the lawsuit in October 1964, and the label filed one last appeal to the Court of Appeals, New York's highest court. That appeal was rejected in November 1966. It meant that absent a settlement, Mercury would have to answer the estate's allegations in court and perhaps be required to open the company books. The lawsuit was settled a year later, in early December 1967. Mercury agreed to pay the estate $15,000 for a period up to June 30, 1967, and then to pay further royalties on a regular basis after that date. However, those funds were put in escrow because of the IRS lien.

More hearings were held through 1968 and most of 1969 on the various disputes over Dinah's estate. Finally in December 1969, Dick, the IRS, and Mercury returned to Wayne County Probate Court to approve a settlement on the Mercury royalties. Since the June 1967 agreement, Mercury had paid another $8,737 in royalties that went into the escrow account. The key provision in this new agreement provided for a lump-sum payment of $25,000 from Mercury, which ended the label's obligation to pay any future royalties to Dinah's estate.

Dick had said through his lawyers that he wanted "to settle in a lump sum all royalties that are due or may become due" from Mercury. George and Bobby had each turned twenty-one by this time, and the lawyer assigned to represent their interests had been dismissed. Not surprisingly Mercury told the court it, too, wanted a lump-sum settlement, allowing the label to be free and clear of any obligation to Dinah's estate.

The total that Mercury paid in royalties after Dinah died was $48,737—$15,000 at the time of the December 1967 agreement, $8,737 in royalties accrued from that time until December 1969, and then the $25,000 lump sum. A portion of that total went to Martin Machat for handling the litigation for the estate against Mercury and to pay the estate's administrative expenses. The rest of the money—roughly $32,000—went to the IRS, which removed the lien against Mercury. However, the agency held out the possibility that it would seek to recover other funds if they came into the estate.

The language in the 1969 settlement was as broad as it was clear. The $25,000 would be considered "in full and final settlement of any claims of whatsoever kind or nature that Dinah Washington or the Estate of Dinah Washington or Richard Lane individually and as administrator of the Estate of Dinah Washington has, may have or will have against Mercury." The next provision confirmed that Dick as an individual and administrator of the estate "hereby releases, remises and discharges Mercury of any and all obligations of any kind or nature that may be due or become due and owing by Mercury to Dinah Washington or the Estate of Dinah Washington . . . and Mercury shall have no further obligation to make any further payments with respect to royalties that would otherwise have become due and payable to Dinah Washington, the Estate of Dinah Washington or Richard Lane, administrator of the Estate of Dinah Washington."

The settlement meant that neither George nor Bobby would get any money from their mother's fifteen years of recording for Mercury either now or in the future, nor would any of the creditors who had filed their claims right after Dinah died be paid anything.

Over the next two years, various other amounts of money came into the estate from performance royalties and other miscellaneous sources, and that money was used to cover administrative expenses. The estate was finally closed March 7, 1973. The final account showed a cash balance of $5,987, almost all of it from the portion of the Mercury settlement in 1969 that went to the estate. There was nothing in the probate documents that reflected income from Dinah's Roulette recordings or any agreement about those royalties.

Viewed thirty-five years later, the royalty provisions in the 1969 agreement are stunning even when one tries to imagine the scenario at the time—a huge IRS lien, all kinds of claims, a wish to close the estate. Moreover, an agreement was made affecting Dinah's sons by someone who was married to their mother for only five months and was not their father. For whatever reason, neither George nor Bobby interceded nor did anyone on their behalf.

Given that Mercury had paid $23,700 in royalties between 1967 and 1969, the lump-sum payment of $25,000 at the end of 1969 to end all future royalty obligations appeared to be very small. It was certainly to Mercury's advantage to close off any obligation to pay future royalties, and on Dick's side there perhaps was a failure to realize how a record company could mine its catalogue long after an artist had died and how significant the resulting royalty income could be.

Five years after Dinah's death, though, Mercury seemed uninterested in Dinah. From 1970 through the early 1980s her music was not often heard, her place in music history uncertain. It was easy to forget that when she died, Dinah was a fixture in the homes of so many black Americans, the beat and the melody for their days and nights, and was growing in popularity in white America. But in death she was lost in the large corporate culture of Philips, the music company that had bought Mercury in 1960 and then was absorbed into the even larger Polygram in 1973. She was overshadowed in memory by Bessie Smith and Billie Holiday and barely an afterthought when music lovers talked of Ella Fitzgerald and Sarah Vaughan, her contemporaries who were still alive, still performing, and still recording.

In 1983 the Ballantine Belles celebrated Dinah's memory in Detroit on the twentieth anniversary of her death; Keter Betts and Jimmy Cobb, her bassist and drummer from the glory days of the early 1950s, came to play and honor her. That same year Sasha Dalton, a Chicago singer, put together a one-woman show about Dinah that had an extended run at a small New York theater.

By 1984 Polygram was rediscovering Dinah's music. The company started to repackage some of her material on LPs as part of its "classics" series. But it was the company's representative in Japan, Kiyoshi Koyama, who did the most to revive Dinah's legacy. He decided that Dinah was long overdue for attention, and he convinced Polygram to begin reissuing her entire Mercury output. The advent of the compact disc, which provided a sharper sound and was easier to handle, made the effort that much more manageable. The complete Dinah on Mercury, which was released in stages between 1987 and 1989, required twenty-one CDs, three in each of seven boxes arranged in chronological order and including everything that was available—tracks released only as singles, alternate tracks of songs that had been released, some songs never released at all, Dinah telling a joke.

Now a new generation could hear for themselves what a distinctive stylist Dinah was, whether she sang a soulful blues, an uptempo swing, or a deeply felt ballad, how she could make even treacly material sound interesting, that precise diction and innate feel for the phrase overcoming the saccharine strings and too-busy vocals that threatened to get in her way.

Dinah was not shy about her distaste for rock 'n' roll. But rock 'n' rollers felt their debt to her. She was inducted into the Rock and Roll Hall of Fame in 1993 as an early influence, and when the organization's permanent collection formally opened in Cleveland, her picture was hung on the wall right next to Bessie Smith's. That same year the United States Postal Service honored her with a stamp as a Legend of Rhythm and Blues.

AT THE END OF January 1994, George Jenkins hired a lawyer in Chicago to reopen his mother's estate. The underlying argument was simple: that Dinah's estate was due royalties from her earnings. Howard Linden, a probate attorney in Detroit, was hired by George's lawyer in Chicago, Jay Ross, to manage the affairs. At the same time Ross hired lawyers in California who specialized in retrieving past royalties to sue Polygram. They filed a suit in 1996 to get back royalties for the previous six years—the longest period allowed under New York law. However, the lawyers voluntarily agreed to dismiss the suit after they learned about the 1969 agreement.

In 1998, Seagram, which had expanded greatly from its origins as a distillery, acquired Polygram and renamed the music operations Universal Music Group. Verve Music Group was a division within the larger music section and took over Dinah's catalogue. Since the Koyama CD project, a much more aggressive reissue program had been in place, and that continued under the new corporate organization. Between 1995 and the spring of 2004 twelve new Dinah CDs had been reissued to go along with seven that had been released in the early 1990s.

Roulette, which was now part of EMI, also had a reissue program, though more modest than the Universal/Verve program, which had the bulk of Dinah's creative output.

Although EMI apparently was under no legal obligation to pay Dinah's estate any royalties, the company and Ross, the Chicago lawyer, worked out an arrangement for royalties from the Roulette material. The importance of that deal was never more apparent than in 1996, when EMI paid the estate $60,321, much of that coming from the use of "I'll Close My Eyes" in the movie *The Bridges of Madison County*. Two other songs from Dinah's Mercury years were also in the movie, but estate documents showed that no royalty income was paid to her. Over the next four years another $45,000 in royalties from EMI came into the estate. According to estate documents most of that money went to pay taxes on the yearly income, attorneys' fees for Ross and Linden, and other related expenses. None of it went to Dinah's sons.

As of February 2004, Universal Music Group was not paying any royalties to Dinah's estate.

EVERY DAY OF HER LIFE Dinah had to negotiate the racial divide, often difficult and always demeaning. She died only months before she could experience what had been the unthinkable— staying at the elegant Peabody Hotel in Memphis or even Chicago's own Palmer House, buying gas at any station along Mississippi's highways, or eating lunch wherever she wanted in Alabama, the routine activities made possible by the 1964 Civil Rights Act. But if Dinah was of her time, she was, sadly, ahead of it in her obsession to be model-thin, obsessed with meeting some arbitrary standard of attractiveness well before white women turned the obsession into a medical category all its own. It is hardly a stretch to say that Dinah's desire to be thin, which drove her to diet pills to lose weight and tranquilizers to sleep, ultimately killed her.

But those private demons that so often played out in public, and the husbands, the boyfriends, the penchant for mink—all of it was Dinah, woven into the tapestry of her music. "When you get inside of a tune, the soul in you should come out," Dinah once said. "You should just be able to step back and let that soul come right out." And Dinah always did when she was standing in her favorite place, center stage, head back and hands outstretched, declaring in that pitch-perfect voice, "I don't hurt anymore."

DISCOGRAPHY

DINAH WASHINGTON ON RECORD

The information below is a listing in rough chronological order of Dinah's output in the nineteen years of her recording career, 1944–1963. The bulk of it was with Mercury. Though she was known as Queen of the Blues and Queen of the Juke Boxes on the strength of her rhythm and blues hits, and also had success in the jazz arena, Dinah, once established, sang whatever she wanted. She never abandoned the blues, however. In 1958 she recorded an album of all Bessie Smith tunes, and when she went to Roulette in 1962, her second album was *Back to the Blues*.

A more detailed session discography that includes recording dates and session players where known can be found in the published discographies listed in the Bibliography.

Keynote Singles (1944)
605 Evil Gal Blues/Homeward Bound
606 Salty Papa Blues/I Know How to Do It

Decca Single (1945)
23792 Blowtop Blues/(Lionel Hampton instrumental)
   (This was not released until May 1947.)

Apollo Singles (1945)
368 Wise Woman Blues/No Voot—No Boot
371 My Lovin' Papa/Mellow Mama Blues
374 Walking Blues/Rich Man's Blues
388 My Voot Is Really Vout/Blues for a Day
396 Pacific Coast Blues/Chewin' Mama Blues

Seven of the Apollo titles were issued on Grand Award 33-18 circa 1957. The rest of the album was Earl Hines. (Wise Woman Blues; Chewin' Mama Blues;

Rich Man's Blues; Beggin' Mama Blues; All or Nothing Blues; Blues for a Day; Pacific Coast Blues)

Beggin' Woman Blues and All or Nothing were released on Parrot 20-001 (78rpm).

Mercury Singles (1946–1961)

In its singles category, Mercury used several numbering sequences. In the early days of the company, 8000 was the "race" series; 5000 was for the "pop" releases. Sometime in 1952 Mercury combined all releases into the 70000 series and for about three years made distinctions in the type of release by the color of the label. By the end of 1955, however, the company had gone to a uniform label.

These singles were recorded between 1946 and 1961, when Dinah left Mercury to go to the Roulette label. In the beginning the singles were 78s; gradually they became 45s, though there was a period when the company issued singles in both formats.

2052 I Can't Get Started with You/Joy Juice
2053 Embraceable You/When a Woman Loves a Man
8010 Oo-wee Walkie Talkie/When a Woman Loves a Man
8024 A Slick Chick (on the Mellow Side)/Postman Blues
8030 That's Why a Woman Loves a Heel/Embraceable You
8035 Stairway to the Stars/I Want to Be Loved
8043 Evil Gal Blues/Homeward Bound
8044 Salty Papa Blues/I Know How to Do It
8050 Fool That I Am/Mean and Evil Blues
8057 You Can Depend on Me/Since I Fell for You
8061 There's Got to Be a Change/Early in the Morning
8065 I Love You, Yes I Do/Don't Come Knockin' at My Door
8072 No More Lonely Gal Blues/Ain't Misbehavin'
8079 Walkin' and Talkin' and Crying My Blues Away/West Side Baby
8082 I Want to Cry/Resolution Blues
8094 Tell Me So/In the Rain
8095 Am I Asking Too Much/I Sold My Heart to the Junk Man
8102 You Satisfy/Laughing Boy
8107 It's Too Soon to Know/I'll Wait
8114 Why Can't You Behave/It's Funny
8133 What Can I Say After I Say I'm Sorry/Pete
8148 Long John Blues/Baby Get Lost
8154 Good Daddy Blues/ Richest Man in the Graveyard
8163 I Only Know/New York, Chicago and Los Angeles
8169 It Isn't Fair/Journey's End
8181 I Wanna Be Loved/Love with Misery
8187 I'll Never Be Free/Big Deal
8192 Why Don't You Think Things Over/How Deep Is the Ocean
5488 Harbor Lights/I Cross My Fingers
5503 Time Out for Tears/Only a Moment Ago
5521 Why Can't You Behave/So in Love (Patti Page is the singer)

8206 My Kind of Man/If I Loved You
8207 Juicehead Man/Fast Movin' Mama
8209 My Heart Cries for You/I Apologize
8231 Please Send Me Someone to Love/Ain't Nobody's Business
8232 Fine, Fine Daddy/I'm So Lonely I Could Cry
5445 I'm a Fool/If You Don't Believe
8249 Saturday Night/Be Fair to Me
5728 Mixed Emotions/Cold, Cold Heart
5736 Baby, Did You Hear/Just One More Chance
8211 I Won't Cry Anymore/Don't Say You're Sorry
8257 Out in the Cold Again/Hey, Good Lookin' (with the Ravens on both sides)
8267 Tell Me Why/Wheel of Fortune
8269 Trouble in Mind/New Blowtop Blues
5842 Mad About the Boy/I Can't Face the Music
8292 Pillow Blues/Double Dealing Daddy
8294 My Song/Half as Much
5904 Stormy Weather/Make Believe Dreams
70046 Gamblers' Blues/I Cried for You
70125 Ain't Nothin' Good/You Let My Love Grow Cold
70175 My Lean Baby/Never, Never
70214 TV Is the Thing (This Year)/Fat Daddy
70263 The Lord's Prayer/Silent Night
70284 Since My Man Has Gone and Went/My Man's an Undertaker
70329 Short John/Feel like I Wanna Cry
70334 Such a Night/Until Sunrise
70392 (No, No, No) You Can't Love Two/Big Long Slidin' Thing
16014 Love for Sale/Pennies from Heaven (EmArcy 45)
70439 Dream/I Don't Hurt Anymore
70497 Teach Me Tonight/Wishing Well
70537 That's All I Want from You/You Stay on My Mind
70600 I Diddle/If It's the Last Thing I Do
70653 I Hear Those Bells/The Cheat
70694 Not Without You/I Concentrate on You
70728 You Might Have Told Me/I'm Lost Without You Tonight
70776 The Show Must Go On/I Just Couldn't Stand It No More
70833 Let's Get Busy Too/Let's Go Around Together
70868 Cat on a Hot Tin Roof/The First Time
70906 Soft Winds/Tears to Burn
70968 Relax Max/The Kissing Way Home
71018 To Love and Be Loved/All Because of You
71043 You Let My Love Grow Cold/I Know
71087 I'm Gonna Keep My Eyes on You/Ain't Nobody Home
71220 Everybody Loves My Baby/Blues Down Home
71317 Never Again/Ring-a My Phone
71377 Make Me a Present of You/All of Me
71389 Honky Tonky/Somewhere Along the Line (as "The Queen")
71435 What a Diff'rence a Day Makes/Come on Home (also 30078)
71508 Unforgettable/Nothing in the World
71557 Ol' Santa/The Light

71560 It Could Happen to You/Age of Miracles
71565 Baby (You've Got What It Takes)/I Do (duet with Brook Benton)
71629 A Rockin' Good Way (To Mess Around and Fall in Love)/I Believe (duet with Brook Benton)
71635 This Bitter Earth/I Understand
71696 Love Walked In/I'm in Heaven
30032 Cold, Cold Heart/Harbor Lights
30033 Salty Papa Blues/Long John Blues
30078 What a Diff'rence a Day Makes/Come on Home
30090 Baby (You've Got What It Takes)/Rockin' Good Way (To Mess Around and Fall in Love)
30091 Unforgettable/Love Walked In
30114 Love for Sale/Cottage for Sale
71744 We Have Love/Looking Back
71778 Early Every Morning/Do You Want It That Way
71812 Our Love Is Here to Stay/Congratulations to Someone
71876 September in the Rain/Wake the Town and Tell the People
71922 Tears and Laughter/If I Should Lose You
71958 Such a Night/Dream
72015 I Wanna Be Loved/Am I Blue
72040 Cold, Cold Heart/I Don't Hurt Anymore

Roulette Singles 1962–1963
4424 You're Nobody 'Til Somebody Loves You/Where Are You
4444 For All We Know/I Wouldn't Know
4455 You're a Sweetheart/It's a Mean Old Man's World
4476 No Hard Feelings/Romance in the Dark
4490 Soulville/Let Me Be the First to Know

Mercury Albums
These include ten-inch and twelve-inch albums and "extended plays" or EPs. Typically a ten-inch LP had eight tracks, a twelve-inch would have ten to twelve tracks, and an EP, which was seven inches, had four tracks. The SR numbers are the stereo versions, starting in 1959.

1024 Dinah Sings
MG 25060 Dinah Washington
MG 25138 Dynamic Dinah
MG 25140 Blazing Ballads
EP-1-3023 Dinah Washington (this is made up of four tracks from MG 25060)
MG 20119 Music for a First Love
MG 20120 Music for Late Hours
EP-1-3205 Blues in Fashion
MG 20247 The Best in Blues
EP-1-3207 Blues
EP-1-3208 Singing with Strings
EP 1-3395 Dinah Washington
MG 203-C Dinah Washington
EP-1-4006 Tops in Pops

EP 1-4035 Dinah Washington
MG 20439 (SR60111) The Queen
MG 20479 (SR60158) What a Diff'rence a Day Makes!
MGW 12140 Late Late Show (the Wing subsidiary)
MG 20572 (SR60232) Unforgettable
MG 20588 (SR60244) The Two of Us (with Brook Benton) (EP-1-4028 with four tracks)
MG 20604 (SR60604) I Concentrate on You
MG 20614 (SR 60614) For Lonely Lovers (EP 1-4041 with four tracks)
MG 20638 (SR60638) September in the Rain
MG 20661(SR60661) Tears and Laughter
MG 20729 (SR60729) I Wanna Be Loved
MG 20788 (SR60788) This Is My Story (Vol. 1)
MG 20789 (SR60789) This Is My Story (Vol. 2)
MG 20829 (SR60829) Good Old Days

EmArcy Albums (ten-inch and twelve-inch)
MG 26032 After Hours with Miss D (10 inch; Also issued as 12 inch, MG 36028 and as EP 1-6054/6055—5 A.M. with Dinah)
MG 36000 Dinah Jams (EP 1-6080; EP 6081; EP 6082)*
MG 36011 For Those in Love (EP 1-6118/6120/6121)
MG 36065 Dinah
MG 36073 Dinah Washington in the Land of Hi-Fi
MG 36104 The Swingin' Miss D
MG 36119 (SR 80011) Dinah Sings Fats Waller (also released later as MG 20525 [SR60202])
MG 36130 Dinah Sings Bessie Smith
MG 36141 (SR 80009) Newport '58 (also released later as MG 20523 ([SR60200])

*MG 36002 Jam Session. (This album is credited to Clifford Brown, with two vocals by Dinah—Darn that Dream and Don't Worry 'Bout Me.)

Roulette Albums
25170 Dinah '62
25183 Drinking Again
25180 In Love
25189 Back to the Blues
25220 Dinah '63
25244 In Tribute*
25253 A Stranger on Earth*
52108 We Three (with Sarah Vaughan and Joe Williams)*

*Released after Dinah died on December 14, 1963.

Dinah Washington on CD
Between 1987 and 1989, Polygram, which then owned the Mercury masters, reissued all of Dinah's Mercury recordings in a project overseen by Kiyoshi Koyama, head of the Japanese division. Twenty-one CDs were packaged chronologically in seven box sets. As of 2004 only a few of the boxes were still available.

Separate CD reissues of Dinah's music continued through 2004, including several albums, some with additional material and new liner notes.

EMI, which controls the Roulette material, has reissued four CDs.

Delmark Records has reissued all of Dinah's Apollo material on one CD.

Apollo Material on CD
Mellow Mama (Delmark Records—DD401)

Mercury Albums on CD
Verve B0000094-02 After Hours with Miss D
Verve 814 639-2 Dinah Jams
Verve 314 538 635-2 Dinah Sings Bessie Smith
Verve 314 514 073-2 For Those in Love
Verve 314 558 074-2 The Swingin' Miss D
Verve 314 537 811-2 The Best in Blues
Verve 314 543 300-2 What a Diff'rence a Day Makes!
Verve 314 510 602-2 Unforgettable
Verve 314 526 467-2 The Two of Us (with Brook Benton)

Mercury Compilations Since 2000
These compilations include at least one or more of Dinah's biggest hits What a Diff'rence a Day Makes, Unforgettable, This Bitter Earth—and her two hits with Brook Benton, Baby (You've Got What It Takes) and A Rockin' Good Way (To Mess Around and Fall in Love). The other tracks include Dinah in all her modes—straight blues, rhythm and blues, and jazz, particularly the tracks from the 1954 live album, *Dinah Jams*.

Verve 314 543 596-2 Dinah's Finest Hour
Verve 314 489 839-2 The Definitive Dinah Washington
Hip-O 314 586 913-2 The Best of Dinah Washington—The Millenium Collection—
    Hip-O
Verve 440 065 215-2 Dinah Washington—Diva Series

Roulette Material on CD
Roulette Jazz 7243 5 81831 2 2 Dinah '62
Roulette Jazz CDP 7972732 In Love
Roulette Jazz CDP 7243 B 543342 9 Back to the Blues
Roulette Jazz CDP 7945762 Dinah '63

Dinah Live on CD
The music is from radio broadcasts.

BJH 310 Queen of the Juke Box Live—1948–55 (Baldwin Street Music)
BJH 301 Dinah Washington and Her Trio—Live at Birdland (Baldwin Street
    Music)
High Note HCD 7068 Arnett Cobb—Cobb and His Mob in Concert Featuring
    Dinah Washington
Compact Classics SR5014 Lionel Hampton and His Orchestra—1944–45.
    This CD includes six tracks with Dinah in the second full year of her career.

NOTES

The majority of the interviews are my own. The interviews conducted for *Queen of the Blues* by James Haskins are among the Haskins papers at Boston University's Special Collections, and information taken from those interviews is cited as "Haskins papers." All American Guild of Variety Artists (AGVA) material comes from the AGVA files, New York University Tamiment Library, Robert F. Wagner Labor Archives.

1 · Tuscaloosa, 1900–1928

6 *"many beautiful homes":* Information on Tuscaloosa from the 1923–24 Tuscaloosa Chamber of Commerce report, "For Tuscaloosa This Record of Achievement Is Written," *Polk's Tuscaloosa Directory,* 1924–25; *"A Historical Sketch of Tuscaloosa, Alabama,"* by Thomas Chalmers McCorvey; see also the pamphlet at the University of Alabama Special Collections, *Tuscaloosa—In Alabama's Great Mineral District,* 1920.

6 *Rufus and Matilda Williams:* Information on Rufus and Matilda Williams from the U.S. Census, 1920, Tuscaloosa, Precinct (ib)—Courthouse; Clarissa Smith interview, October 6, 2001; James Doss interview, October 30, 2001; information on Ike and Mattie Jones and their children from the U.S. Census, 1910, Tuscaloosa, Precinct 7, Cowden; interviews with Evelyn Jones Banks, Sam and Willie Lawrence Jones, children of Chap Jones, October 24, 2001.

7 *marriage license:* Marriage license of Ollie Jones and Azalea (sic) Williams from Tuscaloosa County records; interviews with Debra Gamble, October 15, 2001; "Dinah's Talent Celebrated," *Tuscaloosa News,* July 15, 1993.

7 *peaches, pears:* Interviews with Debra Gamble, October 15, 16, 30, 2001.

8 *Elizabeth Baptist Church:* Information on 24th Street and the church neighborhood from Debra Gamble interviews, October 15, 16, 2001.

8 *new demands:* Hubbs, *Tuscaloosa: Portrait of an Alabama County,* pp. 65–66; Drake and Clayton, *Black Metropolis,* pp. 58–60.

9 **Ku Klux Klan:** Rogers et al., *Alabama: The History of a Deep South State,* pp. 430–31; *Tuscaloosa News and Times Gazette,* February 28, 1924, p. 4; August 20, 1924, p. 4.

9 **Ollie's older brother Snow:** Interview with George Albert Jones, October 29, 2001; Clarissa Smith interviews.

2 · Lift Every Voice, 1929–July 1942

10 **black belt:** See Gareth Canaan, "Part of the Loaf: Economic Conditions of Chicago's African-American Working Class During the 1920s," pp. 160–62, *Journal of Social History,* Fall 2001, Vol. 35; George Jones interviews, October 29, November 8, 14, 2001; Drake and Clayton, *Black Metropolis,* pp. 62–64; 384–85, for maps showing black belt boundaries; James Doss interview; 1930 Census, which showed the Jones family at Aldine Square, House Number 502, Dwelling 101, and listed Ollie's occupation as a minister.

11 **shared a bed:** George Jones interviews.

11 **Aldine Square:** 1930 U.S. Census, which shows that Ollie Jones's nephew, Walter Sutherland, also lived with the family for a time. Drake and Clayton, *Black Metropolis,* pp. 78–79; George Jones interview, January 8, 2002; Estrellita Dukes, Clarissa Smith, Vera Hamb Payne interviews, January 9, 2001.

12 **St. Luke Baptist:** St. Luke history, Ruth Roudez interviews, August 30, November 20, 2001; *Chicago Defender,* January 29, 1938, p. 22; June 17, 1939; April 26, 1941, p. 9; November 1, 1941.

12 **28th and Indiana:** Drake and Clayton, *Black Metropolis,* pp. 413–16; George Jones interviews; the address of 2832 Indiana Avenue is noted on Clarissa Smith's birth certificate of December 1939 (Clarissa Jones). This is the same address Ruth listed on her first Social Security card application, made October 1, 1940.

13 **Thomas A. Dorsey:** Heilbut, *The Gospel Sound; Good News and Bad Times,* pp. 42–44, 62–65; Harris, *The Rise of Gospel Blues: The Music of Thomas A. Dorsey in the Urban Church,* pp. 126–28, 256–57; Johnny Lloyd interview, November 16, 2001; *Atlanta Daily World,* May 20, 1940, p. 2; *Chicago Defender,* August 3, 1940, p. 6; George Jones interviews; Clarissa Smith interviews.

In 1940 the National Convention of Gospel Choirs and Choruses, the group Dorsey and Martin had started, held a five-day affair in Chicago that brought seven hundred delegates from out of town to meet and sing.

14 **all the choirs:** *Chicago Defender,* March 4, 1939, p. 8; May 6, 1939, p .8; May 13, 1939, p. 10.

15 **"my little cousins":** Evelyn Doss Dorsey interview, October 18, 2002.

15 **Morningstar Baptist Church:** *Chicago Defender,* May 27, 1939, p. 11; July 8, 1939, p. 8; November 4, 1939, p. 11; December 16, 1939, p. 11.

16 **Roberta Martin:** *Atlanta Daily World,* August 31, 1940, p. 3; October 19, 1940; Dinah Washington interview with Leonard Feather cited in Feather's liner notes for Mercury Record *Dinah Discovered,* MG-21119; for information on Brooklyn gospel meeting, *Chicago Defender,* May 13, 1939, p. 10.

Sallie Martin and Roberta Martin occasionally performed together in this period, billing themselves as "Martin and Martin." The theme for their recitals came from one of the gospel favorites, "It's a Highway to Heaven." Heilbut, *The Gospel Sound*, pp. 42–44, p. 193; Clarissa Smith interviews.

16 **Sallie Martin Singers:** Sallie Martin's performing career after she left Thomas Dorsey can be gleaned from articles in the *Chicago Defender* and the *Atlanta Daily World*: *Defender*, August 3, 1940, p.6—working with Thomas Dorsey on a meeting of the National Convention of Gospel Choirs and Choruses; *Daily World*, August 31, 1940, p. 3, with Roberta Martin as Martin and Martin in an Atlanta recital at Springfield Baptist Church and Antioch Baptist Church; *Defender*, September 7, 1940, p. 9, Sallie Martin in recital at DuSable High School; *Daily World*, October 19, 1940, in Atlanta again with Roberta Martin as Martin and Martin at Flipper Temple AME; *Defender*, February 1, 1941, p. 9, appears with Roberta Martin at Jubilee Temple Church; March 1, 1941, p. 7, assists Roberta Martin in recital at Monumental Baptist Church; July 11, 1942, p. 10, Sallie Martin is guest singer with the Ebenezer Baptist Church; August 1, 1942, p. 10, Sallie Martin and Kenneth Morris and their singers perform at the People's Church of America; March 13, 1943, p. 10, Sallie Martin in recital at the Pilgrim Baptist Church, her first musical program after returning from a "western tour"; May 29, 1943, Sallie Martin, assisted by Roberta Martin in recital at the Monumental Baptist Church; June 26, 1943, p. 5, Sallie Martin performs at DuSable High School "song fest" along with Roberta Martin and "her famous group of 'Martin singers.' " The first clear reference to the Sallie Martin Singers comes from a January 1944 item, cited in *The Gospel Sound*, p. 12, in the *King's Ambassador*, a white Los Angeles Baptist newspaper, which notes an upcoming musical program.

16 **"Uncle Ted:"** Dr. Lena Johnson McLin interview, November 20, 2001; Ann Littles interviews, September 10, 12, 2001.

17 **"I wanna":** Clarissa Smith interviews.

17 **Wendell Phillips High:** Melvin Gaynor interviews, May 31, July 7, 2001; Travis, *Autobiography of Black Chicago*, pp. 71–73; Vera Hamb Payne interview, November 8, 2001; Charles Walton interviews; various *Chicago Defenders* entertainment pages, 1937–1940.

18 **radio:** Barlow, *Voice Over: The Making of Black Radio*, pp. 50–58; Clarissa Smith interviews; *Chicago Defender*, February 11, 193, p. 5, and February 18, 1939, p. 19; Eugene Smith interview, October 10, 2001; Yvonne Buckner Storey interviews, January 2, 11, 2002; James "Duke" Davis interview, May 31, 2001.

20 **"itched to get away:"** *Sepia*, December 1959; Ruth Jones's Social Security card application signed October 1, 1940, listed Dave's Café as her place of employment. *Chicago Defender*, June 29, 1940, p. 13; July 13, 1940, p. 11.

21 **amateur hour:** *Sepia*, December 1959, p. 9; Dance, *The World of Earl Hines*, p. 165; for the Grand Terrace, see *Chicago Defender*, September 28, 1940, p. 13; October 12, 1940, p. 11; November 30, 1940, p. 13; December 28, 1940, p. 9; *Chicago Defender*, June 4–August 13, 1938, specifically July 9, 1938, p. 10, for a detailed story on the kind of acts that were presented on amateur night; *Tan*, September 1957, p. 38.

22 **Sarah Vaughan:** *Chicago Defender*, January 17, 1948, p. 30. *Chicago Defender*, April 5, 1941, p. 10. This *Defender* article noted that among the singers would be "Mrs. Jones and daughter of St. Luke Baptist."

22 **Ida B. Wells Homes:** *Chicago Defender,* August 10, 1940, p. 7; October 26, 1940, Section III, p. 7; Bowly, *The Poorhouse: Subsidized Housing in Chicago, 1895–1976,* pp. 30–33.

Though by this time the two Jones families had moved to different neighborhoods, Lela, Snow Jones's wife, and their son, George, regularly came to see Alice and Ruth on Sundays to have dinner together, according to George.

23 **John Young:** Marriage license of John M. Young and Ruth Jones, from Cook County, Illinois, Vital Statistics, #11786463; Washington-Hepburn, "Me and My Six Husbands," *Sepia,* December 1959; wedding picture of John Young and Ruth Jones from Berna Dean Jones Brown.

3 · Is There Anyone Finer?, August–December 1942

24 **Mrs. John Young:** *Sepia,* December 1959, p. 10.

There is little reliable information about Ruth's life in this period, including where she and John Young lived and where exactly she worked after leaving Dave's Café. Many stories have circulated about her playing at one club or another but none of them can be verified. One story touts Fats Waller's support of her when he played at the Downbeat Room of the Sherman. The author of this story most likely meant the Panther Room of the Sherman. But the one documented time Waller played the Panther Room was November 1940, when Ruth, just sixteen years old, was most likely still singing gospel music and not performing in hotel showrooms.

25 **Garrick Building:** Minutes from Chicago Local 208, March 16, 1944; see also comments from Johnny Board in Travis, *An Autobiography of Black Jazz,* p. 212.

26 **Three Deuces:** *Down Beat,* December 15, 1942, p. 5; *Down Beat,* July– December 1942, the "Chicago Band Briefs" column, specifically October 1, 1942, p. 5; *Down Beat,* November 1, 1942, p. 5; November 15, 1942, p. 5.

27 **Lionel Hampton:** Hampton information from *Hamp: An Autobiography,* with James Haskins, pp. 51, 63, 68, 72–74; *Down Beat,* October 1, 1941, p. 3; December 12, 1941, p. 14; January 15, 1942, p. 7. Jimmy Cobb interview, February 16, 2002, for information about Dinah listening to Billie Holiday at the Downbeat Room of the Garrick.

30 **"rich liquor":** *Ebony,* June 1950, p. 62.

There are many stories with conflicting information about what Ruth was doing in 1942, how she met Hampton, and how she got her stage name. The *Down Beat* article of January 15, 1943, and previous items in the magazine's "Chicago Band Briefs" column from October 1942 to January 1943 are critical to a better understanding of this pivotal moment. Though Hampton often said Ruth was working as a washroom attendant at the Garrick in December 1942, she in fact was singing with the Cats and the Fiddle.

In Dempsey Travis's *An Autobiography of Black Jazz* (p. 304), Dorothy Donegan, the piano player, claimed that she "befriended a washroom attendant named Ruth Jones" while she—Donegan—was playing at the Garrick. However, contemporaneous accounts show this was not possible.

Donegan, according to *Down Beat* notices at the time, was playing at Elmer's on State Street when Ruth was at the Garrick.

The matter of who gave Ruth the name Dinah Washington is more problematic. But it could not have happened as Hampton said. In *Hamp*, he recounted that "I said 'Ladies and gentlemen, here's Ruth Jones, Chicago girl Ruth Jones' " (p. 86). The *Down Beat* article of January 15, 1943, indicates that she already had the name "Dinah Washington" when she went out onstage to sing, suggesting that it was probably Sherman who had come up with it sometime before the Regal event. For a good hypothesis on the name, see Leonard Feather liner notes on *The Complete Dinah Washington on Mercury*, Vol. 1, p. 9. Another source for Joe Sherman giving Ruth her new name is Eddie Plique, a boxing promoter and announcer, who knew Ruth as a teenager. In a 1968 interview with Jack Thompson, another Chicagoan and amateur boxer, Plique said, "When Joe Sherman hired her to sing at the Garrick downtown, he changed her name. Joe and her both told me that, and although I love Lionel Hampton, he didn't change it." Interview courtesy of Jack Thompson. Dinah herself gave credit to Joe Sherman. Red Allen comment, Balliett, *Improvisation: Sixteen Jazz Musicians and Their Art*, pp. 11–12.

4 · The "Find" of the Year, January–July 1943

32 **Mount Joy Baptist:** *Chicago Defender*, December 19, 1942, p. 10, on Alice Jones in recital.

32 **luggage:** "Feather's Nest" in *Down Beat*, May 21, 1952, p. 16.

33 **headed to Detroit:** *Down Beat*, January 15, 1943, p. 4; *Michigan Chronicle*, January 2, 1943, p. 17.

33 **"covered their head up":** Dance, *The World of Earl Hines*, pp. 283–84; Haskins, *Hamp*, p. 87; Slappy White interview, Haskins papers; Joe Wilder interview, March 29, 2004.

Though George Dixon talks about the "covered their heads" incident as occurring in Washington, D.C., he is likely mistaken. The Hampton band did not play Washington in January or the first week in February, when Dinah joined the band. The band went from Detroit to Boston (*Variety*, January 27, 1943, p. 37, reviewing a January 22 performance), on to Newark, (*Washington Afro-American*, January 30, 1943, p. 14), and then to Camp Edwards, Massachusetts (*Washington Afro-American*, February 6, 1943, p. 15, citing a February 4 performance), before heading to the Apollo on February 12. And the Hines itinerary, according to *Down Beat*'s semiweekly listing January 15 and February 1, showed no dates in Washington. It is probable that the bands crossed paths when Hines and his group were heading from the Royal in Baltimore to the Paradise Theater in Detroit.

34 **Buzzard's Roost:** Schiffman, *Uptown: The Story of Harlem's Apollo Theatre*, pp. 15–16.

34 **"new girl singer":** *Metronome*, March 1943, p. 16; *Variety*, February 17, 1943, p. 30; the *Variety* review offered another version of how Hampton and Dinah met: the bandleader "found her singing spirituals in a choir." *Newark Afro-American*, February 27, 1943, p. 8.

35 **her place in the lineup:** *Hamp,* p. 87; see also Slappy White interview, Haskins papers.

35 **billing:** *Cleveland Call & Post,* April 10, 1948, p. 9. The Philadelphia date was publicized in the April 3, 1943, *Philadelphia Tribune,* p. 12; *New York Amsterdam News,* March 13, 1943, p. 17.

37 **" 'Legs' ":** *Hamp,* p. 87; see also Slappy White interview, Haskins papers; Wilder interview.

37 **Spotlight Bands:** *Norfolk Virginian-Pilot,* June 5, 1943; *Amsterdam News,* June 5, 1943; *Norfolk Journal and Guide,* June 12, 1943, p. 12; *Spotlight Bands* description from Library of Congress file on the program, Recorded Sound Reference Room; *Wise Women Blues: Dinah Washington,* 1984 LP from Rosetta Records, RR1313.

The *Spotlight Bands* program had an interesting history. According to Robert Carneal, who had been the chief of the magnetic recording laboratory of the Library of Congress and who compiled a history of the series, and independent collector Jerry Valburn, who did another history of the series, Coca-Cola launched the program in November 1941 to feature big band music. Prior to this moment, the big bands were heard only via late night remote broadcasts most often from hotel showrooms and on once-a-week special shows. But the Coca-Cola program allowed a radio audience to hear a different band each night on a specific radio show in prime time. Coca-Cola sponsored the first year under an arrangement with the Mutual Broadcasting System, and when that arrangement ended, the company contracted with NBC's Blue Network, changed the name to *Victory Parade of Spotlight Bands,* and went on the air September 21, 1942, six nights a week. Now the show originated directly from various military installations, hospitals, and war plants, and the shows were geared to entertain soldiers at home and overseas. The Armed Forces Radio Service began to record the programs in March 1943 from direct radio feeds. They then created acetates and processed them into sixteen-inch transcriptons for use by the Armed Forces Radio Network for later broadcasting. (From Carneal's history of the *Spotlight Bands* programs; see also Jerry Valburn's compilation on the *Spotlight Bands* program.)

38 **"she sounded better":** *Metronome,* July 1943, p. 22, *Variety,* June 23, 1943, p. 36.

5 · I Know How to Do It, August 1943–November 1945

40 **moving nonstop:** Hampton itinerary from weekly listings in *Down Beat,* "Where the Bands Are Playing"; *Variety,* September 1, 1943, p. 26.

41 **"Shucks":** Slappy White interview, Haskins papers.

41 **"We gravitated":** Toni Thompson Brazington interviews, May 4, October 2003.

42 **Famous Door:** See Shaw, *The Street That Never Slept: New York's Fabled 52nd Street,* specifically p. 126, though there are several sections that talk about the Famous Door. See also *Variety,* November 3, 1943, p. 36.

42 **Leonard Feather:** *Amsterdam News,* April 7, 1945, p. 7; Feather, *The Jazz Years,* pp. 183–84; *Down Beat,* December 1994, p. 12; www.leonard-feather.com, pp. 2–3, a Web site put together by Feather's wife and daugh-

ter from his scrapbooks, which are in the Lionel Hampton School of Music, University of Idaho in Moscow. See also *Melody Maker,* July 29, August 26, October 7, 1933, for Feather's letters to the editor.

43 **ban on recording:** Seltzer, *Music Matters: The Performer and the American Federation of Musicians,* pp. 39–45, noting specifically *International Musician,* October 1955, and Seltzer's interviews with Petrillo; see also *Down Beat,* August 1, 1942, p. 1; *New York Times,* October 25, 1984, p. B22.

45 **Keynote Records:** Seltzer, *Music Matters,* pp. 42–44, *Down Beat,* October 1, 1943, p. 1; *Variety,* October 13, 1943, p. 1; Hammond, *John Hammond on Record,* p. 200; *Metronome,* June 1944, p. 18; see Buhle, Buhle, and Georgkas, *The Encyclopedia of the American Left,* pp. 554–55, for a discussion of *New Masses.*

45 **Christmas week:** *Billboard,* February 5, 1944, p. 15; Dan Morgenstern interview, March 5, 2002; Feather, *The Jazz Years,* pp. 184–85.

47 **printing glitch:** *Billboard,* February 5, 1944, p. 15; *Down Beat,* February 15, 1944, p. 1.

Hampton's recollection of the recording date is slightly different from some other accounts. While he said in his 1989 autobiography that the session took place at the RKO studio in Radio City, contemporaneous accounts placed it at the WOR radio station studio. He recalled the controversy with Decca over recording for another label but had reasoned that the Decca pact "was for big-band instrumentals. With Dinah, we were backing up a singer" (p. 88).

48 **recording artist:** *Down Beat,* March 15, 1944, p. 9; *Metronome,* March 1944, p. 26; *Metronome,* January 1944, p. 32.

48 **"one inning":** *Variety,* February 16, 1944, p. 18. *Variety's* review of the Hampton show at the Earle in Philadelphia (May 3, 1944, p. 30) was one of the few less-than-glowing accounts of Dinah's singing: "Dinah Washington, femme singer, was not quite up to standard on 'Do Nothing Till You Hear from Me' and 'There'll Be a Jubilee.' "

49 **One Night Stand:** Mackenzie and Polomski, *One Night Stand Series, 1-1001,* pp. xiii–xxiii, for a history of the program; Lotz, Rainer E., and Ulrich Neuert, *The AFRS "Jubilee Transcription Programs: An Exploratory Discography.* See especially the foreword by Richard S. Sears, pp. vii–ix.

The introductions to both of these volumes offer detailed explanations of the Armed Forces Radio Services programs. The listing of the programs themselves provides information about dates and set lists of each one. The music, some available on CD, is invaluable because it is the first professional singing of Dinah Washington.

There appears to be an error in the location of *One Night Stand* #329, when Dinah sang "Was It Like That." The Mackenzie-Polomski book lists the location as the Civic Auditorium in Oakland, California, June 4, 1944. That is almost surely incorrect. Hampton was in Chicago at the Regal Theater May 26 to June 1, and he and the revue were in Louisville at the National June 9–11. Ads from the *Chicago Defender* and the *Louisville Courier Journal* and *Down Beat's* weekly band listings confirm the dates. It appears impossible, given travel in 1944, that Hampton and the band could have gone from Chicago to Oakland and made it back to Louisville in time for the show.

49 ***one or two songs:*** Hampton itinerary comes from weekly *Down Beat* listing and then confirmed when possible by ads and stories in newspapers in the cities mentioned. The Hampton discography in his autobiography lists a June 16, 1944, date at the Trianon in South Gate, but this is incorrect. The Hampton group was in Milwaukee on this date at the Riverside in a performance transcribed for *One Night Stand.* Dinah sang "There'll Be a Jubilee" and "No Love No Nothin'."

50 ***"recess in heaven":*** See *Big Band Jazz: the Jubilee Sessions, 1943–46*, Hindsight HBCD 504. See also *Lionel Hampton and His Orchestra: 1944–45 Broadcasts*, Soundcraft SC-5014; routines with Ernie "Bubbles" Whitman taken from *Lionel Hampton and His Orchestra* CD; Jubilee Program 53, courtesy of Harry Mackenzie archives, Glasgow, Scotland, and David S. Siegel archives, Yorktown Heights, New York.

51 ***"Girl Singer (With Band)":*** *Down Beat*, January 1, 1945, p. 13; *Metronome*, January 1945, pp. 18, 29. *Down Beat* put Billie Holiday in a different category than Dinah—"Girl Singer (Not Band)," where she placed fourth, well behind Dinah Shore, Helen Forrest, and Jo Stafford.

A full-page ad Hampton's manager, Joe Glaser, took out in the December 1944 *Metronome* for his Associated Booking Corporation was illuminating. The ad first named the bands ABC represented, and Hampton was listed along with Louis Armstrong, Red Norvo, Andy Kirk, and several others. Then the ad named "personalities," who included Mildred Bailey, the popular singer now divorced from Norvo, Billie Holiday, and piano great Mary Lou Williams. Dinah, who was not under contract to Glaser directly but only through the Hampton band, was not mentioned.

52 ***"almost no singing":*** *Down Beat*, May 21, 1952, p. 16; see the following issues of *Variety* for an understanding of Dinah's limited singing time and what she sang: December 20, 1944, p. 38; February 28, 1945, p. 23; March 12, 1945, p. 25; April 11, 1945, p. 42; August 22, 1945, p. 24; September 12, 1945, p. 50; October 13, 1945, p. 20.

53 ***Carnegie Hall:*** *Metronome*, May 1945, p. 9; *Down Beat*, May 1, 1945, p. 1. Paradise Theater: *Metronome*, July 1945, p. 23.

54 ***Theresa Hotel:*** Statement of living expenses on a form from the Essex Amusement Corporation signed by Dinah Washington. The statement says the expenses were incurred "on behalf of my employer, Essex Amusement Corporation, in connection with my employment at the Adams Theater, Newark, N.J. and are claimed as a deduction in computing the amount of Federal Income Tax to be withheld." Document in personal collection of the author.

54 ***pulled a gun:*** *Ebony*, November 1956, pp. 37–42.

6 · Stairway to a Star, December 1945–December 1947

55 ***Apollo Records:*** *California Eagle*, November 25, 1945, p. 16; $1,800 figure from "Feather's Nest," Leonard Feather's *Down Beat* column, May 21, 1952, p. 16. Sam Schneider information comes from Gart, *The American Record Label Directory and Dating Guide*, 1940–1959; Jack McVea liner notes in *Jack McVea and His Door Openers: Two Timin' Baby*, Jukebox Lil LP JB612; Lee Young interview, May 2, 2002.

A sense of the vibrant recording scene in Los Angeles in this period is apparent from such Apollo releases as the Lucky Thompson All-Stars backing singer Rabon Tarrant, a different group of Thompson All-Stars recording on Bel-Tone behind Bob Mosely and billed this time as "Bob Mosely & His All-Stars." Thompson had also recorded under his own name for Excelsior, one of the few labels operated by a black man, Otis Rene. Lee Young put it best when he said, "We were trying to go from one job to another. That's all I was doing—recording, and I had a band at night."

56 *recording procedure:* Session personnel from Apollo #368 and #371, which lists the musicians on the record label, Library of Congress, Recorded Sound Reference Room. In *Queen of the Blues,* Haskins erroneously states that these sessions were sponsored jointly by Apollo, ABC, Grand Award, and Parrot, each paying part of the costs. The original records were solely for Apollo. Reissues that came much later were on the other labels, who had licensed or bootlegged the masters. Haskins also incorrectly stated that Dinah made her first trip to California for the record session. She had been in California fifteen months earlier with the Hampton band on one of its West Coast swings.

The precise source for the recording dates and tracks recorded on each date is not known, but according to veteran discographer and jazz enthusiast Kurt Mohr, the information probably came from Apollo owner Bess Berman in correspondence with Charles DeLauney, founder of the French Vogue label, who had licensed early Apollo tracks (Mohr interview, April 25, 2002). All available discographies—Walter Bruyninckx, Jorgen Jepsen, and Tom Lord—say these sessions were held December 10, 12, 13, 1945, in Los Angeles. Lee Young recalled that they were done at Radio Recorders, which was a prominent studio at that time. It is likely that the musicians—or most of them—were members of Local 767, the black chapter of the American Federation of Musicians in Los Angeles. Local 767 merged with Local 47, the white union, in 1953, and if there had been time sheets for these sessions, they were lost in the transition, according to Debra Fresquez, the Local 47 archivist.

56 *Mercury Records:* Mercury Records information from Berle Adams interview, November 2000; Adams, *A Sucker for Talent,* pp. 97–100; *Billboard,* October 13, 1945, p. 24; February 11, 1946, p. 6; January 25, 1946, p. 32; *Variety,* January 23, 1946, p. 36; *Down Beat,* January 28, 1946, p. 4; February 11, 1946, p. 6. Michel Ruppli's Mercury discography, pp. 1–2.

Mercury almost lost its name before the company got started. In his self-published autobiography, Adams wrote that the fledgling company was sued by Mercury Transcriptions, "a company none of us had ever heard of." The transcription company provided ad agencies with off-the-air transcriptions and commercials of radio shows They had no contact with the general public. When the case went to court, Adams argued that Mercury Records was not in competition with the transcription service, but the judge considered them to be in the same business. Adams subsequently bought the name Mercury for $5,000 (p. 98).

59 *"sultry princess of song":* *Billboard,* February 23, 1946, p. 189; March 2, 1946, p. 27.

59 *write-ups:* *Down Beat,* March 25, 1946, p. 16; *Metronome,* April 1946, p. 33.

59 **George Jenkins:** George Jenkins and the Hampton band, *Metronome,* August 1944, p. 11; *Variety,* August 22, 1945, p. 24; Beatrice Buck interview, June 3, 2002. *Sepia,* December 1959, p. 10.

60 **Rhumboogie:** *Chicago Defender,* March 23, 1946, p. 25; April 6, 1949, p. 26, for the Rhumboogie show, produced by Leonard Reed, who had helped the teenage Ruth Jones get on the Regal amateur hour. The other acts were exotic dancer Delores Alvarado, the dance and comedy team of Rogers and Collins, and a choral group, the Golden Tones. The Eddie Mallory Orchestra provided the music.

60 **Gerald Wilson:** Gerald Wilson interview, April 16, 2002; *California Eagle,* January 24, 1946, p. 13; NPR Jazz Profiles; "Gerald Wilson's Bronzeville Memories," interview with Charles Walton for the Jazz Institute of Chicago Web site; Snooky Young interview via fax, May 6, 2002.

61 **Pershing in early May:** *Chicago Defender,* May 4, 1946, p. 26, for the Pershing date with Eugene Wright's "Dukes of Swing"; *Billboard,* May 18, 1946, p. 41; June 8, 1946, p. 32; *Billboard,* June 29, 1946, p. 30.

62 **married:** George Jenkins–Ruth Jones marriage license from Cook County, Illinois, Vital Records, #1910978; *Jenkins v. Jenkins,* No. 47S15542, Cook County Superior Court, Complaint for Annulment of Marriage. Beatrice Buck interview, June 11, 2002.

62 **West Side on the:** *Chicago Defender,* July 13, 1946, p. 24; July 20, 1946, p. 26; July 27, 1946, p. 26. There were no stories in the *Defender* at this time noting that Dinah had to cancel anything because she was about to give birth to her first child.

63 **George Kenneth Jenkins:** Birth certificate of George Kenneth Jenkins, Illinois Department of Public Health. Picture of Dinah, George, and George Kenneth courtesy of Clarissa Smith.

63 **" 'Race' locations":** *Cash Box,* August 26, 1946, p. 10; *Billboard,* September 7, 1946, p. 33; *Cash Box,* September 22, 1946, p. 12.

64 **"A Slick Chick":** *Billboard,* December 7, 1946, p. 112, Mercury ad, December 21, 1946, p. 25, review, p. 27; December 14, 1946, p. 19.

65 **raise money:** *Daily Worker,* January 4, 1947, p. 8. Dinah Washington FBI file, #100-43795-A.

66 **Ben Bart:** Interviews with Jack Bart, Ben Bart's son, August 8, 9, 2001, April 30, 2002; *Chicago Defender,* May 21, 1947, p. 25; *Variety,* August 14, 1968, p. 71.

67 **Colosimo's:** *Chicago Defender,* June 7, 1947, p. 27, June 14, 1947, p. 28; *Variety,* October 14, 1921, p. 9; *Variety,* June 5, 1946, p. 46; May 7, 1947, p. 60; *Chicago Defender,* June 21, 1947, p. 24; June 28, 1947, p. 29, for Colosimo's show, produced by Joe "Ziggy" Johnson and featuring Carmencita Romero and Her Dancers, Frenchie Bascombe, and Johnson's regular group, which he billed as "the dancing, darling Ziggyettes." Interviews with Eloise Hughes, January 10, February, April 5 and 23, 2002.

67 **"Blowtop Blues":** *Billboard,* May 24, 1947, p. 28.

68 **Ritz Lounge:** Travis, *An Autobiography of Black Jazz,* pp. 494–97; interview with Dave Young, courtesy of Charles Walton; Eddie Plique interview, June 1968, courtesy of Jack Thompson.

69 **Robert Grayson:** Marriage license from Cook County, Illinois, Vital Records #1986817; *Sepia,* December 1959, pp. 8–11. See also, *Jenkins v. Jenkins,*

#47S15542, Cook Superior Court Complaint for Annulment of Marriage; photo courtesy of Charles Walton.

70 **She was livid:** Artie Frazier, Jr., interview, June 17, 2002.

71 **John Hammond:** *Cash Box,* September 1, 1947, p. 11; Hammond, *John Hammond on Record,* pp. 278–81; *Down Beat,* May 7, 1947, p. 3.

71 **Dave Garroway:** *Dave Garroway Show,* RWB 4823 A2-3, Library of Congress Recorded Sound Collection.

71 **Rudy Martin Trio:** Bill Settles on bass and Curtis Walker on drums filled out the Martin Trio.

71 **"Fool That I Am":** *Metronome,* November 1947, p. 49; October 1947, p. 32; *Billboard,* September 6, 1947, p. 20. "Fool That I Am"/"Mean and Evil Blues," Mercury 8050.

7 · Queen of the Juke Boxes, 1948–1949

73 **1518 South Trumbull:** Black home ownership, U.S. Census information from 1950; black Chicagoans' income level, Drake and Cayton, *Black Metropolis,* p. 816.

Cook County Recorder of Deeds, Chicago, Illinois: Warranty Deed 1488220, Book 43187, p. 51, John Salerno and Letitia Salerno to Alice L. Jones, March 22, 1948; first mortgage of $6,500 with Illinois Federal Savings and Loan, 14288221, Box 43187, p. 58, March 22, 1948; second mortgage of $2,800 with George Spatuzza, 14288222, Book 441844, p. 149, March 26, 1948.

The first mortgage, co-signed by Ruth Jones, carried a 5 percent interest rate, with the first payment of $87 due on the first of each month beginning May 1948. The second mortgage, signed only by Alice Jones, also carried a 5 percent interest rate. That loan was to be paid up by March 26, 1951.

74 **backyard:** Estrellita Dukes interview, May 28, 2002; Clarissa Smith interviews.

75 **at number six:** *Billboard,* March 27, 1948, p. 181; *Billboard* liked "Pacific Coast Blues" better than the flip side, noting of "Chewin' Woman" that "Dinah sings well but the material is sub-par." Mercury had also released "No More Lonely Gal Blues"/"Ain't Misbehavin," Mercury 8072.

75 **Viola Battles:** William Battles interviews, April 10, October 16, 2003.

Dinah was at the Powelton Cafe in Philadelphia for a week starting March, *Philadelphia Tribune,* March 5, 1948, p. 12; in Newark at Laurel Garden with Cootie Williams on March 12, and then at Elates in Philadelphia on March 19, 1948, *Philadelphia Tribune,* March 20, 1948, p. 12.

76 **Newport News:** *Philadelphia Tribune,* March 20, 1948, p. 12; *Chicago Defender,* April 17, 1948, p. 28; *Washington Afro-American,* April 24, 1948, p. 17; *Norfolk Journal and Guide,* April 24, 1948, p. 17.

76 **"Queen of the Juke Box":** *Atlanta Daily World,* May 2, 1948, p. 2; *Billboard,* May 15, 1948, p. 36.

77 **LaRue Manns:** *Washington Afro-American,* May 8, 1948, p. 6; May 29, 1948, p. 8; *Washington Afro-American,* May 29, 1948, p. 8; LaRue Manns interview, September 8, 1985, Haskins papers.

78 **another record ban:** *Billboard* articles from September through December,

when the recording ban was finally lifted, provide information about what some of the labels were doing and how the negotiations were proceeding. One sticking point had been the royalty structure and when any new structure would be put in place. The eventual agreement provided for a five-year pact between the American Federation of Musicians and the industry. Previous agreements had been for one or two. *Billboard,* September 25 through November 13, 1948, and also December 1948.

78 *last session before the ban:* In her last session in 1947, on December 31 in New York, Dinah had recorded the witty "Record Ban Blues," which she co-wrote. One pointed line talks about recording a tune that was "grand." "The union man said go ahead but you'll have to do it without the band." When would Dinah record again? "Only Petrillo knows."

The copyrights on "Record Ban Blues" and "Resolution Blues" were filed February 26, 1948, listing Margo Music as the publisher. Dinah shared a writing credit on the "Ban" tune with Leonard Swain (EU118669), and on "Resolution" with Joseph D. Newman and Joseph B. Wilder (EU118670). "Record Ban Blues" was never released as a single. It appeared several years later on compilations.

Although the ban was still in place, Mercury scheduled another session for Dinah in New York the second week in June 1948. A few musicians—a clarinet player and a rhythm section—were recruited to bolster a vocal group that backed Dinah on two numbers, "In the Rain" and "I Sold My Heart to the Junk Man." They were either nonunion or apparently not concerned about flouting Petrillo, though no discography ever identified them.

78 *quick rapport:* Clarissa Smith interview, June 16, 2002.

79 *"West Side Baby":* Chicago Defender, June 12, 1948, p. 26; *Billboard,* June 19, 1948, p. 4; June 26, 1948, p. 29. Earlier in the year, the magazine had started a second chart for race music to go along with the most-played jukebox record, "best selling retail race record."

79 *moved upstairs:* Clarissa Smith interview, June 16, 2002; LaRue Manns interview, Haskins papers.

80 *"She was a natural":* Mitch Miller interview, April 30, 2002.

80 *twenty thousand copies:* Billboard, September 11, 1948, p. 30. "Am I Asking Too Much" had been recorded in Chicago in 1947 with the Dave Young Orchestra. *Chicago Defender,* September 18, 1948, p. 28.

81 *"an energetic worker":* Variety, September 15, 1948, p. 51. For Dinah's other fall dates see also *Chicago Defender,* August 28, 1948, p. 26; *New York Post,* September 9, 1948, p. 36; *Billboard,* October 9, 1948, p. 35, see *Billboard* race music charts from mid-October to mid-November 1948, for "Am I Asking Too Much."

81 *"She had no airs":* Billboard, December 4, 1948, p. 20; Richard "Dickie" Harris interview, January 2, 2002; *Chicago Defender,* December 4, 1948, p. 28.

82 *in the middle of Mississippi:* Chicago Defender, December 25, 1948, p. 26; Clarissa Smith interview, June 16, 2002; Clark Terry interview, October 4, 2002.

83 *Dinah's commercial appeal:* Billboard, January 1, 1949, pp. 14, 20; *Cash Box,* November 20, 1948, p. 5; *Down Beat,* December 29, 1948, p. 12; *Metronome,* January 1949, p. 32.

Dinah and the Orioles had been neck and neck in the charts with their respective recordings of "It's Too Soon to Know," with Dinah one notch ahead for several weeks. But like a good horse race, the Orioles nudged her at the end, winding up the year among black singers one notch ahead at number eighteen.

In the year-end magazine polls, only Ella Fitzgerald among black singers registered on *Billboard*'s all-important "best selling female vocalist" chart— she was sixth of seven, well behind Peggy Lee in the top spot. In *Down Beat* and *Metronome*, Sarah Vaughan topped each magazine's polls. Vaughan booking, *Chicago Defender*, January 8, 1949, p. 24.

84 *"genuinely gratified":* Chicago Defender, January 15, 1949, p. 24.

84 *due in Cleveland:* Cleveland Call & Post, January 8, 1949, p. 4A; January 15, 1949, p. 4A.

84 *mail-order stores:* See the *Chicago Defender*, January 29, 1949, p. 28, and the *Newark Afro-American*, March 5, 1949, p. 6, as examples of mail order record store ads that featured Dinah's records.

Dinah's newest release was "Laughing Boy"/"You Satisfy" (Mercury 8102) and one instance where two different takes were tried in the studio and each preserved. "Laughing Boy" was about a man who always has "a smile on his face" and who always has "a laugh to share" but cries when he's alone. Dinah sang both versions almost identically, but at the beginning of the second she starts with a laugh that sounds forced at best. Her old friend Leonard Feather called the idea "a very questionable tactic" though it apparently was the version Mercury released. *Cash Box* spotlighted "Laughing Boy" in its February 26, 1949, issue.

85 *a major tour:* Sylvia Weinberg interview, August 27, 2001; Jack Bart interviews, May 30, June 18, 2002.

87 *Camp Fire Girls:* Baltimore Sun, February 13, 1949, Section A, p. 5.

87 *speak out:* Chicago Defender, January 1, 1949, p. 20; Washington Afro-American, February 12, 1949, p. 7; February 26, 1949, p. 1.

88 *Memorial Auditorium:* News and Observer, March 6, 1949, Section IV, p. 8; Jack Bart interviews, August 8, 2002; May 30, 2002.

88 *Asheville:* Asheville Citizen Times, March 20, 1949, p. 8B; *Columbia State*, March 11, 1949, p. 2B; *Chattanooga Times*, March 20, 1949, p. 27. The ad in the *Times* was the most explicit: "Concert-Dance for Colored." The population figures for Buncombe County are from *County Population Trends*, North Carolina, 1790–1960, courtesy of Zoe Rhine in the Asheville-Buncombe Library; Keter Betts interview, June 28, 2002.

89 *terrific start:* Billboard, March 21, 1949, p. 20; *Chicago Defender*, March 26, 1949, p. 35; *Atlanta Daily World*, March 10, 1949, p. 3.

The full tour, gleaned from schedules printed in New Jersey's *Newark Afro-American* and the *Chicago Defender*, was announced as: March 4, Philadelphia; March 5, Newark; March 6, Washington; March 7, Raleigh; March 10, Atlanta; March 11, Columbia, South Carolina; March 12, Tuskegee, Alabama; March 14, Jacksonville, Florida; March 16, New Orleans; March 18, Nashville; March 21, Chattanooga; March 22, Asheville, North Carolina; March 23, Danville, Virginia; April 1, Norfolk, Virginia; April 2, Fayetteville, North Carolina; April 4, Roanoke, Virginia; April 5, Huntingon, West Virginia. There were apparently performances in two other cities,

Maxton, North Carolina, and Charleston, South Carolina, because information about the attendance and the amount collected in those two cities is included in the *Billboard* and *Defender* stories.

The *Defender* of March 26, 1949, was particularly detailed, providing attendance figures and door proceeds—before taxes were taken out—for several cities in addition to Atlanta: Philadelphia, 2,960 payees and $4,440.50; Newark, 2,165 and $3,994.50; Washington, 1,549 and $2,323.50; Raleigh, 2,220 and $3,875.83; Maxton, 1,023 and $1,955.86; Charleston, 2,640 and $4,423.80.

See also *Billboard*, April 2, 1949, p. 41; *Cash Box*, April 2, 1949, p. 13. "You Satisfy" moved to number five on the Los Angeles chart the next week, *Cash Box*, April 9, 1949, p. 15; *Roanoke Times*, April 4, 1949, p. 4.

89 *"We had everything":* Clarissa Smith interview, June 16, 2002.

90 *midnight concert: Pittsburgh Courier*, April 16, 1940, p. 1; April 23, 1949, p. 19.

90 *Flame Show Bar: Michigan Chronicle*, August 12, 1949, p. 2; August 13, 1949, p. 21; *Indiana Recorder*, August 6, 1949.

91 *"Baby Get Lost":* "Baby Get Lost," Mercury 8148 ("Long John Blues"), had been recorded in New York with an orchestra headed by Teddy Stewart. Mercury's discography and Tom Lord's, which was put together from a combination of sources, list the date as March 4, but that is questionable. On March 4, Dinah, the Ravens, and Cootie Williams were supposed to be performing in Philadelphia, and it is likely that the session was actually a week or two earlier, while Dinah was playing the Royal Roost at night. The discographies list "Long John Blues" as being recorded in New York on July 1, 1948, and that date, too, is questionable. Dinah was eight months pregnant with her second child, and there is evidence that she had returned to Chicago from Washington, after a playing the Howard Theater and then the Crystal Cavern nightclub. It is highly unlikely that she went back to New York for a session that was only one song. It is more probable that "Long John Blues," if it was recorded in July 1948, was recorded in Chicago.

91 *staying with Mercury: Chicago Defender*, August 13, 1949.

92 *"a short comedy gag": Variety*, September 7, 1949, p. 27; *New York Amsterdam News*, September 10, 1949, p. 21.

92 *joined the Ravens: Chicago Defender*, September 10, 1949, pp. 26–27.

92 *rhythm and blues exacta: Billboard*, September 24, 1949, p. 31; *Cash Box*, September 24, 1949, p. 15.

92 *"Thanks, baby":* Leonard Feather interview, Haskins papers. Feather, *The Jazz Years*, p. 185.

93 *"hefty": Chicago Defender*, September 24, 1949, p. 30. The subhead to "No More Dieting for Dinah" had particular punch: "Reason? Bed Replaces Her Table."

93 *on the road again: Philadelphia Recorder*, November 5, 1949, p. 13; see also *Philadelphia Tribune*, October 22, 1949, p. 12.

An October 29, 1949, story in the *Defender* about the tour (p. 27) noted that the Joe Thomas band won the job of backing Dinah and the Ravens, though seven other groups had bid for the chance to go on the tour. The *Defender* story, which was written out of New York, said that Dinah and the

Ravens were "the current box office champion of the nation," but that was most likely press agent hyperbole.

94 **broke a record:** *Chicago Defender,* December 3, 1949, p. 26. The *Defender* story gave an indication of what kind of money the tour was making. In South Bend, Indiana, the audience of 1,867 brought in $2,951; in Louisville, the 4,164 patrons accounted for $5,816.25; and in Indianapolis, the 2,019 in the audience brought in $3,666.06.

94 **"if the dog goes":** *Chicago Defender,* December 24, 1949, p. 33; *Billboard,* December 24, 1949, p. 43.

95 **end of the year:** *Cash Box,* December 3, 1949, p. 7; *Billboard,* January 14, 1950, p. 17; *Down Beat,* December 29, 1949, p. 12; *Metronome,* January 1950, p. 31.

8 · No Time for Tears, 1950–1951

96 **a girlfriend:** *Sepia,* December 1959, p. 10; *Ebony,* March 1964, pp. 140–51; Artie Frazier, Jr., interview; Charles Walton interviews.

Fifty years later it was more a matter of interest rather than dispositive of legal technicalities that there was no record in the Cook County files of Dinah's divorce from Robert Grayson nor one from her first husband, John Young.

97 **a Sunday evening:** *Washington Afro-American,* February 28, 1950, p. 8; *Chicago Defender,* March 25, 1950, p. 35.

98 **"I Only Know":** There is no copyright for "I Only Know" that lists Dinah Washington or Ruth Jones as a writer. The flip side was "New York, Chicago and Los Angeles," Mercury 8163.

98 **Café Society:** *Chicago Defender,* April 1, 1950, p. 34; see *Chicago Defender,* May 13, 1950, p. 36 for Bop City.

99 **"I Wanna Be Loved":** See *Billboard,* May 20, June 3, June 17, 1950, music chart pages; *Cash Box,* July, August 1950 chart pages. "I Wanna Be Loved"/"Love with Misery," Mercury 8181.

100 **"top interpreter of blues":** *Ebony,* June 1950, pp. 59–64.

102 **Teddy Stewart:** *New York Amsterdam News,* May 26, 1950, p. 12; *Kansas City Call,* May 26, 1950, p. 12; Keter Betts interviews.

103 **"I have no intention":** *New York Amsterdam News,* June 10, 1950, p. 25; *Chicago Defender,* June 17, 1950, p. 36. Both of these stories have Kansas City datelines and almost surely came from an interview Dinah gave while performing at the nearby Junction City Municipal Auditorium.

104 **Los Angeles:** *Los Angeles Sentinel,* June 23, 1950, p. B2; June 15, 1950, p. B1; *Chicago Defender,* June 24, 1950, p. 27; *California Eagle,* June 16, 1950, p. 14; *Sepia,* March 1953, p. 22, on the Oasis. See also *Los Angeles Sentinel,* June 27, 1950, p. A2; June 29, 1950, p. B2; *California Eagle,* June 30, 1950, p. 4.

105 **making movies:** *Chicago Defender,* July 1, 1950, p. 30.

105 **fish diet:** *Chicago Defender,* July 15, 1950, p. 30.

105 **Denver:** *Denver Post,* July 16, 1950, p. 4E, Julia Lee article; July 19, 1950, p. 30, Dinah Washington ad; see also *Rocky Mountain News,* July 16, 1950, p. 4A, July 19, 1950, p. 18.

The *Defender* reported July 29, 1950 (p. 30), that while Dinah was appearing at the Rossonian, she was informed that she had won "a precedent shattering first by hanging up the first 'grand slam' ever registered by a girl singer" because "I Wanna Be Loved" had registered in first place in all the cities the magazine polled. The issues of *Cash Box* for the first three weeks in July, however, do not support that contention. While "I Wanna Be Loved" registers on the charts in Harlem, Chicago's South Side, New Orleans, and Central Avenue in Los Angeles, it was first only in Harlem for three weeks and in first place in Chicago for one week (July 22, 1950, pp. 14–15; July 29, 1950, pp. 14–15).

  Before heading to Denver, Dinah had returned to Los Angeles to play a well-publicized dance at the Avodon Ballroom July 14.

106 ***Howard Johnson restaurant chain:*** *California Eagle,* July 21, 1950, p. 15; Gart, *First Pressings,* July 1950, p. 86.

107 ***Pompton Lakes:*** *Philadelphia Tribune,* August 15, 1950, p. 12; August 22, 1950, p. 12; August 29, 1950, p. 12; *New York Amsterdam News,* August 26, 1950, p. 22.

107 ***Wynton Kelly:*** *Down Beat,* January 1963, p. 16; Keter Betts interview, August 20, 2002. It is probable that Dinah first heard Wynton when he was playing with Eddie "Cleanhead" Vinson on the same bill at the Earle Theater in Philadelphia in late August 1950. *Philadelphia Tribune,* August 22, 1950, p. 12; August 22, 1950, p. 12, on birthday party. See also *Chicago Defender,* August 24, 1950, p. 36.

108 ***sore throat:*** *New York Post,* September 27, 1950, p. 67; *Variety,* October 4, 1950, p. 61.

  The item in the *New York Amsterdam News* (September 30, 1950, p. 24) announcing the show read as if it were a press release from Universal Attractions, asserting that Dinah was "riding a new and unprecedented popularity wave which has reached such proportions in the sales division as to make even veteran record promoters scratch their heads in wonder. And little wonder that this dynamic young miss has achieved such prominence; she is a package of dynamite on the stage and off. Possessor of one of the most unique of all song styles, the 'Queen of the Juke Boxes' is also queen of the blues and reigns as high as any in the ballad department."

108 ***number five slot:*** The Andrews Sisters' version of "I Wanna Be Loved" was number six in the "Top Pop Records" of the year. It was a tribute to Nat King Cole's popularity that he was number one on the pop chart with "Mona Lisa" and number six on the R&B chart. *Billboard,* October 1, 1950, p. 27.

108 ***Walter Buchanan:*** State of Maryland marriage license, #10687, Maryland State Archives; *Baltimore Afro-American,* October 10, 1950, p. 9; October 14, 1950, p. 17; October 21, 1950, p. 11. Though the *Pittsburgh Courier* advertised that Dinah would play October 10, 1950, at the American Legion Hall with Calvin Boze and his orchestra, that date almost surely didn't happen because Dinah was in Baltimore (October 7, 1950, p. 14).

109 ***chitchat columns:*** *First Pressings: The History of Rhythm and Blues, 1950 Special Issue,* November, p. 140; Vivian Hunter testimony, May 25, 1953, in *Dinah Buchanan v. Walter Buchanan,* divorce proceedings involving Dinah's fourth husband, Superior Court of Cook County, Illinois, #52S2736.

109 ***"Time Out for Tears":*** As Dinah's fourth song hit the charts, "Time Out for Tears," Mercury 5503 ("Only a Moment Ago"), it was no surprise when

Dinah was invited to be part of the star-studded cast on hand in Harlem in mid-December to celebrate the twenty-fifth anniversary of Small's Paradise, a well-known bistro. Several nights of shows were packaged to include the biggest stars—Duke Ellington, Ella Fitzgerald, Nat Cole, and even a few white entertainers including Frank Sinatra and Stan Kenton. Dinah either cringed or laughed if she saw the December 16 issue of the *New York Amsterdam News,* which ran pictures of a dozen or so of the stars and used that first publicity shot she had taken with Hampton in the spring of 1943. It was seven years old, and now she hardly looked like the teenager who wore a gardenia in her hair.

110 *gave her a ring:* Clarissa Smith interview, August 24, 2002.

110 *marriage was in trouble:* Walter Buchanan information from *Dinah Buchanan v. Walter Buchanan,* "Report of Proceedings," filed June 10, 1953, Superior Court of Cook County. It is a transcript of the May 26, 1953, divorce proceedings, #52S2736.

111 *Morris Levy:* Dannen, *Hit Men: Power Brokers and Fast Money Inside the Music Business,* pp. 35–37; Wade and Picardie, *Music Man: Ahmet Ertegun, Atlantic Records and the Triumph of Rock 'n' Roll,* pp. 252–56.

   The FBI had Levy under surveillance for many years for alleged racketeering activities. His file is extensive, and includes monitoring by several other federal agencies, including the Internal Revenue Service, the Postal Service, and the Customs Service. Dannen reports that several years after Birdland opened, authorities believed that Morris and his brother Irving took over the location from mobster Joseph "Joe the Wop" Cataldo (p. 37).

112 *"Go wail one":* From *Queen of the Jukebox Live,* Baldwin Street Music, BJH 310.

113 *Detroit: Michigan Chronicle,* February 17, 1951, p. 20. Dinah was on a bill with Amos Milburn, who was atop the blues charts with "Chicken Shack Boogie," and the comedian Moms Mabley. The backing band was headed by local musician Candy Johnson, suggesting that this was a solo date for Dinah that Bart had booked rather than the packages he had put together for a tour. The *Chronicle* ad gave Dinah her customary billing, "Juke Box Queen."

113 *Earl Bostic's hand: Chicago Defender,* February 10, 1951, p. 34.

   Dinah and Bostic got a little extra publicity during the Apollo run when they were invited to a party honoring singer-dancer Josephine Baker, who had come to the city to play the Strand Theater. The two were photographed by the *New York Amsterdam News* (March 10, 1951, p. 27), and the caption noted that among the other musicians at the party was Dinah's husband, Walter.

114 *Cadillac:* Keter Betts interviews, March 30, July 12, August 1, 2001.

114 *"marriage was doomed": Sepia,* December 1959, p. 12; transcript of hearing in *Dinah Buchanan v. Walter Buchanan.* Although Dinah and her maid, Vivian Hunter, testified that the couple split up January 11, 1951, and that Dinah didn't see him again except for a brief encounter at a party, Keter Betts remembered in detail that Walter was with Dinah in Washington in March 1951 and in St. Louis, when they split up for good. Betts interviews, 2001–02.

   For information on the St. Louis performances, which were for the

Royal Scot Social Club, see *St. Louis Argus*, April 13, 1951, p. 22; April 20, 1951, p. 22.

116 ***Jimmy Cobb:*** Jimmy Cobb interview; Keter Betts interviews.

117 ***"point of departure":*** *Variety*, March 7, 1951, p. 54; see *Los Angeles Sentinel*, May 17, 1951, p. B4, for Elks Hall performance; "I Won't Cry Any More," Mercury 8211 ("Don't Say You're Sorry"), *Billboard*, May 26, 1951, p. 32.

118 ***Ike Carpenter:*** The contract for the musicians, all from Los Angeles AFM Local 47 except Wynton (who was in the New York local), provided a glimpse of what musicians earned. Each sideman got $41.25 for each session; Carpenter, as the leader, got double. Contract from the archives of Local 47.

119 ***Dinah flew back east:*** *Philadelphia Tribune*, June 16, 1951, p. 12; *Chicago Defender*, June 16, 1951, p. 33; July 14, 1951, pp. 33, 34.

119 ***"Let's have a great big hand":*** *Queen of the Juke Box Live*, BJH 310.

119 ***farblondjet:*** See Leo Rosten, *The Joys of Yiddish*, p. 112; Keter Betts interviews for Jimmy Cobb's driving lessons.

121 ***Tabernacle Baptist Church:*** *Chicago Defender*, August 4, 1951, p. 10; August 11, 1951, p. 11.

121 ***Gleason's:*** *Cleveland Call & Post*, August 27, 1951, p. 4D.

122 ***contract with Mercury:*** *Billboard*, October 13, 1951, p. 13, on Bobby Shad; October 20, 1951, p. 20, on Mercury deal with Bart and Dinah's extension. The mink coat episode was noted by Dave Young in an interview with Charles Walton, also Irving Green interview, June 14, 2001, and it was referred to in Ziggy Johnson's *Michigan Chronicle* column, "Zagging with Ziggy," October 20, 1951, p. 19. See also the October 13, 1951, *Chronicle*, p. 19. The mink coat was mentioned in a *Down Beat* article February 22, 1952, p. 12; Mitch Miller interview, April 30, 2002, for other mink coat story.

    Mercury took out an ad for Dinah October 20, 1950 (p. 28), to promote a new single, "Baby, Did You Hear?" Mercury 5736 ("Just One More Chance"), an unusual song with very little instrumental accompaniment and one that evoked Eastern European dance music. Jazz critic Dan Morgenstern, calling it "exotic trivia," thought it might have been inspired by Peggy Lee's "pseudo Gypsy" hit "Golden Earrings." Dinah sang the song without kitsch, however.

123 ***"Cold, Cold Heart":*** Clark Terry interview October 4, 2002; Keter Betts interviews. Wynton Kelly had told Keter how the "Cold, Cold Heart" session unfolded. Mercury 5728 ("Mixed Emotions").

123 ***Nook Shrier:*** Nook Shrier interview, August 26, 2002.

124 s***eventeen one-nighters:*** *Philadelphia Tribune*, October 16, 1951, p. 12; *Variety*, November 14, 1951, p. 56; *Chicago Defender*, November 10, 1951, p. 15, for a discussion of the recording session with the Ravens, which was at the Reeves studio.

    Dinah also made a quick trip to Philadelphia to work the Club Harlem for the nightspot's one-year anniversary. Perhaps the money was too good to pass up, and perhaps, too, she liked the owner and was willing to do him a favor. When she returned to Philadelphia a few weeks later to play the Earle, a reviewer from *Variety* wondered in print whether her return along with others on the bill reflected "a scarcity of talent or the popularity of the acts."

124 *Holiday canceled:* New York Amsterdam News, June 24, 1950, p. 29; July 22, 1950, p. 20.

125 *"spectators":* News and Observer, November 11, p. IV-11, 1951; November 18, 1951, p. IV-7; Keter Betts interviews.

125 *Tifton, Georgia:* Washington Afro-American, December 16, 1951, p. 7; Los Angeles Sentinel, January 10, 1952, p. B3; Keter Betts interviews. There were enough accidents among black entertainers that *Sepia* wrote an article about the problem in its March 1957 issue (p. 24). The Bostic incident was mentioned prominently.

9 · Keter, Wynton, and Jimmy, 1952

126 *"Wheel of Fortune":* Mercury 8267 ("Tell Me Why"). The song had been a pop hit for Kay Starr. Dinah's version went on the *Billboard* sales and juke-box charts March 8 and stayed there for five weeks. Sunny Gale and Eddie Wilcox also had an R&B hit with their versions. "Tell Me Why," which was a pop hit for the Four Aces, went on the charts a week later and stayed for three weeks. "Trouble in Mind," Mercury 8269 ("New Blowtop Blues"), registered March 29 and stayed on the charts for two weeks. *Cash Box,* February 2, 1952, p. 16. The magazine ran a picture of Dinah, dressed in a handsome blazer, standing at the microphone with Shad. *Cash Box,* March 22, 1952, p. 20.

126 *"She opened up my head":* Keter Betts interviews; Jimmy Cobb interview, June 6, 2001.

128 *"easier to handle":* Jet, July 30, 1953, p. 40.

128 *"Queen, can I buy you a drink?":* Keter Betts interviews.

128 *in the Los Angeles area:* Dinah started the new year in Los Angeles at the Elks Club, the opening West Coast date, on a package with Cootie Williams. She also played the Club Alabam the first week in February and then went south to San Diego to perform at the Mission Beach Ballroom. Dinah and the trio headed north, winding up their tour in Oakland around February 15. *California Eagle,* January 3, 1952, p. 8; *Los Angeles Sentinel,* January 10, 1952, p. B3; *California Eagle,* February 4, 1952, p. 12; *Down Beat,* February 22, 1952, p. 13, which refers to the San Diego date. Cotten, *Shake, Rattle and Roll,* p. 5; see also *Los Angeles Sentinel,* February 7, 1952, p. B2; February 21, 1952, p. 32. On the bill with Dinah at the Club Alabam were Mabel Scott, advertised as the "Brown Bombshell," and Slappy White and Redd Foxx. The *Sentinel* also reported that Dinah performed with Cootie Williams February 3 at the Long Beach Municipal Auditorium.

129 *fit right in:* picture courtesy of Clarissa Smith. While Dinah was in Chicago, she and the trio joined Cootie Williams March 8 to perform at the Union Park Temple.

129 *a solo harp:* The discographies credit the "Walter Rodell Orchestra." Rodell was the professional name of Nook Shrier, the Mercury producer who had worked with Dinah earlier. Shrier interview, October 4, 2002. In 1955, three years after Dinah recorded "I Thought About You," Frank Sinatra

recorded the song, and his version came to be considered the definitive one.

The "New Blowtop Blues" had been recorded a year earlier, in the same session as "Cold, Cold Heart."

Variety reviewed the Apollo show, devoting a paragraph to Dinah: "Warbler is fave here and sustains rep with a top songalog. She drives hard on 'Tell Me Why,' 'Cold Cold Heart,' 'Wheel of Fortune.' Closes big with 'Blow Top Blues' and has to beg off. Her hard hitting song styling keeps house rocking throughout the set" (April 16, 1952, p. 60).

The *Cash Box* mentions about Dinah and Jimmy appeared in the March 8 "Rhythm & Blues Ramblins" (p. 16) and in Sam Evans's "Kickin' the Blues Around," p. 19.

130 ***three-foot-high trophy:*** See *Pittsburgh Courier,* all of April 1952, entertainment pages, and May 3, 1952, p. 22, for a roundup of the concert. Picture of Dinah and her mother with the trophy, courtesy of Clarissa Smith. Beatrice Buck interviews.

131 ***carefully coordinated:*** Rose Snow interview, October 22, 2002. Snow worked for Dinah in 1951–52, introduced to her by Dinah's Washington, D.C., friend Georgia Mae Scott; Robert Mitchum, *Chicago Defender,* July 26, 1952, p. 18; see also *Sepia,* March 1953, p. 23.

131 ***"boosters":*** Jimmy Cobb interview; Keter Betts interviews; Ann Littles interviews; Tammy Graves Foster interview, 1981, courtesy of Jack Thompson.

132 ***"had no shape":*** LaRue Manns interview, Haskins papers; see also *Washington Afro-American,* April 8, 1952, p. 6; *Jet,* December 27, 1951, p. 33; *Chicago Defender,* July 26, 1952, p. 18; *Sepia,* March 1953, p. 23.

133 ***interracial bill:*** *Chicago Defender,* March 15, 1952, p. 13; *New York Amsterdam News,* July 15, 1952, p. 26, on "Biggest Show" lineup; *Baltimore Afro-American,* May 24, 1952, p. 21, on "Caravan of Stars; *Chicago Defender,* October 4, 1952, p. 24, on "Jazz at the Philharmonic"; *Chicago Defender,* March 15, 1952, p. 14, on Billy Eckstine and Count Basie.

Dinah and the "Caravan of Stars" played the Philadelphia Armory on May 18, the Baltimore Coliseum on May 21, and the Syria Mosque in Pittsburgh on May 23.

The "Caravan" tour reunited in July to play Carnegie Hall. Dinah sang "Wheel of Fortune" and "Blowtop Blues." The *Down Beat* reviewer liked her, Woody Herman, Chubby Jackson, and the Mills Brothers but complained that the rest of the show, singer Tommy Edwards and comedian Herkie Styles, in particular, "could have been dispensed with" (July 12, 1952, p. 14).

For Dinah's other summer events see *Baltimore Afro-American,* May 24, 1952, p. 21; *Philadelphia Tribune,* May 31, 1952, p. 12; *Washington Afro-American,* July 9, 1952, p. 6; *Baltimore Afro-American,* July 15, 2002. The bills included Arnett Cobb's orchestra, the dancer Harold King, the Ravens, and Slappy White and Redd Foxx.

135 ***Blue Note:*** *Cash Box,* April 26, 1952, p. 15; *Chicago Defender,* May 24, 1952, p. 20; January 17, 1953, p. 14.

136 ***Beryl Booker:*** *Philadelphia Tribune,* March 5, 1949, p. 12, Beryl Booker ad; *Chicago Defender,* June 28, 1952, p. 18, Al Monroe's column noting Booker

in Los Angeles. *Down Beat,* April 4, 1952, p. 8, Leonard Feather profile of Booker; *Down Beat,* August 27, 1952, p. 11.

136 *"Now you're being corny":* Dinah Washington: Queen of the Juke Box Live.

The liner notes say that Wynton Kelly played the piano on this date and that Ed Shaughnessy may have been the drummer. However, Keter Betts and Jimmy Cobb, who listened to the tracks independently, said Beryl Booker was the piano player. "The whole thing was different," Jimmy said, adding that when Wynton played, "he was all over Dinah when she sang." Jimmy said he played drums on the date.

137 *"Skeeter":* Keter Betts interviews; Jimmy Cobb interviews; *Washington Post,* March 19, 2002, p. C2, a reminiscence about Birdland. Crow, *From Birdland to Broadway: Scenes from a Jazz Life,* pp. 87–90; *New York Times,* June 23–26, 1952, sports pages for Sugar Ray Robinson fight coverage.

138 *"Sepia Hit Parade":* Cash Box, July 5, 1952, p. 7.

138 *"Oh, that friend":* Arnett Cobb–Dinah Washington, High Note 7068. The liner notes say Dinah's personnel were Keter Betts, bass, Jimmy Cobb, drums, and Johnny Acea on piano, though at this time Beryl Booker was also playing for Dinah. Wynton Kelly had been drafted into the army.

138 *"So after three nights":* Wein, with Chinen, *Myself Among Others: A Life in Music,* pp. 94–95; Wein interviews. "Mad About the Boy"/"I Could Face the Music," Mercury 5842.

139 *missed her siblings:* Robert Grayson, Jr., interviews, Clarissa Smith interviews; Estrellita Dukes interview, October 7, 2002.

140 *"the traditions of jazz":* San Francisco Chronicle, October 5, 1952, p. 18; *Down Beat,* October 8, 1952, p. 3; *California Eagle,* October 16, 1952, p. 10; October 23, 1952, p. 14.

141 *Rose Snow:* Rose Snow interview, October 28, 2002.

142 *back in Chicago:* Philadelphia Tribune, November 22, 1952, p. 10; *Chicago Defender,* December 27, 1952, p. 13.

142 *"the outstanding performer":* Down Beat, December 31, 1952, p. 8; *Metronome,* February 1953, p. 24; *Chicago Defender,* November 22, 1952, p. 18; *Tan,* February 1953, p. 12. In September (12th) a *Billboard* poll of jukebox operators had picked Dinah as one of the top ten artists to have a hit in the fall, one notch below Sarah Vaughan (p. 67).

10 · Love for Sale, 1953

143 *flew to Honolulu:* Los Angeles Sentinel, January 6, 1953, p. A10 on the Elks Hall. Dinah also performed January 15 in a big stage show at the Lincoln Theatre, *Sentinel,* January 15, 1953, p. B2; *Honolulu Advertiser,* January 18, 1953, Section 3, p. 6. The paper ran ads for Dinah's stay through February 3, 1953; Keter Betts interview, October 10, 2002; *Honolulu Star Bulletin,* January 15, 1953, p. C3.

144 *Blackhawk:* Tape of Blackhawk performance February 1953, courtesy of Keter Betts; Slappy White interview, Haskins papers; Keter Betts interviews; *San Francisco Chronicle,* February 8, 1953, p. 13; February 14, 1953, p. 5.

145 *returned to Los Angeles:* California Eagle, January 15, 1953, p. 9; March 12, 1953, p.7; April 2, 1953, p. 14, in "People and Places" column. Dinah always

stayed at the Watkins Hotel, the city's most upscale hotel for blacks. It was to Los Angeles as the Theresa was to Harlem and the Gotham to Detroit. Dinah liked a suite with at least a kitchenette so she could cook—or have cooked—her favorite things. Before she and the trio left, according to the *Eagle,* she threw a party at the hotel where the liquor—ten bottles of scotch, five of bourbon, gin, and wine—far overshadowed the two baked hams.

145 *"Sing it, Billie":* **California Eagle,** March 5, 1953, p. 9, March 12, 1953, p. 9.

146 *"Anything she sings":* **Jet,** March 26, 1953, pp. 58–59.

147 *"All I know":* **Dinah Buchanan v. Walter Buchanan.** The official divorce decree was filed July 10, 1953, in Superior Court of Cook County.

149 **back in New York:** See *Chicago Defender,* June 18, 1953, p. 32; *Amsterdam News,* June 27, 1953, p. 24, for Apollo date; *Washington Afro-American,* July 7, 1953, p. 6; *Michigan Chronicle,* August 15, 1953, p. 20.

　　Cash Box spotlighted "Never Never"/"My Lean Baby," Mercury 70175, June 20 (p. 20). The reviewer liked "Never Never" better than the flip side. "Her impassioned and sexy reading of this slow shuffle item brings life and color to the plate." Of "My Lean Baby," the reviewer wrote: "Dinah sings the quick beat bounce expertly, but it falls short of the upper etching." *Cash Box,* July 11, 1953, p. 16, is an example of a Mercury ad for the record.

150 *"Sleepy" Anderson:* **Atlanta Daily World,** August 8, 1953, p. 1. See July 26, 1953, p. 3, and August 6, 1953, p. 2, for information about the disc jockey's ball. Ann Littles interviews.

　　Though it would be an exaggeration to say that all or even most musicians were users, drugs were rampant, and the Sleepy Anderson problem was the second episode in ten months that Dinah had witnessed. The first, the previous October, was in Salt Lake City, when three members of the Woody Herman band were arrested on narcotics charges when they returned to their downtown hotel after the performance. The band and Dinah and her trio were on the same bill. Police acting on a tip searched the musicians' room and confiscated a stash of marijuana hidden in a dental powder can, a Vapo-Rub jar, and a Kodak film container. One of the men tried to flush an envelope filled with drugs down the toilet, but the police were able to confiscate the material. *Salt Lake Tribune,* October 27, 1952, p. 17; *Deseret News,* October 21, 1952, p. F7; October 27, 1952, p. B1.

　　Down Beat took the issue of drugs seriously enough to run a series, "Narcotics and Music," that featured a letter from Stan Getz about his habit that was written from the Los Angeles County Jail. April 7, 1954, p. 1; April 21, 1954, p. 3.

150 **twenty-ninth birthday:** *Our World,* December 1953, pp. 75–76, which describes Dinah's birthday party four months earlier in Detroit. *Michigan Chronicle,* August 15, 1953, p. 20, for the Graystone Ballroom date.

151 *"Miss Juke-box":* **Our World,** August 1953, p. 41. Dinah had also been featured in a Perma-Strate ad with Illinois Jacquet in the *Los Angeles Sentinel,* January 24, 1952, p. B2.

151 *"the possibility":* **Cash Box,** March 8, 1952, p. 16.

152 **James Kimbrough:** Marriage license of James Kimbrough and Alice Jones from Cook County Illinois Vital Statistics. The date of marriage was July 2, 1953. Farris Kimbrough interview, August 1, 2002; Alfreda Kimbrough interview, August 19, 2002. Robert Grayson interviews.

152 **West Side skating rink:** *Chicago Defender,* August 13, 1953, p. 27; August 27, 1953, p. 13; *The Complete Dinah Washington,* vol. 3, liner notes by Dan Morgenstern, p. 7; Milt Gabler story courtesy of Charles McGovern, Smithsonian Institution cultural historian/College of William and Mary.

153 **"Silent Night":** *Cash Box,* November 14, 1953, p. 28. Mercury 70263. The flip side was "The Lord's Prayer."

154 **Ducky Moore:** *Jet,* December 26, 1952, p. 65; January 15, 1953, p. 64.

154 **"She just went off":** Jimmy Cobb interviews; Keter Betts interviews; *Sepia,* December 1959, p. 12.

155 **momentary diversion:** See *Pittsburgh Courier,* September 12, 19, 26, 1953, entertainment pages; *Cash Box,* July 18, 1953, p. 43.

155 **"She's a nice girl":** Keter Betts interviews; pictures courtesy of Keter Betts.

156 **"They pushed us into a cab":** Larry Wrice interviews.

156 **"TV Is the Thing":** Mercury 70214 ("Fat Daddy"). See *Cash Box* rhythm and blues pages for October and November 1953. *Cash Box* had given Dinah another "award-of-the-week" October 3, predicting correctly that "TV" could be "one of Dinah's big ones." And a summer *Billboard* poll of jukebox operators had listed Dinah as one of the top ten artists likely to have an R&B hit in the fall.

"Fat Daddy" reached the charts the second week in November, though it didn't have quite the appeal of "TV."

157 **"Worst record":** Bobby Shad interview, courtesy of the Shad family and Derrick Ray.

157 **"I did her hair":** Ann Littles interviews, July 10, September 10, 2002.

158 **"She's the only woman":** Larry Wrice interviews, June 30, September 12, 2001, November 18, 2002; Charles Walton interviews; *Jet,* December 10, 1953, p. 14.

159 **Dizzy Gillespie:** *Michigan Chronicle,* December 26, 1953, p. 25. Before leaving Chicago for the Graystone Ballroom performance, Dinah and the trio played one night at the Madison Rink on the West Side. *Chicago Defender,* December 26, 1953, p. 14.

11 · Dinah Jams, 1954

160 **Her first 1954 session:** Dinah played a week at the Apollo starting January 22 and then went to Washington for another engagement at the Howard. *New York Amsterdam News,* January 23, 1954, p. 23; *Washington Afro-American,* January 30, 1954, p. 16.

The details of this early 1954 session are murky. Larry Wrice remembered that the session was in Chicago and that Sleepy Anderson played the piano. The existing discographies list the session in New York on February 5, and that makes sense given that Dinah had just finished several days at the Howard in Washington. However, there could have been enough time to finish in Washington and get back to Chicago to record there.

161 **"hogging the show":** *Baltimore Afro-American,* February 6, 1954, late city and five star editions for Royal Performance, p. 16; *Jet,* February 25, 1954, p. 17; March 11, 1954, p. 18; April 15, 1954, p. 64.

While Dinah sings about a "Mr. Rice" in "My Man's an Undertaker" (Mercury 70284), as some liner notes spell it, she may have been referring to Larry. According to discographies she actually recorded the song before she and Larry were together, in August 1953. Mercury did not release the song until December. *Cash Box* caught up with it in the January 2, 1954, issue (p. 18), giving it their R&B "award-o-the-week." The magazine predicted that the "chuckley lyrics were going to stir up swift sales. A solemn idea is given a light twist."

Mercury paired "Undertaker" with the calypso "Since My Man Has Gone and Went," which *Cash Box* proclaimed "zestfully performed." See also *Jet*, March 10, 1954, pp. 18–19, on Harold "Killer" Johnson.

162 *"I had never:"* Ed Thigpen interview, November 19, 2002.

163 *"trumpet tones":* *Michigan Chronicle*, February 27, 1954, pp. 23, 29; *Detroit Free Press*, February 28, 1954, section C, p. 13; March 6, 1954, p. 12.

163 **Prophet Jones:** Information on Prophet Jones, *Hue*, April 14, 1953, p. 55; *Sepia*, January 1953, p. 31; *Washington Afro-American*, December 12, 1953, p. 23. Beatrice Buck interview, December 4, 2002; references to Dinah's behavior, *Hue*, July 14, 1954, p. 43; *Tan*, September 1957, p. 22; Eddie Plique interview from 1968, courtesy of Jack Thompson.

164 *"I conked her":* The incident was first mentioned in *Hue*, July 14, 1954 (p. 44), and a few years later, Dinah provided more details in a story about her in *Tan*, August 1957, p. 24. The December 24, 1953, *Jet* (p. 65) had an item about Ruby Hines opening her own club in St. Louis.

164 *"uninhibited":* *Down Beat*, March 24, 1954, p. 3; *Cash Box*, April 24, 1954, p. 26. Shad had left Mercury in the fall of 1953 to join Decca but abruptly changed course and returned to his old employer, presumably to handle to the new EmArcy line.

Mercury 1024, *Dinah Sings*, released early in 1951 was apparently the first "album" for Dinah. The tracks were "It Isn't Fair, "I Wanna Be Loved," "I Only Know," "I'll Never Be Free," Harbor Lights," and "How Deep Is the Ocean." Eighteen months later four of the songs were repackaged a second time into Dinah's first EP (EP-1-3023) called simply *Dinah Washington*. The cover was a picture of her in a black evening gown, the lettering of her name as elegant as a wedding invitation. The songs were "It Isn't Fair," "I Wanna Be Loved," "How Deep Is the Ocean," "I Can't Get Started with You."

Another album (MG 25060), Dinah's first in the 33⅓ "long playing microgroove" series, was released in October 1951 and included "I Want to Cry," "I Can't Get Started with You," and "Why Don't You Think Things Over." Her second record in the series was *Dynamic Dinah*, Mercury 25138, and the third was *Blazing Ballads*, Mercury 25140, and included "Baby, Did Ya Hear," "My Heart Cries for You," "I Won't Cry Anymore," "Don't Say You're Sorry Again," "Mixed Emotions," "Cold Cold Heart," "Just One More Chance," and "I Apologize."

Release dates come from the monthly reports of *Popular Recordaid*.

164 *"goes her shouting way":* *Metronome*, October 1954, p. 26.

165 *"Juke Box Sociology":* *Ebony*, March 1954, p. 88.

168 **Club 86:** Al Colizzi interview, November 23, 2002. See *Finger Lakes Times*, December 15, 1996, p. 1A, for information on Club 86 on its fiftieth anniversary.

169 *"You need good ears":* Ed Thigpen interview, November 19, 2002.

170 *"offered me the job":* Junior Mance interview, August 15, 2001.

170 *"Bye Bye Blues":* Dan Morgenstern, *The Complete Dinah Washington,* volume 3, p. 9.

While discographies say the possible musicians included Jimmy Cobb and Wynton Kelly, this may not be correct. The best evidence is that Wynton was not yet out of the army, and Jimmy Cobb did not remember playing with Dinah after they split up until they had a professional rapprochement later in the year. Jimmy Cobb interview, December 9, 2002. "Big Long Slidin' Thing," Mercury 70392 ("No, No, No, You Can't Love Two" was the flip side.)

171 **Kiel Opera House:** The chronology of Dinah's itinerary prior to the June 29 Las Vegas date is unclear. *Billboard* reported June 26 (p. 38) that Dinah and the Bostic orchestra were on tour through the Midwest and would play Kansas City and St. Louis "this weekend." However, the Kiel Auditorium date in St. Louis was June 18. According to the *Chicago Defender,* Dinah and the trio and Earl Bostic played the Trianon in Chicago on June 25, which would have meant that they were booked a few hundred miles west (St. Louis and Kansas City) and then turned around to come east to Chicago, before heading west again to Las Vegas. Keter Betts said that such things occasionally happened, when booking agents accepted jobs without much thought to the travel involved. Sloppy White interview, Haskins papers; Mance interview, August 15, 2001.

172 **watermelon:** Junior Mance recounting the tale at a birthday party for Keter Betts, August 3, 2003.

172 **Las Vegas:** See Claytee D. White, "The Role of African American Women in the Las Vegas Gaming Industry, 1940–1980," master's thesis for the University of Nevada, Las Vegas, Department of History; Horne and Schickel, *Lena,* pp. 202–04; Las *Vegas Review Journal,* January 13, 1947, p. 9; *Sepia,* April 1953, p. 12; *Ebony,* March 1954, p. 45.

174 **half-page ad:** Whoever was handling Dinah's publicity didn't get the Patio the correct information. The ad listed Keter Betts as the drummer, Jimmy Cobb on the bass, and misspelled the name of the piano player, Al Jarvis, a New York musician who was sitting in for Junior Mance. Ed Thigpen, hired in February, was still the drummer, however, not Jimmy Cobb.

175 **served an attachment:** *Las Vegas Review Journal,* June 28, 1954, p. 9; July 4, 1954, p. 3. Some businessmen criticized the Patio's owners for overemphasis on the restaurant. The kitchen was overstaffed, they said, and the overhead continued to climb. Other critics said the gambling operation was poorly run.

Concerns about money were constant throughout the country, prompting some performers, if they had the clout, to demand their fees up front. For instance, in May pianist Hazel Scott had refused to perform in Memphis at a benefit for a local church and the Collins Chapel Negro Hospital because the sponsor failed to provide the $1,000 guarantee ahead of time. *Sepia,* June 1954, p. 39. Keter Betts and Ed Thigpen interviews.

176 *"If you don't":* Keter Betts interview, October 21, 2002. Keter remembered the union official's name as Elmer Fain.

177 **a black eye:** Keter Betts interviews; Slappy White interview, Haskins papers; Ed Thigpen interview, November 25, 2002. Clark Terry interview, Oc-

tober 4, 2002. Charles Walton interviews, especially January 2004. See *California Eagle,* July 8, 1954, pp. 9, 10; July 15, 1954, p. 10, *Los Angeles Sentinel,* July 15, 1954, p. A11, for ads and stories about the Los Angeles club dates.

178 **Mooney brought in horns:** In addition to Keter Betts, Junior Mance, and Ed Thigpen, the session also included Maynard Ferguson on trumpet, Milton Bernhart on trombone, Joseph "Cook" Koch and Don Lodice on saxophone, and Alton Hendrickson on guitar. Hal Mooney was listed as the leader, earning $82.50 for the three-hour session. The other sidemen each received $41.25. Contract from Los Angeles Local 47 of the American Federation of Musicians. Although discographies put this session on August 3, 1954, the AFM contract shows it to be August 4, from 3:00 to 6:00 P.M. Slappy White interview, Haskins papers.

    After finishing the Oasis engagement, Dinah and the trio performed a one-night gala August 1 at the Elks Club, which was an award show for the area's top disc jockeys.

178 **weeklong swing:** *Cash Box,* August 7, 1954, p. 21.

    At Slim Jenkins Showbar in Oakland, which started her first stop on the Northern California swing, Dinah was the first to perform under the club's new policy of hiring only "big-name" performers.

178 **a jam with Dinah:** Junior Mance interviews; Clark Terry interview, October 4, 2002, Ed Thigpen interview, November 19, 2002.

182 **Showtime at the Apollo:** *New York Amsterdam News,* September 4, 1954, p. 22; *Down Beat,* December 15, 1954, p. 15.

182 **Hucklebuckers:** Dinah in performance courtesy of Ted Ono, Paul Vernon. Among the other numbers Dinah performed were "My Lean Baby," "Such a Night," and "Only a Moment." She changed clothes for the other performances, wearing a satiny evening gown for "Lean Baby," and a sleeveless blouse trimmed with lace and a skirt for the other two numbers. She wore a single strand of white beads and a matching bracelet.

183 **Hear America Swingin':** NBC radio collection of the Library of Congress, RGA 0797 2, September 3, 1954; RWD 4192 A2, September 10, 1954; see also *Tan,* October 1954, p. 13; Gart, *First Pressings,* September 1954, p. 98. Keter Betts interviews; Ed Thigpen interview, November 19, 2002.

184 **"I just can't find":** December 1954 article from an unnamed publication based on an interview shortly after Dinah's thirtieth birthday. Dinah Washington file at the Institute for Jazz Studies, Rutgers University.

184 **Diamond Skating Rink:** The specific East Coast dates after Birdland included an engagement at the Howard Theater in Washington, billed as "Clarence Robinson's Tropicana Review," which also included Slappy White and a women's singing group, the Honey Girls. *Washington Afro-American,* September 14, 1954, p. 6. Dinah was back at the Apollo September 24, with Peg Leg Bates joining the show. *New York Post,* September 24, 1954, p. 50. The Pittsburgh date with saxophonist James Moody was October 4. *Pittsburgh Courier,* September 25, 1954, p. 19.

185 **"I Don't Hurt Anymore":** Mercury 70439 ("Dream").

185 **Blues in Fashion:** Mercury EP-1-3205: "My Song," "Feel Like I Wanna Cry," "Half as Much," "Trouble in Mind."

185 **"Mother":** Robert Grayson interviews.

186 *Comedy Club:* Rose Snow interview, October 28, 2002; photograph of opening at the Comedy Club courtesy of Rose Snow; *Baltimore Afro-American,*
October 30, 1954, pp. 19, 21; November 6, 1954, p. 18; Evelyn Dorsey interview, November 7, 2002.

186 *"Teach Me Tonight":* Mercury 70407 ("Wishing Well"). Discographies have
put this recording date on November 2, 1954, in New York, but that is
probably a week too early. Dinah and the trio were booked at the Comedy
Club in Baltimore for a week that began November 1, and the November 6
Baltimore Afro-American made reference to their being in town beyond November 1.

187 *DeCastro Sisters: Down Beat,* December 29, 1954, p. 5.

188 *Pacific Northwest:* The end-of-the-year tour was announced in the November 20, 1954, *Billboard* (p. 18), which described the route as heading
south until December and then going to the Midwest. Keter Betts remembered stops in Vancouver, Seattle, and Spokane. The group stopped in Denver December 13, 1954, to play one night at the Rainbow Ballroom,
probably on the way back to Chicago. *Rocky Mountain News,* December 12,
1954, p. 51; December 13, 1954, p. 77. *Billboard* reported the participation
of the Honeytones December 11, 1954, p. 47.

188 *"Mama, Mama":* Chicago Defender, December 4, 1954, p. 16, noting Dinah
filling in for an ailing Ruth Brown. Brown, *Miss Rhythm,* pp. 104–05; 246–47;
Ruth Brown interview, July 2002.

189 *"we didn't get home":* Alfreda and Farris Kimbrough interviews; information about Dinah offstage from a December 1954 article, "The Marrying
Kind," from an unnamed magazine, Dinah Washington file at the Institute
for Jazz Studies, Rutgers University.

190 *the Honeytones: Louisville Defender,* December 16, 1954, p. 14. Tickets for
the New Year's Eve show were $1.50 per person in advance, $2.00 at the
door. Table reservations were 50 cents extra per person; Eloise Hughes interviews.

191 *holiday gift:* "Teach Me Tonight" entered the *Billboard* chart December 18,
1954, and stayed on the sales and jukebox tallies for two months. It entered the *Cash Box* "R&B Top 15" the same week and stayed there two
months.

In the year-end *Cash Box* tally, Dinah was third on the "Best R&B Female
Artist" tally behind Ruth Brown and Faye Adams.

Billboard ran its disc jockey poll November 13, and in the R&B category,
which mixed female and male vocalists, Dinah was sixteenth of twenty-
five in the list of deejays' favorite artists. Ruth Brown was number one.
Dinah barely made the readers' poll in *Down Beat*'s tally for 1954, garnering
eighteen votes, three above the minimum. Ella Fitzgerald was first, with
1,093 (December 20, 1954, p. 6). *Metronome* stopped polling vocalists, re-
stricting its year-end voting to instrumentalists.

12 · Much More Than a Blues Singer, 1955

192 *"A Foggy Day":* Dinah's first EmArcy release, *After Hours with Miss D*
(MG26032) was issued as a ten-inch LP and later a twelve-inch LP
(MG36028). There were also two EPs, 1-6054 and 1-6055.

193 *"How come":* Bobby Shad interview courtesy of the Shad family and Derrick Ray.

193 *smiling and hands outstretched:* New York Amsterdam News, January 29, 1955, p. 24; see also *Billboard,* December 11, 1954, p. 47; *Variety,* January 19, 1955, p. 61. "Warbler has her usual excellent act," the review said in the part devoted to Dinah. "Unfortunately, there has been so much singing prior to her closing spot that the audience understandably is a bit tired of ballads."

194 *Joe Glaser:* Keter Betts interview; Ann Littles interviews; Shad interview courtesy of the Shad family/Derrick Ray; Molly Shad interview, July 21, 2003; Joe Glaser obituary, *New York Times,* June 8, 1969, p. 92.

195 *"That's All I Want":* Mercury 70537. The flip side was "You Stay on My Mind." *Billboard,* February 5, 1955, p. 45; *Cash Box,* January 29, 1955, p. 30. Both magazines, but *Cash Box* in particular, received new records from the labels before their official release dates in the hope of getting good advance publicity.

196 *"I was in a bad marriage":* Junior Mance interview, August 15, 2001.

197 **Dinah Jams:** EmArcy 36000. *Billboard,* February 5, 1955, p. 22; *Cash Box,* January 29, 1955, p. 18; *Down Beat,* March 9, 1955, p. 18.

198 *Steve Allen:* NBC Masterbooks for February 15, 1955, at the Library of Congress Television–Motion Picture Collection. Dinah appeared right after an up-and-coming white singer, Andy Williams, who did two songs. According to the production notes, his second number, "Here Comes That Dream," was lip-synced.

198 *Quincy Jones:* Jones interview, December 19, 2003; Jones, *Q,* pp. 102–04; see also Jones comments on a compilation *This Is My Story,* Vols. 1 and 2, Mercury 20788, 20789; Ann Littles interviews; Buddy Collette interview, Haskins papers.

Before the March recording session in New York, Dinah played a few days in Toronto at the Colonial Tavern, *Cash Box,* February 26, 1955, p. 34; March 5, 1955, p. 30.

200 *David Heard:* Dave Heard interviews; LaRue Manns interview, Haskins papers.

200 *a sad moment:* Carnegie Hall program courtesy of Carnegie Hall archives. Thirty-nine musicians were listed in the program—a who's who of jazz that included Dizzy Gillespie, Stan Getz, Billie Holiday, Lena Horne, Sarah Vaughan, Mary Lou Williams, and Lester Young.

201 *session on the 28th:* Although discographies put the April 28, 1955, session in New York, it took place at Capitol Studios in Hollywood from 3:00 to 6:00 P.M. Wynton Kelly did not play. Isaac Royal filled in with Keter Betts and Jimmy Cobb. The five sax players were Skeets Herfurt, Wilbur Schwartz, Georgie Auld, Babe Russin, and Mort Friedman. The three trumpeters were Conrad Gozzo, Maynard Ferguson, and Zeke Zarchy. Simon Zentner, Ed Kusby, and Joe Howard played trombone. Barney Kessel played the guitar. Local 47 AFM contract, from the Local 47 archives. "I Hear Those Bells"/"The Cheat," Mercury 70653.

202 *"green things":* Jimmy Cobb interview; Keter Betts interviews; Toots Thielemans interview, January 30, 2003.

202 *Berkeley: Variety,* May 11, 1955, p. 47.

203 *"Rock 'n' Roll Revue":* On her way back from California and before the Boston performance, Dinah stopped in Chicago to see the family and play again at the Trianon May 13; *Chicago Defender,* May 14, 1955, p. 29. She was in Detroit the next night to perform at Olympia Stadium as part of the *Pittsburgh Courier*'s concert to honor its annual music competition. *Detroit Free Press,* May 14, 1955, p. 12; *Michigan Chronicle,* May 14, 1955 p. 12, *Pittsburgh Courier,* May 21, 1955, p. 16; *Boston Globe,* May 21, 1955, p. 12; *Down Beat,* June 1, 1955, p. 15, which talks about other dates for the revue.

204 *"I Diddle":* Mercury 70600 ("If It's the Last Thing I Do"). *Cash Box* April 9, 1955, p. 28. In its review, the magazine said: "a cutie of middle tempo that has the gal bouncing along to the aid of handclaps and strong ork support . . . A captivating jump that should pull in large sales and possibly Dinah's most impressive push into the pop department. The flip, 'If It's the Last Thing I Do,' is a slow pretty ballad that Miss Washington does straight and with proper emotional projection. . . ."

The *Cash Box* rhythm and blues page captured a genre in transition. Dinah's new record was noted along with the latest from Atlantic star LaVern Baker. Like Mercury with Dinah, Atlantic had packaged a conventional tune, "That's All I Need," with a novelty number like "I Diddle"— here "Bop-Ting-A-Ling." But also on the page in an equally prominent spot were Bo Diddley's breakout hits, "Bo Diddley" and "I'm a Man."

See also Ralph J. Gleason's "Perspective" column in *Down Beat,* March 9, 1955, p. 18, for his view on the changes in rhythm and blues.

204 *"You can say that again":* Dinah Washington—Queen of the Juke Box, BJH 310; *Variety,* July 13, 1955, p. 53. The magazine's reviewer had taken in another of the Birdland shows that included a different eclectic set: Dinah's two weather songs, "Come Rain or Come Shine" and "A Foggy Day" and the crowd-pleasing "TV Is the Thing This Year." He singled out the trio for giving Dinah "fine support."

205 **Newport:** Newport Jazz Festival, July 16, 1955, from Voice of America collection at the Library of Congress, RGA 0016 (RWD 5003 A3-B1); *Billboard,* July 30, 1955, p. 15; *Variety,* July 20, 1955, p. 44; *Down Beat,* August 24, 1955, p. 13, *Metronome,* September 1955, p. 15.

For information on the first Newport festival, see *Down Beat,* June 16, 1954, p. 1; August 25, 1954, p. 2.

206 *"Wynton played":* Keter Betts interviews.

207 *"Simultaneous":* Liner notes from *For Those in Love,* EmArcy MG 36011. See also *Billboard,* June 25, 1955, p. 24, which said, "Miss D continues to surprise and to amaze." It predicted the record would appeal to jazz, pop, and R&B fans. *Cash Box* said, "The sensational Miss Dinah Washington is in rare form" (June 18, 1955, p. 20); *Down Beat,* July 13, 1955, p. 32; *Metronome,* October 1955, p. 39.

209 *"Happy Birthday":* Marva Scott-Starks interview, November 11, 2002.

209 *"Received a call":* *Michigan Chronicle,* August 6, 1955, p. 11; *Chicago Defender,* August 20, 1966, p. 27; *Chicago Defender,* July 30, 1955, p. 14; Beatrice Buck interview, July 8, 2002.

210 **stand in the back:** *Jet,* February 17, 1955, p. 4.

211 **New Orleans:** *Louisiana Weekly,* July 1, 1955, p. 16; August 19, 1955, p. 3B; Information about Curley's Neutral Corner from the 1955 and 1956 New

Orleans city directories. The first band to play at Curley's was the Dixieland Knock-Outs led by the young trumpeter Al Hirt; Jimmy Cobb interview; Keter Betts interviews.

212 **Moulin Rouge:** In addition to the articles cited, see *Sepia,* February 1955, p. 17, and *Our World,* August 1955, p. 24, for articles on the Moulin Rouge. The Moulin Rouge Preservation Association put out a brochure about the storied hotel in 1966 that includes a history and several photos. It is on file at the Nevada State Museum and Historical Society in Las Vegas.

214 **Joe Davis:** Keter Betts interviews; see also *Ebony,* November 1956, p. 40.

216 **"You got to give me":** Dinah's joke from *The Complete Dinah Washington,* vol. 4. The songs that Dinah recorded at this session featured the central themes of romance gone awry and broken hearts. "You Might Have Told Me"/"I'm Lost Without You Tonight" (Mercury 70728) were released as a single right away.

217 **Mocambo:** Keter Betts interviews; *Jet,* October 20, 1955, p. 60.

218 **"She's slimmed down":** *San Francisco Chronicle,* October 15, 1955, p. 7; October 22, 1955, p. 7.

218 **Johnny Mathis:** Keter Betts interviews; Ann Littles interviews; Slappy White interview, Haskins papers. See also www.johnnymathis.com, official Web site, biography section.

218 **Rock 'n' Roll Revue:** *Chicago Defender,* October 1, 1955, p. 36, as an example of the ads for the *Rock 'n' Roll Revue.* The ad described the movie as "Breezy—Bouncy—Screen Treat! Rhythm Packed and Star Studded."

219 **"I Concentrate on You":** Mercury 70694 ("Not Without You"). *Billboard,* October 1, 1955, p. 70.

219 **mix of standards:** The personnel on the November 11 session, likely the same for the other days, were Hal Mooney, leader; David Klein, orchestra manager; William R. Guy, Ray S. Linvi, Mannie Klein, trumpet; Si Zentner, Frank Rosolino, Joe Howard, trombone; Gus Birona, Herb Geller, Georgie Auld, Mort Friedman, saxophone; Barney Kessel, Tony Rizzi, guitar; Wynton Kelly, piano; Keter Betts, bass; Jimmy Cobb, drums. The total for the musicians' fees was $877.80.

See rhythm and blues pages in *Billboard,* November 26, 1955, and December 7, 1955.

220 **Sahara:** *Las Vegas Review Journal,* October 6, 1952, for its opening; October 4, 1959, for a special seventh anniversary celebration. *Las Vegas Sun Magazine,* June 3, 1979, p. 6. The article on the Sahara was part of a series, "The Great Resorts of Las Vegas—How They Began!" See also *Las Vegas Review Journal,* October 6, 1952, pp. 13, 20, 24, for the opening of the Sahara; November 22, 1955, p. 11, for ads about Dinah's performance. LaRue Manns interview, Haskins papers; Bob Bailey interview, September 12, 2001.

Contrary to some accounts, Dinah was not the first black woman to perform on the Strip. Lena Horne had played Las Vegas nine years earlier. For the demise of the Moulin Rouge see *Jet,* October 27, 1955, p. 18.

221 **"all he had":** *Billboard,* October 1, 1955, p. 38.

In the year-end *Cash Box* poll Dinah was second in the female rhythm and blues category behind Ruth Brown. She had 51,547 votes, Dinah, 39,748. December 3, 1955, p. 6.

13 · "Hot, Fresh and Invigorating," 1956

222 *"Jazz is a touchy subject":* Down Beat, January 25, 1956, pp. 14, 18–19.

222 *"Big Show of 1956":* Michigan Chronicle, January 14, 1956, p. 16. Frank Brown's Big Show of 1956 was at the Graystone Ballroom in Detroit Monday, January 16. It was a concert and dance over five hours, 8:30 P.M. to 1:30 A.M. The Toledo show a few days later at the Sports Arena was a concert for only three hours. Washington Afro-American, January 24, 1956, p. 6.

"I Just Couldn't Stand It No More"/"The Show Must Go On" (Mercury 70776).

223 *Safari Room:* New Orleans Times-Picayune, February 16, 1956, p. 1; February 17, 1956, p. 12; Dinah on Joe Glaser, Tan, May 1956, p. 27.

When Lionel Hampton played a concert at the University of Mississippi in Oxford, a bastion of segregation and a training ground for white southern leaders, he was so enthusiastically received that the Daily Mississippian, the student newspaper, published a review on the front page. "Ole Miss was ready for The Hamp. And The Hamp was ready for them," the reviewer wrote. The musicians, however, were not permitted to stay on the campus, and none of them could have attended the school; Keter Betts interview.

224 *"What do I do?":* Beatrice Buck interviews; Michigan Chronicle, February 25, 1956, p. 13, "Zagging with Ziggy" column mentioning Buck's southern trip with Rev. Franklin.

224 *"Jazz vs. Rock 'n Roll":* For more information on the Graystone and its racial policy see Smith, Dancing in the Street.

225 *"Week by week":* Cash Box, May 12, 1956, p. 56; Down Beat, May 30, 1956, p. 12, for Billy Taylor.

225 **The Tonight Show:** NBC Masterbooks, Library of Congress Television–Motion Picture Collection.

"Let's Get Busy"/"Let's Go Get Around Together" (Mercury 70833).

226 *Herzl Auditorium:* Chicago Defender, April 16, 1956, pp. 5, 14.

226 *"Cat on a Hot Tin Roof":* Mercury 70868 ("The First Time") was released the week of May 12, 1955.

227 *"We met":* Gordon Austin interview, Haskins papers.

227 *"I'm Patti Austin":* Patti Austin interview, Haskins papers; Austin interview, September 10, 2003; New York Amsterdam News, May 5, 1956, p. 15, for the Apollo ad that includes "The Princess"—Patti Austin.

Austin recalled that Sammy Davis, Jr., had been rehearsing his show at the Apollo the night she first sang with Dinah and asked the Austins to let her sing on his show.

There were other occasional problems with being a child star. Jet reported July 12, 1956 (p. 65), that Patti—described as Dinah's protegée—was scratched from a July 14 date on the CBS-TV Stage Show because she was too young for a work permit. But she was able to do her song and dance routine by the fall on another network show, Star Time, before she signed her RCA contract. Jet, October 18, 1955, p. 59.

Patti first made the R&B top fifty list in 1969 with the single for United Artists, "Family Tree." She made her debut LP, End of the Rainbow, in 1976 for the CTI label and made two more after that. She made several other albums over the next twenty-five years for a variety of labels and continued to perform live throughout the United States and overseas.

228 *the Reverend Russell Roberts: Sepia,* September 1956, pp. 43–47.

229 *Pete Buck: Jet,* April 19, 1956, pp. 44, 63. The magazine quoted Dinah saying, "While I was getting a new love, I got a new pianist too." *Jet* said that Kenny Drew was replacing Wynton Kelly. This is incorrect, according to discographies and other information about Dinah's work through the rest of 1956. Keter Betts did not remember any time Wynton was not with the trio except for his stint in the army.

230 *"I'm through":* Beatrice Buck interviews; Ann Littles interviews; *Michigan Chronicle,* May 19, 1956, p. 13; May 26, 1956, p. 17; *Ebony,* November 1956, p. 41. This is a feature on Dinah that alludes to the Detroit incident.

232 *"square meal": Cleveland Call & Post,* June 2, 1956, p. 7C; June 9, 1956, p. 1D.

232 *"Dinah has not lost":* Ann Littles interviews; LaRue Manns interview, Haskins papers; *New York Amsterdam News,* May 5, 1956, p. 16.

233 *"Bosom Secrets of Women": Sepia,* May 1956, pp. 5–8. The four-page article focused entirely on women and their bodies and was filled with pictures of celebrities in strapless gowns showing various amounts of cleavage. The only noncelebrities were five models, pictured on the first page and shot from above so that the view was straight down the front of their dresses. Ella Fitzgerald, dynamic but coolly professional on stage, was shown in an off-the-shoulder dress just at the moment the left strap slid down her arm to reveal more skin than she showed in public, onstage or off-. The picture of Dinah was comparatively tasteful—a three-year-old photo of her in a strapless appliquéd dress that had been one of her publicity shots. The caption was the written equivalent of a leer: "King size Queen: Married four times, she proves her claim, 'the bigger you are, the harder they fall.' " It was not clear whether this was Dinah's comment and if so whether she had made it for the article or in some other context.

233 *"Okay, Juanita":* Fox, *Showtime at the Apollo,* p. 185.

234 *threw Ann a party: Kansas City Call,* June 22, 1956, p. 9; see also Haskins, *Queen of the Blues,* LaRue Manns picture; Ann Littles interviews.

234 *Budland:* Dinah was in Chicago for more than a month, opening at Budland the first time on June 26, 1956, for a week, returning July 18 for another eight days, and then coming back for a third time for five days starting July 31. Slappy White joined her on this engagement, which was billed as an early birthday celebration. *Chicago Defender,* June 30, 1956, pp. 14–15; July 14, 1956, p. 14; July 21, 1956, p. 14; July 27, 1956, p. 12; July 28, 1956, p. 12; Farris Kimbrough interviews. See also Pruter, *Doowop: The Chicago Scene,* p. 14.

235 *"slim, trim": San Francisco Chronicle,* August 5, 1956, p. 11; August 11, 1956, p. 7; *Los Angeles Sentinel,* August 9, 1956, p. 14.

If Dinah read Schaefer's column, she might have cringed that he referred to her as "wearing a slim, trim size 14 evening gown." As Ann Littles knew, Dinah was conscious of dress sizes, and if she had lost weight, she was probably down to a size 10.

The most recent *Cash Box* R&B disc jockey poll (July 14, 1956, p. 28) was confirmation of *Chronicle* columnist Hal Schaefer's observation that Dinah's weight loss had not diminished her singing. She was third in the most pro-grammed female vocalist tally, right behind Ruth Brown and LaVern Baker.

235 *"A new small sized Dinah":* Los Angeles Sentinel, August 16, 1956, p. 14; Au-gust 23, 1956, p. 17; August 30, 1956, p. 16; California Eagle, August 23, 1956, p. 9; August 30, 1956, p. 9.

The August 1956 Sepia had a different take on the whole appearance issue, devoting its cover story to the issue of skin color—"There's No Heaven Up North—The Real Truth About Dark Negroes." Sarah Vaughan, who was on the cover, and Eartha Kitt were featured prominently as ex-amples of dark-skinned entertainers who had done well.

236 *"Tristan and Isolde":* Jet, September 27, 1956, p. 46; see also September 13, 1956, p. 31, for bathing suit picture.

236 *"Happy Birthday":* Los Angeles Sentinel, September 6, 1956, p. 15.

237 *Disneyland:* Pictures of Dinah and her sons at Disneyland, courtesy of Ann Littles; Ebony, November 1956; Keter Betts interviews; Ann Littles inter-views.

237 *Los Angeles Cavalcade of Jazz:* Los Angeles Sentinel, August 23, 1956, p. 16. The other acts on the bill, all from the Los Angeles area, were the Chuck Higgins Orchestra, Bo Rhambo, the Dots, and Jerry Grey and His Orchestra.

The presence of Little Richard—born Richard Wayne Penniman and raised on church singing in Macon, Georgia—was telling, suggesting that rock 'n' roll was popular enough to drown out its critics. Earlier in the year, self-proclaimed white supremacists in the South sought to ban the music, arguing that it was a tool of integrationists. Asa Carter of Birmingham, Al-abama, head of the North Alabama White Citizens Council, argued that the integrationists were using rock 'n' roll as a means of "pulling the white man down to the level of the Negro" and "to undermine the morals of the youth of our nation." He called the music "sexualistic, unmoralistic and the best way to bring young people of both races together." Down Beat, May 2, 1956, p. 7.

See also Jet, August 2, 1956, p. 58, "Dixie Racists Call It 'Savage'; Inte-grated Teens Call It Crazy."

238 *"Her new figure":* St. Louis Argus, September 28, 1956, p. 22. Dinah was on the bill with local musician Eddie Johnson and his band.

238 *"Losing 40 pounds":* The Call, Kansas City, August 24, 1956, p. 9; Novem-ber 2, 1956, p. 1.

239 *Bowery Bank Building:* LaRue Manns interviews, September 8, 1985, March 23, 1986, Haskins papers; Farris Kimbrough interviews, 2002–2003.

While it is correct that Dinah moved out of the Theresa and into the Bowery Bank Building sometime in the summer of 1956, there are some discrepancies about when and how the move took place and when George and Bobby moved to New York. LaRue said in a 1985 interview for the Haskins book that she helped Dinah move into the Bowery Building July 15, 1956, and that they left for California July 18 until September 14. Con-temporaneous information about Dinah's engagement shows that this is not exactly right. Dinah could have come back to New York for a day or two between engagements at Budland in Chicago, but she did not finish there until the first week in August. She wasn't in San Francisco until Au-gust 6, where she and the trio opened the next day at the Blackhawk.

In an interview on March 23, 1986, LaRue said she had been in Chicago helping Alice take care of the children when Dinah flew to sing at an affair for her mother and told LaRue to have the kids packed so that they could all go back to New York with her. Dinah was in Chicago April 22 to sing for an American Boys Commonwealth Club benefit that included Alice, and it could be that LaRue was talking about this event. That would mean that Dinah took her sons back to New York before the school year was out and while she was still living in her apartment at the Theresa Hotel. Though Dinah was in Chicago the last week in June and most of July, she did not go back in August or early September because she was in California, and George, Bobby, and LaRue were with her. See also *Jet*, November 29, 1956, p. 65.

240 *released another album: Dinah,* EmArcy MG36065, *Cash Box,* May 26, 1956, p. 23; *Down Beat,* July 25 through September 1956 album chart listings.

From *Cash Box:* "Here's a waxing where the vocals by Dinah Washington, the arrangements of Hal Mooney and material from the evergreen library fall perfectly into place. Dinah, whose singles keep the charts busy, has a vocal expression that can settle firmly on a blues type number like 'Goodbye' or react with vitality on an oldie like 'There'll Be a Jubilee.' The arrangements of Hal Mooney superbly meet each occasion. . . . But the plot still revolves around Dinah and how expertly it does. . . ."

Ella Fitzgerald had done a well-received version of "Sunday Kind of Love" in 1947, and the song reemerged six years later as a favorite of doo-wop groups.

241 *first appearance:* "Soft Winds"/"Tears to Burn," Mercury 70906.

242 *"Oh, it was emotional":* Keter Betts interview, January 20, 2003. The band probably stopped in Chicago on their way back to New York. The October 10, 1956, *Defender* (p. 15) ran a picture of Dinah visiting a club on Oakwood Boulevard to hear sax player Johnny Griffin. Her offstage outfit was striking—a dark dress with a white shawl collar accentuated by a large tassel.

243 *domino effect:* Jimmy Cobb interviews; see the Tom Lord discography for specific information about Wynton Kelly and Jimmy Cobb.

243 *national exposure: Jet,* November 15, 1956, p. 66, citing the Robert Q. Lewis CBS radio show; NBC Masterbooks.

244 *Storyville: Boston Globe,* November 22, 1956, p. 54; *Chicago Defender,* November 19, 1956, p. 23.

Prior to the week in Boston, Dinah played at Basin Street in New York on a bill with Gene Krupa, though it is not clear what personnel she used on either date.

244 **Bandstand U.S.A.:** *Variety,* December 5, 1956, p. 60. *Bandstand U.S.A.* was produced by bandleader Tommy Reynolds, and *Variety* said the program provided "a potent outlet both for the jazz spots and combos. Part of a recent marked growth in the number of jazz clubs is credited to the Mutual show for its promotional boost to the jazz market as a whole." Among the clubs featured on the show were the Blue Note in Philadelphia, the Patio Lounge in Washington, D.C., the Red Hill Inn in Pennsauken, New Jersey, and Café Bohemia in Greenwich Village.

Though Dinah's backing band wasn't publicized, she might have convinced Milt Hinton and Jimmy Crawford to make this trip with her given that they were in the studio with her right before the engagement. Hinton was also scheduled for another two-day session with Dinah December 4–5 in New York.

245 **"a 100-proof bonded antidote":** *Dinah Washington in the Land of Hi-Fi,* EmArcy 36073. *Down Beat,* December 12, 1956, p. 21. In its review, *Billboard* (November 24, 1956, p. 20) pointedly noted that Dinah "ignores her 'Queen of the Blues' tag in this album but the results are superior just the same." The magazine even complimented EmArcy on the picture it chose for the cover.

Cash Box also reviewed the album, giving it glowing praise in the December 23, 1956, issue (p. 31): "Her ringing tones always make an exciting hi-fi experience and on this EmArcy issue, the stylist makes the visit a romp. She belts engagingly through the usually sentimental 'Our Love Is Here to Stay,' and stays sentimental with the usual sentimental 'Say It Isn't So.' Whatever the method of handling a song, Miss Washington's voice is always underlined with vitality. . . ."

"All Because of You"/ "To Love and Be Loved," Mercury 71018. *Billboard* (December 22, 1956, p. 44) said "All Because of You" is "a ballad with a strong beat, and she rides it with ease. Her suave vocal style is sharply etched by vocal chorus in the background." Of the flip side, the magazine said it was "a big song that builds to a big climax . . . The singer puts a lot of power in her presentation."

246 **Chatterbox Cafe:** *Cleveland Call & Post,* December 15, 1956, p. 6C; *Chicago Defender,* December 10, 1956, p. 18.

246 **8125 South Vernon:** Trust documents from the Cook County, Illinois, Recorder of Deeds, Book 54399, p. 498, December 20, 1956. The property had been owned previously by Hans and Ina Gustafson.

Jet alluded to the purchase in a February 21, 1957, item: "Dinah Washington's new manager is Brooklyn attorney Harold Lovette, who has put her on a budget of $50 weekly and is investing her money in Chicago apartment houses" (p. 63).

14 · "You've Got to Lay It on Charisma," 1957

248 **"she's just too much":** Undated Eddie Chamblee interview, Haskins papers; Gourse, *Louis's Children,* pp. 226–27; *Washington Afro-American,* February 23, 1957, p. 1; *Ebony,* March 1964, pp. 140–51.

249 **Dinah's busy schedule:** *New York Age,* January 12, 1957, p. 23; *Variety,* January 23, 1957, p. 49, mentioning Pep's; *Detroit Free Press,* January 25, 1957, p. 6; *Michigan Chronicle,* January 26, 1957, section 2, p. 5.

Variety reviewed the Apollo show January 15, 1957, p. 63: "Dinah Washington, the blues singer, takes over the Apollo stage before the curtain, and in real pro fashion gives the vaude layout a smart off-the-beat lift. . . . Miss Washington, using a portable mike, takes command with a blues songalog. She has poise, a sense of rapport with the audience, a voice which she knows how to use, and arrangements tailored to her need. Result, pleasurable listening."

249 **ailing Ella Fitzgerald:** *New York Amsterdam News,* February 2, 1957, p. 11; *Cash Box,* February 9, 1957, p. 40: "From what we hear Dinah and Ruth

were sensational and while the management regretted the absence of Ella they were elated with the way the two gals sold themselves." Nat King Cole and Count Basie were also on the bill. Abyssinian benefit, *Billboard,* February 2, 1957, p. 24; *Tan,* May 1957, p. 65.

250 **Molly loved it:** Bobby Shad interview; Molly Shad interviews, June, July 2003.

250 **the evening of the 23rd:** Details on Dinah's marriage to Eddie Chamblee come from several sources: *Washington Afro-American,* February 23, 1957, p. 1; March 2, 1957, p. 13; *New York Amsterdam News,* March 2, 1957, p. 13; *Philadelphia Tribune,* March 19, 1957, p. 5; *Jet,* March 7, 1957; *Baltimore Afro-American,* March 2, 1957, p. 2; Robert Grayson, May 2, 2003; Molly Shad interviews, May 19, 20, 2003; Application for license, #409631, for Ruth Jones and Eddie Chamblee, issued February 23, 1957, District of Columbia Superior Court, Family Division, Marriage Bureau.

252 **"When we got back to the hotel room":** Eddie Chamblee interview, Haskins papers; Gourse, *Louis's Children,* p. 231; Farris Kimbrough interviews; Ruth Bowen interview, June 2, 2003; Toni Brazington interview, October 16, 2003.

252 **Zardi's:** *California Eagle,* February 28, 1957, p. 10; March 7, 1957, p. 10; *Los Angeles Sentinel,* February 28, 1957, p. 7; *California Eagle,* March 14, 1957, p. 1; *Los Angeles Sentinel,* March 14, p. 1; *New York Amsterdam News,* March 23, 1957, p. 1; *Birmingham World,* March 23, 1957, p. 1.

253 **"It's true":** *Billboard,* March 23, 1957, p. 23.

254 **Dinah gave Eddie a kiss:** *Jet,* March 21, 1957, p. 61.

254 **up to San Francisco:** See also *San Francisco Chronicle,* March 16, 1957, p. 9. Besides Eddie Chamblee, Dinah's musicians at the Blackhawk were Sonny Clark, piano, Jimmy Rowser, bass, and Arthur Edgehill on drums. *Oakland Tribune,* March 31, 1957, p. 12B.

256 **"Mister Kelly's is kind of":** Slappy White interview, Haskins papers; Dinah's comments, *Tan,* September 1957, p. 58.

Between California and Chicago, Dinah, Eddie, and his group stopped in Denver to play at the Rainbow Theater May 1. Eddie was given separate billing—"Dinah Washington plus Eddie Chamblee Orchestra." Although Dinah liked playing Birdland in New York and considered Morris Levy a good friend, for some reason she was not part of the Birdland Stars of '57 that the club had put together and who, by coincidence, were coming to Denver May 3. The Birdland show this year featured Billy Eckstine, Count Basie with Joe Williams, Sarah Vaughan, and Jeri Southern. *Rocky Mountain News,* April 21, 1957, p. 48; April 29, 1957, p. 31; *Chicago Sun Times,* May 16, 1957, p. 70.

258 **"Police":** Charles Davis interview, June 12, 2001; Richard Evans interview, April 26, 2001; Dinah at Pep's, *Philadelphia Inquirer,* June 1957, p. 19; *Philadelphia Evening Bulletin,* June 3, 1957, p. 31.

258 **Roberts Show Lounge:** *Chicago Defender,* February 5, 1955, p. 31 for club opening; *Ebony,* June 1956, p. 88.

259 **the Comeback Trail:** *Chicago Defender,* June 6, 1957, p. 18; June 8, 1957, p. 14; *Jet,* June 27, 1957, p. 65.

259 **Cook County Jail:** *Chicago Defender,* June 24, 1957, p. 18.

260 **"I'd be walking":** Herman Roberts interview, April 2, 2001; *Jet,* July 18,

1957, p. 33; for Dinah onstage see *Chicago Defender,* June 18, 1957, p. 19; party after last performance, *Chicago Defender,* July 2, 1957, p. 19.

Dinah's show was typical of a Roberts lineup. In addition to her and Eddie's band, the bill featured Slappy White, DeConge, an exotic dancer, the Roberts Dansations, Dave Green, who sang and played the organ, and Pickney Roberts, who told jokes and also served as the master of ceremonies.

260 *Club Tijuana: Baltimore Afro-American,* July 20, 1957, pp. 20–21; July 27, 1957, p. 12.

261 *"Jazz Under the Stars": New York Age,* August 3, 1957, pp. 16, 17.

261 **The Swingin' Miss D:** Mercury 36104. *Billboard,* September 2, 1957, p. 23: "Swingin' is correct. Dinah's outstanding technical equipment and quality is matched to a set of swinging modern arrangements by Quincy Jones. The material comprises great show tunes as 'They Didn't Believe Me,' 'Makin' Whoopee,' some Latin-flavored standards as 'Caravan' and 'Perdido,' etc. Knowledgable jocks and buyers will be especially interested in the instrumentation. It's a big band with a flock of class musicians, and dealers' clerks should be aware of this fact. The liner note material is very informative in this regard." Quincy Jones interview, December 19, 2003.

262 *return to the Apollo: Variety,* September 18, 1957, p. 54: "Vet songstress, backed by Eddie Chamblee's band, does a batch of numbers from one of her albums tagged *Swingin' Miss D.* Sparkplug of the session, Miss Washington can do no wrong here whether she's warbling 'Teach Me to Love,' or dueting 'The More I See You' with Chamblee. She also demonstrates her versatility by thumping out an instrumental piece on the piano accompanied by Chamblee's sax. She wins deserved plaudits."

264 *"I want to be a mother": New York Age,* October 2, 1957, p. 21; *Baltimore Afro-American,* November 9, 1957, p. 1; *Tan,* September 1957, p. 58; Robert Grayson interview.

266 *Eddie's former wife: Chicago Defender,* May 15, 1957, p. 3; *Jet,* May 30, 1957, p. 20.

267 **DuPont Show of the Month:** Among the other performers with Dinah on the September 29, 1957, *DuPont Show* were Louis Armstrong, Diahann Carroll, Lizzie Miles, Mahalia Jackson, Stubby Kaye, Carol Channing, Peggy Lee, Eddie Arnold, and Julie Andrews. Video courtesy of the Hagley Museum, Special Collections; *New York Amsterdam News,* August 3, 1957, p. 12; comments on rehearsal, *Toronto Daily Star,* March 21, 1959, section 2, p. 1.

268 *Nat King Cole: Jet,* April 26, 1956, p. 60; see also *Michigan Chronicle,* April 21, 1956, p. 16, for commentary. Louis Armstrong, *Jet,* October 3, 1957, pp. 6–9.

269 *racial awareness:* Norman Granz, Dave Brubeck, *Jet,* September 26, 1957, p. 61; Morris Levy, "Birdland Stars," *New York Amsterdam News,* October 12, 1957, p. 12; *Variety,* September 26, 1956, p. 1, Leonard Feather, *Jet,* October 17, 1957.

A reminder of the barriers that still existed came from Louisiana. *Jet* reported October 24, 1957 (p. 62), that Barbara Ann Remo, a twelve-year-old black girl from Baton Rouge, was unable to appear with the New Orleans Symphony Orchestra even though she won a statewide audition because of the state law banning interracial activities. She was given a $50 prize instead.

See also *Variety,* December 19, 1956, p. 58, "Frisco Columnist Raps White Tooters for Nixing Merger with Negro Local." The short article discusses Ralph Gleason's *San Francisco Chronicle* column criticizing the white Local 669 of the American Federation of Musicians for voting down a proposed consolidation with the black local. Gleason noted that "mixed groups" appear everywhere and that "jazz clubs, theatres, recording studios, accept musicians, by and large, on their ability and their drawing power and not on their color. . . . The action has been taken now and it is something to be regretted. Unless musicians open their eyes as well as their ears, music will lose its place as a force for human rights."

271 **Jack Wilson:** Jack Wilson interviews, June 28, 29, 2001; earlier interview, Haskins papers. Julian Priester interview, March 12, 2001.

272 **Town Hill:** *New York Amsterdam News,* November 2, 1957, p. 12.

272 **"the mink and white tie set":** *Hue,* November 1957, pp. 54–56.

272 **"No, I'm not":** *New York Age,* October 2, 1957, p. 21; *Dinah Washington Sings the Best in* Blues (Mercury 20247), *Cash Box,* October 12, 1957, p. 34.

274 **"The joint was packed":** *Jet,* December 19, 1957, p. 43; January 2, 1958, p. 49. This story explained that "the real reason" Dinah missed the show at Pep's was because of her son's illness.

274 **"Dinah's Last Man":** *Baltimore Afro-American,* December 3, 1957, p. 1 of magazine, five-star edition.

274 **Brass Rail:** *Milwaukee Journal,* November 22, 1957, p. 1, "The Green Sheet"; Charles Walton interviews.

275 **"I grew quickly to respect her":** James Slaughter interview, April 2, 2001.

277 **veterans hospital:** *Jet,* December 26, 1957, p. 58; January 9, 1958, p. 51.

277 **"It took four people":** *Sepia,* December 1959, p. 12.

15 · "Ah, I Got You," 1958

278 **shake dancer:** *Jet,* January 23, 1958, p. 33. Moms Mabley was also on the bill with her and Eddie Chamblee's band.

279 **white jazz audience:** *Down Beat,* December 26, 1957, p. 21. In contrast to the jazz poll, Dinah had not registered in *Cash Box*'s year-end poll of top female rhythm and blues singers.

279 **Black Orchid:** *Variety,* January 15, 1958, p. 67. Comedian Herkie Styles was also on the bill along with a surprise addition, Slim Gaillard, who *Variety* said "fairly steals the honors with a diverting turn that instantly warms up the house. He is a prepossessing fellow with an amusing line of hipster double talk, impressive songwriting credits, and a pair of enormous hands that help him to cut up in madcap fashion on a variety of instruments."

279 **first anniversary:** *Michigan Chronicle,* February 8, 1958, section 2, p. 5; February 15, 1958, p. 10; March 1, 1958, section 2, pp. 4–5; March 8, 1958, p. 10; Mabel Page interview, May 27, 2003; Ruth Bowen interviews. Dinah actually did two stints at the Frolic. The second, which started the second week in March, paired her with Little Jimmy Scott.

281 **owed her $900:** *Michigan Chronicle,* March 15, 1958, p. 1. The *Chronicle*'s headline was particularly pointed: "Dinah, a Salty Mama Wants $$ Honey." The kicker said "No Frolic at Frolic." *Jet,* March 27, 1958, p. 60.

282 **engagement in Florida:** Though it seemed unusual that Dinah would go

back to New York from Atlanta, Farris Kimbrough said Dinah liked to go back home between jobs even if it was just for a couple of days. Charles Davis, the baritone saxophone player, remembered that the band went from Atlanta to Miami. Interview, June 12, 2001.

282 **Harry Belafonte:** *Baltimore Afro-American,* April 28, 1956, p. 1; July 16, 1957, p. 15.

282 **Sir John:** Bud Ward interview, April 16, 2001.

284 **"I used to meet her":** Farris Kimbrough interviews; King Coleman interview, May 26, 2003.

285 **"Night after night":** Accounts of the fight between Dinah and Eddie come from a number of interviews and news accounts. *Chicago Defender,* April 21, 1958, p. 19; *Miami Times,* April 12, 1958, pp. 3, 5; April 19, 1958, pp. 7, 10; Farris Kimbrough interviews; Julian Priester interview, March 12, 2001; Jody Williams interview, spring 2003.

288 **"I'll decide":** *New York Amsterdam News,* April 19, 1958, p. 16; *Chicago Defender,* April 21, 1958, p. 19; *Jet,* April 24, 1958, p. 58. *Los Angeles Sentinel,* April 24, 1958, p. 12. While the stories said that Dinah had fired Jack Wilson, the piano player, and Paul West, the bass player, that was not the case, according to both men. Paul West, July 20, 2001; Jack Wilson interviews, June 28, 29, 2001.

288 **"I was just exhausted":** Eddie Chamblee interview, Haskins papers; Gourse, *Louis's Children,* p. 231; Farris Kimbrough interviews.

289 **"her sincerity":** Paul West interview, July 20, 2001.

289 **Jacksonville:** Keter Betts interviews; Teddy Washington interview, June 9, 2003; information on the Two Spot, Mason, *African-American Life in Jacksonville,* pp. 47, 71–73; *The Crisis,* January 1942, p. 14; "The James Craddock Enterprise," which is a profile of the original owner of the Two Spot, p. 18; Farris Kimbrough interviews; picture from her photo collection. See also *Jacksonville Journal,* February 7, 1983, p. 1; *Florida Times Union,* January 2, 1992, Section B, p. 1; *Tour of Black Historical Sites, Metropolitan Jacksonville,"* a pamphlet prepared early in 1979 by the Gamma Rho chapter of the Alpha Kappa Sorority, Jacksonville Public Library, Florida Collection.

No doubt it was comforting to see a familiar face April 27 when Dinah went back in the studio in New York. Hal Mooney, who had produced "Wheel of Fortune" and "Trouble in Mind" and a half-dozen other hits, was called in for this session. Four songs were recorded. The arrangements were unusually fussy, though, with a vocal group backing Dinah on three of the tunes. One of them was the novelty "Ring-a My Phone," which Mercury released a few weeks after the session with "Never Again" on the B side (71317). The record didn't get much attention, though "Never Again" showed up briefly on the *Cash Box* pop one hundred at number seventy-four.

291 **she mixed genres:** *Chicago Defender,* June 7, 1958, p. 16; *Variety,* May 21, 1958, p. 72. In its review of the Apollo show, *Variety* said Dinah "delivers a songa-log with impact. Warbler once again proves her versatility by moving from r&r tunes to the blues and tosses in a touch of Latin America. Miss Washington, an accomplished songstress with an easy delivery and poise, scores with 'Crazy Love,' 'Electric Chair,' and winds up with 'Blue Gardenia.' "

Before the Apollo show, Dinah was in Baltimore May 9 to be part of the

"Cavalcade of Jazz" at the city's Coliseum. The publicity for the event still listed her performing with the Eddie Chamblee Band. *Baltimore Afro-American*, May 3, 1958, p. 30.

291 **"I hate men":** *New York Amsterdam News*, May 31, 1958, p. 13.

293 **"eating my cooking":** Farris Kimbrough interviews.

293 **Negro Labor Relations League:** *Chicago Defender*, May 31, 1958, p. 12.

293 **Mahalia Jackson:** *Chicago Defender*, May 28, 1958, p. 18; May 31, 1958, p. 13; *Jet*, March 13, 1958, p. 30; *Jet*, July 31, 1958, p. 65.

294 **"a 15-room house":** *Houston Informer*, June 7, 1958, p. 12; June 14, 1958, p. 12.

294 **Laurel, Mississippi:** Farris Kimbrough interviews, especially June 2, 2003; *Variety*, June 14, 1958, p. 60; Jack Wilson interviews, June 2001, Haskins papers; Paul West interview, July 20, 2001.

295 **"There are certain things":** James Slaughter interview, April 2, 2001. Paul West recalled that Dinah took only a trio on the road with her after the breakup with Eddie, but Charles Davis and Slaughter remember being on the road with her after she and Eddie separated.

296 **Bessie Smith tributes:** *Down Beat* reviewed the three Smith tributes all at once and found the RCA collection with vocals by Ronnie Gilbert, the folksinger with the Weavers, wanting. "I suppose the best thing to say about the Victor collection is that they sent a girl in to do a woman's work," the reviewer wrote. "The situation is almost the reverse on the Dinah Washington set. She sings excellently, with respect and understanding. She adopts the very slow tempos that Bessie Smith favored but remains thoroughly herself. . . . Dinah's way has constant direct reference to gospel singing. Bessie's of course, did not. Perhaps there really was a strong distinction made between the sacred and the secular." The *Down Beat* writer, though, did not care for the accompaniment behind Dinah.

When *Cash* Box reviewed *Dinah Sings Bessie Smith*, EmArcy MG36130, April 19, 1958 (p. 32), the writer was more forgiving: "The Chamblee orchestra supplies a smooth, pleasing background as Miss Washington gives impressive readings of the familiar blues items. . . . Top jazz vocals." LaVern Baker's Bessie Smith tribute was reviewed on the same page in a similar vein.

On May 17 (p. 34), *Cash Box* reviewed *Dinah Washington Sings Fats Waller*, Mercury MG36119. The magazine noted that on this album Dinah was backed by "an all star band conducted by Ernie Wilkins. . . . Miss Washington, one of the best jazz inspired vocalists around, has here a set due for lots of sales action. Stock well."

296 **"two dressmakers":** *Chicago Defender*, June 14, 1958, p. 16.

296 **"Honey, you're ruining the boys":** LaRue Manns interview, Haskins papers.

297 **Dinah and Davis:** Pictures of Dinah with Miles Davis at Newport from Goldblatt, *Newport Jazz Festival: The Illustrated History; Chicago Defender*, July 19, 1958, p. 15, Ziggy Johnson column.

297 **"Are you scared of me?":** Jack Tracy interviews, especially November 18, 2000. *Down Beat*, April 3, 1958, p. 5, for Tracy's farewell column in *Down Beat*.

297 **Dinah took the stage:** The other personnel with Dinah at Newport July 6 were, in addition to Roach, Kelly, and West, Melba Liston, trombone,

Harold Ousley, tenor sax, and Sahib Shihab, baritone sax, on the Bessie Smith tunes. On "All of Me" the band was Roach, Kelly, West, Terry Gibbs, vibraphone, Don Elliott, melophone, and Urbie Green, trombone. Dinah received good if brief notices in reviews of the Newport festival. See *Down Beat*, August 1, 1958, pp. 33–34; *Metronome*, September 1958, p. 17; *Chicago Defender*, July 12, 1958, p. 16; July 18, 1958, p. 58. The *Defender* said Dinah's singing was the "highlight" of the radio broadcast. See also *Sepia*, July 1958, pp. 8–12.

299 **Bermuda:** Paul West interview; Harold Ousley interview, March 12, 2001; Benny Pope interview, July 10, 2001.

300 **"I'm a singer":** *Baltimore Afro-American*, August 23, 1958, p. 1 (late city edition); August 30, 1958, p. 1; *New York Amsterdam News*, August 30, 1958, p. 1. *Variety* (September 8, 1958), the *New York Times* (August 21), and *Jet* (September 4, 1958) also had brief stories about the Baltimore episode.

By coincidence Dinah had found herself in the middle of a dispute between a club owner and local police earlier in the year. In March, she was supposed to play three days in Cleveland at Skateland, which was a new venue for her in the city. The promoter planned an ambitious late night schedule—two shows Friday, March 28, to run from 11:00 P.M. to 3:00 A.M., two shows Saturday, March 29, from midnight to 4:00 A.M., and then Sunday, again from 11:00 P.M. to 3:00 A.M.

Dinah played the first show on the 28th to a big crowd, but when she got ready to go on again shortly after 2:00 A.M., the police, for some inexplicable reason, came in at 2:15 and told everyone they had to leave immediately. They ignored the promoter's protestations that he was allowed to stay open another forty-five minutes. The customers initially refused to leave, screaming at the police with such intensity that the riot squad was called to make sure there was no further disturbance while the crowd exited. *Cleveland Call & Post*, March 22, 1958, p. 58; *Pittsburgh Courier*, April 12, 1958, p. 23.

301 **Newport, Kentucky:** *Variety*, July 30, 1958, p. 110. Messick, *Razzle Dazzle*, pp. 112–14, about Newport; see also Messick, *Syndicate Wife*, especially pp. 116–17.

301 **two extended engagements:** *Chicago Defender*, entertainment pages, October 6, 9, 11, 13, 25, 1958. Dinah and Slappy took time out from Roberts one evening to perform for the annual "Bartenders and Waiters Ball."

302 **Chess Records studio:** Jack Tracy interview, November 18, 2000; *Jet*, November 6, 1958, p. 37.

302 **"bewildering mixture":** *Down Beat*, October 30, 1958, p. 24. *Doodlin,'* EmArcy 36131.

302 **whirlwind late fall:** *Louisiana Weekly*, November 6, 1958; *California Eagle*, November 6, 1958, p. 10, November 13, 1958, p. 9; *Los Angeles Sentinel*, November 6, 1958, p. 3B; *Jet*, December 12, 1958, p. 64; *Variety*, October 22, 1958, p. 62, talking about the Showboat; *Chicago Defender*, December 27, 1958, p. 12. Dinah was backed once again by Red Saunders, and performing with Dinah were the Dyerettes, Pee Wee Crayton, and Freddie Gordon, who was the emcee. Mabel Page interview, May 27, 2000.

303 **a new pink Chrysler:** *Jet*, January 8, 1959, p. 57; January 15, 1959, p. 58; January 22, 1959, p. 33. The magazine said Dinah's coat came from "an ad-

mirer," which was probably Dinah's sly way of saying she got the coat for herself with help either from Mercury or Joe Glaser.

Dinah's presence in the year-end polls reconfirmed her status even though she hadn't had a song on the charts for over two years. In mid-December "Make Me a Present of You" made a brief appearance on the *Billboard* tally, Mercury 71377 ("All of Me"). In the *Down Beat* readers poll (December 5, 1958, p. 25), Dinah was fifteenth of twenty-five. Ella Fitzgerald was first. In *Cash Box* (December 6, 1958, p. 57), Dinah was third on the "Best R&B Female Vocalist" list, behind LaVern Baker and Ruth Brown.

16 · What a Diff'rence a Day Makes, 1959

304 **return to the studio:** *Chicago Defender,* January 14, 1959, p. 19; *Jet,* February 5, 1959, p. 64; *New York Age,* January 31, 1959, p. 16.

Writing about Dinah's stay at Roberts, the *Defender* noted that she was a big draw, having been held over twice, even though it was the holiday time and the city was full of other stars and the fact that she had been at Roberts a few months earlier. "One big thing Dinah has going for her, of course, is the fact that Chicago is a blues town. Give 'em blues and watch the turnstiles click. However, the blues must be of the top variety such as La Washington dishes out. Otherwise the singing becomes just some more vocalizing without much patron appeal. That it must be admitted is the main reason Dinah Washington always clicks in Chicago regardless of how often she appears."

304 **Ernestine Anderson:** Ruth Bowen interviews. *Jet,* February 5, 1959, p. 64; January 9, 1964, pp. 59–60. In an interview for the Haskins book twenty years later, Bowen told a similar story but said it had been Gloria Lynne who went to the Apollo. In Lynne's book, *I Wish You Love: A Memoir,* pp. 108–10, she said Dinah had invited her to sing at the Village Vanguard.

305 **at the Flame:** *Michigan Chronicle,* January 31, 1959, p. 10. Dinah got sick during her stay at the Flame and was treated by Dr. Bob Bennett. Whatever Bennett gave Dinah, Ziggy Johnson joked in his *Chronicle* column, "She should try to get more of it cause she sounded like Lily Pons, good voice and shape." He was referring to the diminutive opera star famous for her coloratura roles (February 7, 1959, p. 13).

New York Amsterdam News, February 7, 1959, p. 17; *Pittsburgh Courier,* February 7, 1959, p. 23. These stories refer to the following dates for Dinah: a concert at Symphony Hall in Boston February 6 and then two concerts on the 7th, an early performance at the Mosque in Newark and then a midnight concert at Carnegie Hall. Saxophonist James Moody, the singer Eddie Jefferson, and Ray Charles were on the bill, too. Dinah and Mulligan's quartet teamed up again later in the month to play the Academy of Music in Philadelphia as part of the "Jazz Showcase" (*Variety,* February 18, 1959, p. 46).

305 **Bobby Shad:** *Billboard,* October 6, 1958, p. 9; October 30, 1958, p. 2; *Chicago Defender,* December 30, 1958, p. 18.

305 **Clyde Otis:** Clyde Otis interview, June 24, 2003; September 25, 2002; see also Escott, "Clyde Otis—Looking Back," *Goldmine,* October 1, 1993, pp. 42–44.

307 **Newport '58:** MG36141; *Tan,* March 1959, p. 11. *Tan* devoted most of a page to the record in its regular monthly feature on new music. It was a complimentary review though not a rave. "As far as most of her fans are concerned, the queen of the blues can do no wrong, vocally speaking," *Tan* said, "and while Dinah may have been finer on other occasions, she here still handles a lyric as no one else quite can."

308 *both shows: Billboard,* March 9, 1959, p. 10; *Variety,* March 11, 1959, p. 74; *Chicago Defender,* March 23, 1959, p. 19; *Variety,* April 8, 1959, p. 60; *Down Beat,* May 28, 1959, p. 45, on Beryl Booker; *New York Amsterdam News,* May 2, 1959, p. 13. Beryl Booker continued to back Dinah at the Vanguard, where she sang three forty-five-minute sets each night. Jazz guitarist Kenny Burrell was also on the bill.

   Dinah got some added exposure on radio when she appeared March 15 on Jackie Robinson's half-hour radio show on WRCA. Known as the *Rheingold Show* because of its sponsor, the show ran from 6:30 to 7:00 P.M. *New York Amsterdam News,* February 21, 1959, p. 14; February 28, 1959, p. 14.

309 *"And just who are you?":* Sepia, February 1964, p. 78.

   The singer Jackie Cain recalled that Dinah was also generous with her dressmaker. Cain, who had first seen Dinah when she was a teenager in Milwaukee and Dinah performed there with Hampton, got to know her when they crossed paths in New York. Cain need some work done on a dress, and Dinah told her whom to call. "It worked out great," Cain said. July 17, 2002, interview.

309 **Here's Duffy:** *Toronto Daily Star,* March 21, 1959, section 2.

310 *"an honest and competent listener":* Down Beat, April 30, 1959, p. 39. "Cry Me a River": Dinah's comment, *The Complete Dinah Washington,* vol. 6.

312 *"She had a great way":* Maynard Ferguson interview, July 22, 2003.

312 *"What a Diff'rence a Day Makes":* Mercury 71435 ("Come on Home"). *Variety,* June 3, 1959, p. 46; June 10, 1959, p. 58.

313 *judo lessons: Jet,* May 7, 1959, p. 42; Robert Grayson interviews; Farris Kimbrough interviews.

314 *"Queen's Jesters":* Variety, May 27, 1959, p. 60, on Pep's date; *New York Age,* June 6, 1959, p. 12; *New York Amsterdam News,* May 23, 1959, p. 14. On the Apollo bill with Dinah were Thelonious Monk, the Axidentals, and Gil Evans. Symphony Sid was the host.

314 *"I went down and spoke":* Ruth Bowen interview, Haskins papers; Bowen interviews.

315 *"I had heard":* In his telling essay about Dinah in *Talking Jazz,* Max Jones remembered that Leonard Feather had handed Dinah a sheet of paper, perhaps with lyrics on it, that she took up on the stand at the BBC studio. "And she announced, before naming her closing number, that Leonard had asked her to do such-and-such a song but she wasn't going to. Possibly this was typical Dinah conduct, too" (p. 273).

   Leonard did not cite that moment in his recollections of the BBC program, saying only that Dinah performed well. Beryl Bryden comment, *Talking Jazz,* p. 275.

319 *Before Dinah left:* Jones, *Talking Jazz,* pp. 265–76; *New Musical Express,* June 19, 1959, p. 6; *Melody Maker,* June 20, 1959, p. 2, p. 9; Leonard Feather interview, Haskins papers.

320 **Known as "Rusty":** *Jet,* January 15, 1959, p. 64; *New York Age,* February 14, 1959, p. 16; Ruth Bowen interviews; Max Jones comments, *Talking Jazz,* p. 275.

Some of the reports about Rusty Maillard described him as "well to do" and coming from a family that owned the property in Harlem that became the Bowery Bank Building. However, this information appears to be incorrect.

321 **"the spiritual guidance":** *Dagens Nyheter,* July 2, 1959. Translation courtesy of the Embassy of Sweden, Washington, D.C.

321 **"more than 250,000 fans":** *Michigan Chronicle,* August 29, 1959, p. 5; *Sepia,* December 1959, pp. 9–12; *Jet,* August 20, 1959, pp. 60–61; *New York Age,* August 9, 1959, p. 1.

321 **"I finally got a hit":** *Billboard, Cash Box,* and *Variety* chart listings for July and August, in particular, *Cash Box,* August 15, 1959, top one hundred page. *Variety,* July 20, 1959, p. 62; August 26, 1959, p. 59. See also Whitburn, *Top Pop Singles, 1955–1993; Cash Box, Pop Singles Charts,* 1950–1993.

322 **Auburn Casino:** *Atlanta Daily World,* July 29, 1959, p. 3. The Auburn Casino featured an eclectic bill. Joining Dinah were Eugene Church, Spo-Dee-Odee, the Pips, and Dan Carmichael and his band. For Detroit and Chicago dates see *Michigan Chronicle,* August 8, 1959, p. 9; August 15, 1959, p. 5; August 22, 1959, p. 5; *Chicago Defender,* August 29, 1959, p. 14. Lois Green dispute, *Baltimore Afro-American,* September 19, 1959, p. 1.

324 **"A shiver":** Wein, *Myself Among Others,* pp. 94–95.

324 **celebration with Rusty:** *Jet,* October 1, 1959, p. 32; *Chicago Defender,* September 26, 1959, p. 15; *Down Beat,* October 29, 1959, p. 46; *New York Amsterdam News,* September 19, 1959, p. 13; October 9, 1959, p. 16.

324 **"Unforgettable":** Mercury 71508 ("Nothing in the World"). *Cash Box,* September 26, 1959, p. 10. The magazine named "Unforgettable" the "Pick of the Week." "The one-time Nat Cole success, 'Unforgettable,' gets that 'What a Diff'rence a Day Makes' touch from the stylist, giving the song a beautiful strong chart come-back. Warm and lovely instrumental setting. 'Nothing in the World' (sometimes a reminder of 'Maybe You'll Be There') receives a similar approach. Might be active."

See *Cash Box* and *Variety* weekly charts for October–November 1959.

324 **"People are talking":** *The Queen,* Mercury MG20439, SR60111. *Billboard,* October 5, 1959 (p. 28), put the album in its "Spotlight Winners of the Week." "The Queen has a package here of much vocal craftsmanship. There are four blues, including 'Trouble in Mind' and 'Back Water Blues' and a number of ballads and sophisticated songs including 'All of Me,' 'I Remember Clifford,' etc. The backing is tastefully smart jazz. For those who are fond of wonderful phrasing and sensitive vocal nuance, here it is."

Cash Box, October 17, 1959 (p. 30), was similarly praiseworthy, designating the album a popular pick of the week. "Tagged the 'Queen of Blues' Miss Washington brings to her pop singing the warmth, earthy passion and soulful expressiveness that she communicates in her blues singing."

325 **Dinah was nominated:** *Billboard,* October 5, 1959, p. 9. The other nominees in the "Best Rhythm and Blues Performance" category were Elvis Presley, "A Big Hunk o' Love"; The Coasters, "Charlie Brown"; Jesse Belvin, "Guess Who"; and Nat King Cole, "Midnight Flyer."

For a brief history of NARAS see the Grammy Web site, www.grammy.com/academy/history. Clyde Otis, *Jet*, June 25, 1959, p. 63.

325 *Joe Zawinul:* Joe Zawinul interview, January 22, 2003; see also *Down Beat*, May 2002, pp. 21–24; Jimmy Rowser interview, September 25, 2002.

326 *Copa Club: Billboard*, October 5, 1959, p. 20; October 12, 1959, p. 20; October 19, 1959, p. 33.

326 *Odessa, Texas:* Joe Zawinal interview, January 22, 2003.

327 *a busy couple of weeks: Michigan Chronicle*, November 14, 1959, pp. 4–5, for Dinah's brief stop in Detroit, which was to open a new ballroom at the 20 Grand Club. The rest of Dinah's schedule from *Cash Box* listings, November 14, 1959, p. 28; November 21, 1959, p. 22; Carnegie Hall program for November 25, 1959, Carnegie Hall Archives. The Carnegie performance was billed as the "Golden Anniversary Sound of Jazz," and headlining the bill was Count Basie and his band. The singer Joe Williams also appeared. Dinah performed with a trio.

327 *police organization: Tan*, June 1959, p. 8.

327 *Basin Street East: New York Amsterdam News*, October 10, 1959, p. 16. Two other acts were on the Basin Street bill when Dinah played, a piano trio headed by the young Chicago artist Ramsey Lewis, and Chubby Jackson's quartet.

328 **What a Diff'rence a Day Makes:** Mercury 60158. *Cash Box* cited the album in its November 21, 1959, issue (p. 44): "The great blues singer has embarked on a new pop career and this is her first LP attempt in this vein. . . . Miss Washington brings to these love ballads the soulful, earthy quality that's found in her blues singing, a personal warmth unattainable by many pop singers. Hot item."

In keeping with the holiday season, Mercury also released a single with the appropriate theme, "Ol' Santa"/"The Light" (Mercury 71557). Neither captured much attention, though *Cash Box* cited the record in its Christmas roundup. *Cash Box*, December 5, 1959, p. 16.

329 *"Me and My Six Husbands": Sepia*, December 1959, p. 12, Robert Grayson interviews.

330 *year-end polls: Cash Box*, December 5, 1959, p. 22; *Variety*, December 30, 1959, p. 43; *Billboard*, December 14, 1959, pp. 40–42; *Down Beat*, December 24, 1959, p. 23; *Los Angeles Sentinel*, December 17, 1959, p. C1, on Christmas gift list; December 31, 1959, p. A13, winning jazz poll.

17 · Baby, You've Got What It Takes, 1960

331 *Cloister: Los Angeles Sentinel*, December 17, 1959, p. 12; December 24, 1959, p. A13; *California Eagle*, December 24, 1959, pp. 9, 12; *Down Beat*, March 1, 1960, p. 45.

332 *prescription diet pills: California Eagle*, January 7, 1960, p. 1; January 21, 1960, p. 10; *Pittsburgh Courier*, January 23, 1960, p. 4; *Los Angeles Sentinel*, January 21, 1960, p. 1; *New York Amsterdam News*, January 16, 1960, p. 15; *Jet*, March 3, 1960, p. 63.

332 *$60,000 contract suit: Tri-State Defender*, September 19, 1959, p. 10; *Memphis Commercial Appeal*, September 20, 1959, section IV, p. 8, announcing the Memphis concert.

333 **Clark Hotel:** *California Eagle,* January 14, 1960, p. 7; *Los Angeles Sentinel,* January 14, 1960, p. 2B; January 28, 1960, p. C1; *New York Amsterdam News,* January 16, 1960, p. 16; Ann Littles interview; picture courtesy of Ann Littles.

333 **Pasadena Civic Auditorium:** *California Eagle,* January 14, 1960, p. 9; *Los Angeles Sentinel,* January 21, 1960, p. 10; *San Francisco Chronicle,* January 31, 1960, p. 23. Hal Lederman and Peter Ekstein were the promoters of the Pasadena Jazz Festival.

334 **Brook Benton:** For extensive information on Brook Benton see *Tan,* May 1960, p. 15; *Sepia,* March 1961, p. 22; *Sepia,* September 1963, p. 25; Clyde Otis interviews, Escott, "Clyde Otis—Looking Back," *Goldmine,* October 1, 1993, p. 121.

334 **"Baby (You've Got What It Takes)":** Mercury 71565 ("I Do"). Dinah and Brook Benton comments are on the recording, Benton comments, Jones, *Talking Jazz,* p. 274.

   Billboard, January 11, 1960, p. 45, January 25, 1960, p. 36 (as an example of chart position): "The artists team up for powerful outings on two likely big tunes. Top side is blues-ballad. Flip is a slower ballad with strong teen-appeal lyrics. Ork support on both complements strongly."

   Cash Box, January 16, 1960, p. 10: "Mercury has teamed two of its star vocalists for a delightful string-filled rhythmic 'Baby (You've Got What It Takes)' (not the current Marv Johnson click). One of the most engaging vocal meetings in years and a bid for a smash chart position. 'I Do' opens with a wedding-march gimmick and goes on to an almost reverent duo by the pair. Can move, too."

   Variety, January 10, 1960, p. 60; February 10, 1960, pp. 56 (title change), 59 (as an example of chart position): " 'Baby (You've Got What It Takes)' has an energetic beat that fits right into the duo's styling. 'I Do' sets up an okay ballad mood that Miss Washington and Benton build for good spinning results."

336 **"a late husband":** *Jet,* February 25, 1960, p. 58.

336 **"causing her great concern":** *Washington Post,* January 17, 1960, p. G8; *Jet,* March 10, 1960, p. 29; April 21, 1960, p. 59.

337 **"Mr. Dinah Washington":** *Chicago Defender,* March 9, 1960, p. 6; *Jet,* March 17, 1960, p. 29; August 27, 1959, p. 64; June 2, 1960, p. 64; *Tan,* June 1960, p. 8.

337 **The Swingin' Singin' Years:** Berle Adams interview, November 2000.

338 **opened at the Regal:** See *Chicago Defender* entertainment pages for March 8–16, 1960. See also "The Swinging Singing Years," Classic TV. Hollywood's Attic Burbank, CA.

   "It Could Happen to You," Mercury 71560 ("Age of Miracles") went on the *Cash Box* pop one hundred chart March 19, where it would stay for nine weeks, rising to number forty-seven. The record went on the *Billboard* pop one hundred chart March 25, where it would stay for six weeks and reach number fifty-three. See Downey et al., *Cash Box* pop singles charts, *1950–1993;* Whitburn, *Top Pop Singles, 1955–1993—Billboard.*

339 **placed high in the music poll:** See the *Washington Post*'s "This Week's Pop Poll" in February and early March 1960 and the "Tops in Pops" column. See also *Chicago Defender,* March 7, 1960, p. 17.

339 *"Soul 60":* Chicago Tribune, March 25, 1960, p. 19; Detroit Free Press, March 26, 1960, p. 9; Chicago Defender, March 22, 1960, p. 16.

Dinah was honored March 15 at an after-hours party thrown by popular local disc jockey McKie Fitzhugh at his club, the Disc Jockey Lounge. Fitzhugh frequently invited top stars to the club where the house band performed for the visiting entertainer. For Dinah, the band had worked up a blues tribute. *Chicago Defender,* March 15, 1960, p. 17.

340 *"I make hit records, too":* Jet, April 7, 1960, p. 64. Robert Grayson interviews; Variety, April 20, 1960, p. 144. The promoter was Sid Bernstein. Also on the bill were Maynard Ferguson and his big band, Dion and the Belmonts, Leo DeLyon, Lambert, Hendricks & Ross, the Jazztet, which featured Benny Golson, the Cha Cha Taps, and William B. Williams. According to the *Chicago Defender* (May 2, 1960, p. 16), the show grossed $66,000.

Variety said of Dinah: "Working solo, Miss Washington displays her vocal flair with 'Give Me Gin, Instead,' 'A Foggy Day,' 'Unforgettable,' and 'What a Diff'rence a Day Makes.' The style is effortless, but it carries a lot of punch." (*Variety* probably meant "Me and My Gin.")

340 *"She had no respect":* Otis interviews; Shelby Singleton interview, August 13, 2003. Singleton's and Otis's memories of Dinah snapping at Brook Benton are quite different from Benton's genial coments. In addition to his cheerful memories about making "Baby," Benton told writer Stan Britt that he had no problems with her. "We had fun, I'll tell you that. I never laughed so much in my life—really. She was a very funny woman."

340 *Redd Foxx:* Dan Morgenstern interview, October 22, 2001.

341 *"A Rockin' Good Way (To Mess Around and Fall in Love)":* Mercury 71629 ("I Believe"). *Cash Box* (May 14, 1960, p. 14) said that "Rockin' " "should prove another fortunate pairing of the talents who recently teamed up on the smash 'Baby.' . . . Here the two and rock-a-string support offer an infectious cut in the 'Baby' manner." See *New York Amsterdam News,* April 16, 1960, p. 17; *Jet,* April 7, 1960, p. 64. "Rockin' " also did well in the *Variety* charts. See *Variety* charts in the music section for June 1960, especially June 8, p. 48.

341 *Unforgettable:* Mercury MR20572; Variety, May 11, 1960, p. 42.

341 *returned to Birdland:* Dinah Washington and Her Trio—Live at Birdland, Baldwin Street Music BJH 301. Dinah was joined at Birdland through May 11 by the John Handy Quintet, *Down Beat,* May 12, 1960, p. 46.

342 *"She didn't even say 'good-bye' ":* Winston-Salem Journal, May 14, 1960, p. 1; Variety, May 18, 1960, p. 64.

343 *Jackie Hayes:* Chicago Defender, May 19, 1960, p. 3; New York Amsterdam News, May 7, 1960, p. 16; May 14, 1960, p. 17; Jet, May 26, 1960, p. 26; July 14, 1960, p. 30, for the "millionaire fan."

345 *mink-trimmed sofa bed:* Chicago Defender, June 21, 1960, p. 16.

345 *Queen Artists:* Philadelphia Tribune, March 8, 1960, p. 5; Down Beat, June 23, 1960, p. 11; Ruth Bowen interviews; Bowen interview, Haskins papers.

345 *Eddie Chamblee:* Michigan Chronicle, June 25, 1960, p. 5; July 2, 1960, section 2, p. 5; July 9, 1960, p. 11; July 30, 1960, section 3, p. 8; Ziggy Johnson's column on July 11 discussed the acts in Dinah's revue at the Flame.

Beyond the packed club every night, Dinah had the added pleasure of seeing "This Bitter Earth," Mercury 71635 ("I Understand") in the number one slot on the top ten records published weekly by disc jockey Frantic Ernie Durham of WJLB.

345 **cancel her performance:** *New York Amsterdam News,* June 25, 1960, p. 17; *Down Beat,* July 7, 1960, p. 46; *Cash Box,* July 2, 1960, p. 25, *Berkshire Eagle,* July 9, 1960, p. 11A, July 11, 1960, p. 9.

Though Dinah's Newport date was canceled and her illness prevented her from singing at the Berkshire festival, she apparently performed at a festival in Atlantic City with Count Basie, Sarah Vaughan, and Cannonball Adderley. *Chicago Defender,* July 11, 1960, p. 21; *Atlantic City Press,* June 26, July 1, 1960. Later in July, according to *Down Beat,* she played other dates in Mattapoisett, Massachusett, and back in the Boston area (July 21, 1960, p. 69). *Boston Globe,* July 6, 1960, p. 1, and *Variety,* July 6, 1960, p. 1, for articles about the fracas at Newport.

346 **"getting 'cold feet' ":** *Chicago Defender,* July 5, 1960, p. 16; *Los Angeles Sentinel,* July 7, 1960, p. 2C; *Jet,* July 21, 1960, p. 59.

346 **"shopping for a mate":** Clark Terry interview; Ruth Bowen interviews; George Dixon interviews.

347 **"it ain't easy":** *Michigan Chronicle,* October 1, 1960, Section 2, p. 4.

347 **The Two of Us:** Mercury 20588. *Cash Box* (July 9, 1960, p. 32), reviewed the album: "Teaming the label's top artists was a brainstorm proven by the sucess of 'Baby' and 'A Rockin' Good Way.' They should have no trouble chart-selling their initial LP together. It includes the two hits, a couple of other duet numbers and several solo performances. . . . A truly worthy meeting of two outstanding artists."

347 **"She started swearing":** Carrie Taylor interview, 1967, courtesy of Jack Thompson; Clyde Otis interview by Robert Pruter, reproduced in liner notes for a reissue of *The Two of Us,* Verve 3145264672, confirms Taylor's account. *Down Beat,* September 29, 1960, p. 48; August 4, 1960, p. 20.

348 **Bud Billiken:** *Chicago Defender,* August 1, 1960, p. 17; August 9, 1960, pp. 16–17; *Los Angeles Sentinel,* August 11, 1960, p. 4, Doc Young column from Chicago; for Roberts "gala" breakfast, see *Chicago Defender,* August 15, 1960, p. 16; September 7, 1960, p. 16.

349 **Randall's Island:** *Down Beat,* September 29, 1960, p. 20; *New York Amsterdam News,* August 27, 1960, p. 14.

349 **"j.a.m.f.":** Schiffman, *Uptown: The Story of Harlem's Apollo Theatre,* pp. 106–07, 145, 157–58; Fox, *Showtime at the Apollo,* pp. 150–51; *New York Amsterdam News,* September 10, 1960, p. 15; Ruth Bowen interviews.

Prior to her week at the Apollo September 9–15, Dinah had returned to the Boston area to play a festival sponsored by George Wein at Pleasure Island and also played the Frolic at Revere Beach. *Down Beat,* September 1, 1960, p. 46.

351 **Wayne County sheriff:** *Jet,* October 13, 1960, p. 56.

352 **"corporation of friends":** *Michigan Chronicle,* October 1, 1960, section 2, p. 4; October 20, 1960, section 2, p. 4; *Jet,* October 13, 1960, p. 31, ballet picture; George Dixon interviews.

In the *Chronicle,* Paul R. Adams gave a detailed account of one of the Flame shows, and at the end, he provided a personal account of Dinah's last numbers: "Her soul poured into the mike with genuine sincerity. She sang without effort, without regard for harmonics, pitch or tone—but her voice was in control, always true. Even the most insensible boor in the audience got the message when she sang 'This Bitter Earth' with trembling lips and tears streaking her makeup."

353 **Flamingo:** *Las Vegas Sun Magazine,* April 22, 1979, which includes a feature on the Flamingo as part of the series, "The Great Resorts of Las Vegas— How They Began!"; *Las Vegas Review Journal,* October 12, 1960, p. 3; *Sepia,* December 1960; Joe Zawinul interview, January 22, 2003.

As was her custom, Dinah worked her way west to Las Vegas, with one of the main jobs a three-day stand in Oklahoma City at the Bryant Recreation Center, *Oklahoma Black Dispatch,* October 7, 1960.

354 **"I guess I just flipped him":** *Jet,* December 8, 1960, p. 58. The article was based on an interview Dinah gave in the hotel while performing at the Bali Hai in Portland, Oregon.

354 **"sent me a telegram":** UPI telephoto, showing Dinah, Peter Lawford, and Frank Sinatra as they wait outside Sammy Davis Jr.'s house, courtesy of the Los Angeles Public Library Photo Department; *Philadelphia Tribune,* November 19, 1960, p. 5; *Jet,* December 1, 1960, p. 56; December 8, 1960, p. 58.

355 **"Families welcome":** *Oregonian,* November 12, 1960, p. 5; November 14, 1960, p. 5; November 21, 1960, p. 9; Jack Tracy interviews.

355 **"New York style revue":** *California Eagle,* December 8, 1960, p. 7, for a review of the Pasadena Civic Center Auditorium show.

355 **I Concentrate on You:** Mercury MG20604. *Down Beat,* December 8, 1960, p. 52; *Cash Box,* November 5, 1960, p. 46.

355 **Ciro's:** *California Eagle* and *Los Angeles Sentinel* entertainment pages for December 1960 for ads and short articles about Dinah at Ciro's. *Los Angeles Times,* November 7, 1959, for purchase of Ciro's by Frank Sennes.

Variety reviewed the December 5 Ciro's show: "In the blues spectrum extant, there's no one finah than Dinah Washington, that is. That fact is amply demonstrated in the course of her appearance as a sort of 'queen mother' presiding over the ambitious revue with which she has surrounded herself for a four-week stand at Ciro's."

355 **black entertainers:** "Jazz for Civil Rights," *New York Amsterdam News,* September 26, 1959, p. 15; Sarah Vaughan, *Jet,* July 14, 1960, p. 63; Harry Belafonte, *Jet,* December 22, 1960, p. 8; Clyde McPhatter, *Jet,* December 22, 1960, p. 37.

356 **jettisoned the black acts:** *Jet,* December 22, 1960, p. 54. Major Robinson's article, "The Big Rock 'n' Roll Package—How Dixie Race Tension Is Killing Mixed Shows," provides important detail about black entertainers and the South.

356 **"I just couldn't take":** *Los Angeles Sentinel,* December 8, 1960, p. 1; *Jet,* December 15, 1960, p. 44.

Among the other stars at the May benefit, which was at the Majestic Theater, were Sarah Vaughan, Cannonball Adderley, Ahmad Jamal, Gerry Mulligan, and Buddy Rich.

18 · September in the Rain, 1961

358 **Rafael Campos:** *Jet,* January 12, 1961, p. 59; *Sepia,* April 1961, pp. 20–23; *Chicago Daily Defender,* January 7, 1961, p. 17; *Pittsburgh Courier,* January 14,

1961, p. 7; *New York Amsterdam News,* January 14, 1961, p. 14; *Jet,* January 12, 1961, p. 59; January 19, 1961, p. 58; February 16, 1961, p. 56; "Dinah W. Campos" check, January 18, 1961, to Donald Smith for $291 from the Estate of Dinah Washington, #529465, Wayne County, Michigan, Probate Court.

361 *"Where's Dinah?":* Clyde Otis interviews; Colin Escott interview with Otis, *Goldmine,* October 1, 1993.

In the interviews, Otis spoke of only one session in Los Angeles in January 1961, describing how he had to scramble to find studio time for an hour of Dinah's vocals after she agreed to record. The files of Local 47, however, indicate that five sessions took place between January 21 and January 24, 1961, for Dinah's recording. All were at United Recording Corporation at 6050 Sunset Boulevard. The session on the 21st was scheduled from 7:30 to 10:30 P.M., with eighteen musicians; the sessions on the 22nd were scheduled for 2:00 to 5:00 P.M. and 6:30 to 9:30 P.M., with twenty-five musicians at each; the session on the 23rd was from 7:30 to 10:30 P.M. with nineteen musicians; and the one on the 24th was scheduled from 7:30 to 10:30 P.M. with eighteen musicians.

Belford Hendricks, the arranger, and Herman Clabanoff, the contractor who hired the musicians, each got $103, double scale. The other musicians received $51.50 for each session.

Although Joe Zawinul, the piano player, and bassist Jimmy Rowser were still working with Dinah on her live dates, neither played these sessions, perhaps because Dinah did no live dates after she finished her Ciro's run at the end of 1960 and was not scheduled for a club date until January 27, 1961, at the Tivoli Theater in Chicago. Ernie Freeman played the piano and George "Red" Callender played bass on the sessions.

The musicians for each session are listed on the AFM Local 47 contracts, #23810 for January 21, 23809 and 23808 for January 22, #23807 for January 23, and #23806 for January 24. Some combination of the following, in addition to Freeman and Callender, played on the sessions: Earl C. Palmer, Sr., Benny Gill, Erno Neufield, Ambrose Russo, Bernard Senescu, Sarah Kreindler, Lou Raderman, Alex Murray, Ralph Schaeffer, Leonard Malarsky, Joseph Stepansky, William Miller, Gerald Vinci, Alvin Dinkin, Joseph DiFiore, Eleanor Slatkin, Raphael Kramer, James Decker, Katherine Julye, Barney Kessel, and Rene Hall.

Palmer was the drummer; Kessel and Hall split the guitar work; the others were string players.

363 *on the shelf:* Early in 1961 Mercury put out a single from a fall session in New York, "Looking Back"/"We Have Love," Mercury 71744, and it was "We Have Love" that generated some attention. The up-tempo song made it onto the *Cash Box* and *Billboard* top one hundred charts for a few weeks, though in the lower half of the tallies. Dinah also made *Jet's* annual poll of the top five female singers, which was published January 26, 1961.

Cash Box highlighted the record in the December 10, 1960, issue (p. 6): "Lark's long hit chain (which currently lists 'Love Walked In') should include both ends of her new Mercury outing. ["Looking Back"] is an ultra-lovely ballad offering while the other's from the bright jump school. Sock choral-ork support on both."

363 *"Dinah always said":* Jet, February 9, 1961, p. 31; February 16, 1961, pp. 56–59; *Chicago Defender,* city edition, February 4–10, 1961, p. 12; Robert Grayson interviews. The full revue at the Tivoli as advertised included: Dinah, Ray Sneed, Five Hi-Fis, Perri Lee Trio, Celeste, Lady Bird, and the Dinahettes, Dinah's chorus line.

364 *appendicitis:* Chicago Defender, city edition, January 28–February 3, 1961, p. 15; *Daily Defender,* February 15, 1961, p. 17; February 16, 1961, p. 23; *New York Amsterdam News,* February 14, 1961, p. 15; Jet, February 23, 1961, p. 33.

365 *"I'm getting tired":* Joe Zawinul, Jimmy Rowser interviews.

365 *"Celebrity Night":* Cash Box, March 18, 1961, p. 40, guest nights; Jet, April 4, 1961, p. 32; James and Ritz, *Rage to Survive,* pp. 102–03; George Kirby interview, 1987, from Jack Thompson.

367 *"Rafael went berserk":* Farris Kimbrough interviews, in particular May 14, 2003; LaRue Manns interview, Haskins papers; *Chicago Daily Defender,* March 22, 1961, p. 17; March 29, 1961, p. 17; *Chicago Defender*, city edition, April 8–16, 1961, p. 6; *Michigan Chronicle*, April 8, 1961, p. 1; *Jet*, April 6, 1961, p. 23; *Pittsburgh Courier*, April 8, 1961, p. 22; *Sepia*, April 1961, p. 23.

369 *"I had to pay fifty people":* See *Chicago Defender* entertainment pages, daily and city editions, through April for ads and stories about Dinah's show at Roberts/Dinahland. *Jet*, April 13, 1961, p. 42; Drake Tolbert, undated article in the *National Enquirer,* "The Dinah Washington I Know," probably early 1962.

While Dinah was in Chicago, Mercury released another single, though it had only a modest run: "Early Every Morning"/"Do You Want It That Way," Mercury 71778. *Cash Box,* February 25, 1961, p. 8, made the record a "Pick of the Week." "The coming weeks ahead should find Dinah Washington's name plastered all over the hit lists. Her latest for Mercury has that double-barreled smash look. 'Early Every Morning' is a sparkling rockin' rhythm affair colorfully backed by the Fred Norman outfit. 'Do You Want It That Way' features Dinah's beautiful ballad stylings against a lush Nat Goodman ork-chorus backdrop."

"Early Every Morning" went on the *Cash Box* pop singles chart March 4 and stayed there five weeks, rising to number seventy-five. The record went on the *Billboard* pop singles chart March 13 at number ninety-five and stayed on the tally only one week.

370 *"The Parade of Stars":* Chicago Defender, city edition, May 6–12, p. 20; May 13–19, p. 20.

Variety, May 10, 1961, p. 79, reported in its "On the Upbeat" column that Dinah and her revue were going to play Pep's in Philadelphia May 1–6, but that was probably in error. Stories and ads in the *Defender* indicated that she was still at Roberts.

370 *"should be chided":* Variety, May 17, 1961, p. 68; *New York Amsterdan News,* May 20, 1961, p. 19.

The full bill at the Apollo included Dinah, the Hi-Fis, the Dells, Arnold Dover, a mimic, the Perri Lee organ trio, the dancing Kit-Kats, and Dinah's Mink-Clad chorus.

New York Amsterdam News, July 15, 1961, p. 17, Rafael Campos remarriage; *Jet,* June 22, 1961, p. 42, on book with Dave Hepburn.

371 ***"Our Love Is Here to Stay"/"Congratulations to Someone":*** Mercury
71812. *Cash Box,* May 6, 1961, p. 8, a "Pick of the Week," said the song "is
properly treated to a fabulous ballad performance by Dinah. Belford Hendricks' outfit warmly assists as the thrush makes each word come alive.
More stellar ballad results on the 'Congratulations' side (a chartmaker for
Tony Bennett awhile back)."

371 ***The Dells:*** Charles "Chuck" Barksdale interview, September 2, 2002, also
Barksdale video interview, 2000, courtesy of the Chicago-based Historymakers project, www.historymakers.com; see Pruter, *Chicago Doowop,*
pp. 120–25, for an extensive discussion of the Dells. The other singers in
1961 were Vern Allison, Johnny Carter, Marvin Junior, and Mickey
McGill; Marvin Junior interview, August 26, 2003; Mickey McGill interview, August 26, 2002; undated article in the *National Enquirer* by Drake
Tolbert, "The Dinah Washington I Know," probably early 1962 based on
the information in the article.

373 ***She decided to sue:*** *Jet,* July 13, 1961, p. 61. *Dinah Washington v. Andrew C.
Baird, Sheriff of Wayne County, Stephen Book, and Walter Bates, Jr., Deputy Sheriffs,* Case #61-21402, U.S. District Court for the Eastern District of Michigan.
      Order to Dismiss, May 3, 1962, part of the file in *Dinah Washington v. An-
drew C. Baird.*
      While she was in Detroit, Dinah hustled back to New York to sing at the
funeral of seven-year-old Gregory Randolph, the son of Luther "Red" Randolph, who owned the Shalimar, a club in New York. The boy was on his
bicycle when he rode into the path of a large truck. *Norfolk Journal and
Guide,* July 15, 1961, p. 18. Slappy White joke, *Jet,* July 12, 1961, p. 64.

374 ***abruptly resigned:*** Clyde Otis resignation, *Cash Box,* April 27, 1961, p. 32; *Jet,*
May 11, 1961, p. 61; joining Liberty Records, *Cash Box,* May 6, 1961, p. 28;
Quincy Jones to Mercury, *Cash Box,* July 15, 1961, p. 30; *Variety,* July 12,
1961, p. 49; see also *New York Amsterdam News,* July 24, 1961, p. 17, Cannonball Adderley column about Jones; Jack Tracy return, *Cash Box,* July 1,
1961, p. 6. Quincy Jones interview, December 19, 2003.
      In his 1993 interview with Colin Escott in *Goldmine,* Otis gave this ac-
count of his departure from Mercury: "Irving Green came to New York,
and he said he was going to start a publishing company and he wanted all
of his A&R people to put their songs into that company. I said I already had
a publishing company. 'I told you when I came here I was a song man,' I
told him. They kept putting the pressure on me, so my attorney put me in
touch with Al Bennett at Liberty Records. I went out to Los Angeles to
meet him and came back and told Irving Green that I couldn't go along
with what he wanted." (Otis left Liberty in July 1964 to become a producer
in Columbia's pop division [*Cash Box,* March 28, 1964, p. 32].)
      In July 1961 Green announced that Mercury would become part of the
international firm Consolidated Electronics Corp., which was known in the
United States through Philips records. The deal was intended to allow an
exchange of record libraries between the two companies. According to *Cash
Box* (July 1, 1961, p. 34), "Mercury plans an expansion program based on
the acquisition of a part of this vast classical and foreign popular catalog."

374 ***"Is this Sophie Tucker's date?":*** Clark Terry interview, October 4, 2002; Joe
Wilder interview, March 29, 2004.

376 **Dave Bondu:** *Miami Times,* August 12, 1961; August 19, 1961.

376 **"We're poor little lambs":** Mickey McGill interview.

377 **"freedom riders":** *Chicago Defender,* city edition, January 21–27, 1961, p. 12; *Pittsburgh Courier,* April 1, 1961, p. 23; *New York Amsterdam News,* May 27, 1961, p. 1; *Sepia,* September 1961, p. 42.

377 **benefit for the NAACP:** *Florida Star,* September 2, 1961, pp. 3, 8; September 9, 1961, pp. 3, 5; see also Jay Jay's column, "Chips off the Blocks," p. 8; Vern Allison interview, September 9, 2003; Farris Kimbrough interviews.

378 **a little fox terrier:** James and Bertha Foreman interview, May 15, 2003.

378 **Roulette:** Ruth Bowen interviews; Jack Tracy interviews.

379 **"September in the Rain"/"Wake the Town and Tell the People":** Mercury 71876. *Cash Box,* September 30, 1961, p. 6, "Pick of the Week: "Dinah's ear-arresting style should have 'September in the Rain' all over the airwaves once again. The beautiful oldie never sounded better than it does under the lark's expert vocal guidance that rests happily against the lovely string-filled shuffle-ballad backdrop painted by Clyde Otis & Co. It's Quincy Jones' outfit brightly backing up on the excellent 'Wake the Town,' rock-blues revival flipside."

379 **She hadn't been feeling well:** *Jet,* October 26, 1961, p. 58; *Pittsburgh Courier,* November 4, 1961, p. 22. This story, dated in November, seems to refer to the early October hospitalization. It was not unusual for these weekly papers to report on events that had happened a week or two beforehand.

The Dells were still with Dinah on the Apollo bill along with some new acts, including Dave Turner, billed as "singer/mimic," Nate Nelson, former lead singer with the Flamingos, another Chicago singing group, and Cecilia Cooper, advertised as "Cannes Beauty Winner." The *New York Amsterdam News* explained that Cooper, a model, had won first prize in France, "winning over Europe's most beautiful girls." She also studied dance with Cholly Atkins, who had taught George and Bobby. Pep's engagement, *Philadelphia Inquirer,* September 8, 1961. p. 27

379 **Lois Green:** The account of Dinah's disagreement with Lois Green, which included Dinah's arrest for allegedly pulling a gun, is drawn from the *New York Post,* October 22, 1961, p. 4; *New York Daily News,* October 24, 1961, p. 10; *Jet,* November 9, 1961, p. 58; *New York Amsterdam News,* October 28, 1961, p. 1; *Jet,* November 16, 1961, p. 63; *Down Beat,* December 7, 1961, p. 10; and from Farris Kimbrough interviews, Ruth Bowen interviews, and David Dinkins interview, October 19, 2003.

382 **the Cave:** the *Sun,* Vancouver, Canada, October 21, 1961, p. 12; October 26, 1961, p. 12. Dinah was billed as "The Exciting Queen of Song!" Also on the bill were Jimmy Troy, the Cordettes, and the Dave Robbins Band.

382 **the Birdhouse:** *Chicago Tribune,* November 21, 1961, p. 8; *Cash Box,* December 2, 1961, p. 30; December 9, 1961, p. 26; Art Sheridan interview, August 22, 2003. Sheridan's partner in the Birdhouse, Basin Street, and the Sutherland Lounge was Ewart Abner, who also operated Vee-Jay Records.

383 **"We'll cancel the session":** Boris Zlatich interview, October 24, 2003.

384 **"good booze:"** Jack Tracy interviews; Quincy Jones interview, December 19, 2003. Patti Austin interview, Haskins papers; Patti Austin interview, September 10, 2003.

384 **"I hung up":** Gourse, *Louis's Children,* pp. 228–29; Patti Bown interviews.

385 **John the Baptist:** Jack Wilson interview, Haskins papers; Wilson interviews June 28, 29, 2001; Jack Tracy interviews; Boris Zlatich interview; Quincy Jones interview, December 19, 2003. Clarissa Smith interviews; Bill Jackson interview, January 26, 2004.

387 **September in the Rain:** MG20638.

According to the usual year-end polls, Dinah was still popular and selling well. She was fourteenth out of twenty in *Down Beat*'s annual "Female Singer" poll. Ella Fitzgerald was the runaway in first place with Sarah Vaughan a distant second (December 21, 1961, p. 29). In *Cash Box,* Dinah was sixth of ten among the best-selling female vocalists of singles. Connie Francis was in first place. December 30, 1961, p. 56.

19 · Roulette Wheel, 1962

388 **Miami Beach:** *Cash Box,* January 27, 1962, p. 11; February 10, 1962, p. 37; February 17, 1962, p. 20.

Tears and Laughter, Mercury 206611; *Cash Box* review, January 20, 1962, p. 22: "The inimitable Dinah Washington dishes up a potent collection of evergreens in this wax teaming up with orkster Quincy Jones. Dinah starts things off by taking off full steam into 'Bewitched.' Thrush goes on to create a lot of excitement as she delivers moving renditions of 'Am I Blue' and the title song. . . . The Jones sound is a perfect match for the lark's talents. Session as a hot noise-maker."

"Tears and Laughter"/"If I Should Lose You," Mercury 71922. "Tears" stayed on the *Billboard* chart for five weeks, reaching number seventy-one. The record stayed on the *Cash Box* chart for seven weeks, reaching fifty-six.

389 **"I loved her":** Patti Bown interview, August 26, 2003; Farris Kimbrough interviews; Drake Tolbert, "The Dinah Washington I Know," *National Enquirer;* LaRue Manns interview, Haskins papers.

390 **"She's hitting on me":** Jack Wilson interviews, in particular June 29, 2001.

390 **Bluebird Club:** *Panorama,* the newsletter of the U.S. Naval Base in Naples, January 12, 1962, Volume 7, Number 2, pp. 2–3, courtesy of Daniel Smithyman, JOC (NSANAP 10); Jack Wilson interviews.

391 **Thunderbird:** *Las Vegas Sun* magazine, May 6, 1979, pp. 6–10, part of a series "The Great Resorts of Las Vegas—How They Began!" Thunderbird opening, September 3, 1948. Dinah's opening, February 2, 1962, pp. 3, 7; Dinah's contract, AGVA files; Jimmy Sigler interviews for Allegros information.

The *Las Vegas Sun* was particularly effusive in welcoming Dinah back to Las Vegas: "An amazing sidelight to the career of this terrific singer . . . is that very few people are aware of her talents as a musician, composer and arranger. She plays the organ, piano, vibes, bass fiddle and French horn." While it was true that Dinah played the piano and could play the organ, when she "played" the bass it was more for fun, slapping away at the strings. The vibes reference was probably a nod to her impromptu turn with Terry Gibbs at Newport in 1958. This was the first time Dinah had ever been linked to the French horn.

Sigler interviews on Tony Bennett, Earl Edwards, and Buddy Rich, particularly January 14, 19, 27, 2004. Richmond Auditorium, *San Francisco Chronicle,* February 25, 1962, "Sunday Datebook," p. 8.

In addition to the Richmond date, according to Sigler, Dinah and the group also played the Fillmore Lounge and then made an appearance as a favor to someone at the Red Carpet, which was a club.

Picture of Dinah Washington and Tony Bennett courtesy of Ann Littles.

393 **week at Pep's:** March 9, 1962, letter from Associated Booking Corporation to AGVA contains the details of Dinah's March 19, 1962, engagement at Pep's. She was paid $3,000 for the week according to the AGVA contract. See also *Philadelphia Inquirer,* March 19, 1962, p. 15.

393 **"Dinah commanded":** *Variety,* April 4, 1962, p. 76.

393 **Masco Young:** *Carolinian,* April 21, 1962; Jimmy Sigler interview, September 6, 2003.

393 **"Such a Night"/"Dream":** Mercury 71958. *Cash Box,* April 14, 1962, p. 14: "Dinah, whose most recent chart appearance was *Tears and Laughter,* could be all over the airwaves with her new Mercury pairing. They're two oldies, 'Such a Night' and 'Dream,' that the lark and the Quincy Jones ork put across with coin-catching authority. Former takes an inviting jump-a-twist route while the latter follows an ear-arresting best-ballad path. Two goodies."

"Where Are You"/"You're Nobody 'Til Somebody Loves You," Roulette 4424: *Cash Box,* May 5, 1962, p. 14: "Dinah Washington's bow on Roulette should be filling the airwaves in no time flat. It's the lovely sentimental oldie 'Where Are You' that the outsanding stylist puts across with telling ballad effect. Also first rate is her swinging-to-a-big-finish up-dating of 'You're Nobody 'Til Somebody Loves You.' Excellent ork-choral showcases supplied by Fred Norman's crew. Both sides are in her "Dinah '62 LP.' "

Roulette took out a full-page ad for Dinah and "Where Are You," in the April 21, 1962, *Cash Box,* p. 25. A full-page ad for the album also ran on the last page of *Down Beat,* July 5, 1962.

395 **"Won't somebody—please":** *Down Beat,* September 27, 1962, p. 40.

395 **"all of the label's expectations":** Bud Katzel, *Cash Box,* May 5, 1962, pp. 6, 13.

396 **"so much aggravation":** *Jet,* May 17, 1962, p. 60; Jimmy Sigler interviews; *Flint Journal,* April 27, 1962, p. 25; AGVA contract for the Palladium, made April 13, 1962. This contract included a rider that specified that Dinah would receive $4,650 for the three-day performance, half paid up-front, the rest before the first show on the last day. While the club agreed to rent and install a Hammond organ, Dinah was required to cover the cost, which was not to exceed $115. See also *Oakland Tribune,* May 11, 1962, p. 14D.

396 **"Where Are You":** *Chicago Defender,* City Edition, May 19–25, 1962, p. 16; *Jet,* May 31, 1962, p. 64.

397 **International Jazz Festival:** *Variety,* November 4, 1961, p. 59, announcing the festival; *Jet,* April 12, 1962, p. 58; *Washington Afro-American,* June 2, 1962, p. 15; *Jet,* June 14, 1962, p. 56; *Down Beat,* July 19, 1962, p. 20; Dinah and Duke Ellington, Voice of America collection, RGA0114, Library of Congress.

399 **acute anemia:** *Philadelphia Tribune,* June 5, 1962, p. 1; *Pittsburgh Courier,* June 17, 1962, p. 17. Dinah was paid $2,850 for the Erie Social Club; she was paid $3,000 for the six-day week at Pep's. Associated Booking had lined up a performance June 9 at the Mosque in Newark. Correspondence relating to these three dates from the AGVA files; Sigler interviews, especially September 5, 2003.

399 *"pep pills":* LaRue Manns interview, Haskins papers; Ann Littles interviews; Beatrice Buck interviews; Keter Betts interviews.

400 *"extremely tired":* Birdland contract from AGVA files; *New York Amsterdam News,* July 7, 1962, p. 19; short review, "Birdland Has Dinah Quintet," July 2, 1962, in Haskins papers.

401 *$2,800 Chevrolet: Jet,* July 26, 1962, p. 63.

401 *Carr's Beach: Baltimore Afro-American,* July 14, 1962, p. 18; Jimmy Sigler interview, September 5, 1962.

According to *Cash Box,* Dinah returned for another two weeks at Birdland starting July 28. Dave Turner was still on the bill and received an enthusiastic write-up in the *New York Amsterdam News,* September 15, 1962, p. 16. Ruth Bowen interviews; Jimmy Sigler interviews.

402 *argued with Costa:* Ann Littles interviews; Jimmy Sigler interviews.

402 *"an alarming decline": Down Beat,* December 20, 1962, pp. 34–35.

Right around the time of the critical *Down Beat* review, Dinah received unflattering attention in the normally generous *Chicago Defender.* On August 2 the *Daily Defender* (p. 3) published an acerbic full-page feature by one of its newer writers, Bob Hunter, under the headline "The Lives and Loves of Miss Dinah Washington." He said she was like "Jezebel or a Delilah, mainly because she is cunning, evil and is really heartbroken." Hunter said Dinah "cannot keep a husband" because "the men themselves grew tired of being referred to as Mr. Dinah Washington."

Drinking Again: Roulette R25183; *I Wanna Be Loved,* Mercury, MG20729, SR60729; *Cash Box,* September 15, 1962, p. 31, on *Drinking Again:* "Dinah Washington . . . unleashes her distinctive, full-bodied vocal charms full blast on this tasteful session of Don Costa arranged sturdies. The lark, whose highly personal emotionally-charged style has won her many laurels in the past, should attract a legion of her many admirers with this top rung effort. Some of the best sides here include 'Just Friends,' 'I'll Be Around,' and 'For All We Know.' Plenty of sales potential here."

Billboard, September 13, 1962, p. 22, was equally enthusiastic: "Dinah is at the top of her form and is backed by Don Costa arrangements that are highly sensitive both to her personal style and to the music. Some great standards get the full Washington treatment, making them sound fresh and new. Those include 'Just Friends,' 'I'll Be Around,' 'Baby Won't You Please Come Home,' and 'For All We Know.' Should get a solid sales response."

403 *Frolic in Revere Beach:* Associated Booking correspondence in the 1962 AGVA files. A contract in the same AGVA files showed that Dinah was supposed to have traveled with six others to the Caribbean. The promoter or operator was Danny Sims Associates. The word "Cancelled" was scrawled across the front of the contract and referred to a letter that apparently explained the circumstances. An entertainment column in the July 7 *Miami Times* referred to an upcoming Dinah performance at the King O'Hearts but nothing more about the date appeared the rest of July or August.

403 *a surprise party: Jet,* September 27, 1962, p. 33; *Jet,* January 9, 1964, pp. 57–58; Robert Grayson interviews.

The canceled Caribbean trip apparently afforded Dinah the chance to go back in the studio with Don Costa, according to discographical information from Blue Note/Mosaic, courtesy of Michael Cuscuna.

403 *"For All We Know" /"I Wouldn't Know":* Roulette 4444.
 The differences in a record's chart placement between *Billboard* and *Cash Box* largely reflected the differences in the way the two magazines conducted their weekly surveys. *Cash Box* was considered among record sellers to reflect the buying practices of the black community much more reliably than *Billboard*.

404 *"too busy raising her two sons":* Chicago Daily Defender, September 6, 1962, p. 2; *Carolinian*, September 15, 1962, p. 14; *Jet*, September 20, 1962, p. 63.

404 **Flower Drum Song:** Las Vegas Review, September 13, 1962, p. 18; *Las Vegas Sun*, September 29, 1962, p. 15; *Hollywood Reporter*, October 1, 1962, p. 6.

404 *"Ladies and gentlemen":* Jimmy Sigler interviews, January 2004.

405 **In Love:** Roulette 25180; see also *Dinah Washington and Her Trio—Live at Birdland, 1962*, Baldwin Street Music BJH 301; *Billboard*, November 2, 1962, p. 14. "Dinah sings of love and things on this dreamy, warm album that also spotlights lush arrangements by Don Costa. This is the Queen at her most soulful, and it's a wonderful listening experience. Tunes include 'You're a Sweetheart,' 'Fly Me to the Moon,' 'If It's the Last Thing I Do,' and 'Do Nothin' Till You Hear from Me.' Fine wax."

406 *"Cold Cold Heart,"/ "I Don't Hurt Anymore":* Mercury 72040; "You're a Sweetheart" "It's a Mean Old Man's World," Roulette 4455. Neither record registered on the *Cash Box* top one hundred.

407 *"For reasons unknown to me":* Pittsburgh Press, December 2, 1962, p. 38; December 4, 1962, p. 38; *Pittsburgh Courier*, December 8, 1962, p. 15; December 15, 1962, p. 15; *Billboard*, December 22, 1962, p. 25; John Bertera's letter is part of the file in *Holiday House, Inc. v. American Guild of Variety Artists*, Civil Action 63-57, U.S. District Court for the Western District of Pennsylvania.

408 *fur toilet seat cover: Jet*, January 17, 1963, p. 62; Ruth Bowen interviews.

408 *year-end music tallies: Down Beat*, December 20, 1962, p. 22; *Cash Box*, December 29, 1962, pp. 48, 54.

20 · For All We Know, January–November 1963

409 **Back to the Blues:** Roulette 25189. *Cash Box*, February 9, 1963 (p. 26), said: "Here is an emotion-packed session of blues tunes by Dinah Washington with some very effective backing from arranger-conductor Fred Norman. The lark gives some feelingful treatments of these numbers as she belts them out in her own distinctive style."
 Don Costa arranged two tracks on the album, one with strings. Fred Norman was probably mistaken in his comment about "You've Been a Good Old Wagon." It was "Nobody Knows the Way I Feel This Morning" that went on for several minutes.
 Down Beat also reviewed the album (April 25, 1963, p. 34), comparing it in the same review to a two-record set from Mercury, *This Is My Story*, MG 20788 (SR 60288); MG 20789 (SR 60789), which included remakes she had done with Quincy Jones and re-releases. The reviewer said that "while Miss Washington generally performs well, she is handicapped by some undistinguished ballads and inappropriate string-and-vocal-group accompaniments. . . . The Roulette album is another matter. Here Miss Washing-

ton switches to a much more earthy approach. The intensity of 'Blues Ain't Nothin' ' puts it above anything on the Mercury release. This vocal is, I think, one of Miss Washington's finest on record. . . . The quality of arrangements ranges from unobtrusive to ludicrous."

According to Bob Porter's liner notes for the CD reissue of *Back to the Blues,* the musicians on the sessions from November 1962 are Eddie Chamblee, Dinah's fifth husband, on tenor saxophone, Illinois Jacquet also on tenor sax, and Billy Butler on guitar.

See also Dance, *The World of Swing,* for Fred Norman comments, p. 239; *Chicago Defender,* April 26, 1962, p. 17.

410 *"he tried to play":* Jet, February 28, 1963, p. 58; *Chicago Daily Defender,* February 4, 1963, p. 13; *Jet,* February 14, 1963, p. 61.

411 *Nipsey Russell: Chicago Daily Defender,* February 4, 1963, p. 13.

411 *Kriegsmann Photo Studios: New York Amsterdam News,* February 9, 1963, p. 16; Jimmy Sigler interviews.

Back to the Blues would stay on the *Billboard* album chart for twelve weeks, reaching number sixty-one.

411 *AGVA threatened: Holiday House, Inc. v. American Guild of Variety Artists,* Civil Action 63-57. This file contains the complaint from the club against AGVA, the temporary restraining order, motions in support of the order, the order of dismissal, and John Bertera's December 14, 1962, letter to AGVA complaining about Dinah's behavior.

Variety, February 6, 1963, p. 55; *Billboard,* February 9, 1962, p. 10; *Chicago Daily Defender,* February 21, 1963, p. 21.

412 *Stay at the airport: Norfolk Journal and Guide,* January 12, 1963, for ad on February 10 recital; January 19, 1963, p. 23; January 26, 1963, p. 9, advance stories; February 16, 1963, p. 1, stories in several editions of the paper; *Pittsburgh Courier,* February 16, 1963, section 2, p. 1; *Chicago Defender,* February 29, 1963, p. 13; *Carolinian,* Feburary 16, 1963; Jimmy Sigler interview, September 16, 2003; President Kennedy, *New York Times,* February 11, 1963, p. 1.

Not only had Dinah disappointed the Delta Sigma Thetas and the audience, she also angered the Norfolk musicians union. Apparently her managers had failed to file a copy of her contract with the union as the organization's rules required to make sure union standards were adhered to.

Ruth Bowen said in interviews in 2003 that while she had no specific recollection of the missed Norfolk concert, she was sure Dinah would have returned the advance fee. That was a standard requirement in the business for a missed performance, she said.

413 *Bill Jackson:* Bill Jackson interview, October 2003; *Chicago Defender,* city edition, March 23–30, 1963, p. 11. Claim of Decker Airways on the Estate of Ruth Jones Lane, a/k/a Dinah Washington, Wayne County Michigan Probate Court, #529465.

414 *Waldorf-Astoria: Chicago Defender,* March 6, 1963, p. 13, referring to Dinah's hospitalization; Ruth Bowen interviews; Bill Jackson, Waldorf-Astoria event, *Chicago Defender,* city edition, March 22–30, 1963, p. 11; Robert Grayson interviews; week at the Galaxy, *New York Amsterdam News,* March 16, 1963, p. 17; *Norfolk Journal and Guide,* March 2, 1963, p. 1, national edition;

Apollo performance, *New York Amsterdam News*, March 2, 1963, p. 17. Tito Puente and his band were also on the bill.

According to an ad in *Variety* (March 6, 1963, p. 50), a story in the *Chicago Daily Defender* (March 20, 1963, p. 16), and the March 16 *New York Amsterdam News* item, Stan Allen had put together an ambitious itinerary for Dinah and Don Sherman that included mid-March dates in Miami Beach, Miami, and Nassau in the Bahamas and then a date at Brooklyn College right before the Waldorf benefit. Jimmy Sigler, the organist with the Allegros, did not remember the Miami or Nassau dates, and it is not clear whether they ever took place, especially since Dinah had the unexpected hospitalization.

415 *"Dinah is constantly getting engaged":* Washington Afro-American, April 6, 1963, p. 15.

415 *De Havilland's forced landing:* Chicago Daily Defender, April 18, 1963, p. 13; El Rancho, Jimmy Sigler interviews; ice cube, *Carolinian,* June 8, 1963; see also *Las Vegas Review Journal,* April 4, 1963, p. 46. Ruth Bowen's pay from document filed in the Estate of Ruth Jones a/k/a Dinah Washington.

Just after Dinah opened in Las Vegas, she was mentioned in *Down Beat* (April 11, 1963, p. 33) as part of Leonard Feather's "Blindfold Test" with Anita O'Day. The song was "You're Crying" from *I Wanna Be Loved* on Mercury. O'Day gave it three and a half stars out of four. "Dinah sang very well on this," O'Day said. "I like it because it's an easygoing type of blues."

416 *bungalow:* Robert Grayson interview, February 13, 2004; Jimmy Sigler interview, February 13, 2004.

417 *"You big SOB":* Bobby Shad interview courtesy of the Shad family.

417 *"If the sound":* Joe Delaney interview, September 12, 2001; Jimmy Sigler interviews.

418 *Clara Ward:* Jimmy Sigler interview January 3, 2004. Royster, *How I Got Over, Clara Ward and the World Famous Ward Singers,* pp. 134–35; *Las Vegas Review Journal,* October 9, 1962, p. 3.

419 *"Throw her a fish":* Bud Katzel interview, May 31, 2002.

419 *"Hey, Dinah:"* Ebony, March 1964, p. 146.

420 *"tipped me gorgeously":* Artie Frazier, Jr., interview, April 15, 2002; Charles Walton interview, Jimmy Sigler interviews; Sutherland performances, *Chicago Daily Defender,* May 8, 1963, p. 24; May 9, 1963, p. 24.

420 *"practically camped in my office":* David Dinkins interview, October 19, 2003; *Dinah Washington v. Mercury Record Corporation,* New York Supreme Court, #9803/63.

422 *"For a long time now":* Chicago Daily Defender, April 16, 1963, p. 24; *Chicago Defender,* national edition, May 11–17, 1963, p. 11; *Jet,* May 30, 1963, p. 64, for Eartha Kitt. Over the summer other stars raised money at benefits, including Ella Fitzgerald, who brought in $5,000 for the Southern Christian Leadership Conference at a Hollywood club, *Jet,* July 11, 1963, p. 62; Jackie and Rachel Robinson, who hosted a "jazz afternoon" that raised $15,000, *Jet,* July 11, 1963, p. 60; Dinah contribution at Sutherland, *New York Amsterdam News,* May 18, 1963, p. 15.

422 *McCormick Place:* Chicago Daily Defender, May 27, 1963, p. 4; May 28, 1963, p. 3; *New York Amsterdam News,* June 15, 1963, p. 15; *Chicago Daily News,*

May 28, 1963, p. 14; *Chicago Tribune*, May 28, 1963, section 2, p. 6; Jimmy Sigler interviews.

423 *"You know I'm so bad"*: *Michigan Chronicle*, May 18, 1963, section 3, p. 10; June 8, 1963, section 2, p. 4.

423 *"and that's no joke"*: *Jet*, May 30, 1962, p. 36; Bill Jackson interview, September 25, 2003.

See also *Chicago Daily Defender*, March 11, 1963, p. 13; *Chicago Defender*, June 3, 1963, p. 16; *New York Amsterdam News*, June 8, 1963, p. 15, for Dinah's spring schedule.

Though Dinah had talked about doing a Carnegie Hall concert in June, it fell through, probably because of scheduling given her West Coast engagement at Basin Street West. But the *Defender* noted that before she could play Carnegie, she would "have to straighten out her problems with the musicians union, which claims she owes a wad of dough to accompanists after her most recent tour."

423 **Dick "Night Train" Lane:** *Michigan Chronicle*, June 8, 1953, p. 4; June 15, 1963, section 2, p. 4; June 15, 1963, section 3, p. 10; June 29, 1963, p. 1; July 6, 1963, p. 1; *Los Angeles Sentinel*, July 4, 1963, which featured a picture of the couple together just before they went to Las Vegas; *Sepia*, "Queen Dinah Takes a New King," September 1963, pp. 18–22; *Las Vegas Sun*, July 3, 1963, p. 1; December 15, 1963, p. 2; *Jet*, July 18, 1963, p. 61, noting that Dinah was miffed when someone reported that Lane was her tenth husband; Beatrice Buck interviews; Basin Street, *Los Angeles Sentinel*, June 20, 1963, p. A19; July 4, 1963, p. 1.

These contemporaneous accounts are at variance with the way Dick Lane remembered events leading up to his marriage to Dinah in an interview for the Haskins book. In the interview, which was conducted twenty-three years after the wedding, Lane said Dinah pursued him, calling regularly from Los Angeles, where she was at Basin Street West. "Next thing I know I get a call and somebody from some press, I guess she told Ruth she was gonna marry me. So I called out there, and I cussed her out. I said, 'I told you before, I make my own decisions. I ain't said nothing about this. You forget about that. You tell them to retract all that stuff.' "

Lane said Dinah called his attorney and urged him to tell Lane: "It's a good deal and I'll obey him and I'll do this and that." Lane's lawyer, Chauncey Estridge, followed up, telling Lane he had two plane tickets and that they were going out to meet with Dinah. Lane said he was upset by all the press calls: "I'm very mad at you," he said he told her. "I told you before I'm not one of these little kids you play around with. You're getting yourself into very serious areas here."

According to Lane, Dinah then said, "If I tell you I love you and you come out, if you don't wanna go through with it you don't have to."

In a later recollection, however, Lane had much gentler memories. He claimed to his biographer, Mike Burns, that he used to play Dinah's records all the time, so loudly sometimes that he couldn't hear when his teammates knocked on his door. By the time he and Dinah reconnected in Detroit, he said, "She was more famous than ever. I felt fortunate to be able to call her, much less date her. We had known each other for many years, but the time just wasn't right" (p. 83).

427 ***Hugh Hefner:*** *Jet,* August 18, 1963, p. 65.

427 ***"I am happy to be thirty-nine":*** *Chicago Defender,* city edition, August 24–30, 1963, p. 15; Robert Grayson interviews.

From Chicago, Dinah and the Allegros continued on to New Jersey, where they played the Beachcomber, a popular club on Schellenger Avenue in Wildwood. Then came the event at the Club Harlem, to celebrate Dinah's birthday a week early. The fourteen-piece house band at the club was led by Johnny Lynch, and the group provided the music for all the stars who came in to perform; Jimmy Sigler interviews.

428 ***"Mama" Ethel Harrison:*** El Taco menu and flyer, Burns, *Night Train Lane: Life of Hall of Famer Richard "Night Train" Lane. Michigan Chronicle,* September 14, 1963, section 3, p. 5; Beatrice Buck interviews.

429 ***"double her size":*** Nate Holloway interview, 1993, courtesy of Jack Thompson; *Dinah '63,* Roulette R25220.

430 ***"things better be running":*** *Michigan Chronicle,* August 24, 1963, p. 1; October 5, 1963, section B, p. 5. Dinah's one performance in Detroit in early fall was for three days, October 4–6, at Maury Baker's Grand Bar. According to the *New York Amsterdam News* (September 28, 1963, p. 15), she went to New York to perform September 29 as the featured guest of the Rinky-dinks, who were hosting their annual party at the Americana Hotel. She apparently returned to New York in time for a session October 15 with Marty Manning directing the orchestra and vocal choir, Roulette discography from Michael Cuscuna. Ballantine Belles, Beatrice Buck interviews; Richard Lane interview, Haskins papers; *Michigan Chronicle,* November 16, 1963, section B, p. 5.

430 ***Jazz Temple:*** *Cleveland Press,* October 12, 1963; *Cleveland Plain Dealer,* October 9, 1963, p. 38.

430 ***General Dealers Services, Inc.*** See *General Dealer Services, Inc., Assignee v. Regina Productions, Inc., Defendant and Dinah Washington, Co-Guarantor,* Case No. 542, August Term, 1963, Court of Common Pleas, Berks County, Pa., September 5, 1963.

430 ***Regina Productions:*** *Jet,* January 9, 1964, p. 60.

431 ***"There's a lovely lady":*** Molly Shad interview, June 2003; Shelby Singleton interview, August 13, 2003.

431 ***"looking like two wet rats":*** *Las Vegas Sun,* October 17, 1963, p. 31; November 2, 1963, p. 14; *Las Vegas Review Journal,* November 13, 1963, p. 1; *Isadore J. Marion . . . and Continental Coiffures v. Dinah Washington, also known as Ruth Jones,* Case #5985, Eighth Judicial District Court of the State of Nevada, Clark County, from the Estate of Ruth Jones a/k/a Dinah Washington. Jimmy Sigler interviews, January 2004; entertainment listings courtesy of the Nevada State Museum and Historical Society.

432 ***Sam Cooke:*** *Los Angeles Sentinel,* December 17, 1964, p. D1.

432 ***"I'm calling my girlfriend":*** Beatrice Buck interviews.

432 ***"I bought a gun":*** Jimmy Sigler interviews; Basin Street, *California Eagle, Los Angeles Sentinel* entertainment pages for November, especially November 21, 1963, p. 16A, of the *Sentinel.*

432 ***"She's made history":*** Steve Allen show details from the November 27, 1963, show, courtesy of Bill Allen and Meadowlane Enterprises; Jimmy Sigler interviews.

21 · "Move Me a Little Higher," December 1963

434 **Maggie Hathaway:** *Los Angeles Sentinel,* December 5, 1963, p. 18A.
434 **"Unbelievable, in the ghetto":** *Michigan Chronicle,* December 21, 1963; December 7, 1963, section B, p. 1; December 14, 1963, section B, p. 1, Dick Lane interview, Haskins papers.
437 **slumped on the floor:** Certificate of Death, #68248, local file #17629, Michigan Department of Health, Vital Records Section; Autopsy Case No. 8670-63, Autopsy No. A63-1801, Wayne County Morgue, Detroit, Michigan; *Jet,* January 2, 1964, pp. 53–54.

Information about Dinah's death and funeral services in Detroit and Chicago is drawn from many sources. These events were front-page news in the major black dailies and in the mainstream Detroit papers as well as in Las Vegas. See especially the *Michigan Chronicle,* December 21, 1963; the *Chicago Daily Defender,* December 16–20, 1963; the *Las Vegas Sun,* December 16, 1963; *Jet,* January 2, 9, 1964. Information also came from interviews with Dick Lane and LaRue Manns, Haskins papers, Ruth Bowen, Beatrice Buck, Estrellita Dukes, Robert Grayson, Bill Jackson, Ann Littles, Herman Roberts, and Jimmy Sigler.

Many news reports said that Dinah accompanied Lane December 13 to pick up her sons at the airport. But this is incorrect, according to Beatrice Buck, who was with Dinah at the house waiting for Lane and the boys to return.

Funeral program courtesy of the Chicago Blues Museum archives.

Apparently at least one reporter covering the funeral didn't stay into the night at Burr Oak. In the *Detroit Free Press,* Van G. Sauter wrote: "From the church, the procession went to snow-covered Burr Oak Cemetery, where Dinah's records of religious songs were played as the casket was lowered into the ground" (December 19, 1963, section A, p. 3).

22 · Long Live the Queen

443 **"I had my instructions":** Interviews with Ruth Bowen, Beatrice Buck, Farris Kimbrough, Dick Lane, Haskins papers; *Jet,* January 2, 9, 1964; *Michigan Chronicle, Chicago Defender,* December 1963.
444 **Tributes to Dinah poured in:** *Jazz* magazine, January 1964, p. 17; *Jazz Hot,* January 1964, pp. 8–9; *Down Beat,* January 16, 1964, p. 11; February 13, 1964, p. 15; *Melody Maker,* December 21, 1963, p. 5; *Jazz Journal,* February 1964, p. 9; *Orkester Journalen,* January 1964, pp. 18–19; *Sepia,* February 1964, pp. 78–79; *Ebony,* March 1964, p. 146; *Tan,* February 1964, p. 16; *Billboard,* February 15, 1964, p. 16; Joey Livingston, Brooklyn, New York, letter to *Sepia,* April 1964, p. 7; *San Francisco Chronicle,* December 16, 1963, p. 57; *Chicago Defender,* city edition, December 28, 1963–January 3, 1964, p. 11.
445 **Ballantine Belles:** *Michigan Chronicle,* January 11, 1964, p. 5. Freda Payne, an up-and-coming singer in 1964, went on to considerable success in soul music. Quincy Jones interview, December 19, 2003.
446 **A Stranger on Earth:** Roulette 25253; *In Tribute,* Roulette, 25244; *This Is My Story:* Mercury MG 20788, MG 20789, *Down Beat* April 25, 1963, p. 34.

We Three, with Sarah Vaughan and Joe Williams, Roulette, 52108; Aretha Franklin, *Unforgettable: A Tribute to Dinah Washington,* Columbia CS8963, released as a CD as part of the Legacy Series, CK 66201.

> *Cash Box* reviewed *We Three* April 4, 1964 (p. 22), calling the album a "top notch package." The mood here is relaxed and easy-going and the artists perform the evergreens with all of their expected poise."

446 **first notice:** All documents and information referred to come from the Estate of Ruth Jones a/k/a Dinah Washington.

447 **8125 South Vernon:** See documents in *Joe Glaser v. Chicago Title and Trust Co.,* as Trustee under Trust #38846, Case #64Ch3913.

449 **lawsuit against Mercury:** *Richard Lane as Administrator of the Estate of Dinah Washington v. Mercury Record Corporation,* Supreme Court of the State of New York, County of New York, Index #9803-1963. See especially the Motion for Summary Judgment filed by Martin J. Machat, the estate's lawyer, which gives a clear chronology of events in the litigation.

451 **twentieth anniversary:** For Sasha Dalton information see *New York Times,* September 11, 1983, p. 68; January 12, 1984, p. C32; October 14, 1983, p. C4.

452 **Rock and Roll Hall of Fame:** In addition to the Rock and Roll Hall of Fame, Dinah has been honored by the Alabama Music Hall of Fame and the Jazz Museum in Birmingham, Alabama. In 1998, the play *Dinah Was,* by Oliver Goldstick, opened in New York. Over the next six years various productions were mounted in several cities including Atlanta, Baltimore, Chicago, Los Angeles, and Washington, D.C. The play features several of Dinah's biggest hits.

> In 2003 Dinah was inducted into the Blues Hall of Fame.

452 **probate attorney:** *Howard T. Linden, in his capacity as Special Fiduciary of the Estate of Ruth J. Lane, aka Dinah Washington, deceased v. Polygram Records, Inc., and Does 1 to 100, inclusive,* #BC172766, 1997, Superior Court of Los Angeles County. Weinstein and Hart were paid $10,000 in 1997 to cover their fees and the costs of the litigation, document filed May 23, 1997, in the Estate of Dinah Washington, #529465, Wayne County, Michigan, Probate Court.

453 **paid the estate $60,321:** See the accountings for the Estate of Dinah Washington from 1996 to 2000, #529465, Wayne County, Michigan, Probate Court.

BIBLIOGRAPHY

BOOKS

Adams, Berle, with Gordon Cohn. *A Sucker for Talent: From Cocktail Lounges to MCA: 50 Years as Agent, Manager, and Executive.* Los Angeles: self-published, 1995.

Albert, George, and Frank Hoffman with Lee Ann Hoffman. *Black Contemporary Singles Charts, 1960–1984,* Metuchen, N.J.: Scarecrow Press, 1986.

Atkins, Cholly, and Jacqui Malone. *Class Act: The Jazz Life of Choreographer Cholly Atkins.*

Balliett, Whitney. *Improvising: Sixteen Jazz Musicians and Their Art.* New York: Oxford University Press, 1977.

Barlow, William. *Voice Over: The Making of Black Radio.* Philadelphia: Temple University Press, 1999.

Barr, Steven C. *The Almost Complete 78 RPM Record Dating Guide,* vol. 2. Huntington Beach, Calif.: Yesterday Once Again, 1992.

Bowly, Devereux Jr. *The Poorhouse: Subsidized Housing in Chicago, 1895–1976.* Carbondale, Ill.: Southern Illinois University Press, 1978.

Brown, Ruth, and Andrew Yule. *Miss Rhythm: The Autobiography of Ruth Brown, Rhythm and Blues Legend.* New York: Donald I. Fine, 1996.

Bruyninckx, Walter. *50 Years of Recorded Jazz, 1917–1967.* Mechelen, Belgium: self-published, 1967–1975.

Buhle, Mari Jo, et al. *Encyclopedia of the American Left,* 2nd Ed. New York: Oxford University Press, 1998.

Burns, Mike. *Night Train Lane: Life of Hall of Famer Richard "Night Train" Lane.* Austin, Tx: Eakin Press, 2000.

Carmer, Carl. *Stars Fell on Alabama.* Tuscaloosa: University of Alabama Press, 1995.

Clinton, Matthew. *Matt Clinton's Scrapbook.* Portals, 1979.

Cotten, Lee. *Shake, Rattle and Roll: The Golden Age of American Rock 'n Roll, Volume 1.* Ann Arbor, Mich.: Pierian Press, 1989.

_____. *Reelin' and Rockin': The Golden Age of American Rock 'n Roll, Volume 2*. Ann Arbor, Mich.: Popular Culture Ink [sic], 1995.

Crow, Bill. *From Birdland to Broadway: Scenes from a Jazz Life*. New York: Oxford University Press, 1992.

Dahl, Linda. *Morning Glory: A Biography of Mary Lou Williams*. New York: Pantheon, 1999.

_____. *Stormy Weather: The Music and Lives of a Century of Jazzwomen*. New York: Pantheon, 1989.

Dance, Stanley. *The World of Earl Hines*. New York: DaCapo, 1983.

Dannen, Frederic. *Hit Men: Power Brokers and Fast Money Inside the Music Business*. New York: Vintage, 1991.

Downey, Pat, George Albert, and Frank Hoffman. *Cash Box Pop Singles Charts, 1950–1993*. Englewood, Colo.: Libraries Unlimited, 1994.

Drake, St. Clair, and Horace R. Clayton. *Black Metropolis: A Study of Negro Life in a Northern City*. New York: Harcourt, Brace & World, 1970.

Feather, Leonard. *From Satchmo to Miles*, New York: DaCapo, 1984.

_____. *The Jazz Years: Earwitness to an Era*. New York: DaCapo, 1987.

_____. *The Pleasures of Jazz*. New York: Horizon Press, 1976.

Fox, Ted. *Showtime at the Apollo*. New York: Holt, Rinehart, and Winston, 1983.

Gart, Galen, ed. *First Pressings: The History of Rhythm & Blues*, 11 volumes. Milford, N.H.: Big Nickel, 1993–2002.

_____. *The American Record Label Directory and Dating Guide, 1940–1959*. Milford, N.H.: Big Nickel, 1995.

Giddins, Gary. *Visions of Jazz*. New York: Oxford University Press, 1998.

Gillespie, Dizzy. *To BE, or not . . . to BOP*. New York: DaCapo, 1979.

Gioia, Ted. *The History of Jazz*. New York: Oxford University Press, 1997.

Glynn, Robert L. *How Firm a Foundation: A History of the First Black Church in Tuscaloosa County, Alabama*. Tuscaloosa: Friends of the Hunter's Chapel African Methodist Episcopal Zion Church and the City of Tuscaloosa, Alabama Bicentennial Committee, 1976.

Goldblatt, Burt, *Newport Jazz Festival—The Illustrated History*. New York: Dial, 1977.

Gourse, Leslie. *Louis's Children*. New York: Morrow, 1984.

Guralnick, Peter. *Careless Love: The Unmaking of Elvis Presley*. Boston: Back Bay Books, 2000.

Hammond, John, with Irving Townsend. *John Hammond on Record: An Autobiography*. New York: Penguin, 1981.

Hampton, Lionel, with James Haskins. *Hamp: An Autobiography*. New York: Warner, 1989.

Harris, Michael W. *The Rise of Gospel Blues: The Music of Thomas A. Dorsey in the Urban Church*. New York: Oxford University Press, 1992.

Haskins, James. *Queen of the Blues: A Biography of Dinah Washington*. New York: Morrow, 1987.

Heilbut, Anthony. *The Gospel Sound: Good News and Bad Times*. New York: Simon & Schuster, 1971.

Hoffmann, Frank, and George Albert, with Lee Ann Hoffmann. *The Cash Box Album Charts, 1955–1974*. Metuchen, N.J.: Scarecrow Press, 1988.

Horne, Lena, and Richard Schickel. *Lena*. New York: Limelight, 1986.

Hubbs, G. Ward. *Tuscaloosa: Portrait of an Alabama County*. Northridge, Calif.: Windsor Publications, 1987.

Hughes, McDonald. *A History and Personal Account of Secondary Education for Blacks in the Tuscaloosa City School System, 1889–1976.* Tuscaloosa: self-published, 1979.

James, Etta, and David Ritz. *Rage to Survive: The Etta James Story.* New York: Villard, 1995.

Jepsen, Jørgen Grunnet. *Jazz Records, 1942–1965: A Discography.* Holte, Denmark: K. E. Knudsen, 1964.

Jones, Max. *Talking Jazz.* Houndmills, Basingstoke, Hampshire: Macmillan, 1987.

Jones, Quincy. *Q: The Autobiography of Quincy Jones.* New York: Doubleday, 2001.

Lewis, David Levering. *When Harlem Was in Vogue.* New York: Vintage, 1982.

Lord, Tom. *The Jazz Discography.* vols. 1–23. West Vancouver, B.C., Canada: Lord Music Reference; Redwood, N.Y.: Distributed by North Country Distributors, 2000.

Lydon, Michael. *Ray Charles: Man and Music.* New York: Riverhead Books, 2000.

Lynne, Gloria, with Karen Chilton. *I Wish You Love: A Memoir.* New York: Tom Doherty Associates, 2000.

Mackenzie, Harry, and Lother Polomski. *One Night Stand Series, 1–1001.* New York: Greenwood Press, 1991.

Mason, Herman. *African-American Life in Jacksonville.* Dover, N.H.: Arcadia, 1997.

Messick, Hank. *Razzle Dazzle.* Covington, KY.: For the Love of Books, 1995.

———. *Syndicate Wife: The Story of Ann Drahmann Coppola.* New York: MacMillan, 1968.

Moore, Sam, and Dave Marsh. *Sam and Dave: An Oral History.* New York: Avon, 1990.

Nicholson, Stuart. *Billie Holiday.* Boston: Northeastern University Press, 1995.

Polk's Tuscaloosa Directory, 1924–25. Birmingham, Ala.: R. L. Polk, 1924.

Pruter, Robert. *Chicago Soul.* Urbana: University of Illinois Press, 1996.

———. *Doowop: The Chicago Scene.* Urbana: University of Illinois Press, 1992.

Rogers, Ward, et al. *Alabama: The History of a Deep South State.* Tuscaloosa: University of Alabama Press, 1994.

Rosten, Leo. *The Joys of Yiddish.* New York: Pocket Books, 1970.

Ruppli, Michel, and Ed Novitsky. *The Mercury Labels.* Westport, Conn.: Greenwood Press, 1993.

Schiffman, Jack. *Uptown: The Story of Harlem's Apollo Theatre.* New York: Cowles, 1971.

Scott, Jimmy, with David Ritz. *Faith in Time: The Life of Jimmy Scott.* Cambridge, Mass.: Da Capo, 2002.

Seltzer, George. *Music Matters: The Performer and the American Federation of Music.* Meteuchen, NJ.: Scarecrow, 1989.

Shaw, Arnold. *Black Popular Music in America: From Spirituals, Minstrels, and Ragtime to Soul, Disco, and Hip-Hop.* New York: Schirmer, 1986.

———. *Honkers and Shouters: The Golden Years of Rhythm and Blues,* New York: Macmillan, 1978.

———. *The Street That Never Slept: New York's Fabled 52nd Street.* New York: Da-Capo, 1971.

Smith, Suzanne E. *Dancing in the Street: Motown and the Cultural Politics of Detroit.* Cambridge: Harvard University Press, 1999.

Travis, Dempsey. *Autobiography of Black Chicago.* Chicago: Urban Research Institute, 1981.

————. *An Autobiography of Black Jazz.* Chicago: Urban Research Institute, 1983.

Wade, Dorothy, and Justine Picardie. *Music Man: Ahmet Ertegun, Atlantic Records and the Triumph of Rock 'n' Roll.* New York: Norton, 1990.

Walker, Lewis, and Ben C. Wilson. *Black Eden: The Idlewild Community.* East Lansing: Michigan State University Press, 2002.

Ward, Elijah. *Escaping the Delta: Robert Johnson and the Invention of the Blues.* New York: Amistad, 2004.

Wein, George, with Nate Chinen. *Myself Among Others: A Life in Music.* New York: DaCapo, 2003.

Whitburn, Joel. *Joel Whitburn's Top LPs 1945–72.* Menomonee Falls, Wis.: Record Research, 1996.

————. *Joel Whitburn's Top Pop Artists and Singles.* Menomonee Falls, Wis.: Record Research, 1979.

————. *Joel Whitburn's Top R&B Singles, 1942–95.* Menomonee Falls, Wis.: Record Research, 1996.

PERIODICALS

The specific articles, both major and minor, from these publications are cited in the notes, which begin on page 461.

Billboard	*Hue*	*Our World*
Cash Box	*Jet*	*Sepia*
Down Beat	*Melody Maker*	*Tan*
Ebony	*Metronome*	*Variety*
Essence		

NEWSPAPERS

Most of the newspapers listed below are devoted to the black communities in their cities. They were an invaluable research tool; the black press paid regular attention to where Dinah Washington was and what she was doing. In addition, the newspapers yielded insights into the black communities across the country, covering and commenting on events often ignored in the mainstream white papers. For specific articles cited, see the chapter-by-chapter notes, which begin on p. 461.

Atlanta Daily News	*Florida Star*	*New York Times*
Baltimore Afro-American	*Houston Informer*	*Newark Afro-American*
California Eagle	Kansas City *Call*	*Norfolk Journal and Guide*
Carolinian	*Louisiana Weekly*	*Oakland Tribune*
Chicago American	*Louisville Defender*	*Philadelphia Tribune*
Chicago Defender	*Los Angeles Sentinel*	*Pittsburgh Courier*
Chicago Tribune	*Miami Times*	*Richmond Afro-American*
Cleveland Call & Post	*Michigan Chronicle*	*Rocky Mountain News*
Denver Post	*New Orleans Times-Picayune*	*San Francisco Chronicle*
Detroit Free Press	*New York Amsterdam News*	*Tri-State Defender*
Detroit News	*New York Post*	*Washington Afro-American*

LEGAL DOCUMENTS*

Dinah Buchanan v. Walter Buchanan, #52S2736, Superior Court of Cook County, 1952.

Dinah Washington v. Andrew C. Baird, Sheriff of Wayne County, Stephen Book, and Walter Bates, Jr., Deputy Sheriffs, Case #61-21402, U.S. District Court for the Eastern District of Michigan, 1961.

Dinah Washington v. Mercury Record Corporation, New York Supreme Court, #9803/63. The plaintiff's name was later changed to *Richard Lane as the Administrator of the Estate of Dinah Washington.*

Estate of Ruth Jones Lane, AKA Ruth Grayson, Ruth Jones, Ruth Lee Jones, Dinah Lane, Dinah Washington, #529465, Wayne County, Michigan, Probate Court.

General Dealers Services, Inc., Assignee, v. Regina Productions, Inc. and Dinah Washington, co-guarantor, # 542, August Term, 1963 Berks County, Pennsylvania Court of Common Pleas.

Holiday House, Inc. v. American Guild of Variety Artists, Civil Action 63-57, U.S. District Court for the Western District of Pennsylvania, 1962.

Isadore J. Marion . . . and Continental Coiffures v. Dinah Washington, also known as Ruth Jones, Case #5985, Eighth Judicial District Court of the State of Nevada, Clark County, 1963.

Howard T. Linden, in his capacity as Special Fidcuciary of the Estate of Ruth J. Lane aka Dinah Washington, deceased, v. Polygram Records, Inc., and Does 1 to 100, inclusive, Case #BC172766, 1997, Superior Court of Los Angeles County.

* Five of Dinah's marriage licenses are cited in the notes, as are her official death certificate and autopsy report.

ACKNOWLEDGMENTS

Many individuals helped make this book possible. They have my everlasting thanks.

I began this project before meeting any of Dinah Washington's family. When I introduced myself after the first few months of research, they were welcoming and patient during my many phone calls and visits. I am grateful to Clarissa Smith and Estrellita Dukes, Dinah's sisters, her son Robert Grayson, and stepsister Farris Kimbrough, for their insights and wonderful stories. Thanks, too, to Alfreda Kimbrough, another stepsister, and to Dinah's cousins on her father's side, the Jones family: Sam, Willie Lawrence, George, Berna Dean Jones Brown, and Mattie Nevels.

Keter Betts, Dinah's bass player for five years and the anchor of her trio during the early 1950s, was my guide through those years, remembering dates, places, people, and stories. Jimmy Sigler, Dinah's organ player during the last two years of her life, was my guide through the end of her career, helping me figure out where she was, what she sang, what she said, and, when possible, why. My appreciation to both men is endless. Thanks, too, to the many other musicians and producers who worked with Dinah and were willing to share their stories: Beryl Adams, Vern Allison, Patti Austin, Chuck Barksdale, Patti Bown, Jackie Cain, Jimmy Cobb, King Coleman, Charles Davis, Richard Evans, Maynard Ferguson, Richard "Dicky" Harris, Quincy Jones, Marvin Junior, Junior Mance, Mickey McGill, Mitch Miller, Clyde Otis, Harold Ousley, Julian Priester, Jimmy Rowser, Nook Shrier, James Slaughter, Clark Terry, Toots Thielemans, Ed Thigpen, Teddy Washington, Paul West, Jody Williams, Joe Wilder, Gerald Wilson, Jack Wilson, Larry Wrice, Lee Young, Joe Zawinul, and Boris Zlatich.

Dinah's close friends and confidants, Ruth Bowen, Beatrice Buck, and Ann Littles, were invaluable, always patient and willing to talk when I called to ask yet another question.

Charles Walton, to whom this book is dedicated, opened many doors for me in ways large and small. Tim Samuelson helped me find my way through the world of Cook County real estate and Chicago's South Side. Donnie Falls and Ruby Haynes on South Trumbull and Juanita and Hershell Mhoon on South Vernon graciously welcomed us into the homes once occupied by Dinah and some of her family in Chicago. And Michele Wallace in New York was equally kind in allowing me to spend time in what had been Dinah's apartment.

Thanks are also due to several others who knew Dinah offstage: Bob Bailey, William and Ruth Battles, Onameega Doris Bluitt, Toni Brazington, Al Colizzi, James "Duke" Davis, Joe Delaney, David Dinkins, George Dixon, James and Bertha Foreman, the late Artie Frazier, Jr., the late Melvin Gaynor, the late Eloise Hughes, Bud Katzel, Vera Hamb Payne, Benny Pope, Herman Roberts, Billie Shepperd, Art Sheridan, Eugene Smith, Rose Snow, Marva Scott Starks, Yvonne Buckner Storey, Dempsey Travis, Bud Ward, and Walt Wright.

In Tuscaloosa my thanks to Debra Gamble, who kindly took me around the city and invited me to the Sweet Hour of Prayer at Elizabeth Baptist Church, Lisa Reams, and Jessica Lacher-Feldman at the University of Alabama Special Collections, and Robert Heath at Stillman College. And thanks to James Doss and his daughters, Joan Doss Anderson, Evelyn Doss Dorsey, and Helen Doss Johnson, now in Chicago but full of memories of Dinah's early life.

More thanks to Molly Shad for her delicious stories about Dinah and Dinah's relationship with Bobby Shad and to Tamara Shad and Derrick Ray. Thanks also to Jack Bart for telling me about the business and how his father, Ben, got started, and to Edna and Mark Albert for the use of *Cash Box*.

Ken Druker and Bryan Koniarz at the Verve Music Group were generous and patient with all my requests. Most important they have helped keep Dinah's music alive.

Jack Thompson shared my enthusiasm for this project and provided many helpful tips, copies of photographs, and record jacket covers.

Special thanks to the invaluable Emily Kelley in Chicago for filling the research gaps, and to Judith Bethea in New Orleans; Donna Clark in Odessa, Texas; Barbara Crissman in Jacksonville, Florida; Jim Cole in Memphis; Michael Lydon and Audrey Warren in New York; and Jean Morris in Pittsburgh. Thanks, too, to Nicholas Bachand, Sholnn Freeman, and Sharon Barksdale for help with the Wayne County, Michigan, Probate Court files. Thanks also to the staff at the Howard Gotlieb Archival Research Center at Boston University when I used the papers of James Haskins that relate to Dinah. I am grateful that he made available the interviews of individuals important to Dinah but no longer alive when I began this project. And thanks to Debra Fresquez, the archivist at the American Federation of Musicians Local 47 in Los Angeles, who filled in so many blanks about Dinah's recording in L.A. More thanks to Daniel Smithyman of the U.S. Navy for his help with Dinah's 1962 visit to the naval base in Naples, Italy.

I owe additional thanks to several reference librarians at the Library of Congress who were unfailingly resourceful in handling my requests: Rosemary Hanes in the Motion Picture and Television Reading Room; Bryan Cornell and Jan McKee in the Recorded Sound Reference Center; Carl Cephas, Bill Harvey, Karen Moses, Robert Ivan Schellenbarger, and Charles Sens in the Music Division; and Jim Schneider in Microforms. Thanks also to the staff at Howard University's Moorland Springarn Research Center and to Jeannie Child and Philip Costello at the Cook County Illinois Clerk of Court Archives.

A number of public librarians around the country patiently answered my requests to search local newspapers for Dinah sightings. Great thanks to Marty Sugden and Glenn Emery in Jacksonville, Florida; Zoe Rhine in Asheville; North Carolina; Jan Henick-Kling in Geneva, New York; Michael Fluge, Cynthia Fife Townsend, and Tammy Hampton at the Vivian Harsh Research Collection in Chicago; and these librarians at other public libraries: Richard C. Leab at the Berkshire Athenaenum in Pittsfield, Massachusetts; Heather Garrison in Flint, Michigan; Paul Schiesser in Oakland; Glenn Creason and Glenna Dunning in Los Angeles; Eleanor Krell in Baltimore at the Enoch Pratt Free Library; Rhonda Green and Bob Murnan in Cleveland and Lynn Bycko at Cleveland State University; Irene Breedlove in Kansas City, Missouri; Bratis Roseboro in Winston-Salem, North Carolina; Janis Young in Newport, Kentucky; Jean Wallace in Beaumont, Texas; Susan Hays in Roanoke, Virginia; David Smith at the New York Public Library; and Dolores Henry at the New Bedford Free Library, New Bedford, Massachusetts; the reference librarians at the Carnegie Library of Pittsburgh and the Broward County, Florida, public library; and Cary Schneider at the *Los Angeles Times*. Thanks also to Beverly Bower and Tracey Dowling at Florida State University, Ethan Manning at the University of Louisville, Hal Rothman at the University of Nevada—Las Vegas, Michael Tarabulski at the University of Idaho's Lionel Hampton School of Music, Thonni Morikawa and the late Frank Wright at the Nevada State Museum and Historical Society, Gino Francesconi at the Carnegie Hall archives, Carolyn Clark at the Auburn Avenue Research Center in Atlanta, Dan Morgenstern at the Institute of Jazz Studies, Rutgers University, Crystal Foster at the HistoryMakers project in Chicago, and Bill Allen at Meadowlane Enterprises.

Additional thanks to Harry Mackenzie and David Segal for their help with Dinah and Lionel Hampton on radio, to Ted Ono for additional help with radio and for video clips of Dinah, and to Victor Pearlin for all the discographical help. Thanks, too, to Eric LeBlanc.

Once I started writing the manuscript, I turned to my informal editorial board, Ron Elving, Phil Kuntz, Charlie McGovern, and Bob Pruter. Their suggestions, observations, and constructive criticism chapter by chapter helped immensely. More than once they saved me from myself. They have my enduring gratitude for their attention and interest over so many months and in so many conversations. One couldn't ask for more.

Jack Tracy not only remembered great stories and helped me understand how the studio worked, he also read the completed manuscript and made valuable suggestions and corrections, as did Bob Porter. Peter Guralnick was a source of inspiration, offering kind words when they were most needed and taking time from his own work to read the chapters.

Thanks to Joe Davis, my valued technical adviser, and to Norman Schneider for his patience and good humor in excising all the formatting gremlins and for giving me the short course on probate.

I would not have had this grand and absorbing adventure without Philippa Brophy, my agent since 1988, who believed in the Dinah Washington project from the start. Her good instincts led me to Deborah Garrison at Pantheon. Deb's enthusiasm and encouragement every step of the way were so important, and even more so were her astute observations and penetrating insights about how to tell this story. Additional thanks to Ilana Kurshan, for her kind and welcoming spirit and her patience in attending to all the details to get a finished product, to copy editor Fred Chase for going over all the pages with such diligence, and to production editor Kathleen Fridella for making sure there was a book.

Finally, eternal thanks to my father, the late Arnold Cohodas, and to my constant cheerleaders on the sidelines, my mother, Sylvia Cohodas, and my brother, Howard Cohodas.

A B O U T   T H E   A U T H O R

Nadine Cohodas is the author of *Strom Thurmond and the Politics of Southern Change; The Band Played Dixie: Race and the Liberal Conscience at Ole Miss;* and *Spinning Blues into Gold: The Chess Brothers and the Legendary Chess Records.* She lives in Washington, D.C.

A NOTE ON THE TYPE

The text of this book was set in a typeface called Méridien,
a classic roman designed by Adrian Frutiger for the French
type foundry Deberny et Peignot in 1957. Méridien, as well
as his other typeface of world renown, Univers, was
created for the Lumitype photo-set machine.

Composed by Creative Graphics,
Allentown, Pennsylvania

Printed and bound by Berryville Graphics,
Berryville, Virginia

Designed by Iris Weinstein